STUDENT'S SOLUTIONS MANUAL

JUDITH A. PENNA

Indiana University Purdue University Indianapolis

to accompany

COLLEGE ALGEBRA

SECOND EDITION

Judith A. Beecher

Indiana University Purdue University Indianapolis

Judith A. Penna

Indiana University Purdue University Indianapolis

Marvin L. Bittinger

Indiana University Purdue University Indianapolis

PEARSON
Addison
Wesley

Boston San Francisco New York
London Toronto Sydney Tokyo Singapore Madrid
Mexico City Munich Paris Cape Town Hong Kong Montreal

Reproduced by Pearson Addison-Wesley from electronic files supplied by the author.

Publishing as Pearson Addison-Wesley, 75 Arlington Street, Boston, MA 02116

ISBN 0-321-23698-X

8 9 BRG 08 07 06

PEARSON
Addison
Wesley

Contents

Chapter R 1

Chapter 1 17

Chapter 2 51

Chapter 3 85

Chapter 4 125

Chapter 5 149

Chapter 6 197

Chapter 7 223

Chapter R

Basic Concepts of Algebra

Exercise Set R.1

1. Whole numbers: $\sqrt[3]{8}$, 0, 9, $\sqrt{25}$ $\quad(\sqrt[3]{8}=2,\ \sqrt{25}=5)$

3. Irrational numbers: $\sqrt{7}$, 5.242242224..., $-\sqrt{14}$, $\sqrt[5]{5}$, $\sqrt[3]{4}$
(Although there is a pattern in 5.242242224..., there is no repeating block of digits.)

5. Rational numbers: -12, $5.\overline{3}$, $-\frac{7}{3}$, $\sqrt[3]{8}$, 0, -1.96, 9, $4\frac{2}{3}$, $\sqrt{25}$, $\frac{5}{7}$

7. Rational numbers but not integers: $5.\overline{3}$, $-\frac{7}{3}$, -1.96, $4\frac{2}{3}$, $\frac{5}{7}$

9. Integers but not rational numbers: -12, 0

11. This is a closed interval, so we use brackets. Interval notation is $[-3, 3]$.

13. This is a half-open interval. We use a bracket on the left and a parenthesis on the right. Interval notation is $[-4, -1)$.

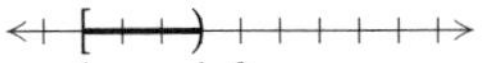

15. This interval is of unlimited extent in the negative direction, and the endpoint -2 is included. Interval notation is $(-\infty, -2]$.

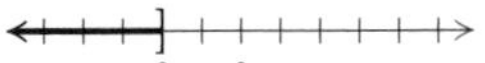

17. This interval is of unlimited extent in the positive direction, and the endpoint 3.8 is not included. Interval notation is $(3.8, \infty)$.

19. $\{x|7 < x\}$, or $\{x|x > 7\}$.
This interval is of unlimited extent in the positive direction and the endpoint 7 is not included. Interval notation is $(7, \infty)$.

21. The endpoints 0 and 5 are not included in the interval, so we use parentheses. Interval notation is $(0, 5)$.

23. The endpoint -9 is included in the interval, so we use a bracket before the -9. The endpoint -4 is not included, so we use a parenthesis after the -4. Interval notation is $[-9, -4)$.

25. Both endpoints are included in the interval, so we use brackets. Interval notation is $[x, x+h]$.

27. The endpoint p is not included in the interval, so we use a parenthesis before the p. The interval is of unlimited extent in the positive direction, so we use the infinity symbol ∞. Interval notation is (p, ∞).

29. Since 6 is an element of the set of natural numbers, the statement is true.

31. Since 3.2 is not an element of the set of integers, the statement is false.

33. Since $-\frac{11}{5}$ is an element of the set of rational numbers, the statement is true.

35. Since $\sqrt{11}$ is an element of the set of real numbers, the statement is false.

37. Since 24 is an element of the set of whole numbers, the statement is false.

39. Since 1.089 is not an element of the set of irrational numbers, the statement is true.

41. Since every whole number is an integer, the statement is true.

43. Since every rational number is a real number, the statement is true.

45. Since there are real numbers that are not integers, the statement is false.

47. The sentence $6x = x6$ illustrates the commutative property of multiplication.

49. The sentence $-3 \cdot 1 = -3$ illustrates the multiplicative identity property.

51. The sentence $5(ab) = (5a)b$ illustrates the associative property of multiplication.

53. The sentence $2(a+b) = (a+b)2$ illustrates the commutative property of multiplication.

55. The sentence $-6(m+n) = -6(n+m)$ illustrates the commutative property of addition.

57. The sentence $8 \cdot \frac{1}{8} = 1$ illustrates the multiplicative inverse property.

59. The distance of -7.1 from 0 is 7.1, so $|-7.1| = 7.1$.

61. The distance of 347 from 0 is 347, so $|347| = 347$.

63. The distance of $-\sqrt{97}$ from 0 is $\sqrt{97}$, so $|-\sqrt{97}| = \sqrt{97}$.

65. The distance of 0 from 0 is 0, so $|0| = 0$.

67. The distance of $\frac{5}{4}$ from 0 is $\frac{5}{4}$, so $\left|\frac{5}{4}\right| = \frac{5}{4}$.

69. $|-5-6| = |-11| = 11$, or
$|6-(-5)| = |6+5| = |11| = 11$

71. $|-2-(-8)| = |-2+8| = |6| = 6$, or
$|-8-(-2)| = |-8+2| = |-6| = 6$

73. $|12.1-6.7| = |5.4| = 5.4$, or
$|6.7-12.1| = |-5.4| = 5.4$

75. $\left|-\frac{3}{4}-\frac{15}{8}\right| = \left|-\frac{6}{8}-\frac{15}{8}\right| = \left|-\frac{21}{8}\right| = \frac{21}{8}$, or
$\left|\frac{15}{8}-\left(-\frac{3}{4}\right)\right| = \left|\frac{15}{8}+\frac{3}{4}\right| = \left|\frac{15}{8}+\frac{6}{8}\right| = \left|\frac{21}{8}\right| = \frac{21}{8}$

77. $|-7-0| = |-7| = 7$, or
$|0-(-7)| = |0+7| = |7| = 7$

79. Discussion and Writing

81. Answers may vary. One such number is $0.124124412444\ldots$.

83. Answers may vary. Since $-\frac{1}{101} = 0.\overline{0099}$ and $-\frac{1}{100} = -0.01$, one such number is -0.00999.

85. Since $1^2 + 3^2 = 10$, the hypotenuse of a right triangle with legs of lengths 1 unit and 3 units has a length of $\sqrt{10}$ units.

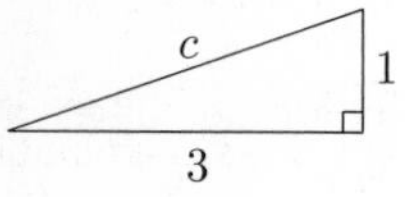

$$c^2 = 1^2 + 3^2$$
$$c^2 = 10$$
$$c = \sqrt{10}$$

Exercise Set R.2

1. $18^\circ = 1$ (For any nonzero real number, $a^0 = 1$.)

3. $x^9 \cdot x^0 = x^{9+0} = x^9$

5. $5^8 \cdot 5^{-6} = 5^{8+(-6)} = 5^2$, or 25

7. $m^{-5} \cdot m^5 = m^{-5+5} = m^0 = 1$

9. $y^3 \cdot y^{-7} = y^{3+(-7)} = y^{-4}$, or $\frac{1}{y^4}$

11. $7^3 \cdot 7^{-5} \cdot 7 = 7^{3+(-5)+1} = 7^{-1}$, or $\frac{1}{7}$

13. $2x^3 \cdot 3x^2 = 2 \cdot 3 \cdot x^{3+2} = 6x^5$

15. $(-3a^{-5})(5a^{-7}) = -3 \cdot 5 \cdot a^{-5+(-7)} = -15a^{-12}$, or $-\frac{15}{a^{12}}$

17. $(5a^2b)(3a^{-3}b^4) = 5 \cdot 3 \cdot a^{2+(-3)} \cdot b^{1+4} = 15a^{-1}b^5$, or $\frac{15b^5}{a}$

19. $(6x^{-3}y^5)(-7x^2y^{-9}) = 6(-7)x^{-3+2}y^{5+(-9)} = -42x^{-1}y^{-4}$, or $-\frac{42}{xy^4}$

21. $(2x)^3(3x)^2 = 2^3x^3 \cdot 3^2x^2 = 8 \cdot 9 \cdot x^{3+2} = 72x^5$

23. $(-2n)^3(5n)^2 = (-2)^3n^3 \cdot 5^2n^2 = -8 \cdot 25 \cdot n^{3+2} = -200n^5$

25. $\frac{b^{40}}{b^{37}} = b^{40-37} = b^3$

27. $\frac{x^{-5}}{x^{16}} = x^{-5-16} = x^{-21}$, or $\frac{1}{x^{21}}$

29. $\frac{x^2y^{-2}}{x^{-1}y} = x^{2-(-1)}y^{-2-1} = x^3y^{-3}$, or $\frac{x^3}{y^3}$

31. $\frac{32x^{-4}y^3}{4x^{-5}y^8} = \frac{32}{4}x^{-4-(-5)}y^{3-8} = 8xy^{-5}$, or $\frac{8x}{y^5}$

33. $(2ab^2)^3 = 2^3a^3(b^2)^3 = 2^3a^3b^{2\cdot 3} = 8a^3b^6$

35. $(-2x^3)^5 = (-2)^5(x^3)^5 = (-2)^5x^{3\cdot 5} = -32x^{15}$

37. $(-5c^{-1}d^{-2})^{-2} = (-5)^{-2}c^{-1(-2)}d^{-2(-2)} = \frac{c^2d^4}{(-5)^2} = \frac{c^2d^4}{25}$

39. $(3m^4)^3(2m^{-5})^4 = 3^3m^{12} \cdot 2^4m^{-20} = 27 \cdot 16m^{12+(-20)} = 432m^{-8}$, or $\frac{432}{m^8}$

41. $\left(\frac{2x^{-3}y^7}{z^{-1}}\right)^3 = \frac{(2x^{-3}y^7)^3}{(z^{-1})^3} = \frac{2^3x^{-9}y^{21}}{z^{-3}} = \frac{8x^{-9}y^{21}}{z^{-3}}$, or $\frac{8y^{21}z^3}{x^9}$

43. $\left(\frac{24a^{10}b^{-8}c^7}{12a^6b^{-3}c^5}\right)^{-5} = (2a^4b^{-5}c^2)^{-5} = 2^{-5}a^{-20}b^{25}c^{-10}$, or $\frac{b^{25}}{32a^{20}c^{10}}$

45. Convert 405,000 to scientific notation.

We want the decimal point to be positioned between the 4 and the first 0, so we move it 5 places to the left. Since 405,000 is greater than 10, the exponent must be positive.

$$405,000 = 4.05 \times 10^5$$

47. Convert 0.00000039 to scientific notation.

We want the decimal point to be positioned between the 3 and the 9, so we move it 7 places to the right. Since 0.00000039 is a number between 0 and 1, the exponent must be negative.

$$0.00000039 = 3.9 \times 10^{-7}$$

49. Convert 234,600,000,000 to scientific notation. We want the decimal point to be positioned between the 2 and the 3, so we move it 11 places to the left. Since 234,600,000,000 is greater than 10, the exponent must be positive.

$$234,600,000,000 = 2.346 \times 10^{11}$$

51. Convert 0.00104 to scientific notation. We want the decimal point to be positioned between the 1 and the last 0, so we move it 3 places to the right. Since 0.00104 is a number between 0 and 1, the exponent must be negative.

$$0.00104 = 1.04 \times 10^{-3}$$

53. Convert 0.000016 to scientific notation.

We want the decimal point to be positioned between the 1 and the 6, so we move it 5 places to the right. Since 0.000016 is a number between 0 and 1, the exponent must be negative.

$$0.000016 = 1.6 \times 10^{-5}$$

55. Convert 8.3×10^{-5} to decimal notation.

The exponent is negative, so the number is between 0 and 1. We move the decimal point 5 places to the left.

$$8.3 \times 10^{-5} = 0.000083$$

57. Convert 2.07×10^{7} to decimal notation.

The exponent is positive, so the number is greater than 10. We move the decimal point 7 places to the right.

$$2.07 \times 10^{7} = 20,700,000$$

59. Convert 3.496×10^{10} to decimal notation.

The exponent is positive, so the number is greater than 10. We move the decimal point 10 places to the right.

$$3.496 \times 10^{10} = 34,960,000,000$$

61. Convert 5.41×10^{-8} to decimal notation.

The exponent is negative, so the number is between 0 and 1. We move the decimal point 8 places to the left.

$$5.41 \times 10^{-8} = 0.0000000541$$

63. Convert 2.319×10^{8} to decimal notation.

The exponent is positive, so the number is greater than 10. We move the decimal point 8 places to the right.

$$2.319 \times 10^{8} = 231,900,000$$

65.

$$(3.1 \times 10^5)(4.5 \times 10^{-3})$$
$$= (3.1 \times 4.5) \times (10^5 \times 10^{-3})$$
$$= 13.95 \times 10^2 \quad \text{This is not scientific notation.}$$
$$= (1.395 \times 10) \times 10^2$$
$$= 1.395 \times 10^3 \quad \text{Writing scientific notation}$$

67.

$$(2.6 \times 10^{-18})(8.5 \times 10^7)$$
$$= (2.6 \times 8.5) \times (10^{-18} \times 10^7)$$
$$= 22.1 \times 10^{-11} \quad \text{This is not scientific notation.}$$
$$= (2.21 \times 10) \times 10^{-11}$$
$$= 2.21 \times 10^{-10}$$

69.

$$\frac{6.4 \times 10^{-7}}{8.0 \times 10^6} = \frac{6.4}{8.0} \times \frac{10^{-7}}{10^6}$$
$$= 0.8 \times 10^{-13} \quad \text{This is not scientific notation.}$$
$$= (8 \times 10^{-1}) \times 10^{-13}$$
$$= 8 \times 10^{-14} \quad \text{Writing scientific notation}$$

71.

$$\frac{1.8 \times 10^{-3}}{7.2 \times 10^{-9}}$$
$$= \frac{1.8}{7.2} \times \frac{10^{-3}}{10^{-9}}$$
$$= 0.25 \times 10^6 \quad \text{This is not scientific notation.}$$
$$= (2.5 \times 10^{-1}) \times 10^6$$
$$= 2.5 \times 10^5$$

73. The average cost per mile is the total cost divided by the number of miles.

$$\frac{\$210 \times 10^6}{17.6}$$
$$= \frac{\$210 \times 10^6}{1.76 \times 10}$$
$$\approx \$119 \times 10^5$$
$$\approx (\$1.19 \times 10^2) \times 10^5$$
$$\approx \$1.19 \times 10^7$$

The average cost per mile was about $\$1.19 \times 10^7$.

75. First find the number of seconds in 1 hour:

$$1 \text{ hour} = 1 \cancel{\text{hr}} \times \frac{60 \cancel{\text{min}}}{1 \cancel{\text{hr}}} \times \frac{60 \text{ sec}}{1 \cancel{\text{min}}} = 3600 \text{ sec}$$

The number of disintegrations produced in 1 hour is the number of disintegrations per second times the number of seconds in 1 hour.

$$37 \text{ billion} \times 3600$$
$$= 37,000,000,000 \times 3600$$
$$= 3.7 \times 10^{10} \times 3.6 \times 10^3 \quad \text{Writing scientific notation}$$
$$= (3.7 \times 3.6) \times (10^{10} \times 10^3)$$
$$= 13.32 \times 10^{13} \quad \text{Multiplying}$$
$$= (1.332 \times 10) \times 10^{13}$$
$$= 1.332 \times 10^{14}$$

One gram of radium produces 1.332×10^{14} disintegrations in 1 hour.

77. $3\cdot 2-4\cdot 2^2+6(3-1)$

$= 3\cdot 2-4\cdot 2^2+6\cdot 2$ Working inside parentheses

$= 3\cdot 2-4\cdot 4+6\cdot 2$ Evaluating 2^2

$= 6-16+12$ Multiplying

$= -10+12$ Adding in order

$= 2$ from left to right

79. $16\div 4\cdot 4\div 2\cdot 256$

$= 4\cdot 4\div 2\cdot 256$ Multiplying and dividing in order from left to right

$= 16\div 2\cdot 256$

$= 8\cdot 256$

$= 2048$

81. $\dfrac{4(8-6)^2-4\cdot 3+2\cdot 8}{3^1+19^0}$

$= \dfrac{4\cdot 2^2-4\cdot 3+2\cdot 8}{3+1}$ Calculating in the numerator and in the denominator

$= \dfrac{4\cdot 4-4\cdot 3+2\cdot 8}{4}$

$= \dfrac{16-12+16}{4}$

$= \dfrac{4+16}{4}$

$= \dfrac{20}{4}$

$= 5$

83. Since interest is compounded semiannually, $n = 2$. Substitute \$2125 for P, 6.2% or 0.062 for i, 2 for n, and 5 for t in the compound interest formula.

$A = P\left(1+\dfrac{i}{n}\right)^{nt}$

$= \$2125\left(1+\dfrac{0.062}{2}\right)^{2\cdot 5}$ Substituting

$= \$2125(1+0.031)^{2\cdot 5}$ Dividing

$= \$2125(1.031)^{2\cdot 5}$ Adding

$= \$2125(1.031)^{10}$ Multiplying 2 and 5

$\approx \$2125(1.357021264)$ Evaluating the exponential expression

$\approx \$2883.670185$ Multiplying

$\approx \$2883.67$ Rounding to the nearest cent

85. Since interest is compounded quarterly, $n = 4$. Substitute \$6700 for P, 4.5% or 0.045 for i, 4 for n, and 6 for t in the compound interest formula.

$A = P\left(1+\dfrac{i}{n}\right)^{nt}$

$= \$6700\left(1+\dfrac{0.045}{4}\right)^{4\cdot 6}$ Substituting

$= \$6700(1+0.01125)^{4\cdot 6}$ Dividing

$= \$6700(1.01125)^{4\cdot 6}$ Adding

$= \$6700(1.01125)^{24}$ Multiplying 4 and 6

$\approx \$6700(1.307991226)$ Evaluating the exponential expression

$\approx \$8763.541217$ Multiplying

$\approx \$8763.54$ Rounding to the nearest cent

87. Discussion and Writing

89. Substitute \$250 for P, 0.05 for r and 27 for t and perform the resulting computation.

$$S = P\left[\frac{\left(1+\frac{r}{12}\right)^{12\cdot t}-1}{\frac{r}{12}}\right]$$

$$= \$250\left[\frac{\left(1+\frac{0.05}{12}\right)^{12\cdot 27}-1}{\frac{0.05}{12}}\right]$$

$\approx \$170,797.30$

91. Substitute \$120,000 for S, 0.06 for r, and 18 for t and solve for P.

$$S = P\left[\frac{\left(1+\frac{r}{12}\right)^{12\cdot t}-1}{\frac{r}{12}}\right]$$

$$\$120,000 = P\left[\frac{\left(1+\frac{0.06}{12}\right)^{12\cdot 18}-1}{\frac{0.06}{12}}\right]$$

$$\$120,000 = P\left[\frac{(1.005)^{216}-1}{0.05}\right]$$

$\$120,000 \approx P(387.3532)$

$\$309.79 \approx P$

93. $(x^t\cdot x^{3t})^2 = (x^{4t})^2 = x^{4t\cdot 2} = x^{8t}$

95. $(t^{a+x}\cdot t^{x-a})^4 = (t^{2x})^4 = t^{2x\cdot 4} = t^{8x}$

97. $\left[\dfrac{(3x^ay^b)^3}{(-3x^ay^b)^2}\right]^2 = \left[\dfrac{27x^{3a}y^{3b}}{9x^{2a}y^{2b}}\right]^2$

$= \left[3x^ay^b\right]^2$

$= 9x^{2a}y^{2b}$

Exercise Set R.3

1. $-5y^4+3y^3+7y^2-y-4=$
$-5y^4+3y^3+7y^2+(-y)+(-4)$

Terms: $-5y^4$, $3y^3$, $7y^2$, $-y$, -4

The degree of the term of highest degree, $-5y^4$, is 4. Thus, the degree of the polynomial is 4.

3. $3a^4b-7a^3b^3+5ab-2=3a^4b+(-7a^3b^3)+5ab+(-2)$

Terms: $3a^4b$, $-7a^3b^3$, $5ab$, -2

The degrees of the terms are 5, 6, 2, and, 0, respectively, so the degree of the polynomial is 6.

5. $(5x^2y-2xy^2+3xy-5)+$
$(-2x^2y-3xy^2+4xy+7)$
$=(5-2)x^2y+(-2-3)xy^2+(3+4)xy+$
$(-5+7)$
$=3x^2y-5xy^2+7xy+2$

7. $(2x+3y+z-7)+(4x-2y-z+8)+$
$(-3x+y-2z-4)$
$=(2+4-3)x+(3-2+1)y+(1-1-2)z+$
$(-7+8-4)$
$=3x+2y-2z-3$

9. $(3x^2-2x-x^3+2)-(5x^2-8x-x^3+4)$
$=(3x^2-2x-x^3+2)+(-5x^2+8x+x^3-4)$
$=(3-5)x^2+(-2+8)x+(-1+1)x^3+(2-4)$
$=-2x^2+6x-2$

11. $(x^4-3x^2+4x)-(3x^3+x^2-5x+3)$
$=(x^4-3x^2+4x)+(-3x^3-x^2+5x-3)$
$=x^4-3x^3+(-3-1)x^2+(4+5)x-3$
$=x^4-3x^3-4x^2+9x-3$

13. $(a-b)(2a^3-ab+3b^2)$
$=(a-b)(2a^3)+(a-b)(-ab)+(a-b)(3b^2)$ Using the distributive property
$=2a^4-2a^3b-a^2b+ab^2+3ab^2-3b^3$ Using the distributive property three more times
$=2a^4-2a^3b-a^2b+4ab^2-3b^3$ Collecting like terms

15. $(x+5)(x-3)$
$=x^2-3x+5x-15$ Using FOIL
$=x^2+2x-15$ Collecting like terms

17. $(x+6)(x+4)$
$=x^2+4x+6x+24$ Using FOIL
$=x^2+10x+24$ Collecting like terms

19. $(2a+3)(a+5)$
$=2a^2+10a+3a+15$ Using FOIL
$=2a^2+13a+15$ Collecting like terms

21. $(2x+3y)(2x+y)$
$=4x^2+2xy+6xy+3y^2$ Using FOIL
$=4x^2+8xy+3y^2$

23. $(y+5)^2$
$=y^2+2\cdot y\cdot 5+5^2$
$[(A+B)^2=A^2+2AB+B^2]$
$=y^2+10y+25$

25. $(x-4)^2$
$=x^2-2\cdot x\cdot 4+4^2$
$[(A-B)^2=A^2-2AB+B^2]$
$=x^2-8x+16$

27. $(5x-3)^2$
$=(5x)^2-2\cdot 5x\cdot 3+3^2$
$[(A-B)^2=A^2-2AB+B^2]$
$=25x^2-30x+9$

29. $(2x+3y)^2$
$=(2x)^2+2(2x)(3y)+(3y)^2$
$[(A+B)^2=A^2+2AB+B^2]$
$=4x^2+12xy+9y^2$

31. $(2x^2-3y)^2$
$=(2x^2)^2-2(2x^2)(3y)+(3y)^2$
$[(A-B)^2=A^2-2AB+B^2]$
$=4x^4-12x^2y+9y^2$

33. $(a+3)(a-3)$
$=a^2-3^2$ $[(A+B)(A-B)=A^2-B^2]$
$=a^2-9$

35. $(2x-5)(2x+5)$
$=(2x)^2-5^2$ $[(A+B)(A-B)=A^2-B^2]$
$=4x^2-25$

37. $(3x-2y)(3x+2y)$
$=(3x)^2-(2y)^2$ $[(A-B)(A+B)=A^2-B^2]$
$=9x^2-4y^2$

39. $(2x+3y+4)(2x+3y-4)$
$=[(2x+3y)+4][(2x+3y)-4]$
$=(2x+3y)^2-4^2$
$=4x^2+12xy+9y^2-16$

41. $(x+1)(x-1)(x^2+1)$
$=(x^2-1)(x^2+1)$
$=x^4-1$

43. Discussion and Writing

45. $(a^n + b^n)(a^n - b^n) = (a^n)^2 - (b^n)^2$
$= a^{2n} - b^{2n}$

47. $(a^n + b^n)^2 = (a^n)^2 + 2 \cdot a^n \cdot b^n + (b^n)^2$
$= a^{2n} + 2a^n b^n + b^{2n}$

49. $(x-1)(x^2+x+1)(x^3+1)$
$= [(x-1)x^2 + (x-1)x + (x-1) \cdot 1](x^3+1)$
$= (x^3 - x^2 + x^2 - x + x - 1)(x^3+1)$
$= (x^3-1)(x^3+1)$
$= (x^3)^2 - 1^2$
$= x^6 - 1$

51. $(x^{a-b})^{a+b}$
$= x^{(a-b)(a+b)}$
$= x^{a^2-b^2}$

53. $(a+b+c)^2$
$= (a+b+c)(a+b+c)$
$= (a+b+c)(a) + (a+b+c)(b) + (a+b+c)(c)$
$= a^2 + ab + ac + ab + b^2 + bc + ac + bc + c^2$
$= a^2 + b^2 + c^2 + 2ab + 2ac + 2bc$

Exercise Set R.4

1. $2x - 10 = 2 \cdot x - 2 \cdot 5 = 2(x-5)$

3. $3x^4 - 9x^2 = 3x^2 \cdot x^2 - 3x^2 \cdot 3 = 3x^2(x^2-3)$

5. $4a^2 - 12a + 16 = 4 \cdot a^2 - 4 \cdot 3a + 4 \cdot 4 = 4(a^2 - 3a + 4)$

7. $a(b-2) + c(b-2) = (b-2)(a+c)$

9. $x^3 + 3x^2 + 6x + 18$
$= x^2(x+3) + 6(x+3)$
$= (x+3)(x^2+6)$

11. $y^3 - y^2 + 3y - 3$
$= y^2(y-1) + 3(y-1)$
$= (y-1)(y^2+3)$

13. $24x^3 - 36x^2 + 72x - 108$
$= 12(2x^3 - 3x^2 + 6x - 9)$
$= 12[x^2(2x-3) + 3(2x-3)]$
$= 12(2x-3)(x^2+3)$

15. $a^3 - 3a^2 - 2a + 6$
$= a^2(a-3) - 2(a-3)$
$= (a-3)(a^2-2)$

17. $x^3 - x^2 - 5x + 5$
$= x^2(x-1) - 5(x-1)$
$= (x-1)(x^2-5)$

19. $p^2 + 6p + 8$

We look for two numbers with a product of 8 and a sum of 6. By trial, we determine that they are 2 and 4.

$$p^2 + 6p + 8 = (p+2)(p+4)$$

21. $x^2 + 8x + 12$

We look for two numbers with a product of 12 and a sum of 8. By trial, we determine that they are 2 and 6.

$$x^2 + 8x + 12 = (x+2)(x+6)$$

23. $t^2 + 8t + 15$

We look for two numbers with a product of 15 and a sum of 8. By trial, we determine that they are 3 and 5.

$$t^2 + 8t + 15 = (t+3)(t+5)$$

25. $x^2 - 6xy - 27y^2$

We look for two numbers with a product of -27 and a sum of -6. By trial, we determine that they are 3 and -9.

$$x^2 - 6xy - 27y^2 = (x+3y)(x-9y)$$

27. $2n^2 - 20n - 48 = 2(n^2 - 10n - 24)$

Now factor $n^2 - 10n - 24$. We look for two numbers with a product of -24 and a sum of -10. By trial, we determine that they are 2 and -12. Then $n^2 - 10n - 24 = (n+2)(n-12)$. We must include the common factor, 2, to have a factorization of the original trinomial.

$$2n^2 - 20n - 48 = 2(n+2)(n-12)$$

29. $y^4 - 4y^2 - 21 = (y^2)^2 - 4y^2 - 21$

We look for two numbers with a product of -21 and a sum of -4. By trial, we determine that they are 3 and -7.

$$y^4 - 4y^2 - 21 = (y^2+3)(y^2-7)$$

31. $2n^2 + 9n - 56$

We use the FOIL method.

1. There is no common factor other than 1 or -1.
2. The factorization must be of the form $(2n+\quad)(n+\quad)$.
3. Factor the constant term, -56. The possibilities are $-1 \cdot 56$, $1(-56)$, $-2 \cdot 28$, $2(-28)$, $-4 \cdot 16$, $4(-16)$, $-7 \cdot 8$, and $7(-8)$. The factors can be written in the opposite order as well: $56(-1)$, $-56 \cdot 1$, $28(-2)$, $-28 \cdot 2$, $16(-4)$, $-16 \cdot 4$, $8(-7)$, and $-8 \cdot 7$.
4. Find a pair of factors for which the sum of the outside and the inside products is the middle term, $9n$. By trial, we determine that the factorization is $(2n-7)(n+8)$.

33. $12x^2 + 11x + 2$

We use the grouping method.

1. There is no common factor other than 1 or -1.
2. Multiply the leading coefficient and the constant: $12 \cdot 2 = 24$.

3. Try to factor 24 so that the sum of the factors is the coefficient of the middle term, 11. The factors we want are 3 and 8.

4. Split the middle term using the numbers found in step (3):

$$11x = 3x + 8x$$

5. Factor by grouping.

$$\begin{aligned} 12x^2 + 11x + 2 &= 12x^2 + 3x + 8x + 2 \\ &= 3x(4x+1) + 2(4x+1) \\ &= (4x+1)(3x+2) \end{aligned}$$

35. $4x^2 + 15x + 9$

We use the FOIL method.

1. There is no common factor other than 1 or -1.

2. The factorization must be of the form $(4x+ \quad)(x+ \quad)$ or $(2x+ \quad)(2x+ \quad)$.

3. Factor the constant term, 9. The possibilities are $1 \cdot 9$, $-1(-9)$, $3 \cdot 3$, and $-3(-3)$. The first two pairs of factors can be written in the opposite order as well: $9 \cdot 1$, $-9(-1)$.

4. Find a pair of factors for which the sum of the outside and the inside products is the middle term, $15x$. By trial, we determine that the factorization is $(4x+3)(x+3)$.

37. $2y^2 + y - 6$

We use the grouping method.

1. There is no common factor other than 1 or -1.

2. Multiply the leading coefficient and the constant: $2(-6) = -12$.

3. Try to factor -12 so that the sum of the factors is the coefficient of the middle term, 1. The factors we want are 4 and -3.

4. Split the middle term using the numbers found in step (3):

$$y = 4y - 3y$$

5. Factor by grouping.

$$\begin{aligned} 2y^2 + y - 6 &= 2y^2 + 4y - 3y - 6 \\ &= 2y(y+2) - 3(y+2) \\ &= (y+2)(2y-3) \end{aligned}$$

39. $6a^2 - 29ab + 28b^2$

We use the FOIL method.

1. There is no common factor other than 1 or -1.

2. The factorization must be of the form $(6x+ \quad)(x+ \quad)$ or $(3x+ \quad)(2x+ \quad)$.

3. Factor the coefficient of the last term, 28. The possibilities are $1 \cdot 28$, $-1(-28)$, $2 \cdot 14$, $-2(-14)$, $4 \cdot 7$, and $-4(-7)$. The factors can be written in the opposite order as well: $28 \cdot 1$, $-28(-1)$, $14 \cdot 2$, $-14(-2)$, $7 \cdot 4$, and $-7(-4)$.

4. Find a pair of factors for which the sum of the outside and the inside products is the middle term, -29. Observe that the second term of each binomial factor will contain a factor of b. By trial, we determine that the factorization is $(3a-4b)(2a-7b)$.

41. $12a^2 - 4a - 16$

We will use the grouping method.

1. Factor out the common factor, 4.

$$12a^2 - 4a - 16 = 4(3a^2 - a - 4)$$

2. Now consider $3a^2 - a - 4$. Multiply the leading coefficient and the constant: $3(-4) = -12$.

3. Try to factor -12 so that the sum of the factors is the coefficient of the middle term, -1. The factors we want are -4 and 3.

4. Split the middle term using the numbers found in step (3):

$$-a = -4a + 3a$$

5. Factor by grouping.

$$\begin{aligned} 3a^2 - a - 4 &= 3a^2 - 4a + 3a - 4 \\ &= a(3a-4) + (3a-4) \\ &= (3a-4)(a+1) \end{aligned}$$

We must include the common factor to get a factorization of the original trinomial.

$$12a^2 - 4a - 16 = 4(3a-4)(a+1)$$

43. $$\begin{aligned} m^2 - 4 &= m^2 - 2^2 \\ &= (m+2)(m-2) \end{aligned}$$

45. $$\begin{aligned} 9x^2 - 25 &= (3x)^2 - 5^2 \\ &= (3x+5)(3x-5) \end{aligned}$$

47. $6x^2 - 6y^2 = 6(x^2 - y^2) = 6(x+y)(x-y)$

49. $$\begin{aligned} 4xy^4 - 4xz^2 &= 4x(y^4 - z^2) \\ &= 4x[(y^2)^2 - z^2] \\ &= 4x(y^2+z)(y^2-z) \end{aligned}$$

51. $$\begin{aligned} 7pq^4 - 7py^4 &= 7p(q^4 - y^4) \\ &= 7p[(q^2)^2 - (y^2)^2] \\ &= 7p(q^2+y^2)(q^2-y^2) \\ &= 7p(q^2+y^2)(q+y)(q-y) \end{aligned}$$

53. $$\begin{aligned} y^2 - 6y + 9 &= y^2 - 2 \cdot y \cdot 3 + 3^2 \\ &= (y-3)^2 \end{aligned}$$

55. $$\begin{aligned} 4z^2 + 12z + 9 &= (2z)^2 + 2 \cdot 2z \cdot 3 + 3^2 \\ &= (2z+3)^2 \end{aligned}$$

57. $$\begin{aligned} 1 - 8x + 16x^2 &= 1^2 - 2 \cdot 1 \cdot 4x + (4x)^2 \\ &= (1-4x)^2 \end{aligned}$$

59. $a^3 + 24a^2 + 144a$
$= a(a^2 + 24a + 144)$
$= a(a^2 + 2 \cdot a \cdot 12 + 12^2)$
$= a(a + 12)^2$

61. $4p^2 - 8pq + 4q^2$
$= 4(p^2 - 2pq + q^2)$
$= 4(p - q)^2$

63. $x^3 + 8 = x^3 + 2^3$
$= (x + 2)(x^2 - 2x + 4)$

65. $m^3 - 1 = m^3 - 1^3$
$= (m - 1)(m^2 + m + 1)$

67. $2y^3 - 128 = 2(y^3 - 64)$
$= 2(y^3 - 4^3)$
$= 2(y - 4)(y^2 + 4y + 16)$

69. $3a^5 - 24a^2 = 3a^2(a^3 - 8)$
$= 3a^2(a^3 - 2^3)$
$= 3a^2(a - 2)(a^2 + 2a + 4)$

71. $t^6 + 1 = (t^2)^3 + 1^3$
$= (t^2 + 1)(t^4 - t^2 + 1)$

73. $18a^2b - 15ab^2 = 3ab \cdot 6a - 3ab \cdot 5b$
$= 3ab(6a - 5b)$

75. $x^3 - 4x^2 + 5x - 20 = x^2(x - 4) + 5(x - 4)$
$= (x - 4)(x^2 + 5)$

77. $8x^2 - 32 = 8(x^2 - 4)$
$= 8(x + 2)(x - 2)$

79. $4y^2 - 5$

There are no common factors. We might try to factor this polynomial as a difference of squares, but there is no integer which yields 5 when squared. Thus, the polynomial is prime.

81. $m^2 - 9n^2 = m^2 - (3n)^2$
$= (m + 3n)(m - 3n)$

83. $x^2 + 9x + 20$

We look for two numbers with a product of 20 and a sum of 9. They are 4 and 5.

$$x^2 + 9x + 20 = (x + 4)(x + 5)$$

85. $y^2 - 6y + 5$

We look for two numbers with a product of 5 and a sum of −6. They are −5 and −1.

$$y^2 - 6y + 5 = (y - 5)(y - 1)$$

87. $2a^2 + 9a + 4$

We use the FOIL method.

1. There is no common factor other than 1 or −1.
2. The factorization must be of the form $(2a+\quad)(a+\quad)$.
3. Factor the constant term, 4. The possibilities are $1 \cdot 4$, $-1(-4)$, and $2 \cdot 2$. The first two pairs of factors can be written in the opposite order as well: $4 \cdot 1$, $-4(-1)$.
4. Find a pair of factors for which the sum of the outside and the inside products is the middle term, $9a$. By trial, we determine that the factorization is $(2a + 1)(a + 4)$.

89. $6x^2 + 7x - 3$

We use the grouping method.

1. There is no common factor other than 1 or −1.
2. Multiply the leading coefficient and the constant: $6(-3) = -18$.
3. Try to factor −18 so that the sum of the factors is the coefficient of the middle term, 7. The factors we want are 9 and −2.
4. Split the middle term using the numbers found in step (3):
$$7x = 9x - 2x$$
5. Factor by grouping.
$$6x^2 + 7x - 3 = 6x^2 + 9x - 2x - 3$$
$$= 3x(2x + 3) - (2x + 3)$$
$$= (2x + 3)(3x - 1)$$

91. $y^2 - 18y + 81 = y^2 - 2 \cdot y \cdot 9 + 9^2$
$= (y - 9)^2$

93. $9z^2 - 24z + 16 = (3z)^2 - 2 \cdot 3z \cdot 4 + 4^2$
$= (3z - 4)^2$

95. $x^2y^2 - 14xy + 49 = (xy)^2 - 2 \cdot xy \cdot 7 + 7^2$
$= (xy - 7)^2$

97. $4ax^2 + 20ax - 56a = 4a(x^2 + 5x - 14)$
$= 4a(x + 7)(x - 2)$

99. $3z^3 - 24 = 3(z^3 - 8)$
$= 3(z^3 - 2^3)$
$= 3(z - 2)(z^2 + 2z + 4)$

101. $16a^7b + 54ab^7$
$= 2ab(8a^6 + 27b^6)$
$= 2ab[(2a^2)^3 + (3b^2)^3]$
$= 2ab(2a^2 + 3b^2)(4a^4 - 6a^2b^2 + 9b^4)$

103. $y^3 - 3y^2 - 4y + 12$
$= y^2(y - 3) - 4(y - 3)$
$= (y - 3)(y^2 - 4)$
$= (y - 3)(y + 2)(y - 2)$

105. $x^3 - x^2 + x - 1$
$= x^2(x-1) + (x-1)$
$= (x-1)(x^2+1)$

107. $5m^4 - 20 = 5(m^4 - 4)$
$= 5(m^2+2)(m^2-2)$

109. $2x^3 + 6x^2 - 8x - 24$
$= 2(x^3 + 3x^2 - 4x - 12)$
$= 2[x^2(x+3) - 4(x+3)]$
$= 2(x+3)(x^2-4)$
$= 2(x+3)(x+2)(x-2)$

111. $4c^2 - 4cd - d^2 = (2c)^2 - 2 \cdot 2c \cdot d - d^2$
$= (2c-d)^2$

113. $m^6 + 8m^3 - 20 = (m^3)^2 + 8m^3 - 20$

We look for two numbers with a product of -20 and a sum of 8. They are 10 and -2.

$m^6 + 8m^3 - 20 = (m^3+10)(m^3-2)$

115. $p - 64p^4 = p(1 - 64p^3)$
$= p[1^3 - (4p)^3]$
$= p(1+4p)(1-4p+16p^2)$

117. Discussion and Writing

119. $y^4 - 84 + 5y^2$
$= y^4 + 5y^2 - 84$
$= u^2 + 5u - 84$ Substituting u for y^2
$= (u+12)(u-7)$
$= (y^2+12)(y^2-7)$ Substituting y^2 for u

121. $y^2 - \frac{8}{49} + \frac{2}{7}y = y^2 + \frac{2}{7}y - \frac{8}{49}$
$= \left(y + \frac{4}{7}\right)\left(y - \frac{2}{7}\right)$

123. $x^2 + 3x + \frac{9}{4} = x^2 + 2 \cdot x \cdot \frac{3}{2} + \left(\frac{3}{2}\right)^2$
$= \left(x + \frac{3}{2}\right)^2$

125. $x^2 - x + \frac{1}{4} = x^2 - 2 \cdot x \cdot \frac{1}{2} + \left(\frac{1}{2}\right)^2$
$= \left(x - \frac{1}{2}\right)^2$

127. $(x+h)^3 - x^3$
$= [(x+h) - x][(x+h)^2 + x(x+h) + x^2]$
$= (x+h-x)(x^2 + 2xh + h^2 + x^2 + xh + x^2)$
$= h(3x^2 + 3xh + h^2)$

129. $(y-4)^2 + 5(y-4) - 24$
$= u^2 + 5u - 24$ Substituting u for $y-4$
$= (u+8)(u-3)$
$= (y-4+8)(y-4-3)$ Substituting $y-4$ for u
$= (y+4)(y-7)$

131. $x^{2n} + 5x^n - 24 = (x^n)^2 + 5x^n - 24$
$= (x^n+8)(x^n-3)$

133. $x^2 + ax + bx + ab = x(x+a) + b(x+a)$
$= (x+a)(x+b)$

135. $25y^{2m} - (x^{2n} - 2x^n + 1)$
$= (5y^m)^2 - (x^n - 1)^2$
$= [5y^m + (x^n - 1)][5y^m - (x^n - 1)]$
$= (5y^m + x^n - 1)(5y^m - x^n + 1)$

137. $(y-1)^4 - (y-1)^2$
$= (y-1)^2[(y-1)^2 - 1]$
$= (y-1)^2[y^2 - 2y + 1 - 1]$
$= (y-1)^2(y^2 - 2y)$
$= y(y-1)^2(y-2)$

Exercise Set R.5

1. Since $-\frac{3}{4}$ is defined for all real numbers, the domain is $\{x|x \text{ is a real number}\}$.

3. $\frac{3x-3}{x(x-1)}$

The denominator is 0 when the factor $x = 0$ and also when $x - 1 = 0$, or $x = 1$. The domain is $\{x|x \text{ is a real number } and\ x \neq 0\ and\ x \neq 1\}$.

5. $\frac{x+5}{x^2+4x-5} = \frac{x+5}{(x+5)(x-1)}$

We see that $x + 5 = 0$ when $x = -5$ and $x - 1 = 0$ when $x = 1$. Thus, the domain is $\{x|x \text{ is a real number } and\ x \neq -5\ and\ x \neq 1\}$.

7. We first factor the denominator completely.

$\frac{7x^2 - 28x + 28}{(x^2-4)(x^2+3x-10)} = \frac{7x^2 - 28x + 28}{(x+2)(x-2)(x+5)(x-2)}$

We see that $x + 2 = 0$ when $x = -2$, $x - 2 = 0$ when $x = 2$, and $x + 5 = 0$ when $x = -5$. Thus, the domain is $\{x|x \text{ is a real number } and\ x \neq -2\ and\ x \neq 2\ and\ x \neq -5\}$.

9. $\frac{x^2-y^2}{(x-y)^2} \cdot \frac{1}{x+y}$
$= \frac{(x^2-y^2) \cdot 1}{(x-y)^2(x+y)}$
$= \frac{\cancel{(x+y)}\cancel{(x-y)} \cdot 1}{\cancel{(x-y)}(x-y)\cancel{(x+y)}}$
$= \frac{1}{x-y}$

11. $\frac{x^2-2x-35}{2x^3-3x^2}\cdot\frac{4x^3-9x}{7x-49}$

$=\frac{\cancel{(x-7)}(x+5)\cancel{(x)}(2x+3)\cancel{(2x-3)}}{\cancel{x}\cdot x\cancel{(2x-3)}(7)\cancel{(x-7)}}$

$=\frac{(x+5)(2x+3)}{7x}$

13. $\frac{a^2-a-6}{a^2-7a+12}\cdot\frac{a^2-2a-8}{a^2-3a-10}$

$=\frac{\cancel{(a-3)}(a+2)\cancel{(a-4)}\cancel{(a+2)}}{\cancel{(a-4)}\cancel{(a-3)}(a-5)\cancel{(a+2)}}$

$=\frac{a+2}{a-5}$

15. $\frac{m^2-n^2}{r+s}\div\frac{m-n}{r+s}$

$=\frac{m^2-n^2}{r+s}\cdot\frac{r+s}{m-n}$

$=\frac{(m+n)\cancel{(m-n)}\cancel{(r+s)}}{\cancel{(r+s)}\cancel{(m-n)}}$

$=m+n$

17. $\frac{3x+12}{2x-8}\div\frac{(x+4)^2}{(x-4)^2}$

$=\frac{3x+12}{2x-8}\cdot\frac{(x-4)^2}{(x+4)^2}$

$=\frac{3\cancel{(x+4)}\cancel{(x-4)}(x-4)}{2\cancel{(x-4)}\cancel{(x+4)}(x+4)}$

$=\frac{3(x-4)}{2(x+4)}$

19. $\frac{x^2-y^2}{x^3-y^3}\cdot\frac{x^2+xy+y^2}{x^2+2xy+y^2}$

$=\frac{(x+y)(x-y)(x^2+xy+y^2)}{(x-y)(x^2+xy+y^2)(x+y)(x+y)}$

$=\frac{1}{x+y}\cdot\frac{(x+y)(x-y)(x^2+xy+y^2)}{(x+y)(x-y)(x^2+xy+y^2)}$

$=\frac{1}{x+y}\cdot 1$ Removing a factor of 1

$=\frac{1}{x+y}$

21. $\frac{(x-y)^2-z^2}{(x+y)^2-z^2}\div\frac{x-y+z}{x+y-z}$

$=\frac{(x-y)^2-z^2}{(x+y)^2-z^2}\cdot\frac{x+y-z}{x-y+z}$

$=\frac{(x-y+z)(x-y-z)(x+y-z)}{(x+y+z)(x+y-z)(x-y+z)}$

$=\frac{(x-y+z)(x+y-z)}{(x-y+z)(x+y-z)}\cdot\frac{x-y-z}{x+y+z}$

$=1\cdot\frac{x-y-z}{x+y+z}$ Removing a factor of 1

$=\frac{x-y-z}{x+y+z}$

23. $\frac{5}{2x}+\frac{1}{2x}=\frac{5+1}{2x}$

$=\frac{6}{2x}$

$=\frac{\cancel{2}\cdot 3}{\cancel{2}\cdot x}$

$=\frac{3}{x}$

25. $\frac{3}{2a+3}+\frac{2a}{2a+3}$

$=\frac{3+2a}{2a+3}$

$=1$

27. $\frac{5}{4z}-\frac{3}{8z}$, LCD is $8z$

$=\frac{5}{4z}\cdot\frac{2}{2}-\frac{3}{8z}$

$=\frac{10}{8z}-\frac{3}{8z}$

$=\frac{7}{8z}$

29. $\frac{3}{x+2}+\frac{2}{x^2-4}$

$=\frac{3}{x+2}+\frac{2}{(x+2)(x-2)}$, LCD is $(x+2)(x-2)$

$=\frac{3}{x+2}\cdot\frac{x-2}{x-2}+\frac{2}{(x+2)(x-2)}$

$=\frac{3x-6}{(x+2)(x-2)}+\frac{2}{(x+2)(x-2)}$

$=\frac{3x-4}{(x+2)(x-2)}$

31. $\frac{y}{y^2-y-20}-\frac{2}{y+4}$

$=\frac{y}{(y+4)(y-5)}-\frac{2}{y+4}$, LCD is $(y+4)(y-5)$

$=\frac{y}{(y+4)(y-5)}-\frac{2}{y+4}\cdot\frac{y-5}{y-5}$

$=\frac{y}{(y+4)(y-5)}-\frac{2y-10}{(y+4)(y-5)}$

$=\frac{y-(2y-10)}{(y+4)(y-5)}$

$=\frac{y-2y+10}{(y+4)(y-5)}$

$=\frac{-y+10}{(y+4)(y-5)}$

33. $$\frac{3}{x+y}+\frac{x-5y}{x^2-y^2}$$
$$=\frac{3}{x+y}+\frac{x-5y}{(x+y)(x-y)},\text{ LCD is }(x+y)(x-y)$$
$$=\frac{3}{x+y}\cdot\frac{x-y}{x-y}+\frac{x-5y}{(x+y)(x-y)}$$
$$=\frac{3x-3y}{(x+y)(x-y)}+\frac{x-5y}{(x+y)(x-y)}$$
$$=\frac{4x-8y}{(x+y)(x-y)}$$

35. $$\frac{y}{y-1}+\frac{2}{1-y}$$
$$=\frac{y}{y-1}+\frac{-1}{-1}\cdot\frac{2}{1-y}$$
$$=\frac{y}{y-1}+\frac{-2}{y-1}$$
$$=\frac{y-2}{y-1}$$

37. $$\frac{x}{2x-3y}-\frac{y}{3y-2x}$$
$$=\frac{x}{2x-3y}-\frac{-1}{-1}\cdot\frac{y}{3y-2x}$$
$$=\frac{x}{2x-3y}-\frac{-y}{2x-3y}$$
$$=\frac{x+y}{2x-3y}\qquad[x-(-y)=x+y]$$

39. $$\frac{9x+2}{3x^2-2x-8}+\frac{7}{3x^2+x-4}$$
$$=\frac{9x+2}{(3x+4)(x-2)}+\frac{7}{(3x+4)(x-1)},$$
LCD is $(3x+4)(x-2)(x-1)$
$$=\frac{9x+2}{(3x+4)(x-2)}\cdot\frac{x-1}{x-1}+\frac{7}{(3x+4)(x-1)}\cdot\frac{x-2}{x-2}$$
$$=\frac{9x^2-7x-2}{(3x+4)(x-2)(x-1)}+\frac{7x-14}{(3x+4)(x-1)(x-2)}$$
$$=\frac{9x^2-16}{(3x+4)(x-2)(x-1)}$$
$$=\frac{\cancel{(3x+4)}(3x-4)}{\cancel{(3x+4)}(x-2)(x-1)}$$
$$=\frac{3x-4}{(x-2)(x-1)}$$

41. $$\frac{5a}{a-b}+\frac{ab}{a^2-b^2}+\frac{4b}{a+b}$$
$$=\frac{5a}{a-b}+\frac{ab}{(a+b)(a-b)}+\frac{4b}{a+b},$$
LCD is $(a+b)(a-b)$
$$=\frac{5a}{a-b}\cdot\frac{a+b}{a+b}+\frac{ab}{(a+b)(a-b)}+\frac{4b}{a+b}\cdot\frac{a-b}{a-b}$$
$$=\frac{5a^2+5ab}{(a+b)(a-b)}+\frac{ab}{(a+b)(a-b)}+\frac{4ab-4b^2}{(a+b)(a-b)}$$
$$=\frac{5a^2+10ab-4b^2}{(a+b)(a-b)}$$

43. $$\frac{7}{x+2}-\frac{x+8}{4-x^2}+\frac{3x-2}{4-4x+x^2}$$
$$=\frac{7}{x+2}-\frac{x+8}{(2+x)(2-x)}+\frac{3x-2}{(2-x)^2},$$
LCD is $(2+x)(2-x)^2$
$$=\frac{7}{2+x}\cdot\frac{(2-x)^2}{(2-x)^2}-\frac{x+8}{(2+x)(2-x)}\cdot\frac{2-x}{2-x}+\frac{3x-2}{(2-x)^2}\cdot\frac{2+x}{2+x}$$
$$=\frac{28-28x+7x^2-(16-6x-x^2)+3x^2+4x-4}{(2+x)(2-x)^2}$$
$$=\frac{28-28x+7x^2-16+6x+x^2+3x^2+4x-4}{(2+x)(2-x)^2}$$
$$=\frac{11x^2-18x+8}{(2+x)(2-x)^2},\text{ or }\frac{11x^2-18x+8}{(x+2)(x-2)^2}$$

45. $$\frac{1}{x+1}+\frac{x}{2-x}+\frac{x^2+2}{x^2-x-2}$$
$$=\frac{1}{x+1}+\frac{x}{2-x}+\frac{x^2+2}{(x+1)(x-2)}$$
$$=\frac{1}{x+1}+\frac{-1}{-1}\cdot\frac{x}{2-x}+\frac{x^2+2}{(x+1)(x-2)}$$
$$=\frac{1}{x+1}+\frac{-x}{x-2}+\frac{x^2+2}{(x+1)(x-2)},$$
LCD is $(x+1)(x-2)$
$$=\frac{1}{x+1}\cdot\frac{x-2}{x-2}+\frac{-x}{x-2}\cdot\frac{x+1}{x+1}+\frac{x^2+2}{(x+1)(x-2)}$$
$$=\frac{x-2}{(x+1)(x-2)}+\frac{-x^2-x}{(x+1)(x-2)}+\frac{x^2+2}{(x+1)(x-2)}$$
$$=\frac{x-2-x^2-x+x^2+2}{(x+1)(x-2)}$$
$$=\frac{0}{(x+1)(x-2)}$$
$$=0$$

47. $$\frac{\dfrac{x^2-y^2}{xy}}{\dfrac{x-y}{y}}=\frac{x^2-y^2}{xy}\cdot\frac{y}{x-y}$$
$$=\frac{(x+y)\cancel{(x-y)}\cancel{y}}{x\cancel{y}\cancel{(x-y)}}$$
$$=\frac{x+y}{x}$$

49. $$\frac{\frac{x}{y}-\frac{y}{x}}{\frac{1}{y}+\frac{1}{x}} = \frac{\frac{x}{y}-\frac{y}{x}}{\frac{1}{y}+\frac{1}{x}}\cdot\frac{xy}{xy}, \text{ LCM is } xy$$
$$= \frac{\left(\frac{x}{y}-\frac{y}{x}\right)(xy)}{\left(\frac{1}{y}+\frac{1}{x}\right)(xy)}$$
$$= \frac{x^2-y^2}{x+y}$$
$$= \frac{\cancel{(x+y)}(x-y)}{\cancel{(x+y)}\cdot 1}$$
$$= x-y$$

51. $$\frac{c+\frac{8}{c^2}}{1+\frac{2}{c}} = \frac{c\cdot\frac{c^2}{c^2}+\frac{8}{c^2}}{1\cdot\frac{c}{c}+\frac{2}{c}}$$
$$= \frac{\frac{c^3+8}{c^2}}{\frac{c+2}{c}}$$
$$= \frac{c^3+8}{c^2}\cdot\frac{c}{c+2}$$
$$= \frac{\cancel{(c+2)}(c^2-2c+4)\cancel{c}}{\cancel{c}\cdot c\cancel{(c+2)}}$$
$$= \frac{c^2-2c+4}{c}$$

53. $$\frac{x^2+xy+y^2}{\frac{x^2}{y}-\frac{y^2}{x}} = \frac{x^2+xy+y^2}{\frac{x^2}{y}\cdot\frac{x}{x}-\frac{y^2}{x}\cdot\frac{y}{y}}$$
$$= \frac{x^2+xy+y^2}{\frac{x^3-y^3}{xy}}$$
$$= (x^2+xy+y^2)\cdot\frac{xy}{x^3-y^3}$$
$$= \frac{(x^2+xy+y^2)(xy)}{(x-y)(x^2+xy+y^2)}$$
$$= \frac{x^2+xy+y^2}{x^2+xy+y^2}\cdot\frac{xy}{x-y}$$
$$= 1\cdot\frac{xy}{x-y}$$
$$= \frac{xy}{x-y}$$

55. $$\frac{a-a^{-1}}{a+a^{-1}} = \frac{a-\frac{1}{a}}{a+\frac{1}{a}} = \frac{a\cdot\frac{a}{a}-\frac{1}{a}}{a\cdot\frac{a}{a}+\frac{1}{a}}$$
$$= \frac{\frac{a^2-1}{a}}{\frac{a^2+1}{a}}$$
$$= \frac{a^2-1}{a}\cdot\frac{a}{a^2+1}$$
$$= \frac{a^2-1}{a^2+1}$$

57. $$\frac{\frac{1}{x-3}+\frac{2}{x+3}}{\frac{3}{x-1}-\frac{4}{x+2}} = \frac{\frac{1}{x-3}\cdot\frac{x+3}{x+3}+\frac{2}{x+3}\cdot\frac{x-3}{x-3}}{\frac{3}{x-1}\cdot\frac{x+2}{x+2}-\frac{4}{x+2}\cdot\frac{x-1}{x-1}}$$
$$= \frac{\frac{x+3+2(x-3)}{(x-3)(x+3)}}{\frac{3(x+2)-4(x-1)}{(x-1)(x+2)}}$$
$$= \frac{\frac{x+3+2x-6}{(x-3)(x+3)}}{\frac{3x+6-4x+4}{(x-1)(x+2)}}$$
$$= \frac{\frac{3x-3}{(x-3)(x+3)}}{\frac{-x+10}{(x-1)(x+2)}}$$
$$= \frac{3x-3}{(x-3)(x+3)}\cdot\frac{(x-1)(x+2)}{-x+10}$$
$$= \frac{(3x-3)(x-1)(x+2)}{(x-3)(x+3)(-x+10)}, \text{ or}$$
$$\frac{3(x-1)^2(x+2)}{(x-3)(x+3)(-x+10)}$$

59. $$\frac{\frac{a}{1-a}+\frac{1+a}{a}}{\frac{1-a}{a}+\frac{a}{1+a}} = \frac{\frac{a}{1-a}\cdot\frac{a}{a}+\frac{1+a}{a}\cdot\frac{1-a}{1-a}}{\frac{1-a}{a}\cdot\frac{1+a}{1+a}+\frac{a}{1+a}\cdot\frac{a}{a}}$$
$$= \frac{\frac{a^2+(1-a^2)}{a(1-a)}}{\frac{(1-a^2)+a^2}{a(1+a)}}$$
$$= \frac{1}{\cancel{a}(1-a)}\cdot\frac{\cancel{a}(1+a)}{1}$$
$$= \frac{1+a}{1-a}$$

61. $$\frac{\frac{1}{a^2}+\frac{2}{ab}+\frac{1}{b^2}}{\frac{1}{a^2}-\frac{1}{b^2}} = \frac{\frac{1}{a^2}+\frac{2}{ab}+\frac{1}{b^2}}{\frac{1}{a^2}-\frac{1}{b^2}}\cdot\frac{a^2b^2}{a^2b^2},$$

LCM is a^2b^2

$$= \frac{b^2+2ab+a^2}{b^2-a^2}$$
$$= \frac{(b+a)(b+a)}{(b+a)(b-a)}$$
$$= \frac{b+a}{b-a}$$

63. Discussion and Writing

65. $$\frac{(x+h)^2-x^2}{h} = \frac{x^2+2xh+h^2-x^2}{h}$$
$$= \frac{2xh+h^2}{h}$$
$$= \frac{h(2x+h)}{h\cdot 1}$$
$$= 2x+h$$

67. $$\frac{(x+h)^3-x^3}{h} = \frac{x^3+3x^2h+3xh^2+h^3-x^3}{h}$$
$$= \frac{3x^2h+3xh^2+h^3}{h}$$
$$= \frac{h(3x^2+3xh+h^2)}{h\cdot 1}$$
$$= 3x^2+3xh+h^2$$

69. $$\left[\frac{\frac{x+1}{x-1}+1}{\frac{x+1}{x-1}-1}\right]^5 = \left[\frac{\frac{(x+1)+(x-1)}{x-1}}{\frac{(x+1)-(x-1)}{x-1}}\right]^5$$
$$= \left[\frac{2x}{x-1}\cdot\frac{x-1}{2}\right]^5$$
$$= \left[\frac{2x(x-1)}{1\cdot 2(x-1)}\right]^5$$
$$= x^5$$

71. $$\frac{n(n+1)(n+2)}{2\cdot 3}+\frac{(n+1)(n+2)}{2}$$
$$= \frac{n(n+1)(n+2)}{2\cdot 3}+\frac{(n+1)(n+2)}{2}\cdot\frac{3}{3},$$

LCD is $2\cdot 3$

$$= \frac{n(n+1)(n+2)+3(n+1)(n+2)}{2\cdot 3}$$
$$= \frac{(n+1)(n+2)(n+3)}{2\cdot 3}$$ Factoring the numerator by grouping

73. $$\frac{x^2-9}{x^3+27}\cdot\frac{5x^2-15x+45}{x^2-2x-3}+\frac{x^2+x}{4+2x}$$
$$= \frac{(x+3)(x-3)(5)(x^2-3x+9)}{(x+3)(x^2-3x+9)(x-3)(x+1)}+\frac{x^2+x}{4+2x}$$
$$= \frac{(x+3)(x-3)(x^2-3x+9)}{(x+3)(x-3)(x^2-3x+9)}\cdot\frac{5}{x+1}+\frac{x^2+x}{4+2x}$$
$$= 1\cdot\frac{5}{x+1}+\frac{x^2+x}{4+2x}$$
$$= \frac{5}{x+1}+\frac{x^2+x}{2(2+x)}$$
$$= \frac{5\cdot 2(2+x)+(x^2+x)(x+1)}{2(x+1)(2+x)}$$
$$= \frac{20+10x+x^3+2x^2+x}{2(x+1)(2+x)}$$
$$= \frac{x^3+2x^2+11x+20}{2(x+1)(2+x)}$$

Exercise Set R.6

1. $\sqrt{(-11)^2} = |-11| = 11$

3. $\sqrt{16y^2} = \sqrt{(4y)^2} = |4y| = 4|y|$

5. $\sqrt{(b+1)^2} = |b+1|$

7. $\sqrt[3]{-27x^3} = \sqrt[3]{(-3x)^3} = -3x$

9. $\sqrt[4]{81x^8} = \sqrt[4]{(3x^2)^4} = |3x^2| = 3x^2$

11. $\sqrt[5]{32} = \sqrt[5]{2^5} = 2$

13. $\sqrt{180} = \sqrt{36\cdot 5} = \sqrt{36}\cdot\sqrt{5} = 6\sqrt{5}$

15. $\sqrt{72} = \sqrt{36\cdot 2} = \sqrt{36}\cdot\sqrt{2} = 6\sqrt{2}$

17. $\sqrt[3]{54} = \sqrt[3]{27\cdot 2} = \sqrt[3]{27}\cdot\sqrt[3]{2} = 3\sqrt[3]{2}$

19. $\sqrt{128c^2d^4} = \sqrt{64c^2d^4\cdot 2} = |8cd^2|\sqrt{2} = 8\sqrt{2}\,|c|d^2$

21. $\sqrt[4]{48x^6y^4} = \sqrt[4]{16x^4y^4\cdot 3x^2} = |2xy|\sqrt[4]{3x^2} = 2|x||y|\sqrt[4]{3x^2}$

23. $\sqrt{x^2-4x+4} = \sqrt{(x-2)^2} = |x-2|$

25. $\sqrt{10}\sqrt{30} = \sqrt{10\cdot 30} = \sqrt{300} = \sqrt{100\cdot 3} = \sqrt{100}\cdot\sqrt{3} = 10\sqrt{3}$

27. $\sqrt{12}\sqrt{33} = \sqrt{12\cdot 33} = \sqrt{3\cdot 4\cdot 3\cdot 11} = \sqrt{3^2\cdot 4\cdot 11} = 3\cdot 2\sqrt{11} = 6\sqrt{11}$

29. $\sqrt{2x^3y}\sqrt{12xy} = \sqrt{24x^4y^2} = \sqrt{4x^4y^2\cdot 6} = 2x^2y\sqrt{6}$

31. $\sqrt[3]{3x^2y}\sqrt[3]{36x} = \sqrt[3]{108x^3y} = \sqrt[3]{27x^3\cdot 4y} = 3x\sqrt[3]{4y}$

33. $$\sqrt[3]{2(x+4)}\,\sqrt[3]{4(x+4)^4} = \sqrt[3]{8(x+4)^5}$$
$$= \sqrt[3]{8(x+4)^3\cdot(x+4)^2}$$
$$= 2(x+4)\sqrt[3]{(x+4)^2}$$

35. $\sqrt[6]{\dfrac{m^{12}n^{24}}{64}} = \sqrt[6]{\left(\dfrac{m^2n^4}{2}\right)^6} = \dfrac{m^2n^4}{2}$

37. $\dfrac{\sqrt[3]{40m}}{\sqrt[3]{5m}} = \sqrt[3]{\dfrac{40m}{5m}} = \sqrt[3]{8} = 2$

39. $\dfrac{\sqrt[3]{3x^2}}{\sqrt[3]{24x^5}} = \sqrt[3]{\dfrac{3x^2}{24x^5}} = \sqrt[3]{\dfrac{1}{8x^3}} = \dfrac{1}{2x}$

41.
$$\sqrt[3]{\frac{64a^4}{27b^3}} = \sqrt[3]{\frac{64\cdot a^3\cdot a}{27\cdot b^3}}$$
$$= \frac{\sqrt[3]{64a^3}\,\sqrt[3]{a}}{\sqrt[3]{27b^3}}$$
$$= \frac{4a\sqrt[3]{a}}{3b}$$

43.
$$\sqrt{\frac{7x^3}{36y^6}} = \sqrt{\frac{7\cdot x^2\cdot x}{36\cdot y^6}}$$
$$= \frac{\sqrt{x^2}\sqrt{7x}}{\sqrt{36y^6}}$$
$$= \frac{x\sqrt{7x}}{6y^3}$$

45.
$$9\sqrt{50} + 6\sqrt{2} = 9\sqrt{25\cdot 2} + 6\sqrt{2}$$
$$= 9\cdot 5\sqrt{2} + 6\sqrt{2}$$
$$= 45\sqrt{2} + 6\sqrt{2}$$
$$= (45+6)\sqrt{2}$$
$$= 51\sqrt{2}$$

47.
$$6\sqrt{20} - 4\sqrt{45} + \sqrt{80} = 6\sqrt{4\cdot 5} - 4\sqrt{9\cdot 5} + \sqrt{16\cdot 5}$$
$$= 6\cdot 2\sqrt{5} - 4\cdot 3\sqrt{5} + 4\sqrt{5}$$
$$= 12\sqrt{5} - 12\sqrt{5} + 4\sqrt{5}$$
$$= (12-12+4)\sqrt{5}$$
$$= 4\sqrt{5}$$

49.
$$8\sqrt{2x^2} - 6\sqrt{20x} - 5\sqrt{8x^2}$$
$$= 8x\sqrt{2} - 6\sqrt{4\cdot 5x} - 5\sqrt{4x^2\cdot 2}$$
$$= 8x\sqrt{2} - 6\cdot 2\sqrt{5x} - 5\cdot 2x\sqrt{2}$$
$$= 8x\sqrt{2} - 12\sqrt{5x} - 10x\sqrt{2}$$
$$= -2x\sqrt{2} - 12\sqrt{5x}$$

51.
$$(\sqrt{3}-\sqrt{2})(\sqrt{3}+\sqrt{2})$$
$$= (\sqrt{3})^2 - (\sqrt{2})^2$$
$$= 3 - 2$$
$$= 1$$

53.
$$(2\sqrt{3}+\sqrt{5})(\sqrt{3}-3\sqrt{5})$$
$$= 2\sqrt{3}\cdot\sqrt{3} - 2\sqrt{3}\cdot 3\sqrt{5} + \sqrt{5}\cdot\sqrt{3} - \sqrt{5}\cdot 3\sqrt{5}$$
$$= 2\cdot 3 - 6\sqrt{15} + \sqrt{15} - 3\cdot 5$$
$$= 6 - 6\sqrt{15} + \sqrt{15} - 15$$
$$= -9 - 5\sqrt{15}$$

55.
$$(1+\sqrt{3})^2 = 1^2 + 2\cdot 1\cdot\sqrt{3} + (\sqrt{3})^2$$
$$= 1 + 2\sqrt{3} + 3$$
$$= 4 + 2\sqrt{3}$$

57.
$$(\sqrt{5}-\sqrt{6})^2 = (\sqrt{5})^2 - 2\sqrt{5}\cdot\sqrt{6} + (\sqrt{6})^2$$
$$= 5 - 2\sqrt{30} + 6$$
$$= 11 - 2\sqrt{30}$$

59. We use the Pythagorean theorem to find b, the airplane's horizontal distance from the airport. We have $a = 3700$ and $c = 14,200$.

$$c^2 = a^2 + b^2$$
$$14,200^2 = 3700^2 + b^2$$
$$201,640,000 = 13,690,000 + b^2$$
$$187,950,000 = b^2$$
$$13,709.5 \approx b$$

The airplane is about 13,709.5 ft horizontally from the airport.

61. a) $h^2 + \left(\dfrac{a}{2}\right)^2 = a^2$ Pythagorean theorem

$$h^2 + \frac{a^2}{4} = a^2$$
$$h^2 = \frac{3a^2}{4}$$
$$h = \sqrt{\frac{3a^2}{4}}$$
$$h = \frac{a}{2}\sqrt{3}$$

b) Using the result of part (a) we have

$$A = \frac{1}{2}\cdot \text{ base } \cdot \text{ height}$$
$$A = \frac{1}{2}a\cdot\frac{a}{2}\sqrt{3} \quad \left(\frac{a}{2}+\frac{a}{2}=a\right)$$
$$A = \frac{a^2}{4}\sqrt{3}$$

63.

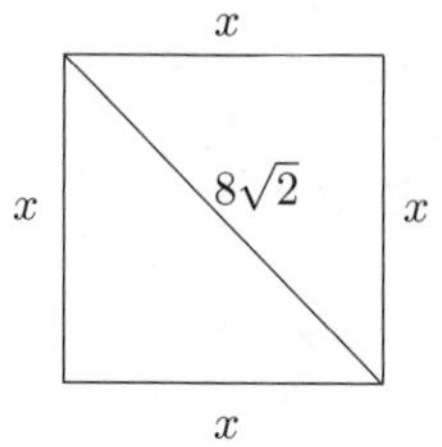

$$x^2 + x^2 = (8\sqrt{2})^2 \quad \text{Pythagorean theorem}$$
$$2x^2 = 128$$
$$x^2 = 64$$
$$x = 8$$

65. $\sqrt{\dfrac{2}{3}} = \sqrt{\dfrac{2}{3}\cdot\dfrac{3}{3}} = \sqrt{\dfrac{6}{9}} = \dfrac{\sqrt{6}}{\sqrt{9}} = \dfrac{\sqrt{6}}{3}$

67. $\dfrac{\sqrt[3]{5}}{\sqrt[3]{4}} = \dfrac{\sqrt[3]{5}}{\sqrt[3]{4}}\cdot\dfrac{\sqrt[3]{2}}{\sqrt[3]{2}} = \dfrac{\sqrt[3]{10}}{\sqrt[3]{8}} = \dfrac{\sqrt[3]{10}}{2}$

69. $\sqrt[3]{\dfrac{16}{9}} = \sqrt[3]{\dfrac{16}{9}\cdot\dfrac{3}{3}} = \sqrt[3]{\dfrac{48}{27}} = \dfrac{\sqrt[3]{48}}{\sqrt[3]{27}} =$

$\dfrac{\sqrt[3]{8\cdot 6}}{3} = \dfrac{2\sqrt[3]{6}}{3}$

71. $\dfrac{6}{3+\sqrt{5}} = \dfrac{6}{3+\sqrt{5}} \cdot \dfrac{3-\sqrt{5}}{3-\sqrt{5}}$
$= \dfrac{6(3-\sqrt{5})}{9-5}$
$= \dfrac{6(3-\sqrt{5})}{4}$
$= \dfrac{3(3-\sqrt{5})}{2} = \dfrac{9-3\sqrt{5}}{2}$

73. $\dfrac{1-\sqrt{2}}{2\sqrt{3}-\sqrt{6}} = \dfrac{1-\sqrt{2}}{2\sqrt{3}-\sqrt{6}} \cdot \dfrac{2\sqrt{3}+\sqrt{6}}{2\sqrt{3}+\sqrt{6}}$
$= \dfrac{2\sqrt{3}+\sqrt{6}-2\sqrt{6}-\sqrt{12}}{4\cdot 3-6}$
$= \dfrac{2\sqrt{3}+\sqrt{6}-2\sqrt{6}-2\sqrt{3}}{12-6}$
$= \dfrac{-\sqrt{6}}{6}$, or $-\dfrac{\sqrt{6}}{6}$

75. $\dfrac{6}{\sqrt{m}-\sqrt{n}} = \dfrac{6}{\sqrt{m}-\sqrt{n}} \cdot \dfrac{\sqrt{m}+\sqrt{n}}{\sqrt{m}+\sqrt{n}}$
$= \dfrac{6(\sqrt{m}+\sqrt{n})}{(\sqrt{m})^2-(\sqrt{n})^2}$
$= \dfrac{6\sqrt{m}+6\sqrt{n}}{m-n}$

77. $\dfrac{\sqrt{12}}{5} = \dfrac{\sqrt{12}}{5} \cdot \dfrac{\sqrt{3}}{\sqrt{3}} = \dfrac{\sqrt{36}}{5\sqrt{3}} = \dfrac{6}{5\sqrt{3}}$

79. $\sqrt[3]{\dfrac{7}{2}} = \sqrt[3]{\dfrac{7}{2}\cdot\dfrac{49}{49}} = \sqrt[3]{\dfrac{343}{98}} = \dfrac{\sqrt[3]{343}}{\sqrt[3]{98}} = \dfrac{7}{\sqrt[3]{98}}$

81. $\dfrac{\sqrt{11}}{\sqrt{3}} = \dfrac{\sqrt{11}}{\sqrt{3}} \cdot \dfrac{\sqrt{11}}{\sqrt{11}} = \dfrac{\sqrt{121}}{\sqrt{33}} = \dfrac{11}{\sqrt{33}}$

83. $\dfrac{9-\sqrt{5}}{3-\sqrt{3}} = \dfrac{9-\sqrt{5}}{3-\sqrt{3}} \cdot \dfrac{9+\sqrt{5}}{9+\sqrt{5}}$
$= \dfrac{9^2-(\sqrt{5})^2}{27+3\sqrt{5}-9\sqrt{3}-\sqrt{15}}$
$= \dfrac{81-5}{27+3\sqrt{5}-9\sqrt{3}-\sqrt{15}}$
$= \dfrac{76}{27+3\sqrt{5}-9\sqrt{3}-\sqrt{15}}$

85. $\dfrac{\sqrt{a}+\sqrt{b}}{3a} = \dfrac{\sqrt{a}+\sqrt{b}}{3a} \cdot \dfrac{\sqrt{a}-\sqrt{b}}{\sqrt{a}-\sqrt{b}}$
$= \dfrac{(\sqrt{a})^2-(\sqrt{b})^2}{3a(\sqrt{a}-\sqrt{b})}$
$= \dfrac{a-b}{3a\sqrt{a}-3a\sqrt{b}}$

87. $x^{3/4} = \sqrt[4]{x^3}$

89. $16^{3/4} = (16^{1/4})^3 = \left(\sqrt[4]{16}\right)^3 = 2^3 = 8$

91. $125^{-1/3} = \dfrac{1}{125^{1/3}} = \dfrac{1}{\sqrt[3]{125}} = \dfrac{1}{5}$

93. $a^{5/4}b^{-3/4} = \dfrac{a^{5/4}}{b^{3/4}} = \dfrac{\sqrt[4]{a^5}}{\sqrt[4]{b^3}} = \dfrac{a\sqrt[4]{a}}{\sqrt[4]{b^3}}$, or $a\sqrt[4]{\dfrac{a}{b^3}}$

95. $m^{5/3}n^{7/3} = \sqrt[3]{m^5}\sqrt[3]{n^7} = \sqrt[3]{m^5n^7} = mn^2\sqrt[3]{m^2n}$

97. $\left(\sqrt[4]{13}\right)^5 = \sqrt[4]{13^5} = 13^{5/4}$

99. $\sqrt[3]{20^2} = 20^{2/3}$

101. $\sqrt[3]{\sqrt{11}} = \left(\sqrt{11}\right)^{1/3} = (11^{1/2})^{1/3} = 11^{1/6}$

103. $\sqrt{5}\sqrt[3]{5} = 5^{1/2}\cdot 5^{1/3} = 5^{1/2+1/3} = 5^{5/6}$

105. $\sqrt[5]{32^2} = 32^{2/5} = (32^{1/5})^2 = 2^2 = 4$

107. $(2a^{3/2})(4a^{1/2}) = 8a^{3/2+1/2} = 8a^2$

109. $\left(\dfrac{x^6}{9b^{-4}}\right)^{1/2} = \left(\dfrac{x^6}{3^2b^{-4}}\right)^{1/2} = \dfrac{x^3}{3b^{-2}}$, or $\dfrac{x^3b^2}{3}$

111. $\dfrac{x^{2/3}y^{5/6}}{x^{-1/3}y^{1/2}} = x^{2/3-(-1/3)}y^{5/6-1/2} = xy^{1/3} = x\sqrt[3]{y}$

113. $(m^{1/2}n^{5/2})^{2/3} = m^{\frac{1}{2}\cdot\frac{2}{3}}n^{\frac{5}{2}\cdot\frac{2}{3}} = m^{1/3}n^{5/3} =$
$\sqrt[3]{m}\sqrt[3]{n^5} = \sqrt[3]{mn^5} = n\sqrt[3]{mn^2}$

115. $a^{3/4}(a^{2/3}+a^{4/3}) = a^{3/4+2/3}+a^{3/4+4/3} =$
$a^{17/12}+a^{25/12} = \sqrt[12]{a^{17}}+\sqrt[12]{a^{25}} =$
$a\sqrt[12]{a^5}+a^2\sqrt[12]{a}$

117. $\sqrt[3]{6}\sqrt{2} = 6^{1/3}2^{1/2} = 6^{2/6}2^{3/6}$
$= (6^22^3)^{1/6}$
$= \sqrt[6]{36\cdot 8}$
$= \sqrt[6]{288}$

119. $\sqrt[4]{xy}\sqrt[3]{x^2y} = (xy)^{1/4}(x^2y)^{1/3} = (xy)^{3/12}(x^2y)^{4/12}$
$= \left[(xy)^3(x^2y)^4\right]^{1/12}$
$= \left[x^3y^3x^8y^4\right]^{1/12}$
$= \sqrt[12]{x^{11}y^7}$

121. $\sqrt[3]{a^4\sqrt{a^3}} = \left(a^4\sqrt{a^3}\right)^{1/3} = (a^4a^{3/2})^{1/3}$
$= (a^{11/2})^{1/3}$
$= a^{11/6}$
$= \sqrt[6]{a^{11}}$
$= a\sqrt[6]{a^5}$

123. $\dfrac{\sqrt{(a+x)^3}\sqrt[3]{(a+x)^2}}{\sqrt[4]{a+x}} = \dfrac{(a+x)^{3/2}(a+x)^{2/3}}{(a+x)^{1/4}}$
$= \dfrac{(a+x)^{26/12}}{(a+x)^{3/12}}$
$= (a+x)^{23/12}$
$= \sqrt[12]{(a+x)^{23}}$
$= (a+x)\sqrt[12]{(a+x)^{11}}$

125. Discussion and Writing

127. $\sqrt{1+x^2}+\dfrac{1}{\sqrt{1+x^2}}$

$$= \sqrt{1+x^2}\cdot\frac{1+x^2}{1+x^2}+\frac{1}{\sqrt{1+x^2}}\cdot\frac{\sqrt{1+x^2}}{\sqrt{1+x^2}}$$

$$= \frac{(1+x^2)\sqrt{1+x^2}}{1+x^2}+\frac{\sqrt{1+x^2}}{1+x^2}$$

$$= \frac{(2+x^2)\sqrt{1+x^2}}{1+x^2}$$

129. $\left(\sqrt{a^{\sqrt{a}}}\right)^{\sqrt{a}} = \left(a^{\sqrt{a}/2}\right)^{\sqrt{a}} = a^{a/2}$

Chapter 1

Graphs, Functions, and Models

Exercise Set 1.1

1. To graph $(4, 0)$ we move from the origin 4 units to the right of the y-axis. Since the second coordinate is 0, we do not move up or down from the x-axis.

To graph $(-3, -5)$ we move from the origin 3 units to the left of the y-axis. Then we move 5 units down from the x-axis.

To graph $(-1, 4)$ we move from the origin 1 unit to the left of the y-axis. Then we move 4 units up from the x-axis.

To graph $(0, 2)$ we do not move to the right or the left of the y-axis since the first coordinate is 0. From the origin we move 2 units up.

To graph $(2, -2)$ we move from the origin 2 units to the right of the y-axis. Then we move 2 units down from the x-axis.

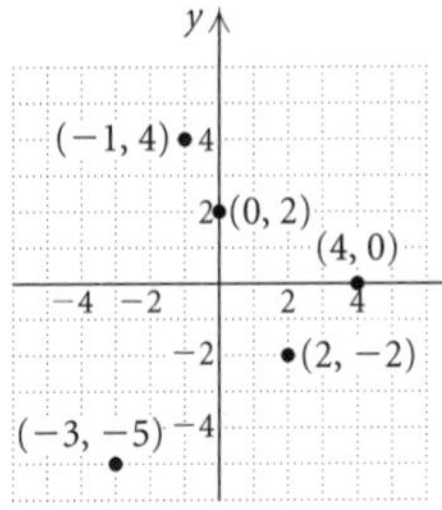

3. To graph $(-5, 1)$ we move from the origin 5 units to the left of the y-axis. Then we move 1 unit up from the x-axis.

To graph $(5, 1)$ we move from the origin 5 units to the right of the y-axis. Then we move 1 unit up from the x-axis.

To graph $(2, 3)$ we move from the origin 2 units to the right of the y-axis. Then we move 3 units up from the x-axis.

To graph $(2, -1)$ we move from the origin 2 units to the right of the y-axis. Then we move 1 unit down from the x-axis.

To graph $(0, 1)$ we do not move to the right or the left of the y-axis since the first coordinate is 0. From the origin we move 1 unit up.

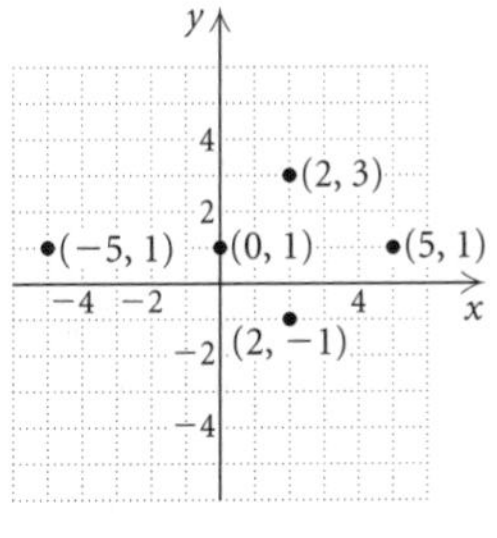

5. The first coordinate represents the year and the corresponding second coordinate represents the amount of sales. The ordered pairs are (1998, \$14 billion), (1999, \$19 billion), (2000, \$25 billion), (2001, \$32 billion), and (2002, \$38 billion).

7. To determine whether $(1, -1)$ is a solution, substitute 1 for x and -1 for y.

$$\begin{array}{c|c} \multicolumn{2}{c}{y = 2x - 3} \\ \hline -1 \ ? & 2 \cdot 1 - 3 \\ & 2 - 3 \\ -1 & -1 \quad \text{TRUE} \end{array}$$

The equation $-1 = -1$ is true, so $(1, -1)$ is a solution.

To determine whether $(0, 3)$ is a solution, substitute 0 for x and -3 for y.

$$\begin{array}{c|c} \multicolumn{2}{c}{y = 2x - 3} \\ \hline 3 \ ? & 2 \cdot 0 - 3 \\ & 0 - 3 \\ 3 & -3 \quad \text{FALSE} \end{array}$$

The equation $3 = -3$ is false, so $(0, 3)$ is not a solution.

9. To determine whether $\left(\frac{2}{3}, \frac{3}{4}\right)$ is a solution, substitute $\frac{2}{3}$ for x and $\frac{3}{4}$ for y.

$$\begin{array}{c|c} \multicolumn{2}{c}{6x - 4y = 1} \\ \hline 6 \cdot \frac{2}{3} - 4 \cdot \frac{3}{4} & ? \ 1 \\ 4 - 3 & \\ 1 & 1 \quad \text{TRUE} \end{array}$$

The equation $1 = 1$ is true, so $\left(\frac{2}{3}, \frac{3}{4}\right)$ is a solution.

To determine whether $\left(1, \frac{3}{2}\right)$ is a solution, substitute 1 for x and $\frac{3}{2}$ for y.

$$\begin{array}{c|c} \multicolumn{2}{c}{6x - 4y = 1} \\ \hline 6 \cdot 1 - 4 \cdot \frac{3}{2} & ? \ 1 \\ 6 - 6 & \\ 0 & 1 \quad \text{FALSE} \end{array}$$

The equation $0 = 1$ is false, so $\left(1, \frac{3}{2}\right)$ is not a solution.

11. To determine whether $\left(-\frac{1}{2}, -\frac{4}{5}\right)$ is a solution, substitute $-\frac{1}{2}$ for a and $-\frac{4}{5}$ for b.

$$\begin{array}{c|l} 2a+5b & = 3 \\ \hline 2\left(-\frac{1}{2}\right)+5\left(-\frac{4}{5}\right) & ?\ 3 \\ -1-4 & \\ -5 & 3 \quad \text{FALSE} \end{array}$$

The equation $-5 = 3$ is false, so $\left(-\frac{1}{2}, -\frac{4}{5}\right)$ is not a solution.

To determine whether $\left(0, \frac{3}{5}\right)$ is a solution, substitute 0 for a and $\frac{3}{5}$ for b.

$$\begin{array}{c|l} 2a+5b & = 3 \\ \hline 2\cdot 0+5\cdot\frac{3}{5} & ?\ 3 \\ 0+3 & \\ 3 & 3 \quad \text{TRUE} \end{array}$$

The equation $3 = 3$ is true, so $\left(0, \frac{3}{5}\right)$ is a solution.

13. To determine whether $(-0.75, 2.75)$ is a solution, substitute -0.75 for x and 2.75 for y.

$$\begin{array}{c|l} x^2-y^2 & = 3 \\ \hline (-0.75)^2-(2.75)^2 & ?\ 3 \\ 0.5625-7.5625 & \\ -7 & 3 \quad \text{FALSE} \end{array}$$

The equation $-7 = 3$ is false, so $(-0.75, 2.75)$ is not a solution.

To determine whether $(2, -1)$ is a solution, substitute 2 for x and -1 for y.

$$\begin{array}{c|l} x^2-y^2 & = 3 \\ \hline 2^2-(-1)^2 & ?\ 3 \\ 4-1 & \\ 3 & 3 \quad \text{TRUE} \end{array}$$

The equation $3 = 3$ is true, so $(2, -1)$ is a solution.

15. Graph $y = 3x + 5$.

We choose some values for x and find the corresponding y-values.

When $x = -3$, $y = 3x + 5 = 3(-3) + 5 = -9 + 5 = -4$.

When $x = -1$, $y = 3x + 5 = 3(-1) + 5 = -3 + 5 = 2$.

When $x = 0$, $y = 3x + 5 = 3 \cdot 0 + 5 = 0 + 5 = 5$

We list these points in a table, plot them, and draw the graph.

x	y	(x, y)
-3	-4	$(-3, -4)$
-1	2	$(-1, 2)$
0	5	$(0, 5)$

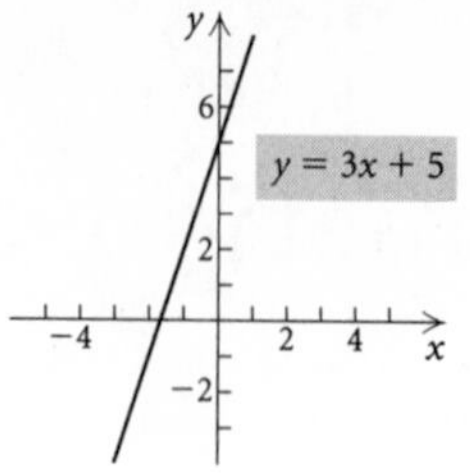

17. Graph $x - y = 3$.

Make a table of values, plot the points in the table, and draw the graph.

x	y	(x, y)
-2	-5	$(-2, -5)$
0	-3	$(0, -3)$
3	0	$(3, 0)$

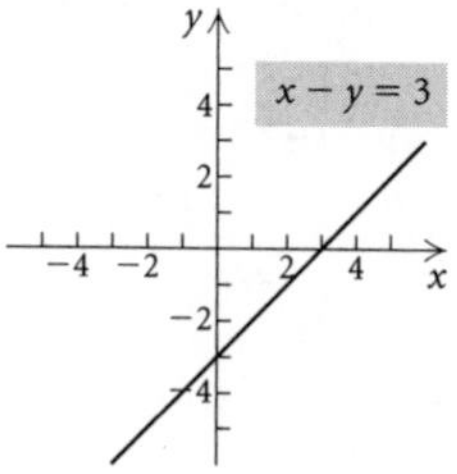

19. Graph $2x + y = 4$.

We could solve for y first.

$2x + y = 4$

$y = -2x + 4$ Subtracting $2x$ on both sides

Make a table of values, plot the points in the table, and draw the graph.

x	y	(x, y)
-1	6	$(-1, 6)$
0	4	$(0, 4)$
2	0	$(2, 0)$

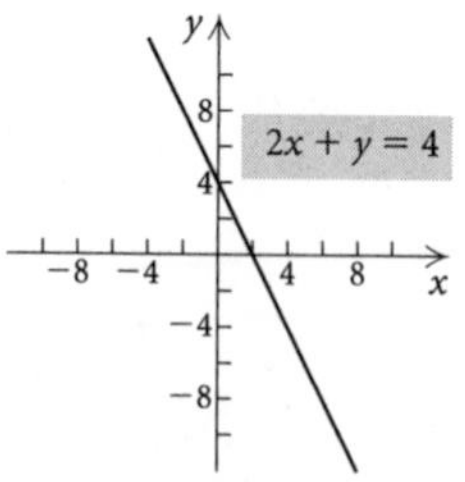

21. Graph $y = -\frac{3}{4}x + 3$.

By choosing multiples of 4 for x, we can avoid fraction values for y. Make a table of values, plot the points in the table, and draw the graph.

x	y	(x,y)
-4	6	$(-4,6)$
0	3	$(0,3)$
4	0	$(4,0)$

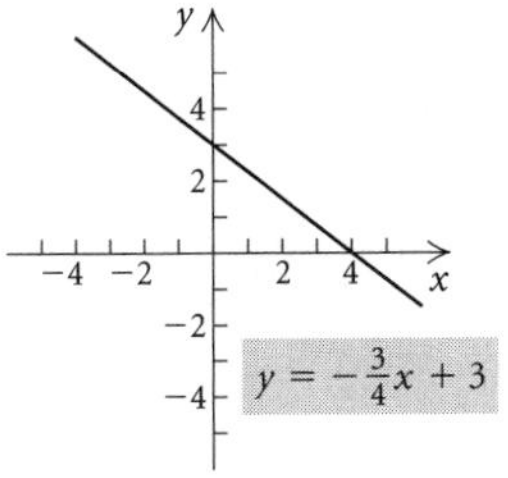

23. Graph $5x - 2y = 8$.

We could solve for y first.

$5x - 2y = 8$

$-2y = -5x + 8$ Subtracting $5x$ on both sides

$y = \frac{5}{2}x - 4$ Multiplying by $-\frac{1}{2}$ on both sides

By choosing multiples of 2 for x we can avoid fraction values for y. Make a table of values, plot the points in the table, and draw the graph.

x	y	(x,y)
0	-4	$(0,-4)$
2	1	$(2,1)$
4	6	$(4,6)$

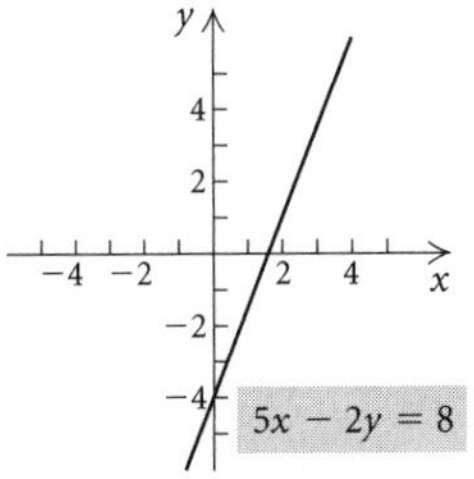

25. Graph $x - 4y = 5$.

Make a table of values, plot the points in the table, and draw the graph.

x	y	(x,y)
-3	-2	$(-3,-2)$
1	-1	$(1,-1)$
5	0	$(5,0)$

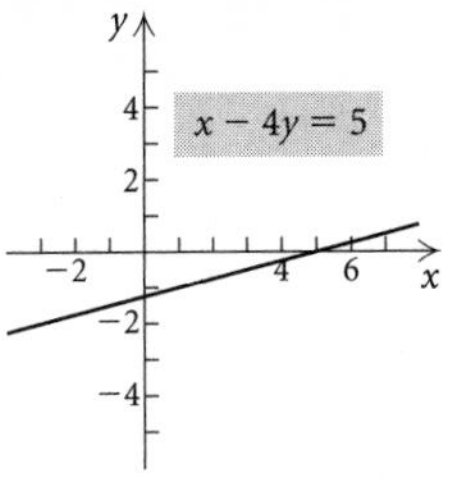

27. Graph $3x - 4y = 12$.

In this case, it is convenient to find the intercepts along with a third point on the graph. Make a table of values, plot the points in the table, and draw the graph.

x	y	(x,y)
4	0	$(4,0)$
0	-3	$(0,-3)$
-4	-6	$(-4,-6)$

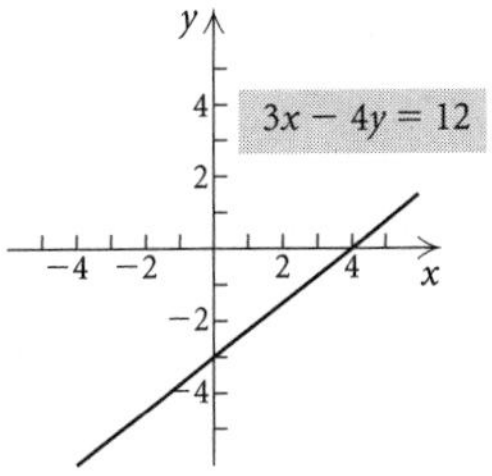

29. Graph $2x + 5y = -10$.

In this case, it is convenient to find the intercepts along with a third point on the graph. Make a table of values, plot the points in the table, and draw the graph.

x	y	(x,y)
-5	0	$(-5,0)$
0	-2	$(0,-2)$
5	-4	$(5,-4)$

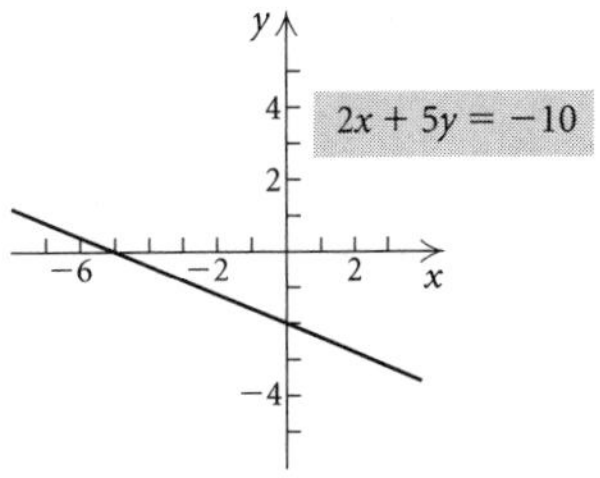

31. Graph $y = -x^2$.

Make a table of values, plot the points in the table, and draw the graph.

x	y	(x, y)
-2	-4	$(-2, -4)$
-1	-1	$(-1, -1)$
0	0	$(0, 0)$
1	-1	$(1, -1)$
2	-4	$(2, -4)$

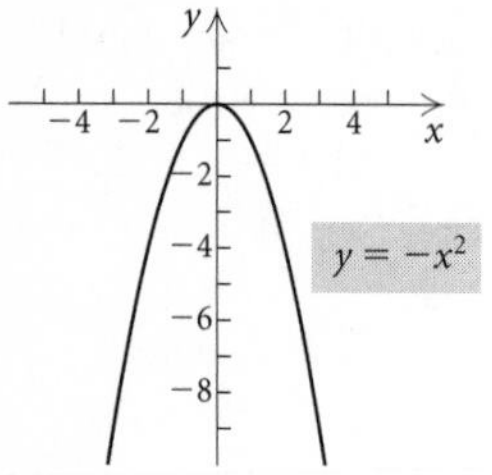

33. Graph $y = x^2 - 3$.

Make a table of values, plot the points in the table, and draw the graph.

x	y	(x, y)
-3	6	$(-3, 6)$
-1	-2	$(-1, -2)$
0	-3	$(0, -3)$
1	-2	$(1, -2)$
3	6	$(3, 6)$

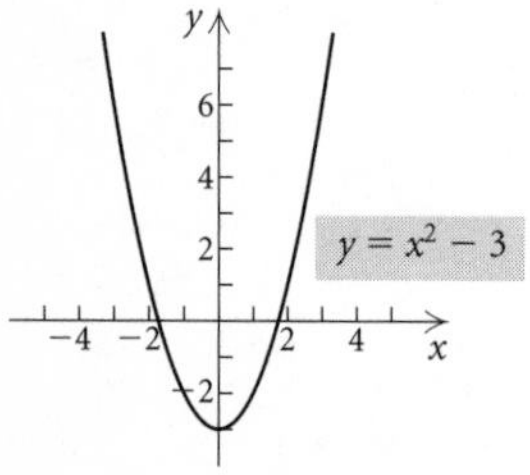

35. Graph $y = -x^2 + 2x + 3$.

Make a table of values, plot the points in the table, and draw the graph.

x	y	(x, y)
-2	-5	$(-2, -5)$
-1	0	$(-1, 0)$
0	3	$(0, 3)$
1	4	$(1, 4)$
2	3	$(2, 3)$
3	0	$(3, 0)$
4	-5	$(4, -5)$

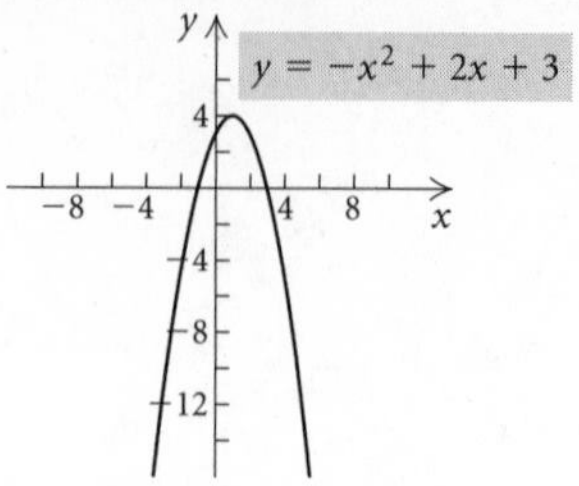

37. Either point can be considered as (x_1, y_1).

$$d = \sqrt{(4-5)^2 + (6-9)^2}$$
$$= \sqrt{(-1)^2 + (-3)^2} = \sqrt{10} \approx 3.162$$

39. Either point can be considered as (x_1, y_1).

$$d = \sqrt{(6-9)^2 + (-1-5)^2}$$
$$= \sqrt{(-3)^2 + (-6)^2} = \sqrt{45} \approx 6.708$$

41. Either point can be considered as (x_1, y_1).

$$d = \sqrt{(-4.2-2.1)^2 + [3-(-6.4)]^2}$$
$$= \sqrt{(-6.3)^2 + (9.4)^2} = \sqrt{128.05} \approx 11.316$$

43. Either point can be considered as (x_1, y_1).

$$d = \sqrt{\left(-\frac{1}{2} - \frac{5}{2}\right)^2 + (4-4)^2}$$
$$= \sqrt{(-3)^2 + 0^2} = \sqrt{9} = 3$$

45. Either point can be considered as (x_1, y_1).

$$d = \sqrt{(-\sqrt{6} - \sqrt{3})^2 + (0 - (-\sqrt{5}))^2}$$
$$= \sqrt{6 + 2\sqrt{18} + 3 + 5} = \sqrt{14 + 2\sqrt{9 \cdot 2}}$$
$$= \sqrt{14 + 2 \cdot 3\sqrt{2}} = \sqrt{14 + 6\sqrt{2}} \approx 4.742$$

47. Either point can be considered as (x_1, y_1).

$$d = \sqrt{(0-a)^2 + (0-b)^2} = \sqrt{a^2 + b^2}$$

49. First we find the length of the diameter:

$$d = \sqrt{(-3-9)^2 + (-1-4)^2}$$
$$= \sqrt{(-12)^2 + (-5)^2} = \sqrt{169} = 13$$

The length of the radius is one-half the length of the diameter, or $\frac{1}{2}(13)$, or 6.5.

51. First we find the distance between each pair of points.

For $(-4, 5)$ and $(6, 1)$:

$$d = \sqrt{(-4-6)^2 + (5-1)^2}$$
$$= \sqrt{(-10)^2 + 4^2} = \sqrt{116}$$

For $(-4, 5)$ and $(-8, -5)$:

$$d = \sqrt{(-4-(-8))^2 + (5-(-5))^2}$$
$$= \sqrt{4^2 + 10^2} = \sqrt{116}$$

For $(6, 1)$ and $(-8, -5)$:

$$d = \sqrt{(6-(-8))^2 + (1-(-5))^2}$$
$$= \sqrt{14^2 + 6^2} = \sqrt{232}$$

Since $(\sqrt{116})^2 + (\sqrt{116})^2 = (\sqrt{232})^2$, the points could be the vertices of a right triangle.

53. First we find the distance between each pair of points.

For $(-4,3)$ and $(0,5)$:

$$d = \sqrt{(-4-0)^2+(3-5)^2} = \sqrt{(-4)^2+(-2)^2} = \sqrt{20}$$

For $(-4,3)$ and $(3,-4)$:

$$d = \sqrt{(-4-3)^2+[3-(-4)]^2} = \sqrt{(-7)^2+7^2} = \sqrt{98}$$

For $(0,5)$ and $(3,-4)$:

$$d = \sqrt{(0-3)^2+[5-(-4)]^2} = \sqrt{(-3)^2+9^2} = \sqrt{90}$$

The greatest distance is $\sqrt{98}$, so if the points are the vertices of a right triangle, then it is the hypotenuse. But $(\sqrt{20})^2+(\sqrt{90})^2 \neq (\sqrt{98})^2$, so the points are not the vertices of a right triangle.

55. We use the midpoint formula.

$$\left(\frac{4+(-12)}{2}, \frac{-9+(-3)}{2}\right) = \left(-\frac{8}{2}, -\frac{12}{2}\right) = (-4,-6)$$

57. We use the midpoint formula.

$$\left(\frac{6.1+3.8}{2}, \frac{-3.8+(-6.1)}{2}\right) = \left(\frac{9.9}{2}, -\frac{9.9}{2}\right) =$$

$(4.95, -4.95)$

59. We use the midpoint formula.

$$\left(\frac{-6+(-6)}{2}, \frac{5+8}{2}\right) = \left(-\frac{12}{2}, \frac{13}{2}\right) = \left(-6, \frac{13}{2}\right)$$

61. We use the midpoint formula.

$$\left(\frac{-\frac{1}{6}+\left(-\frac{2}{3}\right)}{2}, \frac{-\frac{3}{5}+\frac{5}{4}}{2}\right) = \left(\frac{-\frac{5}{6}}{2}, \frac{\frac{13}{20}}{2}\right) =$$

$$\left(-\frac{5}{12}, \frac{13}{40}\right)$$

63. We use the midpoint formula.

$$\left(\frac{\sqrt{3}+3\sqrt{3}}{2}, \frac{-1+4}{2}\right) = \left(\frac{4\sqrt{3}}{2}, \frac{3}{2}\right) = \left(2\sqrt{3}, \frac{3}{2}\right)$$

65.

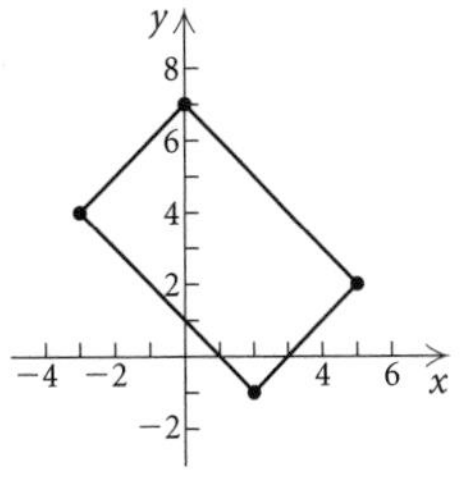

For the side with vertices $(-3,4)$ and $(2,-1)$:

$$\left(\frac{-3+2}{2}, \frac{4+(-1)}{2}\right) = \left(-\frac{1}{2}, \frac{3}{2}\right)$$

For the sides with vertices $(2,-1)$ and $(5,2)$:

$$\left(\frac{2+5}{2}, \frac{-1+2}{2}\right) = \left(\frac{7}{2}, \frac{1}{2}\right)$$

For the sides with vertices $(5,2)$ and $(0,7)$:

$$\left(\frac{5+0}{2}, \frac{2+7}{2}\right) = \left(\frac{5}{2}, \frac{9}{2}\right)$$

For the sides with vertices $(0,7)$ and $(-3,4)$:

$$\left(\frac{0+(-3)}{2}, \frac{7+4}{2}\right) = \left(-\frac{3}{2}, \frac{11}{2}\right)$$

For the quadrilateral whose vertices are the points found above, the diagonals have endpoints

$$\left(-\frac{1}{2}, \frac{3}{2}\right), \left(\frac{5}{2}, \frac{9}{2}\right) \text{ and } \left(\frac{7}{2}, \frac{1}{2}\right), \left(-\frac{3}{2}, \frac{11}{2}\right).$$

We find the length of each of these diagonals.

For $\left(-\frac{1}{2}, \frac{3}{2}\right), \left(\frac{5}{2}, \frac{9}{2}\right)$:

$$d = \sqrt{\left(-\frac{1}{2}-\frac{5}{2}\right)^2+\left(\frac{3}{2}-\frac{9}{2}\right)^2} = \sqrt{(-3)^2+(-3)^2} = \sqrt{18}$$

For $\left(\frac{7}{2}, \frac{1}{2}\right), \left(-\frac{3}{2}, \frac{11}{2}\right)$:

$$d = \sqrt{\left(\frac{7}{2}-\left(-\frac{3}{2}\right)\right)^2+\left(\frac{1}{2}-\frac{11}{2}\right)^2} = \sqrt{5^2+(-5)^2} = \sqrt{50}$$

Since the diagonals do not have the same lengths, the midpoints are not vertices of a rectangle.

67. We use the midpoint formula.

$$\left(\frac{\sqrt{7}+\sqrt{2}}{2}, \frac{-4+3}{2}\right) = \left(\frac{\sqrt{7}+\sqrt{2}}{2}, -\frac{1}{2}\right)$$

69. $(x-h)^2+(y-k)^2 = r^2$

$(x-2)^2+(y-3)^2 = \left(\frac{5}{3}\right)^2$ Substituting

$(x-2)^2+(y-3)^2 = \frac{25}{9}$

71. The length of a radius is the distance between $(-1,4)$ and $(3,7)$:

$$r = \sqrt{(-1-3)^2+(4-7)^2} = \sqrt{(-4)^2+(-3)^2} = \sqrt{25} = 5$$

$$(x-h)^2+(y-k)^2 = r^2$$
$$[x-(-1)]^2+(y-4)^2 = 5^2$$
$$(x+1)^2+(y-4)^2 = 25$$

73. The center is the midpoint of the diameter:

$$\left(\frac{7+(-3)}{2}, \frac{13+(-11)}{2}\right) = (2,1)$$

Use the center and either endpoint of the diameter to find the length of a radius. We use the point $(7,13)$:

$$r = \sqrt{(7-2)^2+(13-1)^2} = \sqrt{5^2+12^2} = \sqrt{169} = 13$$

$$(x-h)^2+(y-k)^2 = r^2$$
$$(x-2)^2+(y-1)^2 = 13^2$$
$$(x-2)^2+(y-1)^2 = 169$$

75. Since the center is 2 units to the left of the y-axis and the circle is tangent to the y-axis, the length of a radius is 2.

$$(x-h)^2+(y-k)^2=r^2$$
$$[x-(-2)]^2+(y-3)^2=2^2$$
$$(x+2)^2+(y-3)^2=4$$

77.
$$x^2+y^2=4$$
$$(x-0)^2+(y-0)^2=2^2$$

Center: $(0,0)$; radius: 2

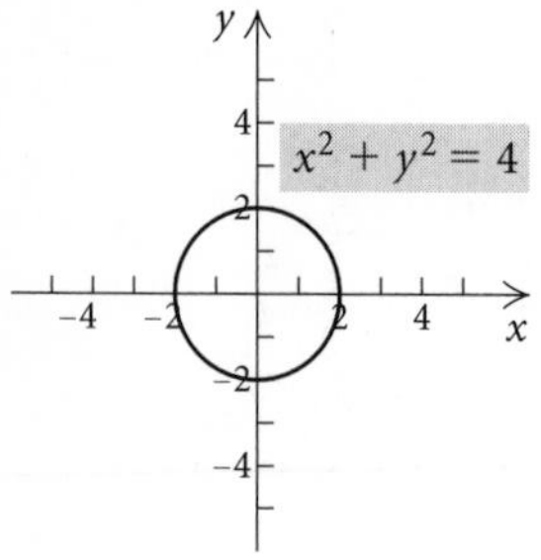

79.
$$x^2+(y-3)^2=16$$
$$(x-0)^2+(y-3)^2=4^2$$

Center: $(0,3)$; radius: 4

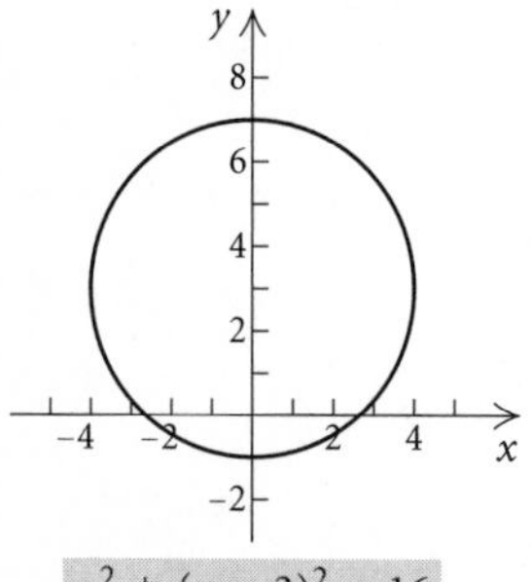

$x^2+(y-3)^2=16$

81.
$$(x-1)^2+(y-5)^2=36$$
$$(x-1)^2+(y-5)^2=6^2$$

Center: $(1,5)$; radius: 6

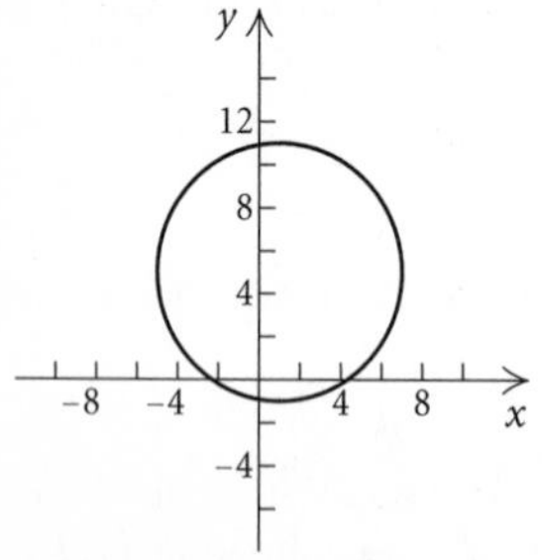

$(x-1)^2+(y-5)^2=36$

83.
$$(x+4)^2+(y+5)^2=9$$
$$[x-(-4)]^2+[y-(-5)]^2=3^2$$

Center: $(-4,-5)$; radius: 3

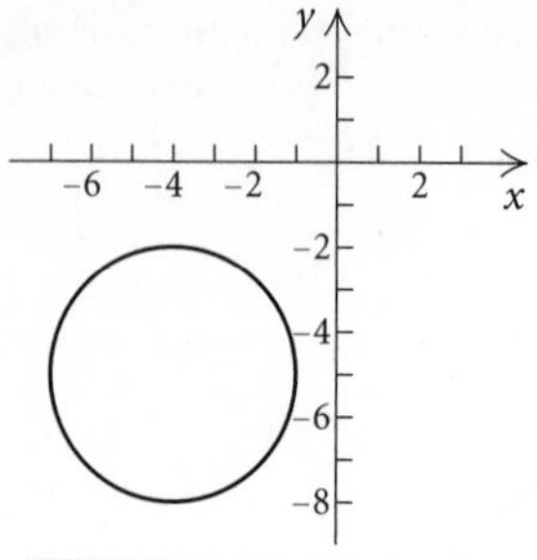

$(x+4)^2+(y+5)^2=9$

85. We regroup the terms and complete the square twice.

$$x^2+y^2-6x-2y-6=0$$
$$(x^2-6x)+(y^2-2y)-6=0$$
$$(x^2-6x+9)+(y^2-2y+1)-9-1-6=0$$
$$\left[\tfrac{1}{2}(-6)=-3 \text{ and } (-3)^2=9;\ \tfrac{1}{2}(-2)=-1 \text{ and } (-1)^2=1\right]$$
$$(x-3)^2+(y-1)^2-16=0$$
$$(x-3)^2+(y-1)^2=16$$
$$(x-3)^2+(y-1)^2=4^2$$

Center: $(3,1)$; radius: 4

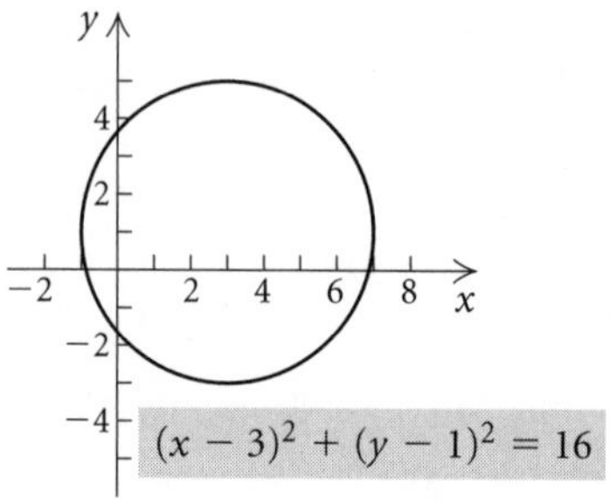

87. We regroup the terms and complete the square twice.

$$x^2+y^2+2x+2y=7$$
$$(x^2+2x)+(y^2+2y)=7$$
$$(x^2+2x+1)+(y^2+2y+1)-1-1=7$$
$$\left[\tfrac{1}{2}\cdot 2=1 \text{ and } 1^2=1\right]$$
$$(x+1)^2+(y+1)^2-2=7$$
$$(x+1)^2+(y+1)^2=9$$
$$[(x-(-1)]^2+[y-(-1)]^2=3^2$$

Center: $(-1,-1)$; radius: 3

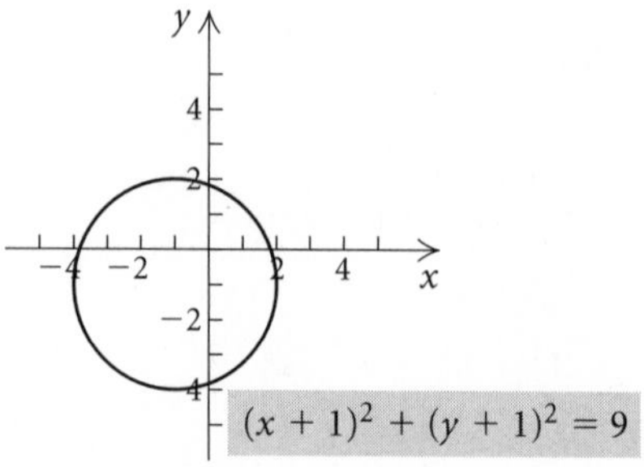

89. From the graph we see that the center of the circle is $(-2, 1)$ and the radius is 3. The equation of the circle is $[x - (-2)]^2 + (y - 1)^2 = 3^2$, or $(x + 2)^2 + (y - 1)^2 = 3^2$.

91. From the graph we see that the center of the circle is $(5, -5)$ and the radius is 15. The equation of the circle is $(x - 5)^2 + [y - (-5)]^2 = 15^2$, or $(x - 5)^2 + (y + 5)^2 = 15^2$.

93. First solve the equation for y: $y = -4x + 7$. Enter the equation in this form, select the standard window, and graph the equation.

$4x + y = 7$

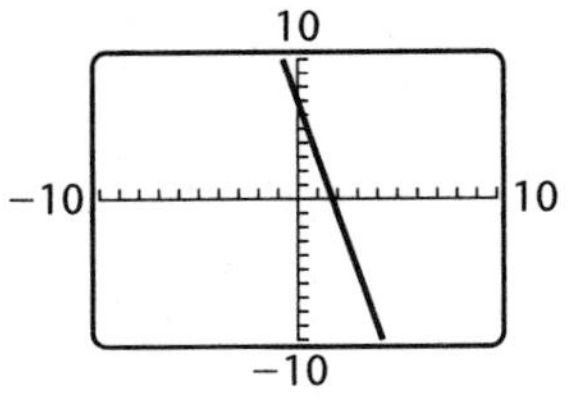

95. Enter the equation, select the standard window, and graph the equation.

$y = \frac{1}{3}x + 2$

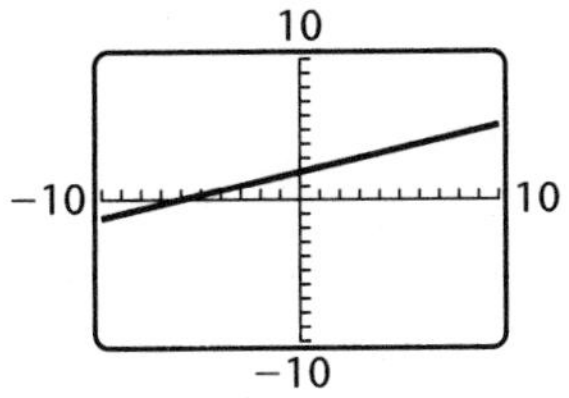

97. Enter the equation, select the standard window, and graph the equation.

$y = x^2 + 6$

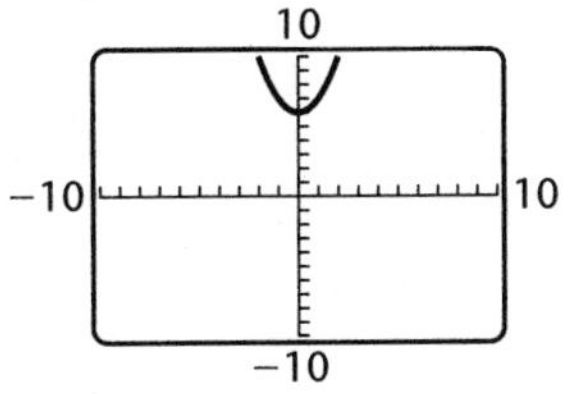

99. Enter the equation, select the standard window, and graph the equation.

$y = 2 - x^2$

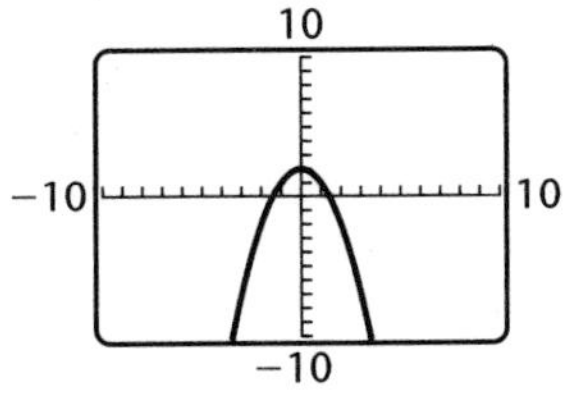

101. Standard window:

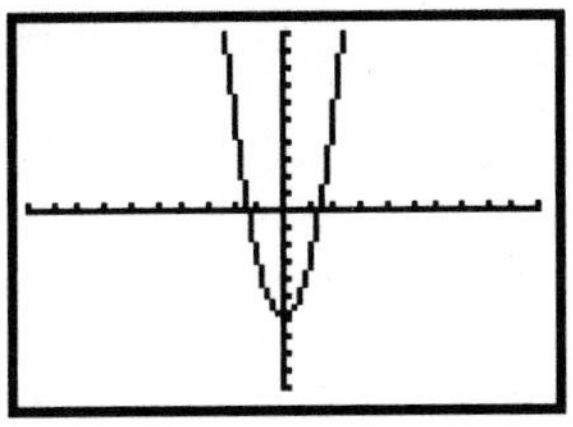

$[-4, 4, -4, 4]$

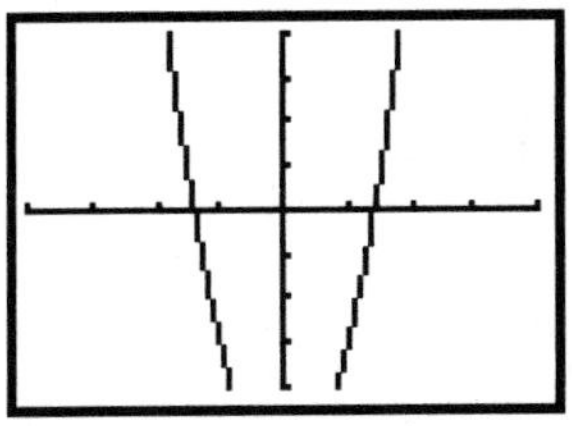

We see that the standard window is a better choice for this graph.

103. Standard window:

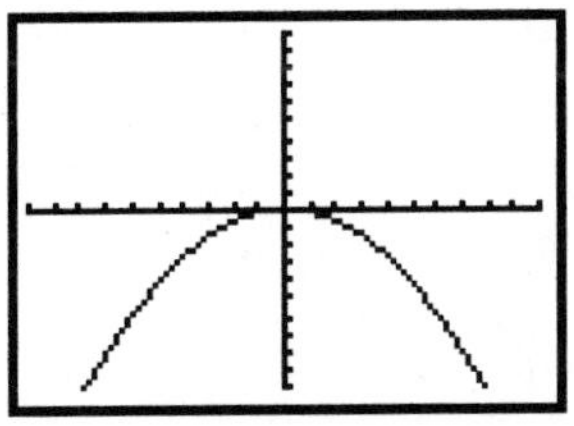

$[-1, 1, -0.3, 0.3]$, Xscl $= 0.1$, Yscl $= 0.1$

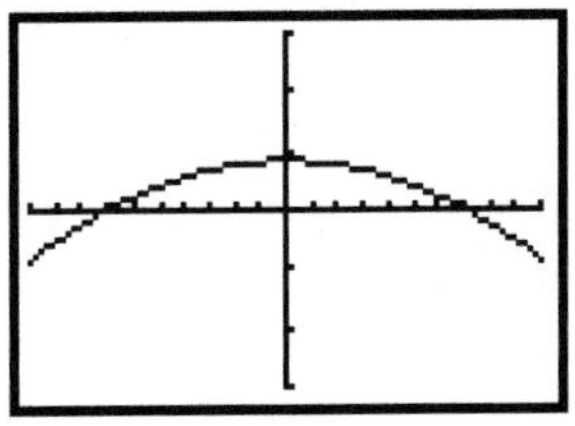

We see that $[-1, 1, -0.3, 0.3]$ is a better choice for this graph.

105. Square the viewing window. For the graph shown, one possibility is $[-12, 9, -4, 10]$.

107.

$x^2 + y^2 = 4$

$y_1 = \sqrt{4 - x^2}$, $y_2 = -\sqrt{4 - x^2}$

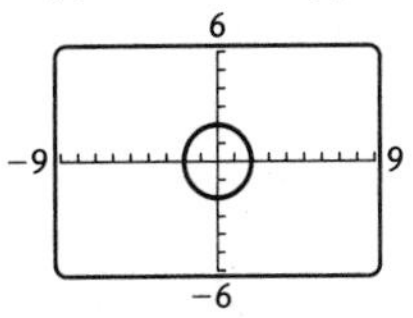

109. $(x-1)^2+(y-5)^2=36$

$y_1 = 5 + \sqrt{36-(x-1)^2}, \quad y_2 = 5 - \sqrt{36-(x-1)^2}$

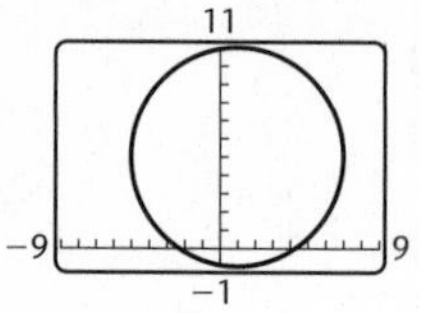

111. We graph $y_1 = 1 + \sqrt{16-(x-3)^2}$ and $y_2 = 1 - \sqrt{16-(x-3)^2}$ in the window $[-9, 9, -6, 6]$.

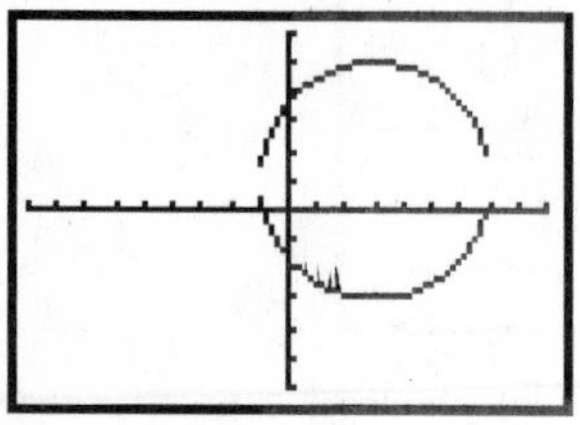

113. Discussion and Writing

115. If the point (p, q) is in the fourth quadrant, then $p > 0$ and $q < 0$. If $p > 0$, then $-p < 0$ so both coordinates of the point $(q, -p)$ are negative and $(q, -p)$ is in the third quadrant.

117. Use the distance formula. Either point can be considered as (x_1, y_1).

$$d = \sqrt{(a+h-a)^2 + (\sqrt{a+h}-\sqrt{a})^2}$$
$$= \sqrt{h^2 + a + h - 2\sqrt{a^2+ah} + a}$$
$$= \sqrt{h^2 + 2a + h - 2\sqrt{a^2+ah}}$$

Next we use the midpoint formula.

$$\left(\frac{a+a+h}{2}, \frac{\sqrt{a}+\sqrt{a+h}}{2}\right) = \left(\frac{2a+h}{2}, \frac{\sqrt{a}+\sqrt{a+h}}{2}\right)$$

119. First use the formula for the area of a circle to find r^2:

$$A = \pi r^2$$
$$36\pi = \pi r^2$$
$$36 = r^2$$

Then we have:

$$(x-h)^2 + (y-k)^2 = r^2$$
$$(x-2)^2 + [y-(-7)]^2 = 36$$
$$(x-2)^2 + (y+7)^2 = 36$$

121. Let $(0, y)$ be the required point. We set the distance from $(-2, 0)$ to $(0, y)$ equal to the distance from $(4, 6)$ to $(0, y)$ and solve for y.

$$\sqrt{[0-(-2)]^2 + (y-0)^2} = \sqrt{(0-4)^2 + (y-6)^2}$$
$$\sqrt{4+y^2} = \sqrt{16+y^2-12y+36}$$
$$4+y^2 = 16+y^2-12y+36$$

Squaring both sides

$$-48 = -12y$$
$$4 = y$$

The point is $(0, 4)$.

123. Label the drawing with additional information and lettering.

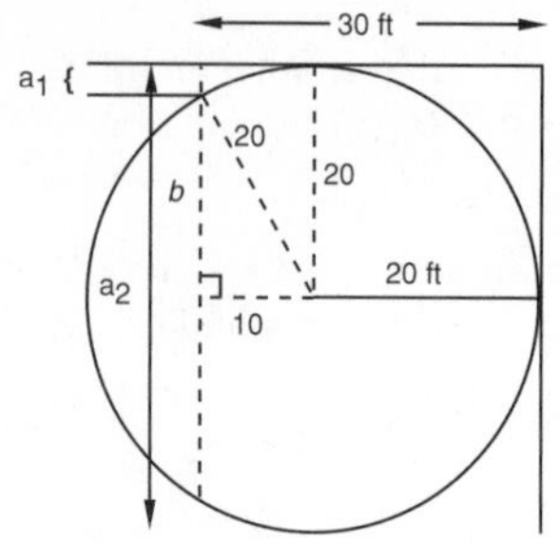

Find b using the Pythagorean theorem.

$$b^2 + 10^2 = 20^2$$
$$b^2 + 100 = 400$$
$$b^2 = 300$$
$$b = 10\sqrt{3}$$
$$b \approx 17.3$$

Find a_1:

$a_1 = 20 - b \approx 20 - 17.3 \approx 2.7$ ft

Find a_2:

$a_2 = 2b + a_1 \approx 2(17.3) + 2.7 \approx 37.3$ ft

125.

$$x^2 + y^2 = 1$$

$$\left(\frac{\sqrt{3}}{2}\right)^2 + \left(-\frac{1}{2}\right)^2 \ ? \ 1$$

$$\frac{3}{4} + \frac{1}{4}$$

$$1 \ \big| \ 1 \quad \text{TRUE}$$

$\left(\frac{\sqrt{3}}{2}, -\frac{1}{2}\right)$ lies on the unit circle.

127.

$$x^2 + y^2 = 1$$

$$\left(\frac{\sqrt{2}}{2}\right)^2 + \left(\frac{\sqrt{2}}{2}\right)^2 \ ? \ 1$$

$$\frac{2}{4} + \frac{2}{4}$$

$$1 \ \big| \ 1 \quad \text{TRUE}$$

$\left(\frac{\sqrt{2}}{2}, \frac{\sqrt{2}}{2}\right)$ lies on the unit circle.

129. a), b) See the answer section in the text.

Exercise Set 1.2

1. This correspondence is a function, because each member of the domain corresponds to exactly one member of the range.

3. This correspondence is a function, because each member of the domain corresponds to exactly one member of the range.

5. This correspondence is not a function, because there is a member of the domain (m) that corresponds to more than one member of the range (A and B).

7. This correspondence is a function, because each member of the domain corresponds to exactly one member of the range.

9. This correspondence is a function, because each car has exactly one license number.

11. This correspondence is a function, because each member of the family has exactly one eye color.

13. This correspondence is not a function, because at least one student will have more than one neighboring seat occupied by another student.

15. The relation is a function, because no two ordered pairs have the same first coordinate and different second coordinates.

The domain is the set of all first coordinates: $\{2, 3, 4\}$.

The range is the set of all second coordinates: $\{10, 15, 20\}$.

17. The relation is not a function, because the ordered pairs $(-2, 1)$ and $(-2, 4)$ have the same first coordinate and different second coordinates.

The domain is the set of all first coordinates: $\{-7, -2, 0\}$.

The range is the set of all second coordinates: $\{3, 1, 4, 7\}$.

19. The relation is a function, because no two ordered pairs have the same first coordinate and different second coordinates.

The domain is the set of all first coordinates: $\{-2, 0, 2, 4, -3\}$.

The range is the set of all second coordinates: $\{1\}$.

21. From the graph we see that, when the input is 1, the output is -2, so $h(1) = -2$. When the input is 3, the output is 2, so $h(3) = 2$. When the input is 4, the output is 1, so $h(4) = 1$.

23. From the graph we see that, when the input is -4, the output is 3, so $s(-4) = 3$. When the input is -2, the output is 0, so $s(-2) = 0$. When the input is 0, the output is -3, so $s(0) = -3$.

25. From the graph we see that, when the input is -1, the output is 2, so $f(-1) = 2$. When the input is 0, the output is 0, so $f(0) = 0$. When the input is 1, the output is -2, so $f(1) = -2$.

27. $g(x) = 3x^2 - 2x + 1$

a) $g(0) = 3 \cdot 0^2 - 2 \cdot 0 + 1 = 1$

b) $g(-1) = 3(-1)^2 - 2(-1) + 1 = 6$

c) $g(3) = 3 \cdot 3^2 - 2 \cdot 3 + 1 = 22$

d) $g(-x) = 3(-x)^2 - 2(-x) + 1 = 3x^2 + 2x + 1$

e) $g(1 - t) = 3(1 - t)^2 - 2(1 - t) + 1 =$

$3(1-2t+t^2)-2(1-t)+1 = 3-6t+3t^2-2+2t+1 =$

$3t^2 - 4t + 2$

29. $g(x) = x^3$

a) $g(2) = 2^3 = 8$

b) $g(-2) = (-2)^3 = -8$

c) $g(-x) = (-x)^3 = -x^3$

d) $g(3y) = (3y)^3 = 27y^3$

e) $g(2 + h) = (2 + h)^3 = 8 + 12h + 6h^2 + h^3$

31. $g(x) = \dfrac{x - 4}{x + 3}$

a) $g(5) = \dfrac{5 - 4}{5 + 3} = \dfrac{1}{8}$

b) $g(4) = \dfrac{4 - 4}{4 + 7} = 0$

c) $g(-3) = \dfrac{-3 - 4}{-3 + 3} = \dfrac{-7}{0}$

Since division by 0 is not defined, $g(-3)$ does not exist.

d) $g(-16.25) = \dfrac{-16.25 - 4}{-16.25 + 3} = \dfrac{-20.25}{-13.25} = \dfrac{81}{53}$

e) $g(x + h) = \dfrac{x + h - 4}{x + h + 3}$

33. $g(x) = \dfrac{x}{\sqrt{1 - x^2}}$

$g(0) = \dfrac{0}{\sqrt{1 - 0^2}} = \dfrac{0}{\sqrt{1}} = \dfrac{0}{1} = 0$

$g(-1) = \dfrac{-1}{\sqrt{1 - (-1)^2}} = \dfrac{-1}{\sqrt{1 - 1}} = \dfrac{-1}{\sqrt{0}} = \dfrac{-1}{0}$

Since division by 0 is not defined, $g(-1)$ does not exist.

$g(5) = \dfrac{5}{\sqrt{1 - 5^2}} = \dfrac{5}{\sqrt{1 - 25}} = \dfrac{5}{\sqrt{-24}}$

Since $\sqrt{-24}$ is not defined as a real number, $g(5)$ does not exist as a real number.

$$g\left(\frac{1}{2}\right) = \frac{\frac{1}{2}}{\sqrt{1 - \left(\frac{1}{2}\right)^2}} = \frac{\frac{1}{2}}{\sqrt{1 - \frac{1}{4}}} = \frac{\frac{1}{2}}{\sqrt{\frac{3}{4}}} =$$

$$\frac{\frac{1}{2}}{\frac{\sqrt{3}}{2}} = \frac{1}{2} \cdot \frac{2}{\sqrt{3}} = \frac{1 \cdot 2}{2\sqrt{3}} = \frac{1}{\sqrt{3}}, \text{ or } \frac{\sqrt{3}}{3}$$

35. We can substitute any real number for x. Thus, the domain is the set of all real numbers, or $(-\infty, \infty)$.

37. The input 0 results in a denominator of 0. Thus, the domain is $\{x|x \neq 0\}$, or $(-\infty, 0) \cup (0, \infty)$.

39. We can substitute any real number in the numerator, but we must avoid inputs that make the denominator 0. We find these inputs.

$2 - x = 0$

$2 = x$

The domain is $\{x|x \neq 2\}$, or $(-\infty, 2) \cup (2, \infty)$.

41. We find the inputs that make the denominator 0:

$$x^2 - 4x - 5 = 0$$
$$(x-5)(x+1) = 0$$
$$x-5=0 \quad or \quad x+1=0$$
$$x=5 \quad or \quad x=-1$$

The domain is $\{x|x \neq 5 \ and \ x \neq -1\}$, or $(-\infty,-1) \cup (-1,5) \cup (5,\infty)$.

43. We can substitute any real number for which the radicand is nonnegative. We see that $8 - x \geq 0$ for $x \leq 8$, so the domain is $\{x|x \leq 8\}$, or $(-\infty, 8]$.

45. We can substitute any real number for x. Thus, the domain is the set of all real numbers, or $(-\infty,\infty)$.

47.

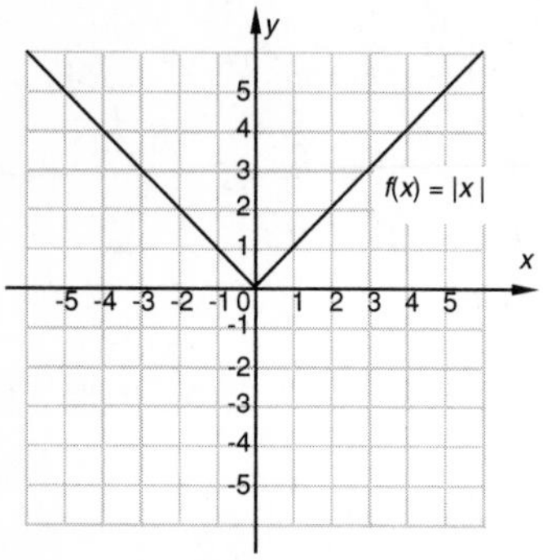

To find the domain we look for the inputs on the x-axis that correspond to a point on the graph. We see that each point on the x-axis corresponds to a point on the graph so the domain is the set of all real numbers, or $(-\infty,\infty)$.

To find the range we look for outputs on the y-axis. The number 0 is the smallest output, and every number greater than 0 is also an output. Thus, the range is $[0,\infty)$.

49.

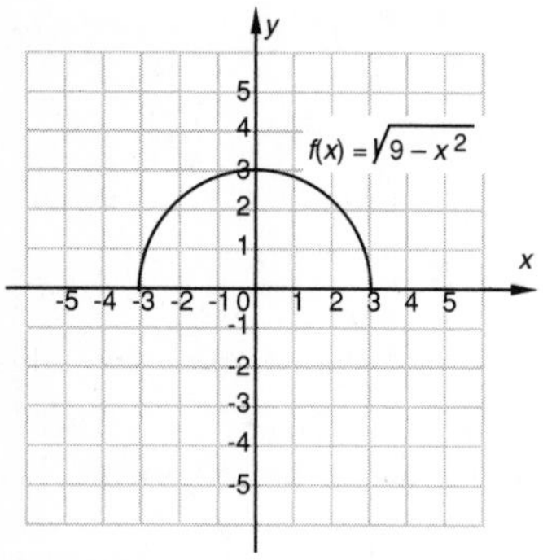

The inputs on the x-axis extend from -3 to 3, so the domain is $[-3,3]$.

The outputs on the y-axis extend from 0 to 3, so the range is $[0,3]$.

51.

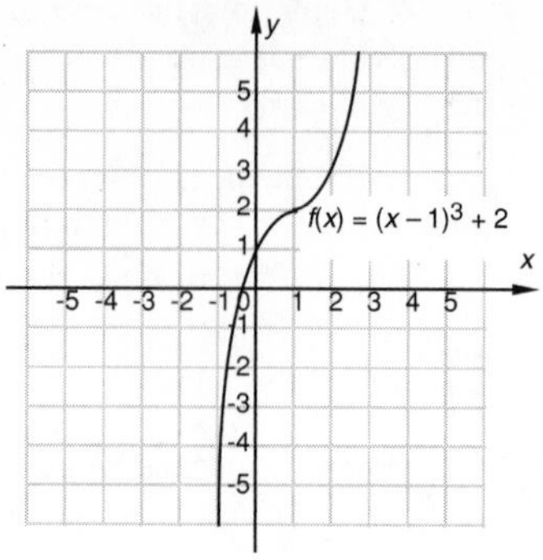

Each point on the x-axis corresponds to a point on the graph, so the domain is the set of all real numbers, or $(-\infty,\infty)$.

Each point on the y-axis also corresponds to a point on the graph, so the range is the set of all real numbers, $(-\infty,\infty)$.

53.

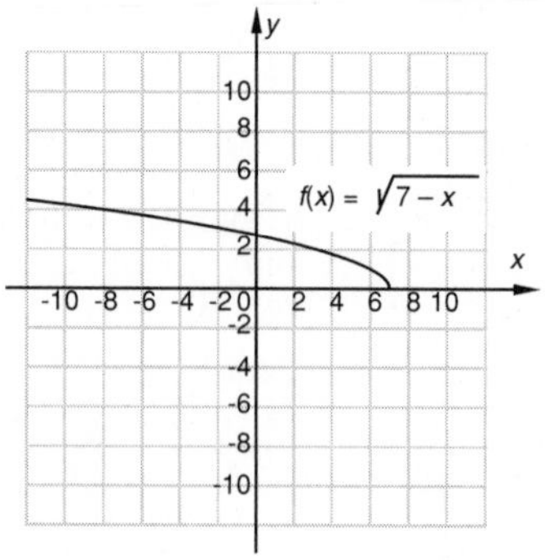

The largest input on the x-axis is 7 and every number less than 7 is also an input. Thus, the domain is $(-\infty,7]$.

The number 0 is the smallest output, and every number greater than 0 is also an output. Thus, the range is $[0,\infty)$.

55.

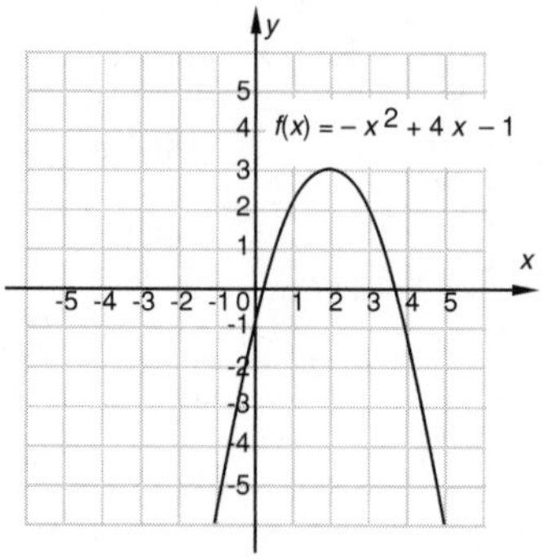

Each point on the x-axis corresponds to a point on the graph, so the domain is the set of all real numbers, or $(-\infty,\infty)$.

The largest output is 3 and every number less than 3 is also an output. Thus, the range is $(-\infty,3]$.

57. This is not the graph of a function, because we can find a vertical line that crosses the graph more than once.

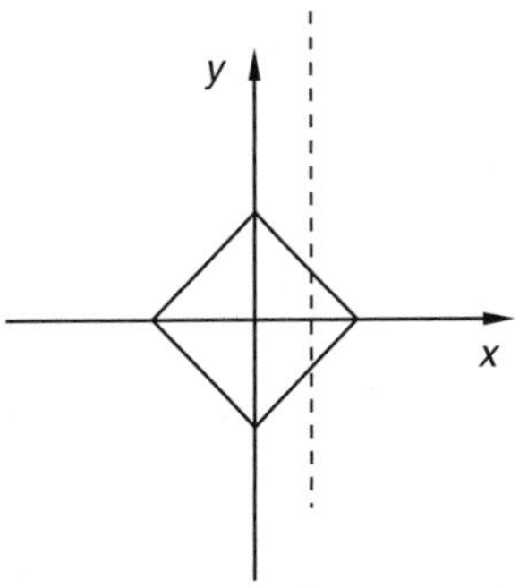

59. This is the graph of a function, because there is no vertical line that crosses the graph more than once.

61. This is the graph of a function, because there is no vertical line that crosses the graph more than once.

63. This is not the graph of a function, because we can find a vertical line that crosses the graph more than once.

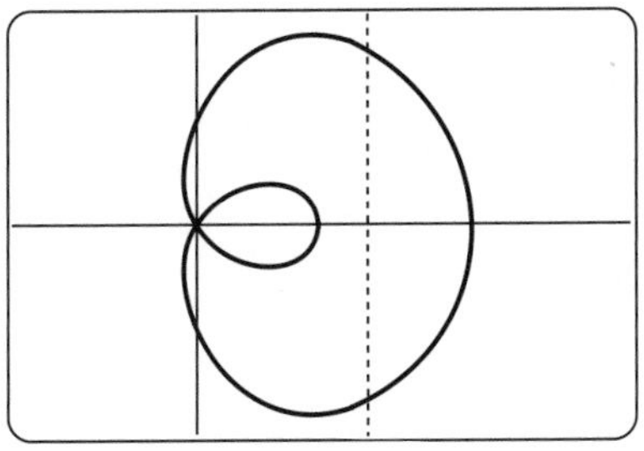

65. This is the graph of a function, because there is no vertical line that crosses the graph more than once.

The inputs on the x-axis that correspond to points on the graph extend from 0 to 5, inclusive. Thus, the domain is $\{x|0 \leq x \leq 5\}$, or $[0, 5]$.

The outputs on the y-axis extend from 0 to 3, inclusive. Thus, the range is $\{y|0 \leq y \leq 3\}$, or $[0, 3]$.

67. This is the graph of a function, because there is no vertical line that crosses the graph more than once.

The inputs on the x-axis that correspond to points on the graph extend from -2π to 2π inclusive. Thus, the domain is $\{x| -2\pi \leq x \leq 2\pi\}$, or $[-2\pi, 2\pi]$.

The outputs on the y-axis extend from -1 to 1, inclusive. Thus, the range is $\{y| -1 \leq y \leq 1\}$, or $[-1, 1]$.

69. $E(t) = 1000(100 - t) + 580(100 - t)^2$

a) $E(99.5) = 1000(100-99.5)+580(100-99.5)^2$
$= 1000(0.5) + 580(0.5)^2$
$= 500 + 580(0.25) = 500 + 145$
$= 645$ m above sea level

b) $E(100) = 1000(100 - 100) + 580(100 - 100)^2$
$= 1000 \cdot 0 + 580(0)^2 = 0 + 0$
$= 0$ m above sea level, or at sea level

71. $T(0.5) = 0.5^{1.31} \approx 0.4$ acre
$T(10) = 10^{1.31} \approx 20.4$ acres
$T(20) = 20^{1.31} \approx 50.6$ acres
$T(100) = 100^{1.31} \approx 416.9$ acres
$T(200) = 200^{1.31} \approx 1033.6$ acres

73.

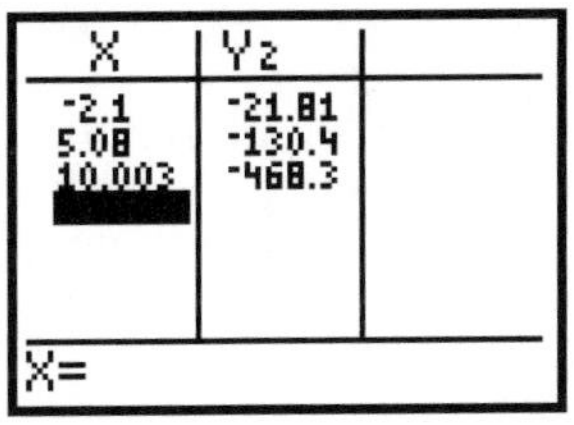

Rounding to the nearest tenth, we see that $g(-2.1) \approx -21.8$, $g(5.08) \approx -130.4$, and $g(10.003) \approx -468.3$.

75. Discussion and Writing

77. To determine whether $(0, -7)$ is a solution, substitute 0 for x and -7 for y.

$$\begin{array}{c|c} \multicolumn{2}{c}{y = 0.5x + 7} \\ \hline -7 \ ? & 0.5(0) + 7 \\ & 0 + 7 \\ -7 & 7 \end{array} \quad \text{FALSE}$$

The equation $-7 = 7$ is false, so $(0, -7)$ is not a solution.

To determine whether $(8, 11)$ is a solution, substitute 8 for x and 11 for y.

$$\begin{array}{c|c} \multicolumn{2}{c}{y = 0.5x + 7} \\ \hline 11 \ ? & 0.5(8) + 7 \\ & 4 + 7 \\ 11 & 11 \end{array} \quad \text{TRUE}$$

The equation $11 = 11$ is true, so $(8, 11)$ is a solution.

79. Graph $y = (x - 1)^2$.

Make a table of values, plot the points in the table, and draw the graph.

x	y	(x, y)
-1	4	$(-1, 4)$
0	1	$(0, 1)$
1	0	$(1, 0)$
2	1	$(2, 1)$
3	4	$(3, 4)$

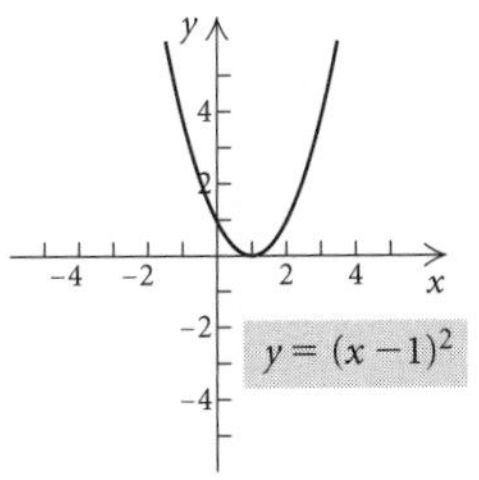

81. Graph $-2x - 5y = 10$.

Make a table of values, plot the points in the table, and draw the graph.

x	y	(x, y)
-5	0	$(-5, 0)$
0	-2	$(0, -2)$
5	-4	$(5, -4)$

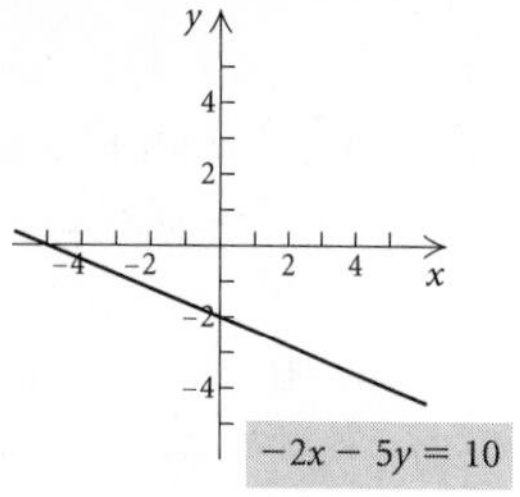

83. Answers may vary. Two possibilities are $f(x) = x$, $g(x) = x + 1$ and $f(x) = x^2$, $g(x) = x^2 - 4$.

85.

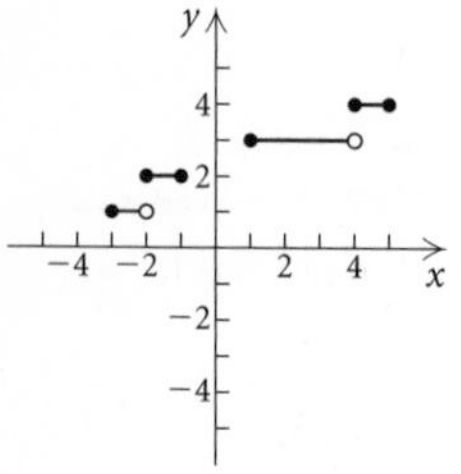

87. First find the value of x for which $x + 3 = -1$.

$$x + 3 = -1$$
$$x = -4$$

Then we have:

$$g(x + 3) = 2x + 1$$
$$g(-1) = g(-4 + 3) = 2(-4) + 1 = -8 + 1 = -7$$

89. $f(x) = |x| + |x - 1|$

a) If x is in the interval $(-\infty, 0)$, then $x < 0$ and $x - 1 < 0$. We have:

$$\begin{aligned} f(x) &= |x| + |x - 1| \\ &= -x - (x - 1) \\ &= -x - x + 1 \\ &= -2x + 1 \end{aligned}$$

b) If x is in the interval $[0, 1)$, then $x \geq 0$ and $x - 1 < 0$. We have:

$$\begin{aligned} f(x) &= |x| + |x - 1| \\ &= x - (x - 1) \\ &= x - x + 1 \\ &= 1 \end{aligned}$$

c) If x is in the interval $[1, \infty)$, then $x > 0$ and $x - 1 \geq 0$. We have:

$$\begin{aligned} f(x) &= |x| + |x - 1| \\ &= x + x - 1 \\ &= 2x + 1 \end{aligned}$$

Exercise Set 1.3

1. a) Yes. Each input is 1 more than the one that precedes it.

b) Yes. Each output is 3 more than the one that precedes it.

c) Yes. Constant changes in inputs result in constant changes in outputs.

3. a) Yes. Each input is 15 more than the one that precedes it.

b) No. The change in the outputs varies.

c) No. Constant changes in inputs do not result in constant changes in outputs.

5. Two points on the line are $(0, 3)$ and $(5, 0)$.

$$m = \frac{y_2 - y_1}{x_2 - x_1} = \frac{0 - 3}{5 - 0} = \frac{-3}{5}, \text{ or } -\frac{3}{5}$$

7. $m = \dfrac{y_2 - y_1}{x_2 - x_1} = \dfrac{3 - 3}{3 - 0} = \dfrac{0}{3} = 0$

9. $m = \dfrac{y_2 - y_1}{x_2 - x_1} = \dfrac{2 - 4}{-1 - 9} = \dfrac{-2}{-10} = \dfrac{1}{5}$

11. $m = \dfrac{y_2 - y_1}{x_2 - x_1} = \dfrac{6 - (-9)}{-5 - 4} = \dfrac{15}{-9} = -\dfrac{5}{3}$

13. $m = \dfrac{y_2 - y_1}{x_2 - x_1} = \dfrac{-0.4 - (-0.1)}{-0.3 - 0.7} = \dfrac{-0.3}{-1} = 0.3$

15. $m = \dfrac{y_2 - y_1}{x_2 - x_1} = \dfrac{-2 - (-2)}{4 - 2} = \dfrac{0}{2} = 0$

17. $m = \dfrac{y_2 - y_1}{x_2 - x_1} = \dfrac{\frac{3}{5} - \left(-\frac{3}{5}\right)}{-\frac{1}{2} - \frac{1}{2}} = \dfrac{\frac{6}{5}}{-1} = -\dfrac{6}{5}$

19. $m = \dfrac{y_2 - y_1}{x_2 - x_1} = \dfrac{-5 - (-13)}{-8 - 16} = \dfrac{8}{-24} = -\dfrac{1}{3}$

21. $m = \dfrac{y_2 - y_1}{x_2 - x_1} = \dfrac{2 - (-3)}{\pi - \pi} = \dfrac{5}{0}$

Since division by 0 is not defined, the slope is not defined.

23. $y = -\dfrac{1}{2}x + 3$

We find and plot two ordered pairs on the line and connect the points.

When $x = 0$, $y = -\dfrac{1}{2} \cdot 0 + 3 = 3$.

When $x = 2$, $y = -\dfrac{1}{2} \cdot 2 + 3 = -1 + 3 = 2$.

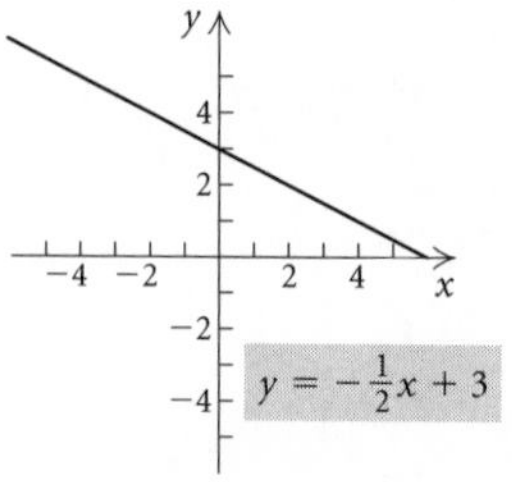

Since the equation is in the form $y = mx+b$ with $m = -\frac{1}{2}$, we know that the slope is $-\frac{1}{2}$.

25. $2y - 3x = -6$

We find and plot two ordered pairs on the line and connect the points.

First let $y = 0$ and solve for x.

$$2 \cdot 0 - 3x = -6$$
$$-3x = -6$$
$$x = 2$$

The point $(2, 0)$ is on the graph.

Next let $x = 0$ and solve for y.

$$2y - 3 \cdot 0 = -6$$
$$2y = -6$$
$$y = -3$$

The point $(0, -3)$ is on the graph.

Plot the points $(2, 0)$ and $(0, -3)$ and connect them.

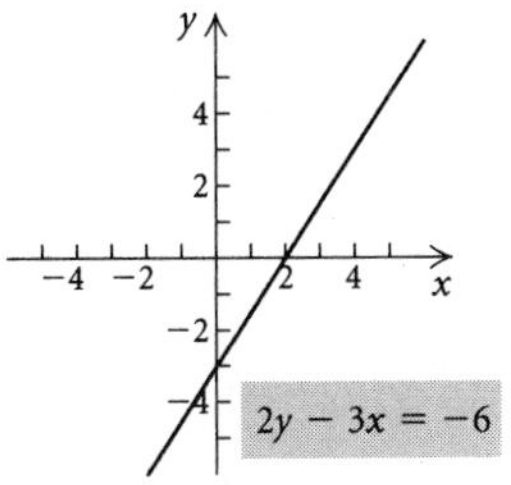

Now find the slope.

$$m = \frac{y_2 - y_1}{x_2 - x_1} = \frac{-3 - 0}{0 - 2} = \frac{-3}{-2} = \frac{3}{2}$$

27. $5x + 2y = 10$

We find and plot two ordered pairs on the line and connect the points.

First let $y = 0$ and solve for x.

$$5x + 2 \cdot 0 = 10$$
$$5x = 10$$
$$x = 2$$

The point $(2, 0)$ is on the graph.

Next let $x = 0$ and solve for y.

$$5 \cdot 0 + 2y = 10$$
$$2y = 10$$
$$y = 5$$

The point $(0, 5)$ is on the graph.

Plot the points $(2, 0)$ and $(0, 5)$ and connect them.

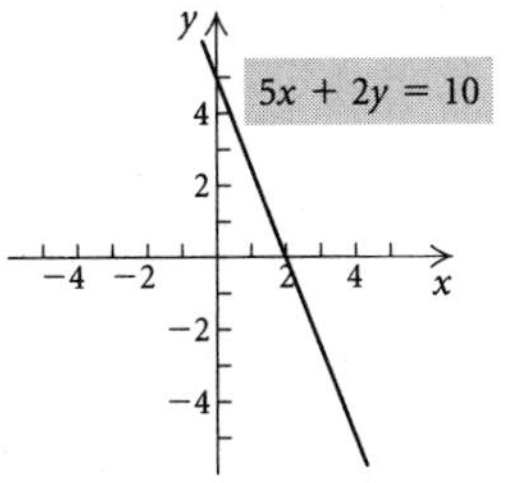

Now find the slope

$$m = \frac{5 - 0}{0 - 2} = \frac{5}{-2} = -\frac{5}{2}$$

29. $y = -\frac{2}{3}$

This is the equation of a horizontal line whose graph is $\frac{2}{3}$ units below the x-axis.

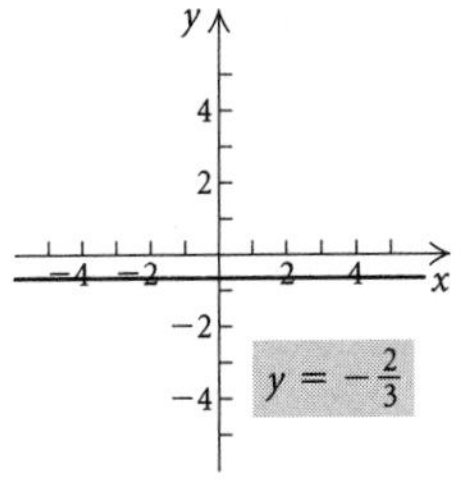

The slope of a horizontal line is 0.

31. We use the points (1992, \$3275) and (2002, \$8940) and find the average rate of change, or slope.

$$m = \frac{\$8940 - \$3275}{2002 - 1992} = \frac{\$5665}{10} = \$566.5$$

The average rate of change was \$566.50 per year.

33. We use the points $(1992, 6472)$ and $(2002, 20,099)$ and find the average rate of change, or slope.

$$m = \frac{20,099 - 6472}{2002 - 1992} = \frac{13,627}{10} = 1362.7 \approx 1363$$

The average rate of change was about 1363 visas per year.

35. First express $1\frac{1}{2}$ hr as 90 min. Then we have the points $(50, 10)$ and $(50 + 90, 25)$, or $(50, 10)$ and $(140, 25)$.

$$\text{Speed} = \text{average rate of change}$$
$$= \frac{25 - 10}{140 - 50}$$
$$= \frac{15}{90}$$
$$= \frac{1}{6}$$

The speed is $\frac{1}{6}$ km per minute.

37. a) $W(h) = 4h - 130$

b) $W(62) = 4 \cdot 62 - 130 = 248 - 130 = 118$ lb

c) Both the height and weight must be positive. Solving $h > 0$ *and* $4h - 130 > 0$, we find that the domain of the function is $\{h|h > 32.5\}$, or $(32.5, \infty)$.

39. $D(F) = 2F + 115$

a) $D(0) = 2 \cdot 0 + 115 = 115$ ft

$D(-20) = 2(-20) + 115 = -40 + 115 = 75$ ft

$D(10) = 2 \cdot 10 + 115 = 20 + 115 = 135$ ft

$D(32) = 2 \cdot 32 + 115 = 64 + 115 = 179$ ft

b) Below $-57.5°$, stopping distance is negative; above $32°$, ice doesn't form.

41. a) $D(r) = \frac{11r+5}{10} = \frac{11}{10}r + \frac{5}{10}$

The slope is $\frac{11}{10}$.

For each mph faster the car travels, it takes $\frac{11}{10}$ ft longer to stop.

b) $D(5) = \frac{11 \cdot 5 + 5}{10} = \frac{60}{10} = 6$ ft

$D(10) = \frac{11 \cdot 10 + 5}{10} = \frac{115}{10} = 11.5$ ft

$D(20) = \frac{11 \cdot 20 + 5}{10} = \frac{225}{10} = 22.5$ ft

$D(50) = \frac{11 \cdot 50 + 5}{10} = \frac{555}{10} = 55.5$ ft

$D(65) = \frac{11 \cdot 65 + 5}{10} = \frac{720}{10} = 72$ ft

c) The speed cannot be negative. $D(0) = \frac{1}{2}$ which says that a stopped car travels $\frac{1}{2}$ ft before stopping. Thus, 0 is not in the domain. The speed can be positive, so the domain is $\{r|r > 0\}$, or $(0, \infty)$.

43. $C(t) = 60 + 29t$

$C(6) = 60 + 29 \cdot 6 = \$234$

45. Let x = the number of shirts produced.

$C(x) = 800 + 3x$

$C(75) = 800 + 3 \cdot 75 = \$1025$

47. Left to the student.

49. Discussion and Writing

51. $f(x) = x^2 - 3x$

$f(-5) = (-5)^2 - 3(-5) = 25 + 15 = 40$

53. $f(x) = x^2 - 3x$

$f(a+h) = (a+h)^2 - 3(a+h) = a^2 + 2ah + h^2 - 3a - 3h$

55. $m = \frac{y_2 - y_1}{x_2 - x_1} = \frac{-2d - (-d)}{9c - (-c)} = \frac{-2d + d}{9c + c} = \frac{-d}{10c} = -\frac{d}{10c}$

57. $m = \frac{y_2 - y_1}{x_2 - x_1} = \frac{z - z}{2 - q - (z + q)} = \frac{0}{z - q - z - q} =$

$\frac{0}{-2q} = 0$

59. $m = \frac{y_2 - y_1}{x_2 - x_1} = \frac{(a+h)^2 - a^2}{a + h - a} = \frac{a^2 + 2ah + h^2 - a^2}{h} =$

$\frac{2ah + h^2}{h} = \frac{h(2a + h)}{h} = 2a + h$

61. False. For example, let $f(x) = x+1$. Then $f(cd) = cd+1$, but $f(c)f(d) = (c+1)(d+1) = cd+c+d+1 \neq cd+1$ for $c \neq -d$.

63. False. For example, let $f(x) = x + 1$. Then $f(c - d) = c - d + 1$, but $f(c) - f(d) = c + 1 - (d + 1) = c - d$.

65.

$$\begin{aligned} f(x) &= mx + b \\ f(x+2) &= f(x) + 2 \\ m(x+2) + b &= mx + b + 2 \\ mx + 2m + b &= mx + b + 2 \\ 2m &= 2 \\ m &= 1 \end{aligned}$$

Thus, $f(x) = 1 \cdot x + b$, or $f(x) = x + b$.

Exercise Set 1.4

1. $y = \frac{3}{5}x - 7$

The equation is in the form $y = mx + b$ where $m = \frac{3}{5}$ and $b = -7$. Thus, the slope is $\frac{3}{5}$, and the y-intercept is $(0, -7)$.

3. $x = -\frac{2}{5}$

This is the equation of a vertical line $\frac{2}{5}$ unit to the left of the y-axis. The slope is not defined, and there is no y-intercept.

5. $f(x) = 5 - \frac{1}{2}x$, or $f(x) = -\frac{1}{2}x + 5$

The second equation is in the form $y = mx + b$ where $m = -\frac{1}{2}$ and $b = 5$. Thus, the slope is $-\frac{1}{2}$ and the y-intercept is $(0, 5)$.

7. Solve the equation for y.

$$\begin{aligned} 3x + 2y &= 10 \\ 2y &= -3x + 10 \\ y &= -\frac{3}{2}x + 5 \end{aligned}$$

Slope: $-\frac{3}{2}$; y-intercept: $(0, 5)$

9. $y = -6 = 0 \cdot x - 6$

Slope: 0; y-intercept: $(0, -6)$

11. Solve the equation for y.

$$\begin{aligned} 5y - 4x &= 8 \\ 5y &= 4x + 8 \\ y &= \frac{4}{5}x + \frac{8}{5} \end{aligned}$$

Slope: $\frac{4}{5}$; y-intercept: $\left(0, \frac{8}{5}\right)$

13. We see that the y-intercept is $(0, -2)$. Another point on the graph is $(1, 2)$. Use these points to find the slope.

$m = \frac{y_2 - y_1}{x_2 - x_1} = \frac{2 - (-2)}{1 - 0} = \frac{4}{1} = 4$

We have $m = 4$ and $b = -2$, so the equation is $y = 4x - 2$.

15. We see that the y-intercept is $(0, 0)$. Another point on the graph is $(3, -3)$. Use these points to find the slope.

$$m = \frac{y_2 - y_1}{x_2 - x_1} = \frac{-3 - 0}{3 - 0} = \frac{-3}{3} = -1$$

We have $m = -1$ and $b = 0$, so the equation is $y = -1 \cdot x + 0$, or $y = -x$.

17. We see that the y-intercept is $(0, -3)$. This is a horizontal line, so the slope is 0. We have $m = 0$ and $b = -3$, so the equation is $y = 0 \cdot x - 3$, or $y = -3$.

19. Graph $y = -\frac{1}{2}x - 3$.

Plot the y-intercept, $(0, -3)$. We can think of the slope as $\frac{-1}{2}$. Start at $(0, -3)$ and find another point by moving down 1 unit and right 2 units. We have the point $(2, -4)$.

We could also think of the slope as $\frac{1}{-2}$. Then we can start at $(0, -3)$ and get another point by moving up 1 unit and left 2 units. We have the point $(-2, -2)$. Connect the three points to draw the graph.

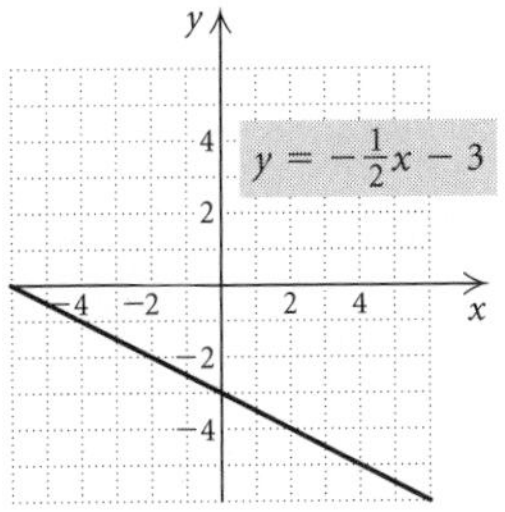

21. Graph $f(x) = 3x - 1$.

Plot the y-intercept, $(0, -1)$. We can think of the slope as $\frac{3}{1}$. Start at $(0, -1)$ and find another point by moving up 3 units and right 1 unit. We have the point $(1, 2)$. We can move from the point $(1, 2)$ in a similar manner to get a third point, $(2, 5)$. Connect the three points to draw the graph.

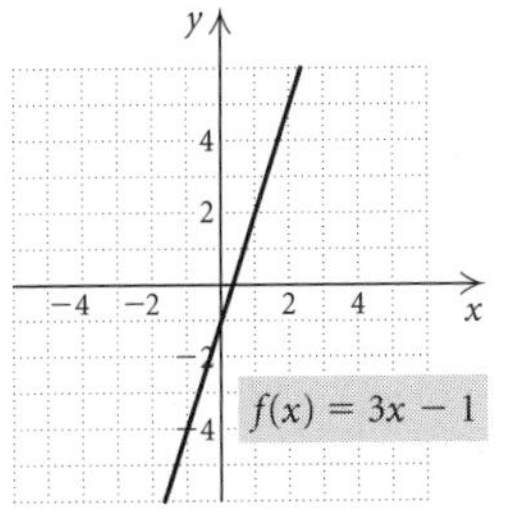

23. First solve the equation for y.

$$3x - 4y = 20$$
$$-4y = -3x + 20$$
$$y = \frac{3}{4}x - 5$$

Plot the y-intercept, $(0, -5)$. Then using the slope, $\frac{3}{4}$, start at $(0, -5)$ and find another point by moving up 3 units and right 4 units. We have the point $(4, -2)$. We can move from the point $(4, -2)$ in a similar manner to get a third point, $(8, 1)$. Connect the three points to draw the graph.

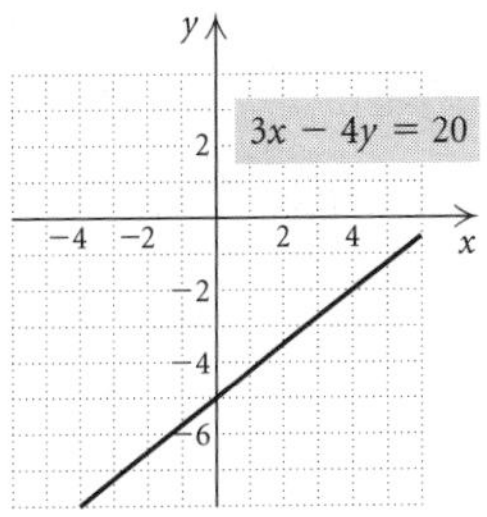

25. First solve the equation for y.

$$x + 3y = 18$$
$$3y = -x + 18$$
$$y = -\frac{1}{3}x + 6$$

Plot the y-intercept, $(0, 6)$. We can think of the slope as $\frac{-1}{3}$. Start at $(0, 6)$ and find another point by moving down 1 unit and right 3 units. We have the point $(3, 5)$. We can move from the point $(3, 5)$ in a similar manner to get a third point, $(6, 4)$. Connect the three points and draw the graph.

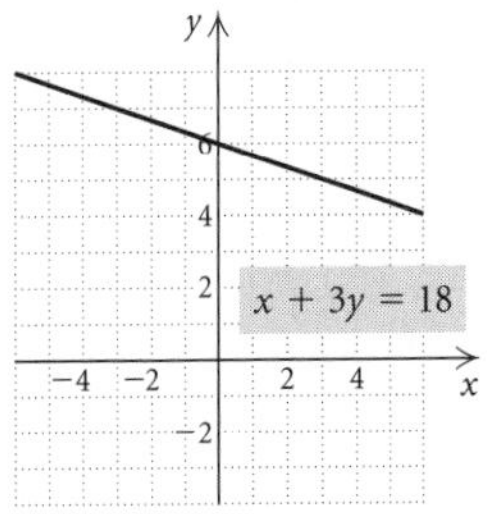

27. We substitute $\frac{2}{9}$ for m and 4 for b in the slope-intercept equation.

$$y = mx + b$$
$$y = \frac{2}{9}x + 4$$

29. We substitute -4 for m and -7 for b in the slope-intercept equation.

$$y = mx + b$$
$$y = -4x - 7$$

31. We substitute -4.2 for m and $\frac{3}{4}$ for b in the slope-intercept equation.

$$y = mx + b$$
$$y = -4.2x + \frac{3}{4}$$

33. Using the point-slope equation:

$$y - y_1 = m(x - x_1)$$
$$y - 7 = \frac{2}{9}(x - 3) \quad \text{Substituting}$$
$$y - 7 = \frac{2}{9}x - \frac{2}{3}$$
$$y = \frac{2}{9}x + \frac{19}{3} \quad \text{Slope-intercept equation}$$

Using the slope-intercept equation:

Substitute $\frac{2}{9}$ for m, 3 for x, and 7 for y in the slope-intercept equation and solve for b.

$$y = mx + b$$
$$7 = \frac{2}{9} \cdot 3 + b$$
$$7 = \frac{2}{3} + b$$
$$\frac{19}{3} = b$$

Now substitute $\frac{2}{9}$ for m and $\frac{19}{3}$ for b in $y = mx + b$.

$$y = \frac{2}{9}x + \frac{19}{3}$$

35. Using the point-slope equation:

$$y - y_1 = m(x - x_1)$$
$$y - (-2) = 3(x - 1)$$
$$y + 2 = 3x - 3$$
$$y = 3x - 5 \quad \text{Slope-intercept equation}$$

Using the slope-intercept equation:

$$y = mx + b$$
$$-2 = 3 \cdot 1 + b$$
$$-2 = 3 + b$$
$$-5 = b$$

Then we have $y = 3x - 5$.

37. Using the point-slope equation:

$$y - y_1 = m(x - x_1)$$
$$y - (-1) = -\frac{3}{5}(x - (-4))$$
$$y + 1 = -\frac{3}{5}(x + 4)$$
$$y + 1 = -\frac{3}{5}x - \frac{12}{5}$$
$$y = -\frac{3}{5}x - \frac{17}{5} \quad \text{Slope-intercept equation}$$

Using the slope-intercept equation:

$$y = mx + b$$
$$-1 = -\frac{3}{5}(-4) + b$$
$$-1 = \frac{12}{5} + b$$
$$-\frac{17}{5} = b$$

Then we have $y = -\frac{3}{5}x - \frac{17}{5}$.

39. First we find the slope.

$$m = \frac{-4 - 5}{2 - (-1)} = \frac{-9}{3} = -3$$

Using the point-slope equation:

Using the point $(-1, 5)$, we get

$$y - 5 = -3(x - (-1)), \text{ or } y - 5 = -3(x + 1).$$

Using the point $(2, -4)$, we get

$$y - (-4) = -3(x - 2), \text{ or } y + 4 = -3(x - 2).$$

In either case, the slope-intercept equation is $y = -3x + 2$.

Using the slope-intercept equation and the point $(-1, 5)$:

$$y = mx + b$$
$$5 = -3(-1) + b$$
$$5 = 3 + b$$
$$2 = b$$

Then we have $y = -3x + 2$.

41. First we find the slope.

$$m = \frac{4 - 0}{-1 - 7} = \frac{4}{-8} = -\frac{1}{2}$$

Using the point-slope equation:

Using the point $(7, 0)$, we get

$$y - 0 = -\frac{1}{2}(x - 7).$$

Using the point $(-1, 4)$, we get

$$y - 4 = -\frac{1}{2}(x - (-1)), \text{ or}$$
$$y - 4 = -\frac{1}{2}(x + 1).$$

In either case, the slope-intercept equation is $y = -\frac{1}{2}x + \frac{7}{2}$.

Using the slope-intercept equation and the point $(7, 0)$:

$$0 = -\frac{1}{2} \cdot 7 + b$$
$$\frac{7}{2} = b$$

Then we have $y = -\frac{1}{2}x + \frac{7}{2}$.

43. First we find the slope.

$$m = \frac{-4 - (-6)}{3 - 0} = \frac{2}{3}$$

We know the y-intercept is $(0, -6)$, so we substitute in the slope-intercept equation.

$$y = mx + b$$
$$y = \frac{2}{3}x - 6$$

45. The equation of the horizontal line through $(0, -3)$ is of the form $y = b$ where b is -3. We have $y = -3$.

The equation of the vertical line through $(0, -3)$ is of the form $x = a$ where a is 0. We have $x = 0$.

47. The equation of the horizontal line through $\left(\frac{2}{11}, -1\right)$ is of the form $y = b$ where b is -1. We have $y = -1$.

The equation of the vertical line through $\left(\frac{2}{11}, -1\right)$ is of the form $x = a$ where a is $\frac{2}{11}$. We have $x = \frac{2}{11}$.

49. The slopes are $\frac{26}{3}$ and $-\frac{3}{26}$. Their product is -1, so the lines are perpendicular.

51. The slopes are $\frac{2}{5}$ and $-\frac{2}{5}$. The slopes are not the same and their product is not -1, so the lines are neither parallel nor perpendicular.

53. We solve each equation for y.

$$x + 2y = 5 \qquad\qquad 2x + 4y = 8$$
$$y = -\frac{1}{2}x + \frac{5}{2} \qquad\qquad y = -\frac{1}{2}x + 2$$

We see that $m_1 = -\frac{1}{2}$ and $m_2 = -\frac{1}{2}$. Since the slopes are the same and the y-intercepts, $\frac{5}{2}$ and 2, are different, the lines are parallel.

55. We solve each equation for y.

$$y = 4x - 5 \qquad 4y = 8 - x$$
$$y = -\frac{1}{4}x + 2$$

We see that $m_1 = 4$ and $m_2 = -\frac{1}{4}$. Since $m_1 m_2 = 4\left(-\frac{1}{4}\right) = -1$, the lines are perpendicular.

57. $y = \frac{2}{7}x + 1$; $m = \frac{2}{7}$

The line parallel to the given line will have slope $\frac{2}{7}$. We use the point-slope equation for a line with slope $\frac{2}{7}$ and containing the point $(3, 5)$:

$$y - y_1 = m(x - x_1)$$
$$y - 5 = \frac{2}{7}(x - 3)$$
$$y - 5 = \frac{2}{7}x - \frac{6}{7}$$
$$y = \frac{2}{7}x + \frac{29}{7} \quad \text{Slope-intercept form}$$

The slope of the line perpendicular to the given line is the opposite of the reciprocal of $\frac{2}{7}$, or $-\frac{7}{2}$. We use the point-slope equation for a line with slope $-\frac{7}{2}$ and containing the point $(3, 5)$:

$$y - y_1 = m(x - x_1)$$
$$y - 5 = -\frac{7}{2}(x - 3)$$
$$y - 5 = -\frac{7}{2}x + \frac{21}{2}$$
$$y = -\frac{7}{2}x + \frac{31}{2} \quad \text{Slope-intercept form}$$

59. $y = -0.3x + 4.3$; $m = -0.3$

The line parallel to the given line will have slope -0.3. We use the point-slope equation for a line with slope -0.3 and containing the point $(-7, 0)$:

$$y - y_1 = m(x - x_1)$$
$$y - 0 = -0.3(x - (-7))$$
$$y = -0.3x - 2.1 \quad \text{Slope-intercept form}$$

The slope of the line perpendicular to the given line is the opposite of the reciprocal of -0.3, or $\frac{1}{0.3} = \frac{10}{3}$.

We use the point-slope equation for a line with slope $\frac{10}{3}$ and containing the point $(-7, 0)$:

$$y - y_1 = m(x - x_1)$$
$$y - 0 = \frac{10}{3}(x - (-7))$$
$$y = \frac{10}{3}x + \frac{70}{3} \quad \text{Slope-intercept form}$$

61. $3x + 4y = 5$

$$4y = -3x + 5$$
$$y = -\frac{3}{4}x + \frac{5}{4};\ m = -\frac{3}{4}$$

The line parallel to the given line will have slope $-\frac{3}{4}$. We use the point-slope equation for a line with slope $-\frac{3}{4}$ and containing the point $(3, -2)$:

$$y - y_1 = m(x - x_1)$$
$$y - (-2) = -\frac{3}{4}(x - 3)$$
$$y + 2 = -\frac{3}{4}x + \frac{9}{4}$$
$$y = -\frac{3}{4}x + \frac{1}{4} \quad \text{Slope-intercept form}$$

The slope of the line perpendicular to the given line is the opposite of the reciprocal of $-\frac{3}{4}$, or $\frac{4}{3}$. We use the point-slope equation for a line with slope $\frac{4}{3}$ and containing the point $(3, -2)$:

$$y - y_1 = m(x - x_1)$$
$$y - (-2) = \frac{4}{3}(x - 3)$$
$$y + 2 = \frac{4}{3}x - 4$$
$$y = \frac{4}{3}x - 6 \quad \text{Slope-intercept form}$$

63. $x = -1$ is the equation of a vertical line. The line parallel to the given line is a vertical line containing the point $(3, -3)$, or $x = 3$.

The line perpendicular to the given line is a horizontal line containing the point $(3, -3)$, or $y = -3$.

65. a) For model 1 we will use the data points $(0, 7.8)$ and $(20, 6.4)$. First we find the slope of the line.

$$m = \frac{6.4 - 7.8}{20 - 0} = \frac{-1.4}{20} = -0.07$$

We know that the y-intercept is $(0, 7.8)$, so we substitute in the slope-intercept equation.

$$y = mx + b$$
$$y = -0.07x + 7.8$$

For model 2 we will use the data points $(10, 7.3)$ and $(31, 4.9)$. First we find the slope of the line.

$$m = \frac{4.9 - 7.3}{31 - 10} = \frac{-2.4}{21} = -\frac{2.4}{21} \cdot \frac{10}{10} = -\frac{24}{210} = -\frac{4}{35}$$

Now we use the slope-intercept equation and the point $(10, 7.3)$.

$$y = mx + b$$
$$7.3 = -\frac{4}{35}(10) + b$$
$$\frac{73}{10} = -\frac{8}{7} + b$$
$$\frac{591}{70} = b$$

Then we have $y = -\frac{4}{35}x + \frac{591}{70}$.

b) In 2005, $x = 2005 - 1970 = 35$.

With model 1: $y = -0.07x + 7.8$
$$y = -0.07(35) + 7.8$$
$$y = 5.35$$

Using model 1, we estimate that in 2005 the average length of a hospital stay will be about 5.4 days.

With model 2: $y = -\frac{4}{35}x + \frac{591}{70}$
$$y = -\frac{4}{35} \cdot 35 + \frac{591}{70}$$
$$y = -4 + \frac{591}{70}$$
$$y = \frac{311}{70} \approx 4.4$$

Using model 2, we estimate that in 2005 the average length of a hospital stay will be about 4.4 days.

c) The estimate found using model 2 is more in keeping with the decreases shown in the graph in the text than is the estimate found using model 1. Thus, model 2 appears to fit the data more closely.

67. Answers will vary depending on the data points used. We will use $(1,\ 10,424)$ and $(3,\ 11,717)$.

$$m = \frac{11,717 - 10,424}{3 - 1} = \frac{1293}{2} = 646.5$$

Use the point-slope equation.

$$y - 10,424 = 646.5(x - 1)$$
$$y - 10,424 = 646.5x - 646.5$$
$$y = 646.5x + 9777.5$$

In 2004-2005, $y = 646.5(7) + 9777.5 = \$14,303$.

In 2006-2007, $y = 646.5(9) + 9777.5 = \$15,596$.

In 2010-2011, $y = 646.5(13) + 9777.5 = \$18,182$.

69. Answers will vary depending on the data points used. We will use $(3, 77.5)$ and $(5, 82.7)$.

$$m = \frac{82.7 - 77.5}{5 - 3} = \frac{5.2}{2} = 2.6$$

Use the slope intercept equation and the point $(3, 77.5)$.

$$y = mx + b$$
$$77.5 = 2.6(3) + b$$
$$77.5 = 7.8 + b$$
$$69.7 = b$$

We have $y = 2.6x + 69.7$.

In 2004, $x = 2004 - 1994 = 10$, and $y = 2.6(10) + 69.7 = 95.7$ billion eggs.

In 2008, $x = 2008 - 1994 = 14$, and $y = 2.6(14) + 69.7 = 106.1$ billion eggs.

In 2012, $x = 2012 - 1994 = 18$, and $y = 2.6(18) + 69.7 = 116.5$ billion eggs.

71. a) Using the linear regression feature on a graphing calculator, we get $M = 0.2H + 156$.

b) For $H = 40$: $M = 0.2(40) + 156 = 164$ beats per minute

For $H = 65$: $M = 0.2(65) + 156 = 169$ beats per minute

For $H = 76$: $M = 0.2(76) + 156 \approx 171$ beats per minute

For $H = 84$: $M = 0.2(84) + 156 \approx 173$ beats per minute

c) $r = 1$; all the data points are on the regression line so it should be a good predictor.

73. a) Using the linear regression feature on a graphing calculator, we get $y = 0.02x + 1.77$, where x is the number of years after 1999 and y is in billions of dollars.

b) In 2005, $x = 2005 - 1999 = 6$, and $y = 0.02(6) + 1.77 = \$1.89$ billion.

In 2010, $x = 2010 - 1999 = 11$,and $y = 0.02(11) + 1.77 = \$1.99$ billion.

c) $r \approx 0.3162$; since there is a low correlation, the regression line does not fit the data closely.

75. a) Using the linear regression feature on a graphing calculator, we get $y = -0.093641074x + 8.028026378$, where x is the number of years after 1970.

b) In 2005, $x = 2005 - 1970 = 35$, so $y = -0.093641074(35) + 8.028026378 \approx 4.8$ days. The value is 0.4 days more than the value found using model 2.

c) $r \approx 0.9786$; the value is close to 1 so the line fits the data well.

77. Discussion and Writing

79. $m = \frac{y_2 - y_1}{x_2 - x_1}$
$$= \frac{-1 - (-8)}{-5 - 2} = \frac{-1 + 8}{-7}$$
$$= \frac{7}{-7} = -1$$

81.
$$(x-h)^2+(y-k)^2=r^2$$
$$[x-(-7)]^2+[y-(-1)]^2=\left(\frac{9}{5}\right)^2$$
$$(x+7)^2+(y+1)^2=\frac{81}{25}$$

83. The slope of the line containing $(-3,k)$ and $(4,8)$ is
$$\frac{8-k}{4-(-3)}=\frac{8-k}{7}.$$
The slope of the line containing $(5,3)$ and $(1,-6)$ is
$$\frac{-6-3}{1-5}=\frac{-9}{-4}=\frac{9}{4}.$$
The slopes must be equal in order for the lines to be parallel:
$$\frac{8-k}{7}=\frac{9}{4}$$
$$32-4k=63 \quad \text{Multiplying by 28}$$
$$-4k=31$$
$$k=-\frac{31}{4},\text{ or }-7.75$$

Exercise Set 1.5

1. a) For x-values from -5 to 1, the y-values increase from -3 to 3. Thus the function is increasing on the interval $(-5,1)$.

b) For x-values from 3 to 5, the y-values decrease from 3 to 1. Thus the function is decreasing on the interval $(3,5)$.

c) For x-values from 1 to 3, y is 3. Thus the function is constant on $(1,3)$.

3. a) For x-values from -3 to -1, the y-values increase from -4 to 4. Also, for x-values from 3 to 5, the y-values increase from 2 to 6. Thus the function is increasing on $(-3,-1)$ and on $(3,5)$.

b) For x-values from 1 to 3, the y-values decrease from 3 to 2. Thus the function is decreasing on the interval $(1,3)$.

c) For x-values from -5 to -3, y is 1. Thus the function is constant on $(-5,-3)$.

5. a) For x-values from $-\infty$ to -8, the y-values increase from $-\infty$ to 2. Also, for x-values from -3 to -2, the y-values increase from -2 to 3. Thus the function is increasing on $(-\infty,-8)$ and on $(-3,-2)$.

b) For x-values from -8 to -6, the y-values decrease from 2 to -2. Thus the function is decreasing on the interval $(-8,-6)$.

c) For x-values from -6 to -3, y is -2. Also, for x-values from -2 to ∞, y is 3. Thus the function is constant on $(-6,-3)$ and on $(-2,\infty)$.

7. The x-values extend from -5 to 5, so the domain is $[-5,5]$.

The y-values extend from -3 to 3, so the range is $[-3,3]$.

9. The x-values extend from -5 to -1 and from 1 to 5, so the domain is $[-5,-1]\cup[1,5]$.

The y-values extend from -4 to 6, so the range is $[-4,6]$.

11. The x-values extend from $-\infty$ to ∞, so the domain is $(-\infty,\infty)$.

The y-values extend from $-\infty$ to 3, so the range

13. From the graph we see that a relative maximum value of the function is 3.25. It occurs at $x=2.5$. There is no relative minimum value.

The graph starts rising, or increasing, from the left and stops increasing at the relative maximum. From this point, the graph decreases. Thus the function is increasing on $(-\infty,2.5)$ and is decreasing on $(2.5,\infty)$.

15. From the graph we see that a relative maximum value of the function is 2.370. It occurs at $x=-0.667$. We also see that a relative minimum value of 0 occurs at $x=2$.

The graph starts rising, or increasing, from the left and stops increasing at the relative maximum. From this point it decreases to the relative minimum and then increases again. Thus the function is increasing on $(-\infty,-0.667)$ and on $(2,\infty)$. It is decreasing on $(-0.667,2)$.

17.

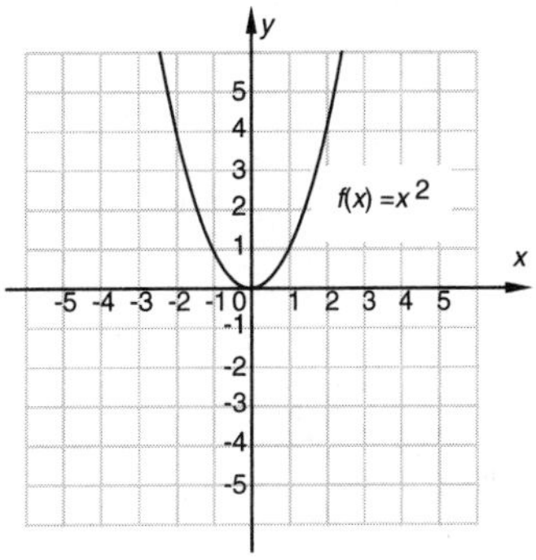

The function is increasing on $(0,\infty)$ and decreasing on $(-\infty,0)$. We estimate that the minimum is 0 at $x=0$. There are no maxima.

19.

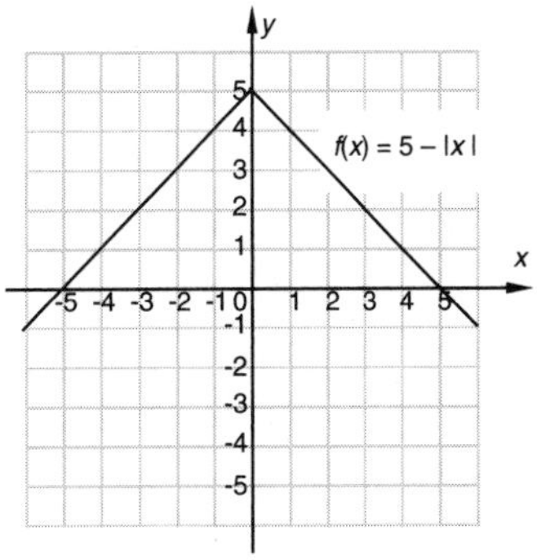

The function is increasing on $(-\infty,0)$ and decreasing on $(0,\infty)$. We estimate that the maximum is 5 at $x=0$. There are no minima.

21.

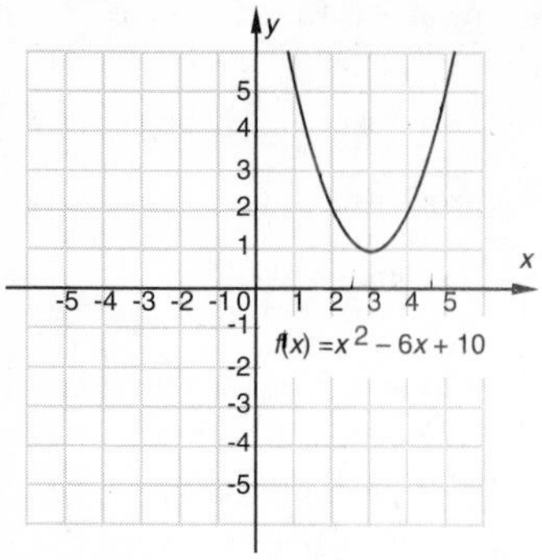

The function is decreasing on $(-\infty, 3)$ and increasing on $(3, \infty)$. We estimate that the minimum is 1 at $x = 3$. There are no maxima.

23. If x = the length of the rectangle, in meters, then the width is $\frac{60-2x}{2}$, or $30 - x$. We use the formula Area = length × width:

$$A(x) = x(30 - x)$$
$$A(x) = 30x - x^2$$

25. After t minutes, the balloon has risen $120t$ ft. We use the Pythagorean theorem.

$$[d(t)]^2 = (120t)^2 + (400)^2$$
$$d(t) = \sqrt{(120t)^2 + (400)^2}$$

We only considered the positive square root since distance must be nonnegative.

27. Let w = the width of the rectangle. Then the length $= \frac{40-2w}{2}$, or $20 - w$. Divide the rectangle into quadrants as shown below.

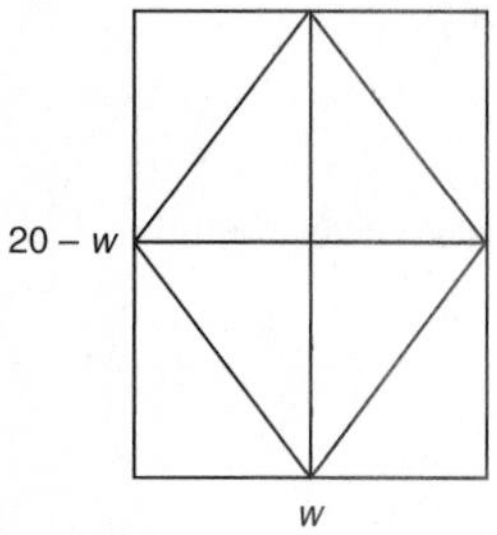

In each quadrant there are two congruent triangles. One triangle is part of the rhombus and both are part of the rectangle. Thus, in each quadrant the area of the rhombus is one-half the area of the rectangle. Then, in total, the area of the rhombus is one-half the area of the rectangle.

$$A(w) = \frac{1}{2}(20 - w)(w)$$
$$A(w) = 10w - \frac{w^2}{2}$$

29. We will use similar triangles, expressing all distances in feet. $\left(6 \text{ in.} = \frac{1}{2} \text{ ft}, s \text{ in.} = \frac{s}{12} \text{ ft, and } d \text{ yd} = 3d \text{ ft}\right)$ We have

$$\frac{3d}{7} = \frac{\frac{1}{2}}{\frac{s}{12}}$$
$$\frac{s}{12} \cdot 3d = 7 \cdot \frac{1}{2}$$
$$\frac{sd}{4} = \frac{7}{2}$$
$$d = \frac{4}{s} \cdot \frac{7}{2}, \text{ so}$$
$$d(s) = \frac{14}{s}.$$

31. a) If the length $= x$ feet, then the width $= 30 - x$ feet.

$$A(x) = x(30 - x)$$
$$A(x) = 30x - x^2$$

b) The length of the rectangle must be positive and less than 30 ft, so the domain of the function is $\{x|0 < x < 30\}$, or $(0, 30)$.

c) We see from the graph that the maximum value of the area function on the interval $(0, 30)$ appears to be 225 when $x = 15$. Then the dimensions that yield the maximum area are length = 15 ft and width $= 30 - 15$, or 15 ft.

33. a) When a square with sides of length x are cut from each corner, the length of each of the remaining sides of the piece of cardboard is $12 - 2x$. Then the dimensions of the box are x by $12-2x$ by $12-2x$. We use the formula Volume = length × width × height to find the volume of the box:

$$V(x) = (12 - 2x)(12 - 2x)(x)$$
$$V(x) = (144 - 48x + 4x^2)(x)$$
$$V(x) = 144x - 48x^2 + 4x^3$$

This can also be expressed as $V(x) = 4x(x-6)^2$, or $V(x) = 4x(6-x)^2$.

b) The length of the sides of the square corners that are cut out must be positive and less than half the length of a side of the piece of cardboard. Thus, the domain of the function is $\{x|0 < x < 6\}$, or $(0, 6)$.

c) We see from the graph that the maximum value of the area function on the interval $(0, 6)$ appears to be 128 when $x = 2$. When $x = 2$, then $12 - 2x = 12 - 2 \cdot 2 = 8$, so the dimensions that yield the maximum volume are 8 cm by 8 cm by 2 cm.

35. $g(x) = \begin{cases} x + 4, & \text{for } x \le 1, \\ 8 - x, & \text{for } x > 1 \end{cases}$

Since $-4 \le 1$, $g(-4) = -4 + 4 = 0$.

Since $0 \le 1$, $g(0) = 0 + 4 = 4$.

Since $1 \le 1$, $g(1) = 1 + 4 = 5$.

Since $3 > 1$, $g(3) = 8 - 3 = 5$.

37. $h(x) = \begin{cases} -3x - 18, & \text{for } x < -5, \\ 1, & \text{for } -5 \le x < 1, \\ x + 2, & \text{for } x \ge 1 \end{cases}$

Since -5 is in the interval $[-5, 1)$, $h(-5) = 1$.

Since 0 is in the interval $[-5, 1)$, $h(0) = 1$.

Since $1 \ge 1$, $h(1) = 1 + 2 = 3$.

Since $4 \ge 1$, $h(4) = 4 + 2 = 6$.

39. $f(x) = \begin{cases} \frac{1}{2}x, & \text{for } x < 0, \\ x + 3, & \text{for } x \ge 0 \end{cases}$

We create the graph in two parts. Graph $f(x) = \frac{1}{2}x$ for inputs x less than 0. The graph $f(x) = x + 3$ for inputs x greater than or equal to 0.

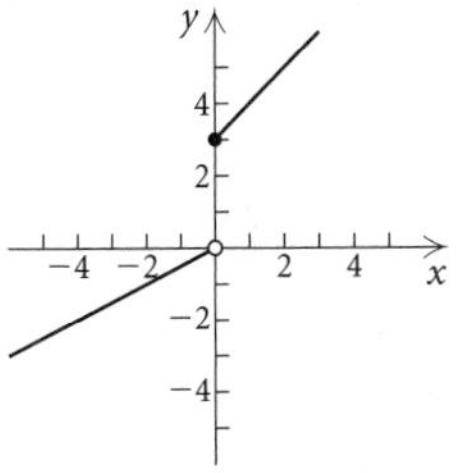

41. $f(x) = \begin{cases} -\frac{3}{4}x + 2, & \text{for } x < 4, \\ -1, & \text{for } x \ge 4 \end{cases}$

We create the graph in two parts. Graph $f(x) = -\frac{3}{4}x + 2$ for inputs x less than 4. The graph $f(x) = -1$ for inputs x greater than or equal to 4.

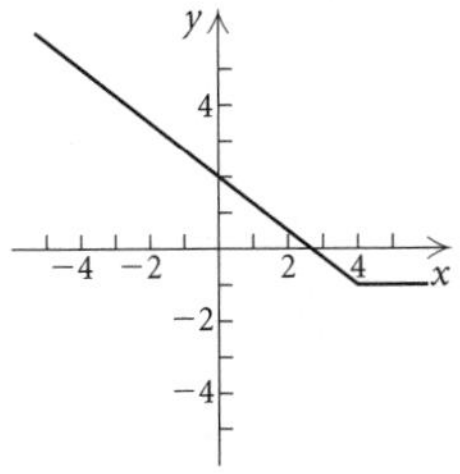

43. $f(x) = \begin{cases} x + 1, & \text{for } x \le -3, \\ -1, & \text{for } -3 < x < 4 \\ \frac{1}{2}x, & \text{for } x \ge 4 \end{cases}$

We create the graph in three parts. Graph $f(x) = x + 1$ for inputs x less than or equal to -3. Graph $f(x) = -1$ for inputs greater than -3 and less than 4. Then graph $f(x) = \frac{1}{2}x$ for inputs greater than or equal to 4.

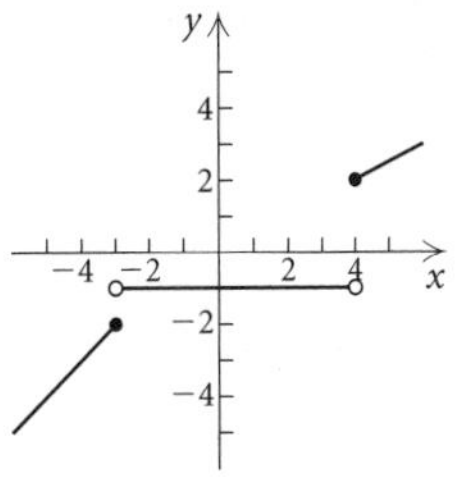

45. $f(x) = \begin{cases} 2, & \text{for } x = 5, \\ \dfrac{x^2 - 25}{x - 5}, & \text{for } x \ne 5 \end{cases}$

When $x \ne 5$, the denominator of $(x^2 - 25)/(x - 5)$ is nonzero so we can simplify:

$$\frac{x^2 - 25}{x - 5} = \frac{(x + 5)(x - 5)}{x - 5} = x + 5.$$

Thus, $f(x) = x + 5$, for $x \ne 5$.

The graph of this part of the function consists of a line with a "hole" at the point $(5, 10)$, indicated by an open dot. At $x = 5$, we have $f(5) = 2$, so the point $(5, 2)$ is plotted below the open dot.

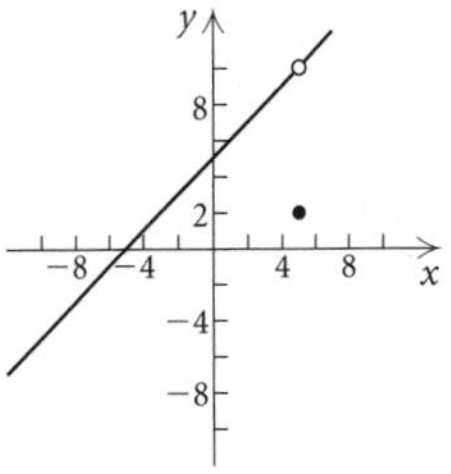

47. $f(x) = \text{int}(x)$

See Example 7.

49. $f(x) = 1 + \text{int}(x)$

This function can be defined by a piecewise function with an infinite number of statements:

$$f(x) = \begin{cases} \vdots \\ -1, & \text{for } -2 \le x < -1, \\ 0, & \text{for } -1 \le x < -0, \\ 1, & \text{for } 0 \le x < 1, \\ 2, & \text{for } 1 \le x < 2, \\ \vdots \end{cases}$$

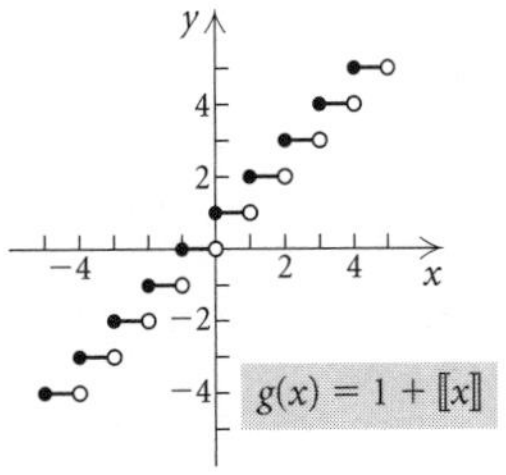

51. From the graph we see that the domain is $(-\infty, \infty)$ and the range is $(-\infty, 0) \cup [3, \infty)$.

53. From the graph we see that the domain is $(-\infty, \infty)$ and the range is $[-1, \infty)$.

55. From the graph we see that the domain is $(-\infty, \infty)$ and the range is $(-\infty, -2] \cup \{-1\} \cup [2, \infty)$, or $\{y | y \leq -2 \text{ or } y = -1 \text{ or } y \geq 2\}$.

57. From the graph we see that the domain is $(-\infty, \infty)$ and the range is $\{-5, -2, 4\}$. An equation for the function is:

$$f(x) = \begin{cases} -2, & \text{for } x < 2, \\ -5, & \text{for } x = 2, \\ 4, & \text{for } x > 2 \end{cases}$$

59. From the graph we see that the domain is $(-\infty, \infty)$ and the range is $(-\infty, -1] \cup [2, \infty)$. Finding the slope of each segment and using the slope-intercept or point-slope formula, we find that an equation for the function is:

$$g(x) = \begin{cases} x, & \text{for } x \leq -1, \\ 2, & \text{for } -1 < x \leq 2, \\ x, & \text{for } x > 2 \end{cases}$$

This can also be expressed as follows:

$$g(x) = \begin{cases} x, & \text{for } x \leq -1, \\ 2, & \text{for } -1 < x < 2, \\ x, & \text{for } x \geq 2 \end{cases}$$

61. From the graph we see that the domain is $[-5, 3]$ and the range is $(-3, 5)$. Finding the slope of each segment and using the slope-intercept or point-slope formula, we find that an equation for the function is:

$$h(x) = \begin{cases} x + 8, & \text{for } -5 \leq x < -3, \\ 3, & \text{for } -3 \leq x \leq 1, \\ 3x - 6, & \text{for } 1 < x \leq 3 \end{cases}$$

63. a)

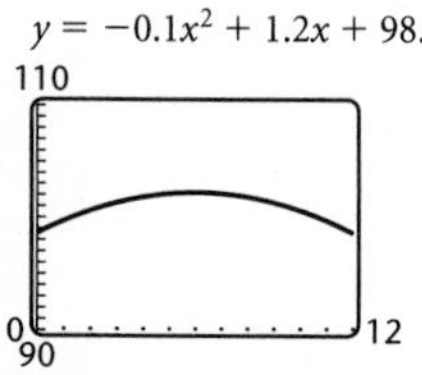

b) Using the MAXIMUM feature we find that the relative maximum is 102.2 at $t = 6$. Thus, we know that the patient's temperature was the highest at $t = 6$, or 6 days after the onset of the illness and that the highest temperature was 102.2°F.

65. Graph $y = \dfrac{8x}{x^2 + 1}$.

Increasing: $(-1, 1)$

Decreasing: $(-\infty, -1)$, $(1, \infty)$

67. Graph $y = x\sqrt{4 - x^2}$, for $-2 \leq x \leq 2$.

Increasing: $(-1.414, 1.414)$

Decreasing: $(-2, -1.414)$, $(1.414, 2)$

69. a) The length of a diameter of the circle (and a diagonal of the rectangle) is $2 \cdot 8$, or 16 ft. Let l = the length of the rectangle. Use the Pythagorean theorem to write l as a function of x.

$$x^2 + l^2 = 16^2$$
$$x^2 + l^2 = 256$$
$$l^2 = 256 - x^2$$
$$l = \sqrt{256 - x^2}$$

Since the length must be positive, we considered only the positive square root.

Use the formula Area = length × width to find the area of the rectangle:

$$A(x) = x\sqrt{256 - x^2}$$

b) The width of the rectangle must be positive and less than the diameter of the circle. Thus, the domain of the function is $\{x | 0 < x < 16\}$, or $(0, 16)$.

c)

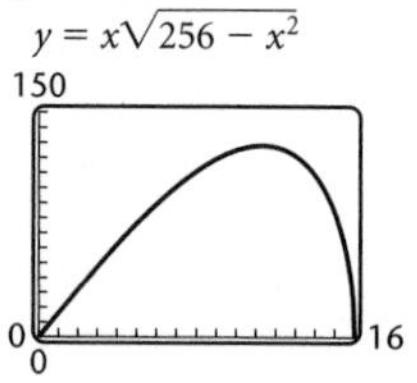

d) Using the MAXIMUM feature, we find that the maximum area occurs when x is about 11.314. When $x \approx 11.314$, $\sqrt{256 - x^2} \approx \sqrt{256 - (11.314)^2} \approx 11.313$. Thus, the dimensions that maximize the area are about 11.314 ft by 11.313 ft. (Answers may vary slightly due to rounding differences.)

71. Discussion and Writing

73. Function; domain; range; domain; exactly one; range

75. x-intercept

77. If $[\text{int}(x)]^2 = 25$, then $\text{int}(x) = -5$ or $\text{int}(x) = 5$. For $-5 \leq x < -4$, $\text{int}(x) = -5$. For $5 \leq x < 6$, $\text{int}(x) = 5$. Thus, the possible inputs for x are $\{x | -5 \leq x < -4 \text{ or } 5 \leq x < 6\}$.

79. a) We add labels to the drawing in the text.

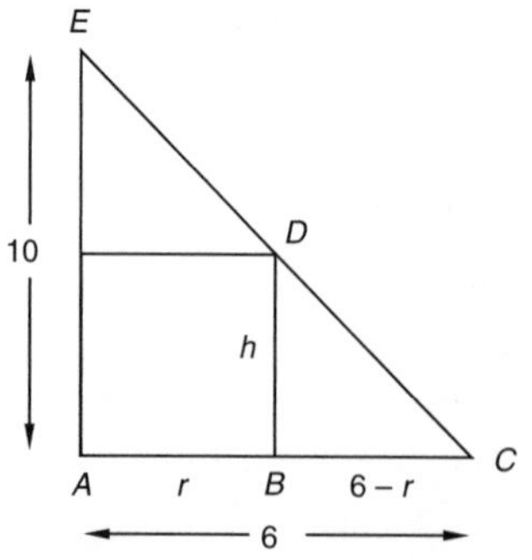

We write a proportion involving the lengths of the sides of the similar triangles BCD and ACE. Then we solve it for h.

$$\frac{h}{6-r} = \frac{10}{6}$$
$$h = \frac{10}{6}(6-r) = \frac{5}{3}(6-r)$$
$$h = \frac{30-5r}{3}$$

Thus, $h(r) = \dfrac{30-5r}{3}$.

b) $V = \pi r^2 h$

$V(r) = \pi r^2 \left(\dfrac{30-5r}{3}\right)$ Substituting for h

c) We first express r in terms of h.

$$h = \frac{30-5r}{3}$$
$$3h = 30 - 5r$$
$$5r = 30 - 3h$$
$$r = \frac{30-3h}{5}$$
$$V = \pi r^2 h$$
$$V(h) = \pi\left(\frac{30-3h}{5}\right)^2 h$$

Substituting for r

We can also write $V(h) = \pi h\left(\dfrac{30-3h}{5}\right)^2$.

Exercise Set 1.6

1. $(f+g)(5) = f(5) + g(5)$
$= (5^2 - 3) + (2 \cdot 5 + 1)$
$= 25 - 3 + 10 + 1$
$= 33$

3. $(f-g)(-1) = f(-1) - g(-1)$
$= ((-1)^2 - 3) - (2(-1) + 1)$
$= -2 - (-1) = -2 + 1$
$= -1$

5. $$(f/g)\left(-\frac{1}{2}\right) = \frac{f\left(-\frac{1}{2}\right)}{g\left(-\frac{1}{2}\right)} = \frac{\left(-\frac{1}{2}\right)^2 - 3}{2\left(-\frac{1}{2}\right)+1} = \frac{\frac{1}{4} - 3}{-1+1} = \frac{-\frac{11}{4}}{0}$$

Since division by 0 is not defined, $(f/g)\left(-\dfrac{1}{2}\right)$ does not exist.

7. $$(fg)\left(-\frac{1}{2}\right) = f\left(-\frac{1}{2}\right)\cdot g\left(-\frac{1}{2}\right) = \left[\left(-\frac{1}{2}\right)^2 - 3\right]\left[2\left(-\frac{1}{2}\right)+1\right] = -\frac{11}{4}\cdot 0 = 0$$

9. $(g-f)(-1) = g(-1) - f(-1)$
$= [2(-1)+1] - [(-1)^2 - 3]$
$= (-2+1) - (1-3)$
$= -1 - (-2)$
$= -1 + 2$
$= 1$

11. $(h-g)(-4) = h(-4) - g(-4)$
$= (-4+4) - \sqrt{-4-1}$
$= 0 - \sqrt{-5}$

Since $\sqrt{-5}$ is not a real number, $(h-g)(-4)$ does not exist.

13. $$(g/h)(1) = \frac{g(1)}{h(1)} = \frac{\sqrt{1-1}}{1+4} = \frac{\sqrt{0}}{5} = \frac{0}{5} = 0$$

15. $(g+h)(1) = g(1) + h(1)$
$= \sqrt{1-1} + (1+4)$
$= \sqrt{0} + 5$
$= 0 + 5 = 5$

17. $f(x) = 2x+3$, $g(x) = 3-5x$

a) The domain of f and of g is the set of all real numbers, or $(-\infty, \infty)$. Then the domain of $f+g$, $f-g$, ff, and fg is also $(-\infty, \infty)$. For f/g we must exclude $\dfrac{3}{5}$ since $g\left(\dfrac{3}{5}\right) = 0$. Then the domain of f/g is $\left(-\infty, \dfrac{3}{5}\right) \cup \left(\dfrac{3}{5}, \infty\right)$. For g/f we must exclude $-\dfrac{3}{2}$ since $f\left(-\dfrac{3}{2}\right) = 0$. The domain of g/f is $\left(-\infty, -\dfrac{3}{2}\right) \cup \left(-\dfrac{3}{2}, \infty\right)$.

b) $(f+g)(x) = f(x) + g(x) = (2x+3) + (3-5x) = -3x + 6$

$(f-g)(x) = f(x) - g(x) = (2x+3) - (3-5x) = 2x + 3 - 3 + 5x = 7x$

$(fg)(x) = f(x)\cdot g(x) = (2x+3)(3-5x) = 6x - 10x^2 + 9 - 15x = -10x^2 - 9x + 9$

$(ff)(x) = f(x)\cdot f(x) = (2x+3)(2x+3) = 4x^2 + 12x + 9$

$(f/g)(x) = \frac{f(x)}{g(x)} = \frac{2x+3}{3-5x}$

$(g/f)(x) = \frac{g(x)}{f(x)} = \frac{3-5x}{2x+3}$

19. $f(x) = x - 3$, $g(x) = \sqrt{x+4}$

a) Any number can be an input in f, so the domain of f is the set of all real numbers, or $(-\infty, \infty)$.

The inputs of g must be nonnegative, so we have $x + 4 \geq 0$, or $x \geq -4$. Thus, the domain of g is $[-4, \infty)$.

The domain of $f+g$, $f-g$, and fg is the set of all numbers in the domains of both f and g. This is $[-4, \infty)$.

The domain of ff is the domain of f, or $(-\infty, \infty)$.

The domain of f/g is the set of all numbers in the domains of f and g, excluding those for which $g(x) = 0$. Since $g(-4) = 0$, the domain of f/g is $(-4, \infty)$.

The domain of g/f is the set of all numbers in the domains of g and f, excluding those for which $f(x) = 0$. Since $f(3) = 0$, the domain of g/f is $[-4, 3) \cup (3, \infty)$.

b) $(f+g)(x) = f(x) + g(x) = x - 3 + \sqrt{x+4}$

$(f-g)(x) = f(x) - g(x) = x - 3 - \sqrt{x+4}$

$(fg)(x) = f(x) \cdot g(x) = (x-3)\sqrt{x+4}$

$(ff)(x) = [f(x)]^2 = (x-3)^2 = x^2 - 6x + 9$

$(f/g)(x) = \frac{f(x)}{g(x)} = \frac{x-3}{\sqrt{x+4}}$

$(g/f)(x) = \frac{g(x)}{f(x)} = \frac{\sqrt{x+4}}{x-3}$

21. $f(x) = 2x - 1$, $g(x) = -2x^2$

a) The domain of f and of g is $(-\infty, \infty)$. Then the domain of $f+g$, $f-g$, fg, and ff is $(-\infty, \infty)$. For f/g, we must exclude 0 since $g(0) = 0$. The domain of f/g is $(-\infty, 0) \cup (0, \infty)$. For g/f, we must exclude $\frac{1}{2}$ since $f\left(\frac{1}{2}\right) = 0$. The domain of g/f is $\left(-\infty, \frac{1}{2}\right) \cup \left(\frac{1}{2}, \infty\right)$.

b) $(f+g)(x) = f(x) + g(x) = (2x-1) + (-2x^2) = -2x^2 + 2x - 1$

$(f-g)(x) = f(x) - g(x) = (2x-1) - (-2x^2) = 2x^2 + 2x - 1$

$(fg)(x) = f(x) \cdot g(x) = (2x-1)(-2x^2) = -4x^3 + 2x^2$

$(ff)(x) = f(x) \cdot f(x) = (2x-1)(2x-1) = 4x^2 - 4x + 1$

$(f/g)(x) = \frac{f(x)}{g(x)} = \frac{2x-1}{-2x^2}$

$(g/f)(x) = \frac{g(x)}{f(x)} = \frac{-2x^2}{2x-1}$

23. $f(x) = \sqrt{x-3}$, $g(x) = \sqrt{x+3}$

a) Since $f(x)$ is nonnegative for values of x in $[3, \infty)$, this is the domain of f. Since $g(x)$ is nonnegative for values of x in $[-3, \infty)$, this is the domain of g. The domain of $f+g$, $f-g$, and fg is the intersection of the domains of f and g, or $[3, \infty)$. The domain of ff is the same as the domain of f, or $[3, \infty)$. For f/g, we must exclude -3 since $g(-3) = 0$. This is not in $[3, \infty)$, so the domain of f/g is $[3, \infty)$. For g/f, we must exclude 3 since $f(3) = 0$. The domain of g/f is $(3, \infty)$.

b) $(f+g)(x) = f(x) + g(x) = \sqrt{x-3} + \sqrt{x+3}$

$(f-g)(x) = f(x) - g(x) = \sqrt{x-3} - \sqrt{x+3}$

$(fg)(x) = f(x) \cdot g(x) = \sqrt{x-3} \cdot \sqrt{x+3} = \sqrt{x^2-9}$

$(ff)(x) = f(x) \cdot f(x) = \sqrt{x-3} \cdot \sqrt{x-3} = |x-3|$

$(f/g)(x) = \frac{\sqrt{x-3}}{\sqrt{x+3}}$

$(g/f)(x) = \frac{\sqrt{x+3}}{\sqrt{x-3}}$

25. $f(x) = x + 1$, $g(x) = |x|$

a) The domain of f and of g is $(-\infty, \infty)$. Then the domain of $f+g$, $f-g$, fg, and ff is $(-\infty, \infty)$. For f/g, we must exclude 0 since $g(0) = 0$. The domain of f/g is $(-\infty, 0) \cup (0, \infty)$. For g/f, we must exclude -1 since $f(-1) = 0$. The domain of g/f is $(-\infty, -1) \cup (-1, \infty)$.

b) $(f+g)(x) = f(x) + g(x) = x + 1 + |x|$

$(f-g)(x) = f(x) - g(x) = x + 1 - |x|$

$(fg)(x) = f(x) \cdot g(x) = (x+1)|x|$

$(ff)(x) = f(x) \cdot f(x) = (x+1)(x+1) = x^2 + 2x + 1$

$(f/g)(x) = \frac{x+1}{|x|}$

$(g/f)(x) = \frac{|x|}{x+1}$

27. $f(x) = x^3$, $g(x) = 2x^2 + 5x - 3$

a) Since any number can be an input for either f or g, the domain of f, g, $f+g$, $f-g$, fg, and ff is the set of all real numbers, or $(-\infty, \infty)$.

Since $g(-3) = 0$ and $g\left(\frac{1}{2}\right) = 0$, the domain of f/g is $(-\infty, -3) \cup \left(-3, \frac{1}{2}\right) \cup \left(\frac{1}{2}, \infty\right)$.

Since $f(0) = 0$, the domain of g/f is $(-\infty, 0) \cup (0, \infty)$.

b) $(f+g)(x) = f(x) + g(x) = x^3 + 2x^2 + 5x - 3$

$(f-g)(x) = f(x) - g(x) = x^3 - (2x^2 + 5x - 3) = x^3 - 2x^2 - 5x + 3$

$(fg)(x) = f(x) \cdot g(x) = x^3(2x^2 + 5x - 3) = 2x^5 + 5x^4 - 3x^3$

$(ff)(x) = f(x) \cdot f(x) = x^3 \cdot x^3 = x^6$

$$(f/g)(x) = \frac{f(x)}{g(x)} = \frac{x^3}{2x^2+5x-3}$$

$$(g/f)(x) = \frac{g(x)}{f(x)} = \frac{2x^2+5x-3}{x^3}$$

29. $f(x) = \frac{4}{x+1}$, $g(x) = \frac{1}{6-x}$

a) Since $x + 1 = 0$ when $x = -1$, we must exclude -1 from the domain of f. It is $(-\infty,-1)\cup(-1,\infty)$. Since $6-x = 0$ when $x = 6$, we must exclude 6 from the domain of g. It is $(-\infty,6)\cup(6,\infty)$. The domain of $f+g$, $f-g$, and fg is the intersection of the domains of f and g, or $(-\infty,-1)\cup(-1,6)\cup(6,\infty)$. The domain of ff is the same as the domain of f, or $(-\infty,-1)\cup(-1,\infty)$. Since there are no values of x for which $g(x) = 0$ or $f(x) = 0$, the domain of f/g and g/f is $(-\infty,-1)\cup(-1,6)\cup(6,\infty)$.

b) $(f+g)(x) = f(x)+g(x) = \frac{4}{x+1} + \frac{1}{6-x}$

$(f-g)(x) = f(x)-g(x) = \frac{4}{x+1} - \frac{1}{6-x}$

$(fg)(x) = f(x)\cdot g(x) = \frac{4}{x+1}\cdot\frac{1}{6-x} = \frac{4}{(x+1)(6-x)}$

$(ff)(x) = f(x)\cdot f(x) = \frac{4}{x+1}\cdot\frac{4}{x+1} = \frac{16}{(x+1)^2}$, or $\frac{16}{x^2+2x+1}$

$$(f/g)(x) = \frac{\frac{4}{x+1}}{\frac{1}{6-x}} = \frac{4}{x+1}\cdot\frac{6-x}{1} = \frac{4(6-x)}{x+1}$$

$$(g/f)(x) = \frac{\frac{1}{6-x}}{\frac{4}{x+1}} = \frac{1}{6-x}\cdot\frac{x+1}{4} = \frac{x+1}{4(6-x)}$$

31. $f(x) = \frac{1}{x}$, $g(x) = x-3$

a) Since $f(0)$ is not defined, the domain of f is $(-\infty,0)\cup(0,\infty)$. The domain of g is $(-\infty,\infty)$. Then the domain of $f+g$, $f-g$, fg, and ff is $(-\infty,0)\cup(0,\infty)$. Since $g(3) = 0$, the domain of f/g is $(-\infty,0)\cup(0,3)\cup(3,\infty)$. There are no values of x for which $f(x) = 0$, so the domain of g/f is $(-\infty,0)\cup(0,\infty)$.

b) $(f+g)(x) = f(x)+g(x) = \frac{1}{x} + x - 3$

$(f-g)(x) = f(x)-g(x) = \frac{1}{x}-(x-3) = \frac{1}{x}-x+3$

$(fg)(x) = f(x)\cdot g(x) = \frac{1}{x}\cdot(x-3) = \frac{x-3}{x}$, or $1-\frac{3}{x}$

$(ff)(x) = f(x)\cdot f(x) = \frac{1}{x}\cdot\frac{1}{x} = \frac{1}{x^2}$

$$(f/g)(x) = \frac{f(x)}{g(x)} = \frac{\frac{1}{x}}{x-3} = \frac{1}{x}\cdot\frac{1}{x-3} = \frac{1}{x(x-3)}$$

$(g/f)(x) = \frac{g(x)}{f(x)} = \frac{x-3}{\frac{1}{x}} = (x-3)\cdot\frac{x}{1} = x(x-3)$, or x^2-3x

33. From the graph, we see that the domain of F is $[0,9]$ and the domain of G is $[3,10]$. The domain of $F+G$ is the set of numbers in the domains of both F and G. This is $[3,9]$.

35. The domain of G/F is the set of numbers in the domains of both F and G (See Exercise 33.), excluding those for which $F = 0$. Since $F(6) = 0$ and $F(8) = 0$, the domain of G/F is $[3,6)\cup(6,8)\cup(8,9]$.

37.

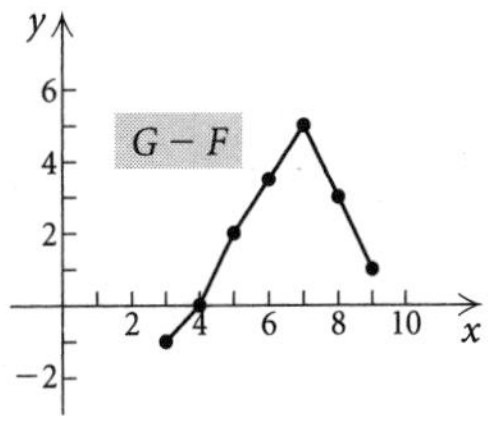

39. a) $P(x) = R(x)-C(x) = 60x-0.4x^2-(3x+13) = 60x-0.4x^2-3x-13 = -0.4x^2+57x-13$

b) $R(100) = 60\cdot100-0.4(100)^2 = 6000-0.4(10{,}000) = 6000-4000 = 2000$

$C(100) = 3\cdot100+13 = 300+13 = 313$

$P(100) = R(100)-C(100) = 2000-313 = 1687$

41. $f(x) = x^2+1$

$f(x+h) = (x+h)^2+1 = x^2+2xh+h^2+1$

$$\begin{aligned}\frac{f(x+h)-f(x)}{h} &= \frac{x^2+2xh+h^2+1-(x^2+1)}{h}\\ &= \frac{x^2+2xh+h^2+1-x^2-1}{h}\\ &= \frac{2xh+h^2}{h}\\ &= \frac{h(2x+h)}{h}\\ &= \frac{h}{h}\cdot\frac{2x+h}{1}\\ &= 2x+h\end{aligned}$$

43. $f(x) = 3x-5$

$f(x+h) = 3(x+h)-5 = 3x+3h-5$

$$\begin{aligned}\frac{f(x+h)-f(x)}{h} &= \frac{3x+3h-5-(3x-5)}{h}\\ &= \frac{3x+3h-5-3x+5}{h}\\ &= \frac{3h}{h} = 3\end{aligned}$$

45. $f(x) = 3x^2 - 2x + 1$

$f(x+h) = 3(x+h)^2 - 2(x+h) + 1 =$

$3(x^2 + 2xh + h^2) - 2(x+h) + 1 =$

$3x^2 + 6xh + 3h^2 - 2x - 2h + 1$

$f(x) = 3x^2 - 2x + 1$

$\dfrac{f(x+h) - f(x)}{h} =$

$\dfrac{(3x^2 + 6xh + 3h^2 - 2x - 2h + 1) - (3x^2 - 2x + 1)}{h} =$

$\dfrac{3x^2 + 6xh + 3h^2 - 2x - 2h + 1 - 3x^2 + 2x - 1}{h} =$

$\dfrac{6xh + 3h^2 - 2h}{h} = \dfrac{h(6x + 3h - 2)}{h \cdot 1} =$

$\dfrac{h}{h} \cdot \dfrac{6x + 3h - 2}{1} = 6x + 3h - 2$

47. $f(x) = 4 + 5|x|$

$f(x+h) = 4 + 5|x+h|$

$\dfrac{f(x+h) - f(x)}{h} = \dfrac{4 + 5|x+h| - (4 + 5|x|)}{h}$

$= \dfrac{4 + 5|x+h| - 4 - 5|x|}{h}$

$= \dfrac{5|x+h| - 5|x|}{h}$

49. $f(x) = x^3$

$f(x+h) = (x+h)^3 = x^3 + 3x^2h + 3xh^2 + h^3$

$f(x) = x^3$

$\dfrac{f(x+h) - f(x)}{h} = \dfrac{x^3 + 3x^2h + 3xh^2 + h^3 - x^3}{h} =$

$\dfrac{3x^2h + 3xh^2 + h^3}{h} = \dfrac{h(3x^2 + 3xh + h^2)}{h \cdot 1} =$

$\dfrac{h}{h} \cdot \dfrac{3x^2 + 3xh + h^2}{1} = 3x^2 + 3xh + h^2$

51. $f(x) = \dfrac{x-4}{x+3}$

$\dfrac{f(x+h) - f(x)}{h} = \dfrac{\dfrac{x+h-4}{x+h+3} - \dfrac{x-4}{x+3}}{h} =$

$\dfrac{\dfrac{x+h-4}{x+h+3} - \dfrac{x-4}{x+3}}{h} \cdot \dfrac{(x+h+3)(x+3)}{(x+h+3)(x+3)} =$

$\dfrac{(x+h-4)(x+3) - (x-4)(x+h+3)}{h(x+h+3)(x+3)} =$

$\dfrac{x^2+hx-4x+3x+3h-12-(x^2+hx+3x-4x-4h-12)}{h(x+h+3)(x+3)} =$

$\dfrac{x^2 + hx - x + 3h - 12 - x^2 - hx + x + 4h + 12}{h(x+h+3)(x+3)} =$

$\dfrac{7h}{h(x+h+3)(x+3)} = \dfrac{h}{h} \cdot \dfrac{7}{(x+h+3)(x+3)} =$

$\dfrac{7}{(x+h+3)(x+3)}$

53. $(f \circ g)(-1) = f(g(-1)) = f((-1)^2 - 2(-1) - 6) =$

$f(1 + 2 - 6) = f(-3) = 3(-3) + 1 = -9 + 1 = -8$

55. $(h \circ f)(1) = h(f(1)) = h(3 \cdot 1 + 1) = h(3+1) =$

$h(4) = 4^3 = 64$

57. $(g \circ f)(5) = g(f(5)) = g(3 \cdot 5 + 1) = g(15 + 1) =$

$g(16) = 16^2 - 2 \cdot 16 - 6 = 218$

59. $(f \circ h)(-3) = f(h(-3)) = f((-3)^3) = f(-27) =$

$3(-27) + 1 = -81 + 1 = -80$

61. $(f \circ g)(x) = f(g(x)) = f(x-3) = x - 3 + 3 = x$

$(g \circ f)(x) = g(f(x)) = g(x+3) = x + 3 - 3 = x$

The domain of f and of g is $(-\infty, \infty)$, so the domain of $f \circ g$ and of $g \circ f$ is $(-\infty, \infty)$.

63. $(f \circ g)(x) = f(g(x)) = f\left(\dfrac{1}{x}\right) = \dfrac{4}{1 - 5 \cdot \dfrac{1}{x}} = \dfrac{4}{1 - \dfrac{5}{x}} =$

$\dfrac{4}{\dfrac{x-5}{x}} = 4 \cdot \dfrac{x}{x-5} = \dfrac{4x}{x-5}$

$(g \circ f)(x) = g(f(x)) = g\left(\dfrac{4}{1-5x}\right) = \dfrac{1}{\dfrac{4}{1-5x}} =$

$1 \cdot \dfrac{1-5x}{4} = \dfrac{1-5x}{4}$

The domain of f is $\left\{x \middle| x \neq \dfrac{1}{5}\right\}$ and the domain of g is $\{x|x \neq 0\}$. Consider the domain of $f \circ g$. Since 0 is not in the domain of g, 0 is not in the domain of $f \circ g$. Since $\dfrac{1}{5}$ is not in the domain of f, we know that $g(x)$ cannot be $\dfrac{1}{5}$. We find the value(s) of x for which $g(x) = \dfrac{1}{5}$.

$\dfrac{1}{x} = \dfrac{1}{5}$

$5 = x$ Multiplying by $5x$

Thus 5 is also not in the domain of $f \circ g$. Then the domain of $f \circ g$ is $\{x|x \neq 0 \textit{ and } x \neq 5\}$, or $(-\infty, 0) \cup (0, 5) \cup (5, \infty)$.

Now consider the domain of $g \circ f$. Recall that $\dfrac{1}{5}$ is not in the domain of f, so it is not in the domain of $g \circ f$. Now 0 is not in the domain of g but $f(x)$ is never 0, so the domain of $g \circ f$ is $\left\{x \middle| x \neq \dfrac{1}{5}\right\}$, or $\left(-\infty, \dfrac{1}{5}\right) \cup \left(\dfrac{1}{5}, \infty\right)$.

65. $(f \circ g)(x) = f(g(x)) = f\left(\dfrac{x+7}{3}\right) =$

$3\left(\dfrac{x+7}{3}\right) - 7 = x + 7 - 7 = x$

$(g \circ f)(x) = g(f(x)) = g(3x - 7) = \dfrac{(3x-7)+7}{3} =$

$\dfrac{3x}{3} = x$

The domain of f and of g is $(-\infty, \infty)$, so the domain of $f \circ g$ and of $g \circ f$ is $(-\infty, \infty)$.

67. $(f \circ g)(x) = f(g(x)) = f(\sqrt{x}) = 2\sqrt{x} + 1$

$(g \circ f)(x) = g(f(x)) = g(2x + 1) = \sqrt{2x + 1}$

The domain of f is $(-\infty, \infty)$ and the domain of g is $\{x|x \geq 0\}$. Thus the domain of $f \circ g$ is $\{x|x \geq 0\}$, or $[0, \infty)$.

Now consider the domain of $g \circ f$. There are no restrictions on the domain of f, but the domain of g is $\{x|x \geq 0\}$. Since $f(x) \geq 0$ for $x \geq -\frac{1}{2}$, the domain of $g \circ f$ is $\left\{x \middle| x \geq -\frac{1}{2}\right\}$, or $\left[-\frac{1}{2}, \infty\right)$.

69. $(f \circ g)(x) = f(g(x)) = f(0.05) = 20$

$(g \circ f)(x) = g(f(x)) = g(20) = 0.05$

The domain of f and of g is $(-\infty, \infty)$, so the domain of $f \circ g$ and of $g \circ f$ is $(-\infty, \infty)$.

71. $(f \circ g)(x) = f(g(x)) = f(x^2 - 5) =$

$\sqrt{x^2 - 5 + 5} = \sqrt{x^2} = |x|$

$(g \circ f)(x) = g(f(x)) = g(\sqrt{x + 5}) =$

$(\sqrt{x + 5})^2 - 5 = x + 5 - 5 = x$

The domain of f is $\{x|x \geq -5\}$ and the domain of g is $(-\infty, \infty)$. Since $x^2 \geq 0$ for all values of x, then $x^2 - 5 \geq -5$ for all values of x and the domain of $g \circ f$ is $(-\infty, \infty)$.

Now consider the domain of $f \circ g$. There are no restrictions on the domain of g, so the domain of $f \circ g$ is the same as the domain of f, $\{x|x \geq -5\}$, or $[-5, \infty)$.

73. $(f \circ g)(x) = f(g(x)) = f(\sqrt{3 - x}) = (\sqrt{3 - x})^2 + 2 =$

$3 - x + 2 = 5 - x$

$(g \circ f)(x) = g(f(x)) = g(x^2 + 2) = \sqrt{3 - (x^2 + 2)} =$

$\sqrt{3 - x^2 - 2} = \sqrt{1 - x^2}$

The domain of f is $(-\infty, \infty)$ and the domain of g is $\{x|x \leq 3\}$, so the domain of $f \circ g$ is $\{x|x \leq 3\}$, or $(-\infty, 3]$.

Now consider the domain of $g \circ f$. There are no restrictions on the domain of f and the domain of g is $\{x|x \leq 3\}$, so we find the values of x for which $f(x) \leq 3$. We see that $x^2 + 2 \leq 3$ for $-1 \leq x \leq 1$, so the domain of $g \circ f$ is $\{x| -1 \leq x \leq 1\}$, or $[-1, 1]$.

75. $(f \circ g)(x) = f(g(x)) = f\left(\frac{1}{1+x}\right) =$

$$\frac{1 - \left(\frac{1}{1+x}\right)}{\frac{1}{1+x}} = \frac{\frac{1+x-1}{1+x}}{\frac{1}{1+x}} =$$

$$\frac{x}{1+x} \cdot \frac{1+x}{1} = x$$

$(g \circ f)(x) = g(f(x)) = g\left(\frac{1-x}{x}\right) =$

$$\frac{1}{1 + \left(\frac{1-x}{x}\right)} = \frac{1}{\frac{x+1-x}{x}} =$$

$$\frac{1}{\frac{1}{x}} = 1 \cdot \frac{x}{1} = x$$

The domain of f is $\{x|x \neq 0\}$ and the domain of g is $\{x|x \neq -1\}$, so we know that -1 is not in the domain of $f \circ g$. Since 0 is not in the domain of f, values of x for which $g(x) = 0$ are not in the domain of $f \circ g$. But $g(x)$ is never 0, so the domain of $f \circ g$ is $\{x|x \neq -1\}$, or $(-\infty, -1) \cup (-1, \infty)$.

Now consider the domain of $g \circ f$. Recall that 0 is not in the domain of f. Since -1 is not in the domain of g, we know that $g(x)$ cannot be -1. We find the value(s) of x for which $f(x) = -1$.

$\frac{1-x}{x} = -1$

$1 - x = -x$ Multiplying by x

$1 = 0$ False equation

We see that there are no values of x for which $f(x) = -1$, so the domain of $g \circ f$ is $\{x|x \neq 0\}$, or $(-\infty, 0) \cup (0, \infty)$.

77. $(f \circ g)(x) = f(g(x)) = f(x + 1) =$

$(x + 1)^3 - 5(x + 1)^2 + 3(x + 1) + 7 =$

$x^3 + 3x^2 + 3x + 1 - 5x^2 - 10x - 5 + 3x + 3 + 7 =$

$x^3 - 2x^2 - 4x + 6$

$(g \circ f)(x) = g(f(x)) = g(x^3 - 5x^2 + 3x + 7) =$

$x^3 - 5x^2 + 3x + 7 + 1 = x^3 - 5x^2 + 3x + 8$

The domain of f and of g is $(-\infty, \infty)$, so the domain of $f \circ g$ and of $g \circ f$ is $(-\infty, \infty)$.

79. $h(x) = (4 + 3x)^5$

This is $4 + 3x$ to the 5th power. The most obvious answer is $f(x) = x^5$ and $g(x) = 4 + 3x$.

81. $h(x) = \frac{1}{(x-2)^4}$

This is 1 divided by $(x - 2)$ to the 4th power. One obvious answer is $f(x) = \frac{1}{x^4}$ and $g(x) = x - 2$. Another possibility is $f(x) = \frac{1}{x}$ and $g(x) = (x - 2)^4$.

83. $f(x) = \frac{x-1}{x+1}$, $g(x) = x^3$

85. $f(x) = x^6$, $g(x) = \frac{2 + x^3}{2 - x^3}$

87. $f(x) = \sqrt{x}$, $g(x) = \frac{x-5}{x+2}$

89. $f(x) = x^3 - 5x^2 + 3x - 1$, $g(x) = x + 2$

91. $f(x) = y(x) \circ s(x) = y(s(x))$

$f(x) = 2(x - 32 + 12) = 2(x - 20)$

93.

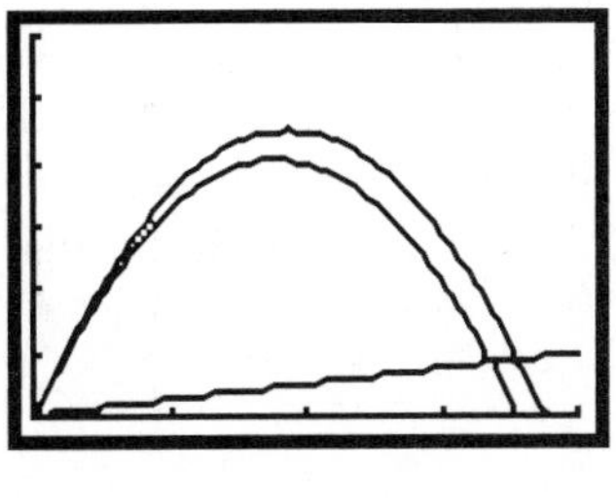

95. Discussion and Writing

97. Equations $(a) - (f)$ are in the form $y = mx + b$, so we can read the y-intercepts directly from the equations. Equations (g) and (h) can be written in this form as $y = \frac{2}{3}x - 2$ and $y = -2x + 3$, respectively. We see that only equation (c) has y-intercept $(0, 1)$.

99. If a line slopes down from left to right, its slope is negative. The equations $y = mx + b$ for which m is negative are (b), (d), (f), and (h). (See Exercise 97.)

101. The only equation that has $(0, 0)$ as a solution is (a).

103. Only equations (c) and (g) have the same slope and different y-intercepts. They represent parallel lines.

105. Answers may vary. One example is $f(x) = 2x + 5$ and $g(x) = \frac{x-5}{2}$. Other examples are found in Exercises 61, 62, 65, 66, 72, and 75.

107. The domain of $h(x)$ is $\left\{x \middle| x \neq \frac{7}{3}\right\}$, and the domain of $g(x)$ is $\{x|x \neq 3\}$, so $\frac{7}{3}$ and 3 are not in the domain of $(h/g)(x)$. We must also exclude the value of x for which $g(x) = 0$.

$$\frac{x^4 - 1}{5x - 15} = 0$$

$$x^4 - 1 = 0 \quad \text{Multiplying by } 5x - 15$$

$$x^4 = 1$$

$$x = \pm 1$$

Then the domain of $(h/g)(x)$ is
$\left\{x \middle| x \neq \frac{7}{3} \text{ and } x \neq 3 \text{ and } x \neq -1 \text{ and } x \neq 1\right\}$, or
$(-\infty, -1) \cup (-1, 1) \cup \left(1, \frac{7}{3}\right) \cup \left(\frac{7}{3}, 3\right) \cup (3, \infty)$.

Exercise Set 1.7

1. If the graph were folded on the x-axis, the parts above and below the x-axis would not coincide, so the graph is not symmetric with respect to the x-axis.

If the graph were folded on the y-axis, the parts to the left and right of the y-axis would coincide, so the graph is symmetric with respect to the y-axis.

If the graph were rotated 180°, the resulting graph would not coincide with the original graph, so it is not symmetric with respect to the origin.

3. If the graph were folded on the x-axis, the parts above and below the x-axis would coincide, so the graph is symmetric with respect to the x-axis.

If the graph were folded on the y-axis, the parts to the left and right of the y-axis would not coincide, so the graph is not symmetric with respect to the y-axis.

If the graph were rotated 180°, the resulting graph would not coincide with the original graph, so it is not symmetric with respect to the origin.

5. If the graph were folded on the x-axis, the parts above and below the x-axis would not coincide, so the graph is not symmetric with respect to the x-axis.

If the graph were folded on the y-axis, the parts to the left and right of the y-axis would not coincide, so the graph is not symmetric with respect to the y-axis.

If the graph were rotated 180°, the resulting graph would coincide with the original graph, so it is symmetric with respect to the origin.

7. Test for symmetry with respect to the x-axis:

$$5x - 5y = 0 \quad \text{Original equation}$$

$$5x - 5(-y) = 0 \quad \text{Replacing } y \text{ by } -y$$

$$5x + 5y = 0 \quad \text{Simplifying}$$

The last equation is not equivalent to the original equation, so the graph is not symmetric with respect to the x-axis.

Test for symmetry with respect to the y-axis:

$$5x - 5y = 0 \quad \text{Original equation}$$

$$5(-x) - 5y = 0 \quad \text{Replacing } x \text{ by } -x$$

$$-5x - 5y = 0 \quad \text{Simplifying}$$

$$5x + 5y = 0$$

The last equation is not equivalent to the original equation, so the graph is not symmetric with respect to the y-axis.

Test for symmetry with respect to the origin:

$$5x - 5y = 0 \quad \text{Original equation}$$

$$5(-x) - 5(-y) = 0 \quad \text{Replacing } x \text{ by } -x \text{ and } y \text{ by } -y$$

$$-5x + 5y = 0 \quad \text{Simplifying}$$

$$5x - 5y = 0$$

The last equation is equivalent to the original equation, so the graph is symmetric with respect to the origin.

9. Test for symmetry with respect to the x-axis:

$$3x^2 - 2y^2 = 3 \quad \text{Original equation}$$

$$3x^2 - 2(-y)^2 = 3 \quad \text{Replacing } y \text{ by } -y$$

$$3x^2 - 2y^2 = 3 \quad \text{Simplifying}$$

The last equation is equivalent to the original equation, so the graph is symmetric with respect to the x-axis.

Test for symmetry with respect to the y-axis:

$$3x^2 - 2y^2 = 3 \quad \text{Original equation}$$

$$3(-x)^2 - 2y^2 = 3 \quad \text{Replacing } x \text{ by } -x$$

$$3x^2 - 2y^2 = 3 \quad \text{Simplifying}$$

The last equation is equivalent to the original equation, so the graph is symmetric with respect to the y-axis.

Test for symmetry with respect to the origin:

$$3x^2 - 2y^2 = 3 \quad \text{Original equation}$$

$$3(-x)^2 - 2(-y)^2 = 3 \quad \text{Replacing } x \text{ by } -x \text{ and } y \text{ by } -y$$

$$3x^2 - 2y^2 = 3 \quad \text{Simplifying}$$

The last equation is equivalent to the original equation, so the graph is symmetric with respect to the origin.

11. Test for symmetry with respect to the x-axis:

$y = |2x|$ Original equation

$-y = |2x|$ Replacing y by $-y$

$y = -|2x|$ Simplifying

The last equation is not equivalent to the original equation, so the graph is not symmetric with respect to the x-axis.

Test for symmetry with respect to the y-axis:

$y = |2x|$ Original equation

$y = |2(-x)|$ Replacing x by $-x$

$y = |-2x|$ Simplifying

$y = |2x|$

The last equation is equivalent to the original equation, so the graph is symmetric with respect to the y-axis.

Test for symmetry with respect to the origin:

$y = |2x|$ Original equation

$-y = |2(-x)|$ Replacing x by $-x$ and y by $-y$

$-y = |-2x|$ Simplifying

$-y = |2x|$

$y = -|2x|$

The last equation is not equivalent to the original equation, so the graph is not symmetric with respect to the origin.

13. Test for symmetry with respect to the x-axis:

$2x^4 + 3 = y^2$ Original equation

$2x^4 + 3 = (-y)^2$ Replacing y by $-y$

$2x^4 + 3 = y^2$ Simplifying

The last equation is equivalent to the original equation, so the graph is symmetric with respect to the x-axis.

Test for symmetry with respect to the y-axis:

$2x^4 + 3 = y^2$ Original equation

$2(-x)^4 + 3 = y^2$ Replacing x by $-x$

$2x^4 + 3 = y^2$ Simplifying

The last equation is equivalent to the original equation, so the graph is symmetric with respect to the y-axis.

Test for symmetry with respect to the origin:

$2x^4 + 3 = y^2$ Original equation

$2(-x)^4 + 3 = (-y)^2$ Replacing x by $-x$ and y by $-y$

$2x^4 + 3 = y^2$ Simplifying

The last equation is equivalent to the original equation, so the graph is symmetric with respect to the origin.

15. Test for symmetry with respect to the x-axis:

$3y^3 = 4x^3 + 2$ Original equation

$3(-y)^3 = 4x^3 + 2$ Replacing y by $-y$

$-3y^3 = 4x^3 + 2$ Simplifying

$3y^3 = -4x^3 - 2$

The last equation is not equivalent to the original equation, so the graph is not symmetric with respect to the x-axis.

Test for symmetry with respect to the y-axis:

$3y^3 = 4x^3 + 2$ Original equation

$3y^3 = 4(-x)^3 + 2$ Replacing x by $-x$

$3y^3 = -4x^3 + 2$ Simplifying

The last equation is not equivalent to the original equation, so the graph is not symmetric with respect to the y-axis.

Test for symmetry with respect to the origin:

$3y^3 = 4x^3 + 2$ Original equation

$3(-y)^3 = 4(-x)^3 + 2$ Replacing x by $-x$ and y by $-y$

$-3y^3 = -4x^3 + 2$ Simplifying

$3y^3 = 4x^3 - 2$

The last equation is not equivalent to the original equation, so the graph is not symmetric with respect to the origin.

17. Test for symmetry with respect to the x-axis:

$xy = 12$ Original equation

$x(-y) = 12$ Replacing y by $-y$

$-xy = 12$ Simplifying

$xy = -12$

The last equation is not equivalent to the original equation, so the graph is not symmetric with respect to the x-axis.

Test for symmetry with respect to the y-axis:

$xy = 12$ Original equation

$-xy = 12$ Replacing x by $-x$

$xy = -12$ Simplifying

The last equation is not equivalent to the original equation, so the graph is not symmetric with respect to the y-axis.

Test for symmetry with respect to the origin:

$xy = 12$ Original equation

$-x(-y) = 12$ Replacing x by $-x$ and y by $-y$

$xy = 12$ Simplifying

The last equation is equivalent to the original equation, so the graph is symmetric with respect to the origin.

19. x-axis: Replace y with $-y$; $(-5, -6)$

y-axis: Replace x with $-x$; $(5, 6)$

Origin: Replace x with $-x$ and y with $-y$; $(5, -6)$

21. x-axis: Replace y with $-y$; $(-10, 7)$

y-axis: Replace x with $-x$; $(10, -7)$

Origin: Replace x with $-x$ and y with $-y$; $(10, 7)$

23. x-axis: Replace y with $-y$; $(0, 4)$

y-axis: Replace x with $-x$; $(0, -4)$

Origin: Replace x with $-x$ and y with $-y$; $(0, 4)$

25. The graph is symmetric with respect to the y-axis, so the function is even.

27. The graph is symmetric with respect to the origin, so the function is odd.

29. The graph is not symmetric with respect to either the y-axis or the origin, so the function is neither even nor odd.

31.
$$f(x) = -3x^3 + 2x$$
$$f(-x) = -3(-x)^3 + 2(-x) = 3x^3 - 2x$$
$$-f(x) = -(-3x^3 + 2x) = 3x^3 - 2x$$
$f(-x) = -f(x)$, so f is odd.

33.
$$f(x) = 5x^2 + 2x^4 - 1$$
$$f(-x) = 5(-x)^2 + 2(-x)^4 - 1 = 5x^2 + 2x^4 - 1$$
$f(x) = f(-x)$, so f is even.

35.
$$f(x) = x^{17}$$
$$f(-x) = (-x)^{17} = -x^{17}$$
$$-f(x) = -x^{17}$$
$f(-x) = -f(x)$, so f is odd.

37.
$$f(x) = \frac{1}{x^2}$$
$$f(-x) = \frac{1}{(-x)^2} = \frac{1}{x^2}$$
$f(x) = f(-x)$, so f is even.

39.
$$f(x) = 8$$
$$f(-x) = 8$$
$f(x) = f(-x)$, so f is even.

41. Shift the graph of $f(x) = x^2$ right 3 units.

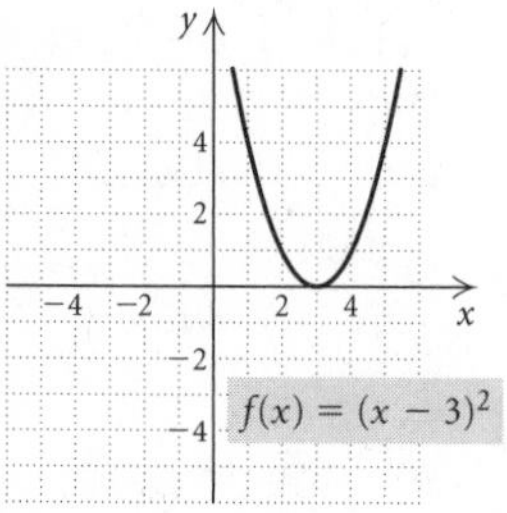

43. Shift the graph of $g(x) = x$ down 3 units.

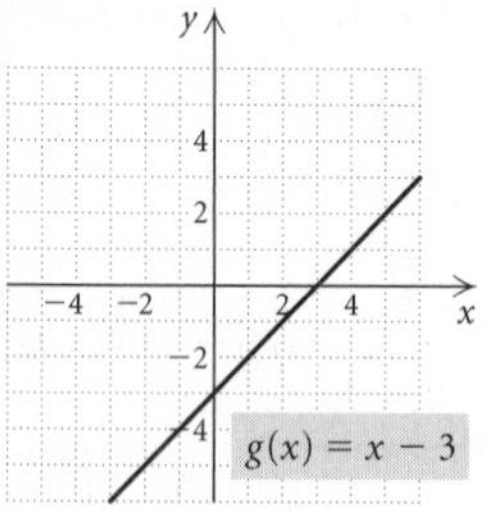

45. Reflect the graph of $h(x) = \sqrt{x}$ across the x-axis.

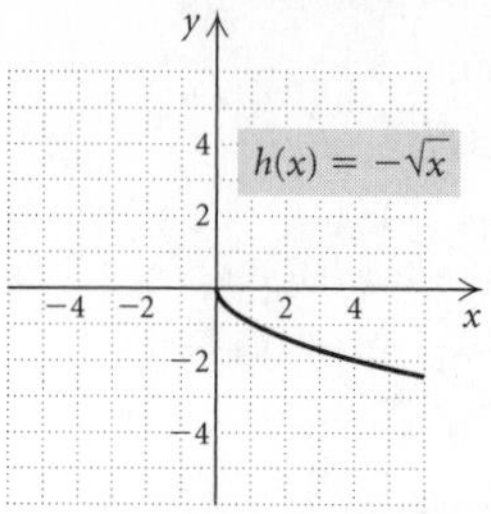

47. Shift the graph of $h(x) = \dfrac{1}{x}$ up 4 units.

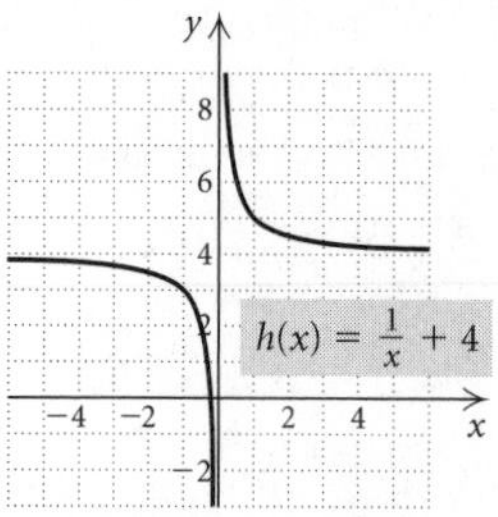

49. First stretch the graph of $h(x) = x$ vertically by multiplying each y-coordinate by 3. Then reflect it across the x-axis and shift it up 3 units.

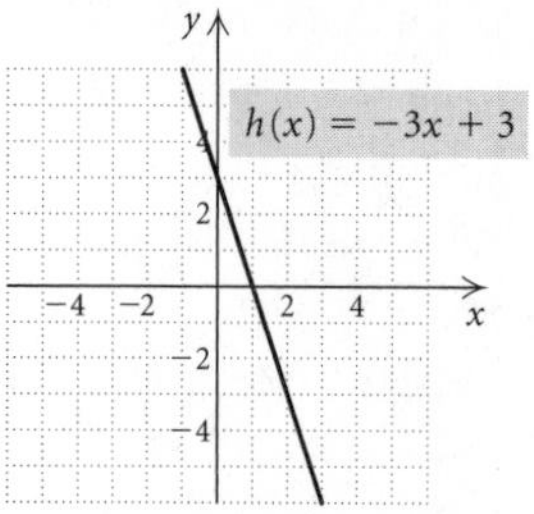

51. First shrink the graph of $h(x) = |x|$ vertically by multiplying each y-coordinate by $\dfrac{1}{2}$. Then shift it down 2 units.

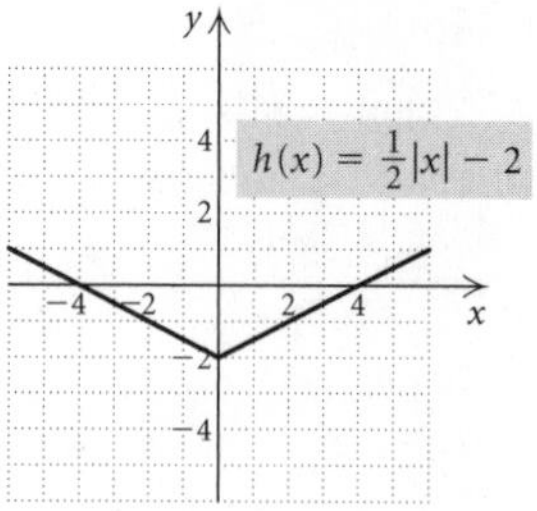

53. Shift the graph of $g(x) = x^3$ right 2 units and reflect it across the x-axis.

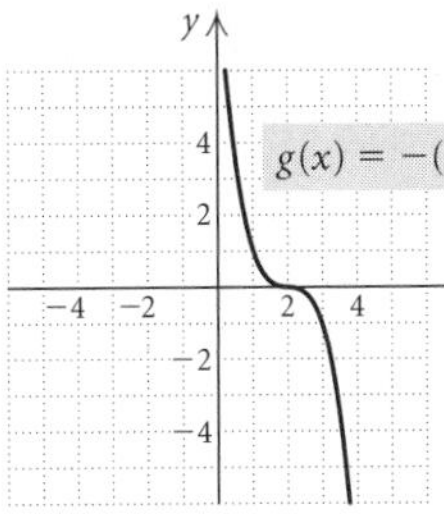

55. Shift the graph of $g(x) = x^2$ left 1 unit and down 1 unit.

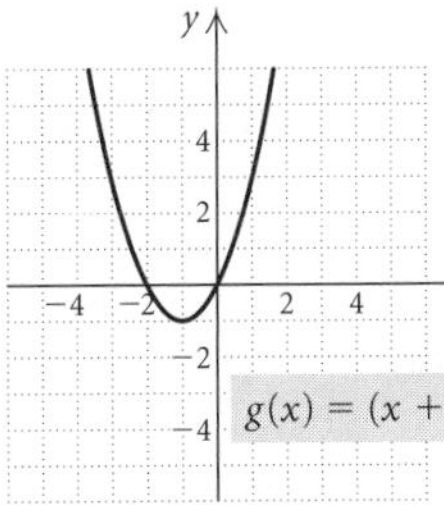

57. First shrink the graph of $g(x) = x^3$ vertically by multiplying each y-coordinate by $\frac{1}{3}$. Then shift it up 2 units.

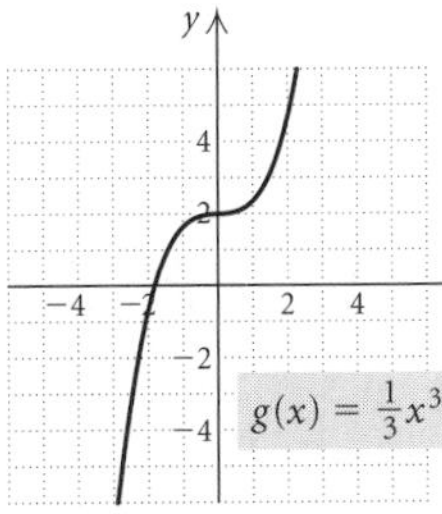

59. Shift the graph of $f(x) = \sqrt{x}$ left 2 units.

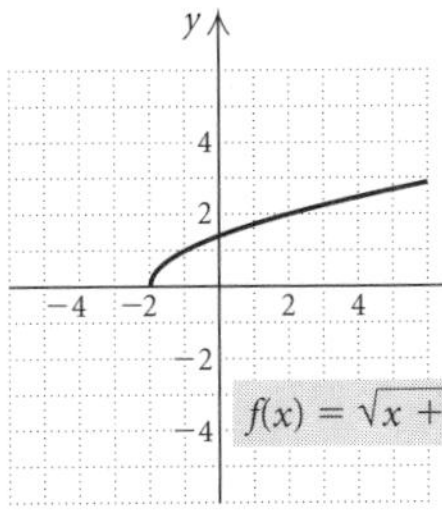

61. Shift the graph of $f(x) = \sqrt[3]{x}$ down 2 units.

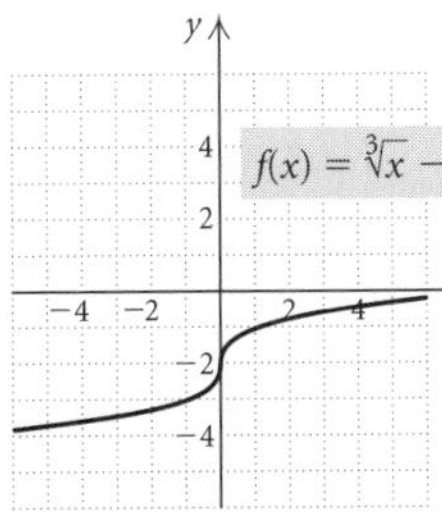

63. Think of the graph of $f(x) = |x|$. Since $g(x) = f(3x)$, the graph of $g(x) = |3x|$ is the graph of $f(x) = |x|$ shrunk horizontally by dividing each x-coordinate by 3 $\left(\text{or multiplying each } x\text{-coordinate by } \frac{1}{3}\right)$.

65. Think of the graph of $f(x) = \frac{1}{x}$. Since $h(x) = 2f(x)$, the graph of $h(x) = \frac{2}{x}$ is the graph of $f(x) = \frac{1}{x}$ stretched vertically by multiplying each y-coordinate by 2.

67. Think of the graph of $g(x) = \sqrt{x}$. Since $f(x) = 3g(x) - 5$, the graph of $f(x) = 3\sqrt{x} - 5$ is the graph of $g(x) = \sqrt{x}$ stretched vertically by multiplying each y-coordinate by 3 and then shifted down 5 units.

69. Think of the graph of $f(x) = |x|$. Since $g(x) = f\left(\frac{1}{3}x\right) - 4$, the graph of $g(x) = \left|\frac{1}{3}x\right| - 4$ is the graph of $f(x) = |x|$ stretched horizontally by multiplying each x-coordinate by 3 and then shifted down 4 units.

71. Think of the graph of $g(x) = x^2$. Since $f(x) = -\frac{1}{4}g(x - 5)$, the graph of $f(x) = -\frac{1}{4}(x - 5)^2$ is the graph of $g(x) = x^2$ shifted right 5 units, shrunk vertically by multiplying each y-coordinate by $\frac{1}{4}$, and reflected across the x-axis.

73. Think of the graph of $g(x) = \frac{1}{x}$. Since $f(x) = g(x + 3) + 2$, the graph of $f(x) = \frac{1}{x + 3} + 2$ is the graph of $g(x) = \frac{1}{x}$ shifted left 3 units and up 2 units.

75. Think of the graph of $f(x) = x^2$. Since $h(x) = -f(x-3) + 5$, the graph of $h(x) = -(x-3)^2 + 5$ is the graph of $f(x) = x^2$ shifted right 3 units, reflected across the x-axis, and shifted up 5 units.

77. The graph of $y = g(x)$ is the graph of $y = f(x)$ shrunk vertically by a factor of $\frac{1}{2}$. Multiply the y-coordinate by $\frac{1}{2}$: $(-12, 2)$.

79. The graph of $y = g(x)$ is the graph of $y = f(x)$ reflected across the y-axis, so we reflect the point across the y-axis: $(12, 4)$.

81. The graph of $y = g(x)$ is the graph of $y = f(x)$ shifted down 2 units. Subtract 2 from the y-coordinate: $(-12, 2)$.

83. The graph of $y = g(x)$ is the graph of $y = f(x)$ stretched vertically by a factor of 4. Multiply the y-coordinate by 4: $(-12, 16)$.

85. Shape: $h(x) = x^2$

Turn $h(x)$ upside-down (that is, reflect it across the x-axis): $g(x) = -h(x) = -x^2$

Shift $g(x)$ right 8 units: $f(x) = g(x - 8) = -(x - 8)^2$

87. Shape: $h(x) = |x|$

Shift $h(x)$ left 7 units: $g(x) = h(x+7) = |x+7|$

Shift $g(x)$ up 2 units: $f(x) = g(x) + 2 = |x+7| + 2$

89. Shape: $h(x) = \dfrac{1}{x}$

Shrink $h(x)$ vertically by a factor of $\dfrac{1}{2}$ $\left(\text{that is, multiply each function value by } \dfrac{1}{2}\right)$:

$g(x) = \dfrac{1}{2}h(x) = \dfrac{1}{2}\cdot\dfrac{1}{x}$, or $\dfrac{1}{2x}$

Shift $g(x)$ down 3 units: $f(x) = g(x) - 3 = \dfrac{1}{2x} - 3$

91. Shape: $m(x) = x^2$

Turn $m(x)$ upside-down (that is, reflect it across the x-axis): $h(x) = -m(x) = -x^2$

Shift $h(x)$ right 3 units: $g(x) = h(x-3) = -(x-3)^2$

Shift $g(x)$ up 4 units: $f(x) = g(x) + 4 = -(x-3)^2 + 4$

93. Shape: $m(x) = \sqrt{x}$

Reflect $m(x)$ across the y-axis: $h(x) = m(-x) = \sqrt{-x}$

Shift $h(x)$ left 2 units: $g(x) = h(x+2) = \sqrt{-(x+2)}$

Shift $g(x)$ down 1 unit: $f(x) = g(x) - 1 = \sqrt{-(x+2)} - 1$

95. Each y-coordinate is multiplied by -2. We plot and connect $(-4,0)$, $(-3,4)$, $(-1,4)$, $(2,-6)$, and $(5,0)$.

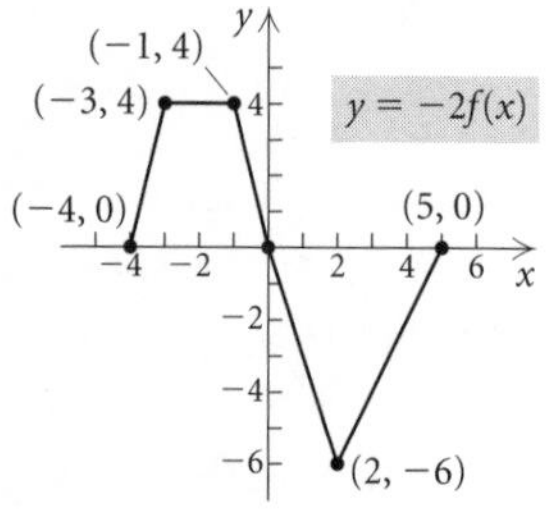

97. The graph is reflected across the y-axis and stretched horizontally by a factor of 2. That is, each x-coordinate is multiplied by -2 $\left(\text{or divided by } -\dfrac{1}{2}\right)$. We plot and connect $(8,0)$, $(6,-2)$, $(2,-2)$, $(-4,3)$, and $(-10,0)$.

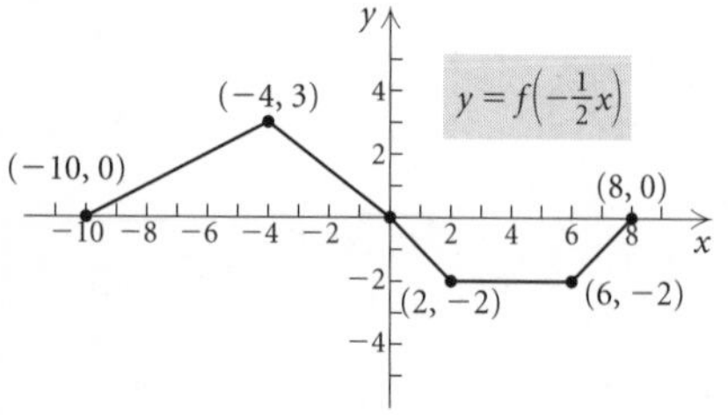

99. The graph is shifted right 1 unit so each x-coordinate is increased by 1. The graph is also reflected across the x-axis, shrunk vertically by a factor of 2, and shifted up 3 units. Thus, each y-coordinate is multiplied by $-\dfrac{1}{2}$ and then increased by 3. We plot and connect $(-3,3)$, $(-2,4)$, $(0,4)$, $(3,1.5)$, and $(6,3)$.

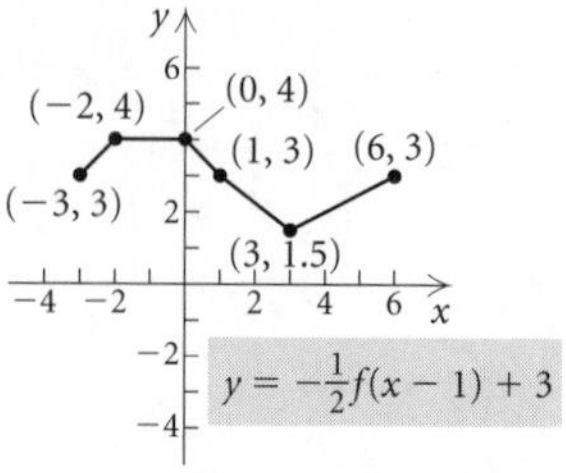

101. The graph is reflected across the y-axis so each x-coordinate is replaced by its opposite.

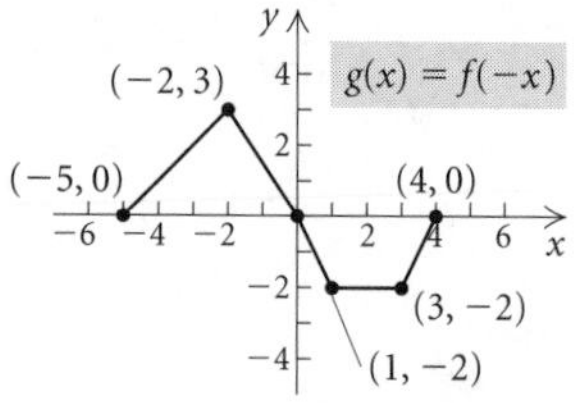

103. The graph is shifted left 2 units so each x-coordinate is decreased by 2. It is also reflected across the x-axis so each y-coordinate is replaced with its opposite. In addition, the graph is shifted up 1 unit, so each y-coordinate is then increased by 1.

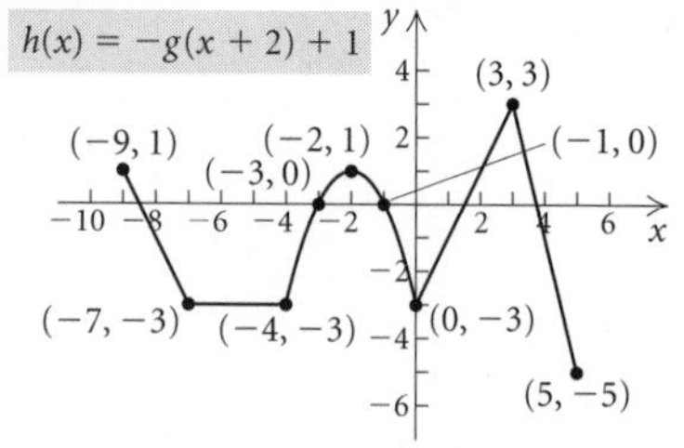

105. The graph is shrunk horizontally. The x-coordinates of $y = h(x)$ are one-half the corresponding x-coordinates of $y = g(x)$.

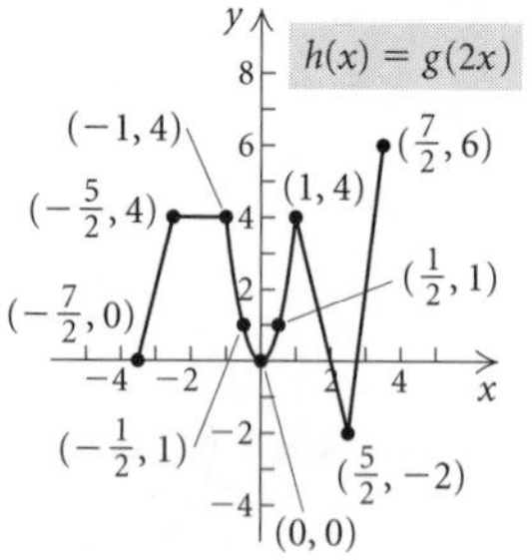

107. $g(x) = f(-x) + 3$

The graph of $g(x)$ is the graph of $f(x)$ reflected across the y-axis and shifted up 3 units. This is graph (f).

109. $g(x) = -f(x) + 3$

The graph of $g(x)$ is the graph of $f(x)$ reflected across the x-axis and shifted up 3 units. This is graph (f).

111. $g(x) = \frac{1}{3}f(x-2)$

The graph of $g(x)$ is the graph of $f(x)$ shrunk vertically by a factor of 3 $\left(\text{that is, each } y\text{-coordinate is multiplied by } \frac{1}{3}\right)$ and then shifted right 2 units. This is graph (d).

113. $g(x) = \frac{1}{3}f(x+2)$

The graph of $g(x)$ is the graph of $f(x)$ shrunk vertically by a factor of 3 $\left(\text{that is, each } y\text{-coordinate is multiplied by } \frac{1}{3}\right)$ and then shifted left 2 units. This is graph (c).

115. $f(-x) = 2(-x)^4 - 35(-x)^3 + 3(-x) - 5 =$
$2x^4 + 35x^3 - 3x - 5 = g(x)$

117. The graph of $f(x) = x^3 - 3x^2$ is shifted up 2 units. A formula for the transformed function is $g(x) = f(x) + 2$, or $g(x) = x^3 - 3x^2 + 2$.

119. The graph of $f(x) = x^3 - 3x^2$ is shifted left 1 unit. A formula for the transformed function is $k(x) = f(x+1)$, or $k(x) = (x+1)^3 - 3(x+1)^2$.

121. Discussion and Writing

123. For every point (x, y) on the graph of $y = f(x)$, its reflection across the y-axis $(-x, y)$ is on the graph of $y = f(-x)$.

125. $f(x) = 5x^2 - 7$

a) $f(-3) = 5(-3)^2 - 7 = 5 \cdot 9 - 7 = 45 - 7 = 38$

b) $f(3) = 5 \cdot 3^2 - 7 = 5 \cdot 9 - 7 = 45 - 7 = 38$

c) $f(a) = 5a^2 - 7$

d) $f(-a) = 5(-a)^2 - 7 = 5a^2 - 7$

127. First find the slope of the given line.

$$8x - y = 10$$
$$8x = y + 10$$
$$8x - 10 = y$$

The slope of the given line is 8. The slope of a line perpendicular to this line is the opposite of the reciprocal of 8, or $-\frac{1}{8}$.

$$y - y_1 = m(x - x_1)$$
$$y - 1 = -\frac{1}{8}[x - (-1)]$$
$$y - 1 = -\frac{1}{8}(x + 1)$$
$$y - 1 = -\frac{1}{8}x - \frac{1}{8}$$
$$y = -\frac{1}{8}x + \frac{7}{8}$$

129. Each point for which $f(x) < 0$ is reflected across the x-axis.

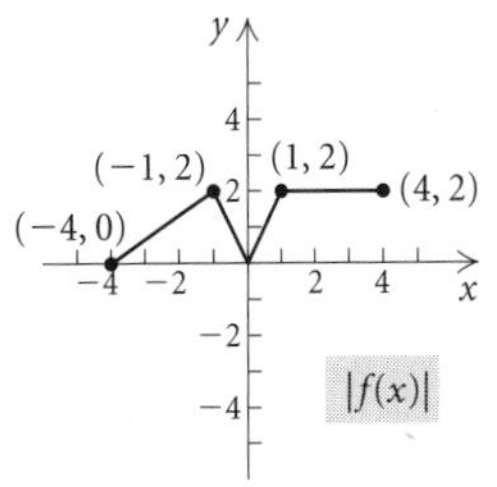

131. Each point for which $g(x) < 0$ is reflected across the x-axis.

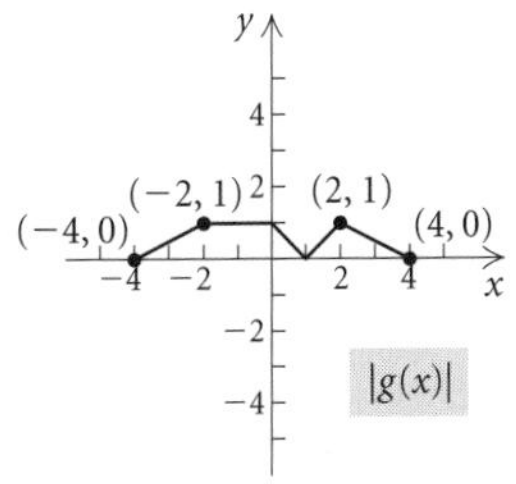

133.
$$f(x) = x\sqrt{10 - x^2}$$
$$f(-x) = -x\sqrt{10 - (-x)^2} = -x\sqrt{10 - x^2}$$
$$-f(x) = -x\sqrt{10 - x^2}$$

Since $f(-x) = -f(x)$, f is odd.

135. If the graph were folded on the x-axis, the parts above and below the x-axis would coincide, so the graph is symmetric with respect to the x-axis.

If the graph were folded on the y-axis, the parts to the left and right of the y-axis would not coincide, so the graph is not symmetric with respect to the y-axis.

If the graph were rotated 180°, the resulting graph would not coincide with the original graph, so it is not symmetric with respect to the origin.

137. If the graph were folded on the x-axis, the parts above and below the x-axis would coincide, so the graph is symmetric with respect to the x-axis.

If the graph were folded on the y-axis, the parts to the left and right of the y-axis would not coincide, so the graph is not symmetric with respect to the y-axis.

If the graph were rotated 180°, the resulting graph would not coincide with the original graph, so it is not symmetric with respect to the origin.

139. $f(2-3) = f(-1) = 5$, so $b = 5$.

(The graph of $y = f(x-3)$ is the graph of $y = f(x)$ shifted right 3 units, so the point $(-1, 5)$ on $y = f(x)$ is transformed to the point $(-1+3, 5)$, or $(2, 5)$ on $y = f(x-3)$.)

141. Let $f(x)$ and $g(x)$ be even functions. Then by definition, $f(x) = f(-x)$ and $g(x) = g(-x)$. Thus, $(f+g)(x) = f(x) + g(x) = f(-x) + g(-x) = (f+g)(-x)$ and $f + g$ is even. The statement is true.

143. See the answer section in the text.

145. a), b) See the answer section in the text.

Chapter 2

Functions, Equations, and Inequalities

Exercise Set 2.1

1. $4x + 5 = 21$

$4x = 16$ Subtracting 5 on both sides

$x = 4$ Dividing by 4 on both sides

The solution is 4.

3. $4x + 3 = 0$

$4x = -3$ Subtracting 3 on both sides

$x = -\frac{3}{4}$ Dividing by 4 on both sides

The solution is $-\frac{3}{4}$.

5. $3 - x = 12$

$-x = 9$ Subtracting 3 on both sides

$x = -9$ Multiplying (or dividing) by -1 on both sides

The solution is -9.

7. $8 = 5x - 3$

$11 = 5x$ Adding 3 on both sides

$\frac{11}{5} = x$ Dividing by 5 on both sides

The solution is $\frac{11}{5}$.

9. $y + 1 = 2y - 7$

$1 = y - 7$ Subtracting y on both sides

$8 = y$ Adding 7 on both sides

The solution is 8.

11. $2x + 7 = x + 3$

$x + 7 = 3$ Subtracting x on both sides

$x = -4$ Subtracting 7 on both sides

The solution is -4.

13. $3x - 5 = 2x + 1$

$x - 5 = 1$ Subtracting $2x$ on both sides

$x = 6$ Adding 5 on both sides

The solution is 6.

15. $4x - 5 = 7x - 2$

$-5 = 3x - 2$ Subtracting $4x$ on both sides

$-3 = 3x$ Adding 2 on both sides

$-1 = x$ Dividing by 3 on both sides

The solution is -1.

17. $5x - 2 + 3x = 2x + 6 - 4x$

$8x - 2 = 6 - 2x$ Collecting like terms

$8x + 2x = 6 + 2$ Adding $2x$ and 2 on both sides

$10x = 8$ Collecting like terms

$x = \frac{8}{10}$ Dividing by 10 on both sides

$x = \frac{4}{5}$, or 0.8 Simplifying

The solution is $\frac{4}{5}$, or 0.8.

19. $7(3x + 6) = 11 - (x + 2)$

$21x + 42 = 11 - x - 2$ Using the distributive property

$21x + 42 = 9 - x$ Collecting like terms

$21x + x = 9 - 42$ Adding x and subtracting 42 on both sides

$22x = -33$ Collecting like terms

$x = -\frac{33}{22}$ Dividing by 22 on both sides

$x = -\frac{3}{2}$, or -1.5 Simplifying

The solution is $-\frac{3}{2}$, or -1.5.

21. $3(x + 1) = 5 - 2(3x + 4)$

$3x + 3 = 5 - 6x - 8$ Removing parentheses

$3x + 3 = -6x - 3$ Collecting like terms

$9x + 3 = -3$ Adding $6x$

$9x = -6$ Subtracting 3

$x = -\frac{2}{3}$ Dividing by 9

The solution is $-\frac{2}{3}$.

23. $2(x - 4) = 3 - 5(2x + 1)$

$2x - 8 = 3 - 10x - 5$ Using the distributive property

$2x - 8 = -10x - 2$ Collecting like terms

$12x = 6$ Adding $10x$ and 8 on both sides

$x = \frac{1}{2}$ Dividing by 12 on both sides

The solution is $\frac{1}{2}$.

25. ***Familiarize.*** Let t = the average tuition at a public college or university in 2001. We know that 9.6% of this amount is \$356.

Translate.

$$\underbrace{\$356}\ \text{is}\ \underbrace{9.6\%}\ \text{of}\ \underbrace{\text{the average tuition in 2001.}}$$
$$356 = 0.096 \cdot t$$

Carry out. We solve the equation.

$$356 = 0.096 \cdot t$$
$$3708 \approx t \qquad \text{Dividing by } 0.096$$

Check. Since 9.6% of \$3708, or 0.096(\$3708), is approximately \$356, the answer checks.

State. In 2001 the average tuition at a public college or university was about \$3708.

27. ***Familiarize.*** Let $d =$ the percent of spending on films in 2002 that went for DVDs.

Translate.

$$\underbrace{\$8.1\text{ billion}}\ \text{is}\ \underbrace{\text{what percent}}\ \text{of}\ \underbrace{\$12.4\text{ billion?}}$$
$$8.1 = d \cdot 12.4$$

Carry out. We solve the equation.

$$8.1 = d \cdot 12.4$$
$$0.653 \approx d \qquad \text{Dividing by } 12.4$$
$$65.3\% \approx d \qquad \text{Writing percent notation}$$

Check. Since 65.3% of \$12.4 billion, or 0.653(\$12.4 billion), is approximately \$8.1 billion, the answer checks.

State. In 2002, about 65.3% of the spending on copies of films for home viewing went for DVDs.

29. ***Familiarize.*** Let $h =$ the number of U.S. households with broadband Internet access in 2003, in millions.

Translate.

$$\underbrace{\text{Number of households in 2006}}\ \text{is}\ \underbrace{25.6\text{ million}}\ \underbrace{\text{more than}}\ \underbrace{\text{number of households in 2003.}}$$
$$54.8 = 25.6 + h$$

Carry out. We solve the equation.

$$54.8 = 25.6 + h$$
$$29.2 = h \qquad \text{Subtracting } 25.6$$

Check. Since 29.2 million more than 25.6 million or 25.6 million + 29.2 million is 54.8 million, the answer checks.

State. In 2003 29.2 million households had broadband Internet access.

31. ***Familiarize.*** Let $c =$ the average daily calorie requirement for many adults.

Translate.

$$\underbrace{1560\text{ calories}}\ \text{is}\ \frac{3}{4}\ \text{of}\ \underbrace{\text{the average dailyrequirement for many adults.}}$$
$$1560 = \frac{3}{4} \cdot c$$

Carry out. We solve the equation.

$$1560 = \frac{3}{4} \cdot c$$
$$\frac{4}{3} \cdot 1560 = c \qquad \text{Multiplying by } \frac{4}{3}$$
$$2080 = c$$

Check. $\frac{3}{4} \cdot 2080 = 1560$, so the answer checks.

State. The average daily calorie requirement for many adults is 2080 calories.

33. ***Familiarize.*** Let $P =$ the amount Tamisha borrowed. We will use the formula $I = Prt$ to find the interest owed. For $r = 5\%$, or 0.05, and $t = 1$, we have $I = P(0.05)(1)$, or $0.05P$.

Translate.

$$\underbrace{\text{Amount borrowed}}\ \text{plus}\ \text{interest}\ \text{is}\ \$1365.$$
$$P + 0.05P = 1365$$

Carry out. We solve the equation.

$$P + 0.05P = 1365$$
$$1.05P = 1365 \qquad \text{Adding}$$
$$P = 1300 \qquad \text{Dividing by } 1.05$$

Check. The interest due on a loan of \$1300 for 1 year at a rate of 5% is \$1300(0.05)(1), or \$65, and \$1300 + \$65 = \$1365. The answer checks.

State. Tamisha borrowed \$1300.

35. ***Familiarize.*** Let $s =$ Ryan's sales for the month. Then his commission is 8% of s, or $0.08s$.

Translate.

$$\underbrace{\text{Base salary}}\ \text{plus}\ \text{commission}\ \text{is}\ \underbrace{\text{total pay.}}$$
$$1500 + 0.08s = 2284$$

Carry out. We solve the equation.

$$1500 + 0.08s = 2284$$
$$0.08s = 784 \qquad \text{Subtracting } 1500$$
$$s = 9800$$

Check. 8% of \$9800, or 0.08(\$9800), is \$784 and \$1500 + \$784 = \$2284. The answer checks.

State. Ryan's sales for the month were \$9800.

37. ***Familiarize.*** Let $d =$ the number of miles Diego traveled in the cab.

Translate.

$$\underbrace{\text{Pickup fee}}\ \text{plus}\ \underbrace{\text{cost per mile}}\ \text{times}\ \underbrace{\text{number of miles traveled}}\ \text{is}\ \$19.75.$$
$$1.75 + 1.50 \cdot d = 19.75$$

Carry out. We solve the equation.

$$1.75 + 1.50 \cdot d = 19.75$$
$$1.5d = 18 \qquad \text{Subtracting } 1.75$$
$$d = 12 \qquad \text{Dividing by } 1.5$$

Check. If Diego travels 12 mi, his fare is \$1.75 + \$1.50 · 12, or \$1.75 + \$18, or \$19.75. The answer checks.

State. Diego traveled 12 mi in the cab.

39. ***Familiarize***. We make a drawing.

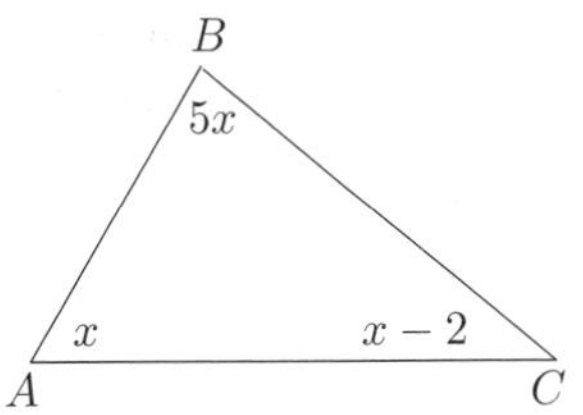

We let x = the measure of angle A. Then $5x$ = the measure of angle B, and $x - 2$ = the measure of angle C. The sum of the angle measures is 180°.

Translate.

Measure of angle A	+	Measure of angle B	+	Measure of angle C	=	180.
x	+	$5x$	+	$x - 2$	=	180

Carry out. We solve the equation.

$$x + 5x + x - 2 = 180$$
$$7x - 2 = 180$$
$$7x = 182$$
$$x = 26$$

If $x = 26$, then $5x = 5 \cdot 26$, or 130, and $x - 2 = 26 - 2$, or 24.

Check. The measure of angle B, 130°, is five times the measure of angle A, 26°. The measure of angle C, 24°, is 2° less than the measure of angle A, 26°. The sum of the angle measures is 26° + 130° + 24°, or 180°. The answer checks.

State. The measure of angles A, B, and C are 26°, 130°, and 24°, respectively.

41. ***Familiarize***. Using the labels on the drawing in the text, we let w = the width of the test plot and $w + 25$ = the length, in meters. Recall that for a rectangle, Perimeter = 2 · length + 2 · width.

Translate.

Perimeter	=	2 · length	+	2 · width
322	=	$2(w + 25)$	+	$2 \cdot w$

Carry out. We solve the equation.

$$322 = 2(w + 25) + 2 \cdot w$$
$$322 = 2w + 50 + 2w$$
$$322 = 4w + 50$$
$$272 = 4w$$
$$68 = w$$

When $w = 68$, then $w + 25 = 68 + 25 = 93$.

Check. The length is 25 m more than the width: $93 = 68 + 25$. The perimeter is $2 \cdot 93 + 2 \cdot 68$, or $186 + 136$, or 322 m. The answer checks.

State. The length is 93 m; the width is 68 m.

43. ***Familiarize***. Let l = the length of the soccer field and $l - 35$ = the width, in yards.

Translate. We use the formula for the perimeter of a rectangle. We substitute 330 for P and $l - 35$ for w.

$$P = 2l + 2w$$
$$330 = 2l + 2(l - 35)$$

Carry out. We solve the equation.

$$330 = 2l + 2(l - 35)$$
$$330 = 2l + 2l - 70$$
$$330 = 4l - 70$$
$$400 = 4l$$
$$100 = l$$

If $l = 100$, then $l - 35 = 100 - 35 = 65$.

Check. The width, 65 yd, is 35 yd less than the length, 100 yd. Also, the perimeter is

$$2 \cdot 100 \text{ yd} + 2 \cdot 65 \text{ yd} = 200 \text{ yd} + 130 \text{ yd} = 330 \text{ yd}.$$

The answer checks.

State. The length of the field is 100 yd, and the width is 65 yd.

45. ***Familiarize***. Let w = the number of pounds of Jocelyn's body weight that is water.

Translate.

50%	of	body weight	is	water.
↓	↓	↓	↓	↓
0.5	×	135	=	w

Carry out. We solve the equation.

$$0.5 \times 135 = w$$
$$67.5 = w$$

Check. Since 50% of 138 is 67.5, the answer checks.

State. 67.5 lb of Jocelyn's body weight is water.

47. ***Familiarize***. We make a drawing. Let r = the speed of the Central Railway freight train. Then $r + 14$ = the speed of the Amtrak passenger train. Also let t = the time the train travels.

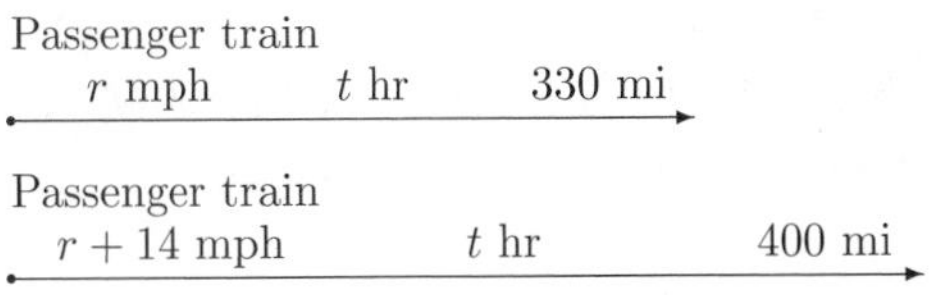

We can also organize the information in a table.

$$d = r \cdot t$$

	Distance	Rate	Time
Freight train	330	r	t
Passenger train	400	$r + 14$	t

Translate. Using the formula $d = rt$ in each row of the table, we get two equations.

$330 = rt$ and $400 = (r+14)t$

Solve each equation for t.

$\frac{330}{r} = t$ and $\frac{400}{r+14} = t$

Thus, we have the equation

$\frac{330}{r} = \frac{400}{r+14}$.

Carry out. We solve the equation.

$$\frac{330}{r} = \frac{400}{r+14}, \text{ LCD is } r(r+14)$$

$$r(r+14)\cdot\frac{330}{r} = r(r+14)\cdot\frac{400}{r+14}$$

$$330(r+14) = 400r$$

$$330r + 4620 = 400r$$

$$4620 = 70r$$

$$66 = r$$

When $r = 66$, $r + 14 = 66 + 14 = 80$.

Check. The freight train travels 330 mi in 330/66, or 5 hr and the passenger train travels 400 mi in 400/80, or 5 hr. Since the times are the same the answer checks.

State. The speed of the Central Railway freight train is 66 mph, and the speed of the Amtrak passenger train is 80 mph.

49. ***Familiarize.*** Let t = the number of hours it takes the paddleboat to travel 36 mi upstream. The boat travels upstream at a rate of $12-4$, or 8 mph.

Translate. We use the formula $d = rt$.

$36 = 8\cdot t$

Carry out. We solve the equation.

$$36 = 8\cdot t$$

$$4.5 = t$$

Check. At a rate of 8 mph, in 4.5 hr the boat travels 8(4.5), or 36 mi. The answer checks.

State. It takes the paddleboat 4.5 hr to travel 36 mi upstream.

51. ***Familiarize.*** Let t = the number of hours it will take Angelo to travel 20 km downstream. The kayak travels downstream at a rate of $14+2$, or 16 km/h.

Translate. We use the formula $d = rt$.

$20 = 16t$

Carry out. We solve the equation.

$$20 = 16t$$

$$1.25 = t$$

Check. At a rate of 16 km/h, in 1.25 hr the kayak will travel 16(1.25), or 20 km. The answer checks.

State. It will take Angelo 1.25 hr to travel 20 km downstream.

53. ***Familiarize.*** Let x = the amount invested at 3% interest. Then $5000 - x$ = the amount invested at 4%. We organize the information in a table, keeping in mind the simple interest formula, $I = Prt$.

	Amount invested	Interest rate	Time	Amount of interest
3% investment	x	3%, or 0.03	1 yr	$x(0.03)(1)$, or $0.03x$
4% investment	$5000-x$	4%, or 0.04	1 yr	$(5000-x)(0.04)(1)$, or $0.04(5000-x)$
Total	5000			176

Translate.

Interest on 3% investment plus interest on 4% investment is \$176.

$$0.03x + 0.04(5000-x) = 176$$

Carry out. We solve the equation.

$$0.03x + 0.04(5000-x) = 176$$

$$0.03x + 200 - 0.04x = 176$$

$$-0.01x + 200 = 176$$

$$-0.01x = -24$$

$$x = 2400$$

If $x = 2400$, then $5000 - x = 5000 - 2400 = 2600$.

Check. The interest on \$2400 at 3% for 1 yr is \$2400(0.03)(1) = \$72. The interest on \$2600 at 4% for 1 yr is \$2600(0.04)(1) = \$104. Since \$72 + \$104 = \$176, the answer checks.

State. \$2400 was invested at 3%, and \$2600 was invested at 4%.

55. ***Familiarize.*** Let w = the number of violations reqported by Division II schools. Then $1989 - v$ = the number of violations reported by Division I schools.

Translate.

Number of Division I violations is 6.5 times number of Division II violations.

$$1989 - v = 6.5 \times v$$

Carry out. We solve the equation.

$$1989 - v = 6.5v$$

$$1989 = 7.5v$$

$$265 \approx v$$

If $v = 265$, then $1989 - v = 1989 - 265 = 1724$.

Check. $6.5(265) = 1722.5 \approx 1724$, so the answer checks.

State. Division I schools reported 1724 violations, and Division II schools reported 265 violations.

57. ***Familiarize.*** Let m = the number of MSM users, in millions. Then $m + 23.1$ = the number of AOL users, in millions.

Translate.

Number of AOL users plus Number of MSN users is 81.9 million.

$$m + 23.1 + m = 81.9$$

Carry out. We solve the equation.

$$m + 23.1 + m = 81.9$$
$$2m + 23.1 = 81.9$$
$$2m = 58.8$$
$$m = 29.4$$

If $m = 29.4$, then $m + 23.1 = 29.4 + 23.1 = 52.5$.

Check. The number of AOL users, 52.5 million, is 23.1 million more than 29.4 million, the number of MSN users. Also, 52.5 million + 29.4 million = 81.9 million, the total number of users. The answer checks.

State. AOL's Instant Messenger Service had 52.5 million users, and MSN's Messenger Service had 29.4 million users.

59. ***Familiarize***. Let x = the number of years it will take Horseshoe Falls to migrate one-fourth mile upstream. We will express one-fourth mile in feet:

$$\frac{1}{4}\text{ mi} \times \frac{5280\text{ ft}}{1\text{ mi}} = 1320\text{ ft}$$

Translate.

$$\underbrace{\text{Rate per year}}_{\downarrow\; 2} \quad \underset{\downarrow\; \cdot}{\text{times}} \quad \underbrace{\text{number of years}}_{\downarrow\; x} \quad \underset{\downarrow\; =}{\text{is}} \quad \underbrace{1320\text{ ft.}}_{\downarrow\; 1320}$$

Carry out. We solve the equation.

$$2x = 1320$$
$$x = 660$$

Check. At a rate of 2 ft per year, in 660 yr the falls will migrate $2 \cdot 660$, or 1320 ft. The answer checks.

State. It will take Horseshoe Falls 660 yr to migrate one-fourth mile upstream.

61. $x + 5 = 0$ Setting $f(x) = 0$

$x + 5 - 5 = 0 - 5$ Subtracting 5 on both sides

$x = -5$

The zero of the function is -5.

63. $-x + 18 = 0$ Setting $f(x) = 0$

$-x + 18 + x = 0 + x$ Adding x on both sides

$18 = x$

The zero of the function is 18.

65. $16 - x = 0$ Setting $f(x) = 0$

$16 - x + x = 0 + x$ Adding x on both sides

$16 = x$

The zero of the function is 16.

67. $x + 12 = 0$ Setting $f(x) = 0$

$x + 12 - 12 = 0 - 12$ Subtracting 12 on both sides

$x = -12$

The zero of the function is -12.

69. $-x + 6 = 0$ Setting $f(x) = 0$

$-x + 6 + x = 0 + x$ Adding x on both sides

$6 = x$

The zero of the function is 6.

71. $20 - x = 0$ Setting $f(x) = 0$

$20 - x + x = 0 + x$ Adding x on both sides

$20 = x$

The zero of the function is 20.

73. $x - 6 = 0$ Setting $f(x) = 0$

$x = 6$ Adding 6 on both sides

The zero of the function is 6.

75. $-x + 15 = 0$ Setting $f(x) = 0$

$15 = x$ Adding x on both sides

The zero of the function is 15.

77. a) The graph crosses the x-axis at $(4, 0)$. This is the x-intercept.

b) The zero of the function is the first coordinate of the x-intercept. It is 4.

79. a) The graph crosses the x-axis at $(-2, 0)$. This is the x-intercept.

b) The zero of the function is the first coordinate of the x-intercept. It is -2.

81. a) The graph crosses the x-axis at $(-4, 0)$. This is the x-intercept.

b) The zero of the function is the first coordinate of the x-intercept. It is -4.

83. $A = \frac{1}{2}bh$

$2A = bh$ Multiplying by 2 on both sides

$\frac{2A}{h} = b$ Dividing by h on both sides

85. $P = 2l + 2w$

$P - 2l = 2w$ Subtracting $2l$ on both sides

$\frac{P - 2l}{2} = w$ Dividing by 2 on both sides

87. $A = \frac{1}{2}h(b_1 + b_2)$

$2A = h(b_1 + b_2)$ Multiplying by 2 on both sides

$\frac{2A}{b_1 + b_2} = h$ Dividing by $b_1 + b_2$ on both sides

89. $V = \frac{4}{3}\pi r^3$

$3V = 4\pi r^3$ Multiplying by 3 on both sides

$\frac{3V}{4r^3} = \pi$ Dividing by $4r^3$ on both sides

91. $F = \frac{9}{5}C + 32$

$F - 32 = \frac{9}{5}C$ Subtracting 32 on both sides

$\frac{5}{9}(F - 32) = C$ Multiplying by $\frac{5}{9}$ on both sides

93. $Ax + By = C$

$$Ax = C - By \quad \text{Subtracting } By \text{ on both sides}$$

$$A = \frac{C - By}{x} \quad \text{Dividing by } x \text{ on both sides}$$

95. $2w + 2h + l = p$

$$2h = p - 2w - l \quad \text{Subtracting } 2w \text{ and } l$$

$$h = \frac{p - 2w - l}{2} \quad \text{Dividing by 2}$$

97. $2x - 3y = 6$

$$-3y = 6 - 2x \quad \text{Subtracting } 2x$$

$$y = \frac{6 - 2x}{-3}, \text{ or } \frac{2x - 6}{3} \quad \text{Dividing by } -3$$

99. $a = b + bcd$

$$a = b(1 + cd) \quad \text{Factoring}$$

$$\frac{a}{1 + cd} = b \quad \text{Dividing by } 1 + cd$$

101. $z = xy - xy^2$

$$z = x(y - y^2) \quad \text{Factoring}$$

$$\frac{z}{y - y^2} = x \quad \text{Dividing by } y - y^2$$

103. Left to the student

105. Discussion and Writing

107. First find the slope of the given line.

$$3x + 4y = 7$$

$$4y = -3x + 7$$

$$y = -\frac{3}{4}x + \frac{7}{4}$$

The slope is $-\frac{3}{4}$. Now write a slope-intersect equation of the line containing $(-1, 4)$ with slope $-\frac{3}{4}$.

$$y - 4 = -\frac{3}{4}[x - (-1)]$$

$$y - 4 = -\frac{3}{4}(x + 1)$$

$$y - 4 = -\frac{3}{4}x - \frac{3}{4}$$

$$y = -\frac{3}{4}x + \frac{13}{4}$$

109. The domain of f is the set of all real numbers as is the domain of g, so the domain of $f + g$ is the set of all real numbers, or $(-\infty, \infty)$.

111. $(f - g)(x) = f(x) - g(x) = 2x - 1 - (3x + 6) = 2x - 1 - 3x - 6 = -x - 7$

113. $f(x) = 7 - \frac{3}{2}x = -\frac{3}{2}x + 7$

The function can be written in the form $y = mx + b$, so it is a linear function.

115. $f(x) = x^2 + 1$ cannot be written in the form $f(x) = mx + b$, so it is not a linear function.

117. $2x - \{x - [3x - (6x + 5)]\} = 4x - 1$

$$2x - \{x - [3x - 6x - 5]\} = 4x - 1$$

$$2x - \{x - [-3x - 5]\} = 4x - 1$$

$$2x - \{x + 3x + 5\} = 4x - 1$$

$$2x - \{4x + 5\} = 4x - 1$$

$$2x - 4x - 5 = 4x - 1$$

$$-2x - 5 = 4x - 1$$

$$-6x - 5 = -1$$

$$-6x = 4$$

$$x = -\frac{2}{3}$$

The solution is $-\frac{2}{3}$.

119. The size of the cup was reduced 8 oz − 6 oz, or 2 oz, and $\frac{2 \text{ oz}}{8 \text{ oz}} = 0.25$, so the size was reduced 25%. The price per ounce of the 8 oz cup was $\frac{89¢}{8 \text{ oz}}$, or 11.25¢/oz. The price per ounce of the 6 oz cup is $\frac{71¢}{6 \text{ oz}}$, or $11.8\overline{3}$¢/oz. Since the price per ounce was not reduced, it is clear that the price per ounce was not reduced by the same percent as the size of the cup. The price was increased by $11.8\overline{3} - 11.125$¢, or $0.708\overline{3}$¢ per ounce. This is an increase of $\frac{0.708\overline{3}¢}{11.8\overline{3}¢} \approx 0.064$, or about 6.4% per ounce.

121. We use a proportion to determine the number of calories c burned running for 75 minutes, or 1.25 hr.

$$\frac{720}{1} = \frac{c}{1.25}$$

$$720(1.25) = c$$

$$900 = c$$

Next we use a proportion to determine how long the person would have to walk to use 900 calories. Let t represent this time, in hours. We express 90 min as 1.5 hr.

$$\frac{1.5}{480} = \frac{t}{900}$$

$$\frac{900(1.5)}{480} = t$$

$$2.8125 = t$$

Then, at a rate of 4 mph, the person would have to walk 4(2.8125), or 11.25 mi.

Exercise Set 2.2

1. $(-5 + 3i) + (7 + 8i)$

$$= (-5 + 7) + (3i + 8i) \quad \text{Collecting the real parts and the imaginary parts}$$

$$= 2 + (3 + 8)i$$

$$= 2 + 11i$$

3. $(4-9i)+(1-3i)$

$=(4+1)+(-9i-3i)$ Collecting the real parts and the imaginary parts

$=5+(-9-3)i$

$=5-12i$

5. $(12+3i)+(-8+5i)$

$=(12-8)+(3i+5i)$

$=4+8i$

7. $(-1-i)+(-3-i)$

$=(-1-3)+(-i-i)$

$=-4-2i$

9. $(3+\sqrt{-16})+(2+\sqrt{-25})=(3+4i)+(2+5i)$

$=(3+2)+(4i+5i)$

$=5+9i$

11. $(10+7i)-(5+3i)$

$=(10-5)+(7i-3i)$ The 5 and the $3i$ are both being subtracted.

$=5+4i$

13. $(13+9i)-(8+2i)$

$=(13-8)+(9i-2i)$ The 8 and the $2i$ are both being subtracted.

$=5+7i$

15. $(6-4i)-(-5+i)$

$=[6-(-5)]+(-4i-i)$

$=(6+5)+(-4i-i)$

$=11-5i$

17. $(-5+2i)-(-4-3i)$

$=[-5-(-4)]+[2i-(-3i)]$

$=(-5+4)+(2i+3i)$

$=-1+5i$

19. $(4-9i)-(2+3i)$

$=(4-2)+(-9i-3i)$

$=2-12i$

21. $7i(2-5i)$

$=14i-35i^2$ Using the distributive law

$=14i+35$ $i^2=-1$

$=35+14i$ Writing in the form $a+bi$

23. $-2i(-8+3i)$

$=16i-6i^2$ Using the distributive law

$=16i+6$ $i^2=-1$

$=6+16i$ Writing in the form $a+bi$

25. $(1+3i)(1-4i)$

$=1-4i+3i-12i^2$ Using FOIL

$=1-4i+3i-12(-1)$ $i^2=-1$

$=1-i+12$

$=13-i$

27. $(2+3i)(2+5i)$

$=4+10i+6i+15i^2$ Using FOIL

$=4+10i+6i-15$ $i^2=-1$

$=-11+16i$

29. $(-4+i)(3-2i)$

$=-12+8i+3i-2i^2$ Using FOIL

$=-12+8i+3i+2$ $i^2=-1$

$=-10+11i$

31. $(8-3i)(-2-5i)$

$=-16-40i+6i+15i^2$

$=-16-40i+6i-15$ $i^2=-1$

$=-31-34i$

33. $(3+\sqrt{-16})(2+\sqrt{-25})$

$=(3+4i)(2+5i)$

$=6+15i+8i+20i^2$

$=6+15i+8i-20$ $i^2=-1$

$=-14+23i$

35. $(5-4i)(5+4i)=5^2-(4i)^2$

$=25-16i^2$

$=25+16$ $i^2=-1$

$=41$

37. $(3+2i)(3-2i)$

$=9-6i+6i-4i^2$

$=9-6i+6i+4$ $i^2=-1$

$=13$

39. $(7-5i)(7+5i)$

$=49+35i-35i-25i^2$

$=49+35i-35i+25$ $i^2=-1$

$=74$

41. $(4+2i)^2$

$=16+2\cdot 4\cdot 2i+(2i)^2$ Recall $(A+B)^2=A^2+2AB+B^2$

$=16+16i+4i^2$

$=16+16i-4$ $i^2=-1$

$=12+16i$

43. $(-2+7i)^2$

$=(-2)^2+2(-2)(7i)+(7i)^2$ Recall $(A+B)^2=A^2+2AB+B^2$

$=4-28i+49i^2$

$=4-28i-49$ $i^2=-1$

$=-45-28i$

45. $(1-3i)^2$

$=1^2-2\cdot 1\cdot(3i)+(3i)^2$

$=1-6i+9i^2$

$=1-6i-9$ $i^2=-1$

$=-8-6i$

47. $(-1-i)^2$

$= (-1)^2 - 2(-1)(i) + i^2$

$= 1 + 2i + i^2$

$= 1 + 2i - 1$ $i^2 = -1$

$= 2i$

49. $(3+4i)^2$

$= 9 + 2\cdot 3\cdot 4i + (4i)^2$

$= 9 + 24i + 16i^2$

$= 9 + 24i - 16$ $i^2 = -1$

$= -7 + 24i$

51. $\frac{3}{5-11i}$

$= \frac{3}{5-11i}\cdot\frac{5+11i}{5+11i}$ $5-11i$ is the conjugate of $5+11i$.

$= \frac{3(5+11i)}{(5-11i)(5+11i)}$

$= \frac{15+33i}{25-121i^2}$

$= \frac{15+33i}{25+121}$ $i^2 = -1$

$= \frac{15+33i}{146}$

$= \frac{15}{146} + \frac{33}{146}i$ Writing in the form $a+bi$

53. $\frac{5}{2+3i}$

$= \frac{5}{2+3i}\cdot\frac{2-3i}{2-3i}$ $2-3i$ is the conjugate of $2+3i$.

$= \frac{5(2-3i)}{(2+3i)(2-3i)}$

$= \frac{10-15i}{4-9i^2}$

$= \frac{10-15i}{4+9}$ $i^2 = -1$

$= \frac{10-15i}{13}$

$= \frac{10}{13} - \frac{15}{13}i$ Writing in the form $a+bi$

55. $\frac{4+i}{-3-2i}$

$= \frac{4+i}{-3-2i}\cdot\frac{-3+2i}{-3+2i}$ $-3+2i$ is the conjugate of the divisor.

$= \frac{(4+i)(-3+2i)}{(-3-2i)(-3+2i)}$

$= \frac{-12+5i+2i^2}{9-4i^2}$

$= \frac{-12+5i-2}{9+4}$ $i^2 = -1$

$= \frac{-14+5i}{13}$

$= -\frac{14}{13} + \frac{5}{13}i$ Writing in the form $a+bi$

57. $\frac{5-3i}{4+3i}$

$= \frac{5-3i}{4+3i}\cdot\frac{4-3i}{4-3i}$ $4-3i$ is the conjugate of $4+3i$.

$= \frac{(5-3i)(4-3i)}{(4+3i)(4-3i)}$

$= \frac{20-27i+9i^2}{16-9i^2}$

$= \frac{20-27i-9}{16+9}$ $i^2 = -1$

$= \frac{11-27i}{25}$

$= \frac{11}{25} - \frac{27}{25}i$ Writing in the form $a+bi$

59. $\frac{2+\sqrt{3}i}{5-4i}$

$= \frac{2+\sqrt{3}i}{5-4i}\cdot\frac{5+4i}{5+4i}$ $5+4i$ is the conjugate of the divisor.

$= \frac{(2+\sqrt{3}i)(5+4i)}{(5-4i)(5+4i)}$

$= \frac{10+8i+5\sqrt{3}i+4\sqrt{3}i^2}{25-16i^2}$

$= \frac{10+8i+5\sqrt{3}i-4\sqrt{3}}{25+16}$ $i^2 = -1$

$= \frac{10-4\sqrt{3}+(8+5\sqrt{3})i}{41}$

$= \frac{10-4\sqrt{3}}{41} + \frac{8+5\sqrt{3}}{41}i$ Writing in the form $a+bi$

61. $\frac{1+i}{(1-i)^2}$

$= \frac{1+i}{1-2i+i^2}$

$= \frac{1+i}{1-2i-1}$ $i^2 = -1$

$= \frac{1+i}{-2i}$

$= \frac{1+i}{-2i}\cdot\frac{2i}{2i}$ $2i$ is the conjugate of $-2i$.

$= \frac{(1+i)(2i)}{(-2i)(2i)}$

$= \frac{2i+2i^2}{-4i^2}$

$= \frac{2i-2}{4}$ $i^2 = -1$

$= -\frac{2}{4} + \frac{2}{4}i$

$= -\frac{1}{2} + \frac{1}{2}i$

63. $\dfrac{4-2i}{1+i}+\dfrac{2-5i}{1+i}$

$=\dfrac{6-7i}{1+i}$ Adding

$=\dfrac{6-7i}{1+i}\cdot\dfrac{1-i}{1-i}$ $1-i$ is the conjugate of $1+i$.

$=\dfrac{(6-7i)(1-i)}{(1+i)(1-i)}$

$=\dfrac{6-13i+7i^2}{1-i^2}$

$=\dfrac{6-13i-7}{1+1}$ $i^2=-1$

$=\dfrac{-1-13i}{2}$

$=-\dfrac{1}{2}-\dfrac{13}{2}i$

65. $i^{11}=i^{10}\cdot i=(i^2)^5\cdot i=(-1)^5\cdot i=-1\cdot i=-i$

67. $i^{35}=i^{34}\cdot i=(i^2)^{17}\cdot i=(-1)^{17}\cdot i=-1\cdot i=-i$

69. $i^{64}=(i^2)^{32}=(-1)^{32}=1$

71. $(-i)^{71}=(-1\cdot i)^{71}=(-1)^{71}\cdot i^{71}=-i^{70}\cdot i=$
$-(i^2)^{35}\cdot i=-(-1)^{35}\cdot i=-(-1)i=i$

73. $(5i)^4=5^4\cdot i^4=625(i^2)^2=625(-1)^2=625\cdot 1=625$

75. Left to the student

77. Discussion and Writing

79. First find the slope of the given line.

$3x-6y=7$

$-6y=-3x+7$

$y=\dfrac{1}{2}x-\dfrac{7}{6}$

The slope is $\dfrac{1}{2}$. The slope of the desired line is the opposite of the reciprocal of $\dfrac{1}{2}$, or -2. Write a slope-intercept equation of the line containing $(3,-5)$ with slope -2.

$y-(-5)=-2(x-3)$

$y+5=-2x+6$

$y=-2x+1$

81. The domain of f is the set of all real numbers as is the domain of g. When $x=-\dfrac{5}{3}$, $g(x)=0$, so the domain of f/g is $\left(-\infty,-\dfrac{5}{3}\right)\cup\left(-\dfrac{5}{3},\infty\right)$.

83. $(f/g)(2)=\dfrac{f(2)}{g(2)}=\dfrac{2^2+4}{3\cdot 2+5}=\dfrac{4+4}{6+5}=\dfrac{8}{11}$

85. $(a+bi)+(a-bi)=2a$, a real number. Thus, the statement is true.

87. $(a+bi)(c+di)=(ac-bd)+(ad+bc)i$. The conjugate of the product is $(ac-bd)-(ad+bc)i=$
$(a-bi)(c-di)$, the product of the conjugates of the individual complex numbers. Thus, the statement is true.

89. $z\bar{z}=(a+bi)(a-bi)=a^2-b^2i^2=a^2+b^2$

Exercise Set 2.3

1. $(2x-3)(3x-2)=0$

$2x-3=0$ *or* $3x-2=0$ Using the principle of zero products

$2x=3$ *or* $3x=2$

$x=\dfrac{3}{2}$ *or* $x=\dfrac{2}{3}$

The solutions are $\dfrac{3}{2}$ and $\dfrac{2}{3}$.

3. $x^2-8x-20=0$

$(x-10)(x+2)=0$ Factoring

$x-10=0$ *or* $x+2=0$ Using the principle of zero products

$x=10$ *or* $x=-2$

The solutions are 10 and -2.

5. $3x^2+x-2=0$

$(3x-2)(x+1)=0$ Factoring

$3x-2=0$ *or* $x+1=0$ Using the principle of zero products

$x=\dfrac{2}{3}$ *or* $x=-1$

The solutions are $\dfrac{2}{3}$ and -1.

7. $4x^2-12=0$

$4x^2=12$

$x^2=3$

$x=\sqrt{3}$ *or* $x=-\sqrt{3}$ Using the principle of square roots

The solutions are $\sqrt{3}$ and $-\sqrt{3}$.

9. $3x^2=21$

$x^2=7$

$x=\sqrt{7}$ *or* $x=-\sqrt{7}$ Using the principle of square roots

The solutions are $\sqrt{7}$ and $-\sqrt{7}$.

11. $5x^2+10=0$

$5x^2=-10$

$x^2=-2$

$x=\sqrt{2}i$ *or* $x=-\sqrt{2}i$

The solutions are $\sqrt{2}i$ and $-\sqrt{2}i$.

13. $2x^2-34=0$

$2x^2=34$

$x^2=17$

$x=\sqrt{17}$ *or* $x=-\sqrt{17}$

The solutions are $\sqrt{17}$ and $-\sqrt{17}$.

15. $2x^2 = 6x$

$2x^2 - 6x = 0$ Subtracting $6x$ on both sides

$2x(x-3) = 0$

$2x = 0$ *or* $x - 3 = 0$

$x = 0$ *or* $x = 3$

The solutions are 0 and 3.

17. $3y^3 - 5y^2 - 2y = 0$

$y(3y^2 - 5y - 2) = 0$

$y(3y+1)(y-2) = 0$

$y = 0$ *or* $3y + 1 = 0$ *or* $y - 2 = 0$

$y = 0$ *or* $y = -\frac{1}{3}$ *or* $y = 2$

The solutions are $-\frac{1}{3}$, 0 and 2.

19. $7x^3 + x^2 - 7x - 1 = 0$

$x^2(7x+1) - (7x+1) = 0$

$(x^2-1)(7x+1) = 0$

$(x+1)(x-1)(7x+1) = 0$

$x + 1 = 0$ *or* $x - 1 = 0$ *or* $7x + 1 = 0$

$x = -1$ *or* $x = 1$ *or* $x = -\frac{1}{7}$

The solutions are -1, $-\frac{1}{7}$, and 1.

21. a) The graph crosses the x-axis at $(-4, 0)$ and at $(2, 0)$. These are the x-intercepts.

b) The zeros of the function are the first coordinates of the x-intercepts of the graph. They are -4 and 2.

23. a) The graph crosses the x-axis at $(-1, 0)$ and at $(3, 0)$. These are the x-intercepts.

b) The zeros of the function are the first coordinates of the x-intercepts of the graph. They are -1 and 3.

25. a) The graph crosses the x-axis at $(-2, 0)$ and at $(2, 0)$. These are the x-intercepts.

b) The zeros of the function are the first coordinates of the x-intercepts of the graph. They are -2 and 2.

27. $x^2 + 6x = 7$

$x^2 + 6x + 9 = 7 + 9$ Completing the square: $\frac{1}{2} \cdot 6 = 3$ and $3^2 = 9$

$(x+3)^2 = 16$ Factoring

$x + 3 = \pm 4$ Using the principle of square roots

$x = -3 \pm 4$

$x = -3 - 4$ *or* $x = -3 + 4$

$x = -7$ *or* $x = 1$

The solutions are -7 and 1.

29. $x^2 = 8x - 9$

$x^2 - 8x = -9$ Subtracting $8x$

$x^2 - 8x + 16 = -9 + 16$ Completing the square: $\frac{1}{2}(-8) = -4$ and $(-4)^2 = 16$

$(x-4)^2 = 7$ Factoring

$x - 4 = \pm\sqrt{7}$ Using the principle of square roots

$x = 4 \pm \sqrt{7}$

The solutions are $4 - \sqrt{7}$ and $4 + \sqrt{7}$, or $4 \pm \sqrt{7}$.

31. $x^2 + 8x + 25 = 0$

$x^2 + 8x = -25$ Subtracting 25

$x^2 + 8x + 16 = -25 + 16$ Completing the square: $\frac{1}{2} \cdot 8 = 4$ and $4^2 = 16$

$(x+4)^2 = -9$ Factoring

$x + 4 = \pm 3i$ Using the principle of square roots

$x = -4 \pm 3i$

The solutions are $-4 - 3i$ and $-4 + 3i$, or $-4 \pm 3i$.

33. $3x^2 + 5x - 2 = 0$

$3x^2 + 5x = 2$ Adding 2

$x^2 + \frac{5}{3}x = \frac{2}{3}$ Dividing by 3

$x^2 + \frac{5}{3}x + \frac{25}{36} = \frac{2}{3} + \frac{25}{36}$ Completing the square: $\frac{1}{2} \cdot \frac{5}{3} = \frac{5}{6}$ and $(\frac{5}{6})^2 = \frac{25}{36}$

$\left(x + \frac{5}{6}\right)^2 = \frac{49}{36}$ Factoring and simplifying

$x + \frac{5}{6} = \pm\frac{7}{6}$ Using the principle of square roots

$x = -\frac{5}{6} \pm \frac{7}{6}$

$x = -\frac{5}{6} - \frac{7}{6}$ *or* $x = -\frac{5}{6} + \frac{7}{6}$

$x = -\frac{12}{6}$ *or* $x = \frac{2}{6}$

$x = -2$ *or* $x = \frac{1}{3}$

The solutions are -2 and $\frac{1}{3}$.

35. $x^2 - 2x = 15$

$x^2 - 2x - 15 = 0$

$(x-5)(x+3) = 0$ Factoring

$x - 5 = 0$ *or* $x + 3 = 0$

$x = 5$ *or* $x = -3$

The solutions are 5 and -3.

37.
$$5m^2 + 3m = 2$$
$$5m^2 + 3m - 2 = 0$$
$$(5m - 2)(m + 1) = 0 \quad \text{Factoring}$$
$$5m - 2 = 0 \quad or \quad m + 1 = 0$$
$$m = \frac{2}{5} \quad or \quad m = -1$$

The solutions are $\frac{2}{5}$ and -1.

39.
$$3x^2 + 6 = 10x$$
$$3x^2 - 10x + 6 = 0$$

We use the quadratic formula. Here $a = 3$, $b = -10$, and $c = 6$.

$$x = \frac{-b \pm \sqrt{b^2 - 4ac}}{2a}$$
$$= \frac{-(-10) \pm \sqrt{(-10)^2 - 4 \cdot 3 \cdot 6}}{2 \cdot 3} \quad \text{Substituting}$$
$$= \frac{10 \pm \sqrt{28}}{6} = \frac{10 \pm 2\sqrt{7}}{6}$$
$$= \frac{2(5 \pm \sqrt{7})}{2 \cdot 3} = \frac{5 \pm \sqrt{7}}{3}$$

The solutions are $\frac{5 - \sqrt{7}}{3}$ and $\frac{5 + \sqrt{7}}{3}$, or $\frac{5 \pm \sqrt{7}}{3}$.

41. $x^2 + x + 2 = 0$

We use the quadratic formula. Here $a = 1$, $b = 1$, and $c = 2$.

$$x = \frac{-b \pm \sqrt{b^2 - 4ac}}{2a}$$
$$= \frac{-1 \pm \sqrt{1^2 - 4 \cdot 1 \cdot 2}}{2 \cdot 1} \quad \text{Substituting}$$
$$= \frac{-1 \pm \sqrt{-7}}{2}$$
$$= \frac{-1 \pm \sqrt{7}i}{2} = -\frac{1}{2} \pm \frac{\sqrt{7}}{2}i$$

The solutions are $-\frac{1}{2} - \frac{\sqrt{7}}{2}i$ and $-\frac{1}{2} + \frac{\sqrt{7}}{2}i$, or $-\frac{1}{2} \pm \frac{\sqrt{7}}{2}i$.

43.
$$5t^2 - 8t = 3$$
$$5t^2 - 8t - 3 = 0$$

We use the quadratic formula. Here $a = 5$, $b = -8$, and $c = -3$.

$$t = \frac{-b \pm \sqrt{b^2 - 4ac}}{2a}$$
$$= \frac{-(-8) \pm \sqrt{(-8)^2 - 4 \cdot 5(-3)}}{2 \cdot 5}$$
$$= \frac{8 \pm \sqrt{124}}{10} = \frac{8 \pm 2\sqrt{31}}{10}$$
$$= \frac{2(4 \pm \sqrt{31})}{2 \cdot 5} = \frac{4 \pm \sqrt{31}}{5}$$

The solutions are $\frac{4 - \sqrt{31}}{5}$ and $\frac{4 + \sqrt{31}}{5}$, or $\frac{4 \pm \sqrt{31}}{5}$.

45.
$$3x^2 + 4 = 5x$$
$$3x^2 - 5x + 4 = 0$$

We use the quadratic formula. Here $a = 3$, $b = -5$, and $c = 4$.

$$x = \frac{-b \pm \sqrt{b^2 - 4ac}}{2a}$$
$$= \frac{-(-5) \pm \sqrt{(-5)^2 - 4 \cdot 3 \cdot 4}}{2 \cdot 3}$$
$$= \frac{5 \pm \sqrt{-23}}{6} = \frac{5 \pm \sqrt{23}i}{6}$$
$$= \frac{5}{6} \pm \frac{\sqrt{23}}{6}i$$

The solutions are $\frac{5}{6} - \frac{\sqrt{23}}{6}i$ and $\frac{5}{6} + \frac{\sqrt{23}}{6}i$, or $\frac{5}{6} \pm \frac{\sqrt{23}}{6}i$.

47. $x^2 - 8x + 5 = 0$

We use the quadratic formula. Here $a = 1$, $b = -8$, and $c = 5$.

$$x = \frac{-b \pm \sqrt{b^2 - 4ac}}{2a}$$
$$= \frac{-(-8) \pm \sqrt{(-8)^2 - 4 \cdot 1 \cdot 5}}{2 \cdot 1}$$
$$= \frac{8 \pm \sqrt{44}}{2} = \frac{8 \pm 2\sqrt{11}}{2}$$
$$= \frac{2(4 \pm \sqrt{11})}{2} = 4 \pm \sqrt{11}$$

The solutions are $4 - \sqrt{11}$ and $4 + \sqrt{11}$, or $4 \pm \sqrt{11}$.

49.
$$3x^2 + x = 5$$
$$3x^2 + x - 5 = 0$$

We use the quadratic formula. We have $a = 3$, $b = 1$, and $c = -5$.

$$x = \frac{-b \pm \sqrt{b^2 - 4ac}}{2a}$$
$$= \frac{-1 \pm \sqrt{1^2 - 4 \cdot 3 \cdot (-5)}}{2 \cdot 3}$$
$$= \frac{-1 \pm \sqrt{61}}{6}$$

The solutions are $\frac{-1 - \sqrt{61}}{6}$ and $\frac{-1 + \sqrt{61}}{6}$, or $\frac{-1 \pm \sqrt{61}}{6}$.

51.
$$2x^2 + 1 = 5x$$
$$2x^2 - 5x + 1 = 0$$

We use the quadratic formula. We have $a = 2$, $b = -5$, and $c = 1$.

$$x = \frac{-b \pm \sqrt{b^2 - 4ac}}{2a}$$
$$= \frac{-(-5) \pm \sqrt{(-5)^2 - 4 \cdot 2 \cdot 1}}{2 \cdot 2} = \frac{5 \pm \sqrt{17}}{4}$$

The solutions are $\frac{5-\sqrt{17}}{4}$ and $\frac{5+\sqrt{17}}{4}$, or $\frac{5\pm\sqrt{17}}{4}$.

53. $5x^2+2x=-2$

$5x^2+2x+2=0$

We use the quadratic formula. We have $a=5$, $b=2$, and $c=2$.

$$x=\frac{-b\pm\sqrt{b^2-4ac}}{2a}$$
$$=\frac{-2\pm\sqrt{2^2-4\cdot 5\cdot 2}}{2\cdot 5}$$
$$=\frac{-2\pm\sqrt{-36}}{10}=\frac{-2\pm 6i}{10}$$
$$=\frac{2(-1\pm 3i)}{2\cdot 5}=\frac{-1\pm 3i}{5}$$
$$=-\frac{1}{5}\pm\frac{3}{5}i$$

The solutions are $-\frac{1}{5}-\frac{3}{5}i$ and $-\frac{1}{5}+\frac{3}{5}i$, or $-\frac{1}{5}\pm\frac{3}{5}i$.

55. $4x^2=8x+5$

$4x^2-8x-5=0$

$a=4,\ b=-8,\ c=-5$

$b^2-4ac=(-8)^2-4\cdot 4(-5)=144$

Since $b^2-4ac>0$, there are two different real-number solutions.

57. $x^2+3x+4=0$

$a=1,\ b=3,\ c=4$

$b^2-4ac=3^2-4\cdot 1\cdot 4=-7$

Since $b^2-4ac<0$, there are two different imaginary-number solutions.

59. $5t^2-7t=0$

$a=5,\ b=-7,\ c=0$

$b^2-4ac=(-7)^2-4\cdot 5\cdot 0=49$

Since $b^2-4ac>0$, there are two different real-number solutions.

61. $x^2+6x+5=0$ Setting $f(x)=0$

$(x+5)(x+1)=0$ Factoring

$x+5=0$ *or* $x+1=0$

$x=-5$ *or* $x=-1$

The zeros of the function are -5 and -1.

63. $x^2-3x-3=0$

$a=1,\ b=-3,\ c=-3$

$$x=\frac{-b\pm\sqrt{b^2-4ac}}{2a}$$
$$=\frac{-(-3)\pm\sqrt{(-3)^2-4\cdot 1\cdot(-3)}}{2\cdot 1}$$
$$=\frac{3\pm\sqrt{9+12}}{2}$$
$$=\frac{3\pm\sqrt{21}}{2}$$

The zeros of the function are $\frac{3-\sqrt{21}}{2}$ and $\frac{3+\sqrt{21}}{2}$, or $\frac{3\pm\sqrt{21}}{2}$.

65. $x^2-5x+1=0$

$a=1,\ b=-5,\ c=1$

$$x=\frac{-b\pm\sqrt{b^2-4ac}}{2a}$$
$$=\frac{-(-5)\pm\sqrt{(-5)^2-4\cdot 1\cdot 1}}{2\cdot 1}$$
$$=\frac{5\pm\sqrt{25-4}}{2}$$
$$=\frac{5\pm\sqrt{21}}{2}$$

The zeros of the function are $\frac{5-\sqrt{21}}{2}$ and $\frac{5+\sqrt{21}}{2}$, or $\frac{5\pm\sqrt{21}}{2}$.

67. $x^2+2x-5=0$

$a=1,\ b=2,\ c=-5$

$$x=\frac{-b\pm\sqrt{b^2-4ac}}{2a}$$
$$=\frac{-2\pm\sqrt{2^2-4\cdot 1\cdot(-5)}}{2\cdot 1}$$
$$=\frac{-2\pm\sqrt{4+20}}{2}=\frac{-2\pm\sqrt{24}}{2}$$
$$=\frac{-2\pm 2\sqrt{6}}{2}=-1\pm\sqrt{6}$$

The zeros of the function are $-1+\sqrt{6}$ and $-1-\sqrt{6}$, or $-1\pm\sqrt{6}$.

69. $2x^2-x+4=0$

$a=2,\ b=-1,\ c=4$

$$x=\frac{-b\pm\sqrt{b^2-4ac}}{2a}$$
$$=\frac{-(-1)\pm\sqrt{(-1)^2-4\cdot 2\cdot 4}}{2\cdot 2}$$
$$=\frac{1\pm\sqrt{-31}}{4}=\frac{1\pm\sqrt{31}i}{4}$$
$$=\frac{1}{4}\pm\frac{\sqrt{31}}{4}i$$

The zeros of the function are $\frac{1}{4}-\frac{\sqrt{31}}{4}i$ and $\frac{1}{4}+\frac{\sqrt{31}}{4}i$, or $\frac{1}{4}\pm\frac{\sqrt{31}}{4}i$.

71. $3x^2-x-1=0$

$a=3,\ b=-1,\ c=-1$

$$x=\frac{-b\pm\sqrt{b^2-4ac}}{2a}$$
$$=\frac{-(-1)\pm\sqrt{(-1)^2-4\cdot 3\cdot(-1)}}{2\cdot 3}$$
$$=\frac{1\pm\sqrt{13}}{6}$$

The zeros of the function are $\frac{1-\sqrt{13}}{6}$ and $\frac{1+\sqrt{13}}{6}$, or $\frac{1\pm\sqrt{13}}{6}$.

73. $5x^2 - 2x - 1 = 0$

$a = 5,\ b = -2,\ c = -1$

$$x = \frac{-b\pm\sqrt{b^2-4ac}}{2a}$$
$$= \frac{-(-2)\pm\sqrt{(-2)^2-4\cdot 5\cdot(-1)}}{2\cdot 5}$$
$$= \frac{2\pm\sqrt{24}}{10} = \frac{2\pm 2\sqrt{6}}{10}$$
$$= \frac{2(1\pm\sqrt{6})}{2\cdot 5} = \frac{1\pm\sqrt{6}}{5}$$

The zeros of the function are $\frac{1-\sqrt{6}}{5}$ and $\frac{1+\sqrt{6}}{5}$, or $\frac{1\pm\sqrt{6}}{5}$.

75. $4x^2 + 3x - 3 = 0$

$a = 4,\ b = 3,\ c = -3$

$$x = \frac{-b\pm\sqrt{b^2-4ac}}{2a}$$
$$= \frac{-3\pm\sqrt{3^2-4\cdot 4\cdot(-3)}}{2\cdot 4}$$
$$= \frac{-3\pm\sqrt{57}}{8}$$

The zeros of the function are $\frac{-3-\sqrt{57}}{8}$ and $\frac{-3+\sqrt{57}}{8}$, or $\frac{-3\pm\sqrt{57}}{8}$.

77. $x^4 - 3x^2 + 2 = 0$

Let $u = x^2$.

$u^2 - 3u + 2 = 0$ Substituting u for x^2

$(u-1)(u-2) = 0$

$u - 1 = 0$ *or* $u - 2 = 0$

$u = 1$ *or* $u = 2$

Now substitute x^2 for u and solve for x.

$x^2 = 1$ *or* $x^2 = 2$

$x = \pm 1$ *or* $x = \pm\sqrt{2}$

The solutions are -1, 1, $-\sqrt{2}$, and $\sqrt{2}$.

79. $x^4 + 3x^2 = 10$

$x^4 + 3x^2 - 10 = 0$

Let $u = x^2$.

$u^2 + 3u - 10 = 0$ Substituting u for x^2

$(u+5)(u-2) = 0$

$u + 5 = 0$ *or* $u - 2 = 0$

$u = -5$ *or* $u = 2$

Now substitute x^2 for u and solve for x.

$x^2 = -5$ *or* $x^2 = 2$

$x = \pm\sqrt{5}i$ *or* $x = \pm\sqrt{2}$

The solutions are $-\sqrt{5}i$, $\sqrt{5}i$, $-\sqrt{2}$, and $\sqrt{2}$.

81. $y^6 - 9y^3 + 8 = 0$

Let $u = y^3$.

$u^2 - 9u + 8 = 0$ Substituting u for y^3

$(u-1)(u-8) = 0$

$u - 1 = 0$ *or* $u - 8 = 0$

$u = 1$ *or* $u = 8$

Now substitute y^3 for u and solve for y.

$y^3 = 1$ *or* $y^3 = 8$

$y = 1$ *or* $y = 2$

The solutions are 1 and 2.

83. $x - 3\sqrt{x} - 4 = 0$

Let $u = \sqrt{x}$.

$u^2 - 3u - 4 = 0$ Substituting u for $\sqrt{x}$

$(u+1)(u-4) = 0$

$u + 1 = 0$ *or* $u - 4 = 0$

$u = -1$ *or* $u = 4$

Now substitute $\sqrt{x}$ for u and solve for x.

$\sqrt{x} = -1$ *or* $\sqrt{x} = 4$

No solution $\quad x = 16$

Note that $\sqrt{x}$ must be nonnegative, so $\sqrt{x} = -1$ has no solution. The number 16 checks and is the solution. The solution is 16.

85. $m^{2/3} - 2m^{1/3} - 8 = 0$

Let $u = m^{1/3}$.

$u^2 - 2u - 8 = 0$ Substituting u for $m^{1/3}$

$(u+2)(u-4) = 0$

$u + 2 = 0$ *or* $u - 4 = 0$

$u = -2$ *or* $u = 4$

Now substitute $m^{1/3}$ for u and solve for m.

$m^{1/3} = -2$ *or* $m^{1/3} = 4$

$(m^{1/3})^3 = (-2)^3$ *or* $(m^{1/3})^3 = 4^3$ Using the principle of powers

$m = -8$ *or* $m = 64$

The solutions are -8 and 64.

87. $x^{1/2} - 3x^{1/4} + 2 = 0$

Let $u = x^{1/4}$.

$u^2 - 3u + 2 = 0$ Substituting u for $x^{1/4}$

$(u-1)(u-2) = 0$

$u - 1 = 0$ *or* $u - 2 = 0$

$u = 1$ *or* $u = 2$

Now substitute $x^{1/4}$ for u and solve for x.

$$x^{1/4} = 1 \quad or \quad x^{1/4} = 2$$
$$(x^{1/4})^4 = 1^4 \quad or \quad (x^{1/4})^4 = 2^4$$
$$x = 1 \quad or \quad x = 16$$

The solutions are 1 and 16.

89. $(2x-3)^2 - 5(2x-3) + 6 = 0$

Let $u = 2x - 3$.

$u^2 - 5u + 6 = 0$ Substituting u for $2x - 3$

$$(u-2)(u-3) = 0$$
$$u - 2 = 0 \quad or \quad u - 3 = 0$$
$$u = 2 \quad or \quad u = 3$$

Now substitute $2x - 3$ for u and solve for x.

$$2x - 3 = 2 \quad or \quad 2x - 3 = 3$$
$$2x = 5 \quad or \quad 2x = 6$$
$$x = \frac{5}{2} \quad or \quad x = 3$$

The solutions are $\frac{5}{2}$ and 3.

91. $(2t^2 + t)^2 - 4(2t^2 + t) + 3 = 0$

Let $u = 2t^2 + t$.

$u^2 - 4u + 3 = 0$ Substituting u for $2t^2 + t$

$$(u-1)(u-3) = 0$$
$$u - 1 = 0 \quad or \quad u - 3 = 0$$
$$u = 1 \quad or \quad u = 3$$

Now substitute $2t^2 + t$ for u and solve for t.

$$2t^2 + t = 1 \quad or \quad 2t^2 + t = 3$$
$$2t^2 + t - 1 = 0 \quad or \quad 2t^2 + t - 3 = 0$$
$$(2t-1)(t+1) = 0 \quad or \quad (2t+3)(t-1) = 0$$
$$2t-1=0 \quad or \quad t+1=0 \quad or \quad 2t+3=0 \quad or \quad t-1 = 0$$
$$t=\frac{1}{2} \quad or \quad t=-1 \quad or \quad t=-\frac{3}{2} \quad or \quad t = 1$$

The solutions are $\frac{1}{2}$, -1, $-\frac{3}{2}$ and 1.

93. ***Familiarize and Translate.*** We will use the formula $s = 16t^2$, substituting 2120 for s.

$$2120 = 16t^2$$

Carry out. We solve the equation.

$$2120 = 16t^2$$

$132.5 = t^2$ Dividing by 16 on both sides

$11.5 \approx t$ Taking the square root on both sides

Check. When $t = 11.5$, $s = 16(11.5)^2 = 2116 \approx 2120$. The answer checks.

State. It would take an object about 11.5 sec to reach the ground.

95. Substitute 9.7 for $w(x)$ and solve for x.

$$-0.01x^2 + 0.27x + 8.60 = 9.7$$
$$-0.01x^2 + 0.27x - 1.1 = 0$$

$a = -0.01,\ b = 0.27,\ c = -1.1$

$$x = \frac{-b \pm \sqrt{b^2 - 4ac}}{2a}$$
$$= \frac{-0.27 \pm \sqrt{(0.27)^2 - 4(-0.01)(-1.1)}}{2(-0.01)}$$
$$= \frac{-0.27 \pm \sqrt{0.0289}}{-0.02}$$

$x \approx 5$ *or* $x \approx 22$

There were 9.7 million self-employed workers in the United States 5 years after 1980 and also 22 years after 1980, or in 1985 and in 2002.

97. ***Familiarize.*** Let w = the width of the rug. Then $w+1$ = the length.

Translate. We use the Pythagorean equation.

$$w^2 + (w+1)^2 = 5^2$$

Carry out. We solve the equation.

$$w^2 + (w+1)^2 = 5^2$$
$$w^2 + w^2 + 2w + 1 = 25$$
$$2w^2 + 2w + 1 = 25$$
$$2w^2 + 2w - 24 = 0$$
$$2(w+4)(w-3) = 0$$
$$w + 4 = 0 \quad or \quad w - 3 = 0$$
$$w = -4 \quad or \quad w = 3$$

Since the width cannot be negative, we consider only 3. When $w = 3$, $w + 1 = 3 + 1 = 4$.

Check. The length, 4 ft, is 1 ft more than the width, 3 ft. The length of a diagonal of a rectangle with width 3 ft and length 4 ft is $\sqrt{3^2 + 4^2} = \sqrt{9+16} = \sqrt{25} = 5$. The answer checks.

State. The length is 4 ft, and the width is 3 ft.

99. ***Familiarize.*** Let n = the smaller number. Then $n + 5$ = the larger number.

Translate.

$$\underbrace{\text{The product of the numbers}}_{n(n+5)} \ \underset{=}{\text{is}} \ \underset{36}{36.}$$

Carry out.

$$n(n+5) = 36$$
$$n^2 + 5n = 36$$
$$n^2 + 5n - 36 = 0$$
$$(n+9)(n-4) = 0$$
$$n + 9 = 0 \quad or \quad n - 4 = 0$$
$$n = -9 \quad or \quad n = 4$$

If $n = -9$, then $n + 5 = -9 + 5 = -4$. If $n = 4$, then $n + 5 = 4 + 5 = 9$.

Check. The number -4 is 5 more than -9 and $(-4)(-9) = 36$, so the pair -9 and -4 check. The number 9 is 5 more than 4 and $9 \cdot 4 = 36$, so the pair 4 and 9 also check.

State. The numbers are -9 and -4 or 4 and 9.

101. ***Familiarize***. We add labels to the drawing in the text.

We let x represent the length of a side of the square in each corner. Then the length and width of the resulting base are represented by $20-2x$ and $10-2x$, respectively. Recall that for a rectangle, Area = length × width.

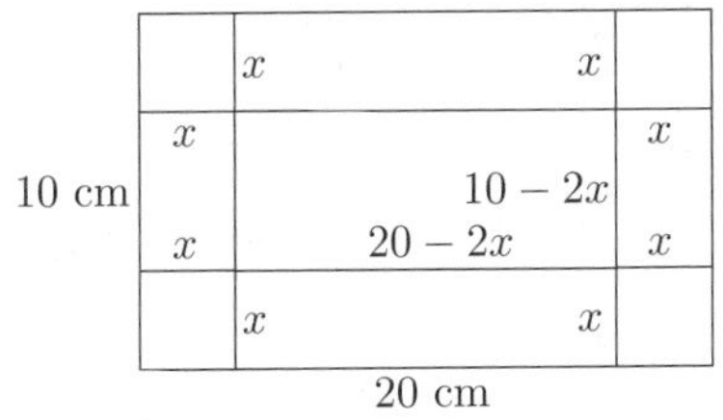

Translate.

$$\underbrace{\text{The area of the base}} \text{ is } \underbrace{96 \text{ cm}^2}.$$

$$(20-2x)(10-2x) \quad = \quad 96$$

Carry out. We solve the equation.

$$200-60x+4x^2=96$$
$$4x^2-60x+104=0$$
$$x^2-15x+26=0$$
$$(x-13)(x-2)=0$$
$$x-13=0 \quad or \quad x-2=0$$
$$x=13 \quad or \quad x=2$$

Check. When $x=13$, both $20-2x$ and $10-2x$ are negative numbers, so we only consider $x=2$. When $x=2$, then $20-2x=20-2\cdot 2=16$ and $10-2x=10-2\cdot 2=6$, and the area of the base is $16\cdot 6$, or 96 cm^2. The answer checks.

State. The length of the sides of the squares is 2 cm.

103. ***Familiarize***. We have $P=2l+2w$, or $28=2l+2w$. Solving for w, we have

$$28=2l+2w$$
$$14=l+w \quad \text{Dividing by 2}$$
$$14-l=w.$$

Then we have l = the length of the rug and $14-l$ = the width, in feet. Recall that the area of a rectangle is the product of the length and the width.

Translate.

$$\underbrace{\text{The area}} \text{ is } \underbrace{48 \text{ ft}^2}.$$

$$\downarrow \qquad \downarrow \qquad \downarrow$$

$$l(14-l) \quad = \quad 48$$

Carry out. We solve the equation.

$$l(14-l)=48$$
$$14l-l^2=48$$
$$0=l^2-14l+48$$
$$0=(l-6)(l-8)$$
$$l-6=0 \quad or \quad l-8=0$$
$$l=6 \quad or \quad l=8$$

If $l=6$, then $14-l=14-6=8$.

If $l-8$, then $14-l=14-8=6$.

In either case, the dimensions are 8 ft by 6 ft. Since we usually consider the length to be greater than the width, we let 8 ft = the length and 6 ft = the width.

Check. The perimeter is $2\cdot 8$ ft$+2\cdot 6$ ft $=16$ ft $+12$ ft $=28$ ft. The answer checks.

State. The length of the rug is 8 ft, and the width is 6 ft.

105. $f(x)=4-5x=-5x+4$

The function can be written in the form $y=mx+b$, so it is a linear function.

107. $f(x)=7x^2$

The function is in the form $f(x)=ax^2+bx+c$, $a\neq 0$, so it is a quadratic function.

109. $f(x)=1.2x-(3.6)^2$

The function is in the form $f(x)=mx+b$, so it is a linear function.

111. Graph $y=x^2-8x+12$ and use the Zero feature twice.

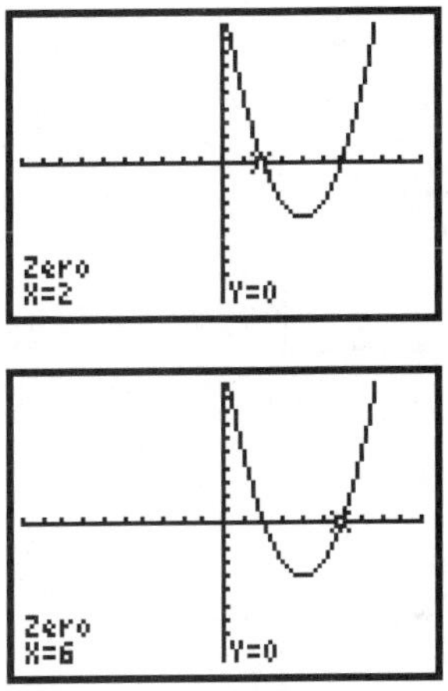

The solutions are 2 and 6.

113. Graph $y=7x^2-43x+6$ and use the Zero feature twice.

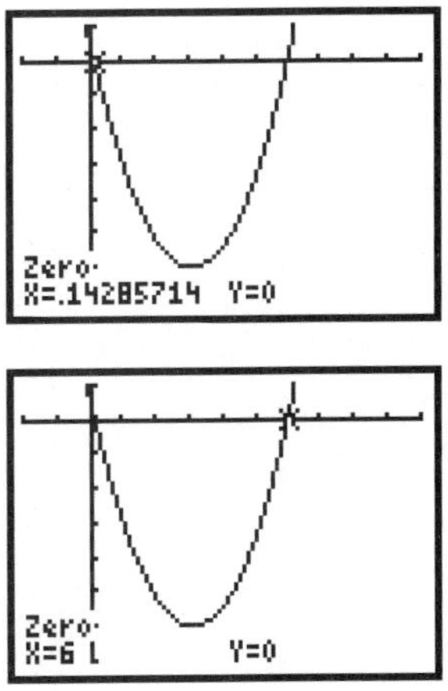

One solution is approximately 0.143 and the other is 6.

115. Graph $y_1 = 6x + 1$ and $y_2 = 4x^2$ and use the Intersect feature twice.

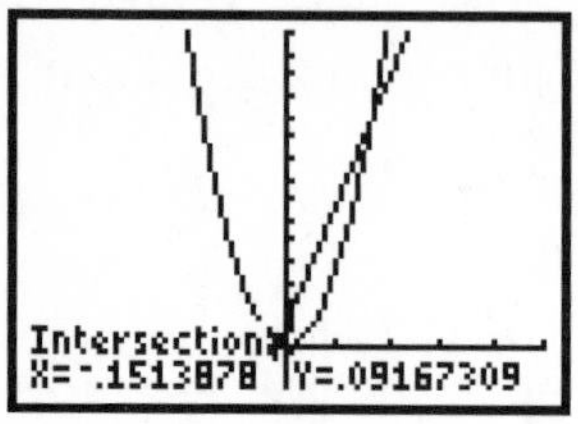

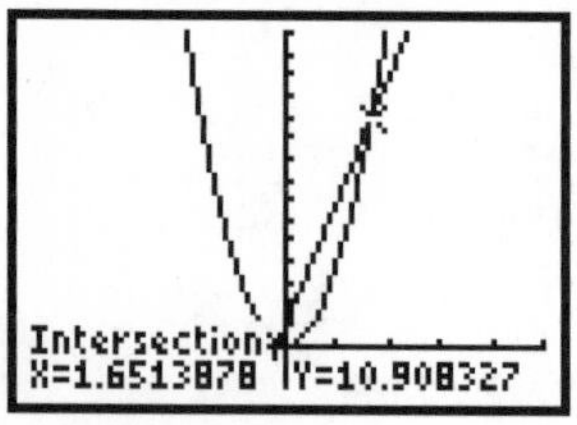

The solutions are approximately -0.151 and 1.651.

117. Graph $y = 2x^2 - 5x - 4$ and use the Zero feature twice.

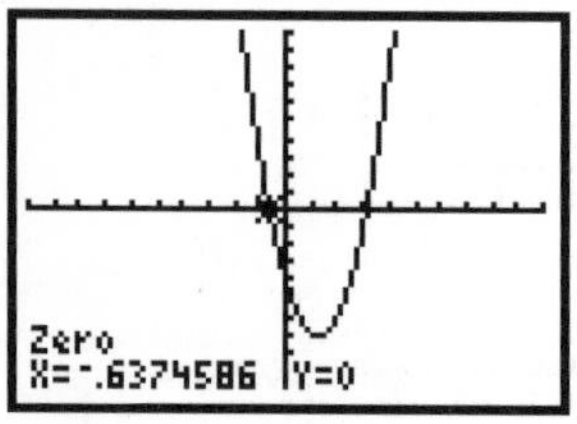

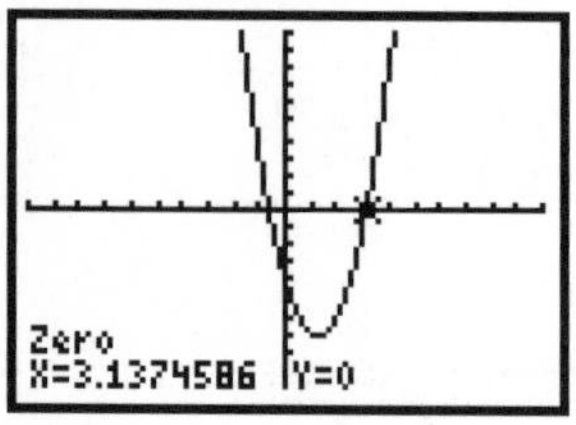

The zeros are approximately -0.637 and 3.137.

119. Graph $y = 3x^2 + 2x - 4$ and use the Zero feature twice.

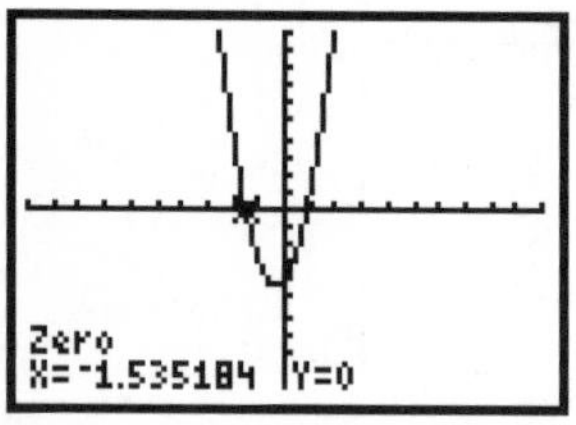

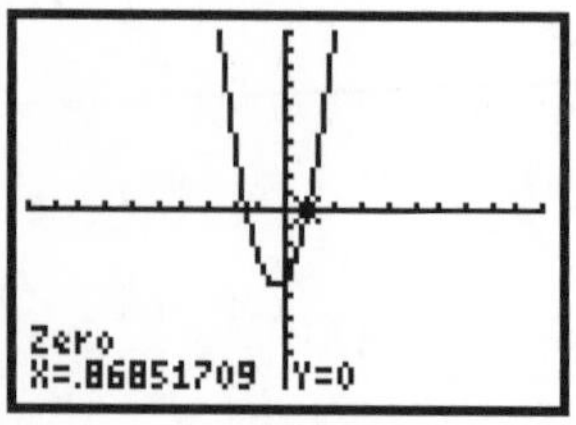

The zeros are approximately -1.535 and 0.869.

121. Graph $y = 5.02x^2 - 4.19x - 2.057$ and use the Zero feature twice.

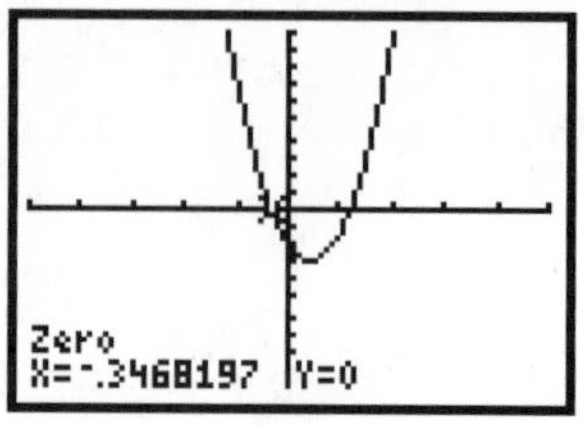

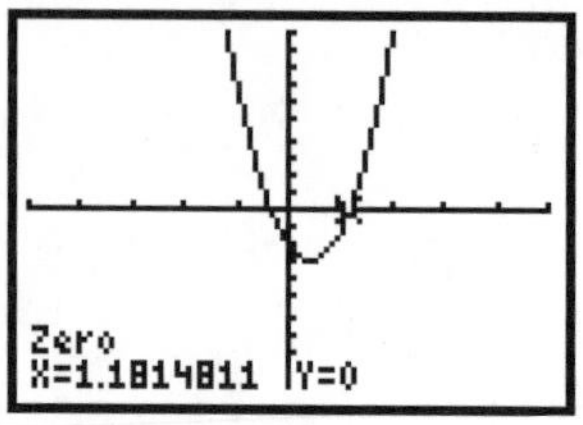

The zeros are approximately -0.347 and 1.181.

123. Discussion and Writing

125. $1998 - 1980 = 18$, so we substitute 18 for x.
$a(18) = 9096(18) + 387,725 = 551,453$ associate's degrees

127. Test for symmetry with respect to the x-axis:

$$\begin{aligned} 3x^2 + 4y^2 &= 5 \quad \text{Original equation} \\ 3x^2 + 4(-y)^2 &= 5 \quad \text{Replacing } y \text{ by } -y \\ 3x^2 + 4y^2 &= 5 \quad \text{Simplifying} \end{aligned}$$

The last equation is equivalent to the original equation, so the graph is symmetric with respect to the x-axis.

Test for symmetry with respect to the y-axis:

$$\begin{aligned} 3x^2 + 4y^2 &= 5 \quad \text{Original equation} \\ 3(-x)^2 + 4y^2 &= 5 \quad \text{Replacing } x \text{ by } -x \\ 3x^2 + 4y^2 &= 5 \quad \text{Simplifying} \end{aligned}$$

The last equation is equivalent to the original equation, so the equation is symmetric with respect to the y-axis.

Test for symmetry with respect to the origin:

$$\begin{aligned} 3x^2 + 4y^2 &= 5 \quad \text{Original equation} \\ 3(-x)^2 + 4(-y)^2 &= 5 \quad \text{Replacing } x \text{ by } -x \\ & \qquad\quad \text{and } y \text{ by } -y \\ 3x^2 + 4y^2 &= 5 \quad \text{Simplifying} \end{aligned}$$

The last equation is equivalent to the original equation, so the equation is symmetric with respect to the origin.

129.

$$\begin{aligned} f(x) &= 2x^3 - x \\ f(-x) &= 2(-x)^3 - (-x) = -2x^3 + x \\ -f(x) &= -2x^3 + x \end{aligned}$$

$f(x) \neq f(-x)$ so f is not even

$f(-x) = -f(x)$, so f is odd.

131. a)

$$\begin{aligned} kx^2 - 17x + 33 &= 0 \\ k(3)^2 - 17(3) + 33 &= 0 \quad \text{Substituting 3 for } x \\ 9k - 51 + 33 &= 0 \\ 9k &= 18 \\ k &= 2 \end{aligned}$$

b) $2x^2 - 17x + 33 = 0$ Substituting 2 for k

$(2x-11)(x-3) = 0$

$2x - 11 = 0$ *or* $x - 3 = 0$

$x = \frac{11}{2}$ *or* $x = 3$

The other solution is $\frac{11}{2}$.

133. a) $(1+i)^2 - k(1+i) + 2 = 0$ Substituting $1+i$ for x

$1 + 2i - 1 - k - ki + 2 = 0$

$2 + 2i = k + ki$

$2(1+i) = k(1+i)$

$2 = k$

b) $x^2 - 2x + 2 = 0$ Substituting 2 for k

$$x = \frac{-(-2) \pm \sqrt{(-2)^2 - 4\cdot 1\cdot 2}}{2\cdot 1}$$

$$= \frac{2 \pm \sqrt{-4}}{2}$$

$$= \frac{2 \pm 2i}{2} = 1 \pm i$$

The other solution is $1 - i$.

135. $(x-2)^3 = x^3 - 2$

$x^3 - 6x^2 + 12x - 8 = x^3 - 2$

$0 = 6x^2 - 12x + 6$

$0 = 6(x^2 - 2x + 1)$

$0 = 6(x-1)(x-1)$

$x - 1 = 0$ *or* $x - 1 = 0$

$x = 1$ *or* $x = 1$

The solution is 1.

137. $(6x^3 + 7x^2 - 3x)(x^2 - 7) = 0$

$x(6x^2 + 7x - 3)(x^2 - 7) = 0$

$x(3x-1)(2x+3)(x^2-7) = 0$

$x=0$ *or* $3x - 1=0$ *or* $2x+3=0$ *or* $x^2 - 7 = 0$

$x=0$ *or* $x=\frac{1}{3}$ *or* $x=-\frac{3}{2}$ *or* $x = \sqrt{7}$ *or* $x = -\sqrt{7}$

The exact solutions are $-\sqrt{7}$, $-\frac{3}{2}$, 0, $\frac{1}{3}$, and $\sqrt{7}$.

139. $x^2 + x - \sqrt{2} = 0$

$$x = \frac{-b \pm \sqrt{b^2 - 4ac}}{2a}$$

$$= \frac{-1 \pm \sqrt{1^2 - 4\cdot 1(-\sqrt{2})}}{2\cdot 1} = \frac{-1 \pm \sqrt{1 + 4\sqrt{2}}}{2}$$

The solutions are $\frac{-1 \pm \sqrt{1 + 4\sqrt{2}}}{2}$.

141. $2t^2 + (t-4)^2 = 5t(t-4) + 24$

$2t^2 + t^2 - 8t + 16 = 5t^2 - 20t + 24$

$0 = 2t^2 - 12t + 8$

$0 = t^2 - 6t + 4$ Dividing by 2

Use the quadratic formula.

$$t = \frac{-b \pm \sqrt{b^2 - 4ac}}{2a}$$

$$= \frac{-(-6) \pm \sqrt{(-6)^2 - 4\cdot 1\cdot 4}}{2\cdot 1}$$

$$= \frac{6 \pm \sqrt{20}}{2} = \frac{6 \pm 2\sqrt{5}}{2}$$

$$= \frac{2(3 \pm \sqrt{5})}{2} = 3 \pm \sqrt{5}$$

The solutions are $3 \pm \sqrt{5}$.

143. $\sqrt{x-3} - \sqrt[4]{x-3} = 2$

Substitute u for $\sqrt[4]{x-3}$.

$u^2 - u - 2 = 0$

$(u-2)(u+1) = 0$

$u - 2 = 0$ *or* $u + 1 = 0$

$u = 2$ *or* $u = -1$

Substitute $\sqrt[4]{x-3}$ for u and solve for x.

$\sqrt[4]{x-3} = 2$ *or* $\sqrt[4]{x-3} = 1$

$x - 3 = 16$ No solution

$x = 19$

The value checks. The solution is 19.

145. $$\left(y + \frac{2}{y}\right)^2 + 3y + \frac{6}{y} = 4$$

$$\left(y + \frac{2}{y}\right)^2 + 3\left(y + \frac{2}{y}\right) - 4 = 0$$

Substitute u for $y + \frac{2}{y}$.

$u^2 + 3u - 4 = 0$

$(u+4)(u-1) = 0$

$u = -4$ *or* $u = 1$

Substitute $y + \frac{2}{y}$ for u and solve for y.

$y + \frac{2}{y} = -4$ *or* $y + \frac{2}{y} = 1$

$y^2 + 2 = -4y$ *or* $y^2 + 2 = y$

$y^2 + 4y + 2 = 0$ *or* $y^2 - y + 2 = 0$

$$y = \frac{-4 \pm \sqrt{4^2 - 4\cdot 1\cdot 2}}{2\cdot 1} \quad or$$

$$y = \frac{-(-1) \pm \sqrt{(-1)^2 - 4\cdot 1\cdot 2}}{2\cdot 1}$$

$$y = \frac{-4 \pm \sqrt{8}}{2} \quad or \quad y = \frac{1 \pm \sqrt{-7}}{2}$$

$$y = \frac{-4 \pm 2\sqrt{2}}{2} \quad or \quad y = \frac{1 \pm \sqrt{7}i}{2}$$

$$y = -2 \pm \sqrt{2} \quad or \quad y = \frac{1}{2} \pm \frac{\sqrt{7}}{2}i$$

The solutions are $-2 \pm \sqrt{2}$ and $\frac{1}{2} \pm \frac{\sqrt{7}}{2}i$.

147. $\frac{1}{2}at + v_0t + x_0 = 0$

Use the quadratic formula. Here $a = \frac{1}{2}a$, $b = v_0$, and $c = x_0$.

$$t = \frac{-v_0 \pm \sqrt{(v_0)^2 - 4 \cdot \frac{1}{2}a \cdot x_0}}{2 \cdot \frac{1}{2}a}$$

$$t = \frac{-v_0 \pm \sqrt{v_0^2 - 2ax_0}}{a}$$

Exercise Set 2.4

1. a) The minimum function value occurs at the vertex, so the vertex is $\left(-\frac{1}{2}, -\frac{9}{4}\right)$.

b) The line of symmetry is a vertical line through the vertex. It is $x = -\frac{1}{2}$.

c) The minimum value of the function is $-\frac{9}{4}$.

3. $f(x) = x^2 - 8x + 12$ — 16 completes the square for $x^2 - 8x$.

$= x^2 - 8x + 16 - 16 + 12$ — Adding $16 - 16$ on the right side

$= (x^2 - 8x + 16) - 16 + 12$

$= (x - 4)^2 - 4$ — Factoring and simplifying

$= (x - 4)^2 + (-4)$ — Writing in the form $f(x) = a(x - h)^2 + k$

a) Vertex: $(4, -4)$

b) Line of symmetry: $x = 4$

c) Minimum value: -4

d) We plot the vertex and find several points on either side of it. Then we plot these points and connect them with a smooth curve.

x	$f(x)$
4	-4
2	0
1	5
5	-3
6	0

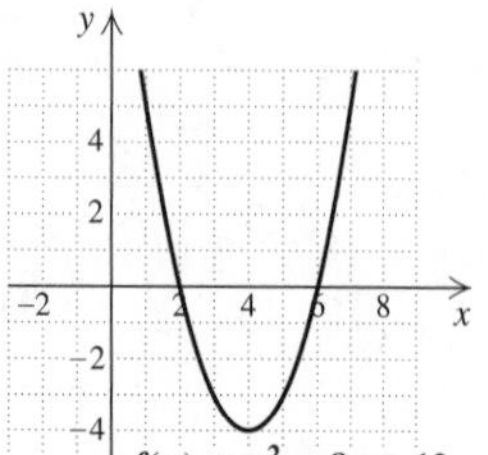

$f(x) = x^2 - 8x + 12$

5. $f(x) = x^2 - 7x + 12$ — $\frac{49}{4}$ completes the square for $x^2 - 7x$.

$= x^2 - 7x + \frac{49}{4} - \frac{49}{4} + 12$ — Adding $\frac{49}{4} - \frac{49}{4}$ on the right side

$= \left(x^2 - 7x + \frac{49}{4}\right) - \frac{49}{4} + 12$

$= \left(x - \frac{7}{2}\right)^2 - \frac{1}{4}$ — Factoring and simplifying

$= \left(x - \frac{7}{2}\right)^2 + \left(-\frac{1}{4}\right)$ — Writing in the form $f(x) = a(x - h)^2 + k$

a) Vertex: $\left(\frac{7}{2}, -\frac{1}{4}\right)$

b) Line of symmetry: $x = \frac{7}{2}$

c) Minimum value: $-\frac{1}{4}$

d) We plot the vertex and find several points on either side of it. Then we plot these points and connect them with a smooth curve.

x	$f(x)$
$\frac{7}{2}$	$-\frac{1}{4}$
4	0
5	2
3	0
1	6

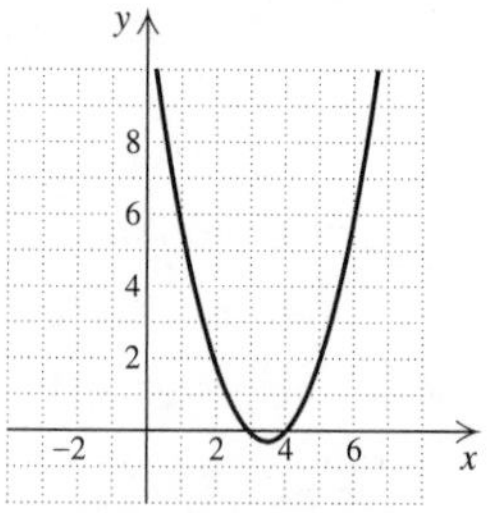

$f(x) = x^2 - 7x + 12$

7. $f(x) = x^2 + 4x + 5$ — 4 completes the square for $x^2 + 4x$

$= x^2 + 4x + 4 - 4 + 5$ — Adding $4 - 4$ on the right side

$= (x + 2)^2 + 1$ — Factoring and simplifying

$= [x - (-2)]^2 + 1$ — Writing in the form $f(x) = a(x - h)^2 + k$

a) Vertex: $(-2, 1)$

b) Line of symmetry: $x = -2$

c) Minimum value: 1

d) We plot the vertex and find several points on either side of it. Then we plot these points and connect them with a smooth curve.

x	$f(x)$
-2	1
-1	2
0	5
-3	2
-4	5

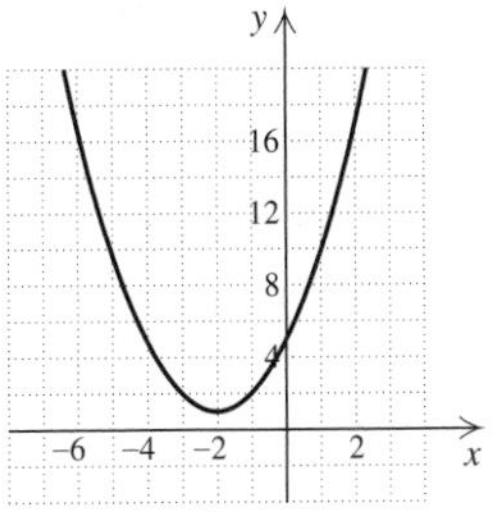

$f(x) = x^2 + 4x + 5$

9. $f(x) = -x^2 - 6x + 3$

$= -(x^2 + 6x) + 3$ 9 completes the square for $x^2 + 6x$.

$= -(x^2 + 6x + 9 - 9) + 3$

$= -(x+3)^2 - (-9) + 3$ Removing -9 from the parentheses

$= -(x+3)^2 + 9 + 3$

$= -[x - (-3)]^2 + 12$

a) Vertex: $(-3, 12)$

b) Line of symmetry: $x = -3$

c) Maximum value: 12

d) We plot the vertex and find several points on either side of it. Then we plot these points and connect them with a smooth curve.

x	$f(x)$
-3	12
0	3
1	-4
-6	3
-7	-4

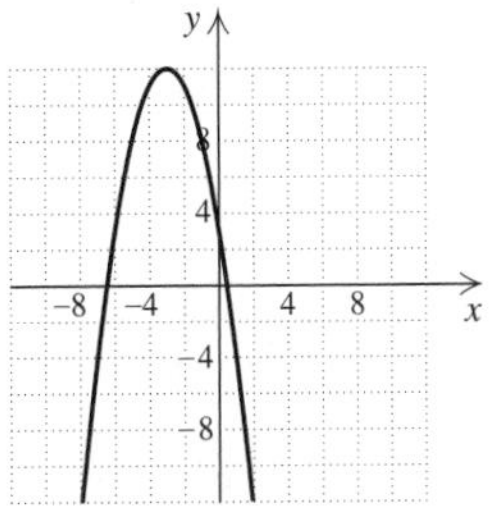

$f(x) = -x^2 - 6x + 3$

11. $g(x) = 2x^2 + 6x + 8$

$= 2(x^2 + 3x) + 8$ Factoring 2 out of the first two terms

$= 2\left(x^2 + 3x + \frac{9}{4} - \frac{9}{4}\right) + 8$ Adding $\frac{9}{4} - \frac{9}{4}$ inside the parentheses

$= 2\left(x^2 + 3x + \frac{9}{4}\right) - 2 \cdot \frac{9}{4} + 8$ Removing $-\frac{9}{4}$ from within the parentheses

$= 2\left(x + \frac{3}{2}\right)^2 + \frac{7}{2}$ Factoring and simplifying

$= 2\left[x - \left(-\frac{3}{2}\right)\right]^2 + \frac{7}{2}$

a) Vertex: $\left(-\frac{3}{2}, \frac{7}{2}\right)$

b) Line of symmetry: $x = -\frac{3}{2}$

c) Minimum value: $\frac{7}{2}$

d) We plot the vertex and find several points on either side of it. Then we plot these points and connect them with a smooth curve.

x	$f(x)$
$-\frac{3}{2}$	$\frac{7}{2}$
-1	4
0	8
-2	4
-3	8

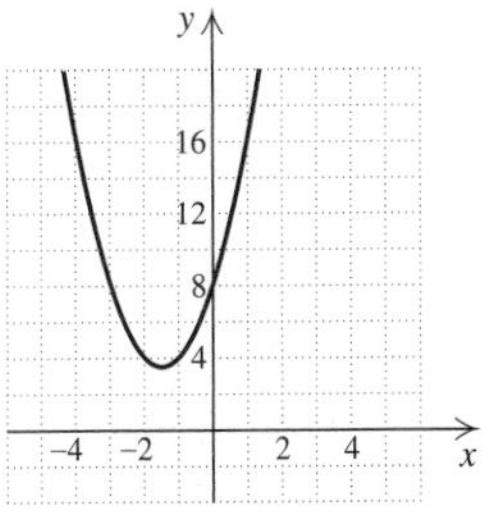

$g(x) = 2x^2 + 6x + 8$

13. $g(x) = -2x^2 + 2x + 1$

$= -2(x^2 - x) + 1$ Factoring -2 out of the first two terms

$= -2\left(x^2 - x + \frac{1}{4} - \frac{1}{4}\right) + 1$ Adding $\frac{1}{4} - \frac{1}{4}$ inside the parentheses

$= -2\left(x^2 - x + \frac{1}{4}\right) - 2\left(-\frac{1}{4}\right) + 1$

Removing $-\frac{1}{4}$ from within the parentheses

$= -2\left(x - \frac{1}{2}\right)^2 + \frac{3}{2}$

a) Vertex: $\left(\frac{1}{2}, \frac{3}{2}\right)$

b) Line of symmetry: $x = \frac{1}{2}$

c) Maximum value: $\frac{3}{2}$

d) We plot the vertex and find several points on either side of it. Then we plot these points and connect them with a smooth curve.

x	$f(x)$
$\frac{1}{2}$	$\frac{3}{2}$
1	1
2	-3
0	1
-1	-3

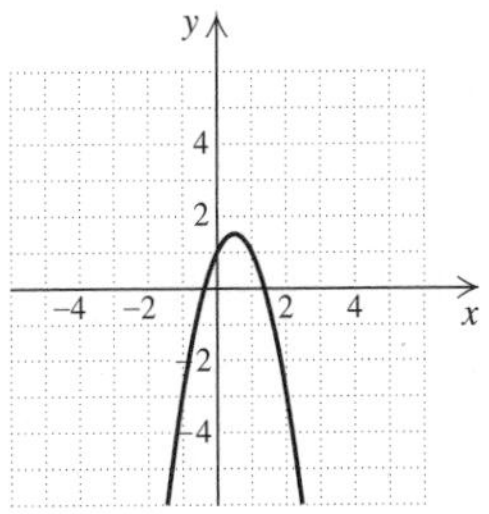

$g(x) = -2x^2 + 2x + 1$

15. The graph of $y = (x+3)^2$ has vertex $(-3, 0)$ and opens up. It is graph (f).

17. The graph of $y = 2(x-4)^2 - 1$ has vertex $(4, -1)$ and opens up. It is graph (b).

19. The graph of $y = -\frac{1}{2}(x+3)^2 + 4$ has vertex $(-3, 4)$ and opens down. It is graph (h).

21. The graph of $y = -(x+3)^2 + 4$ has vertex $(-3, 4)$ and opens down. It is graph (c).

23. $f(x) = x^2 - 6x + 5$

a) The x-coordinate of the vertex is
$$-\frac{b}{2a} = -\frac{-6}{2 \cdot 1} = 3.$$
Since $f(3) = 3^2 - 6 \cdot 3 + 5 = -4$, the vertex is $(3, -4)$.

b) Since $a = 1 > 0$, the graph opens up so the second coordinate of the vertex, -4, is the minimum value of the function.

c) The range is $[-4, \infty)$.

d) Since the graph opens up, function values decrease to the left of the vertex and increase to the right of the vertex. Thus, $f(x)$ is increasing on $(3, \infty)$ and decreasing on $(-\infty, 3)$.

25. $f(x) = 2x^2 + 4x - 16$

a) The x-coordinate of the vertex is
$$-\frac{b}{2a} = -\frac{4}{2 \cdot 2} = -1.$$
Since $f(-1) = 2(-1)^2 + 4(-1) - 16 = -18$, the vertex is $(-1, -18)$.

b) Since $a = 2 > 0$, the graph opens up so the second coordinate of the vertex, -18, is the minimum value of the function.

c) The range is $[-18, \infty)$.

d) Since the graph opens up, function values decrease to the left of the vertex and increase to the right of the vertex. Thus, $f(x)$ is increasing on $(-1, \infty)$ and decreasing on $(-\infty, -1)$.

27. $f(x) = -\frac{1}{2}x^2 + 5x - 8$

a) The x-coordinate of the vertex is
$$-\frac{b}{2a} = -\frac{5}{2\left(-\frac{1}{2}\right)} = 5.$$
Since $f(5) = -\frac{1}{2} \cdot 5^2 + 5 \cdot 5 - 8 = \frac{9}{2}$, the vertex is $\left(5, \frac{9}{2}\right)$.

b) Since $a = -\frac{1}{2} < 0$, the graph opens down so the second coordinate of the vertex, $\frac{9}{2}$, is the maximum value of the function.

c) The range is $\left(-\infty, \frac{9}{2}\right]$.

d) Since the graph opens down, function values increase to the left of the vertex and decreases to the right of the vertex. Thus, $f(x)$ is increasing on $(-\infty, 5)$ and decreasing on $(5, \infty,)$.

29. $f(x) = 3x^2 + 6x + 5$

a) The x-coordinate of the vertex is
$$-\frac{b}{2a} = -\frac{6}{2 \cdot 3} = -1.$$
Since $f(-1) = 3(-1)^2 + 6(-1) + 5 = 2$, the vertex is $(-1, 2)$.

b) Since $a = 3 > 0$, the graph opens up so the second coordinate of the vertex, 2, is the minimum value of the function.

c) The range is $[2, \infty)$.

d) Since the graph opens up, function values decrease to the left of the vertex and increase to the right of the vertex. Thus, $f(x)$ is increasing on $(-1, \infty)$ and decreasing on $(-\infty, -1)$.

31. $g(x) = -4x^2 - 12x + 9$

a) The x-coordinate of the vertex is
$$-\frac{b}{2a} = -\frac{-12}{2(-4)} = -\frac{3}{2}.$$
Since $g\left(-\frac{3}{2}\right) = -4\left(-\frac{3}{2}\right)^2 - 12\left(-\frac{3}{2}\right) + 9 = 18$, the vertex is $\left(-\frac{3}{2}, 18\right)$.

b) Since $a = -4 < 0$, the graph opens down so the second coordinate of the vertex, 18, is the maximum value of the function.

c) The range is $(-\infty, 18]$.

d) Since the graph opens down, function values increase to the left of the vertex and decrease to the right of the vertex. Thus, $g(x)$ is increasing on $\left(-\infty, -\frac{3}{2}\right)$ and decreasing on $\left(-\frac{3}{2}, \infty\right)$.

33. ***Familiarize and Translate***. The function $s(t) = -16t^2 + 20t + 6$ is given in the statement of the problem.

Carry out. The function $s(t)$ is quadratic and the coefficient of t^2 is negative, so $s(t)$ has a maximum value. It occurs at the vertex of the graph of the function. We find the first coordinate of the vertex. This is the time at which the ball reaches its maximum height.
$$t = -\frac{b}{2a} = -\frac{20}{2(-16)} = 0.625$$
The second coordinate of the vertex gives the maximum height.
$$s(0.625) = -16(0.625)^2 + 20(0.625) + 6 = 12.25$$

Check. Completing the square, we write the function in the form $s(t) = -16(t - 0.625)^2 + 12.25$. We see that the coordinates of the vertex are $(0.625, 12.25)$, so the answer checks.

State. The ball reaches its maximum height after 0.625 seconds. The maximum height is 12.25 ft.

35. ***Familiarize and Translate***. The function $s(t) = -16t^2 + 120t + 80$ is given in the statement of the problem.

Carry out. The function $s(t)$ is quadratic and the coefficient of t^2 is negative, so $s(t)$ has a maximum value. It occurs at the vertex of the graph of the function. We find the first coordinate of the vertex. This is the time at which the rocket reaches its maximum height.
$$t = -\frac{b}{2a} = -\frac{120}{2(-16)} = 3.75$$

The second coordinate of the vertex gives the maximum height.

$s(3.75) = -16(3.75)^2 + 120(3.75) + 80 = 305$

Check. Completing the square, we write the function in the form $s(t) = -16(t - 3.75)^2 + 305$. We see that the coordinates of the vertex are $(3.75, 305)$, so the answer checks.

State. The rocket reaches its maximum height after 3.75 seconds. The maximum height is 305 ft.

37. ***Familiarize.*** Using the label in the text, we let x = the height of the file. Then the length = 10 and the width = $18 - 2x$.

Translate. Since the volume of a rectangular solid is length × width × height we have

$V(x) = 10(18 - 2x)x$, or $-20x^2 + 180x$.

Carry out. Since $V(x)$ is a quadratic function with $a = -20 < 0$, the maximum function value occurs at the vertex of the graph of the function. The first coordinate of the vertex is

$$-\frac{b}{2a} = -\frac{180}{2(-20)} = 4.5.$$

Check. When $x = 4.5$, then $18 - 2x = 9$ and $V(x) = 10 \cdot 9(4.5)$, or 405. As a partial check, we can find $V(x)$ for a value of x less than 4.5 and for a value of x greater than 4.5. For instance, $V(4.4) = 404.8$ and $V(4.6) = 404.8$. Since both of these values are less than 405, our result appears to be correct.

State. The file should be 4.5 in. tall in order to maximize the volume.

39. ***Familiarize.*** Let b = the length of the base of the triangle. Then the height $= 20 - b$.

Translate. Since the area of a triangle is $\frac{1}{2} \times$ base × height, we have

$A(b) = \frac{1}{2}b(20 - b)$, or $-\frac{1}{2}b^2 + 10b$.

Carry out. Since $A(b)$ is a quadratic function with $a = -\frac{1}{2} < 0$, the maximum function value occurs at the vertex of the graph of the function. The first coordinate of the vertex is

$$-\frac{b}{2a} = -\frac{10}{2\left(-\frac{1}{2}\right)} = 10.$$

When $b = 10$, then $20 - b = 20 - 10 = 10$, and the area is $\frac{1}{2} \cdot 10 \cdot 10 = 50$ cm^2.

Check. As a partial check, we can find $A(b)$ for a value of b less than 10 and for a value of b greater than 10. For instance, $V(9.9) = 49.995$ and $V(10.1) = 49.995$. Since both of these values are less than 50, our result appears to be correct.

State. The area is a maximum when the base and the height are both 10 cm.

41. $C(x) = 0.1x^2 - 0.7x + 2.425$

Since $C(x)$ is a quadratic function with $a = 0.1 > 0$, a minimum function value occurs at the vertex of the graph of $C(x)$. The first coordinate of the vertex is

$$-\frac{b}{2a} = -\frac{-0.7}{2(0.1)} = 3.5.$$

Thus, 3.5 hundred, or 350 bicycles should be built to minimize the average cost per bicycle.

43. $P(x) = R(x) - C(x)$

$P(x) = (50x - 0.5x^2) - (10x + 3)$

$P(x) = -0.5x^2 + 40x - 3$

Since $P(x)$ is a quadratic function with $a = -0.5 < 0$, a maximum function value occurs at the vertex of the graph of the function. The first coordinate of the vertex is

$$-\frac{b}{2a} = -\frac{40}{2(-0.5)} = 40.$$

$P(40) = -0.5(40)^2 + 40 \cdot 40 - 3 = 797$

Thus, the maximum profit is \$797. It occurs when 40 units are sold.

45. ***Familiarize.*** We let s = the height of the elevator shaft, t_1 = the time it takes the screwdriver to reach the bottom of the shaft, and t_2 = the time it takes the sound to reach the top of the shaft.

Translate. We know that $t_1 + t_2 = 5$. Using the information in Example 4 we also know that

$$s = 16t_1^2, \quad \textit{or} \quad t_1 = \frac{\sqrt{s}}{4} \text{ and}$$

$$s = 1100t_2, \quad \textit{or} \quad t_2 = \frac{s}{1100}.$$

Then $\frac{\sqrt{s}}{4} + \frac{s}{1100} = 5$.

Carry out. We solve the last equation above.

$$\frac{\sqrt{s}}{4} + \frac{s}{1100} = 5$$

$$275\sqrt{s} + s = 5500 \quad \text{Multiplying by 1100}$$

$$s + 275\sqrt{s} - 5500 = 0$$

Let $u = \sqrt{s}$ and substitute.

$$u^2 + 275u - 5500 = 0$$

$$u = \frac{-b + \sqrt{b^2 - 4ac}}{2a} \quad \text{We only want the positive solution.}$$

$$= \frac{-275 + \sqrt{275^2 - 4 \cdot 1(-5500)}}{2 \cdot 1}$$

$$= \frac{-275 + \sqrt{97,625}}{2} \approx 18.725$$

Since $u \approx 18.725$, we have $\sqrt{s} = 18.725$, so $s \approx 350.6$.

Check. If $s \approx 350.6$, then $t_1 = \frac{\sqrt{s}}{4} = \frac{\sqrt{350.6}}{4} \approx 4.68$ and $t_2 = \frac{s}{1100} = \frac{350.6}{1100} \approx 0.32$, so $t_1 + t_2 = 4.68 + 0.32 = 5$.

The result checks.

State. The elevator shaft is about 350.6 ft tall.

47. ***Familiarize***. Using the labels on the drawing in the text, we let x = the width of each corral and $240 - 3x$ = the total length of the corrals.

Translate. Since the area of a rectangle is length × width, we have

$$A(x) = (240 - 3x)x = -3x^2 + 240x.$$

Carry out. Since $A(x)$ is a quadratic function with $a = -3 < 0$, the maximum function value occurs at the vertex of the graph of $A(x)$. The first coordinate of the vertex is

$$-\frac{b}{2a} = -\frac{240}{2(-3)} = 40.$$

$A(40) = -3(40)^2 + 240(40) = 4800$

Check. As a partial check we can find $A(x)$ for a value of x less than 40 and for a value of x greater than 40. For instance, $A(39.9) = 4799.97$ and $A(40.1) = 4799.97$. Since both of these values are less than 4800, our result appears to be correct.

State. The largest total area that can be enclosed is 4800 yd^2.

49. Left to the student

51. Left to the student

53. Discussion and Writing

55. Discussion and Writing

57. $f(x) = 2x^2 - x + 4$

$$\begin{aligned} f(x+h) &= 2(x+h)^2 - (x+h) + 4 \\ &= 2(x^2 + 2xh + h^2) - (x+h) + 4 \\ &= 2x^2 + 4xh + 2h^2 - x - h - 4 \end{aligned}$$

$$\begin{aligned} &\frac{f(x+h) - f(x)}{h} \\ &= \frac{2x^2 + 4xh + 2h^2 - x - h - 4 - (2x^2 - x + 4)}{h} \\ &= \frac{2x^2 + 4xh + 2h^2 - x - h - 4 - 2x^2 + x - 4}{h} \\ &= \frac{4xh + 2h^2 - h}{h} = \frac{h(4x + 2h - 1)}{h} \\ &= 4x + 2h - 1 \end{aligned}$$

59. The graph of $f(x)$ is stretched vertically and reflected across the x-axis.

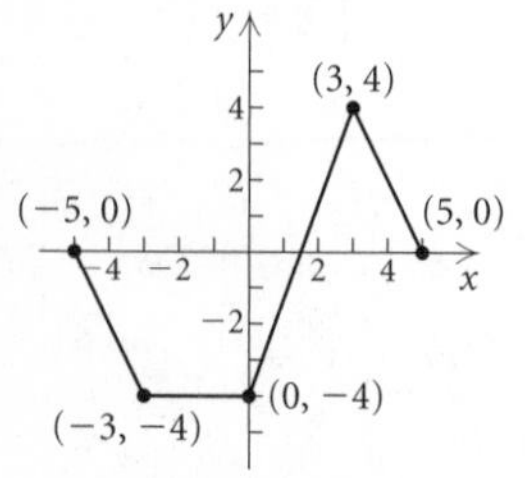

$g(x) = -2f(x)$

61. $f(x) = -0.2x^2 - 3x + c$

The x-coordinate of the vertex of $f(x)$ is $-\frac{b}{2a} = -\frac{-3}{2(-0.2)} = -7.5$. Now we find c such that $f(-7.5) = -225$.

$$\begin{aligned} -0.2(-7.5)^2 - 3(-7.5) + c &= -225 \\ -11.25 + 22.5 + c &= -225 \\ c &= -236.25 \end{aligned}$$

63.

$y = (|x| - 5)^2 - 3$

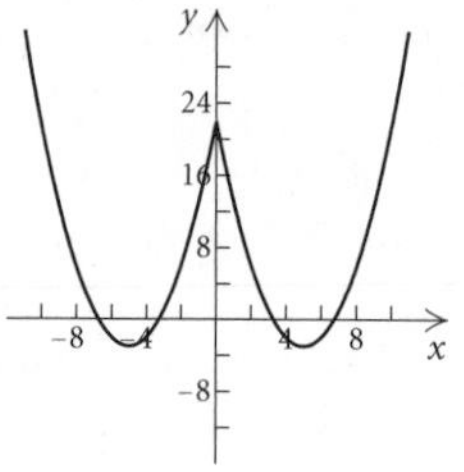

Exercise Set 2.5

1.

$$\begin{aligned} \frac{1}{4} + \frac{1}{5} &= \frac{1}{t}, \text{ LCD is } 20t \\ 20t\left(\frac{1}{4} + \frac{1}{5}\right) &= 20t \cdot \frac{1}{t} \\ 20t \cdot \frac{1}{4} + 20t \cdot \frac{1}{5} &= 20t \cdot \frac{1}{t} \\ 5t + 4t &= 20 \\ 9t &= 20 \\ t &= \frac{20}{9} \end{aligned}$$

Check:

$$\frac{1}{4} + \frac{1}{5} = \frac{1}{t}$$

$\frac{1}{4} + \frac{1}{5}$?	$\frac{1}{\frac{20}{9}}$
$\frac{5}{20} + \frac{4}{20}$	$1 \cdot \frac{9}{20}$
$\frac{9}{20}$	$\frac{9}{20}$ TRUE

The solution is $\frac{20}{9}$.

3.

$$\begin{aligned} \frac{x+2}{4} - \frac{x-1}{5} &= 15, \text{ LCD is } 20 \\ 20\left(\frac{x+2}{4} - \frac{x-1}{5}\right) &= 20 \cdot 15 \\ 5(x+2) - 4(x-1) &= 300 \\ 5x + 10 - 4x + 4 &= 300 \\ x + 14 &= 300 \\ x &= 286 \end{aligned}$$

The solution is 286.

5. $\frac{1}{2}+\frac{2}{x}=\frac{1}{3}+\frac{3}{x}$, LCD is $6x$

$$6x\left(\frac{1}{2}+\frac{2}{x}\right)=6x\left(\frac{1}{3}+\frac{3}{x}\right)$$
$$3x+12=2x+18$$
$$3x-2x=18-12$$
$$x=6$$

Check:

$\frac{1}{2}+\frac{2}{x}=\frac{1}{3}+\frac{3}{x}$	
$\frac{1}{2}+\frac{2}{6}$?	$\frac{1}{3}+\frac{3}{6}$
$\frac{1}{2}+\frac{1}{3}$	$\frac{1}{3}+\frac{1}{2}$ TRUE

The solution is 6.

7. $\frac{3x}{x+2}+\frac{6}{x}=\frac{12}{x^2+2x}$

$$\frac{3x}{x+2}+\frac{6}{x}=\frac{12}{x(x+2)},\ \text{LCD is } x(x+2)$$
$$x(x+2)\left(\frac{3x}{x+2}+\frac{6}{x}\right)=x(x+2)\cdot\frac{12}{x(x+2)}$$
$$3x\cdot x+6(x+2)=12$$
$$3x^2+6x+12=12$$
$$3x^2+6x=0$$
$$3x(x+2)=0$$

$3x=0$ *or* $x+2=0$

$x=0$ *or* $x=-2$

Neither 0 nor -2 checks, so the equation has no solution.

9. $\frac{4}{x^2-1}-\frac{2}{x-1}=\frac{3}{x+1}$, LCD is $(x+1)(x-1)$

$$(x+1)(x-1)\left(\frac{4}{(x+1)(x-1)}-\frac{2}{x-1}\right)=(x+1)(x-1)\cdot\frac{3}{x+1}$$
$$4-2(x+1)=3(x-1)$$
$$4-2x-2=3x-3$$
$$2-2x=3x-3$$
$$2+3=3x+2x$$
$$5=5x$$
$$1=x$$

Check:

$\frac{4}{x^2-1}-\frac{2}{x-1}=\frac{3}{x+1}$	
$\frac{4}{1^2-1}-\frac{2}{1-1}$?	$\frac{3}{1+1}$
$\frac{4}{0}-\frac{2}{0}$	$\frac{3}{2}$

Division by zero is undefined.

There is no solution.

11. $\frac{490}{x^2-49}=\frac{5x}{x-7}-\frac{35}{x+7}$

$$\frac{490}{(x+7)(x-7)}=\frac{5x}{x-7}-\frac{35}{x+7},$$
LCD is $(x+7)(x-7)$

$$(x+7)(x-7)\left(\frac{490}{(x+7)(x-7)}\right)=(x+7)(x-7)\left(\frac{5x}{x-7}-\frac{35}{x+7}\right)$$
$$490=5x(x+7)-35(x-7)$$
$$490=5x^2+35x-35x+245$$
$$0=5x^2-245$$
$$0=5(x+7)(x-7)$$

$x+7=0$ or $x-7=0$

$x=-7$ or $x=7$

Neither -7 nor 7 checks, so the equation has no solution.

13. $\frac{1}{x-6}-\frac{1}{x}=\frac{6}{x^2-6x}$

$$\frac{1}{x-6}-\frac{1}{x}=\frac{6}{x(x-6)},\ \text{LCD is } x(x-6)$$
$$x(x-6)\left(\frac{1}{x-6}-\frac{1}{x}\right)=x(x-6)\cdot\frac{6}{x(x-6)}$$
$$x-(x-6)=6$$
$$x-x+6=6$$
$$6=6$$

We get an equation that is true for all real numbers. Note, however, that when $x=6$ or $x=0$, division by 0 occurs in the original equation. Thus, the solution set is $\{x|x$ is a real number *and* $x\neq 6$ *and* $x\neq 0\}$, or $(-\infty,0)\cup(0,6)\cup(6,\infty)$.

15. $\frac{x}{x-4}-\frac{4}{x+4}=\frac{32}{x^2-16}$

$$\frac{x}{x-4}-\frac{4}{x+4}=\frac{32}{(x+4)(x-4)},$$
LCD is $(x+4)(x-4)$

$$(x+4)(x-4)\left(\frac{x}{x-4}-\frac{4}{x+4}\right)=(x+4)(x-4)\cdot\frac{32}{(x+4)(x-4)}$$
$$x(x+4)-4(x-4)=32$$
$$x^2+4x-4x+16=32$$
$$x^2+16=32$$
$$x^2=16$$
$$x=\pm 4$$

Neither 4 nor -4 checks, so the equation has no solution.

17.
$$\frac{x}{x+3}+\frac{3}{x-3}=\frac{18}{x^2-9}$$
$$\frac{x}{x+3}+\frac{3}{x-3}=\frac{18}{(x+3)(x-3)},$$
LCD is $(x+3)(x-3)$
$$(x+3)(x-3)\left(\frac{x}{x+3}+\frac{3}{x-3}\right)=(x+3)(x-3)\cdot\frac{18}{(x+3)(x-3)}$$
$$x(x-3)+3(x+3)=18$$
$$x^2-3x+3x+9=18$$
$$x^2+9=18$$
$$x^2=9$$
$$x=\pm 3$$
Neither 3 nor -3 checks, so the equation has no solution.

19.
$$\frac{1}{5x+20}-\frac{1}{x^2-16}=\frac{3}{x-4}$$
$$\frac{1}{5(x+4)}-\frac{1}{(x+4)(x-4)}=\frac{3}{x-4},$$
LCD is $5(x+4)(x-4)$
$$5(x+4)(x-4)\left(\frac{1}{5(x+4)}-\frac{1}{(x+4)(x-4)}\right)=5(x+4)(x-4)\cdot\frac{3}{x-4}$$
$$x-4-5=15(x+4)$$
$$x-9=15x+60$$
$$-14x-9=60$$
$$-14x=69$$
$$x=-\frac{69}{14}$$
$-\frac{69}{14}$ checks, so the solution is $-\frac{69}{14}$.

21.
$$\frac{2}{5x+5}-\frac{3}{x^2-1}=\frac{4}{x-1}$$
$$\frac{2}{5(x+1)}-\frac{3}{(x+1)(x-1)}=\frac{4}{x-1},$$
LCD is $5(x+1)(x-1)$
$$5(x+1)(x-1)\left(\frac{2}{5(x+1)}-\frac{3}{(x+1)(x-1)}\right)=5(x+1)(x-1)\cdot\frac{4}{x-1}$$
$$2(x-1)-5\cdot 3=20(x+1)$$
$$2x-2-15=20x+20$$
$$2x-17=20x+20$$
$$-18x-17=20$$
$$-18x=37$$
$$x=-\frac{37}{18}$$
$-\frac{37}{18}$ checks, so the solution is $-\frac{37}{18}$.

23.
$$\frac{8}{x^2-2x+4}=\frac{x}{x+2}+\frac{24}{x^3+8},$$
LCD is $(x+2)(x^2-2x+4)$
$$(x+2)(x^2-2x+4)\cdot\frac{8}{x^2-2x+4}=$$
$$(x+2)(x^2-2x+4)\left(\frac{x}{x+2}+\frac{24}{(x+2)(x^2-2x+4)}\right)$$
$$8(x+2)=x(x^2-2x+4)+24$$
$$8x+16=x^3-2x^2+4x+24$$
$$0=x^3-2x^2-4x+8$$
$$0=x^2(x-2)-4(x-2)$$
$$0=(x-2)(x^2-4)$$
$$0=(x-2)(x+2)(x-2)$$
$x-2=0$ or $x+2=0$ or $x-2=0$

$x=2$ or $x=-2$ or $x=2$

Only 2 checks. The solution is 2.

25.
$$\sqrt{3x-4}=1$$
$$(\sqrt{3x-4})^2=1^2$$
$$3x-4=1$$
$$3x=5$$
$$x=\frac{5}{3}$$
Check:

$\sqrt{3x-4}=1$	
$\sqrt{3\cdot\frac{5}{3}-4}$	? 1
$\sqrt{5-4}$	
$\sqrt{1}$	
1	1 TRUE

The solution is $\frac{5}{3}$.

27.
$$\sqrt{2x-5}=2$$
$$(\sqrt{2x-5})^2=2^2$$
$$2x-5=4$$
$$2x=9$$
$$x=\frac{9}{2}$$
Check:

$\sqrt{2x-5}=2$	
$\sqrt{2\cdot\frac{9}{2}-5}$	? 2
$\sqrt{9-5}$	
$\sqrt{4}$	
2	2 TRUE

The solution is $\frac{9}{2}$.

29.
$$\sqrt{7-x} = 2$$
$$(\sqrt{7-x})^2 = 2^2$$
$$7-x = 4$$
$$-x = -3$$
$$x = 3$$

Check:

$\sqrt{7-x} = 2$	
$\sqrt{7-3}$	? 2
$\sqrt{4}$	
2	2 TRUE

The solution is 3.

31.
$$\sqrt{1-2x} = 3$$
$$(\sqrt{1-2x})^2 = 3^2$$
$$1-2x = 9$$
$$-2x = 8$$
$$x = -4$$

Check:

$\sqrt{1-2x} = 3$	
$\sqrt{1-2(-4)}$	? 3
$\sqrt{1+8}$	
$\sqrt{9}$	
3	3 TRUE

The solution is -4.

33.
$$\sqrt[3]{5x-2} = -3$$
$$(\sqrt[3]{5x-2})^3 = (-3)^3$$
$$5x-2 = -27$$
$$5x = -25$$
$$x = -5$$

Check:

$\sqrt[3]{5x-2} = -3$	
$\sqrt[3]{5(-5)-2}$	? -3
$\sqrt[3]{-25-2}$	
$\sqrt[3]{-27}$	
-3	-3 TRUE

The solution is -5.

35.
$$\sqrt[4]{x^2-1} = 1$$
$$(\sqrt[4]{x^2-1})^4 = 1^4$$
$$x^2-1 = 1$$
$$x^2 = 2$$
$$x = \pm\sqrt{2}$$

Check:

$\sqrt[4]{x^2-1} = 1$	
$\sqrt[4]{(\pm\sqrt{2})^2-1}$	? 1
$\sqrt[4]{2-1}$	
$\sqrt[4]{1}$	
1	1 TRUE

The solutions are $\pm\sqrt{2}$.

37.
$$\sqrt{y-1}+4 = 0$$
$$\sqrt{y-1} = -4$$

The principal square root is never negative. Thus, there is no solution.

If we do not observe the above fact, we can continue and reach the same answer.

$$(\sqrt{y-1})^2 = (-4)^2$$
$$y-1 = 16$$
$$y = 17$$

Check:

$\sqrt{y-1}+4 = 0$	
$\sqrt{17-1}+4$	? 0
$\sqrt{16}+4$	
$4+4$	
8	0 FALSE

Since 17 does not check, there is no solution.

39.
$$\sqrt{b+3}-2 = 1$$
$$\sqrt{b+3} = 3$$
$$(\sqrt{b+3})^2 = 3^2$$
$$b+3 = 9$$
$$b = 6$$

Check:

$\sqrt{b+3}-2 = 1$	
$\sqrt{6+3}-2$	? 1
$\sqrt{9}-2$	
$3-2$	
1	1 TRUE

The solution is 6.

41.
$$\sqrt{z+2}+3 = 4$$
$$\sqrt{z+2} = 1$$
$$(\sqrt{z+2})^2 = 1^2$$
$$z+2 = 1$$
$$z = -1$$

Check:

$\sqrt{z+2}+3 = 4$	
$\sqrt{-1+2}+3$	? 4
$\sqrt{1}+3$	
$1+3$	
4	4 TRUE

The solution is -1.

43. $\sqrt{2x+1}-3=3$

$$\sqrt{2x+1}=6$$
$$(\sqrt{2x+1})^2=6^2$$
$$2x+1=36$$
$$2x=35$$
$$x=\frac{35}{2}$$

Check:

$$\begin{array}{r|l} \sqrt{2x+1}-3 & 3 \\ \hline \sqrt{2\cdot\frac{35}{2}+1}-3 \ ? & 3 \\ \sqrt{35+1}-3 & \\ \sqrt{36}-3 & \\ 6-3 & \\ 3 & 3 \quad \text{TRUE} \end{array}$$

The solution is $\frac{35}{2}$.

45. $\sqrt{2-x}-4=6$

$$\sqrt{2-x}=10$$
$$(\sqrt{2-x})^2=10^2$$
$$2-x=100$$
$$-x=98$$
$$x=-98$$

Check:

$$\begin{array}{r|l} \sqrt{2-x}-4 & 6 \\ \hline \sqrt{2-(-98)}-4 \ ? & 6 \\ \sqrt{100}-4 & \\ 10-4 & \\ 6 & 6 \quad \text{TRUE} \end{array}$$

The solution is -98.

47. $\sqrt[3]{6x+9}+8=5$

$$\sqrt[3]{6x+9}=-3$$
$$(\sqrt[3]{6x+9})^3=(-3)^3$$
$$6x+9=-27$$
$$6x=-36$$
$$x=-6$$

Check:

$$\begin{array}{r|l} \sqrt[3]{6x+9}+8 & 5 \\ \hline \sqrt[3]{6(-6)+9}+8 \ ? & 5 \\ \sqrt[3]{-27}+8 & \\ -3+8 & \\ 5 & 5 \quad \text{TRUE} \end{array}$$

The solution is -6.

49. $\sqrt{x+4}+2=x$

$$\sqrt{x+4}=x-2$$
$$(\sqrt{x+4})^2=(x-2)^2$$
$$x+4=x^2-4x+4$$
$$0=x^2-5x$$
$$0=x(x-5)$$

$x=0$ *or* $x-5=0$

$x=0$ *or* $x=5$

Check:

For 0:

$$\begin{array}{r|l} \sqrt{x+4}+2 & x \\ \hline \sqrt{0+4}+2 \ ? & 0 \\ 2+2 & \\ 4 & 0 \quad \text{FALSE} \end{array}$$

For 5:

$$\begin{array}{r|l} \sqrt{x+4}+2 & x \\ \hline \sqrt{5+4}+2 \ ? & 5 \\ \sqrt{9}+2 & \\ 3+2 & \\ 5 & 5 \quad \text{TRUE} \end{array}$$

The number 5 checks but 0 does not. The solution is 5.

51. $\sqrt{x-3}+5=x$

$$\sqrt{x-3}=x-5$$
$$(\sqrt{x-3})^2=(x-5)^2$$
$$x-3=x^2-10x+25$$
$$0=x^2-11x+28$$
$$0=(x-4)(x-7)$$

$x-4=0$ *or* $x-7=0$

$x=4$ *or* $x=7$

Check:

For 4:

$$\begin{array}{r|l} \sqrt{x-3}+5 & x \\ \hline \sqrt{4-3}+5 \ ? & 4 \\ \sqrt{1}+5 & \\ 1+5 & \\ 6 & 4 \quad \text{FALSE} \end{array}$$

For 7:

$$\begin{array}{r|l} \sqrt{x-3}+5 & x \\ \hline \sqrt{7-3}+5 \ ? & 7 \\ \sqrt{4}+5 & \\ 2+5 & \\ 7 & 7 \quad \text{TRUE} \end{array}$$

The number 7 checks but 4 does not. The solution is 7.

53. $\sqrt{x+7} = x+1$

$(\sqrt{x+7})^2 = (x+1)^2$

$x+7 = x^2+2x+1$

$0 = x^2+x-6$

$0 = (x+3)(x-2)$

$x+3=0$ *or* $x-2=0$

$x=-3$ *or* $x=2$

Check:

For -3:

$\sqrt{x+7} = x+1$		
$\sqrt{-3+7}$?	$-3+1$	
$\sqrt{4}$	-2	
2	-2	FALSE

For 2:

$\sqrt{x+7} = x+1$		
$\sqrt{2+7}$?	$2+1$	
$\sqrt{9}$	3	
3	3	TRUE

The number 2 checks but -3 does not. The solution is 2.

55. $\sqrt{3x+3} = x+1$

$(\sqrt{3x+3})^2 = (x+1)^2$

$3x+3 = x^2+2x+1$

$0 = x^2-x-2$

$0 = (x-2)(x+1)$

$x-2=0$ *or* $x+1=0$

$x=2$ *or* $x=-1$

Check:

For 2:

$\sqrt{3x+3} = x+1$		
$\sqrt{3\cdot 2+3}$?	$2+1$	
$\sqrt{9}$	3	
3	3	TRUE

For -1:

$\sqrt{3x+3} = x+1$		
$\sqrt{3(-1)+3}$?	$-1+1$	
$\sqrt{0}$	0	
0	0	TRUE

Both numbers check. The solutions are 2 and -1.

57. $\sqrt{5x+1} = x-1$

$(\sqrt{5x+1})^2 = (x-1)^2$

$5x+1 = x^2-2x+1$

$0 = x^2-7x$

$0 = x(x-7)$

$x=0$ *or* $x-7=0$

$x=0$ *or* $x=7$

Check:

For 0:

$\sqrt{5x+1} = x-1$		
$\sqrt{5\cdot 0+1}$?	$0-1$	
$\sqrt{1}$	-1	
1	-1	FALSE

For 7:

$\sqrt{5x+1} = x-1$		
$\sqrt{5\cdot 7+1}$?	$7-1$	
$\sqrt{36}$	6	
6	6	TRUE

The number 7 checks but 0 does not. The solution is 7.

59. $\sqrt{x-3}+\sqrt{x+2} = 5$

$\sqrt{x+2} = 5-\sqrt{x-3}$

$(\sqrt{x+2})^2 = (5-\sqrt{x-3})^2$

$x+2 = 25-10\sqrt{x-3}+(x-3)$

$x+2 = 22-10\sqrt{x-3}+x$

$10\sqrt{x-3} = 20$

$\sqrt{x-3} = 2$

$(\sqrt{x-3})^2 = 2^2$

$x-3 = 4$

$x = 7$

Check:

$\sqrt{x-3}+\sqrt{x+2} = 5$		
$\sqrt{7-3}+\sqrt{7+2}$?	5	
$\sqrt{4}+\sqrt{9}$		
$2+3$		
5	5	TRUE

The solution is 7.

61. $\sqrt{3x-5}+\sqrt{2x+3}+1 = 0$

$\sqrt{3x-5}+\sqrt{2x+3} = -1$

The principal square root is never negative. Thus the sum of two principal square roots cannot equal -1. There is no solution.

63. $\sqrt{x}-\sqrt{3x-3} = 1$

$\sqrt{x} = \sqrt{3x-3}+1$

$(\sqrt{x})^2 = (\sqrt{3x-3}+1)^2$

$x = (3x-3)+2\sqrt{3x-3}+1$

$2-2x = 2\sqrt{3x-3}$

$1-x = \sqrt{3x-3}$

$(1-x)^2 = (\sqrt{3x-3})^2$

$1-2x+x^2 = 3x-3$

$x^2-5x+4 = 0$

$(x-4)(x-1) = 0$

$x=4$ *or* $x=1$

The number 4 does not check, but 1 does. The solution is 1.

65. $\sqrt{2y-5}-\sqrt{y-3}=1$

$$\begin{aligned}\sqrt{2y-5} &= \sqrt{y-3}+1\\ (\sqrt{2y-5})^2 &= (\sqrt{y-3}+1)^2\\ 2y-5 &= (y-3)+2\sqrt{y-3}+1\\ y-3 &= 2\sqrt{y-3}\\ (y-3)^2 &= (2\sqrt{y-3})^2\\ y^2-6y+9 &= 4(y-3)\\ y^2-6y+9 &= 4y-12\\ y^2-10y+21 &= 0\\ (y-7)(y-3) &= 0\end{aligned}$$

$y=7$ *or* $y=3$

Both numbers check. The solutions are 7 and 3.

67. $\sqrt{y+4}-\sqrt{y-1}=1$

$$\begin{aligned}\sqrt{y+4} &= \sqrt{y-1}+1\\ (\sqrt{y+4})^2 &= (\sqrt{y-1}+1)^2\\ y+4 &= y-1+2\sqrt{y-1}+1\\ 4 &= 2\sqrt{y-1}\\ 2 &= \sqrt{y-1} \quad \text{Dividing by 2}\\ 2^2 &= (\sqrt{y-1})^2\\ 4 &= y-1\\ 5 &= y\end{aligned}$$

The answer checks. The solution is 5.

69. $\sqrt{x+5}+\sqrt{x+2}=3$

$$\begin{aligned}\sqrt{x+5} &= 3-\sqrt{x+2}\\ (\sqrt{x+5})^2 &= (3-\sqrt{x+2})^2\\ x+5 &= 9-6\sqrt{x+2}+x+2\\ -6 &= -6\sqrt{x+2}\\ 1 &= \sqrt{x+2} \quad \text{Dividing by } -6\\ 1^2 &= (\sqrt{x+2})^2\\ 1 &= x+2\\ -1 &= x\end{aligned}$$

The answer checks. The solution is -1.

71.

$$\begin{aligned}x^{1/3} &= -2\\ (x^{1/3})^3 &= (-2)^3 \qquad (x^{1/3}=\sqrt[3]{x})\\ x &= -8\end{aligned}$$

The value checks. The solution is -8.

73.

$$\begin{aligned}t^{1/4} &= 3\\ (t^{1/4})^4 &= 3^4 \qquad (t^{1/4}=\sqrt[4]{t})\\ t &= 81\end{aligned}$$

The value checks. The solution is 81.

75. $|x|=7$

The solutions are those numbers whose distance from 0 on a number line is 7. They are -7 and 7. That is,

$x=-7$ *or* $x=7$.

The solutions are -7 and 7.

77. $|x|=-10.7$

The absolute value of a number is nonnegative. Thus, the equation has no solution.

79. $|x-1|=4$

$x-1=-4$ *or* $x-1=4$

$x=-3$ *or* $x=5$

The solutions are -3 and 5.

81. $|3x|=1$

$3x=-1$ *or* $3x=1$

$x=-\frac{1}{3}$ *or* $x=\frac{1}{3}$

The solutions are $-\frac{1}{3}$ and $\frac{1}{3}$.

83. $|x|=0$

The distance of 0 from 0 on a number line is 0. That is,

$x=0$.

The solution is 0.

85. $|3x+2|=1$

$3x+2=-1$ *or* $3x+2=1$

$3x=-3$ *or* $3x=-1$

$x=-1$ *or* $x=-\frac{1}{3}$

The solutions are -1 and $-\frac{1}{3}$.

87. $\left|\frac{1}{2}x-5\right|=17$

$\frac{1}{2}x-5=-17$ *or* $\frac{1}{2}x-5=17$

$\frac{1}{2}x=-12$ *or* $\frac{1}{2}x=22$

$x=-24$ *or* $x=44$

The solutions are -24 and 44.

89. $|x-1|+3=6$

$|x-1|=3$

$x-1=-3$ *or* $x-1=3$

$x=-2$ *or* $x=4$

The solutions are -2 and 4.

91. $|x+3|-2=8$

$|x+3|=10$

$x+3=-10$ *or* $x+3=10$

$x=-13$ *or* $x=7$

The solutions are -13 and 7.

93. $|3x+1|-4=-1$

$|3x+1|=3$

$3x+1=-3$ *or* $3x+1=3$

$3x=-4$ *or* $3x=2$

$x=-\frac{4}{3}$ *or* $x=\frac{2}{3}$

The solutions are $-\frac{4}{3}$ and $\frac{2}{3}$.

95. $|4x-3|+1=7$

$|4x-3|=6$

$4x-3=-6$ *or* $4x-3=6$

$4x=-3$ *or* $4x=9$

$x=-\frac{3}{4}$ *or* $x=\frac{9}{4}$

The solutions are $-\frac{3}{4}$ and $\frac{9}{4}$.

97. $12-|x+6|=5$

$-|x+6|=-7$

$|x+6|=7$ Multiplying by -1

$x+6=-7$ *or* $x+6=7$

$x=-13$ *or* $x=1$

The solutions are -13 and 1.

99. $\frac{P_1V_1}{T_1}=\frac{P_2V_2}{T_2}$

$P_1V_1T_2=P_2V_2T_1$ Multiplying by T_1T_2 on both sides

$\frac{P_1V_1T_2}{P_2V_2}=T_1$ Dividing by P_2V_2 on both sides

101. $\frac{1}{R}=\frac{1}{R_1}+\frac{1}{R_2}$

$RR_1R_2\cdot\frac{1}{R}=RR_1R_2\left(\frac{1}{R_1}+\frac{1}{R_2}\right)$

Multiplying by RR_1R_2 on both sides

$R_1R_2=RR_2+RR_1$

$R_1R_2-RR_2=RR_1$ Subtracting RR_2 on both sides

$R_2(R_1-R)=RR_1$ Factoring

$R_2=\frac{RR_1}{R_1-R}$ Dividing by R_1-R on both sides

103. $\frac{1}{F}=\frac{1}{m}+\frac{1}{p}$

$Fmp\cdot\frac{1}{F}=Fmp\left(\frac{1}{m}+\frac{1}{p}\right)$ Multiplying by Fmp on both sides

$mp=Fp+Fm$

$mp-Fp=Fm$ Subtracting Fp on both sides

$p(m-F)=Fm$ Factoring

$p=\frac{Fm}{m-F}$ Dividing by $m-F$ on both sides

105. Left to the student

107. Discussion and Writing

109. $15-2x=0$ Setting $f(x)=0$

$15=2x$

$\frac{15}{2}=x$, or

$7.5=x$

The zero of the function is $\frac{15}{2}$, or 7.5.

111. ***Familiarize***. Let a = the number of adults who passed the GED test in 1990.

Translate.

Number of adults who passed the test in 2000	was	82,000	more than	number who passed the test in 1990.
↓	↓	↓	↓	↓
501,000	=	82,000	+	a

Carry out. We solve the equation.

$501,000=82,000+a$

$419,000=a$ Subtracting 82,000

Check. 82,000 more than 419,000 is $82,000+419,000$, or 501,000. The answer checks.

State. In 1990, 419,000 adults passed the GED test.

113. $(x-3)^{2/3}=2$

$[(x-3)^{2/3}]^3=2^3$

$(x-3)^2=8$

$x^2-6x+9=8$

$x^2-6x+1=0$

$a=1$, $b=-6$, $c=1$

$x=\frac{-b\pm\sqrt{b^2-4ac}}{2a}$

$=\frac{-(-6)\pm\sqrt{(-6)^2-4\cdot1\cdot1}}{2\cdot1}$

$=\frac{6\pm\sqrt{32}}{2}=\frac{6\pm4\sqrt{2}}{2}$

$=\frac{2(3\pm2\sqrt{2})}{2}=3\pm2\sqrt{2}$

Both values check. The solutions are $3\pm2\sqrt{2}$.

115. $\sqrt{x+5}+1=\frac{6}{\sqrt{x+5}}$, LCD is $\sqrt{x+5}$

$x+5+\sqrt{x+5}=6$ Multiplying by $\sqrt{x+5}$

$\sqrt{x+5}=1-x$

$x+5=1-2x+x^2$

$0=x^2-3x-4$

$0=(x-4)(x+1)$

$x=4$ *or* $x=-1$

Only -1 checks. The solution set is -1.

Exercise Set 2.6

1. $x + 6 < 5x - 6$

$6 + 6 < 5x - x$ Subtracting x and adding 6 on both sides

$12 < 4x$

$\frac{12}{4} < x$ Dividing by 4 on both sides

$3 < x$

This inequality could also be solved as follows:

$x + 6 < 5x - 6$

$x - 5x < -6 - 6$ Subtracting $5x$ and 6 on both sides

$-4x < -12$

$x > \frac{-12}{-4}$ Dividing by -4 on both sides and reversing the inequality symbol

$x > 3$

The solution set is $\{x|x > 3\}$, or $(3, \infty)$. The graph is shown below.

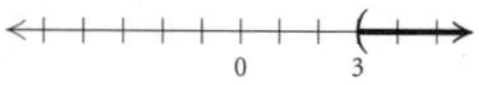

3. $3x - 3 + 2x \geq 1 - 7x - 9$

$5x - 3 \geq -7x - 8$ Collecting like terms

$5x + 7x \geq -8 + 3$ Adding $7x$ and 3 on both sides

$12x \geq -5$

$x \geq -\frac{5}{12}$ Dividing by 12 on both sides

The solution set is $\left\{x \middle| x \geq -\frac{5}{12}\right\}$, or $\left[-\frac{5}{12}, \infty\right)$. The graph is shown below.

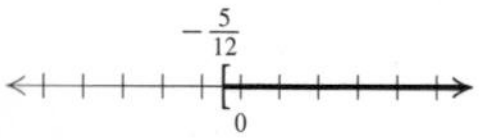

5. $14 - 5y \leq 8y - 8$

$14 + 8 \leq 8y + 5y$

$22 \leq 13y$

$\frac{22}{13} \leq y$

This inequality could also be solved as follows:

$14 - 5y \leq 8y - 8$

$-5y - 8y \leq -8 - 14$

$-13y \leq -22$

$y \geq \frac{22}{13}$ Dividing by -13 on both sides and reversing the inequality symbol

The solution set is $\left\{y \middle| y \geq \frac{22}{13}\right\}$, or $\left[\frac{22}{13}, \infty\right)$. The graph is shown below.

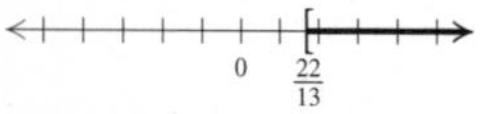

7. $-\frac{3}{4}x \geq -\frac{5}{8} + \frac{2}{3}x$

$\frac{5}{8} \geq \frac{3}{4}x + \frac{2}{3}x$

$\frac{5}{8} \geq \frac{9}{12}x + \frac{8}{12}x$

$\frac{5}{8} \geq \frac{17}{12}x$

$\frac{12}{17} \cdot \frac{5}{8} \geq \frac{12}{17} \cdot \frac{17}{12}x$

$\frac{15}{34} \geq x$

The solution set is $\left\{x \middle| x \leq \frac{15}{34}\right\}$, or $\left(-\infty, \frac{15}{34}\right]$. The graph is shown below.

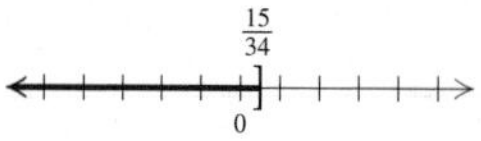

9. $4x(x - 2) < 2(2x - 1)(x - 3)$

$4x(x - 2) < 2(2x^2 - 7x + 3)$

$4x^2 - 8x < 4x^2 - 14x + 6$

$-8x < -14x + 6$

$-8x + 14x < 6$

$6x < 6$

$x < \frac{6}{6}$

$x < 1$

The solution set is $\{x|x < 1\}$, or $(-\infty, 1)$. The graph is shown below.

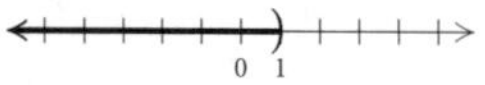

11. $-2 \leq x + 1 < 4$

$-3 \leq x < 3$ Subtracting 1

The solution set is $[-3, 3)$. The graph is shown below.

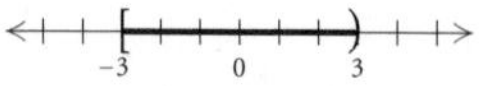

13. $5 \leq x - 3 \leq 7$

$8 \leq x \leq 10$ Adding 3

The solution set is $[8, 10]$. The graph is shown below.

15. $-3 \leq x + 4 \leq 3$

$-7 \leq x \leq -1$ Subtracting 4

The solution set is $[-7, -1]$. The graph is shown below.

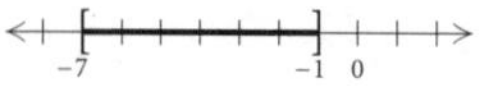

17. $-2 < 2x + 1 < 5$

$-3 < 2x < 4$ Adding -1

$-\frac{3}{2} < x < 2$ Multiplying by $\frac{1}{2}$

The solution set is $\left(-\frac{3}{2}, 2\right)$. The graph is shown below.

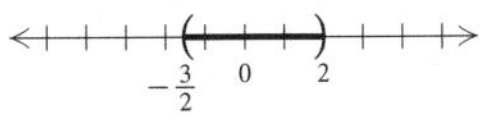

19. $-4 \le 6 - 2x < 4$

$-10 \le -2x < -2$ Adding -6

$5 \ge x > 1$ Multiplying by $-\frac{1}{2}$

or $1 < x \le 5$

The solution set is $(1, 5]$. The graph is shown below.

21. $-5 < \frac{1}{2}(3x + 1) < 7$

$-10 < 3x + 1 < 14$ Multiplying by 2

$-11 < 3x < 13$ Adding -1

$-\frac{11}{3} < x < \frac{13}{3}$ Multiplying by $\frac{1}{3}$

The solution set is $\left(-\frac{11}{3}, \frac{13}{3}\right)$. The graph is shown below.

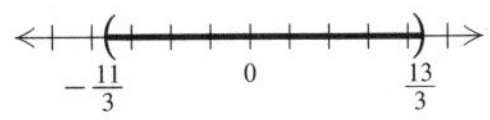

23. $3x \le -6$ *or* $x - 1 > 0$

$x \le -2$ *or* $x > 1$

The solution set is $(-\infty, -2] \cup (1, \infty)$. The graph is shown below.

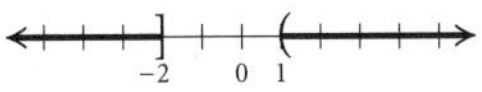

25. $2x + 3 \le -4$ *or* $2x + 3 \ge 4$

$2x \le -7$ *or* $2x \ge 1$

$x \le -\frac{7}{2}$ *or* $x \ge \frac{1}{2}$

The solution set is $\left(-\infty, -\frac{7}{2}\right] \cup \left[\frac{1}{2}, \infty\right)$. The graph is shown below.

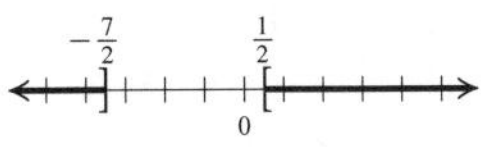

27. $2x - 20 < -0.8$ *or* $2x - 20 > 0.8$

$2x < 19.2$ *or* $2x > 20.8$

$x < 9.6$ *or* $x > 10.4$

The solution set is $(-\infty, 9.6) \cup (10.4, \infty)$. The graph is shown below.

29. $x + 14 \le -\frac{1}{4}$ *or* $x + 14 \ge \frac{1}{4}$

$x \le -\frac{57}{4}$ *or* $x \ge -\frac{55}{4}$

The solution set is $\left(-\infty, -\frac{57}{4}\right] \cup \left[-\frac{55}{4}, \infty\right)$. The graph is shown below.

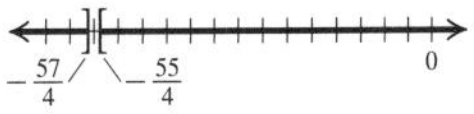

31. $|x| < 7$

To solve we look for all numbers x whose distance from 0 is less than 7. These are the numbers between -7 and 7. That is, $-7 < x < 7$. The solution set and its graph are as follows:

$(-7, 7)$

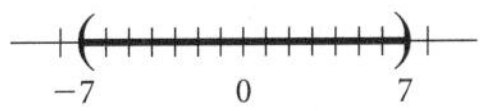

33. $|x| \ge 4.5$

To solve we look for all numbers x whose distance from 0 is greater than or equal to 4.5. That is, $x \le -4.5$ or $x \ge 4.5$. The solution set and its graph are as follows.

$\{x|x \le -4.5 \text{ or } x \ge 4.5\}$, or $(-\infty, -4.5] \cup [4.5, \infty)$

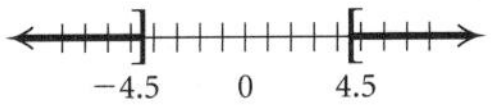

35. $|x + 8| < 9$

$-9 < x + 8 < 9$

$-17 < x < 1$ Subtracting 8

The solution set is $(-17, 1)$. The graph is shown below.

37. $|x + 8| \ge 9$

$x + 8 \le -9$ *or* $x + 8 \ge 9$

$x \le -17$ *or* $x \ge 1$ Subtracting 8

The solution set is $(-\infty, -17] \cup [1, \infty)$. The graph is shown below.

39. $\left|x - \frac{1}{4}\right| < \frac{1}{2}$

$-\frac{1}{2} < x - \frac{1}{4} < \frac{1}{2}$

$-\frac{1}{4} < x < \frac{3}{4}$ Adding $\frac{1}{4}$

The solution set is $\left(-\frac{1}{4}, \frac{3}{4}\right)$. The graph is shown below.

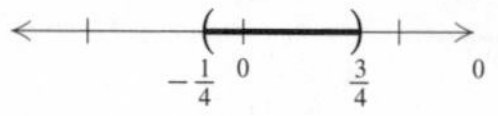

41. $|3x| < 1$

$-1 < 3x < 1$

$-\frac{1}{3} < x < \frac{1}{3}$ Dividing by 3

The solution set is $\left(-\frac{1}{3}, \frac{1}{3}\right)$. The graph is shown below.

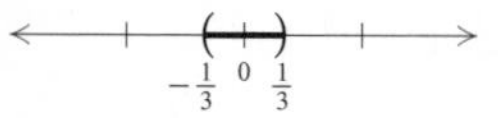

43. $|2x + 3| \le 9$

$-9 \le 2x + 3 \le 9$

$-12 \le 2x \le 6$ Subtracting 3

$-6 \le x \le 3$ Dividing by 2

The solution set is $[-6, 3]$. The graph is shown below.

45. $|x - 5| > 0.1$

$x - 5 < -0.1$ *or* $x - 5 > 0.1$

$x < 4.9$ *or* $x > 5.1$ Adding 5

The solution set is $(-\infty, 4.9) \cup (5.1, \infty)$. The graph is shown below.

47. $|6 - 4x| \le 8$

$-8 \le 6 - 4x \le 8$

$-14 \le -4x \le 2$ Subtracting 6

$\frac{14}{4} \ge x \ge -\frac{2}{4}$ Dividing by -4 and reversing the inequality symbols

$\frac{7}{2} \ge x \ge -\frac{1}{2}$ Simplifying

The solution set is $\left[-\frac{1}{2}, \frac{7}{2}\right]$. The graph is shown below.

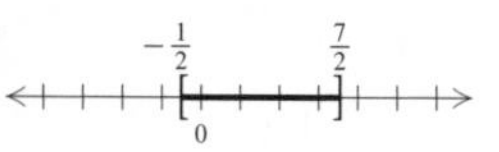

49. $\left|x + \frac{2}{3}\right| \le \frac{5}{3}$

$-\frac{5}{3} \le x + \frac{2}{3} \le \frac{5}{3}$

$-\frac{7}{3} \le x \le 1$ Subtracting $\frac{2}{3}$

The solution set is $\left[-\frac{7}{3}, 1\right]$. The graph is shown below.

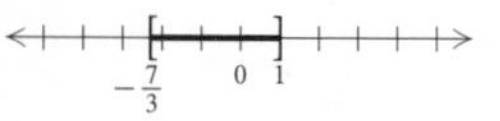

51. $\left|\frac{2x+1}{3}\right| > 5$

$\frac{2x+1}{3} < -5$ *or* $\frac{2x+1}{3} > 5$

$2x + 1 < -15$ *or* $2x + 1 > 15$ Multiplying by 3

$2x < -16$ *or* $2x > 14$ Subtracting 1

$x < -8$ *or* $x > 7$ Dividing by 2

The solution set is $\{x|x < -8 \text{ or } x > 7\}$, or $(-\infty, -8) \cup (7, \infty)$. The graph is shown below.

53. $|2x - 4| < -5$

Since $|2x - 4| \ge 0$ for all x, there is no x such that $|2x - 4|$ would be less than -5. There is no solution.

55. ***Familiarize and Translate***. Spending is given by the equation $y = 12.7x + 15.2$. We want to know when the spending will be more than \$66 billion, so we have

$12.7x + 15.2 > 66.$

Carry out. We solve the inequality.

$12.7x + 15.2 > 66$

$12.7x > 50.8$

$x > 4$

Check. When $x = 4$, the spending is $12.7(4) + 15.2 = 66$. As a partial check, we could try a value of x less than 4 and one greater than 4. When $x = 3.9$, we have $y = 12.7(3.9) + 15.2 = 64.73 < 66$; when $x = 4.1$, we have $y = 12.7(4.1) + 15.2 = 67.27 > 66$. Since $y = 66$ when $x = 4$ and $y > 66$ when $x = 4.1 > 4$, the answer is probably correct.

State. The spending will be more than \$66 billion more than 4 yr after 2002.

57. ***Familiarize***. Let $t =$ the number of hours worked. Then Acme Movers charge $100 + 30t$ and Hank's Movers charge $55t$.

Translate.

Hank's charge is less than Acme's charge.

$55t < 100 + 30t$

Carry out. We solve the inequality.

$55t < 100 + 30t$

$25t < 100$

$t < 4$

Check. When $t = 4$, Hank's Movers charge $55 \cdot 4$, or \$220 and Acme Movers charge $100 + 30 \cdot 4 = 100 + 120 = \$220$, so the charges are the same. As a partial check, we find the charges for a value of $t < 4$. When $t = 3.5$, Hank's Movers charge $55(3.5) = \$192.50$ and Acme Movers charge $100 + 30(3.5) = 100 + 105 = \$205$. Since Hank's charge is less than Acme's, the answer is probably correct.

State. For times less than 4 hr it costs less to hire Hank's Movers.

59. ***Familiarize.*** Let $x =$ the amount invested at 4%. Then $7500 - x =$ the amount invested at 5%. Using the simple-interest formula, $I = Prt$, we see that in one year the 4% investment earns $0.04x$ and the 5% investment earns $0.05(7500 - x)$.

Translate.

$$\underbrace{\text{Interest at 4\%}}_{0.04x}\ \underset{+}{\text{plus}}\ \underbrace{\text{interest at 5\%}}_{0.05(7500-x)}\ \underbrace{\text{is at least}}_{\geq}\ \underset{325}{\$325.}$$

Carry out. We solve the inequality.

$$0.04x + 0.05(7500 - x) \geq 325$$
$$0.04x + 375 - 0.05x \geq 325$$
$$-0.01x + 375 \geq 325$$
$$-0.01x \geq -50$$
$$x \leq 5000$$

Check. When \$5000 is invested at 4%, then \$7500−\$5000, or \$2500, is invested at 5%. In one year the 4% investment earns 0.04(\$5000), or \$200, in simple interest and the 5% investment earns 0.05(\$2500), or \$125, so the total interest is \$200 + \$125, or \$325. As a partial check, we determine the total interest when an amount greater than \$5000 is invested at 4%. Suppose \$5001 is invested at 4%. Then \$2499 is invested at 5%, and the total interest is 0.04(\$5001) + 0.05(\$2499), or \$324.99. Since this amount is less than \$325, the answer is probably correct.

State. The most that can be invested at 4% is \$5000.

61. ***Familiarize.*** Let $c =$ the number of checks written per month. Then the No Frills plan costs $0.35c$ per month and the Simple Checking plan costs $5 + 0.10c$ per month.

Translate.

$$\underbrace{\text{Simple Checking cost}}_{5+0.10c}\ \underbrace{\text{is less than}}_{<}\ \underbrace{\text{No Frills cost.}}_{0.35c}$$

Carry out. We solve the inequality.

$$5 + 0.10c < 0.35c$$
$$5 < 0.25c$$
$$20 < c$$

Check. When 20 checks are written the No Frills plan costs 0.35(20), or \$7 per month and the Simple Checking plan costs 5 + 0.10(20), or \$7, so the costs are the same. As a partial check, we compare the cost for some number of checks greater than 20. When 21 checks are written, the No Frills plan costs 0.35(21), or \$7.35 and the Simple Checking plan costs 5+0.10(21), or \$7.10. Since the Simple Checking plan costs less than the No Frills plan, the answer is probably correct.

State. The Simple Checking plan costs less when more than 20 checks are written per month.

63. ***Familiarize.*** Let $s =$ the monthly sales. Then the amount of sales in excess of \$8000 is $s - 8000$.

Translate.

$$\underbrace{\text{Income from plan B}}_{1200+0.15(s-8000)}\ \underbrace{\text{is greater than}}_{>}\ \underbrace{\text{income from plan A.}}_{900+0.1s}$$

Carry out. We solve the inequality.

$$1200 + 0.15(s - 8000) > 900 + 0.1s$$
$$1200 + 0.15s - 1200 > 900 + 0.1s$$
$$0.15s > 900 + 0.1s$$
$$0.05s > 900$$
$$s > 18,000$$

Check. For sales of \$18,000 the income from plan A is \$900+0.1(\$18,000), or \$2700, and the income from plan B is 1200+0.15(18,000−8000), or \$2700 so the incomes are the same. As a partial check we can compare the incomes for an amount of sales greater than \$18,000. For sales of \$18,001, for example, the income from plan A is \$900 + 0.1(\$18,001), or \$2700.10, and the income from plan B is \$1200 + 0.15(\$18,001 − \$8000), or \$2700.15. Since plan B is better than plan A in this case, the answer is probably correct.

State. Plan B is better than plan A for monthly sales greater than \$18,000.

65. Left to the student

67. Discussion and Writing

69. y-intercept

71. relation

73. horizontal line

75. decreasing

77. $2x \leq 5 - 7x < 7 + x$

$$2x \leq 5 - 7x \quad and \quad 5 - 7x < 7 + x$$
$$9x \leq 5 \quad and \quad -8x < 2$$
$$x \leq \frac{5}{9} \quad and \quad x > -\frac{1}{4}$$

The solution set is $\left(-\frac{1}{4}, \frac{5}{9}\right]$.

79. $|3x - 1| > 5x - 2$

$$3x - 1 < -(5x - 2) \quad or \quad 3x - 1 > 5x - 2$$
$$3x - 1 < -5x + 2 \quad or \quad 1 > 2x$$
$$8x < 3 \quad or \quad \frac{1}{2} > x$$
$$x < \frac{3}{8} \quad or \quad \frac{1}{2} > x$$

The solution set is $\left(-\infty, \frac{3}{8}\right) \cup \left(-\infty, \frac{1}{2}\right)$. This is equivalent to $\left(-\infty, \frac{1}{2}\right)$.

81. $|p-4|+|p+4|<8$

If $p<-4$, then $|p-4|=-(p-4)$ and $|p+4|=-(p+4)$.

Solve: $-(p-4)+[-(p+4)]<8$

$$-p+4-p-4<8$$
$$-2p<8$$
$$p>-4$$

Since this is false for all values of p in the interval $(-\infty,-4)$ there is no solution in this interval.

If $p\geq -4$, then $|p+4|=p+4$.

Solve: $|p-4|+p+4<8$

$$|p-4|<4-p$$

$p-4>-(4-p)$ *and* $p-4<4-p$

$p-4>p-4$ *and* $2p<8$

$-4>-4$ *and* $p<4$

Since $-4>-4$ is false for all values of p, there is no solution in the interval $[-4,\infty)$.

Thus, $|p-4|+|p+4|<8$ has no solution.

83. $|x-3|+|2x+5|>6$

Divide the set of real numbers into three intervals:

$\left(-\infty,-\frac{5}{2}\right)$, $\left[-\frac{5}{2},3\right)$, and $[3,\infty)$.

Find the solution set of $|x-3|+|2x+5|>6$ in each interval. Then find the union of the three solution sets.

If $x<-\frac{5}{2}$, then $|x-3|=-(x-3)$ and $|2x+5|=-(2x+5)$.

Solve: $x<-\frac{5}{2}$ *and* $-(x-3)+[-(2x+5)]>6$

$x<-\frac{5}{2}$ *and* $-x+3-2x-5>6$

$x<-\frac{5}{2}$ *and* $-3x>8$

$x<-\frac{5}{2}$ *and* $x<-\frac{8}{3}$

The solution set in this interval is $\left(-\infty,-\frac{8}{3}\right)$.

If $-\frac{5}{2}\leq x<3$, then $|x-3|=-(x-3)$ and $|2x+5|=2x+5$.

Solve: $-\frac{5}{2}\leq x<3$ *and* $-(x-3)+2x+5>6$

$-\frac{5}{2}\leq x<3$ *and* $-x+3+2x+5>6$

$-\frac{5}{2}\leq x<3$ *and* $x>-2$

The solution set in this interval is $(-2,3)$.

If $x\geq 3$, then $|x-3|=x-3$ and $|2x+5|=2x+5$.

Solve: $x\geq 3$ *and* $x-3+2x+5>6$

$x\geq 3$ *and* $3x>4$

$x\geq 3$ *and* $x>\frac{4}{3}$

The solution set in this interval is $[3,\infty)$.

The union of the above solution sets is $\left(-\infty,-\frac{8}{3}\right)\cup(-2,\infty)$. This is the solution set of $|x-3|+|2x+5|>6$.

Chapter 3

Polynomial and Rational Functions

Exercise Set 3.1

1. $g(x) = \frac{1}{2}x^3 - 10x + 8$

The degree of the polynomial is 3, so the polynomial is cubic. The leading term is $\frac{1}{2}x^3$ and the leading coefficient is $\frac{1}{2}$.

3. $h(x) = 0.9x - 0.13$

The degree of the polynomial is 1, so the polynomial is linear. The leading term is $0.9x$ and the leading coefficient is 0.9.

5. $g(x) = 305x^4 + 4021$

The degree of the polynomial is 4, so the polynomial is quartic. The leading term is $305x^4$ and the leading coefficient is 305.

7. $h(x) = -5x^2 + 7x^3 + x^4 = x^4 + 7x^3 - 5x^2$

The degree of the polynomial is 4, so the polynomial is quartic. The leading term is x^4 and the leading coefficient is 1 ($x^4 = 1 \cdot x^4$).

9. $g(x) = 4x^3 - \frac{1}{2}x^2 + 8$

The degree of the polynomial is 3, so the polynomial is cubic. The leading term is $4x^3$ and the leading coefficient is 4.

11. $f(x) = -3x^3 - x + 4$

The leading term is $-3x^3$. The degree, 3, is odd and the leading coefficient, -3, is negative. Thus the end behavior of the graph is like that of (d).

13. $f(x) = -x^6 + \frac{3}{4}x^4$

The leading term is $-x^6$. The degree, 6, is even and the leading coefficient, -1, is negative. Thus the end behavior of the graph is like that of (b).

15. $f(x) = -3.5x^4 + x^6 + 0.1x^7 = 0.1x^7 + x^6 - 3.5x^4$

The leading term is $0.1x^7$. The degree, 7, is odd and the leading coefficient, 0.1, is positive. Thus the end behavior of the graph is like that of (c).

17. $f(x) = 10 + \frac{1}{10}x^4 - \frac{2}{5}x^3 = \frac{1}{10}x^4 - \frac{2}{5}x^3 + 10$

The leading term is $\frac{1}{10}x^4$. The degree, 4, is even and the leading coefficient, $\frac{1}{10}$, is positive. Thus the end behavior of the graph is like that of (a).

19. $f(x) = \frac{1}{4}x^2 - 5$

The leading term is $\frac{1}{4}x^2$. The sign of the leading coefficient, $\frac{1}{4}$, is positive and the degree, 2, is even, so we would choose either graph (b) or graph (d). Note also that $f(0) = -5$, so the y-intercept is $(0, -5)$. Thus, graph (d) is the graph of this function.

21. $f(x) = x^5 - x^4 + x^2 + 4$

The leading term is x^5. The sign of the leading coefficient, 1, is positive and the degree, 5, is odd. Thus, graph (f) is the graph of this function.

23. $f(x) = x^4 - 2x^3 + 12x^2 + x - 20$

The leading term is x^4. The sign of the leading coefficient, 1, is positive and the degree, 4, is even, so we would choose either graph (b) or graph (d). Note also that $f(0) = -20$, so the y-intercept is $(0, -20)$. Thus, graph (b) is the graph of this function.

25. $f(x) = x^3 - 9x^2 + 14x + 24$

$f(4) = 4^3 - 9 \cdot 4^2 + 14 \cdot 4 + 24 = 0$

Since $f(4) = 0$, 4 is a zero of $f(x)$.

$f(5) = 5^3 - 9 \cdot 5^2 + 14 \cdot 5 + 24 = -6$

Since $f(5) \neq 0$, 5 is not a zero of $f(x)$.

$f(-2) = (-2)^3 - 9(-2)^2 + 14(-2) + 24 = -48$

Since $f(-2) \neq 0$, -2 is not a zero of $f(x)$.

27. $g(x) = x^4 - 6x^3 + 8x^2 + 6x - 9$

$g(2) = 2^4 - 6 \cdot 2^3 + 8 \cdot 2^2 + 6 \cdot 2 - 9 = 3$

Since $g(2) \neq 0$, 2 is not a zero of $g(x)$.

$g(3) = 3^4 - 6 \cdot 3^3 + 8 \cdot 3^2 + 6 \cdot 3 - 9 = 0$

Since $g(3) = 0$, 3 is a zero of $g(x)$.

$g(-1) = (-1)^4 - 6(-1)^3 + 8(-1)^2 + 6(-1) - 9 = 0$

Since $g(-1) = 0$, -1 is a zero of $g(x)$.

29. $f(x) = (x+3)^2(x-1) = (x+3)(x+3)(x-1)$

To solve $f(x) = 0$ we use the principle of zero products, solving $x + 3 = 0$ and $x - 1 = 0$. The zeros of $f(x)$ are -3 and 1.

The factor $x + 3$ occurs twice. Thus the zero -3 has a multiplicity of two.

The factor $x - 1$ occurs only one time. Thus the zero 1 has a multiplicity of one.

31. $f(x) = -2(x-4)(x-4)(x-4)(x+6) = 2(x-4)^3(x+6)$

To solve $f(x) = 0$ we use the principle of zero products, solving $x - 4 = 0$ and $x + 6 = 0$. The zeros of $f(x)$ are 4 and -6.

The factor $x - 4$ occurs three times. Thus the zero 4 has a multiplicity of 3.

The factor $x + 6$ occurs only one time. Thus the zero -6 has a multiplicity of 1.

33. $f(x) = (x^2 - 9)^3 = [(x+3)(x-3)]^3 = (x+3)^3(x-3)^3$

To solve $f(x) = 0$ we use the principle of zero products, solving $x + 3 = 0$ and $x - 3 = 0$. The zeros of $f(x)$ are -3 and 3.

The factors $x+3$ and $x-3$ each occur three times so each zero has a multiplicity of 3.

35. $f(x) = x^3(x-1)^2(x+4)$

To solve $f(x) = 0$ we use the principle of zero products, solving $x = 0$, $x - 1 = 0$, and $x + 4 = 0$. The zeros of $f(x)$ are 0, 1, and -4.

The factor x occurs three times. Thus the zero 0 has a multiplicity of three.

The factor $x - 1$ occurs twice. Thus the zero 1 has a multiplicity of two.

The factor $x + 4$ occurs only one time. Thus the zero -4 has a multiplicity of one.

37. $f(x) = -8(x-3)^2(x+4)^3x^4$

To solve $f(x) = 0$ we use the principle of zero products, solving $x - 3 = 0$, $x + 4 = 0$, and $x = 0$. The zeros of $f(x)$ are 3, -4, and 0.

The factor $x - 3$ occurs twice. Thus the zero 3 has a multiplicity of 2.

The factor $x + 4$ occurs three times. Thus the zero -4 has a multiplicity of 3.

The factor x occurs four times. Thus the zero 0 has a multiplicity of 4.

39. $f(x) = x^4 - 4x^2 + 3$

We factor as follows:

$$\begin{aligned} f(x) &= (x^2-3)(x^2-1) \\ &= (x-\sqrt{3})(x+\sqrt{3})(x-1)(x+1) \end{aligned}$$

The zeros of the function are $\sqrt{3}$, $-\sqrt{3}$, 1, and -1. Each has a multiplicity of 1.

41. $f(x) = x^3 + 3x^2 - x - 3$

We factor by grouping:

$$\begin{aligned} f(x) &= x^2(x+3) - (x+3) \\ &= (x^2-1)(x+3) \\ &= (x-1)(x+1)(x+3) \end{aligned}$$

The zeros of the function are 1, -1, and -3. Each has a multiplicity of 1.

43.
$$\begin{aligned} f(x) &= 2x^3 - x^2 - 8x + 4 \\ &= x^2(2x-1) - 4(2x-1) \\ &= (2x-1)(x^2-4) \\ &= (2x-1)(x+2)(x-2) \end{aligned}$$

The zeros of the function are $\frac{1}{2}$, -2, and 2. Each has a multiplicity of 1.

45. $f(x) = -x^3 - 2x^2$

1. The leading term is $-x^3$. The degree, 3, is odd and the leading coefficient, -1, is negative so as $|x| \to \infty$, $f(x) \to -\infty$ and as $|x| \to -\infty$, $f(x) \to \infty$.

2. We solve $f(x) = 0$.

$$\begin{aligned} -x^3 - 2x^2 &= 0 \\ -x^2(x+2) &= 0 \\ -x^2 = 0 \quad &or \quad x + 2 = 0 \\ x^2 = 0 \quad &or \quad x = -2 \\ x = 0 \quad &or \quad x = -2 \end{aligned}$$

The zeros of the function are 0 and -2, so the x-intercepts of the graph are $(0,0)$ and $(-2,0)$.

3. The zeros divide the x-axis into 3 intervals, $(-\infty,-2)$, $(-2,0)$, and $(0,\infty)$. We choose a value for x from each interval and find $f(x)$. This tells us the sign of $f(x)$ for all values of x in that interval.
In $(-\infty,-2)$, test -3:
$f(-3) = -(-3)^3 - 2(-3)^2 = 9 > 0$
In $(-2,0)$, test -1:
$f(-1) = -(-1)^3 - 2(-1)^2 = -1 < 0$
In $(0,\infty)$, test 1:
$f(1) = -1^3 - 2 \cdot 1^2 = -3 < 0$
Thus the graph lies above the x-axis on $(-\infty,-2)$ and below the x-axis on $(-2,0)$ and $(0,\infty)$. We also know the points $(-3,9)$, $(-1,-1)$, and $(1,-3)$ are on the graph.

4. From Step 2 we see that the y-intercept is $(0,0)$.

5. We find additional points on the graph and then draw the graph.

x	$f(x)$
-2.5	3.125
-1.5	-1.125
1.5	-7.875

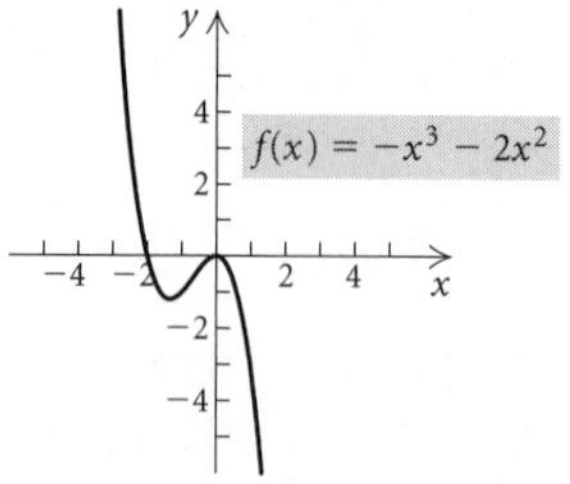

6. Checking the graph as described on page 254 in the text, we see that it appears to be correct.

47. $h(x) = x^5 - 4x^3$

1. The leading term is x^5. The degree, 5, is odd and the leading coefficient, 1, is positive so as $|x| \to \infty$, $h(x) \to \infty$ and as $|x| \to -\infty$, $h(x) \to -\infty$.

2. We solve $h(x) = 0$.

$$x^5 - 4x^3 = 0$$
$$x^3(x^2 - 4) = 0$$
$$x^3(x+2)(x-2) = 0$$
$$x^3 = 0 \quad or \quad x+2 = 0 \quad or \quad x-2 = 0$$
$$x = 0 \quad or \quad x = -2 \quad or \quad x = 2$$

The zeros of the function are 0, -2, and 2 so the x-intercepts of the graph are $(0,0)$, $(-2,0)$, and $(2,0)$.

3. The zeros divide the x-axis into 4 intervals, $(-\infty,-2)$, $(-2,0)$, $(0,2)$, and $(2,\infty)$. We choose a value for x from each interval and find $h(x)$. This tells us the sign of $h(x)$ for all values of x in that interval.

In $(-\infty,-2)$, test -3:

$h(-3) = (-3)^5 - 4(-3)^3 = -135 < 0$

In $(-2,0)$, test -1:

$h(-1) = (-1)^5 - 4(-1)^3 = 3 > 0$

In $(0,2)$, test 1:

$h(1) = 1^5 - 4\cdot 1^3 = -3 < 0$

In $(2,\infty)$, test 3:

$h(3) = 3^5 - 4\cdot 3^3 = 135 > 0$

Thus the graph lies below the x-axis on $(-\infty,-2)$ and on $(0,2)$. It lies above the x-axis on $(-2,0)$ and on $(2,\infty)$. We also know the points $(-3,-135)$, $(-1,3)$, $(1,-3)$, and $(3,135)$ are on the graph.

4. From Step 2 we see that the y-intercept is $(0,0)$.

5. We find additional points on the graph and then draw the graph.

x	$h(x)$
-2.5	-35.2
-1.5	5.9
1.5	-5.9
2.5	35.2

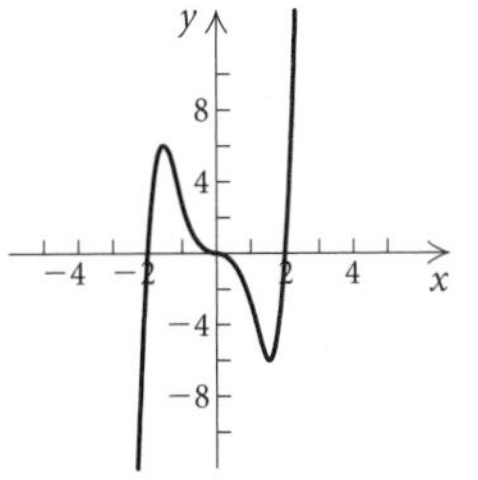

$h(x) = x^5 - 4x^3$

6. Checking the graph as described on page 254 in the text, we see that it appears to be correct.

49. $h(x) = x(x-4)(x+1)(x-2)$

1. The leading term is $x\cdot x\cdot x\cdot x$, or x^4. The degree, 4, is even and the leading coefficient, 1, is positive so as $|x|\to\infty$, $h(x)\to\infty$ and as $|x|\to-\infty$, $h(x)\to\infty$.

2. We see that the zeros of the function are 0, 4, -1, and 2 so the x-intercepts of the graph are $(0,0)$, $(4,0)$, $(-1,0)$, and $(2,0)$.

3. The zeros divide the x-axis into 5 intervals, $(-\infty,-1)$, $(-1,0)$, $(0,2)$, $(2,4)$, and $(4,\infty)$. We choose a value for x from each interval and find $h(x)$. This tells us the sign of $h(x)$ for all values of x in that interval.

In $(-\infty,-1)$, test -2:

$h(-2) = -2(-2-4)(-2+1)(-2-2) = 48 > 0$

In $(-1,0)$, test -0.5:

$h(-0.5) = (-0.5)(-0.5-4)(-0.5+1)(-0.5-2) = -2.8125 < 0$

In $(0,2)$, test 1:

$h(1) = 1(1-4)(1+1)(1-2) = 6 > 0$

In $(2,4)$, test 3:

$h(3) = 3(3-4)(3+1)(3-2) = -12 < 0$

In $(4,\infty)$, test 5:

$h(5) = 5(5-4)(5+1)(5-2) = 90 > 0$

Thus the graph lies above the x-axis on $(-\infty,-1)$, $(0,2)$, and $(4,\infty)$. It lies below the x-axis on $(-1,0)$ and on $(2,4)$. We also know the points $(-2,48)$, $(-0.5,-2.8125)$, $(1,6)$, $(3,-12)$, and $(5,90)$ are on the graph.

4. From Step 2 we see that the y-intercept is $(0,0)$.

5. We find additional points on the graph and then draw the graph.

x	$h(x)$
-1.5	14.4
1.5	4.7
2.5	-6.6
4.5	30.9

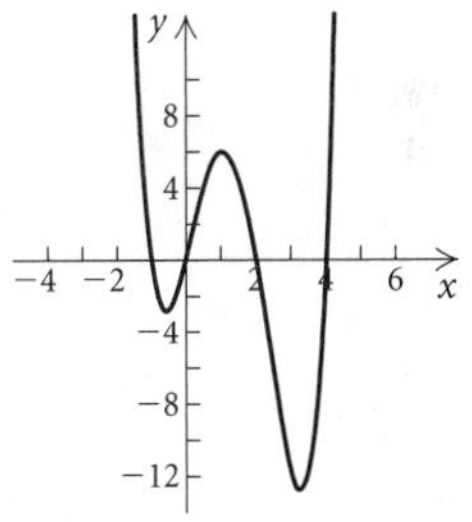

$h(x) = x(x-4)(x+1)(x-2)$

6. Checking the graph as described on page 254 in the text, we see that it appears to be correct.

51. $f(x) = \frac{1}{2}x^3 + \frac{5}{2}x^2$

1. The leading term is $\frac{1}{2}x^3$. The degree, 3, is odd and the leading coefficient, $\frac{1}{2}$, is positive so as $|x|\to\infty$, $f(x)\to\infty$ and as $|x|\to-\infty$, $f(x)\to-\infty$.

2. We solve $f(x) = 0$.

$$\frac{1}{2}x^3 + \frac{5}{2}x^2 = 0$$
$$\frac{1}{2}x^2(x+5) = 0$$
$$\frac{1}{2}x^2 = 0 \quad or \quad x+5 = 0$$
$$x^2 = 0 \quad or \quad x = -5$$
$$x = 0 \quad or \quad x = -5$$

The zeros of the function are 0 and -5, so the x-intercepts of the graph are $(0,0)$ and $(-5,0)$.

3. The zeros divide the x-axis into 3 intervals, $(-\infty,-5)$, $(-5,0)$, and $(0,\infty)$. We choose a value for x from each interval and find $f(x)$. This tells us the sign of $f(x)$ for all values of x in that interval.

In $(-\infty,-5)$, test -6:

$f(-6)=\frac{1}{2}(-6)^3+\frac{5}{2}(-6)^2=-18<0$

In $(-5,0)$, test -1:

$f(-1)=\frac{1}{2}(-1)^3+\frac{5}{2}(-1)^2=2>0$

In $(0,\infty)$, test 1:

$f(1)=\frac{1}{2}\cdot 1^3+\frac{5}{2}\cdot 1^2=3>0$

Thus the graph lies below the x-axis on $(-\infty,-5)$ and above the x-axis on $(-5,0)$ and $(0,\infty)$. We also know the points $(-6,-18)$, $(-1,2)$, and $(1,3)$ are on the graph.

4. From Step 2 we see that the y-intercept is $(0,0)$.
5. We find additional points on the graph and then draw the graph.

x	$f(x)$
-5.5	-7.6
-3	9
-2	6
2	14

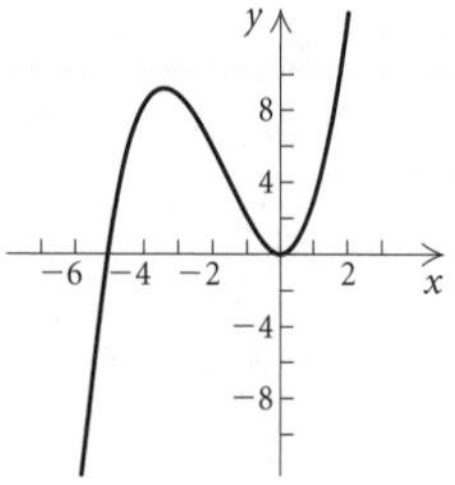

$f(x)=\frac{1}{2}x^3+\frac{5}{2}x^2$

6. Checking the graph as described on page 254 in the text, we see that it appears to be correct.

53. $g(x)=(x-2)^3(x+3)$

1. The leading term is $x\cdot x\cdot x\cdot x$, or x^4. The degree, 4, is even and the leading coefficient, 1, is positive so as $|x|\to\infty$, $g(x)\to\infty$ and as $|x|\to-\infty$, $g(x)\to\infty$.
2. We see that the zeros of the function are 2 and -3 so the x-intercepts of the graph are $(2,0)$ and $(-3,0)$.
3. The zeros divide the x-axis into 3 intervals, $(-\infty,-3)$, $(-3,2)$, and $(2,\infty)$. We choose a value for x from each interval and find $g(x)$. This tells us the sign of $g(x)$ for all values of x in that interval.

In $(-\infty,-3)$, test -4:

$g(-4)=(-4-2)^3(-4+3)=216>0$

In $(-3,2)$, test 0:

$g(0)=(0-2)^3(0+3)=-24<0$

In $(2,\infty)$, test 3:

$g(3)=(3-2)^3(3+3)=6>0$

Thus the graph lies above the x-axis on $(-\infty,-3)$ and on $(2,\infty)$. It lies below the x-axis on $(-3,2)$. We also know the points $(-4,216)$, $(0,-24)$, and $(3,6)$ are on the graph.

4. From Step 3 we know that $g(0)=-24$ so the y-intercept is $(0,-24)$.
5. We find additional points on the graph and then draw the graph.

x	$g(x)$
-3.5	83.2
-2	-64
-1	-54
3.5	23.9

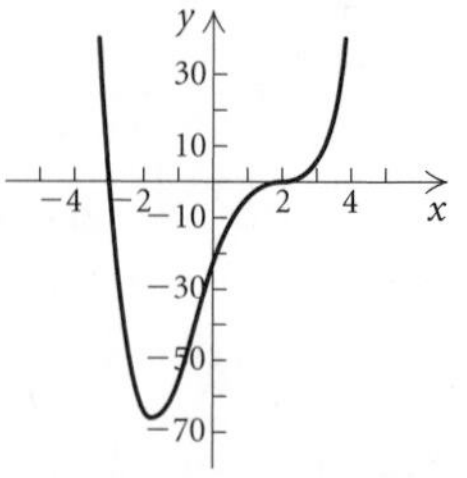

$g(x)=(x-2)^3(x+3)$

6. Checking the graph as described on page 254 in the text, we see that it appears to be correct.

55. $f(x)=x^3-x$

1. The leading term is x^3. The degree, 3, is odd and the leading coefficient, 1, is positive so as $|x|\to\infty$, $f(x)\to\infty$ and as $|x|\to-\infty$, $f(x)\to-\infty$.
2. We solve $f(x)=0$.

$$x^3-x=0$$
$$x(x^2-1)=0$$
$$x(x+1)(x-1)=0$$
$$x=0 \quad or \quad x+1=0 \quad or \quad x-1=0$$
$$x=0 \quad or \quad x=-1 \quad or \quad x=1$$

The zeros of the function are 0, -1, and 1, so the x-intercepts of the graph are $(0,0)$, $(-1,0)$, and $(1,0)$.

3. The zeros divide the x-axis into 4 intervals, $(-\infty,-1)$, $(-1,0)$, $(0,1)$, and $(1,\infty)$. We choose a value for x from each interval and find $f(x)$. This tells us the sign of $f(x)$ for all values of x in that interval.

In $(-\infty,-1)$, test -2:

$f(-2)=(-2)^3-(-2)=-6<0$

In $(-1,0)$, test -0.5:

$f(-0.5)=(-0.5)^3-(-0.5)=0.375>0$

In $(0,1)$, test 0.5:

$f(0.5)=(0.5)^3-0.5=-0.375<0$

In $(1,\infty)$, test 2:

$f(2)=2^3-2=6>0$

Thus the graph lies below the x-axis on $(-\infty,-1)$ and on $(0,1)$. It lies above the x-axis on $(-1,0)$ and on $(1,\infty)$. We also know the points $(-2,-6)$, $(-0.5,0.375)$, $(0.5,-0.375)$, and $(2,6)$ are on the graph.

4. From Step 2 we see that the y-intercept is $(0,0)$.
5. We find additional points on the graph and then draw the graph.

x	$f(x)$
-3	-24
-0.75	0.3
0.25	-0.2
3	24

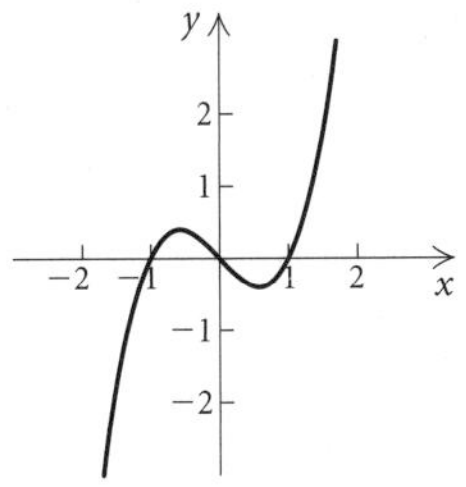

$f(x) = x^3 - x$

6. Checking the graph as described on page 254 in the text, we see that it appears to be correct.

57. $f(x) = (x-2)^2(x+1)^4$

1. The leading term is $x \cdot x \cdot x \cdot x \cdot x \cdot x$, or x^6. The degree, 6, is even and the leading coefficient, 1, is positive so as $|x| \to \infty$, $f(x) \to \infty$ and as $|x| \to -\infty$, $f(x) \to \infty$.
2. We see that the zeros of the function are 2 and -1 so the x-intercepts of the graph are $(2,0)$ and $(-1,0)$.
3. The zeros divide the x-axis into 3 intervals, $(-\infty,-1)$, $(-1,2)$, and $(2,\infty)$. We choose a value for x from each interval and find $f(x)$. This tells us the sign of $f(x)$ for all values of x in that interval.
   In $(-\infty,-1)$, test -2:
   $f(-2) = (-2-2)^2(-2+1)^4 = 16 > 0$
   In $(-1,2)$, test 0:
   $f(0) = (0-2)^2(0+1)^4 = 4 > 0$
   In $(2,\infty)$, test 3:
   $f(3) = (3-2)^2(3+1)^4 = 256 > 0$
   Thus the graph lies above the x-axis on all 3 intervals. We also know the points $(-2,16)$, $(0,4)$, and $(3,256)$ are on the graph.
4. From Step 3 we know that $f(0) = 4$ so the y-intercept is $(0,4)$.
5. We find additional points on the graph and then draw the graph.

x	$f(x)$
-1.5	0.8
-0.5	0.4
1	16
1.5	9.8

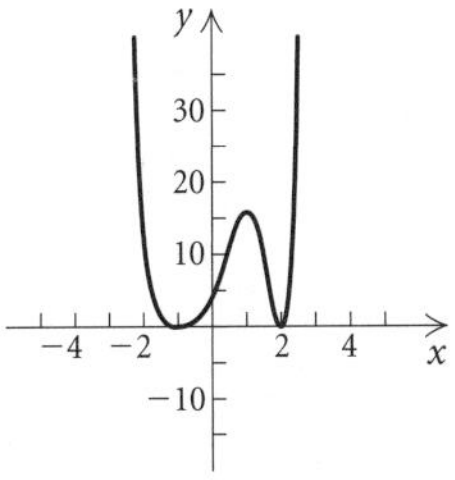

$f(x) = (x-2)^2(x+1)^4$

6. Checking the graph as described on page 254 in the text, we see that it appears to be correct.

59. $g(x) = -(x-1)^4$

1. The leading term is $-1 \cdot x \cdot x \cdot x \cdot x$, or $-x^4$. The degree, 4, is even and the leading coefficient, -1, is negative so as $|x| \to \infty$, $g(x) \to -\infty$ and as $|x| \to -\infty$, $g(x) \to -\infty$.
2. We see that the zero of the function is 1, so the x-intercept is $(1,0)$.
3. The zero divides the x-axis into 2 intervals, $(-\infty,1)$ and $(1,\infty)$. We choose a value for x from each interval and find $g(x)$. This tells us the sign of $g(x)$ for all values of x in that interval.
   In $(-\infty,1)$, test 0:
   $g(0) = -(0-1)^4 = -1 < 0$
   In $(1,\infty)$, test 2:
   $g(2) = -(2-1)^4 = -1 < 0$
   Thus the graph lies below the x-axis on both intervals. We also know the points $(0,-1)$ and $(2,-1)$ are on the graph.
4. From Step 3 we know that $g(0) = -1$ so the y-intercept is $(0,-1)$.
5. We find additional points on the graph and then draw the graph.

x	$g(x)$
-1	-16
-0.5	-5.1
1.5	0.1
3	-16

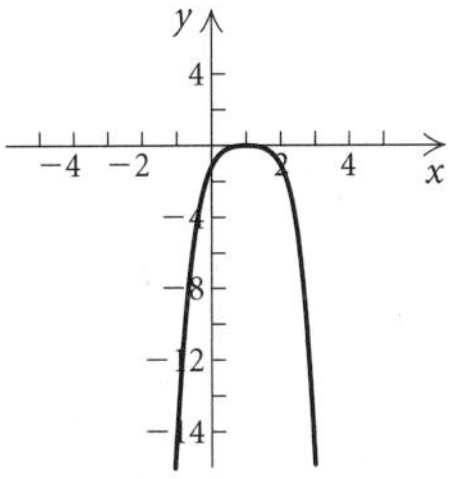

$g(x) = -(x-1)^4$

6. Checking the graph as described on page 254 in the text, we see that it appears to be correct.

61. $h(x) = x^3 + 3x^2 - x - 3$

1. The leading term is x^3. The degree, 3, is odd and the leading coefficient, 1, is positive so as $|x| \to \infty$, $h(x) \to \infty$ and as $|x| \to -\infty$, $h(x) \to -\infty$.
2. We solve $h(x) = 0$.

$$x^3 + 3x^2 - x - 3 = 0$$
$$x^2(x+3) - (x+3) = 0$$
$$(x+3)(x^2-1) = 0$$
$$(x+3)(x+1)(x-1) = 0$$
$$x+3 = 0 \quad or \quad x+1 = 0 \quad or \quad x-1 = 0$$
$$x = -3 \quad or \quad x = -1 \quad or \quad x = 1$$

   The zeros of the function are -3, -1, and 1 so the x-intercepts of the graph are $(-3,0)$, $(-1,0)$, and $(1,0)$.
3. The zeros divide the x-axis into 4 intervals, $(-\infty,-3)$, $(-3,-1)$, $(-1,1)$, and $(1,\infty)$. We choose a value for x from each interval and find $h(x)$. This tells us the sign of $h(x)$ for all values of x in that interval.
   In $(-\infty,-3)$, test -4:
   $h(-4) = (-4)^3 + 3(-4)^2 - (-4) - 3 = -15 < 0$
   In $(-3,-1)$, test -2:
   $h(-2) = (-2)^3 + 3(-2)^2 - (-2) - 3 = 3 > 0$
   In $(-1,1)$, test 0:
   $h(0) = 0^3 + 3 \cdot 0^2 - 0 - 3 = -3 < 0$

In $(1, \infty)$, test 2:

$h(2) = 2^3 + 3 \cdot 2^2 - 2 - 3 = 15 > 0$

Thus the graph lies below the x-axis on $(-\infty, -3)$ and on $(-1, 1)$ and above the x-axis on $(-3, -1)$ and on $(1, \infty)$. We also know the points $(-4, -15)$, $(-2, 3)$, $(0, -3)$, and $(2, 15)$ are on the graph.

4. From Step 3 we know that $h(0) = -3$ so the y-intercept is $(0, -3)$.
5. We find additional points on the graph and then draw the graph.

x	$h(x)$
-4.5	-28.9
-2.5	2.6
0.5	-2.6
2.5	28.9

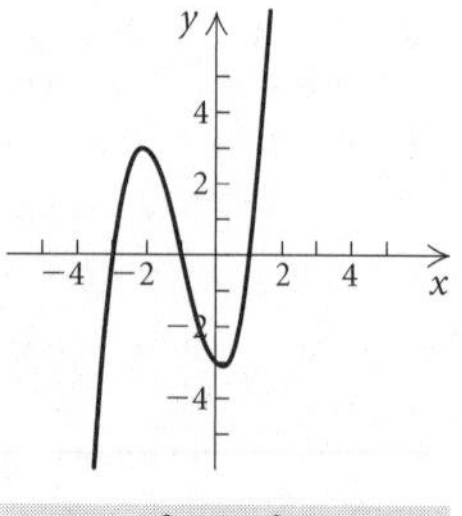

$h(x) = x^3 + 3x^2 - x - 3$

6. Checking the graph as described on page 254 in the text, we see that it appears to be correct.

63. $f(x) = 6x^3 - 8x^2 - 54x + 72$

1. The leading term is $6x^3$. The degree, 3, is odd and the leading coefficient, 6, is positive so as $|x| \to \infty$, $f(x) \to \infty$ and as $|x| \to -\infty$, $f(x) \to -\infty$.
2. We solve $f(x) = 0$.

$$\begin{aligned} 6x^3 - 8x^2 - 54x + 72 &= 0 \\ 2(3x^3 - 4x^2 - 27x + 36) &= 0 \\ 2[x^2(3x - 4) - 9(3x - 4)] &= 0 \\ 2(3x - 4)(x^2 - 9) &= 0 \\ 2(3x - 4)(x + 3)(x - 3) &= 0 \end{aligned}$$

$$3x - 4 = 0 \quad or \quad x + 3 = 0 \quad or \quad x - 3 = 0$$

$$x = \frac{4}{3} \quad or \quad x = -3 \quad or \quad x = 3$$

The zeros of the function are $\frac{4}{3}$, -3, and 3, so the x-intercepts of the graph are $\left(\frac{4}{3}, 0\right)$, $(-3, 0)$, and $(3, 0)$.

3. The zeros divide the x-axis into 4 intervals, $(-\infty, -3)$, $\left(-3, \frac{4}{3}\right)$, $\left(\frac{4}{3}, 3\right)$, and $(3, \infty)$. We choose a value for x from each interval and find $f(x)$. This tells us the sign of $f(x)$ for all values of x in that interval.

In $(-\infty, -3)$, test -4:

$f(-4) = 6(-4)^3 - 8(-4)^2 - 54(-4) + 72 = -224 < 0$

In $\left(-3, \frac{4}{3}\right)$, test 0:

$f(0) = 6 \cdot 0^3 - 8 \cdot 0^2 - 54 \cdot 0 + 72 = 72 > 0$

In $\left(\frac{4}{3}, 3\right)$, test 2:

$f(2) = 6 \cdot 2^3 - 8 \cdot 2^2 - 54 \cdot 2 + 72 = -20 < 0$

In $(3, \infty)$, test 4:

$f(4) = 6 \cdot 4^3 - 8 \cdot 4^2 - 54 \cdot 4 + 72 = 112 > 0$

Thus the graph lies below the x-axis on $(-\infty, -3)$ and on $\left(\frac{4}{3}, 3\right)$ and above the x-axis on $\left(-3, \frac{4}{3}\right)$ and on $(3, \infty)$. We also know the points $(-4, -224)$, $(0, 72)$, $(2, -20)$, and $(4, 112)$ are on the graph.

4. From Step 3 we know that $f(0) = 72$ so the y-intercept is $(0, 72)$.
5. We find additional points on the graph and then draw the graph.

x	$f(x)$
-1	112
1	16
3.5	42.25

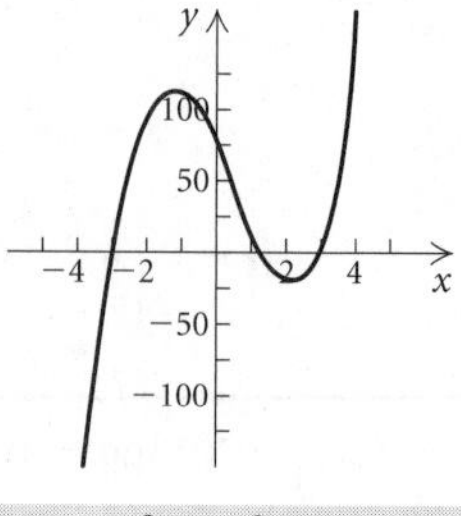

$f(x) = 6x^3 - 8x^2 - 54x + 72$

6. Checking the graph as described on page 254 in the text, we see that it appears to be correct.

65. $f(-5) = (-5)^3 + 3(-5)^2 - 9(-5) - 13 = -18$

$f(-4) = (-4)^3 + 3(-4)^2 - 9(-4) - 13 = 7$

By the intermediate value theorem, since $f(-5)$ and $f(-4)$ have opposite signs then $f(x)$ has a zero between -5 and -4.

67. $f(-3) = 3(-3)^2 - 2(-3) - 11 = 22$

$f(-2) = 3(-2)^2 - 2(-2) - 11 = 5$

Since both $f(-3)$ and $f(-2)$ are positive, we cannot use the intermediate value theorem to determine if there is a zero between -3 and -2.

69. $f(2) = 2^4 - 2 \cdot 2^2 - 6 = 2$

$f(3) = 3^4 - 2 \cdot 3^2 - 6 = 57$

Since both $f(2)$ and $f(3)$ are positive, we cannot use the intermediate value theorem to determine if there is a zero between 2 and 3.

71. $f(4) = 4^3 - 5 \cdot 4^2 + 4 = -12$

$f(5) = 5^3 - 5 \cdot 5^2 + 4 = 4$

By the intermediate value theorem, since $f(4)$ and $f(5)$ have opposite signs then $f(x)$ has a zero between 4 and 5.

73. For 1995, $x = 1995 - 1993 = 2$.

$f(2) = 0.854(2)^4 - 16.115(2)^3 + 86.769(2)^2 - 139.235(2) + 735.664 \approx 689$

In 1995 about 689,000 acres of tobacco were harvested.

For 2000, $x = 2000 - 1993 = 7$.

$f(7) = 0.854(7)^4 - 16.115(7)^3 + 86.769(7)^2 - 139.235(7) + 735.664 \approx 536$

In 2000 about 536,000 acres of tobacco were harvested.

75.
$$V = 48T^2$$
$$36 = 48T^2 \quad \text{Substituting}$$
$$0.75 = T^2$$
$$0.866 \approx T \quad \text{We only want the positive solution.}$$

Anfernee Hardaway's hang time is 0.866 sec.

77. First find the number of games played.

$N(x) = x^2 - x$

$N(9) = 9^2 - 9 = 72$

Now multiply the number of games by the cost per game to find the total cost.

$72 \cdot 45 = 3240$

It will cost \$3240 to play the entire schedule.

79. For 1997, $x = 1997 - 1996 = 1$.

$f(1) = -3.394(1)^4 + 35.838(1)^3 - 98.955(1)^2 + 41.930(1) + 174.974 \approx 150$ bald eagles

For 1999, $x = 1999 - 1996 = 3$.

$f(3) = -3.394(3)^4 + 35.838(3)^3 - 98.955(3)^2 + 41.930(3) + 174.974 \approx 103$ bald eagles

For 2001, $x = 2001 - 1996 = 5$.

$f(5) = -3.394(5)^4 + 35.838(5)^3 - 98.955(5)^2 + 41.930(5) + 174.974 \approx 269$ bald eagles

For 2002, $x = 2002 - 1996 = 6$.

$f(6) = -3.394(6)^4 + 35.838(6)^3 - 98.955(6)^2 + 41.930(6) + 174.974 \approx 207$ bald eagles

81. $A = P(1 + i)^t$

a) $4368.10 = 4000(1 + i)^2$ Substituting

$\frac{4368.10}{4000} = (1 + i)^2$

$\pm 1.045 = 1 + i$ Taking the square root on both sides

$-1 \pm 1.045 = i$

$-1 - 1.045 = i$ *or* $-1 + 1.045 = i$

$-2.045 = i$ *or* $0.045 = i$

Only the positive result has meaning in this application. The interest rate is 0.045, or 4.5%.

b) $13,310 = 10,000(1 + i)^3$ Substituting

$\frac{13,310}{10,000} = (1 + i)^3$

$1.10 \approx 1 + i$ Taking the cube root on both sides

$0.10 \approx i$

The interest rate is 0.1, or 10%.

83. $g(x) = x^3 - 1.2x + 1$

Graph the function and use the Zero, Maximum, and Minimum features.

Relative maximum: 1.506 when $x \approx -0.632$

Relative minimum: 0.494 when $x \approx 0.632$

Range: $(-\infty, \infty)$

85. $f(x) = x^6 - 3.8$

Graph the function and use the Zero and Minimum features.

There is no relative maximum.

Relative minimum: -3.8 when $x = 0$

Range: $[-3.8, \infty)$

87. $f(x) = x^2 + 10x - x^5$

Graph the function and use the Zero, Maximum, and Minimum features.

Relative maximum: 11.012 when $x \approx 1.258$

Relative minimum: -8.183 when $x \approx -1.116$

Range: $(-\infty, \infty)$

89. a) For each function, x represents the number of years after 1900.

Linear: $y = 3.730909091x + 83.72727273$

Quadratic: $y = 0.025011655x^2 + 1.22974359x + 121.2447552$

Cubic: $y = -0.0011822067x^3 + 0.2023426573x^2 - 5.532478632x + 163.8041958$

Quartic: $y = -0.00002634033x^4 + 0.0040858586x^3 - 0.1269114219x^2 + 1.052602953x + 144.8391608$

b) In 2005, $x = 2005 - 1900 = 105$; in 2010, $x = 2010 - 1900 = 110$.

For the linear function: $f(105) \approx 475$ and $f(110) \approx 494$.

For the quadratic function: $f(105) \approx 526$ and $f(110) \approx 559$.

For the cubic function: $f(105) \approx 445$ and $f(110) \approx 430$.

For the power function: $f(105) \approx 384$ and $f(110) \approx 307$.

It is reasonable to assume that the average acreage will continue to decrease as it did from 1990 to 2000. For this reason we rule out the estimates made using the linear and quadratic functions. The rate of decrease appears to be more like that estimated by the cubic function than the quartic function. Thus we say that the esimates of 445 acres and 430 acres given by cubic function are the most realistic. Answers may vary.

91. a) For each function, x represents the number of years after 1992.

Linear: $y = 378.7575758x + 3701.090909$

Quadratic: $y = 43.10227273x^2 - 9.162878788x + 4218.318182$

b) In 2005, $x = 2005 - 1992 = 13$.

For the linear function: $f(13) \approx \$8625$ billion.

For the quadratic function: $f(13) \approx \$11,383$ billion.

The estimate given by the quadratic function seems more consistent with the rate of increase in the table. Answers may vary.

93. Discussion and Writing

95.
$$\begin{aligned} d &= \sqrt{(x_2-x_1)^2+(y_2-y_1)^2} \\ &= \sqrt{[-1-(-5)]^2+(0-3)^2} \\ &= \sqrt{4^2+(-3)^2} = \sqrt{16+9} \\ &= \sqrt{25} = 5 \end{aligned}$$

97.
$$(x-3)^2+(y+5)^2 = 49$$
$$(x-3)^2+[y-(-5)]^2 = 7^2$$

Center: $(3, -5)$; radius: 7

99. $2y-3 \geq 1-y+5$

$2y-3 \geq 6-y$ Collecting like terms

$3y-3 \geq 6$ Adding y

$3y \geq 9$ Adding 3

$y \geq 3$ Dividing by 3

The solution set is $\{y|y \geq 3\}$, or $[3, \infty)$.

101. $|x+6| \geq 7$

$x+6 \leq -7$ *or* $x+6 \geq 7$

$x \leq -13$ *or* $x \geq 1$

The solution set is $\{x|x \leq -13 \text{ or } x \geq 1\}$, or $(-\infty, -13] \cup [1, \infty)$.

103. ***Familiarize***. We will use the compound interest formula. The \$2000 deposit is invested for two years and grows to an amount A_1 given by $A_1 = 2000(1+i)^2$. The \$1200 deposit is invested for one year and grows to an amount A_2 given by $A_2 = 1200(1+i)$.

Translate. There is a total of \$3573.80 in both accounts at the end of the second year, so we have

$A_1 + A_2 = 3573.80$, or

$2000(1+i)^2 + 1200(1+i) = 3573.80.$

Carry out. We solve the equation.

$2000(1+i)^2 + 1200(1+i) - 3573.8 = 0$

Substitute u for $1+i$.

$2000u^2 + 1200u - 3573.8 = 0$

Using the quadratic formula we find that $u = 1.07$ or $u = -3.34$. Only the positive value has meaning in this application. Then since $u = 1.07$, we have $1+i = 1.07$, or $i = 0.07$.

Check. At an interest rate of 0.07, or 7%, in two years \$2000 would grow to $2000(1+0.07)^2$, or \$2289.80. In one year \$1200 would grow to $1200(1+0.07)$, or \$1284. Now \$2289.80 + \$1284 = \$3573.80, so the result checks.

State. The interest rate is 7%.

Exercise Set 3.2

1. a)
$$\begin{array}{r|l} & x^3 - 7x^2 + 8x + 16 \\ \hline x+1 & x^4 - 6x^3 + x^2 + 24x - 20 \\ & x^4 + x^3 \\ \hline & \quad -7x^3 + x^2 \\ & \quad -7x^3 - 7x^2 \\ \hline & \qquad 8x^2 + 24x \\ & \qquad 8x^2 + 8x \\ \hline & \qquad\quad 16x - 20 \\ & \qquad\quad 16x + 16 \\ \hline & \qquad\qquad -4 \end{array}$$

Since the remainder is not 0, $x+1$ is not a factor of $f(x)$.

b)
$$\begin{array}{r|l} & x^3 - 4x^2 - 7x + 10 \\ \hline x-2 & x^4 - 6x^3 + x^2 + 24x - 20 \\ & x^4 - 2x^3 \\ \hline & \quad -4x^3 + x^2 \\ & \quad -4x^3 + 8x^2 \\ \hline & \qquad -7x^2 + 24x \\ & \qquad -7x^2 + 14x \\ \hline & \qquad\quad 10x - 20 \\ & \qquad\quad 10x - 20 \\ \hline & \qquad\qquad 0 \end{array}$$

Since the remainder is 0, $x-2$ is a factor of $f(x)$.

c)
$$\begin{array}{r|l} & x^3 - 11x^2 + 56x - 256 \\ \hline x+5 & x^4 - 6x^3 + x^2 + 24x - 20 \\ & x^4 + 5x^3 \\ \hline & \quad -11x^3 + x^2 \\ & \quad -11x^3 - 55x^2 \\ \hline & \qquad 56x^2 + 24x \\ & \qquad 56x^2 + 280x \\ \hline & \qquad\quad -256x - 20 \\ & \qquad\quad -256x - 1280 \\ \hline & \qquad\qquad 1260 \end{array}$$

Since the remainder is not 0, $x+5$ is not a factor of $f(x)$.

3. a)
$$\begin{array}{r|l} & x^2 + 2x - 3 \\ \hline x-4 & x^3 - 2x^2 - 11x + 12 \\ & x^3 - 4x^2 \\ \hline & \quad 2x^2 - 11x \\ & \quad 2x^2 - 8x \\ \hline & \qquad -3x + 12 \\ & \qquad -3x + 12 \\ \hline & \qquad\quad 0 \end{array}$$

Since the remainder is 0, $x-4$ is a factor of $g(x)$.

b)
$$\begin{array}{r|l} & x^2 + x - 8 \\ \hline x-3 & x^3 - 2x^2 - 11x + 12 \\ & x^3 - 3x^2 \\ \hline & \quad x^2 - 11x \\ & \quad x^2 - 3x \\ \hline & \qquad -8x + 12 \\ & \qquad -8x + 24 \\ \hline & \qquad\quad -12 \end{array}$$

Since the remainder is not 0, $x-3$ is not a factor of $g(x)$.

c)

$$\begin{array}{r} x^2 - x - 12 \\ x-1 \overline{\smash{\big)}\, x^3 - 2x^2 - 11x + 12} \\ \underline{x^3 - x^2 } \\ - x^2 - 11x \\ \underline{- x^2 + x } \\ - 12x + 12 \\ \underline{- 12x + 12} \\ 0 \end{array}$$

Since the remainder is 0, $x - 1$ is a factor of $g(x)$.

5.

$$\begin{array}{r} x^2 - 2x + 4 \\ x+2 \overline{\smash{\big)}\, x^3 + 0x^2 + 0x - 8} \\ \underline{x^3 + 2x^2 } \\ - 2x^2 + 0x \\ \underline{- 2x^2 - 4x } \\ 4x - 8 \\ \underline{4x + 8} \\ -16 \end{array}$$

$x^3 - 8 = (x+2)(x^2 - 2x + 4) - 16$

7.

$$\begin{array}{r} x^2 - 3x + 2 \\ x+9 \overline{\smash{\big)}\, x^3 + 6x^2 - 25x + 18} \\ \underline{x^3 + 9x^2 } \\ - 3x^2 - 25x \\ \underline{- 3x^2 - 27x } \\ 2x + 18 \\ \underline{2x + 18} \\ 0 \end{array}$$

$x^3 + 6x^2 - 25x + 18 = (x+9)(x^2 - 3x + 2) + 0$

9.

$$\begin{array}{r} x^3 - 2x^2 + 2x - 4 \\ x+2 \overline{\smash{\big)}\, x^4 + 0x^3 - 2x^2 + 0x + 3} \\ \underline{x^4 + 2x^3 } \\ - 2x^3 - 2x^2 \\ \underline{- 2x^3 - 4x^2 } \\ 2x^2 + 0x \\ \underline{2x^2 + 4x } \\ - 4x + 3 \\ \underline{- 4x - 8} \\ 11 \end{array}$$

$x^4 - 2x^2 + 3 = (x+2)(x^3 - 2x^2 + 2x - 4) + 11$

11. $(2x^4 + 7x^3 + x - 12) \div (x+3)$

$= (2x^4 + 7x^3 + 0x^2 + x - 12) \div [x - (-3)]$

$$\begin{array}{r|rrrrr} -3 & 2 & 7 & 0 & 1 & -12 \\ & & -6 & -3 & 9 & -30 \\ \hline & 2 & 1 & -3 & 10 & -42 \end{array}$$

The quotient is $2x^3 + x^2 - 3x + 10$. The remainder is -42.

13. $(x^3 - 2x^2 - 8) \div (x+2)$

$= (x^3 - 2x^2 + 0x - 8) \div [x - (-2)]$

$$\begin{array}{r|rrrr} -2 & 1 & -2 & 0 & -8 \\ & & -2 & 8 & -16 \\ \hline & 1 & -4 & 8 & -24 \end{array}$$

The quotient is $x^2 - 4x + 8$. The remainder is -24.

15. $(3x^3 - x^2 + 4x - 10) \div (x+1)$

$= (3x^3 - x^2 + 4x - 10) \div [x - (-1)]$

$$\begin{array}{r|rrrr} -1 & 3 & -1 & 4 & -10 \\ & & -3 & 4 & -8 \\ \hline & 3 & -4 & 8 & -18 \end{array}$$

The quotient is $3x^2 - 4x + 8$. The remainder is -18.

17. $(x^5 + x^3 - x) \div (x-3)$

$= (x^5 + 0x^4 + x^3 + 0x^2 - x + 0) \div (x-3)$

$$\begin{array}{r|rrrrrr} 3 & 1 & 0 & 1 & 0 & -1 & 0 \\ & & 3 & 9 & 30 & 90 & 267 \\ \hline & 1 & 3 & 10 & 30 & 89 & 267 \end{array}$$

The quotient is $x^4 + 3x^3 + 10x^2 + 30x + 89$.

The remainder is 267.

19. $(x^4 - 1) \div (x-1)$

$= (x^4 + 0x^3 + 0x^2 + 0x - 1) \div (x-1)$

$$\begin{array}{r|rrrrr} 1 & 1 & 0 & 0 & 0 & -1 \\ & & 1 & 1 & 1 & 1 \\ \hline & 1 & 1 & 1 & 1 & 0 \end{array}$$

The quotient is $x^3 + x^2 + x + 1$. The remainder is 0.

21. $(2x^4 + 3x^2 - 1) \div \left(x - \frac{1}{2}\right)$

$(2x^4 + 0x^3 + 3x^2 + 0x - 1) \div \left(x - \frac{1}{2}\right)$

$$\begin{array}{r|rrrrr} \frac{1}{2} & 2 & 0 & 3 & 0 & -1 \\ & & 1 & \frac{1}{2} & \frac{7}{4} & \frac{7}{8} \\ \hline & 2 & 1 & \frac{7}{2} & \frac{7}{4} & -\frac{1}{8} \end{array}$$

The quotient is $2x^3 + x^2 + \frac{7}{2}x + \frac{7}{4}$. The remainder is $-\frac{1}{8}$.

23. $f(x) = x^3 - 6x^2 + 11x - 6$

Find $f(1)$.

$$\begin{array}{r|rrrr} 1 & 1 & -6 & 11 & -6 \\ & & 1 & -5 & 6 \\ \hline & 1 & -5 & 6 & 0 \end{array}$$

$f(1) = 0$

Find $f(-2)$.

$$\begin{array}{r|rrrr} -2 & 1 & -6 & 11 & -6 \\ & & -2 & 16 & -54 \\ \hline & 1 & -8 & 27 & -60 \end{array}$$

$f(-2) = -60$

Find $f(3)$.

$$\begin{array}{r|rrrr} 3 & 1 & -6 & 11 & -6 \\ & & 3 & -9 & 6 \\ \hline & 1 & -3 & 2 & 0 \end{array}$$

$f(3) = 0$

25. $f(x) = x^4 - 3x^3 + 2x + 8$

Find $f(-1)$.

$$\begin{array}{r|rrrrr} -1 & 1 & -3 & 0 & 2 & 8 \\ & & -1 & 4 & -4 & 2 \\ \hline & 1 & -4 & 4 & -2 & 10 \end{array}$$

$f(-1) = 10$

Find $f(4)$.

$$\begin{array}{r|rrrrr} 4 & 1 & -3 & 0 & 2 & 8 \\ & & 4 & 4 & 16 & 72 \\ \hline & 1 & 1 & 4 & 18 & 80 \end{array}$$

$f(4) = 80$

Find $f(-5)$.

$$\begin{array}{r|rrrrr} -5 & 1 & -3 & 0 & 2 & 8 \\ & & -5 & 40 & -200 & 990 \\ \hline & 1 & -8 & 40 & -198 & 998 \end{array}$$

$f(-5) = 998$

27. $f(x) = 2x^5 - 3x^4 + 2x^3 - x + 8$

Find $f(20)$.

$$\begin{array}{r|rrrrrr} 20 & 2 & -3 & 2 & 0 & -1 & 8 \\ & & 40 & 740 & 14,840 & 296,800 & 5,935,980 \\ \hline & 2 & 37 & 742 & 14,840 & 296,799 & 5,935,988 \end{array}$$

$f(20) = 5,935,988$

Find $f(-3)$.

$$\begin{array}{r|rrrrrr} -3 & 2 & -3 & 2 & 0 & -1 & 8 \\ & & -6 & 27 & -87 & 261 & -780 \\ \hline & 2 & -9 & 29 & -87 & 260 & -772 \end{array}$$

$f(-3) = -772$

29. $f(x) = x^4 - 16$

Find $f(2)$.

$$\begin{array}{r|rrrrr} 2 & 1 & 0 & 0 & 0 & -16 \\ & & 2 & 4 & 8 & 16 \\ \hline & 1 & 2 & 4 & 8 & 0 \end{array}$$

$f(2) = 0$

Find $f(-2)$.

$$\begin{array}{r|rrrrr} -2 & 1 & 0 & 0 & 0 & -16 \\ & & -2 & 4 & -8 & 16 \\ \hline & 1 & -2 & 4 & -8 & 0 \end{array}$$

$f(-2) = 0$

Find $f(3)$.

$$\begin{array}{r|rrrrr} 3 & 1 & 0 & 0 & 0 & -16 \\ & & 3 & 9 & 27 & 81 \\ \hline & 1 & 3 & 9 & 27 & 65 \end{array}$$

$f(3) = 65$

Find $f(1-\sqrt{2})$.

$$\begin{array}{r|rrrrr} 1-\sqrt{2} & 1 & 0 & 0 & 0 & -16 \\ & & 1-\sqrt{2} & 3-2\sqrt{2} & 7-5\sqrt{2} & 17-12\sqrt{2} \\ \hline & 1 & 1-\sqrt{2} & 3-2\sqrt{2} & 7-5\sqrt{2} & 1-12\sqrt{2} \end{array}$$

$f(1-\sqrt{2}) = 1 - 12\sqrt{2}$

31. $f(x) = 3x^3 + 5x^2 - 6x + 18$

If -3 is a zero of $f(x)$, then $f(-3) = 0$. Find $f(-3)$ using synthetic division.

$$\begin{array}{r|rrrr} -3 & 3 & 5 & -6 & 18 \\ & & -9 & 12 & -18 \\ \hline & 3 & -4 & 6 & 0 \end{array}$$

Since $f(-3) = 0$, -3 is a zero of $f(x)$.

If 2 is a zero of $f(x)$, then $f(2) = 0$. Find $f(2)$ using synthetic division.

$$\begin{array}{r|rrrr} 2 & 3 & 5 & -6 & 18 \\ & & 6 & 22 & 32 \\ \hline & 3 & 11 & 16 & 50 \end{array}$$

Since $f(2) \neq 0$, 2 is not a zero of $f(x)$.

33. $h(x) = x^4 + 4x^3 + 2x^2 - 4x - 3$

If -3 is a zero of $h(x)$, then $h(-3) = 0$. Find $h(-3)$ using synthetic division.

$$\begin{array}{r|rrrrr} -3 & 1 & 4 & 2 & -4 & -3 \\ & & -3 & -3 & 3 & 3 \\ \hline & 1 & 1 & -1 & -1 & 0 \end{array}$$

Since $h(-3) = 0$, -3 is a zero of $h(x)$.

If 1 is a zero of $h(x)$, then $h(1) = 0$. Find $h(1)$ using synthetic division.

$$\begin{array}{r|rrrrr} 1 & 1 & 4 & 2 & -4 & -3 \\ & & 1 & 5 & 7 & 3 \\ \hline & 1 & 5 & 7 & 3 & 0 \end{array}$$

Since $h(1) = 0$, 1 is a zero of $h(x)$.

35. $g(x) = x^3 - 4x^2 + 4x - 16$

If i is a zero of $g(x)$, then $g(i) = 0$. Find $g(i)$ using synthetic division. Keep in mind that $i^2 = -1$.

$$\begin{array}{r|rrrr} i & 1 & -4 & 4 & -16 \\ & & i & -4i-1 & 3i+4 \\ \hline & 1 & -4+i & 3-4i & -12+3i \end{array}$$

Since $g(i) \neq 0$, i is not a zero of $g(x)$.

If $-2i$ is a zero of $g(x)$, then $g(-2i) = 0$. Find $g(-2i)$ using synthetic division. Keep in mind that $i^2 = -1$.

$$\begin{array}{r|rrrr} -2i & 1 & -4 & 4 & -16 \\ & & -2i & 8i-4 & 16 \\ \hline & 1 & -4-2i & 8i & 0 \end{array}$$

Since $g(-2i) = 0$, $-2i$ is a zero of $g(x)$.

37. $f(x) = x^3 - \dfrac{7}{2}x^2 + x - \dfrac{3}{2}$

If -3 is a zero of $f(x)$, then $f(-3) = 0$. Find $f(-3)$ using synthetic division.

$$\begin{array}{r|rrrr} -3 & 1 & -\frac{7}{2} & 1 & -\frac{3}{2} \\ & & -3 & \frac{39}{2} & -\frac{123}{2} \\ \hline & 1 & -\frac{13}{2} & \frac{41}{2} & -63 \end{array}$$

Since $f(-3) \neq 0$, -3 is not a zero of $f(x)$.

If $\dfrac{1}{2}$ is a zero of $f(x)$, then $f\left(\dfrac{1}{2}\right) = 0$.

Find $f\left(\dfrac{1}{2}\right)$ using synthetic division.

$$\begin{array}{r|rrrr} \frac{1}{2} & 1 & -\frac{7}{2} & 1 & -\frac{3}{2} \\ & & \frac{1}{2} & -\frac{3}{2} & -\frac{1}{4} \\ \hline & 1 & -3 & -\frac{1}{2} & -\frac{7}{4} \end{array}$$

Since $f\left(\dfrac{1}{2}\right) \neq 0$, $\dfrac{1}{2}$ is not a zero of $f(x)$.

39. $f(x) = x^3 + 4x^2 + x - 6$

Try $x - 1$. Use synthetic division to see whether $f(1) = 0$.

$$\begin{array}{r|rrrr} 1 & 1 & 4 & 1 & -6 \\ & & 1 & 5 & 6 \\ \hline & 1 & 5 & 6 & 0 \end{array}$$

Since $f(1) = 0$, $x - 1$ is a factor of $f(x)$. Thus $f(x) = (x - 1)(x^2 + 5x + 6)$.

Factoring the trinomial we get

$f(x) = (x - 1)(x + 2)(x + 3)$.

To solve the equation $f(x) = 0$, use the principle of zero products.

$(x - 1)(x + 2)(x + 3) = 0$

$x - 1 = 0$ *or* $x + 2 = 0$ *or* $x + 3 = 0$

$x = 1$ *or* $x = -2$ *or* $x = -3$

The solutions are 1, -2, and -3.

41. $f(x) = x^3 - 6x^2 + 3x + 10$

Try $x - 1$. Use synthetic division to see whether $f(1) = 0$.

$$\begin{array}{r|rrrr} 1 & 1 & -6 & 3 & 10 \\ & & 1 & -5 & -2 \\ \hline & 1 & -5 & -2 & 8 \end{array}$$

Since $f(1) \neq 0$, $x - 1$ is not a factor of $P(x)$.

Try $x+1$. Use synthetic division to see whether $f(-1) = 0$.

$$\begin{array}{r|rrrr} -1 & 1 & -6 & 3 & 10 \\ & & -1 & 7 & -10 \\ \hline & 1 & -7 & 10 & 0 \end{array}$$

Since $f(-1) = 0$, $x + 1$ is a factor of $f(x)$.

Thus $f(x) = (x + 1)(x^2 - 7x + 10)$.

Factoring the trinomial we get

$f(x) = (x + 1)(x - 2)(x - 5)$.

To solve the equation $f(x) = 0$, use the principle of zero products.

$(x + 1)(x - 2)(x - 5) = 0$

$x + 1 = 0$ *or* $x - 2 = 0$ *or* $x - 5 = 0$

$x = -1$ *or* $x = 2$ *or* $x = 5$

The solutions are -1, 2, and 5.

43. $f(x) = x^3 - x^2 - 14x + 24$

Try $x + 1$, $x - 1$, and $x + 2$. Using synthetic division we find that $f(-1) \neq 0$, $f(1) \neq 0$ and $f(-2) \neq 0$. Thus $x + 1$, $x - 1$, and $x + 2$, are not factors of $f(x)$.

Try $x - 2$. Use synthetic division to see whether $f(2) = 0$.

$$\begin{array}{r|rrrr} 2 & 1 & -1 & -14 & 24 \\ & & 2 & 2 & -24 \\ \hline & 1 & 1 & -12 & 0 \end{array}$$

Since $f(2) = 0$, $x - 2$ is a factor of $f(x)$. Thus $f(x) = (x - 2)(x^2 + x - 12)$.

Factoring the trinomial we get

$f(x) = (x - 2)(x + 4)(x - 3)$

To solve the equation $f(x) = 0$, use the principle of zero products.

$(x - 2)(x + 4)(x - 3) = 0$

$x - 2 = 0$ *or* $x + 4 = 0$ *or* $x - 3 = 0$

$x = 2$ *or* $x = -4$ *or* $x = 3$

The solutions are 2, -4, and 3.

45. $f(x) = x^4 - 7x^3 + 9x^2 + 27x - 54$

Try $x + 1$ and $x - 1$. Using synthetic division we find that $f(-1) \neq 0$ and $f(1) \neq 0$. Thus $x + 1$ and $x - 1$ are not factors of $f(x)$. Try $x + 2$. Use synthetic division to see whether $f(-2) = 0$.

$$\begin{array}{r|rrrrr} -2 & 1 & -7 & 9 & 27 & -54 \\ & & -2 & 18 & -54 & 54 \\ \hline & 1 & -9 & 27 & -27 & 0 \end{array}$$

Since $f(-2) = 0$, $x + 2$ is a factor of $f(x)$. Thus $f(x) = (x + 2)(x^3 - 9x^2 + 27x - 27)$.

We continue to use synthetic division to factor $g(x) = x^3 - 9x^2 + 27x - 27$. Trying $x + 2$ again and $x - 2$ we find that $g(-2) \neq 0$ and $g(2) \neq 0$. Thus $x + 2$ and $x - 2$ are not factors of $g(x)$. Try $x - 3$.

$$\begin{array}{r|rrrr} 3 & 1 & -9 & 27 & -27 \\ & & 3 & -18 & 27 \\ \hline & 1 & -6 & 9 & 0 \end{array}$$

Since $g(3) = 0$, $x - 3$ is a factor of $x^3 - 9x^2 + 27x - 27$.

Thus $f(x) = (x + 2)(x - 3)(x^2 - 6x + 9)$.

Factoring the trinomial we get

$f(x) = (x + 2)(x - 3)(x - 3)^2$, or $f(x) = (x + 2)(x - 3)^3$.

To solve the equation $f(x) = 0$, use the principle of zero products.

$(x + 2)(x - 3)(x - 3)(x - 3) = 0$

$x + 2 = 0$ *or* $x - 3 = 0$ *or* $x - 3 = 0$ *or* $x - 3 = 0$

$x = -2$ *or* $x = 3$ *or* $x = 3$ *or* $x = 3$

The solutions are -2 and 3.

47. $f(x) = x^4 - x^3 - 19x^2 + 49x - 30$

Try $x - 1$. Use synthetic division to see whether $f(1) = 0$.

$$\begin{array}{r|rrrrr} 1 & 1 & -1 & -19 & 49 & -30 \\ & & 1 & 0 & -19 & 30 \\ \hline & 1 & 0 & -19 & 30 & 0 \end{array}$$

Since $f(1) = 0$, $x - 1$ is a factor of $f(x)$. Thus $f(x) = (x - 1)(x^3 - 19x + 30)$.

We continue to use synthetic division to factor $g(x) = x^3 - 19x + 30$. Trying $x - 1$, $x + 1$, and $x + 2$ we find that $g(1) \neq 0$, $g(-1) \neq 0$, and $g(-2) \neq 0$. Thus $x - 1$, $x + 1$, and $x + 2$ are not factors of $x^3 - 19x + 30$. Try $x - 2$.

$$\begin{array}{r|rrrr} 2 & 1 & 0 & -19 & 30 \\ & & 2 & 4 & -30 \\ \hline & 1 & 2 & -15 & 0 \end{array}$$

Since $g(2) = 0$, $x - 2$ is a factor of $x^3 - 19x + 30$.

Thus $f(x) = (x - 1)(x - 2)(x^2 + 2x - 15)$.

Factoring the trinomial we get

$f(x) = (x - 1)(x - 2)(x - 3)(x + 5)$.

To solve the equation $f(x) = 0$, use the principle of zero products.

$$(x-1)(x-2)(x-3)(x+5) = 0$$

$$x-1=0 \text{ or } x-2=0 \text{ or } x-3=0 \text{ or } x+5=0$$

$$x=1 \text{ or } \quad x=2 \text{ or } \quad x=3 \text{ or } \quad x=-5$$

The solutions are 1, 2, 3, and -5.

49. $f(x) = x^4 - x^3 - 7x^2 + x + 6$

1. The leading term is x^4. The degree, 4, is even and the leading coefficient, 1, is positive so as $x \to \infty$, $f(x) \to \infty$ and as $x \to -\infty$, $f(x) \to \infty$.
2. Find the zeros of the function. We first use synthetic division to determine if $f(1) = 0$.

$$\begin{array}{r|rrrrr} 1 & 1 & -1 & -7 & 1 & 6 \\ & & 1 & 0 & -7 & -6 \\ \hline & 1 & 0 & -7 & -6 & 0 \end{array}$$

1 is a zero of the function and we have $f(x) = (x-1)(x^3 - 7x - 6)$.

Synthetic division shows that -1 is a zero of $g(x) = x^3 - 7x - 6$.

$$\begin{array}{r|rrrr} -1 & 1 & 0 & -7 & -6 \\ & & -1 & 1 & 6 \\ \hline & 1 & -1 & -6 & 0 \end{array}$$

Then we have $f(x) = (x-1)(x+1)(x^2 - x - 6)$.

To find the other zeros we solve the following equation:

$$x^2 - x - 6 = 0$$

$$(x-3)(x+2) = 0$$

$$x - 3 = 0 \text{ or } x + 2 = 0$$

$$x = 3 \text{ or } \quad x = -2$$

The zeros of the function are 1, -1, 3, and -2 so the x-intercepts of the graph are $(1,0)$, $(-1,0)$, $(3,0)$, and $(-2,0)$.

3. The zeros divide the x-axis into five intervals, $(-\infty,-2)$, $(-2,-1)$, $(-1,1)$, $(1,3)$, and $(3,\infty)$. We choose a value for x from each interval and find $f(x)$. This tells us the sign of $f(x)$ for all values of x in the interval.

In $(-\infty,-2)$, test -3:

$f(-3) = (-3)^4 - (-3)^3 - 7(-3)^2 + (-3) + 6 = 48 > 0$

In $(-2,-1)$, test -1.5:

$f(-1.5) = (-1.5)^4 - (-1.5)^3 - 7(-1.5)^2 + (-1.5) + 6 = -2.8125 < 0$

In $(-1,1)$, test 0:

$f(0) = 0^4 - 0^3 - 7\cdot 0^2 + 0 + 6 = 6 > 0$

In $(1,3)$, test 2:

$f(2) = 2^4 - 2^3 - 7\cdot 2^2 + 2 + 6 = -12 < 0$

In $(3,\infty)$, test 4:

$f(4) = 4^4 - 4^3 - 7\cdot 4^2 + 4 + 6 = 90 > 0$

Thus the graph lies above the x-axis on $(-\infty,-2)$, on $(-1,1)$, and on $(3,\infty)$. It lies below the x-axis on $(-2,-1)$ and on $(1,3)$. We also know the points $(-3,48)$, $(-1.5,-2.8125)$, $(0,6)$, $(2,-12)$, and $(4,90)$ are on the graph.

4. From Step 3 we see that $f(0) = 6$ so the y-intercept is $(0,6)$.
5. We find additional points on the graph and draw the graph.

x	$f(x)$
-2.5	14.3
-0.5	3.9
0.5	4.7
2.5	-11.8

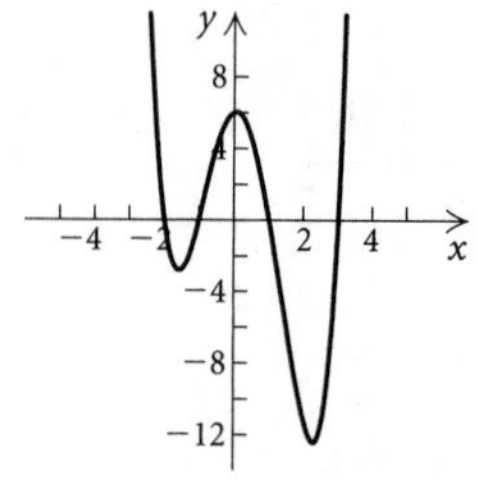

$f(x) = x^4 - x^3 - 7x^2 + x + 6$

6. Checking the graph as described on page 254 in the text, we see that it appears to be correct.

51. $f(x) = x^3 - 7x + 6$

1. The leading term is x^3. The degree, 3, is odd and the leading coefficient, 1, is positive so as $x \to \infty$, $f(x) \to \infty$ and as $x \to -\infty$, $f(x) \to -\infty$.
2. Find the zeros of the function. We first use synthetic division to determine if $f(1) = 0$.

$$\begin{array}{r|rrrr} 1 & 1 & 0 & -7 & 6 \\ & & 1 & 1 & -6 \\ \hline & 1 & 1 & -6 & 0 \end{array}$$

1 is a zero of the function and we have $f(x) = (x-1)(x^2 + x - 6)$. To find the other zeros we solve the following equation.

$$x^2 + x - 6 = 0$$

$$(x+3)(x-2) = 0$$

$$x + 3 = 0 \quad \text{or} \quad x - 2 = 0$$

$$x = -3 \quad \text{or} \quad x = 2$$

The zeros of the function are 1, -3, and 2 so the x-intercepts of the graph are $(1,0)$, $(-3,0)$, and $(2,0)$.

3. The zeros divide the x-axis into four intervals, $(-\infty,-3)$, $(-3,1)$, $(1,2)$, and $(2,\infty)$. We choose a value for x from each interval and find $f(x)$. This tells us the sign of $f(x)$ for all values of x in the interval.

In $(-\infty,-3)$, test -4:

$f(-4) = (-4)^3 - 7(-4) + 6 = -30 < 0$

In $(-3,1)$, test 0:

$f(0) = 0^3 - 7\cdot 0 + 6 = 6 > 0$

In $(1,2)$, test 1.5:

$f(1.5) = (1.5)^3 - 7(1.5) + 6 = -1.125 < 0$

In $(2,\infty)$, test 3:

$f(3) = 3^3 - 7\cdot 3 + 6 = 12 > 0$

Thus the graph lies below the x-axis on $(-\infty,-3)$ and on $(1,2)$. It lies above the x-axis on $(-3,1)$ and on $(2,\infty)$. We also know the points $(-4,-30)$, $(0,6)$, $(1.5,-1.125)$, and $(3,12)$ are on the graph.

4. From Step 3 we see that $f(0) = 6$ so the y-intercept is $(0,6)$.

5. We find additional points on the graph and draw the graph.

x	$f(x)$
-3.5	-12.4
-2	12
2.5	4.1
4	42

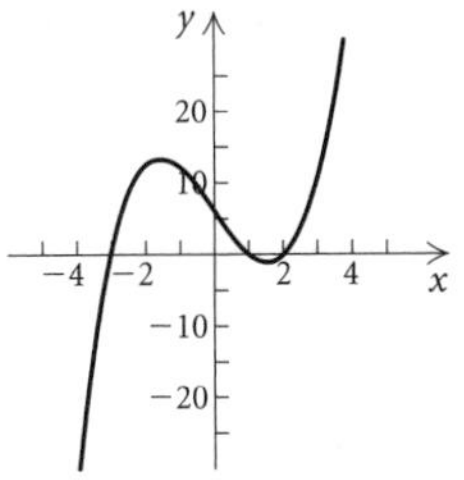

$f(x) = x^3 - 7x + 6$

6. Checking the graph as described on page 254 in the text, we see that it appears to be correct.

53. $f(x) = -x^3 + 3x^2 + 6x - 8$

1. The leading term is $-x^3$. The degree, 3, is odd and the leading coefficient, -1, is negative so as $x \to \infty$, $f(x) \to -\infty$ and as $x \to -\infty$, $f(x) \to \infty$.

2. Find the zeros of the function. We first use synthetic division to determine if $f(1) = 0$.

$$\begin{array}{r|rrrr} 1 & -1 & 3 & 6 & -8 \\ & & -1 & 2 & 8 \\ \hline & -1 & 2 & 8 & 0 \end{array}$$

1 is a zero of the function and we have $f(x) = (x-1)(-x^2+2x+8)$. To find the other zeros we solve the following equation.

$$-x^2 + 2x + 8 = 0$$
$$x^2 - 2x - 8 = 0$$
$$(x-4)(x+2) = 0$$
$$x - 4 = 0 \quad or \quad x + 2 = 0$$
$$x = 4 \quad or \quad x = -2$$

The zeros of the function are 1, 4, and -2 so the x-intercepts of the graph are $(1, 0)$, $(4, 0)$, and $(-2, 0)$.

3. The zeros divide the x-axis into four intervals, $(-\infty, -2)$, $(-2, 1)$, $(1, 4)$, and $(4, \infty)$. We choose a value for x from each interval and find $f(x)$. This tells us the sign of $f(x)$ for all values of x in the interval.

In $(-\infty, -2)$, test -3:

$f(-3) = (-3)^3 + 3(-3)^2 + 6(-3) - 8 = 28 > 0$

In $(-2, 1)$, test 0:

$f(0) = -0^3 + 3 \cdot 0^2 + 6 \cdot 0 - 8 = -8 < 0$

In $(1, 4)$, test 2:

$f(2) = -2^3 + 3 \cdot 2^2 + 6 \cdot 2 - 8 = 8 > 0$

In $(4, \infty)$, test 5:

$f(5) = -5^3 + 3 \cdot 5^2 + 6 \cdot 5 - 8 = -28 < 0$

Thus the graph lies above the x-axis on $(-\infty, -2)$ and on $(1, 4)$. It lies below the x-axis on $(-2, 1)$ and on $(4, \infty)$. We also know the points $(-3, 28)$, $(0, -8)$, $(2, 8)$, and $(5, -28)$ are on the graph.

4. From Step 3 we see that $f(0) = -8$ so the y-intercept is $(0, -8)$.

5. We find additional points on the graph and draw the graph.

x	$f(x)$
-2.5	11.4
-1	-10
3	10
4.5	-11.4

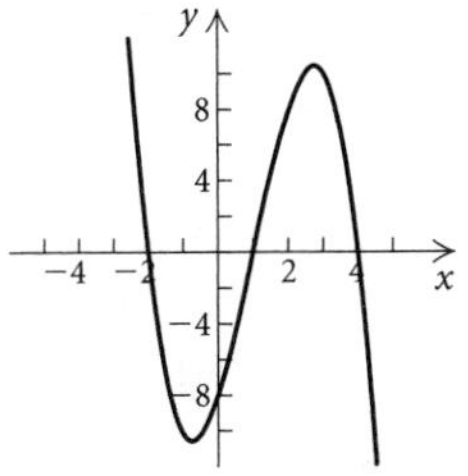

$f(x) = -x^3 + 3x^2 + 6x - 8$

6. Checking the graph as described on page 254 in the text, we see that it appears to be correct.

55. Left to the student

57. Discussion and Writing

59.
$$2x^2 + 12 = 5x$$
$$2x^2 - 5x + 12 = 0$$
$$a = 2,\ b = -5,\ c = 12$$
$$x = \frac{-b \pm \sqrt{b^2 - 4ac}}{2a}$$
$$x = \frac{-(-5) \pm \sqrt{(-5)^2 - 4 \cdot 2 \cdot 12}}{2 \cdot 2}$$
$$= \frac{5 \pm \sqrt{-71}}{4}$$
$$= \frac{5 \pm i\sqrt{71}}{4}$$

The solutions are $\frac{5 + i\sqrt{71}}{4}$ and $\frac{5 - i\sqrt{71}}{4}$, or $\frac{5 \pm i\sqrt{71}}{4}$.

61. We substitute -14 for $g(x)$ and solve for x.

$$-14 = x^2 + 5x - 14$$
$$0 = x^2 + 5x$$
$$0 = x(x + 5)$$
$$x = 0 \quad or \quad x + 5 = 0$$
$$x = 0 \quad or \quad x = -5$$

When the output is -14, the input is 0 or -5.

63. We substitute -20 for $g(x)$ and solve for x.

$$-20 = x^2 + 5x - 14$$
$$0 = x^2 + 5x + 6$$
$$0 = (x + 3)(x + 2)$$
$$x + 3 = 0 \quad or \quad x + 2 = 0$$
$$x = -3 \quad or \quad x = -2$$

When the output is -20, the input is -3 or -2.

65. Let b and h represent the length of the base and the height of the triangle, respectively.

$b + h = 30$, so $b = 30 - h$.

$A = \frac{1}{2}bh = \frac{1}{2}(30 - h)h = -\frac{1}{2}h^2 + 15h$

Find the value of h for which A is a maximum:

$$h = \frac{-15}{2(-1/2)} = 15$$

When $h = 15$, $b = 30 - 15 = 15$.

The area is a maximum when the base and the height are each 15 in.

67. a) -4, -3, 2, and 5 are zeros of the function, so $x+4$, $x+3$, $x-2$, and $x-5$ are factors.

b) We first write the product of the factors:

$P(x) = (x+4)(x+3)(x-2)(x-5)$

Note that $P(0) = 4 \cdot 3(-2)(-5) > 0$ and the graph shows a positive y-intercept, so this function is a correct one.

c) Yes; two examples are $f(x) = c \cdot P(x)$ for any nonzero constant c and $g(x) = (x-a)P(x)$.

d) No; only the function in part (b) has the given graph.

69. Divide $x^3 - kx^2 + 3x + 7k$ by $x+2$.

$$\begin{array}{r|rrrr} -2 & 1 & -k & 3 & 7k \\ & & -2 & 2k+4 & -4k-14 \\ \hline & 1 & -k-2 & 2k+7 & 3k-14 \end{array}$$

Thus $P(-2) = 3k - 14$.

We know that if $x+2$ is a factor of $f(x)$, then $f(-2) = 0$.

We solve $0 = 3k - 14$ for k.

$$0 = 3k - 14$$
$$\frac{14}{3} = k$$

71. $\dfrac{2x^2}{x^2-1} + \dfrac{4}{x+3} = \dfrac{32}{3x^2-x-3}$,

LCM is $(x+1)(x-1)(x+3)$

$$(x+1)(x-1)(x+3)\left[\frac{2x^2}{(x+1)(x-1)} + \frac{4}{x+3}\right] =$$
$$(x+1)(x-1)(x+3) \cdot \frac{32}{(x+1)(x-1)(x+3)}$$
$$2x^2(x+3) + 4(x+1)(x-1) = 32$$
$$2x^3 + 6x^2 + 4x^2 - 4 = 32$$
$$2x^3 + 10x^2 - 36 = 0$$
$$x^3 + 5x^2 - 18 = 0$$

Using synthetic division and several trials, we find that -3 is a factor of $f(x) = x^3 + 5x^2 - 18$:

$$\begin{array}{r|rrrr} -3 & 1 & 5 & 0 & -18 \\ & & -3 & -6 & 18 \\ \hline & 1 & 2 & -6 & 0 \end{array}$$

Then we have:

$(x+3)(x^2+2x-6) = 0$

$x+3 = 0 \quad or \quad x^2 + 2x - 6 = 0$

$x = -3 \quad or \quad x = -1 \pm \sqrt{7}$

Only $-1 \pm \sqrt{7}$ check.

73. Answers may vary. One possibility is $P(x) = x^{15} - x^{14}$.

75.
$$\begin{array}{r|rrr} i & 1 & -3 & 7 \\ & & i & -3i-1 \\ \hline & 1 & -3+i & 6-3i \end{array} \quad (i^2 = -1)$$

The answer is $x - 3 + i$, R $6 - 3i$.

Exercise Set 3.3

1. Find a polynomial function of degree 3 with -2, 3, and 5 as zeros.

Such a function has factors $x+2$, $x-3$, and $x-5$, so we have $f(x) = a_n(x+2)(x-3)(x-5)$.

The number a_n can be any nonzero number. The simplest polynomial will be obtained if we let it be 1. Multiplying the factors, we obtain

$$\begin{aligned} f(x) &= (x+2)(x-3)(x-5) \\ &= (x^2 - x - 6)(x-5) \\ &= x^3 - 6x^2 - x + 30. \end{aligned}$$

3. Find a polynomial function of degree 3 with -3, $2i$, and $-2i$ as zeros.

Such a function has factors $x+3$, $x-2i$, and $x+2i$, so we have $f(x) = a_n(x+3)(x-2i)(x+2i)$.

The number a_n can be any nonzero number. The simplest polynomial will be obtained if we let it be 1. Multiplying the factors, we obtain

$$\begin{aligned} f(x) &= (x+3)(x-2i)(x+2i) \\ &= (x+3)(x^2+4) \\ &= x^3 + 3x^2 + 4x + 12. \end{aligned}$$

5. Find a polynomial function of degree 3 with $\sqrt{2}$, $-\sqrt{2}$, and 3 as zeros.

Such a function has factors $x - \sqrt{2}$, $x + \sqrt{2}$, and $x - 3$, so we have $f(x) = a_n(x-\sqrt{2})(x+\sqrt{2})(x-3)$.

The number a_n can be any nonzero number. The simplest polynomial will be obtained if we let it be 1. Multiplying the factors, we obtain

$$\begin{aligned} f(x) &= (x-\sqrt{2})(x+\sqrt{2})(x-3) \\ &= (x^2-2)(x-3) \\ &= x^3 - 3x^2 - 2x + 6. \end{aligned}$$

7. Find a polynomial function of degree 3 with $1-\sqrt{3}$, $1+\sqrt{3}$, and -2 as zeros.

Such a function has factors $x-(1-\sqrt{3})$, $x-(1+\sqrt{3})$, and $x+2$, so we have

$f(x) = a_n[x-(1-\sqrt{3})][x-(1+\sqrt{3})](x+2)$.

The number a_n can be any nonzero number. The simplest polynomial will be obtained if we let it be 1. Multiplying the factors, we obtain

$$\begin{aligned} f(x) &= [x-(1-\sqrt{3})][x-(1+\sqrt{3})](x+2) \\ &= [(x-1)+\sqrt{3}][(x-1)-\sqrt{3}](x+2) \\ &= [(x-1)^2 - (\sqrt{3})^2](x+2) \\ &= (x^2 - 2x + 1 - 3)(x+2) \\ &= (x^2 - 2x - 2)(x+2) \\ &= x^3 - 2x^2 - 2x + 2x^2 - 4x - 4 \\ &= x^3 - 6x - 4. \end{aligned}$$

9. Find a polynomial function of degree 3 with $1+6i$, $1-6i$, and -4 as zeros.

Such a function has factors $x-(1+6i)$, $x-(1-6i)$, and $x+4$, so we have

$f(x) = a_n[x-(1+6i)][x-(1-6i)](x+4)$.

The number a_n can be any nonzero number. The simplest polynomial will be obtained if we let it be 1. Multiplying the factors, we obtain

$$\begin{aligned} f(x) &= [x-(1+6i)][x-(1-6i)](x+4) \\ &= [(x-1)-6i][(x-1)+6i](x+4) \\ &= [(x-1)^2-(6i)^2](x+4) \\ &= (x^2-2x+1+36)(x+4) \\ &= (x^2-2x+37)(x+4) \\ &= x^3-2x^2+37x+4x^2-8x+148 \\ &= x^3+2x^2+29x+148. \end{aligned}$$

11. Find a polynomial function of degree 3 with $-\frac{1}{3}$, 0, and 2 as zeros.

Such a function has factors $x+\frac{1}{3}$, $x-0$ (or x), and $x-2$ so we have

$f(x) = a_n\left(x+\frac{1}{3}\right)(x)(x-2)$.

The number a_n can be any nonzero number. The simplest polynomial will be obtained if we let it be 1. Multiplying the factors, we obtain

$$\begin{aligned} f(x) &= \left(x+\frac{1}{3}\right)(x)(x-2) \\ &= \left(x^2+\frac{1}{3}x\right)(x-2) \\ &= x^3-\frac{5}{3}x^2-\frac{2}{3}x. \end{aligned}$$

13. A polynomial function of degree 5 has at most 5 zeros. Since 5 zeros are given, these are all of the zeros of the desired function. We proceed as in Exercises 1-11, letting $a_n = 1$.

$$\begin{aligned} f(x) &= (x+1)^3(x-0)(x-1) \\ &= (x^3+3x^2+3x+1)(x^2-x) \\ &= x^5+2x^4-2x^2-x \end{aligned}$$

15. A polynomial function of degree 4 has at most 4 zeros. Since 4 zeros are given, these are all of the zeros of the desired function. We proceed as in Exercises 1-11, letting $a_n = 1$.

$$\begin{aligned} f(x) &= (x+1)^3(x-0) \\ &= (x^3+3x^2+3x+1)(x) \\ &= x^4+3x^3+3x^2+x \end{aligned}$$

17. A polynomial function of degree 4 can have at most 4 zeros. Since $f(x)$ has rational coefficients, in addition to the three zeros given, the other zero is the conjugate of $\sqrt{3}$, or $-\sqrt{3}$.

19. A polynomial function of degree 4 can have at most 4 zeros. Since $f(x)$ has rational coefficients, the other zeros are the conjugates of the given zeros. They are i and $2+\sqrt{5}$.

21. A polynomial function of degree 4 can have at most 4 zeros. Since $f(x)$ has rational coefficients, in addition to the three zeros given, the other zero is the conjugate of $3i$, or $-3i$.

23. A polynomial function of degree 4 can have at most 4 zeros. Since $f(x)$ has rational coefficients, the other zeros are the conjugates of the given zeros. They are $-4+3i$ and $2+\sqrt{3}$.

25. A polynomial function $f(x)$ of degree 5 has at most 5 zeros. Since $f(x)$ has rational coefficients, in addition to the 3 given zeros, the other zeros are the conjugates of $\sqrt{5}$ and $-4i$, or $-\sqrt{5}$ and $4i$.

27. A polynomial function $f(x)$ of degree 5 has at most 5 zeros. Since $f(x)$ has rational coefficients, the other zero is the conjugate of $2-i$, or $2+i$.

29. A polynomial function $f(x)$ of degree 5 has at most 5 zeros. Since $f(x)$ has rational coefficients, in addition to the 3 given zeros, the other zeros are the conjugates of $-3+4i$ and $4-\sqrt{5}$, or $-3-4i$ and $4+\sqrt{5}$.

31. A polynomial function $f(x)$ of degree 5 has at most 5 zeros. Since $f(x)$ has rational coefficients, the other zero is the conjugate of $4-i$, or $4+i$.

33. Find a polynomial function of lowest degree with rational coefficients that has $1+i$ and 2 as some of its zeros. $1-i$ is also a zero.

Thus the polynomial function is

$f(x) = a_n(x-2)[x-(1+i)][x-(1-i)]$.

If we let $a_n = 1$, we obtain

$$\begin{aligned} f(x) &= (x-2)[(x-1)-i][(x-1)+i] \\ &= (x-2)[(x-1)^2-i^2] \\ &= (x-2)(x^2-2x+1+1) \\ &= (x-2)(x^2-2x+2) \\ &= x^3-4x^2+6x-4. \end{aligned}$$

35. Find a polynomial function of lowest degree with rational coefficients that has $4i$ as one of its zeros. $-4i$ is also a zero.

Thus the polynomial function is

$f(x) = a_n(x-4i)(x+4i)$.

If we let $a_n = 1$, we obtain

$f(x) = (x-4i)(x+4i) = x^2+16$.

37. Find a polynomial function of lowest degree with rational coefficients that has $-4i$ and 5 as some of its zeros.

$4i$ is also a zero.

Thus the polynomial function is

$f(x) = a_n(x-5)(x+4i)(x-4i)$.

If we let $a_n = 1$, we obtain

$$\begin{aligned} f(x) &= (x-5)[x^2-(4i)^2] \\ &= (x-5)(x^2+16) \\ &= x^3-5x^2+16x-80 \end{aligned}$$

39. Find a polynomial function of lowest degree with rational coefficients that has $1-i$ and $-\sqrt{5}$ as some of its zeros. $1+i$ and $\sqrt{5}$ are also zeros.

Thus the polynomial function is

$f(x) = a_n[x-(1-i)][x-(1+i)](x+\sqrt{5})(x-\sqrt{5})$.

If we let $a_n = 1$, we obtain

$$\begin{aligned} f(x) &= [x-(1-i)][x-(1+i)](x+\sqrt{5})(x-\sqrt{5}) \\ &= [(x-1)+i][(x-1)-i](x+\sqrt{5})(x-\sqrt{5}) \\ &= (x^2-2x+1+1)(x^2-5) \\ &= (x^2-2x+2)(x^2-5) \\ &= x^4-2x^3+2x^2-5x^2+10x-10 \\ &= x^4-2x^3-3x^2+10x-10 \end{aligned}$$

41. Find a polynomial function of lowest degree with rational coefficients that has $\sqrt{5}$ and $-3i$ as some of its zeros.

$-\sqrt{5}$ and $3i$ are also zeros.

Thus the polynomial function is

$f(x) = a_n(x-\sqrt{5})(x+\sqrt{5})(x+3i)(x-3i)$.

If we let $a_n = 1$, we obtain

$$\begin{aligned} f(x) &= (x^2-5)(x^2+9) \\ &= x^4+4x^2-45 \end{aligned}$$

43. $f(x) = x^3+5x^2-2x-10$

Since -5 is a zero of $f(x)$, we have $f(x) = (x+5)\cdot Q(x)$. We use synthetic division to find $Q(x)$.

$$\begin{array}{r|rrrr} -5 & 1 & 5 & -2 & -10 \\ & & -5 & 0 & 10 \\ \hline & 1 & 0 & -2 & 0 \end{array}$$

Then $f(x) = (x+5)(x^2-2)$. To find the other zeros we solve $x^2-2=0$.

$$\begin{aligned} x^2-2 &= 0 \\ x^2 &= 2 \\ x &= \pm\sqrt{2} \end{aligned}$$

The other zeros are $-\sqrt{2}$ and $\sqrt{2}$.

45. If $-i$ is a zero of $f(x) = x^4-5x^3+7x^2-5x+6$, i is also a zero. Thus $x+i$ and $x-i$ are factors of the polynomial. Since $(x+i)(x-i) = x^2+1$, we know that $f(x) = (x^2+1)\cdot Q(x)$. Divide $x^4-5x^3+7x^2-5x+6$ by x^2+1.

$$\begin{array}{r} x^2 - 5x + 6 \\ x^2+1 \overline{\smash{)}\, x^4 - 5x^3 + 7x^2 - 5x + 6} \\ \underline{x^4 \qquad\quad + x^2} \qquad\qquad \\ -5x^3 + 6x^2 - 5x \qquad \\ \underline{-5x^3 \qquad\quad - 5x} \qquad \\ 6x^2 \qquad + 6 \\ \underline{6x^2 \qquad + 6} \\ 0 \end{array}$$

Thus

$$\begin{aligned} x^4-5x^3+7x^2-5x+6 &= (x+i)(x-i)(x^2-5x+6) \\ &= (x+i)(x-i)(x-2)(x-3) \end{aligned}$$

Using the principle of zero products we find the other zeros to be i, 2, and 3.

47. $x^3-6x^2+13x-20=0$

If 4 is a zero, then $x-4$ is a factor. Use synthetic division to find another factor.

$$\begin{array}{r|rrrr} 4 & 1 & -6 & 13 & -20 \\ & & 4 & -8 & 20 \\ \hline & 1 & -2 & 5 & 0 \end{array}$$

$(x-4)(x^2-2x+5) = 0$

$x-4=0$ *or* $x^2-2x+5=0$ Principle of zero products

$x=4$ *or* $x = \dfrac{2\pm\sqrt{4-20}}{2}$ Quadratic formula

$x=4$ *or* $x = \dfrac{2\pm 4i}{2} = 1\pm 2i$

The other zeros are $1+2i$ and $1-2i$.

49. $f(x) = x^5-3x^2+1$

According to the rational zeros theorem, any rational zero of f must be of the form p/q, where p is a factor of the constant term, 1, and q is a factor of the coefficient of x^5, 1.

$\dfrac{\text{Possibilities for } p}{\text{Possibilities for } q} : \dfrac{\pm 1}{\pm 1}$

Possibilities for p/q: 1, -1

51. $f(x) = 2x^4-3x^3-x+8$

According to the rational zeros theorem, any rational zero of f must be of the form p/q, where p is a factor of the constant term, 8, and q is a factor of the coefficient of x^4, 2.

$\dfrac{\text{Possibilities for } p}{\text{Possibilities for } q} : \dfrac{\pm 1, \pm 2, \pm 4, \pm 8}{\pm 1, \pm 2}$

Possibilities for p/q: 1, -1, 2, -2, 4, -4, 8, -8, $\dfrac{1}{2}$, $-\dfrac{1}{2}$

53. $f(x) = 15x^6+47x^2+2$

According to the rational zeros theorem, any rational zero of f must be of the form p/q, where p is a factor of 2 and q is a factor of 15.

$\dfrac{\text{Possibilities for } p}{\text{Possibilities for } q} : \dfrac{\pm 1, \pm 2}{\pm 1, \pm 3, \pm 5, \pm 15}$

Possibilities for p/q: $1, -1, 2, -2, \dfrac{1}{3}, -\dfrac{1}{3}, \dfrac{2}{3}, -\dfrac{2}{3}, \dfrac{1}{5}, -\dfrac{1}{5}, \dfrac{2}{5}, -\dfrac{2}{5}, \dfrac{1}{15}, -\dfrac{1}{15}, \dfrac{2}{15}, -\dfrac{2}{15}$

55. $f(x) = x^3+3x^2-2x-6$

a) $\dfrac{\text{Possibilities for } p}{\text{Possibilities for } q} : \dfrac{\pm 1, \pm 2, \pm 3, \pm 6}{\pm 1}$

Possibilities for p/q: $1, -1, 2, -2, 3, -3, 6, -6$

From the graph of $y = x^3+3x^2-2x-6$, we see that, of the possibilities above, only -3 might be a zero. We use synthetic division to determine whether -3 is indeed a zero.

$$\begin{array}{r|rrrr} -3 & 1 & 3 & -2 & -6 \\ & & -3 & 0 & 6 \\ \hline & 1 & 0 & -2 & 0 \end{array}$$

Then we have $f(x) = (x+3)(x^2-2)$.

We find the other zeros:

$$x^2 - 2 = 0$$
$$x^2 = 2$$
$$x = \pm\sqrt{2}.$$

There is only one rational zero, -3. The other zeros are $\pm\sqrt{2}$. (Note that we could have used factoring by grouping to find this result.)

b) $f(x) = (x+3)(x-\sqrt{2})(x+\sqrt{2})$

57. $f(x) = x^3 - 3x + 2$

a) $\dfrac{\text{Possibilities for } p}{\text{Possibilities for } q} : \dfrac{\pm 1, \pm 2}{\pm 1}$

Possibilities for p/q: $1, -1, 2, -2$

From the graph of $y = x^3 - 3x + 2$, we see that, of the possibilities above, -2 and 1 might be a zeros. We use synthetic division to determine whether -2 is a zero.

$$\begin{array}{r|rrrr} -2 & 1 & 0 & -3 & 2 \\ & & -2 & 4 & -2 \\ \hline & 1 & -2 & 1 & 0 \end{array}$$

Then we have $f(x) = (x+2)(x^2-2x+1) = (x+2)(x-1)^2$.

Now $(x-1)^2 = 0$ for $x = 1$. Thus, the rational zeros are -2 and 1. (The zero 1 has a multiplicity of 2.) These are the only zeros.

b) $f(x) = (x+2)(x-1)^2$

59. $f(x) = x^3 - 5x^2 + 11x + 17$

a) $\dfrac{\text{Possibilities for } p}{\text{Possibilities for } q} : \dfrac{\pm 1, \pm 17}{\pm 1}$

Possibilities for p/q: $1, -1, 17, -17$

From the graph of $y = x^3 - 5x^2 + 11x + 17$, we see that, of the possibilities above, we see that only -1 might be a zero. We use synthetic division to determine whether -1 is indeed a zero.

$$\begin{array}{r|rrrr} -1 & 1 & -5 & 11 & 17 \\ & & -1 & 6 & -17 \\ \hline & 1 & -6 & 17 & 0 \end{array}$$

Then we have $f(x) = (x+1)(x^2 - 6x + 17)$. We use the quadratic formula to find the other zeros.

$$x^2 - 6x + 17 = 0$$
$$x = \frac{-(-6) \pm \sqrt{(-6)^2 - 4 \cdot 1 \cdot 17}}{2 \cdot 1}$$
$$= \frac{6 \pm \sqrt{-32}}{2} = \frac{6 \pm 4\sqrt{2}i}{2}$$
$$= 3 \pm 2\sqrt{2}i$$

The only rational zero is -1. The other zeros are $3 \pm 2\sqrt{2}i$.

b) $f(x) = (x+1)[x - (3 + 2\sqrt{2}i)][x - (3 - 2\sqrt{2}i)]$
$= (x+1)(x - 3 - 2\sqrt{2}i)(x - 3 + 2\sqrt{2}i)$

61. $f(x) = 5x^4 - 4x^3 + 19x^2 - 16x - 4$

a) $\dfrac{\text{Possibilities for } p}{\text{Possibilities for } q} : \dfrac{\pm 1, \pm 2, \pm 4}{\pm 1, \pm 5}$

Possibilities for p/q: $1, -1, 2, -2, 4, -4, \frac{1}{5}, -\frac{1}{5}, \frac{2}{5}, -\frac{2}{5}, \frac{4}{5}, -\frac{4}{5}$

From the graph of $y = 5x^4 - 4x^3 + 19x^2 - 16x - 4$, we see that, of the possibilities above, only $-\frac{2}{5}$, $-\frac{1}{5}$ and 1 might be zeros. We use synthetic division to determine whether 1 is a zero.

$$\begin{array}{r|rrrrr} 1 & 5 & -4 & 19 & -16 & -4 \\ & & 5 & 1 & 20 & 4 \\ \hline & 5 & 1 & 20 & 4 & 0 \end{array}$$

Then we have

$$f(x) = (x-1)(5x^3 + x^2 + 20x + 4)$$
$$= (x-1)[x^2(5x+1) + 4(5x+1)]$$
$$= (x-1)(5x+1)(x^2+4).$$

We find the other zeros:

$$5x + 1 = 0 \quad or \quad x^2 + 4 = 0$$
$$5x = -1 \quad or \quad x^2 = -4$$
$$x = -\frac{1}{5} \quad or \quad x = \pm 2i$$

The rational zeros are $-\frac{1}{5}$ and 1. The other zeros are $\pm 2i$.

b) From part (a) we see that

$$f(x) = (5x+1)(x-1)(x+2i)(x-2i).$$

63. $f(x) = x^4 - 3x^3 - 20x^2 - 24x - 8$

a) $\dfrac{\text{Possibilities for } p}{\text{Possibilities for } q} : \dfrac{\pm 1, \pm 2, \pm 4, \pm 8}{\pm 1}$

Possibilities for p/q: $1, -1, 2, -2, 4, -4, 8, -8$

From the graph of $y = x^4 - 3x^3 - 20x^2 - 24x - 8$, we see that, of the possibilities above, only -2 and -1 might be zeros. We use synthetic division to determine if -2 is a zero.

$$\begin{array}{r|rrrrr} -2 & 1 & -3 & -20 & -24 & -8 \\ & & -2 & 10 & 20 & 8 \\ \hline & 1 & -5 & -10 & -4 & 0 \end{array}$$

We see that -2 is a zero. Now we determine whether -1 is a zero.

$$\begin{array}{r|rrrr} -1 & 1 & -5 & -10 & -4 \\ & & -1 & 6 & 4 \\ \hline & 1 & -6 & -4 & 0 \end{array}$$

Then we have $f(x) = (x+2)(x+1)(x^2 - 6x - 4)$.

Use the quadratic formula to find the other zeros.

$$x^2 - 6x - 4 = 0$$
$$x = \frac{-(-6) \pm \sqrt{(-6)^2 - 4 \cdot 1 \cdot (-4)}}{2 \cdot 1}$$
$$= \frac{6 \pm \sqrt{52}}{2} = \frac{6 \pm 2\sqrt{13}}{2}$$
$$= 3 \pm \sqrt{13}$$

The rational zeros are -2 and -1. The other zeros are $3 \pm \sqrt{13}$.

b) $f(x) = (x+2)(x+1)[x-(3+\sqrt{13})][x-(3-\sqrt{13})]$
$= (x+2)(x+1)(x-3-\sqrt{13})(x-3+\sqrt{13})$

65. $f(x) = x^3 - 4x^2 + 2x + 4$

a) $\dfrac{\text{Possibilities for } p}{\text{Possibilities for } q} : \dfrac{\pm 1, \pm 2, \pm 4}{\pm 1}$

Possibilities for p/q: $1, -1, 2, -2, 4, -4$

From the graph of $y = x^3 - 4x^2 + 2x + 4$, we see that, of the possibilities above, only -1, 1, and 2 might be zeros. Synthetic division shows that neither -1 nor 1 is a zero. Try 2.

$$\begin{array}{r|rrrr} 2 & 1 & -4 & 2 & 4 \\ & & 2 & -4 & -4 \\ \hline & 1 & -2 & -2 & 0 \end{array}$$

Then we have $f(x) = (x-2)(x^2 - 2x - 2)$. Use the quadratic formula to find the other zeros.

$x^2 - 2x - 2 = 0$

$$x = \frac{-(-2) \pm \sqrt{(-2)^2 - 4 \cdot 1 \cdot (-2)}}{2 \cdot 1}$$
$$= \frac{2 \pm \sqrt{12}}{2} = \frac{2 \pm 2\sqrt{3}}{2}$$
$$= 1 \pm \sqrt{3}$$

The only rational zero is 2. The other zeros are $1 \pm \sqrt{3}$.

b) $f(x) = (x-2)[x - (1+\sqrt{3})][x - (1-\sqrt{3})]$
$= (x-2)(x-1-\sqrt{3})(x-1+\sqrt{3})$

67. $f(x) = x^3 + 8$

a) $\dfrac{\text{Possibilities for } p}{\text{Possibilities for } q} : \dfrac{\pm 1, \pm 2, \pm 4, \pm 8}{\pm 1}$

Possibilities for p/q: $1, -1, 2, -2, 4, -4, 8, -8$

From the graph of $y = x^3 + 8$, we see that, of the possibilities above, only -2 might be a zero. We use synthetic division to see if it is.

$$\begin{array}{r|rrrr} -2 & 1 & 0 & 0 & 8 \\ & & -2 & 4 & -8 \\ \hline & 1 & -2 & 4 & 0 \end{array}$$

We have $f(x) = (x+2)(x^2 - 2x + 4)$. Use the quadratic formula to find the other zeros.

$x^2 - 2x + 4 = 0$

$$x = \frac{-(-2) \pm \sqrt{(-2)^2 - 4 \cdot 1 \cdot 4}}{2 \cdot 1}$$
$$= \frac{2 \pm \sqrt{-12}}{2} = \frac{2 \pm 2\sqrt{3}i}{2}$$
$$= 1 \pm \sqrt{3}i$$

The only rational zero is -2. The other zeros are $1 \pm \sqrt{3}i$.

b) $f(x) = (x+2)[x - (1+\sqrt{3}i)][x - (1-\sqrt{3}i)]$
$= (x+2)(x-1-\sqrt{3}i)(x-1+\sqrt{3}i)$

69. $f(x) = \dfrac{1}{3}x^3 - \dfrac{1}{2}x^2 - \dfrac{1}{6}x + \dfrac{1}{6}$
$= \dfrac{1}{6}(2x^3 - 3x^2 - x + 1)$

a) The second form of the equation is equivalent to the first and has the advantage of having integer coefficients. Thus, we can use the rational zeros theorem for $g(x) = 2x^3 - 3x^2 - x + 1$. The zeros of $g(x)$ are the same as the zeros of $f(x)$. We find the zeros of $g(x)$.

$\dfrac{\text{Possibilities for } p}{\text{Possibilities for } q} : \dfrac{\pm 1}{\pm 1, \pm 2}$

Possibilities for p/q: $1, -1, \dfrac{1}{2}, -\dfrac{1}{2}$

From the graph of $y = 2x^3 - 3x^2 - x + 1$, we see that, of the possibilities above, only $-\dfrac{1}{2}$ and $\dfrac{1}{2}$ might be zeros. Synthetic division shows that $-\dfrac{1}{2}$ is not a zero. Try $\dfrac{1}{2}$.

$$\begin{array}{r|rrrr} \frac{1}{2} & 2 & -3 & -1 & 1 \\ & & 1 & -1 & -1 \\ \hline & 2 & -2 & -2 & 0 \end{array}$$

We have $g(x) = \left(x - \dfrac{1}{2}\right)(2x^2 - 2x - 2) = \left(x - \dfrac{1}{2}\right)(2)(x^2 - x - 1)$. Use the quadratic formula to find the other zeros.

$x^2 - x - 1 = 0$

$$x = \frac{-(-1) \pm \sqrt{(-1)^2 - 4 \cdot 1 \cdot (-1)}}{2 \cdot 1}$$
$$= \frac{1 \pm \sqrt{5}}{2}$$

The only rational zero is $\dfrac{1}{2}$. The other zeros are $\dfrac{1 \pm \sqrt{5}}{2}$.

b) $f(x) = \dfrac{1}{6}g(x)$
$= \dfrac{1}{6}\left(x - \dfrac{1}{2}\right)(2)\left[x - \dfrac{1+\sqrt{5}}{2}\right]\left[x - \dfrac{1-\sqrt{5}}{2}\right]$
$= \dfrac{1}{3}\left(x - \dfrac{1}{2}\right)\left(x - \dfrac{1+\sqrt{5}}{2}\right)\left(x - \dfrac{1-\sqrt{5}}{2}\right)$

71. $f(x) = x^4 + 32$

According to the rational zeros theorem, the possible rational zeros are $\pm 1, \pm 2, \pm 4, \pm 8, \pm 16$, and ± 32. The graph of $y = x^4 + 32$ has no x-intercepts, so $f(x)$ has no real-number zeros and hence no rational zeros.

73. $f(x) = x^3 - x^2 - 4x + 3$

According to the rational zeros theorem, the possible rational zeros are ± 1 and ± 3. The graph of $y = x^3 - x^2 - 4x + 3$ shows that none of these is a zero. Thus, there are no rational zeros.

75. $f(x) = x^4 + 2x^3 + 2x^2 - 4x - 8$

According to the rational zeros theorem, the possible rational zeros are ± 1, ± 2, ± 4, and ± 8. The graph of $y = x^4 + 2x^3 + 2x^2 - 4x - 8$ shows that none of the possibilities is a zero. Thus, there are no rational zeros.

77. $f(x) = x^5 - 5x^4 + 5x^3 + 15x^2 - 36x + 20$

According to the rational zeros theorem, the possible rational zeros are ± 1, ± 2, ± 4, ± 5, ± 10, and ± 20. The graph of $y = x^5 - 5x^4 + 5x^3 + 15x^2 - 36x + 20$ shows that, of these possibilities, only -2, 1 and 2 might be zeros. We try -2.

$$\begin{array}{r|rrrrrr} -2 & 1 & -5 & 5 & 15 & -36 & 20 \\ & & -2 & 14 & -38 & 46 & -20 \\ \hline & 1 & -7 & 19 & -23 & 10 & 0 \end{array}$$

Thus, -2 is a zero. Now try 1.

$$\begin{array}{r|rrrrr} 1 & 1 & -7 & 19 & -23 & 10 \\ & & 1 & -6 & 13 & 10 \\ \hline & 1 & -6 & 13 & -10 & 0 \end{array}$$

1 is also a zero. Try 2.

$$\begin{array}{r|rrrr} 2 & 1 & -6 & 13 & -10 \\ & & 2 & -8 & 10 \\ \hline & 1 & -4 & 5 & 0 \end{array}$$

2 is also a zero.

We have $f(x) = (x+2)(x-1)(x-2)(x^2 - 4x + 5)$. The discriminant of $x^2 - 4x + 5$ is $(-4)^2 - 4 \cdot 1 \cdot 5$, or $4 < 0$, so $x^2 - 4x + 5$ has two nonreal zeros. Thus, the rational zeros are -2, 1, and 2.

79. $f(x) = 3x^5 - 2x^2 + x - 1$

The number of variations in sign in $f(x)$ is 3. Then the number of positive real zeros is either 3 or less than 3 by 2, 4, 6, and so on. Thus, the number of positive real zeros is 3 or 1.

$$\begin{aligned} f(-x) &= 3(-x)^5 - 2(-x)^2 + (-x) - 1 \\ &= -3x^5 - 2x^2 - x - 1 \end{aligned}$$

There are no variations in sign in $f(-x)$, so there are 0 negative real zeros.

81. $h(x) = 6x^7 + 2x^2 + 5x + 4$

There are no variations in sign in $h(x)$, so there are 0 positive real zeros.

$$\begin{aligned} h(-x) &= 6(-x)^7 + 2(-x)^2 + 5(-x) + 4 \\ &= -6x^7 + 2x^2 - 5x + 4 \end{aligned}$$

The number of variations in sign in $h(-x)$ is 3. Thus, there are 3 or 1 negative real zeros.

83. $F(p) = 3p^{18} + 2p^4 - 5p^2 + p + 3$

There are 2 variations in sign in $F(p)$, so there are 2 or 0 positive real zeros.

$$\begin{aligned} F(-p) &= 3(-p)^{18} + 2(-p)^4 - 5(-p)^2 + (-p) + 3 \\ &= 3p^{18} + 2p^4 - 5p^2 - p + 3 \end{aligned}$$

There are 2 variations in sign in $F(-p)$, so there are 2 or 0 negative real zeros.

85. $C(x) = 7x^6 + 3x^4 - x - 10$

There is 1 variation in sign in $C(x)$, so there is 1 positive real zero.

$$\begin{aligned} C(-x) &= 7(-x)^6 + 3(-x)^4 - (-x) - 10 \\ &= 7x^6 + 3x^4 + x - 10 \end{aligned}$$

There is 1 variation in sign in $C(-x)$, so there is 1 negative real zero.

87. $h(t) = -4t^5 - t^3 + 2t^2 + 1$

There is 1 variation in sign in $h(t)$, so there is 1 positive real zero.

$$\begin{aligned} h(-t) &= -4(-t)^5 - (-t)^3 + 2(-t)^2 + 1 \\ &= 4t^5 + t^3 + 2t^2 + 1 \end{aligned}$$

There are no variations in sign in $h(-t)$, so there are 0 negative real zeros.

89. $f(y) = y^4 + 13y^3 - y + 5$

There are 2 variations in sign in $f(y)$, so there are 2 or 0 positive real zeros.

$$\begin{aligned} f(-y) &= (-y)^4 + 13(-y)^3 - (-y) + 5 \\ &= y^4 - 13y^3 + y + 5 \end{aligned}$$

There are 2 variations in sign in $f(-y)$, so there are 2 or 0 negative real zeros.

91. $r(x) = x^4 - 6x^2 + 20x - 24$

There are 3 variations in sign in $r(x)$, so there are 3 or 1 positive real zeros.

$$\begin{aligned} r(-x) &= (-x)^4 - 6(-x)^2 + 20(-x) - 24 \\ &= x^4 - 6x^2 - 20x - 24 \end{aligned}$$

There is 1 variation in sign in $r(-x)$, so there is 1 negative real zero.

93. $R(x) = 3x^5 - 5x^3 - 4x$

There is 1 variation in sign in $R(x)$, so there is 1 positive real zero.

$$\begin{aligned} R(-x) &= 3(-x)^5 - 5(-x)^3 - 4(-x) \\ &= -3x^5 + 5x^3 + 4x \end{aligned}$$

There is 1 variation in sign in $R(-x)$, so there is 1 negative real zero.

95. $f(x) = 4x^3 + x^2 - 8x - 2$

1. The leasing term is $4x^3$. The degree, 3, is odd and the leading coefficient, 4, is positive so as $x \to \infty$, $f(x) \to \infty$ and $x \to -\infty$, $f(x) \to -\infty$.
2. We find the rational zeros p/q of $f(x)$.

   $$\frac{\text{Possibilities for } p}{\text{Possibilities for } q} : \frac{\pm 1, \pm 2}{\pm 1, \pm 2, \pm 4}$$

   Possibilities for p/q: $1, -1, 2, -2, \frac{1}{2}, -\frac{1}{2}, \frac{1}{4}, -\frac{1}{4}$

   Synthetic division shows that $-\frac{1}{4}$ is a zero.

   $$\begin{array}{r|rrrr} -\frac{1}{4} & 4 & 1 & -8 & -2 \\ & & -1 & 0 & 2 \\ \hline & 4 & 0 & -8 & 0 \end{array}$$

We have $f(x) = \left(x + \frac{1}{4}\right)(4x^2 - 8) = 4\left(x + \frac{1}{4}\right)(x^2 - 2)$. Solving $x^2 - 2 = 0$ we get $x = \pm\sqrt{2}$. Thus the zeros of the function are $-\frac{1}{4}$, $-\sqrt{2}$, and $\sqrt{2}$ so the x-intercepts of the graph are $\left(-\frac{1}{4}, 0\right)$, $(-\sqrt{2}, 0)$, and $(\sqrt{2}, 0)$.

3. The zeros divide the x-axis into 4 intervals, $(-\infty, -\sqrt{2})$, $\left(-\sqrt{2}, -\frac{1}{4}\right)$, $\left(-\frac{1}{4}, \sqrt{2}\right)$, and $(\sqrt{2}, \infty)$. We choose a value for x from each interval and find $f(x)$. This tells us the sign of $f(x)$ for all values of x in that interval.
   In $(-\infty, -\sqrt{2})$, test -2:
   $f(-2) = 4(-2)^3 + (-2)^2 - 8(-2) - 2 = -14 < 0$
   In $\left(-\sqrt{2}, -\frac{1}{4}\right)$, test -1:
   $f(-1) = 4(-1)^3 + (-1)^2 - 8(-1) - 2 = 3 > 0$
   In $\left(-\frac{1}{4}, \sqrt{2}\right)$, test 0:
   $f(0) = 4 \cdot 0^3 + 0^2 - 8 \cdot 0 - 2 = -2 < 0$
   In $(\sqrt{2}, \infty)$, test 2:
   $f(2) = 4 \cdot 2^3 + 2^2 - 8 \cdot 2 - 2 = 18 > 0$
   Thus the graph lies below the x-axis on $(-\infty, -\sqrt{2})$ and on $\left(-\frac{1}{4}, \sqrt{2}\right)$. It lies above the x-axis on $\left(-\sqrt{2}, -\frac{1}{4}\right)$ and on $(\sqrt{2}, \infty)$. We also know the points $(-2, -14)$, $(-1, 3)$, $(0, -2)$, and $(2, 18)$ are on the graph.

4. From Step 3 we see that $f(0) = -2$ so the y-intercept is $(0, -2)$.

5. We find additional points on the graph and then draw the graph.

x	$f(x)$
−1.5	−1.25
−0.5	1.75
1	−5
1.5	1.75

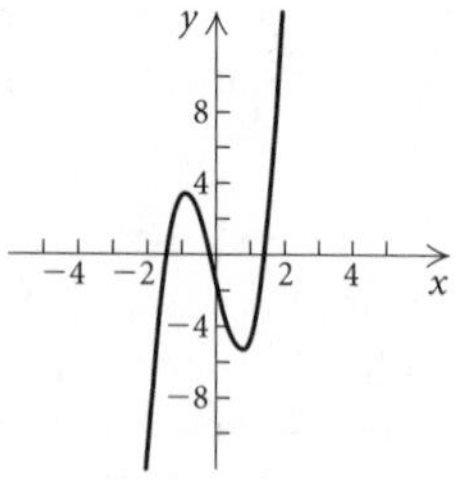

$f(x) = 4x^3 + x^2 - 8x - 2$

6. Checking the graph as described on page 254 in the text, we see that it appears to be correct.

97. $f(x) = 2x^4 - 3x^3 - 2x^2 + 3x$

1. The leading term is $2x^4$. The degree, 4, is even and the leading coefficient, 2, is positive so as $x \to \infty$, $f(x) \to \infty$ and as $x \to -\infty$, $f(x) \to \infty$.

2. We find the rational zeros p/q of $f(x)$. First note that $f(x) = x(2x^3 - 3x^2 - 2x + 3)$, so x is a zero. Now consider $g(x) = 2x^3 - 3x^2 - 2x + 3$.
   $\dfrac{\text{Possibilities for } p}{\text{Possibilities for } q} : \dfrac{\pm 1, \pm 3}{\pm 1, \pm 2}$
   Possibilities for p/q: $1, -1, 3, -3, \frac{1}{2}, -\frac{1}{2}, \frac{3}{2}, -\frac{3}{2}$
   We try 1.
   $$\begin{array}{r|rrrr} 1 & 2 & -3 & -2 & 3 \\ & & 2 & -1 & -3 \\ \hline & 2 & -1 & -3 & 0 \end{array}$$
   Then $f(x) = x(x-1)(2x^2 - x - 3)$. Using the principle of zero products to solve $2x^2 - x - 3 = 0$, we get $x = \frac{3}{2}$ or $x = -1$.
   Thus the zeros of the function are 0, 1, $\frac{3}{2}$, and -1 so the x-intercepts of the graph are $(0, 0)$, $(1, 0)$, $\left(\frac{3}{2}, 0\right)$, and $(-1, 0)$.

3. The zeros divide the x-axis into 5 intervals, $(-\infty, -1)$, $(-1, 0)$, $(0, 1)$, $\left(1, \frac{3}{2}\right)$, and $\left(\frac{3}{2}, \infty\right)$. We choose a value for x from each interval and find $f(x)$. This tells us the sign of $f(x)$ for all values of x in that interval.
   In $(-\infty, -1)$, test -2:
   $f(-2) = 2(-2)^4 - 3(-2)^3 - 2(-2)^2 + 3(2) = 42 > 0$
   In $(-1, 0)$, test -0.5:
   $f(-0.5) = 2(-0.5)^4 - 3(-0.5)^3 - 2(-0.5)^2 + 3(-0.5) = -1.5 < 0$
   In $(0, 1)$, test 0.5:
   $f(0.5) = 2(0.5)^4 - 3(0.5)^3 - 2(0.5)^2 + 3(0.5) = 0.75 > 0$
   In $\left(1, \frac{3}{2}\right)$, test 1.25:
   $f(1.25) = 2(1.25)^4 - 3(1.25)^3 - 2(1.25)^2 + 3(1.25) = -0.3515625 < 0$
   In $\left(\frac{3}{2}, \infty\right)$, test 2:
   $f(2) = 2 \cdot 2^4 - 3 \cdot 2^3 - 2 \cdot 2^2 + 3 \cdot 2 = 6 > 0$
   Thus the graph lies above the x-axis on $(-\infty, -1)$, on $(0, 1)$, and on $\left(\frac{3}{2}, \infty\right)$. It lies below the x-axis on $(-1, 0)$ and on $\left(1, \frac{3}{2}\right)$. We also know the points $(-2, 42)$, $(-0.5, -1.5)$, $(0.5, 0.75)$, $(1.25, -0.3515625)$, and $(2, 6)$ are on the graph.

4. From Step 2 we know that $f(0) = 0$ so the y-intercept is $(0, 0)$.

5. We find additional points on the graph and then draw the graph.

x	$f(x)$
-1.5	11.25
2.5	26.25
3	72

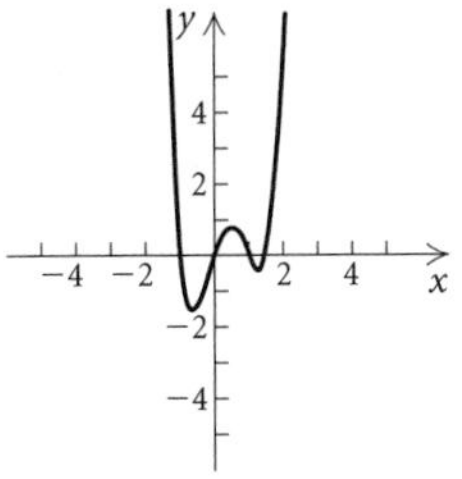

$f(x) = 2x^4 - 3x^3 - 2x^2 + 3x$

6. Checking the graph as described on page 254 in the text, we see that it appears to be correct.

99. Left to the student

101. Discussion and Writing

103. $f(x) = x^2 - 8x + 10$

a) $-\frac{b}{2a} = -\frac{-8}{2 \cdot 1} = -(-4) = 4$

$f(4) = 4^2 - 8 \cdot 4 + 10 = -6$

The vertex is $(4, -6)$.

b) The axis of symmetry is $x = 4$.

c) Since the coefficient of x^2 is positive, there is a minimum function value. It is the second coordinate of the vertex, -6. It occurs when $x = 4$.

105.
$$-\frac{4}{5}x + 8 = 0$$
$$-\frac{4}{5}x = -8 \quad \text{Subtracting 8}$$
$$-\frac{5}{4}\left(-\frac{4}{5}x\right) = -\frac{5}{4}(-8) \quad \text{Multiplying by } -\frac{5}{4}$$
$$x = 10$$

The zero is 10.

107. $g(x) = -x^3 - 2x^2$

The degree is 3, so the function is cubic.

Leading term: $-x^3$; leading coefficient: -1

Since the degree is odd and the leading coefficient is negative, as $x \to \infty$, $g(x) \to -\infty$ and as $x \to -\infty$, $g(x) \to \infty$.

109. $f(x) = -\frac{4}{9}$

The degree is 0, so this is a constant function.

Leading term: $-\frac{4}{9}$; leading coefficient: $-\frac{4}{9}$;

for all x, $f(x) = -\frac{4}{9}$

111. $g(x) = x^4 - 2x^3 + x^2 - x + 2$

The degree is 4, so the function is quartic.

Leading term: x^4; leading coefficient: 1

Since the degree is even and the leading coefficient is positive, as $x \to \infty$, $g(x) \to \infty$ and as $x \to -\infty$, $g(x) \to \infty$.

113.
$$(x^4 - y^4) \div (x - y)$$
$$= (x^4 + 0x^3 + 0x^2 + 0x - y^4) \div (x - y)$$

$$\begin{array}{r|rrrrr} y & 1 & 0 & 0 & 0 & -y^4 \\ & & y & y^2 & y^3 & y^4 \\ \hline & 1 & y & y^2 & y^3 & 0 \end{array}$$

The quotient is $x^3 + x^2y + xy^2 + y^3$. The remainder is 0.

115. $f(x) = 2x^3 - 5x^2 - 4x + 3$

a) $2x^3 - 5x^2 - 4x + 3 = 0$

$\frac{\text{Possibilities for } p}{\text{Possibilities for } q} : \frac{\pm 1, \pm 3}{\pm 1, \pm 2}$

Possibilities for p/q: $1, -1, 3, -3, \frac{1}{2}, -\frac{1}{2}, \frac{3}{2}, -\frac{3}{2}$

The first possibility that is a solution of $f(x) = 0$ is -1:

$$\begin{array}{r|rrrr} -1 & 2 & -5 & -4 & 3 \\ & & -2 & 7 & -3 \\ \hline & 2 & -7 & 3 & 0 \end{array}$$

Thus, -1 is a solution.

Then we have:

$(x + 1)(2x^2 - 7x + 3) = 0$

$(x + 1)(2x - 1)(x - 3) = 0$

The other solutions are $\frac{1}{2}$ and 3.

b) The graph of $y = f(x - 1)$ is the graph of $y = f(x)$ shifted 1 unit right. Thus, we add 1 to each solution of $f(x) = 0$ to find the solutions of $f(x - 1) = 0$. The solutions are $-1 + 1$, or 0; $\frac{1}{2} + 1$, or $\frac{3}{2}$; and $3 + 1$, or 4.

c) The graph of $y = f(x + 2)$ is the graph of $y = f(x)$ shifted 2 units left. Thus, we subtract 2 from each solution of $f(x) = 0$ to find the solutions of $f(x + 2) = 0$. The solutions are $-1 - 2$, or -3; $\frac{1}{2} - 2$, or $-\frac{3}{2}$; and $3 - 2$, or 1.

d) The graph of $y = f(2x)$ is a horizontal shrinking of the graph of $y = f(x)$ by a factor of 2. We divide each solution of $f(x) = 0$ by 2 to find the solutions of $f(2x) = 0$. The solutions are $\frac{-1}{2}$ or $-\frac{1}{2}$; $\frac{1/2}{2}$, or $\frac{1}{4}$; and $\frac{3}{2}$.

117. $P(x) = 2x^5 - 33x^4 - 84x^3 + 2203x^2 - 3348x - 10,080$

a) $2x^5 - 33x^4 - 84x^3 + 2203x^2 - 3348x - 10,080 = 0$

Trying some of the many possibilities for p/q, we find that 4 is a zero.

$$\begin{array}{r|rrrrrr} 4 & 2 & -33 & -84 & 2203 & -3348 & -10,080 \\ & & 8 & -100 & -736 & 5868 & 10,080 \\ \hline & 2 & -25 & -184 & 1467 & 2520 & 0 \end{array}$$

Then we have:

$(x - 4)(2x^4 - 25x^3 - 184x^2 + 1467x + 2520) = 0$

We now use the fourth degree polynomial above to find another zero. Synthetic division shows that 4 is not a double zero, but 7 is a zero.

$$\begin{array}{r|rrrrr} 7 & 2 & -25 & -184 & 1467 & 2520 \\ & & 14 & -77 & -1827 & -2520 \\ \hline & 2 & -11 & -261 & -360 & 0 \end{array}$$

Now we have:

$(x-4)(x-7)(2x^3-11x^2-261x-360)=0$

Use the third degree polynomial above to find a third zero. Synthetic division shows that 7 is not a double zero, but 15 is a zero.

$$\begin{array}{r|rrrr} 15 & 2 & -11 & -261 & -360 \\ & & 30 & 285 & 360 \\ \hline & 2 & 19 & 24 & 0 \end{array}$$

We have:

$$\begin{aligned} P(x) &= (x-4)(x-7)(x-15)(2x^2+19x+24) \\ &= (x-4)(x-7)(x-15)(2x+3)(x+8) \end{aligned}$$

The rational zeros are 4, 7, 15, $-\frac{3}{2}$, and -8.

Exercise Set 3.4

1. Graph (d) is the graph of $f(x)=\dfrac{8}{x^2-4}$.

$x^2-4=0$ when $x=\pm 2$, so $x=-2$ and $x=2$ are vertical asymptotes.

The x-axis, $y=0$, is the horizontal asymptote because the degree of the numerator is less than the degree of the denominator.

There is no oblique asymptote.

3. Graph (e) is the graph of $f(x)=\dfrac{8x}{x^2-4}$.

As in Exercise 1, $x=-2$ and $x=2$ are vertical asymptotes.

The x-axis, $y=0$, is the horizontal asymptote because the degree of the numerator is less than the degree of the denominator.

There is no oblique asymptote.

5. Graph (c) is the graph of $f(x)=\dfrac{8x^3}{x^2-4}$.

As in Exercise 1, $x=-2$ and $x=2$ are vertical asymptotes.

The degree of the numerator is greater than the degree of the denominator, so there is no horizontal asymptote but there is a vertical asymptote. To find it we first divide to find an equivalent expression.

$$\begin{array}{r|l} & 8x \\ \hline x^2-4 & 8x^3 \\ & 8x^3-32x \\ \hline & \quad 32x \end{array}$$

$$\frac{8x^3}{x^2-4}=8x+\frac{32x}{x^2-4}$$

Now we multiply by 1, using $(1/x^2)/(1/x^2)$.

$$\frac{32x}{x^2-4}\cdot\frac{\frac{1}{x^2}}{\frac{1}{x^2}}=\frac{\frac{32}{x}}{1-\frac{4}{x^2}}$$

As $|x|$ becomes very large, each expression with x in the denominator tends toward zero.

Then, as $|x|\to\infty$, we have

$$\frac{\frac{32}{x}}{1-\frac{4}{x^2}}\to\frac{0}{1-0},\text{ or }0.$$

Thus, as $|x|$ becomes very large, the graph of $f(x)$ gets very close to the graph of $y=8x$, so $y=8x$ is the oblique asymptote.

7. $g(x)=\dfrac{1}{x^2}$

The zero of the denominator is 0, so the vertical asymptote is $x=0$.

9. $h(x)=\dfrac{x+7}{2-x}$

$2-x=0$ when $x=2$, so the vertical asymptote is $x=2$.

11. $f(x)=\dfrac{3-x}{(x-4)(x+6)}$

The zeros of the denominator are 4 and -6, so the vertical asymptotes are $x=4$ and $x=-6$.

13. $g(x)=\dfrac{x^2}{2x^2-x-3}=\dfrac{x^2}{(2x-3)(x+1)}$

The zeros of the denominator are $\frac{3}{2}$ and -1, so the vertical asymptotes are $x=\frac{3}{2}$ and $x=-1$.

15. $f(x)=\dfrac{3x^2+5}{4x^2-3}$

The numerator and denominator have the same degree and the ratio of the leading coefficients is $\frac{3}{4}$, so $y=\frac{3}{4}$ is the horizontal asymptote.

17. $h(x)=\dfrac{x^2-4}{2x^4+3}$

The degree of the numerator is less than the degree of the denominator, so $y=0$ is the horizontal asymptote.

19. $g(x)=\dfrac{x^3-2x^2+x-1}{x^2-16}$

The degree of the numerator is greater than the degree of the denominator, so there is no horizontal asymptote.

21. $g(x)=\dfrac{x^2+4x-1}{x+3}$

$$\begin{array}{r|l} & x+1 \\ \hline x+3 & x^2+4x-1 \\ & x^2+3x \\ \hline & \quad\;\; x-1 \\ & \quad\;\; x+3 \\ \hline & \qquad\; -4 \end{array}$$

Then $g(x)=x+1+\dfrac{-4}{x+3}$. The oblique asymptote is $y=x+1$.

23. $h(x) = \dfrac{x^4 - 2}{x^3 + 1}$

$$\begin{array}{r|l} & x \\ x^3+1 & x^4+0x^3+0x^2+0x \\ & x^4 \qquad\qquad\quad +x \\ \hline & \qquad\qquad\qquad -x \end{array}$$

Then $h(x) = x + \dfrac{-x}{x^3+1}$. The oblique asymptote is $y = x$.

25. $f(x) = \dfrac{x^3 - x^2 + x - 4}{x^2 + 2x - 1}$

$$\begin{array}{r|l} & x\ -\ 3 \\ x^2+2x-1 & x^3 - x^2 + x - 4 \\ & x^3 + 2x^2 - x \\ \hline & -3x^2 + 2x - 4 \\ & -3x^2 - 6x + 3 \\ \hline & \qquad\quad 8x - 7 \end{array}$$

Then $f(x) = x - 3 + \dfrac{8x - 7}{x^2 + 2x - 1}$. The oblique asymptote is $y = x - 3$.

27. $f(x) = \dfrac{1}{x}$

1. 0 is the zero of the denominator, so the domain excludes 0. It is $(-\infty, 0) \cup (0, \infty)$. The line $x = 0$, or the y-axis, is the vertical asymptote.
2. Because the degree of the numerator is less than the degree of the denominator, the x-axis, or $y = 0$, is the horizontal asymptote. There are no oblique asymptotes.
3. The numerator has no zeros, so there is no x-intercept.
4. Since 0 is not in the domain of the function, there is no y-intercept.
5. Find other function values to determine the shape of the graph and then draw it.

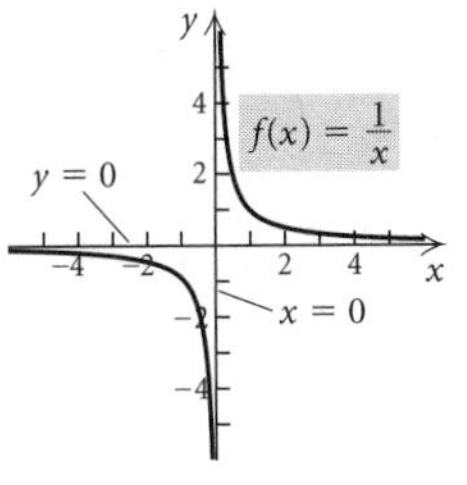

29. $h(x) = -\dfrac{4}{x^2}$

1. 0 is the zero of the denominator, so the domain excludes 0. It is $(-\infty, 0) \cup (0, \infty)$. The line $x = 0$, or the y-axis, is the vertical asymptote.
2. Because the degree of the numerator is less than the degree of the denominator, the x-axis, or $y = 0$, is the horizontal asymptote. There is no oblique asymptote.
3. The numerator has no zeros, so there is no x-intercept.
4. Since 0 is not in the domain of the function, there is no y-intercept.
5. Find other function values to determine the shape of the graph and then draw it.

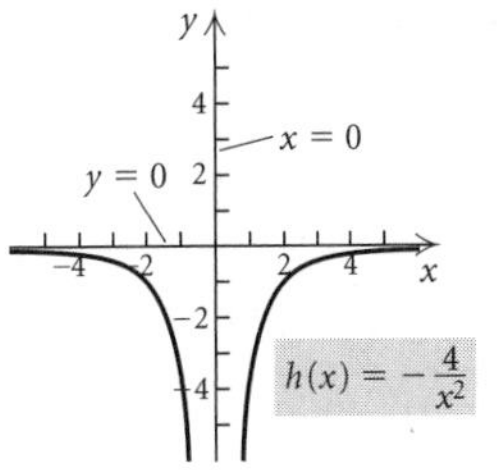

31. $g(x) = \dfrac{x^2 - 4x + 3}{x + 1}$

1. The denominator, $x + 1$, is 0 when $x = -1$, so the domain excludes -1. It is $(-\infty, -1) \cup (-1, \infty)$. The line $x = -1$ is the vertical asymptote.
2. The degree of the numerator is 1 greater than the degree of the denominator, so we divide to find the oblique asymptote.

$$\begin{array}{r|l} & x\ -\ 5 \\ x+1 & x^2 - 4x + 3 \\ & x^2 + x \\ \hline & \quad -5x + 3 \\ & \quad -5x - 5 \\ \hline & \qquad\quad 8 \end{array}$$

The oblique asymptote is $y = x - 5$. There is no horizontal asymptote.

3. $x^2 - 4x + 3 = (x - 1)(x - 3)$, so the zeros of the numerator are 1 and 3. Thus the x-intercepts are $(1, 0)$ and $(3, 0)$.
4. $g(0) = \dfrac{0^2 - 4 \cdot 0 + 3}{0 + 1} = 3$, so the y-intercept is $(0, 3)$.
5. Find other function values to determine the shape of the graph and then draw it.

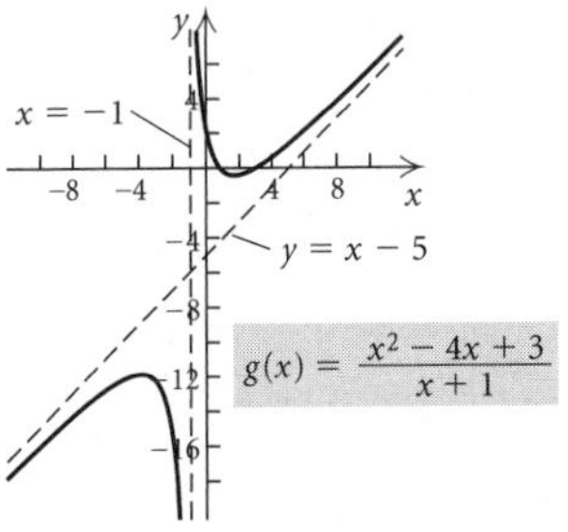

33. $f(x) = \dfrac{1}{x + 3}$

1. -3 is the zero of the denominator, so the domain excludes -3. It is $(-\infty, -3) \cup (-3, \infty)$. The line $x = -3$ is the vertical asymptote.
2. Because the degree of the numerator is less than the degree of the denominator, the x-axis, or $y = 0$, is the horizontal asymptote. There is no oblique asymptote.

3. The numerator has no zeros, so there is no x-intercept.

4. $f(0) = \dfrac{1}{0+3} = \dfrac{1}{3}$, so $\left(0, \dfrac{1}{3}\right)$ is the y-intercept.

5. Find other function values to determine the shape of the graph and then draw it.

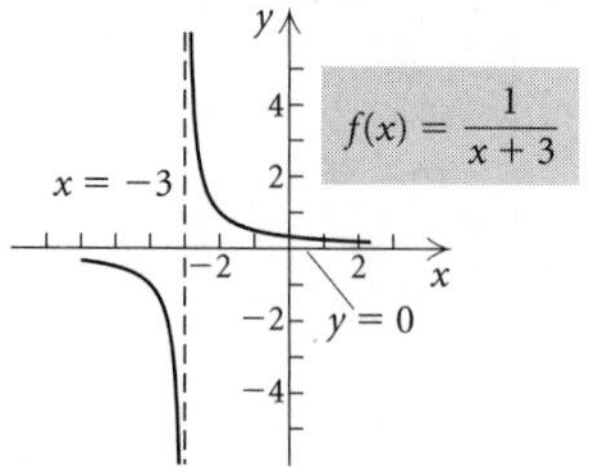

35. $f(x) = \dfrac{-2}{x-5}$

1. 5 is the zero of the denominator, so the domain excludes 5. It is $(-\infty, 5) \cup (5, \infty)$. The line $x = 5$ is the vertical asymptote.

2. Because the degree of the numerator is less than the degree of the denominator, the x-axis, or $y = 0$, is the horizontal asymptote. There is no oblique asymptote.

3. The numerator has no zeros, so there is no x-intercept.

4. $f(0) = \dfrac{-2}{0-5} = \dfrac{2}{5}$, so $\left(0, \dfrac{2}{5}\right)$ is the y-intercept.

5. Find other function values to determine the shape of the graph and then draw it.

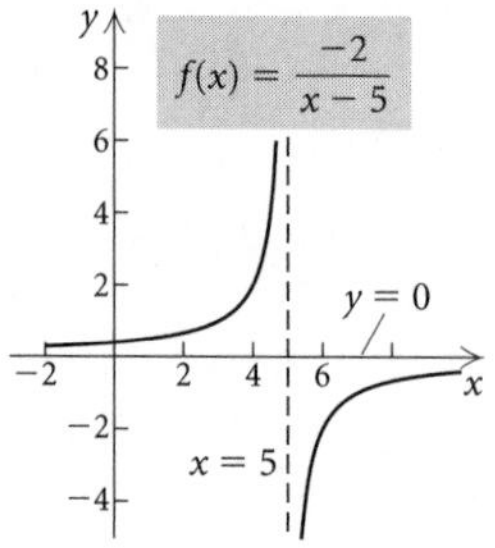

37. $f(x) = \dfrac{2x+1}{x}$

1. 0 is the zero of the denominator, so the domain excludes 0. It is $(-\infty, 0) \cup (0, \infty)$. The line $x = 0$, or the y-axis, is the vertical asymptote.

2. The numerator and denominator have the same degree, so the horizontal asymptote is determined by the ratio of the leading coefficients, $2/1$, or 2. Thus, $y = 2$ is the horizontal asymptote. There is no oblique asymptote.

3. The zero of the numerator is the solution of $2x+1 = 0$, or $-\dfrac{1}{2}$. The x-intercept is $\left(-\dfrac{1}{2}, 0\right)$.

4. Since 0 is not in the domain of the function, there is no y-intercept.

5. Find other function values to determine the shape of the graph and then draw it.

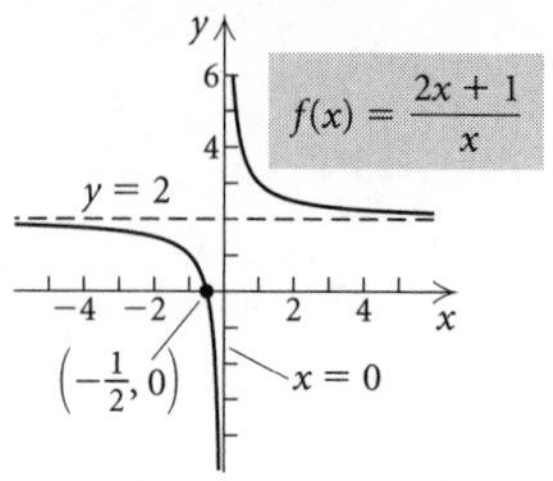

39. $f(x) = \dfrac{1}{(x-2)^2}$

1. 2 is the zero of the denominator, so the domain excludes 2. It is $(-\infty, 2) \cup (2, \infty)$. The line $x = 2$ is the vertical asymptote.

2. Because the degree of the numerator is less than the degree of the denominator, the x-axis, or $y = 0$, is the horizontal asymptote. There is no oblique asymptote.

3. The numerator has no zeros, so there is no x-intercept.

4. $f(0) = \dfrac{1}{(0-2)^2} = \dfrac{1}{4}$, so $\left(0, \dfrac{1}{4}\right)$ is the y-intercept.

5. Find other function values to determine the shape of the graph and then draw it.

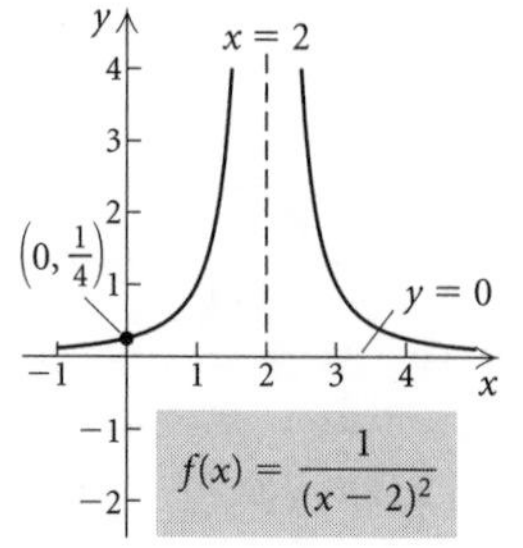

41. $f(x) = -\dfrac{1}{x^2}$

1. 0 is the zero of the denominator, so the domain excludes 0. It is $(-\infty, 0) \cup (0, \infty)$. The line $x = 0$, or the y-axis, is the vertical asymptote.

2. Because the degree of the numerator is less than the degree of the denominator, the x-axis, or $y = 0$, is the horizontal asymptote. There is no oblique asymptote.

3. The numerator has no zeros, so there is no x-intercept.

4. Since 0 is not in the domain of the function, there is no y-intercept.

5. Find other function values to determine the shape of the graph and then draw it.

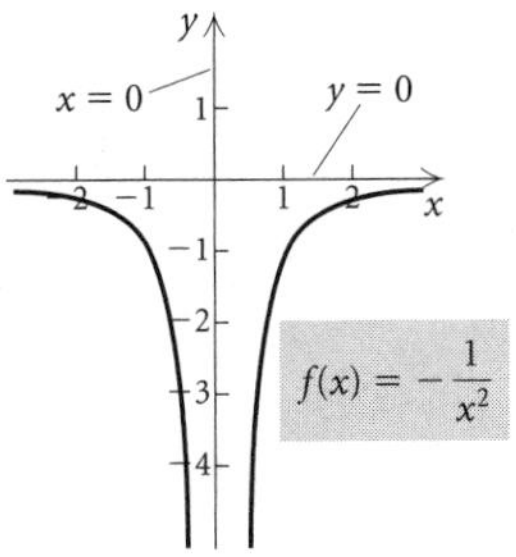

43. $f(x) = \dfrac{1}{x^2+3}$

1. The denominator has no real-number zeros, so the domain is $(-\infty, \infty)$ and there is no vertical asymptote.
2. Because the degree of the numerator is less than the degree of the denominator, the x-axis, or $y = 0$, is the horizontal asymptote. There is no oblique asymptote.
3. The numerator has no zeros, so there is no x-intercept.
4. $f(0) = \dfrac{1}{0^2+3} = \dfrac{1}{3}$, so $\left(0, \dfrac{1}{3}\right)$ is the y-intercept.
5. Find other function values to determine the shape of the graph and then draw it.

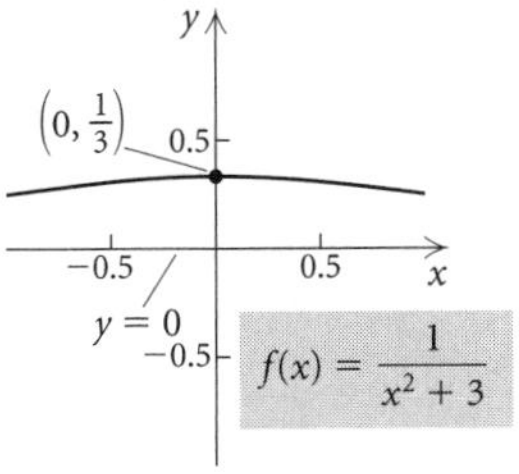

45. $f(x) = \dfrac{x^2-4}{x-2} = \dfrac{(x+2)(x-2)}{x-2} = x+2,\ x \neq 2$

The graph is the same as the graph of $f(x) = x + 2$ except at $x = 2$, where there is a hole. The zero of $f(x) = x + 2$ is -2, so the x-intercept is $(-2, 0)$; $f(0) = 2$, so the y-intercept is $(0, 2)$.

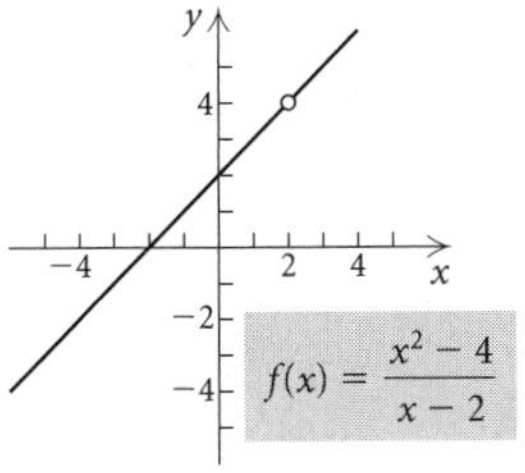

47. $f(x) = \dfrac{x-1}{x+2}$

1. -2 is the zero of the denominator, so the domain excludes -2. It is $(-\infty, -2) \cup (-2, \infty)$. The line $x = -2$ is the vertical asymptote.
2. The numerator and denominator have the same degree, so the horizontal asymptote is determined by the ratio of the leading coefficients, $1/1$, or 1. Thus, $y = 1$ is the horizontal asymptote. There is no oblique asymptote.
3. The zero of the numerator is 1, so the x-intercept is $(1, 0)$.
4. $f(0) = \dfrac{0-1}{0+2} = -\dfrac{1}{2}$, so $\left(0, -\dfrac{1}{2}\right)$ is the y-intercept.
5. Find other function values to determine the shape of the graph and then draw it.

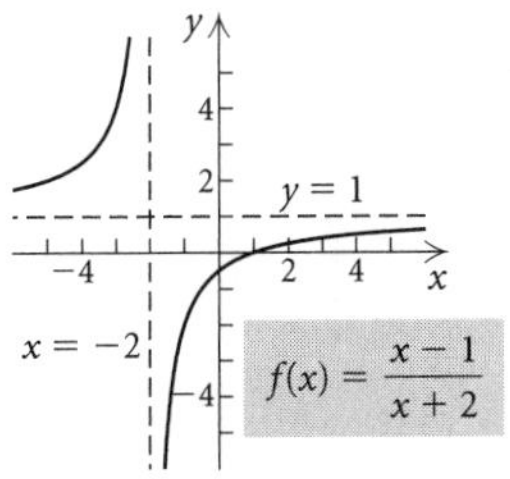

49. $f(x) = \dfrac{x+3}{2x^2-5x-3}$

1. The zeros of the denominator are the solutions of $2x^2 - 5x - 3 = 0$. Since $2x^2 - 5x - 3 = (2x+1)(x-3)$, the zeros are $-\dfrac{1}{2}$ and 3. Thus, the domain is $\left(-\infty, -\dfrac{1}{2}\right) \cup \left(-\dfrac{1}{2}, 3\right) \cup (3, \infty)$ and the lines $x = -\dfrac{1}{2}$ and $x = 3$ are vertical asymptotes.
2. Because the degree of the numerator is less than the degree of the denominator, the x-axis, or $y = 0$, is the horizontal asymptote. There is no oblique asymptote.
3. -3 is the zero of the numerator, so $(-3, 0)$ is the x-intercept.
4. $f(0) = \dfrac{0+3}{2 \cdot 0^2 - 5 \cdot 0 - 3} = -1$, so $(0, -1)$ is the y-intercept.
5. Find other function values to determine the shape of the graph and then draw it.

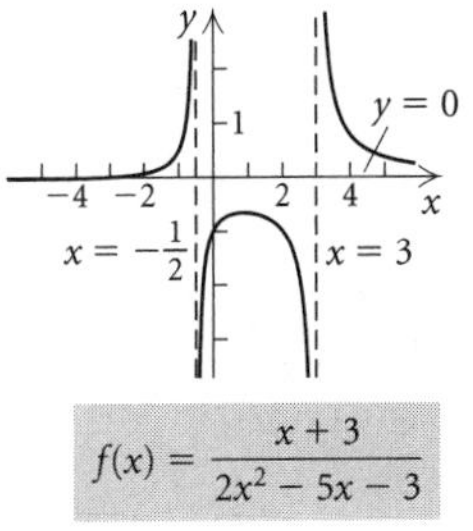

51. $f(x) = \dfrac{x^2-9}{x+1}$

1. -1 is the zero of the denominator, so the domain excludes -1. It is $(-\infty, -1) \cup (-1, \infty)$. The line $x = -1$ is the vertical asymptote.
2. Because the degree of the numerator is one greater than the degree of the denominator, there is an oblique asymptote. Using division, we find that $\dfrac{x^2-9}{x+1} = x - 1 + \dfrac{-8}{x+1}$. As $|x|$ becomes very large, the graph of $f(x)$ gets close to the graph of $y = x - 1$. Thus, the line $y = x - 1$ is the oblique asymptote.

3. Since $x^2 - 9 = (x+3)(x-3)$, the zeros of the numerator are -3 and 3. Thus, the x-intercepts are $(-3, 0)$ and $(3, 0)$.

4. $f(0) = \dfrac{0^2 - 9}{0+1} = -9$, so $(0, -9)$ is the y-intercept.

5. Find other function values to determine the shape of the graph and then draw it.

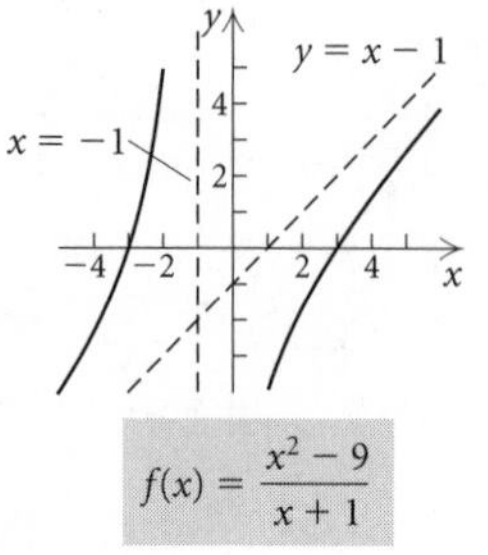

53. $f(x) = \dfrac{x^2 + x - 2}{2x^2 + 1}$

1. The denominator has no real-number zeros, so the domain is $(-\infty, \infty)$ and there is no vertical asymptote.

2. The numerator and denominator have the same degree, so the horizontal asymptote is determined by the ratio of the leading coefficients, $1/2$. Thus, $y = 1/2$ is the horizontal asymptote. There is no oblique asymptote.

3. Since $x^2 + x - 2 = (x+2)(x-1)$, the zeros of the numerator are -2 and 1. Thus, the x-intercepts are $(-2, 0)$ and $(1, 0)$.

4. $f(0) = \dfrac{0^2 + 0 - 2}{2 \cdot 0^2 + 1} = -2$, so $(0, -2)$ is the y-intercept.

5. Find other function values to determine the shape of the graph and then draw it.

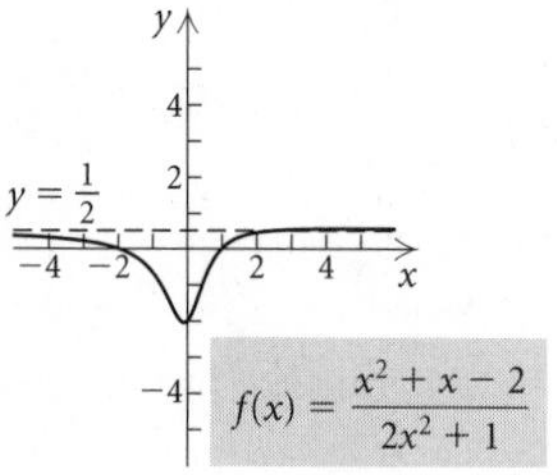

55. $g(x) = \dfrac{3x^2 - x - 2}{x - 1} = \dfrac{(3x+2)(x-1)}{x-1} = 3x + 2$, $x \neq 1$

The graph is the same as the graph of $g(x) = 3x + 2$ except at $x = 1$, where there is a hole.

The zero of $g(x) = 3x + 2$ is $-\dfrac{2}{3}$, so the x-intercept is $\left(-\dfrac{2}{3}, 0\right)$; $g(0) = 2$, so the y-intercept is $(0, 2)$.

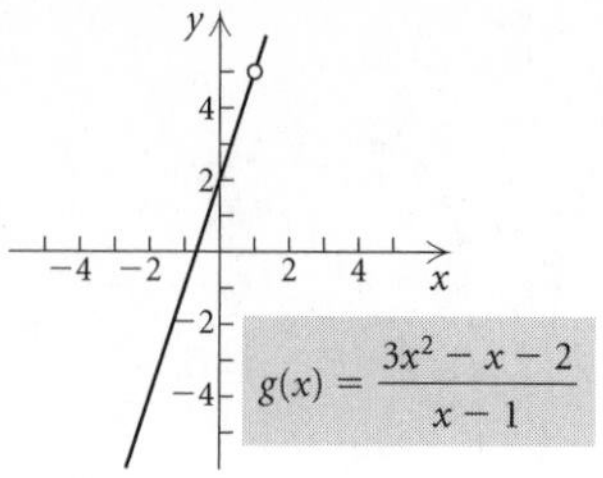

57. $f(x) = \dfrac{x - 1}{x^2 - 2x - 3}$

1. The zeros of the denominator are the solutions of $x^2 - 2x - 3 = 0$. Since $x^2 - 2x - 3 = (x+1)(x-3)$, the zeros are -1 and 3. Thus, the domain is $(-\infty, -1) \cup (-1, 3) \cup (3, \infty)$ and the lines $x = -1$ and $y = 3$ are the vertical asymptotes.

2. Because the degree of the numerator is less than the degree of the denominator, the x-axis, or $y = 0$, is the horizontal asymptote. There is no oblique asymptote.

3. 1 is the zero of the numerator, so $(1, 0)$ is the x-intercept.

4. $f(0) = \dfrac{0 - 1}{0^2 - 2 \cdot 0 - 3} = \dfrac{1}{3}$, so $\left(0, \dfrac{1}{3}\right)$ is the y-intercept.

5. Find other function values to determine the shape of the graph and then draw it.

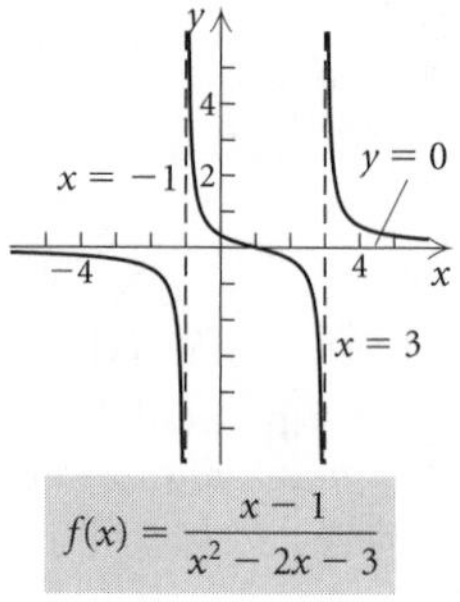

59. $f(x) = \dfrac{x - 3}{(x+1)^3}$

1. -1 is the zero of the denominator, so the domain excludes -1. It is $(-\infty, -1) \cup (-1, \infty)$. The line $x = -1$ is the vertical asymptote.

2. Because the degree of the numerator is less than the degree of the denominator, the x-axis, or $y = 0$, is the horizontal asymptote. There is no oblique asymptote.

3. 3 is the zero of the numerator, so $(3, 0)$ is the x-intercept.

4. $f(0) = \dfrac{0 - 3}{(0+1)^3} = -3$, so $(0, -3)$ is the y-intercept.

5. Find other function values to determine the shape of the graph and then draw it.

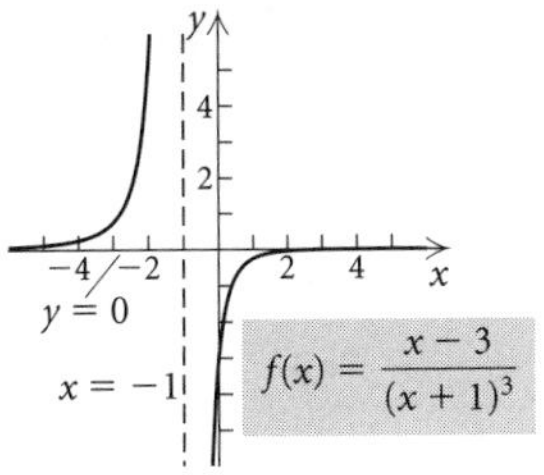

61. $f(x) = \dfrac{x^3+1}{x}$

1. 0 is the zero of the denominator, so the domain excludes 0. It is $(-\infty, 0) \cup (0, \infty)$. The line $x = 0$, or the y-axis, is the vertical asymptote.
2. Because the degree of the numerator is more than one greater than the degree of the denominator, there is no horizontal or oblique asymptote.
3. The real-number zero of the numerator is -1, so the x-intercept is $(-1, 0)$.
4. Since 0 is not in the domain of the function, there is no y-intercept.
5. Find other function values to determine the shape of the graph and then draw it.

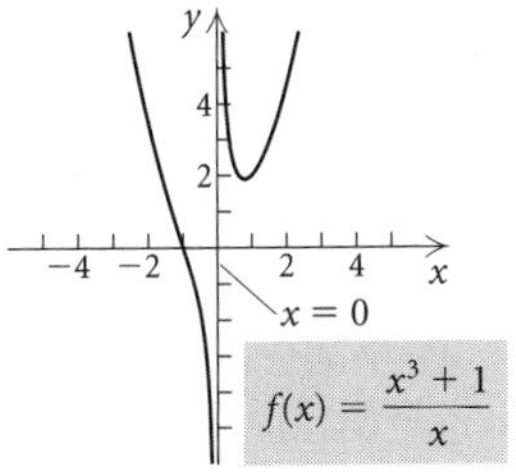

63. $f(x) = \dfrac{x^3+2x^2-15x}{x^2-5x-14}$

1. The zeros of the denominator are the solutions of $x^2-5x-14 = 0$. Since $x^2-5x-14 = (x+2)(x-7)$, the zeros are -2 and 7. Thus, the domain is $(-\infty, -2) \cup (-2, 7) \cup (7, \infty)$ and the lines $x = -2$ and $x = 7$ are the vertical asymptotes.
2. Because the degree of the numerator is one greater than the degree of the denominator, there is an oblique asymptote. Using division, we find that $\dfrac{x^3+2x^2-15x}{x^2-5x-14} = x+7+\dfrac{34x+98}{x^2-5x-14}$. As $|x|$ becomes very large, the graph of $f(x)$ gets close to the graph of $y = x+7$. Thus, the line $y = x+7$ is the oblique asymptote.
3. The zeros of the numerator are the solutions of $x^3+2x^2-15x = 0$. Since $x^3+2x^2-15x = x(x+5)(x-3)$, the zeros are 0, -5, and 3. Thus, the x-intercepts are $(-5, 0)$, $(0, 0)$, and $(3, 0)$.
4. From part (3) we see that $(0, 0)$ is the y-intercept.
5. Find other function values to determine the shape of the graph and then draw it.

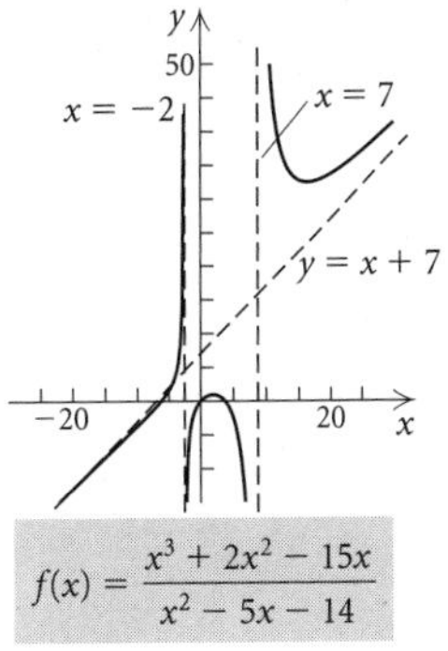

65. $f(x) = \dfrac{5x^4}{x^4+1}$

1. The denominator has no real-number zeros, so the domain is $(-\infty, \infty)$ and there is no vertical asymptote.
2. The numerator and denominator have the same degree, so the horizontal asymptote is determined by the ratio of the leading coefficients, $5/1$, or 5. Thus, $y = 5$ is the horizontal asymptote. There is no oblique asymptote.
3. The zero of the numerator is 0, so $(0, 0)$ is the x-intercept.
4. From part (3) we see that $(0, 0)$ is the y-intercept.
5. Find other function values to determine the shape of the graph and then draw it.

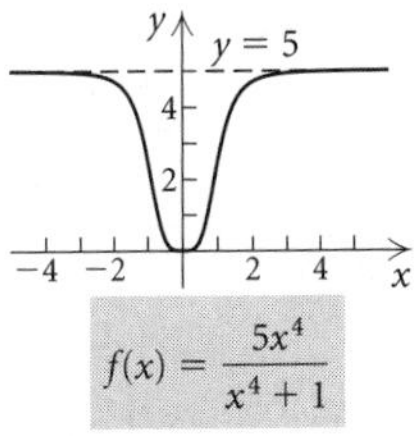

67. $f(x) = \dfrac{x^2}{x^2-x-2}$

1. The zeros of the denominator are the solutions of $x^2-x-2 = 0$. Since $x^2-x-2 = (x+1)(x-2)$, the zeros are -1 and 2. Thus, the domain is $(-\infty, -1) \cup (-1, 2) \cup (2, \infty)$ and the lines $x = -1$ and $x = 2$ are the vertical asymptotes.
2. The numerator and denominator have the same degree, so the horizontal asymptote is determined by the ratio of the leading coefficients, $1/1$, or 1. Thus, $y = 1$ is the horizontal asymptote. There is no oblique asymptote.
3. The zero of the numerator is 0, so the x-intercept is $(0, 0)$.
4. From part (3) we see that $(0, 0)$ is the y-intercept.
5. Find other function values to determine the shape of the graph and then draw it.

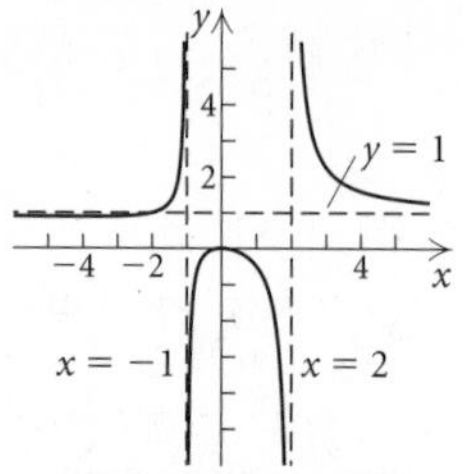

$f(x) = \dfrac{x^2}{x^2 - x - 2}$

69. Answers may vary. The numbers −4 and 5 must be zeros of the denominator. A function that satisfies these conditions is

$$f(x) = \frac{1}{(x+4)(x-5)}, \text{ or } f(x) = \frac{1}{x^2 - x - 20}.$$

71. Answers may vary. The numbers −4 and 5 must be zeros of the denominator and −2 must be a zero of the numerator. In addition, the numerator and denominator must have the same degree and the ratio of their leading coefficients must be 3/2. A function that satisfies these conditions is

$$f(x) = \frac{3x(x+2)}{2(x+4)(x-5)}, \text{ or } f(x) = \frac{3x^2 + 6x}{2x^2 - 2x - 40}.$$

Another function that satisfies these conditions is

$$g(x) = \frac{3(x+2)^2}{2(x+4)(x-5)}, \text{ or } g(x) = \frac{3x^2 + 12x + 12}{2x^2 - 2x - 40}.$$

73. a) The horizontal asymptote of $N(t)$ is the ratio of the leading coefficients of the numerator and denominator, 0.8/5, or 0.16. Thus, $N(t) \to 0.16$ as $t \to \infty$.

b) The medication never completely disappears from the body; a trace amount remains.

75. a) $P(0) = 0$; $P(1) = 45.455$ thousand, or 45,455;

$P(3) = 55.556$ thousand, or 55,556;

$P(8) = 29.197$ thousand, or 29,197

b) The degree of the numerator is less than the degree of the denominator, so the x-axis is the horizontal asymptote. Thus, $P(t) \to 0$ as $t \to \infty$.

c) Eventually, no one will live in Lordsburg.

77. Using the Maximum feature on a graphing calculator, we find that the maximum population is about 58.926 thousand, or 58,926. This occurs when $t \approx 2.12$ months.

79. Discussion and Writing

81. slope

83. point-slope equation

85. $f(-x) = -f(x)$

87. midpoint formula

89. $f(x) = \dfrac{x^5 + 2x^3 + 4x^2}{x^2 + 2} = x^3 + 4 + \dfrac{-8}{x^2 + 2}$

As $|x| \to \infty$, $\dfrac{-8}{x^2 + 2} \to 0$ and the value of $f(x) \to x^3 + 4$. Thus, the nonlinear asymptote is $y = x^3 + 4$.

91.

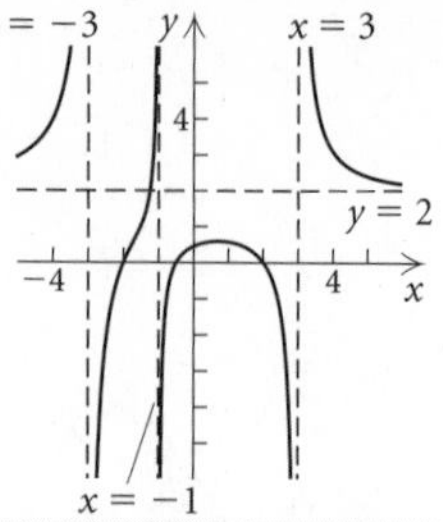

$f(x) = \dfrac{2x^3 + x^2 - 8x - 4}{x^3 + x^2 - 9x - 9}$

93. $f(x) = \sqrt{\dfrac{72}{x^2 - 4x - 21}}$

The radicand must be nonnegative and the denominator must be nonzero. Thus, the values of x for which $x^2 - 4x - 21 > 0$ comprise the domain. By inspecting the graph of $y = x^2 - 4x - 21$ we see that the domain is $\{x | x < -3 \text{ or } x > 7\}$, or $(-\infty, -3) \cup (7, \infty)$.

Exercise Set 3.5

1.
$$x^2 + 2x - 15 = 0$$
$$(x+5)(x-3) = 0$$
$$x + 5 = 0 \quad or \quad x - 3 = 0$$
$$x = -5 \quad or \quad x = 3$$

The solution set is $\{-5, 3\}$.

3. Solve $x^2 + 2x - 15 \le 0$.

From Exercise 2 we know the solution set of $x^2 + 2x - 15 < 0$ is $(-5, 3)$. The solution set of $x^2 + 2x - 15 \le 0$ includes the endpoints of this interval. Thus the solution set is $[-5, 3]$.

5. Solve $x^2 + 2x - 15 \ge 0$.

From Exercise 4 we know the solution set of $x^2 + 2x - 15 > 0$ is $(-\infty, -5) \cup (3, \infty)$. The solution set of $x^2 + 2x - 15 \ge 0$ includes the endpoints −5 and 3. Thus the solution set is $(-\infty, -5] \cup [3, \infty)$.

7. Solve $x^5 - 9x^3 < 0$.

From Exercise 6 we know the solutions of the related equation are −3, 0, and 3. These numbers divide the x-axis into the intervals $(-\infty, -3)$, $(-3, 0)$, $(0, 3)$, and $(3, \infty)$. We test a value in each interval.

$(-\infty, -3)$: $g(-4) = -448 < 0$

$(-3, 0)$: $g(-1) = 8 > 0$

$(0, 3)$: $g(1) = -8 < 0$

$(3, \infty)$: $g(4) = 448 > 0$

Function values are negative on $(-\infty, -3)$ and on $(0, 3)$. The solution set is $(-\infty, -3) \cup (0, 3)$.

9. Solve $x^5 - 9x^3 > 0$.

From our work in Exercise 7 we see that the solution set is $(-3, 0) \cup (3, \infty)$.

11. First we find an equivalent inequality with 0 on one side.

$$x^3 + 6x^2 < x + 30$$
$$x^3 + 6x^2 - x - 30 < 30$$

From the graph we see that the x-intercepts of the related function occur at $x = -5$, $x = -3$, and $x = 2$. They divide the x-axis into the intervals $(-\infty, -5)$, $(-5, -3)$, $(-3, 2)$, and $(2, \infty)$. From the graph we see that the function has negative values only on $(-\infty, -5)$ and $(-3, 2)$. Thus, the solution set is $(-\infty, -5) \cup (-3, 2)$.

13. By observing the graph or the denominator of the function, we see that the function is not defined for $x = -2$ or $x = 2$. We also see that 0 is a zero of the function. These numbers divide the x-axis into the intervals $(-\infty, -2)$, $(-2, 0)$, $(0, 2)$, and $(2, \infty)$. From the graph we see that the function has positive values only on $(-2, 0)$ and $(2, \infty)$. Since the inequality symbol is $\geq$, 0 must be included in the solution set. It is $(-2, 0] \cup (2, \infty)$.

15. $(x - 1)(x + 4) < 0$

The related equation is $(x - 1)(x + 4) = 0$. Using the principle of zero products, we find that the solutions of the related equation are 1 and -4. These numbers divide the x-axis into the intervals $(-\infty, -4)$, $(-4, 1)$, and $(1, \infty)$. We let $f(x) = (x - 1)(x + 4)$ and test a value in each interval.

$(-\infty, -4)$: $f(-5) = 6 > 0$

$(-4, 1)$: $f(0) = -4 < 0$

$(1, \infty)$: $f(2) = 6 > 0$

Function values are negative only in the interval $(-4, 1)$. The solution set is $(-4, 1)$.

17. $(x - 4)(x + 2) \geq 0$

The related equation is $(x - 4)(x + 2) = 0$. Using the principle of zero products, we find that the solutions of the related equation are 4 and -2. These numbers divide the x-axis into the intervals $(-\infty, -2)$, $(-2, 4)$, and $(4, \infty)$. We let $f(x) = (x - 4)(x + 2)$ and test a value in each interval.

$(-\infty, -2)$: $f(-3) = 7 > 0$

$(-2, 4)$: $f(0) = -8 < 0$

$(4, \infty)$: $f(5) = 7 > 0$

Function values are positive on $(-\infty, -2)$ and $(4, \infty)$. Since the inequality symbol is $\geq$, the endpoints of the intervals must be included in the solution set. It is $(-\infty, -2] \cup [4, \infty)$.

19.

$x^2 + x - 2 > 0$ Polynomial inequality

$x^2 + x - 2 = 0$ Related equation

$(x + 2)(x - 1) = 0$ Factoring

Using the principle of zero products, we find that the solutions of the related equation are -2 and 1. These numbers divide the x-axis into the intervals $(-\infty, -2)$, $(-2, 1)$, and $(1, \infty)$. We let $f(x) = x^2 + x - 2$ and test a value in each interval.

$(-\infty, -2)$: $f(-3) = 4 > 0$

$(-2, 1)$: $f(0) = -2 < 0$

$(1, \infty)$: $f(2) = 4 > 0$

Function values are positive on $(-\infty, -2)$ and $(1, \infty)$. The solution set is $(-\infty, -2) \cup (1, \infty)$.

21.

$x^2 > 25$ Polynomial inequality

$x^2 - 25 > 0$ Equivalent inequality with 0 on one side

$x^2 - 25 = 0$ Related equation

$(x + 5)(x - 5) = 0$ Factoring

Using the principle of zero products, we find that the solutions of the related equation are -5 and 5. These numbers divide the x-axis into the intervals $(-\infty, -5)$, $(-5, 5)$, and $(5, \infty)$. We let $f(x) = x^2 - 25$ and test a value in each interval.

$(-\infty, -5)$: $f(-6) = 11 > 0$

$(-5, 5)$: $f(0) = -25 < 0$

$(5, \infty)$: $f(6) = 11 > 0$

Function values are positive on $(-\infty, -5)$ and $(5, \infty)$. The solution set is $(-\infty, -5) \cup (5, \infty)$.

23.

$4 - x^2 \leq 0$ Polynomial inequality

$4 - x^2 = 0$ Related equation

$(2 + x)(2 - x) = 0$ Factoring

Using the principle of zero products, we find that the solutions of the related equation are -2 and 2. These numbers divide the x-axis into the intervals $(-\infty, -2)$, $(-2, 2)$, and $(2, \infty)$. We let $f(x) = 4 - x^2$ and test a value in each interval.

$(-\infty, -2)$: $f(-3) = -5 < 0$

$(-2, 2)$: $f(0) = 4 > 0$

$(2, \infty)$: $f(3) = -5 < 0$

Function values are negative on $(-\infty, -2)$ and $(2, \infty)$. Since the inequality symbol is $\leq$, the endpoints of the intervals must be included in the solution set. It is $(-\infty, -2] \cup [2, \infty)$.

25.

$6x - 9 - x^2 < 0$ Polynomial inequality

$6x - 9 - x^2 = 0$ Related equation

$-(x^2 - 6x + 9) = 0$ Factoring out -1 and rearranging

$-(x - 3)(x - 3) = 0$ Factoring

Using the principle of zero products, we find that the solution of the related equation is 3. This number divides the x-axis into the intervals $(-\infty, 3)$ and $(3, \infty)$. We let $f(x) = 6x - 9 - x^2$ and test a value in each interval.

$(-\infty, 3)$: $f(-4) = -49 < 0$

$(3, \infty)$: $f(4) = -49 < 0$

Function values are negative on both intervals. The solution set is $(-\infty, 3) \cup (3, \infty)$.

27.

$x^2 + 12 < 4x$ Polynomial inequality

$x^2 - 4x + 12 < 0$ Equivalent inequality with 0 on one side

$x^2 - 4x + 12 = 0$ Related equation

Using the quadratic formula, we find that the related equation has no real-number solutions. The graph lies entirely above the x-axis, so the inequality has no solution. We could determine this algebraically by letting $f(x) = x^2 - 4x + 12$ and testing any real number (since there are no real-number solutions of $f(x) = 0$ to divide the x-axis into intervals). For example, $f(0) = 12 > 0$, so we see algebraically that the inequality has no solution. The solution set is $\emptyset$.

29.

$4x^3 - 7x^2 \le 15x$	Polynomial inequality
$4x^3 - 7x^2 - 15x \le 0$	Equivalent inequality with 0 on one side
$4x^3 - 7x^2 - 15x = 0$	Related equation
$x(4x+5)(x-3) = 0$	Factoring

Using the principle of zero products, we find that the solutions of the related equation are 0, $-\frac{5}{4}$, and 3. These numbers divide the x-axis into the intervals $\left(-\infty, -\frac{5}{4}\right)$, $\left(-\frac{5}{4}, 0\right)$, $(0,3)$, and $(3,\infty)$. We let $f(x) = 4x^3 - 7x^2 - 15x$ and test a value in each interval.

$\left(-\infty, -\frac{5}{4}\right)$: $f(-2) = -30 < 0$

$\left(-\frac{5}{4}, 0\right)$: $f(-1) = 4 > 0$

$(0,3)$ $f(1) = -18 < 0$

$(3,\infty)$: $f(4) = 84 > 0$

Function values are negative on $\left(-\infty, -\frac{5}{4}\right)$ and $(0,3)$. Since the inequality symbol is $\le$, the endpoints of the intervals must be included in the solution set. It is $\left(-\infty, -\frac{5}{4}\right] \cup [0,3]$.

31.

$x^3 + 3x^2 - x - 3 \ge 0$	Polynomial inequality
$x^3 + 3x^2 - x - 3 = 0$	Related equation
$x^2(x+3) - (x+3) = 0$	Factoring
$(x^2-1)(x+3) = 0$	
$(x+1)(x-1)(x+3) = 0$	

Using the principle of zero products, we find that the solutions of the related equation are -1, 1, and -3. These numbers divide the x-axis into the intervals $(-\infty,-3)$, $(-3,-1)$, $(-1,1)$, and $(1,\infty)$. We let $f(x) = x^3+3x^2-x-3$ and test a value in each interval.

$(-\infty,-3)$: $f(-4) = -15 < 0$

$(-3,-1)$: $f(-2) = 3 > 0$

$(-1,1)$: $f(0) = -3 < 0$

$(1,\infty)$: $f(2) = 15 > 0$

Function values are positive on $(-3,-1)$ and $(1,\infty)$. Since the inequality symbol is $\ge$, the endpoints of the intervals must be included in the solution set. It is $[-3,-1] \cup [1,\infty)$.

33.

$x^3 - 2x^2 < 5x - 6$	Polynomial inequality
$x^3 - 2x^2 - 5x + 6 < 0$	Equivalent inequality with 0 on one side
$x^3 - 2x^2 - 5x + 6 = 0$	Related equation

Using the techniques of Section 3.3, we find that the solutions of the related equation are -2, 1, and 3. They divide the x-axis into the intervals $(-\infty,-2)$, $(-2,1)$, $(1,3)$, and $(3,\infty)$. Let $f(x) = x^3 - 2x^2 - 5x + 6$ and test a value in each interval.

$(-\infty,-2)$: $f(-3) = -24 < 0$

$(-2,1)$: $f(0) = 6 > 0$

$(1,3)$: $f(2) = -4 < 0$

$(3,\infty)$: $f(4) = 18 > 0$

Function values are negative on $(-\infty,-2)$ and $(1,3)$. The solution set is $(-\infty,-2) \cup (1,3)$.

35.

$x^5 + x^2 \ge 2x^3 + 2$	Polynomial inequality
$x^5 - 2x^3 + x^2 - 2 \ge 0$	Related inequality with 0 on one side
$x^5 - 2x^3 + x^2 - 2 = 0$	Related equation
$x^3(x^2-2) + x^2 - 2 = 0$	Factoring
$(x^3+1)(x^2-2) = 0$	

Using the principle of zero products, we find that the real-number solutions of the related equation are -1, $-\sqrt{2}$, and $\sqrt{2}$. These numbers divide the x-axis into the intervals $(-\infty,-\sqrt{2})$, $(-\sqrt{2},-1)$, $(-1,\sqrt{2})$, and $(\sqrt{2},\infty)$. We let $f(x) = x^5 - 2x^3 + x^2 - 2$ and test a value in each interval.

$(-\infty,-\sqrt{2})$: $f(-2) = -14 < 0$

$(-\sqrt{2},-1)$: $f(-1.3) \approx 0.37107 > 0$

$(-1,\sqrt{2})$: $f(0) = -2 < 0$

$(\sqrt{2},\infty)$: $f(2) = 18 > 0$

Function values are positive on $(-\sqrt{2},-1)$ and $(\sqrt{2},\infty)$. Since the inequality symbol is $\ge$, the endpoints of the intervals must be included in the solution set. It is $[-\sqrt{2},-1] \cup [\sqrt{2},\infty)$.

37.

$2x^3 + 6 \le 5x^2 + x$	Polynomial inequality
$2x^3 - 5x^2 - x + 6 \le 0$	Equivalent inequality with 0 on one side
$2x^3 - 5x^2 - x + 6 = 0$	Related equation

Using the techniques of Section 3.3, we find that the solutions of the related equation are -1, $\frac{3}{2}$, and 2. We can also use the graph of $y = 2x^3 - 5x^2 - x + 6$ to find these solutions. They divide the x-axis into the intervals $(-\infty,-1)$, $\left(-1, \frac{3}{2}\right)$, $\left(\frac{3}{2}, 2\right)$, and $(2,\infty)$. Let $f(x) = 2x^3-5x^2-x+6$ and test a value in each interval.

$(-\infty,-1)$: $f(-2) = -28 < 0$

$\left(-1, \frac{3}{2}\right)$: $f(0) = 6 > 0$

$\left(\frac{3}{2}, 2\right)$: $f(1.6) = -0.208 < 0$

$(2, \infty)$: $f(3) = 12 > 0$

Function values are negative in $(-\infty, -1)$ and $\left(\frac{3}{2}, 2\right)$. Since the inequality symbol is $\leq$, the endpoints of the intervals must be included in the solution set. The solution set is $\left(-\infty, -1\right] \cup \left[\frac{3}{2}, 2\right]$.

39.

$x^3 + 5x^2 - 25x \leq 125$	Polynomial inequality
$x^3 + 5x^2 - 25x - 125 \leq 0$	Equivalent inequality with 0 on one side
$x^3 + 5x^2 - 25x - 125 = 0$	Related equation
$x^2(x+5) - 25(x+5) = 0$	Factoring
$(x^2 - 25)(x+5) = 0$	
$(x+5)(x-5)(x+5) = 0$	

Using the principle of zero products, we find that the solutions of the related equation are -5 and 5. These numbers divide the x-axis into the intervals $(-\infty, -5)$, $(-5, 5)$, and $(5, \infty)$. We let $f(x) = x^3 + 5x^2 - 25x - 125$ and test a value in each interval.

$(-\infty, -5)$: $f(-6) = -11 < 0$

$(-5, 5)$: $f(0) = -125 < 0$

$(5, \infty)$: $f(6) = 121 > 0$

Function values are negative on $(-\infty, -5)$ and $(-5, 5)$. Since the inequality symbol is $\leq$, the endpoints of the intervals must be included in the solution set. It is $(-\infty, -5] \cup [-5, 5]$ or $(-\infty, 5]$.

41. $\frac{1}{x+4} > 0$ Rational inequality

$\frac{1}{x+4} = 0$ Related equation

The denominator of $f(x) = \frac{1}{x+4}$ is 0 when $x = -4$, so the function is not defined for $x = -4$. The related equation has no solution. Thus, the only critical value is -4. It divides the x-axis into the intervals $(-\infty, -4)$ and $(-4, \infty)$. We test a value in each interval.

$(-\infty, -4)$: $f(-5) = -1 < 0$

$(-4, \infty)$: $f(0) = \frac{1}{4} > 0$

Function values are positive on $(-4, \infty)$. This can also be determined from the graph of $y = \frac{1}{x+4}$. The solution set is $(-4, \infty)$.

43. $\frac{-4}{2x+5} < 0$ Rational inequality

$\frac{-4}{2x+5} = 0$ Related equation

The denominator of $f(x) = \frac{-4}{2x+5}$ is 0 when $x = -\frac{5}{2}$, so the function is not defined for $x = -\frac{5}{2}$. The related equation has no solution. Thus, the only critical value is $-\frac{5}{2}$. It divides the x-axis into the intervals $\left(-\infty, -\frac{5}{2}\right)$ and $\left(-\frac{5}{2}, \infty\right)$. We test a value in each interval.

$\left(-\infty, -\frac{5}{2}\right)$: $f(-3) = 4 > 0$

$\left(-\frac{5}{2}, \infty\right)$: $f(0) = -\frac{4}{5} < 0$

Function values are negative on $\left(-\frac{5}{2}, \infty\right)$. The solution set is $\left(-\frac{5}{2}, \infty\right)$.

45. $\frac{x-4}{x+3} - \frac{x+2}{x-1} \leq 0$

The denominator of $f(x) = \frac{x-4}{x+3} - \frac{x+2}{x-1}$ is 0 when $x = -3$ or $x = 1$, so the function is not defined for these values of x. We solve the related equation $f(x) = 0$.

$$\frac{x-4}{x+3} - \frac{x+2}{x-1} = 0$$

$$(x+3)(x-1)\left(\frac{x-4}{x+3} - \frac{x+2}{x-1}\right) = (x+3)(x-1)\cdot 0$$

$$(x-1)(x-4) - (x+3)(x+2) = 0$$

$$x^2 - 5x + 4 - (x^2 + 5x + 6) = 0$$

$$-10x - 2 = 0$$

$$-10x = 2$$

$$x = -\frac{1}{5}$$

The critical values are -3, $-\frac{1}{5}$, and 1. They divide the x-axis into the intervals $(-\infty, -3)$, $\left(3, -\frac{1}{5}\right)$, $\left(-\frac{1}{5}, 1\right)$, and $(1, \infty)$. We test a value in each interval.

$(-\infty, -3)$: $f(-4) = 7.6 > 0$

$\left(-3, -\frac{1}{5}\right)$: $f(-1) = -2 < 0$

$\left(-\frac{1}{5}, 1\right)$: $f(0) = \frac{2}{3} > 0$

$(1, \infty)$: $f(2) = -4.4 < 0$

Function values are negative on $\left(-3, -\frac{1}{5}\right)$ and $(1, \infty)$. Note that since the inequality symbol is $\leq$ and $f\left(-\frac{1}{5}\right) = 0$, then $-\frac{1}{5}$ must be included in the solution set. Note also that since neither -3 nor 1 is in the domain of $f(x)$, they are not included in the solution set. It is $\left(-3, -\frac{1}{5}\right] \cup (1, \infty)$.

47. $\dfrac{2x-1}{x+3} \geq \dfrac{x+1}{3x+1}$ Rational inequality

$\dfrac{2x-1}{x+3} - \dfrac{x+1}{3x+1} \geq 0$ Equivalent inequality with 0 on one side

The denominator of $f(x) = \dfrac{2x-1}{x+3} - \dfrac{x+1}{3x+1}$ is 0 when $x = -3$ or $x = -\dfrac{1}{3}$, so the function is not defined for these values of x. We solve the related equation $f(x) = 0$.

$$\frac{2x-1}{x+3} - \frac{x+1}{3x+1} = 0$$

$$(x+3)(3x+1)\left(\frac{2x-1}{x+3} - \frac{x+1}{3x+1}\right) = (x+3)(3x+1)\cdot 0$$

$$(3x+1)(2x-1) - (x+3)(x+1) = 0$$

$$6x^2 - x - 1 - (x^2 + 4x + 3) = 0$$

$$5x^2 - 5x - 4 = 0$$

Using the quadratic formula we find that $x = \dfrac{5 \pm \sqrt{105}}{10}$. Then the critical values are -3, $\dfrac{5-\sqrt{105}}{10}$, $-\dfrac{1}{3}$, and $\dfrac{5+\sqrt{105}}{10}$. They divide the x-axis into the intervals $(-\infty, -3)$, $\left(-3, \dfrac{5-\sqrt{105}}{10}\right)$, $\left(\dfrac{5-\sqrt{105}}{10}, -\dfrac{1}{3}\right)$, $\left(-\dfrac{1}{3}, \dfrac{5+\sqrt{105}}{10}\right)$, and $\left(\dfrac{5+\sqrt{105}}{10}, \infty\right)$. We test a value in each interval.

$(-\infty, -3)$: $f(-4) \approx 8.7273 > 0$

$\left(-3, \dfrac{5-\sqrt{105}}{10}\right)$: $f(-2) = -5.2 < 0$

$\left(\dfrac{5-\sqrt{105}}{10}, -\dfrac{1}{3}\right)$: $f(-0.4) \approx 2.3077 > 0$

$\left(-\dfrac{1}{3}, \dfrac{5+\sqrt{105}}{10}\right)$: $f(0) \approx -1.333 < 0$

$\left(\dfrac{5+\sqrt{105}}{10}, \infty\right)$: $f(2) \approx 0.1714 > 0$

Function values are positive on $(-\infty, -3)$, $\left(\dfrac{5-\sqrt{105}}{10}, -\dfrac{1}{3}\right)$ and $\left(\dfrac{5+\sqrt{105}}{10}, \infty\right)$. Note that since the inequality symbol is $\geq$ and $f\left(\dfrac{5 \pm \sqrt{105}}{10}\right) = 0$, then $\dfrac{5 \pm \sqrt{105}}{10}$ must be included in the solution set. Note also that since neither -3 nor $-\dfrac{1}{3}$ is in the domain of $f(x)$, they are not included in the solution set. It is

$$(-\infty, -3) \cup \left[\frac{5-\sqrt{105}}{10}, -\frac{1}{3}\right) \cup \left[\frac{5+\sqrt{105}}{10}, \infty\right).$$

49. $\dfrac{x+1}{x-2} \geq 3$ Rational inequality

$\dfrac{x+1}{x-2} - 3 \geq 0$ Equivalent inequality with 0 on one side

The denominator of $f(x) = \dfrac{x+1}{x-2} - 3$ is 0 when $x = 2$, so the function is not defined for this value of x. We solve the related equation $f(x) = 0$.

$$\frac{x+1}{x-2} - 3 = 0$$

$$(x-2)\left(\frac{x+1}{x-2} - 3\right) = (x-2)\cdot 0$$

$$x + 1 - 3(x-2) = 0$$

$$x + 1 - 3x + 6 = 0$$

$$-2x + 7 = 0$$

$$-2x = -7$$

$$x = \frac{7}{2}$$

The critical values are 2 and $\dfrac{7}{2}$. They divide the x-axis into the intervals $(-\infty, 2)$, $\left(2, \dfrac{7}{2}\right)$, and $\left(\dfrac{7}{2}, \infty\right)$. We test a value in each interval.

$(-\infty, 2)$: $f(0) = -3.5 < 0$

$\left(2, \dfrac{7}{2}\right)$: $f(3) = 1 > 0$

$\left(\dfrac{7}{2}, \infty\right)$: $f(4) = -0.5 < 0$

Function values are positive on $\left(2, \dfrac{7}{2}\right)$. Note that since the inequality symbol is $\geq$ and $f\left(\dfrac{7}{2}\right) = 0$, then $\dfrac{7}{2}$ must be included in the solution set. Note also that since 2 is not in the domain of $f(x)$, it is not included in the solution set. It is $\left(2, \dfrac{7}{2}\right]$.

51. $x - 2 > \dfrac{1}{x}$ Rational inequality

$x - 2 - \dfrac{1}{x} > 0$ Equivalent inequality with 0 on one side

The denominator of $f(x) = x - 2 - \dfrac{1}{x}$ is 0 when $x = 0$, so the function is not defined for this value of x. We solve the related equation $f(x) = 0$.

$$x - 2 - \frac{1}{x} = 0$$

$$x\left(x - 2 - \frac{1}{x}\right) = x \cdot 0$$

$$x^2 - 2x - x \cdot \frac{1}{x} = 0$$

$$x^2 - 2x - 1 = 0$$

Using the quadratic formula we find that $x = 1 \pm \sqrt{2}$. The critical values are $1 - \sqrt{2}$, 0, and $1 + \sqrt{2}$. They divide the x-axis into the intervals $(-\infty, 1-\sqrt{2})$, $(1-\sqrt{2}, 0)$, $(0, 1+\sqrt{2})$, and $(1+\sqrt{2}, \infty)$. We test a value in each interval.

$(-\infty, 1-\sqrt{2})$: $f(-1) = -2 < 0$

$(1-\sqrt{2}, 0)$: $f(-0.1) = 7.9 > 0$

$(0, 1+\sqrt{2})$: $f(1) = -2 < 0$

$(1+\sqrt{2}, \infty)$: $f(3) = \frac{2}{3} > 0$

Function values are positive on $(1-\sqrt{2}, 0)$ and $(1+\sqrt{2}, \infty)$. The solution set is $(1-\sqrt{2}, 0) \cup (1+\sqrt{2}, \infty)$.

53.
$$\frac{2}{x^2-4x+3} \le \frac{5}{x^2-9}$$
$$\frac{2}{x^2-4x+3} - \frac{5}{x^2-9} \le 0$$
$$\frac{2}{(x-1)(x-3)} - \frac{5}{(x+3)(x-3)} \le 0$$

The denominator of $f(x) = \frac{2}{(x-1)(x-3)} - \frac{5}{(x+3)(x-3)}$ is 0 when $x = 1$, 3, or -3, so the function is not defined for these values of x. We solve the related equation $f(x) = 0$.

$$\frac{2}{(x-1)(x-3)} - \frac{5}{(x+3)(x-3)} = 0$$
$$(x-1)(x-3)(x+3)\left(\frac{2}{(x-1)(x-3)} - \frac{5}{(x+3)(x-3)}\right) = (x-1)(x-3)(x+3)\cdot 0$$
$$2(x+3) - 5(x-1) = 0$$
$$2x+6-5x+5 = 0$$
$$-3x+11 = 0$$
$$-3x = -11$$
$$x = \frac{11}{3}$$

The critical values are -3, 1, 3, and $\frac{11}{3}$. They divide the x-axis into the intervals $(-\infty, -3)$, $(-3, 1)$, $(1, 3)$, $\left(3, \frac{11}{3}\right)$, and $\left(\frac{11}{3}, \infty\right)$. We test a value in each interval.

$(-\infty, -3)$: $f(-4) \approx -0.6571 < 0$

$(-3, 1)$: $f(0) \approx 1.2222 > 0$

$(1, 3)$: $f(2) = -1 < 0$

$\left(3, \frac{11}{3}\right)$: $f(3.5) \approx 0.6154 > 0$

$\left(\frac{11}{3}, \infty\right)$: $f(4) \approx -0.0476 < 0$

Function values are negative on $(-\infty, -3)$, $(1, 3)$, and $\left(\frac{11}{3}, \infty\right)$. Note that since the inequality symbol is $\le$ and $f\left(\frac{11}{3}\right) = 0$, then $\frac{11}{3}$ must be included in the solution set. Note also that since -3, 1, and 3 are not in the domain of $f(x)$, they are not included in the solution set. It is $(-\infty, -3) \cup (1, 3) \cup \left[\frac{11}{3}, \infty\right)$.

55.
$$\frac{3}{x^2+1} \ge \frac{6}{5x^2+2}$$
$$\frac{3}{x^2+1} - \frac{6}{5x^2+2} \ge 0$$

The denominator of $f(x) = \frac{3}{x^2+1} - \frac{6}{5x^2+2}$ has no real-number zeros. We solve the related equation $f(x) = 0$.

$$\frac{3}{x^2+1} - \frac{6}{5x^2+2} = 0$$
$$(x^2+1)(5x^2+2)\left(\frac{3}{x^2+1} - \frac{6}{5x^2+2}\right) = (x^2+1)(5x^2+2)\cdot 0$$
$$3(5x^2+2) - 6(x^2+1) = 0$$
$$15x^2+6-6x^2-6 = 0$$
$$9x^2 = 0$$
$$x^2 = 0$$
$$x = 0$$

The only critical value is 0. It divides the x-axis into the intervals $(-\infty, 0)$ and $(0, \infty)$. We test a value in each interval.

$(-\infty, 0)$: $f(-1) \approx 0.64286 > 0$

$(0, 0)$: $f(1) \approx 0.64286 > 0$

Function values are positive on both intervals. Note that since the inequality symbol is $\ge$ and $f(0) = 0$, then 0 must be included in the solution set. It is $(-\infty, 0] \cup [0, \infty)$, or $(-\infty, \infty)$.

57.
$$\frac{5}{x^2+3x} < \frac{3}{2x+1}$$
$$\frac{5}{x^2+3x} - \frac{3}{2x+1} < 0$$
$$\frac{5}{x(x+3)} - \frac{3}{2x+1} < 0$$

The denominator of $f(x) = \frac{5}{x(x+3)} - \frac{3}{2x+1}$ is 0 when $x = 0$, -3, or $-\frac{1}{2}$, so the function is not defined for these values of x. We solve the related equation $f(x) = 0$.

$$\frac{5}{x(x+3)} - \frac{3}{2x+1} = 0$$
$$x(x+3)(2x+1)\left(\frac{5}{x(x+3)} - \frac{3}{2x+1}\right) = x(x+3)(2x+1)\cdot 0$$
$$5(2x+1) - 3x(x+3) = 0$$
$$10x+5-3x^2-9x = 0$$
$$-3x^2+x+5 = 0$$

Using the quadratic formula we find that $x = \frac{1\pm\sqrt{61}}{6}$. The critical values are -3, $\frac{1-\sqrt{61}}{6}$, $-\frac{1}{2}$, 0, and $\frac{1+\sqrt{61}}{6}$. They divide the x-axis into the intervals $(-\infty, -3)$, $\left(-3, \frac{1-\sqrt{61}}{6}\right)$, $\left(\frac{1-\sqrt{61}}{6}, -\frac{1}{2}\right)$, $\left(-\frac{1}{2}, 0\right)$, $\left(0, \frac{1+\sqrt{61}}{6}\right)$, and $\left(\frac{1+\sqrt{61}}{6}, \infty\right)$.

We test a value in each interval.

$(-\infty, -3)$: $f(-4) \approx 1.6786 > 0$

$\left(-3, \frac{1-\sqrt{61}}{6}\right)$: $f(-2) = -1.5 < 0$

$\left(\frac{1-\sqrt{61}}{6}, -\frac{1}{2}\right)$: $f(-1) = 0.5 > 0$

$\left(-\frac{1}{2}, 0\right)$: $f(-0.1) \approx -20.99 < 0$

$\left(0, \frac{1+\sqrt{61}}{6}\right)$: $f(1) = 0.25 > 0$

$\left(\frac{1+\sqrt{61}}{6}, \infty\right)$: $f(2) = -0.1 < 0$

Function values are negative on $\left(-3, \frac{1-\sqrt{61}}{6}\right)$, $\left(-\frac{1}{2}, 0\right)$ and $\left(\frac{1+\sqrt{61}}{6}, \infty\right)$. The solution set is $\left(-3, \frac{1-\sqrt{61}}{6}\right) \cup \left(-\frac{1}{2}, 0\right) \cup \left(\frac{1+\sqrt{61}}{6}, \infty\right)$.

59. $\frac{5x}{7x-2} > \frac{x}{x+1}$

$$\frac{5x}{7x-2} - \frac{x}{x+1} > 0$$

The denominator of $f(x) = \frac{5x}{7x-2} - \frac{x}{x+1}$ is 0 when $x = \frac{2}{7}$ or $x = -1$, so the function is not defined for these values of x. We solve the related equation $f(x) = 0$.

$$\frac{5x}{7x-2} - \frac{x}{x+1} = 0$$

$$(7x-2)(x+1)\left(\frac{5x}{7x-2} - \frac{x}{x+1}\right) = (7x-2)(x+1) \cdot 0$$

$$5x(x+1) - x(7x-2) = 0$$

$$5x^2 + 5x - 7x^2 + 2x = 0$$

$$-2x^2 + 7x = 0$$

$$-x(2x-7) = 0$$

$x = 0$ *or* $x = \frac{7}{2}$

The critical values are -1, 0, $\frac{2}{7}$, and $\frac{7}{2}$. They divide the x-axis into the intervals $(-\infty, -1)$, $(-1, 0)$, $\left(0, \frac{2}{7}\right)$, $\left(\frac{2}{7}, \frac{7}{2}\right)$, and $\left(\frac{7}{2}, \infty\right)$. We test a value in each interval.

$(-\infty, -1)$: $f(-2) = -1.375 < 0$

$(-1, 0)$: $f(-0.5) \approx 1.4545 > 0$

$\left(0, \frac{2}{7}\right)$: $f(0.1) \approx -0.4755 < 0$

$\left(\frac{2}{7}, \frac{7}{2}\right)$: $f(1) = 0.5 > 0$

$\left(\frac{7}{2}, \infty\right)$: $f(4) \approx -0.0308 < 0$

Function values are positive on $(-1, 0)$ and $\left(\frac{2}{7}, \frac{7}{2}\right)$. The solution set is $(-1, 0) \cup \left(\frac{2}{7}, \frac{7}{2}\right)$.

61. $\frac{x}{x^2+4x-5} + \frac{3}{x^2-25} \le \frac{2x}{x^2-6x+5}$

$$\frac{x}{x^2+4x-5} + \frac{3}{x^2-25} - \frac{2x}{x^2-6x+5} \le 0$$

$$\frac{x}{(x+5)(x-1)} + \frac{3}{(x+5)(x-5)} - \frac{2x}{(x-5)(x-1)} \le 0$$

The denominator of

$$f(x) = \frac{x}{(x+5)(x-1)} + \frac{3}{(x+5)(x-5)} - \frac{2x}{(x-5)(x-1)}$$

is 0 when $x = -5$, 1, or 5, so the function is not defined for these values of x. We solve the related equation $f(x) = 0$.

$$\frac{x}{(x+5)(x-1)} + \frac{3}{(x+5)(x-5)} - \frac{2x}{(x-5)(x-1)} = 0$$

$$x(x-5) + 3(x-1) - 2x(x+5) = 0$$

Multiplying by $(x+5)(x-1)(x-5)$

$$x^2 - 5x + 3x - 3 - 2x^2 - 10x = 0$$

$$-x^2 - 12x - 3 = 0$$

$$x^2 + 12x + 3 = 0$$

Using the quadratic formula, we find that $x = -6 \pm \sqrt{33}$. The critical values are $-6-\sqrt{33}$, -5, $-6+\sqrt{33}$, 1, and 5. They divide the x-axis into the intervals $(-\infty, -6-\sqrt{33})$, $(-6-\sqrt{33}, -5)$, $(-5, -6+\sqrt{33})$, $(-6+\sqrt{33}, 1)$, $(1, 5)$, and $(5, \infty)$. We test a value in each interval.

$(-\infty, -6-\sqrt{33})$: $f(-12) \approx 0.00194 > 0$

$(-6-\sqrt{33}, -5)$: $f(-6) \approx -0.4286 < 0$

$(-5, -6+\sqrt{33})$: $f(-1) \approx 0.16667 > 0$

$(-6+\sqrt{33}, 1)$: $f(0) = -0.12 < 0$

$(1, 5)$: $f(2) \approx 1.4762 > 0$

$(5, \infty)$: $f(6) \approx -2.018 < 0$

Function values are negative on $(-6-\sqrt{33}, -5)$, $(-6+\sqrt{33}, 1)$, and $(5, \infty)$. Note that since the inequality symbol is $\le$ and $f(-6 \pm \sqrt{33}) = 0$, then $-6-\sqrt{33}$ and $-6+\sqrt{33}$ must be included in the solution set. Note also that since -5, 1, and 5 are not in the domain of $f(x)$, they are not included in the solution set. It is $[-6-\sqrt{33}, -5) \cup [-6+\sqrt{33}, 1) \cup (5, \infty)$.

63. We write and solve a rational inequality.

$$\frac{4t}{t^2+1} + 98.6 > 100$$

$$\frac{4t}{t^2+1} - 1.4 > 0$$

The denominator of $f(t) = \frac{4t}{t^2+1} - 1.4$ has no real-number zeros. We solve the related equation $f(t) = 0$.

$$\frac{4t}{t^2+1} - 1.4 = 0$$

$4t - 1.4(t^2+1) = 0$ Multiplying by t^2+1

$4t - 1.4t^2 - 1.4 = 0$

Using the quadratic formula, we find that $t = \frac{4 \pm \sqrt{8.16}}{2.8}$; that is, $t \approx 0.408$ or $t \approx 2.449$. These numbers divide the t-axis into the intervals $(-\infty, 0.408)$, $(0.408, 2.449)$, and $(2.449, \infty)$. We test a value in each interval.

$(-\infty, 0.408)$: $f(0) = -1.4 < 0$

$(0.408, 2.449)$: $f(1) = 0.6 > 0$

$(2.449, \infty)$: $f(3) = -0.2 < 0$

Function values are positive on $(0.408, 2.449)$. The solution set is $(0.408, 2.449)$.

65. a) We write and solve a polynomial inequality.

$-3x^2 + 630x - 6000 > 0 \quad (x \geq 0)$

We first solve the related equation.

$-3x^2 + 630x - 6000 = 0$

$x^2 - 210x + 2000 = 0$ Dividing by -3

$(x-10)(x-200) = 0$ Factoring

Using the principle of zero products or by observing the graph of $y = -3x^2 + 630 - 6000$, we see that the solutions of the related equation are 10 and 200. These numbers divide the x-axis into the intervals $(-\infty, 10)$, $(10, 200)$, and $(200, \infty)$. Since we are restricting our discussion to nonnegative values of x, we consider the intervals $[0, 10)$, $(10, 200)$, and $(200, \infty)$.

We let $f(x) = -3x^2 + 630x - 6000$ and test a value in each interval.

$[0, 10)$: $f(0) = -6000 < 0$

$(10, 200)$: $f(11) = 567 > 0$

$(200, \infty)$: $f(201) = -573 < 0$

Function values are positive only on $(10, 200)$. The solution set is $\{x|10 < x < 200\}$, or $(10, 200)$.

b) From part (a), we see that function values are negative on $[0, 10)$ and $(200, \infty)$. Thus, the solution set is $\{x|0 < x < 10 \textit{ or } x > 200\}$, or $(0, 10) \cup (200, \infty)$.

67. We write an inequality.

$27 \leq \frac{n(n-3)}{2} \leq 230$

$54 \leq n(n-3) \leq 460$ Multiplying by 2

$54 \leq n^2 - 3n \leq 460$

We write this as two inequalities.

$54 \leq n^2 - 3n \quad \textit{and} \quad n^2 - 3n \leq 460$

Solve each inequality.

$n^2 - 3n \geq 54$

$n^2 - 3n - 54 \geq 0$

$n^2 - 3n - 54 = 0$ Related equation

$(n+6)(n-9) = 0$

$n = -6 \textit{ or } n = 9$

Since only positive values of n have meaning in this application, we consider the intervals $(0, 9)$ and $(9, \infty)$. Let $f(n) = n^2 - 3n - 54$ and test a value in each interval.

$(0, 9)$: $f(1) = -56 < 0$

$(9, \infty)$: $f(10) = 16 > 0$

Function values are positive on $(9, \infty)$. Since the inequality symbol is $\geq$, 9 must also be included in the solution set for this portion of the inequality. It is $\{n|n \geq 9\}$.

Now solve the second inequality.

$n^2 - 3n \leq 460$

$n^2 - 3n - 460 \leq 0$

$n^2 - 3n - 460 = 0$ Related equation

$(n+20)(n-23) = 0$

$n = -20 \textit{ or } n = 23$

We consider only positive values of n as above. Thus, we consider the intervals $(0, 23)$ and $(23, \infty)$. Let $f(n) = n^2 - 3n - 460$ and test a value in each interval.

$(0, 23)$: $f(1) = -462 < 0$

$(23, \infty)$: $f(24) = 44 > 0$

Function values are negative on $(0, 23)$. Since the inequality symbol is $\leq$, 23 must also be included in the solution set for this portion of the inequality. It is $\{n|0 < n \leq 23\}$.

The solution set of the original inequality is $\{n|n \geq 9 \textit{ and } 0 < n \leq 23\}$, or $\{n|9 \leq n \leq 23\}$.

69. Left to the student

71. Discussion and Writing

73. $(x-h)^2 + (y-k)^2 = r^2$

$[x - (-2)]^2 + (y-4)^2 = 3^2$

$(x+2)^2 + (y-4)^2 = 9$

75. $h(x) = -2x^2 + 3x - 8$

a) $-\frac{b}{2a} = -\frac{3}{2(-2)} = \frac{3}{4}$

$h\left(\frac{3}{4}\right) = -2\left(\frac{3}{4}\right)^2 + 3 \cdot \frac{3}{4} - 8 = -\frac{55}{8}$

The vertex is $\left(\frac{3}{4}, -\frac{55}{8}\right)$.

b) The coefficient of x^2 is negative, so there is a maximum value. It is the second coordinate of the vertex, $-\frac{55}{8}$. It occurs at $x = \frac{3}{4}$.

c) The range is $\left(-\infty, -\frac{55}{8}\right]$.

77. $x^4 + 3x^2 > 4x - 15$

$x^4 + 3x^2 - 4x + 15 > 0$

The graph of $y = x^4 + 3x^2 - 4x + 15$ lies entirely above the x-axis. Thus, the solution set is the set of all real numbers, or $(-\infty, \infty)$.

79. $|x^2-5| = |5-x^2| = 5-x^2$ when $5-x^2 \geq 0$. Thus we solve $5-x^2 \geq 0$.

$$5-x^2 \geq 0$$
$$5-x^2 = 0 \quad \text{Related equation}$$
$$5 = x^2$$
$$\pm\sqrt{5} = x$$

Let $f(x) = 5-x^2$ and test a value in each of the intervals determined by the solutions of the related equation.

$(-\infty,-\sqrt{5})$: $f(-3) = -4 < 0$

$(-\sqrt{5},\sqrt{5})$: $f(0) = 5 > 0$

$(\sqrt{5},\infty)$: $f(3) = -4 < 0$

Function values are positive on $(-\sqrt{5},\sqrt{5})$. Since the inequality symbol is $\geq$, the endpoints of the interval must be included in the solution set. It is $\left[-\sqrt{5},\sqrt{5}\right]$.

81.
$$2|x|^2 - |x| + 2 \leq 5$$
$$2|x|^2 - |x| - 3 \leq 0$$
$$2|x|^2 - |x| - 3 = 0 \quad \text{Related equation}$$
$$(2|x|-3)(|x|+1) = 0 \quad \text{Factoring}$$
$$2|x|-3 = 0 \quad \textit{or} \quad |x|+1 = 0$$
$$|x| = \frac{3}{2} \quad \textit{or} \quad |x| = -1$$

The solution of the first equation is $x = -\frac{3}{2}$ or $x = \frac{3}{2}$. The second equation has no solution. Let $f(x) = 2|x|^2 - |x| - 3$ and test a value in each interval determined by the solutions of the related equation.

$\left(-\infty,-\frac{3}{2}\right)$: $f(-2) = 3 > 0$

$\left(-\frac{3}{2},\frac{3}{2}\right)$: $f(0) = -3 < 0$

$\left(\frac{3}{2},\infty\right)$: $f(2) = 3 > 0$

Function values are negative on $\left(-\frac{3}{2},\frac{3}{2}\right)$. Since the inequality symbol is $\leq$, the endpoints of the interval must also be included in the solution set. It is $\left[-\frac{3}{2},\frac{3}{2}\right]$.

83.
$$\left|1+\frac{1}{x}\right| < 3$$
$$-3 < 1+\frac{1}{x} < 3$$
$$-3 < 1+\frac{1}{x} \quad \textit{and} \quad 1+\frac{1}{x} < 3$$

First solve $-3 < 1+\frac{1}{x}$.

$$0 < 4+\frac{1}{x}, \text{ or } \frac{1}{x}+4 > 0$$

The denominator of $f(x) = \frac{1}{x}+4$ is 0 when $x = 0$, so the function is not defined for this value of x. Now solve the related equation.

$$\frac{1}{x}+4 = 0$$
$$1+4x = 0 \quad \text{Multiplying by } x$$
$$x = -\frac{1}{4}$$

The critical values are $-\frac{1}{4}$ and 0. Test a value in each of the intervals determined by them.

$\left(\infty,-\frac{1}{4}\right)$: $f(-1) = 3 > 0$

$\left(-\frac{1}{4},0\right)$: $f(-0.1) = -6 < 0$

$(0,\infty)$: $f(1) = 5 > 0$

The solution set for this portion of the inequality is $\left(-\infty,-\frac{1}{4}\right) \cup (0,\infty)$.

Next solve $1+\frac{1}{x} < 3$, or $\frac{1}{x} - 2 < 0$. The denominator of $f(x) = \frac{1}{x} - 2$ is 0 when $x = 0$, so the function is not defined for this value of x. Now solve the related equation.

$$\frac{1}{x} - 2 = 0$$
$$1-2x = 0 \quad \text{Multiplying by } x$$
$$x = \frac{1}{2}$$

The critical values are 0 and $\frac{1}{2}$. Test a value in each of the intervals determined by them.

$(-\infty,0)$: $f(-1) = -3 < 0$

$\left(0,\frac{1}{2}\right)$: $f(0.1) = 8 > 0$

$\left(\frac{1}{2},\infty\right)$: $f(1) = -1 < 0$

The solution set for this portion of the inequality is $(-\infty,0) \cup \left(\frac{1}{2},\infty\right)$.

The solution set of the original inequality is

$$\left(\left(-\infty,-\frac{1}{4}\right) \cup (0,\infty)\right) \textit{and} \left((-\infty,0) \cup \left(\frac{1}{2},\infty\right)\right),$$

or $\left(-\infty,-\frac{1}{4}\right) \cup \left(\frac{1}{2},\infty\right)$.

85.
$$|x^2+3x-1| < 3$$
$$-3 < x^2+3x-1 < 3$$
$$-3 < x^2+3x-1 \quad \textit{and} \quad x^2+3x-1 < 3$$

First solve $-3 < x^2+3x-1$, or $x^2+3x-1 > -3$.

$$x^2+3x-1 > -3$$
$$x^2+3x+2 > 0$$
$$x^2+3x+2 = 0 \quad \text{Related equation}$$
$$(x+2)(x+1) = 0$$
$$x = -2 \quad \textit{or} \quad x = -1$$

Let $f(x) = x^2+3x+2$ and test a value in each of the intervals determined by the solution of the related equation.

$(-\infty,-2)$: $f(-3)=2>0$

$(-2,-1)$: $f(-1.5)=-0.25<0$

$(-1,\infty)$: $f(0)=2>0$

The solution set for this portion of the inequality is $(-\infty,-2)\cup(-1,\infty)$.

Next solve $x^2+3x-1<3$.

$$x^2+3x-1<3$$
$$x^2+3x-4<0$$
$$x^2+3x-4=0 \quad \text{Related equation}$$
$$(x+4)(x-1)=0$$
$$x=-4 \ \ or\ \ x=1$$

Let $f(x)=x^2+3x-4$ and test a value in each of the intervals determined by the solution of the related equation.

$(-\infty,-4)$: $f(-5)=6>0$

$(-4,1)$: $f(0)=-4<0$

$(1,\infty)$: $f(2)=6>0$

The solution set for this portion of the inequality is $(-4,1)$.

The solution set of the original inequality is $\big((-\infty,-2)\cup(-1,\infty)\big)$ *and* $(-4,1)$, or $(-4,-2)\cup(-1,1)$.

87. First find a quadratic equation with solutions -4 and 3.

$$(x+4)(x-3)=0$$
$$x^2+x-12=0$$

Test a point in each of the three intervals determined by -4 and 3.

$(-\infty,-4)$: $(-5+4)(-5-3)=8>0$

$(-4,3)$: $(0+4)(0-3)=-12<0$

$(3,\infty)$: $(4+4)(4-3)=8>0$

Then a quadratic inequality for which the solution set is $(-4,3)$ is $x^2+x-12<0$. Answers may vary.

Exercise Set 3.6

1.
$$y=kx$$
$$54=k\cdot 12$$
$$\frac{54}{12}=k,\ \text{or}\ k=\frac{9}{2}$$

The variation constant is $\frac{9}{2}$, or 4.5. The equation of variation is $y=\frac{9}{2}x$, or $y=4.5x$.

3.
$$y=\frac{k}{x}$$
$$3=\frac{k}{12}$$
$$36=k$$

The variation constant is 36. The equation of variation is $y=\frac{36}{x}$.

5.
$$y=kx$$
$$1=k\cdot\frac{1}{4}$$
$$4=k$$

The variation constant is 4. The equation of variation is $y=4x$.

7.
$$y=\frac{k}{x}$$
$$32=\frac{k}{\frac{1}{8}}$$
$$\frac{1}{8}\cdot 32=k$$
$$4=k$$

The variation constant is 4. The equation of variation is $y=\frac{4}{x}$.

9.
$$y=kx$$
$$\frac{3}{4}=k\cdot 2$$
$$\frac{1}{2}\cdot\frac{3}{4}=k$$
$$\frac{3}{8}=k$$

The variation constant is $\frac{3}{8}$. The equation of variation is $y=\frac{3}{8}x$.

11.
$$y=\frac{k}{x}$$
$$1.8=\frac{k}{0.3}$$
$$0.54=k$$

The variation constant is 0.54. The equation of variation is $y=\frac{0.54}{x}$.

13.
$$T=\frac{k}{P} \quad T \text{ varies inversely as } P.$$
$$5=\frac{k}{7} \quad \text{Substituting}$$
$$35=k \quad \text{Variation constant}$$
$$T=\frac{35}{P} \quad \text{Equation of variation}$$
$$T=\frac{35}{10} \quad \text{Substituting}$$
$$T=3.5$$

It will take 10 bricklayers 3.5 hr to complete the job.

15. Let F = the number of grams of fat and w = the weight.

$$F=kw \quad F \text{ varies directly as } w.$$
$$60=k\cdot 120 \quad \text{Substituting}$$
$$\frac{60}{120}=k,\ \text{or} \quad \text{Solving for } k$$
$$\frac{1}{2}=k \quad \text{Variation constant}$$

$F = \frac{1}{2}w$ Equation of variation

$F = \frac{1}{2} \cdot 180$ Substituting

$F = 90$

The maximum daily fat intake for a person weighing 180 lb is 90 g.

17. $W = \frac{k}{L}$ W varies inversely as L.

$1200 = \frac{k}{8}$ Substituting

$9600 = k$ Variation constant

$W = \frac{9600}{L}$ Equation of variation

$W = \frac{9600}{14}$ Substituting

$W = 685\frac{5}{7}$

A 14-m beam can support $685\frac{5}{7}$ kg, or about 686 kg.

19. $M = kE$ M varies directly as E.

$38 = k \cdot 95$ Substituting

$\frac{2}{5} = k$ Variation constant

$M = \frac{2}{5}E$ Equation of variation

$M = \frac{2}{5} \cdot 100$ Substituting

$M = 40$

A 100-lb person would weigh 40 lb on Mars.

21. $d = km$ d varies directly as m.

$40 = k \cdot 3$ Substituting

$\frac{40}{3} = k$ Variation constant

$d = \frac{40}{3}m$ Equation of variation

$d = \frac{40}{3} \cdot 5 = \frac{200}{3}$ Substituting

$d = 66\frac{2}{3}$

A 5-kg mass will stretch the spring $66\frac{2}{3}$ cm.

23. $P = \frac{k}{W}$ P varies inversely as W.

$330 = \frac{k}{3.2}$ Substituting

$1056 = k$ Variation constant

$P = \frac{1056}{W}$ Equation of variation

$550 = \frac{1056}{W}$ Substituting

$550W = 1056$ Multiplying by W

$W = \frac{1056}{550}$ Dividing by 550

$W = 1.92$ Simplifying

A tone with a pitch of 550 vibrations per second has a wavelength of 1.92 ft.

25. $y = \frac{k}{x^2}$

$0.15 = \frac{k}{(0.1)^2}$ Substituting

$0.15 = \frac{k}{0.01}$

$0.15(0.01) = k$

$0.0015 = k$

The equation of variation is $y = \frac{0.0015}{x^2}$.

27. $y = kx^2$

$0.15 = k(0.1)^2$ Substituting

$0.15 = 0.01k$

$\frac{0.15}{0.01} = k$

$15 = k$

The equation of variation is $y = 15x^2$.

$y = \frac{2}{3}x^2$

29. $y = kxz$

$56 = k \cdot 7 \cdot 8$ Substituting

$56 = 56k$

$1 = k$

The equation of variation is $y = xz$.

31. $y = kxz^2$

$105 = k \cdot 14 \cdot 5^2$ Substituting

$105 = 350k$

$\frac{105}{350} = k$

$\frac{3}{10} = k$

The equation of variation is $y = \frac{3}{10}xz^2$.

33.
$$\begin{aligned} y &= k\frac{xz}{wp} \\ \frac{3}{28} &= k\frac{3\cdot 10}{7\cdot 8} \quad \text{Substituting} \\ \frac{3}{28} &= k\cdot\frac{30}{56} \\ \frac{3}{28}\cdot\frac{56}{30} &= k \\ \frac{1}{5} &= k \end{aligned}$$

The equation of variation is $y = \frac{xz}{5wp}$.

35.
$$\begin{aligned} I &= \frac{k}{d^2} \\ 90 &= \frac{k}{5^2} \quad \text{Substituting} \\ 90 &= \frac{k}{25} \\ 2250 &= k \end{aligned}$$

The equation of variation is $I = \frac{2250}{d^2}$.

Substitute 40 for I and find d.
$$\begin{aligned} 40 &= \frac{2250}{d^2} \\ 40d^2 &= 2250 \\ d^2 &= 56.25 \\ d &= 7.5 \end{aligned}$$

The distance from 5 m to 7.5 m is $7.5-5$, or 2.5 m, so it is 2.5 m further to a point where the intensity is 40 W/m^2.

37.
$$\begin{aligned} d &= kr^2 \\ 200 &= k\cdot 60^2 \quad \text{Substituting} \\ 200 &= 3600k \\ \frac{200}{3600} &= k \\ \frac{1}{18} &= k \end{aligned}$$

The equation of variation is $d = \frac{1}{18}r^2$.

Substitute 72 for d and find r.
$$\begin{aligned} 72 &= \frac{1}{18}r^2 \\ 1296 &= r^2 \\ 36 &= r \end{aligned}$$

A car can travel 36 mph and still stop in 72 ft.

39. $E = \frac{kR}{I}$

We first find k.
$$\begin{aligned} 2.24 &= \frac{k\cdot 28}{112\frac{1}{3}} \quad \text{Substituting} \\ 2.24\left(\frac{112\frac{1}{3}}{28}\right) &= k \quad \text{Multiplying by } \frac{112\frac{1}{3}}{28} \\ 9 &\approx k \end{aligned}$$

The equation of variation is $E = \frac{9R}{I}$.

Substitute 2.24 for E and 300 for I and solve R.
$$\begin{aligned} 2.24 &= \frac{9R}{300} \\ 2.24\left(\frac{300}{9}\right) &= R \quad \text{Multiplying by } \frac{300}{9} \\ 75 &\approx R \end{aligned}$$

Kevin Brown would have given up 75 earned runs if he had pitched 300 innings.

41. Discussion and Writing

43.

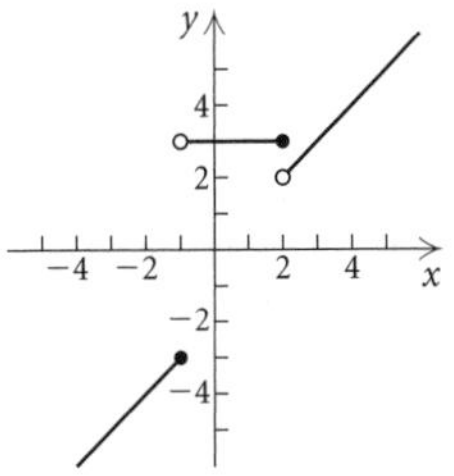

45. Test for symmetry with respect to the x-axis.
$$\begin{aligned} y^2 &= x \quad \text{Original equation} \\ (-y)^2 &= x \quad \text{Replacing } y \text{ by } -y \\ y^2 &= x \quad \text{Simplifying} \end{aligned}$$

The last equation is equivalent to the original equation, so the graph is symmetric with respect to the x-axis.

Test for symmetry with respect to the y-axis:
$$\begin{aligned} y^2 &= x \quad \text{Original equation} \\ y^2 &= -x \quad \text{Replacing } x \text{ by } -x \end{aligned}$$

The last equation is not equivalent to the original equation, so the graph is not symmetric with respect to the y-axis.

Test for symmetry with respect to the origin:
$$\begin{aligned} y^2 &= x \quad \text{Original equation} \\ (-y)^2 &= -x \quad \text{Replacing } x \text{ by } -x \text{ and } y \text{ by } -y \\ y^2 &= -x \quad \text{Simplifying} \end{aligned}$$

The last equation is not equivalent to the original equation, so the graph is not symmetric with respect to the origin.

47. Let V represent the volume and p represent the price of a jar of peanut butter.
$$\begin{aligned} V &= kp \quad V \text{ varies directly as } p. \\ \pi\left(\frac{3}{2}\right)^2(5) &= k(1.8) \quad \text{Substituting} \\ 6.25\pi &= k \quad \text{Variation constant} \\ V &= 6.25\pi p \quad \text{Equation of variation} \\ \pi(1.625)^2(5.5) &= 6.25\pi p \quad \text{Substituting} \\ 2.32 &\approx p \end{aligned}$$

If cost is directly proportional to volume, the larger jar should cost \$2.32.

Now let W represent the weight and p represent the price of a jar of peanut butter.

$W = kp$

$18 = k(1.8)$ Substituting

$10 = k$ Variation constant

$W = 10p$ Equation of variation

$28 = 10p$ Substituting

$2.8 = p$

If cost is directly proportional to weight, the larger jar should cost \$2.80.

49. We are told $A = kd^2$, and we know $A = \pi r^2$ so we have:

$kd^2 = \pi r^2$

$kd^2 = \pi\left(\frac{d}{2}\right)^2$ $\quad r = \frac{d}{2}$

$kd^2 = \frac{\pi d^2}{4}$

$k = \frac{\pi}{4}$ Variation constant

Chapter 4

Exponential and Logarithmic Functions

Exercise Set 4.1

1. We interchange the first and second coordinates of each ordered pair to find the inverse of the relation. It is

$\{(8,7),\ (8,-2),\ (-4,3),\ (-8,8)\}.$

3. We interchange the first and second coordinates of each ordered pair to find the inverse of the relation. It is

$\{(-1,-1),\ (4,-3)\}.$

5. Interchange x and y.

$$\begin{aligned} y &= 4x{-}5 \\ \downarrow\ & \quad \downarrow \\ x &= 4y{-}5 \end{aligned}$$

7. Interchange x and y.

$$\begin{aligned} x^3y &= -5 \\ \downarrow\downarrow & \\ y^3x &= -5 \end{aligned}$$

9. Interchange x and y.

$$\begin{aligned} x &= y^2{-}2y \\ \downarrow\ & \quad \downarrow\ \ \downarrow \\ y &= x^2{-}2x \end{aligned}$$

11. Graph $x = y^2 - 3$. Some points on the graph are $(-3,0)$, $(-2,-1)$, $(-2,1)$, $(1,-2)$, and $(1,2)$. Plot these points and draw the curve. Then reflect the graph across the line $y = x$.

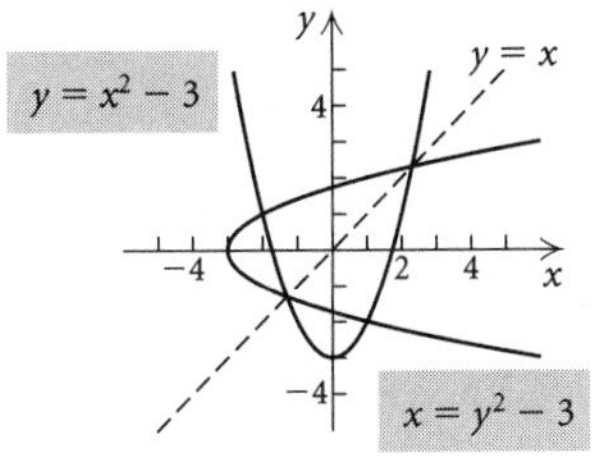

13. Graph $y = 3x - 2$. The intercepts are $(0,-2)$ and $\left(\frac{2}{3}, 0\right)$. Plot these points and draw the line. Then reflect the graph across the line $y = x$.

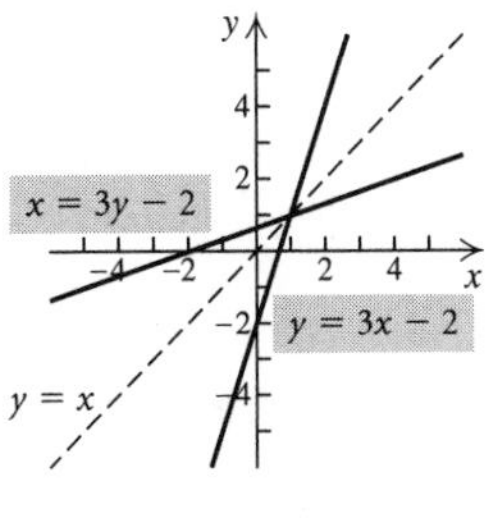

15. Graph $y = |x|$. Some points on the graph are $(0,0)$, $(-2,2)$, $(2,2)$, $(-5,5)$, and $(5,5)$. Plot these points and draw the graph. Then reflect the graph across the line $y = x$.

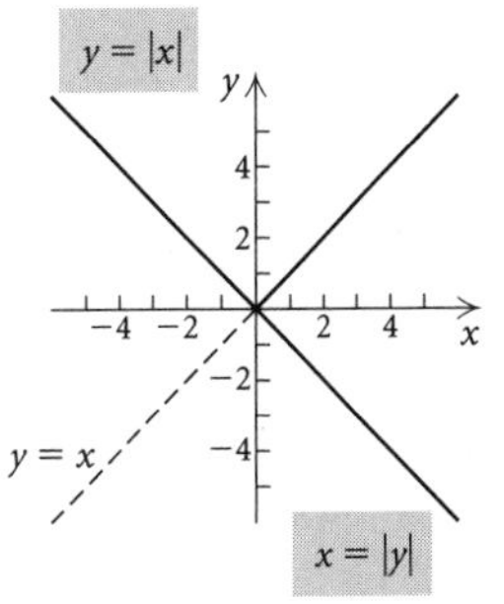

17. We show that if $f(a) = f(b)$, then $a = b$.

$$\begin{aligned} \frac{1}{3}a - 6 &= \frac{1}{3}b - 6 \\ \frac{1}{3}a &= \frac{1}{3}b \qquad \text{Adding 6} \\ a &= b \qquad \text{Multiplying by 3} \end{aligned}$$

Thus f is one-to-one.

19. We show that if $f(a) = f(b)$, then $a = b$.

$$\begin{aligned} a^3 + \frac{1}{2} &= b^3 + \frac{1}{2} \\ a^3 &= b^3 \qquad \text{Subtracting } \frac{1}{2} \\ a &= b \qquad \text{Taking cube roots} \end{aligned}$$

Thus f is one-to-one.

21. $g(-1) = 1 - (-1)^2 = 1 - 1 = 0$ and $g(1) = 1 - 1^2 = 1 - 1 = 0$, so $g(-1) = g(1)$ but $-1 \neq 1$. Thus the function is not one-to-one.

23. $f(-2) = (-2)^4 - (-2)^2 = 16 - 4 = 12$ and $f(2) = 2^4 - 2^2 = 16 - 4 = 12$, so $f(-2) = f(2)$ but $-2 \neq 2$. Thus the function is not one-to-one.

25. The function is one-to-one, because no horizontal line crosses the graph more than once.

27. The function is not one-to-one, because there are many horizontal lines that cross the graph more than once.

29. The function is not one-to-one, because there are many horizontal lines that cross the graph more than once.

31. The function is one-to-one, because no horizontal line crosses the graph more than once.

33. The graph of $f(x) = 5x - 8$ is shown below.

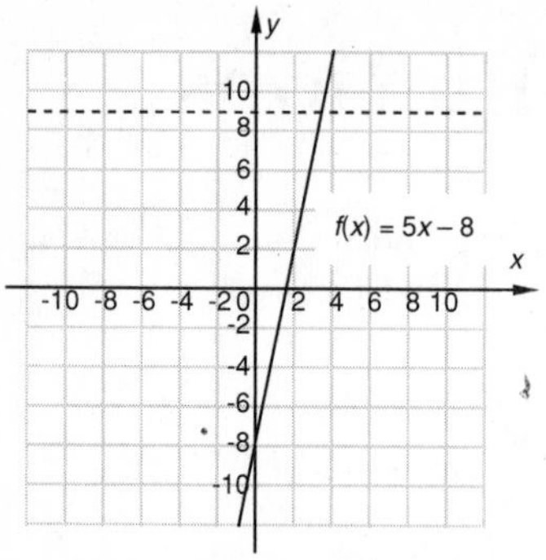

Since there is no horizontal line that crosses the graph more than once, the function is one-to-one.

35. The graph of $f(x) = 1 - x^2$ is shown below.

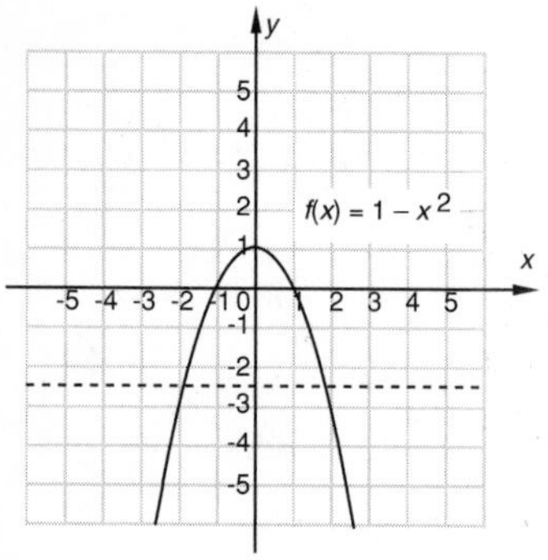

Since there are many horizontal lines that cross the graph more than once, the function is not one-to-one.

37. The graph of $f(x) = |x + 2|$ is shown below.

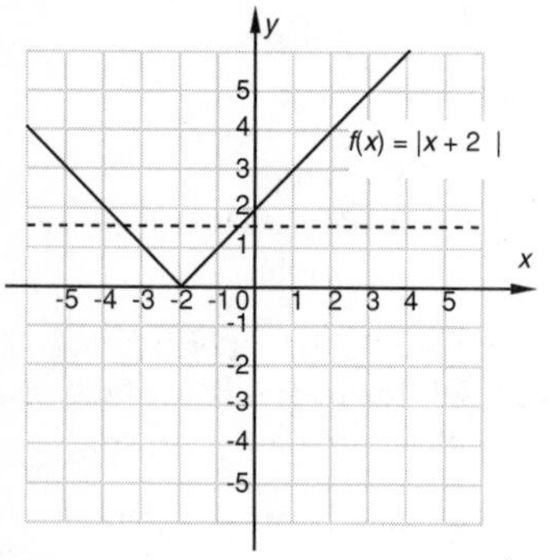

Since there are many horizontal lines that cross the graph more than once, the function is not one-to-one.

39. The graph of $f(x) = -\dfrac{4}{x}$ is shown below.

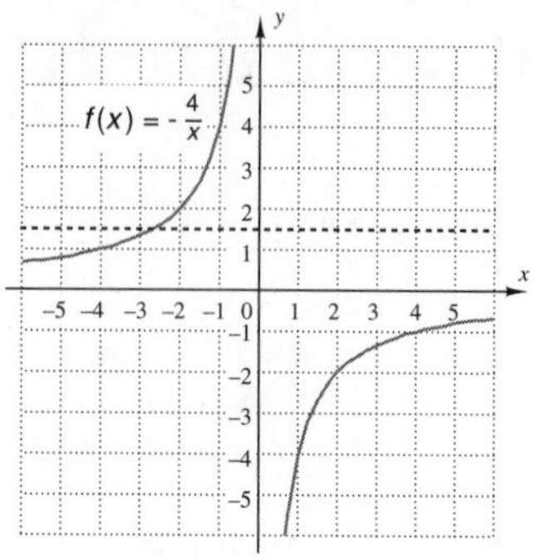

Since there is no horizontal line that crosses the graph more than once, the function is one-to-one.

41. The graph of $f(x) = \dfrac{2}{3}$ is shown below.

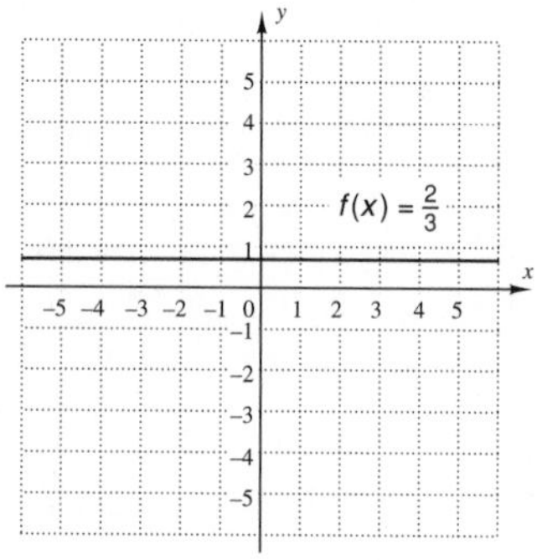

Since the horizontal line $y = \dfrac{2}{3}$ crosses the graph more than once, the function is not one-to-one.

43. The graph of $f(x) = \sqrt{25 - x^2}$ is shown below.

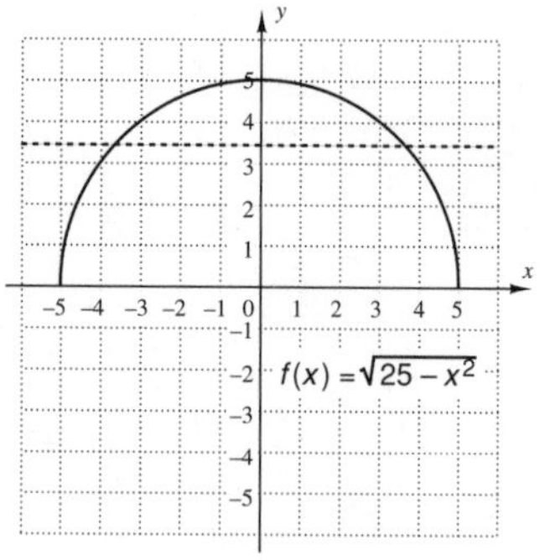

Since there are many horizontal lines that cross the graph more than once, the function is not one-to-one.

45. a) The graph of $f(x) = x + 4$ is shown below. It passes the horizontal line test, so it is one-to-one.

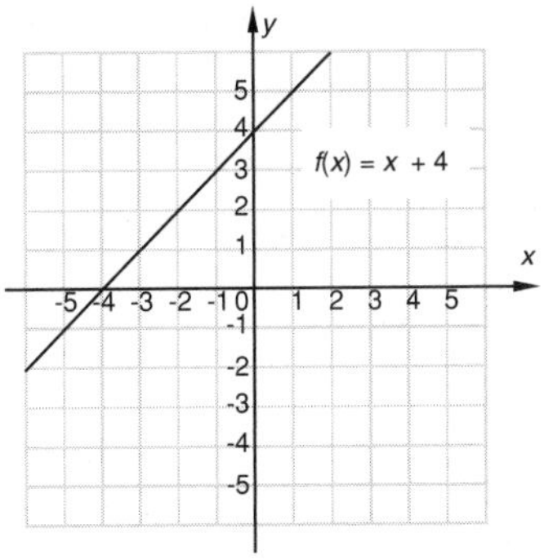

b) Replace $f(x)$ with y: $y = x + 4$

Interchange x and y: $x = y + 4$

Solve for y: $x - 4 = y$

Replace y with $f^{-1}(x)$: $f^{-1}(x) = x - 4$

47. a) The graph of $f(x) = 2x - 1$ is shown below. It passes the horizontal line test, so it is one-to-one.

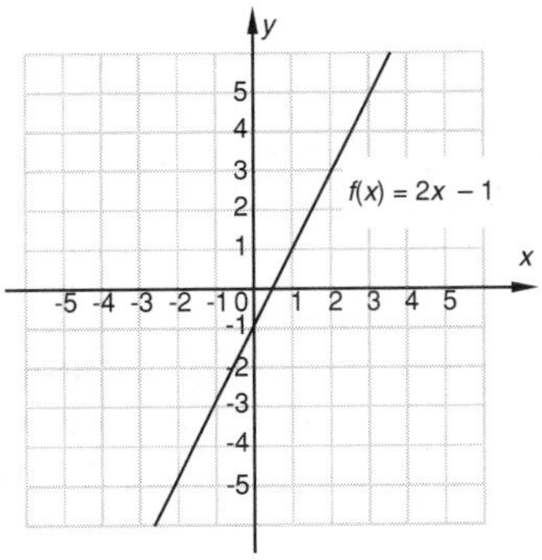

b) Replace $f(x)$ with y: $y = 2x - 1$

Interchange x and y: $x = 2y - 1$

Solve for y: $\dfrac{x+1}{2} = y$

Replace y with $f^{-1}(x)$: $f^{-1}(x) = \dfrac{x+1}{2}$

49. a) The graph of $f(x) = \dfrac{4}{x+7}$ is shown below. It passes the horizontal line test, so the function is one-to-one.

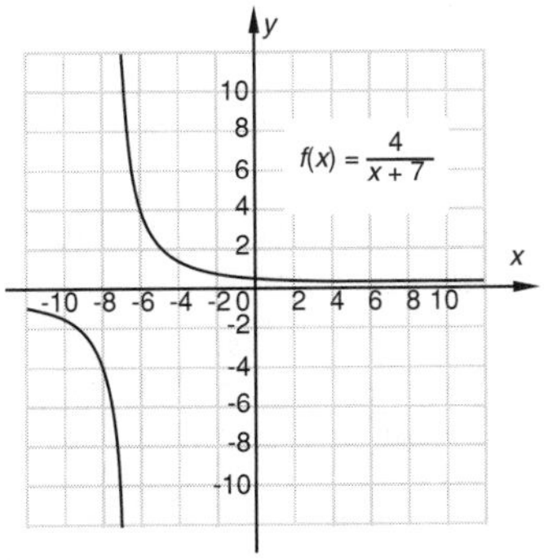

b) Replace $f(x)$ with y: $y = \dfrac{4}{x+7}$

Interchange x and y: $x = \dfrac{4}{y+7}$

Solve for y: $x(y+7) = 4$

$$y + 7 = \frac{4}{x}$$

$$y = \frac{4}{x} - 7$$

Replace y with $f^{-1}(x)$: $f^{-1}(x) = \dfrac{4}{x} - 7$

51. a) The graph of $f(x) = \dfrac{x+4}{x-3}$ is shown below. It passes the horizontal line test, so the function is one-to-one.

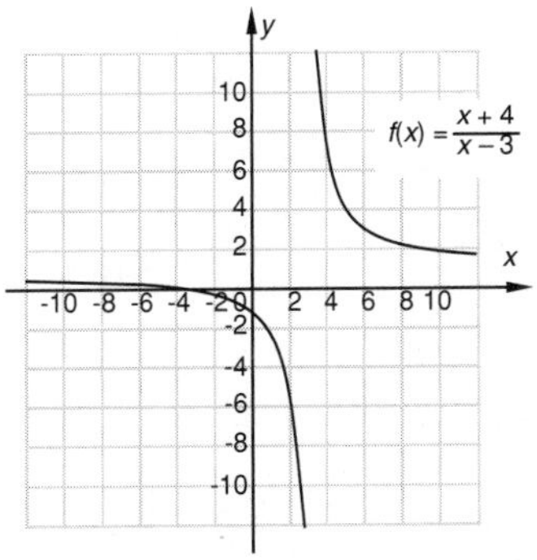

b) Replace $f(x)$ with y: $y = \dfrac{x+4}{x-3}$

Interchange x and y: $x = \dfrac{y+4}{y-3}$

Solve for y: $(y-3)x = y + 4$

$$xy - 3x = y + 4$$

$$xy - y = 3x + 4$$

$$y(x-1) = 3x + 4$$

$$y = \frac{3x+4}{x-1}$$

Replace y with $f^{-1}(x)$: $f^{-1}(x) = \dfrac{3x+4}{x-1}$

53. a) The graph of $f(x) = x^3 - 1$ is shown below. It passes the horizontal line test, so the function is one-to-one.

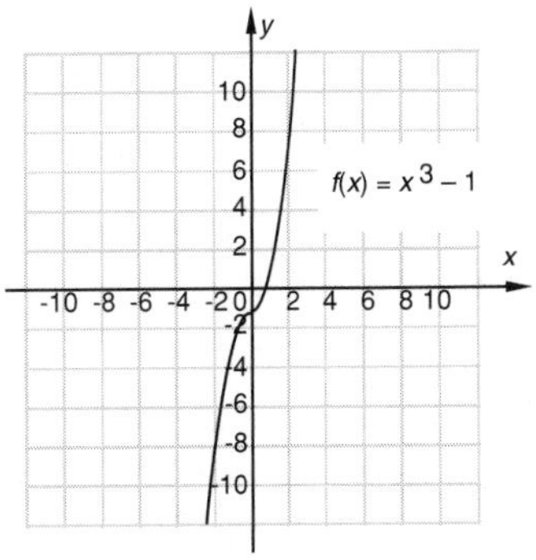

b) Replace $f(x)$ with y: $y = x^3 - 1$

Interchange x and y: $x = y^3 - 1$

Solve for y: $x + 1 = y^3$

$\sqrt[3]{x+1} = y$

Replace y with $f^{-1}(x)$: $f^{-1}(x) = \sqrt[3]{x+1}$

55. a) The graph of $f(x) = x\sqrt{4 - x^2}$ is shown below. Since there are many horizontal lines that cross the graph more than once, the function is not one-to-one and thus does not have an inverse that is a function.

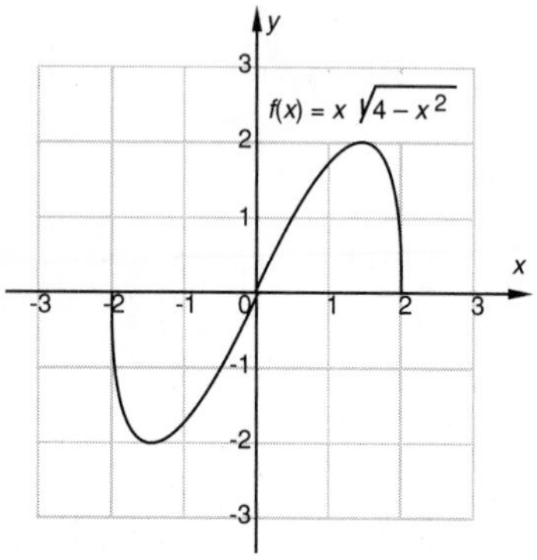

57. a) The graph of $f(x) = 5x^2 - 2$, $x \geq 0$ is shown below. It passes the horizontal line test, so it is one-to-one.

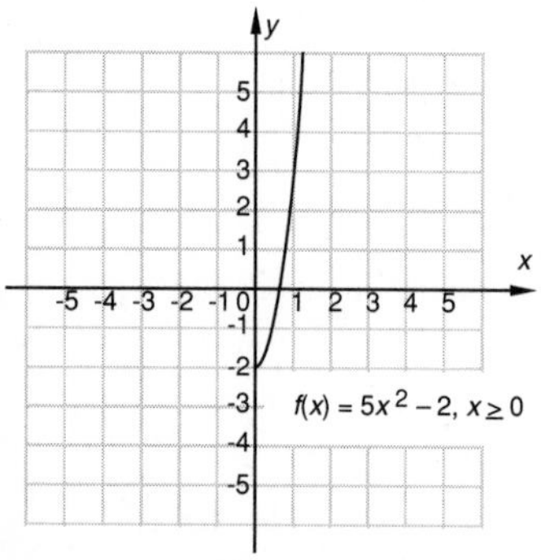

b) Replace $f(x)$ with y: $y = 5x^2 - 2$

Interchange x and y: $x = 5y^2 - 2$

Solve for y: $x + 2 = 5y^2$

$$\frac{x+2}{5} = y^2$$

$$\sqrt{\frac{x+2}{5}} = y$$

(We take the principal square root, because $x \geq 0$ in the original equation.)

Replace y with $f^{-1}(x)$: $f^{-1}(x) = \sqrt{\frac{x+2}{5}}$ for all x in the range of $f(x)$, or $f^{-1}(x) = \sqrt{\frac{x+2}{5}}$, $x \geq -2$

59. a) The graph of $f(x) = \sqrt{x+1}$ is shown below. It passes the horizontal line test, so the function is one-to-one.

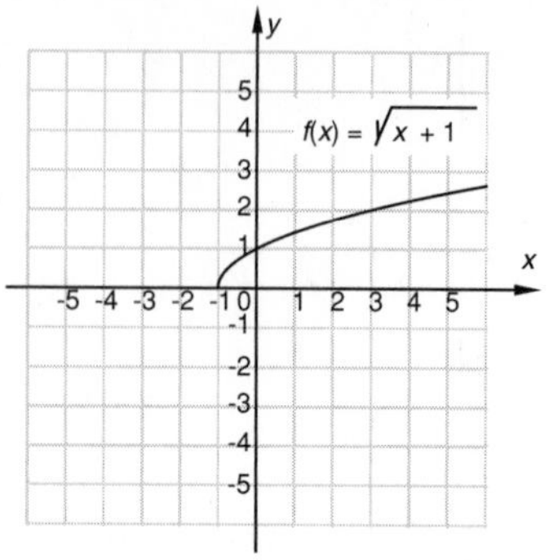

b) Replace $f(x)$ with y: $y = \sqrt{x+1}$

Interchange x and y: $x = \sqrt{y+1}$

Solve for y: $x^2 = y + 1$

$x^2 - 1 = y$

Replace y with $f^{-1}(x)$: $f^{-1}(x) = x^2 - 1$ for all x in the range of $f(x)$, or $f^{-1}(x) = x^2 - 1$, $x \geq 0$.

61. $f(x) = 3x$

The function f multiplies an input by 3. Then to reverse this procedure, f^{-1} would divide each of its inputs by 3. Thus, $f^{-1}(x) = \frac{x}{3}$, or $f^{-1}(x) = \frac{1}{3}x$.

63. $f(x) = -x$

The outputs of f are the opposites, or additive inverses, of the inputs. Then the outputs of f^{-1} are the opposites of its inputs. Thus, $f^{-1}(x) = -x$.

65. $f(x) = \sqrt[3]{x-5}$

The function f subtracts 5 from each input and then takes the cube root of the result. To reverse this procedure, f^{-1} would raise each input to the third power and then add 5 to the result. Thus, $f^{-1}(x) = x^3 + 5$.

67. We reflect the graph of f across the line $y = x$. The reflections of the labeled points are $(-5, -5)$, $(-3, 0)$, $(1, 2)$, and $(3, 5)$.

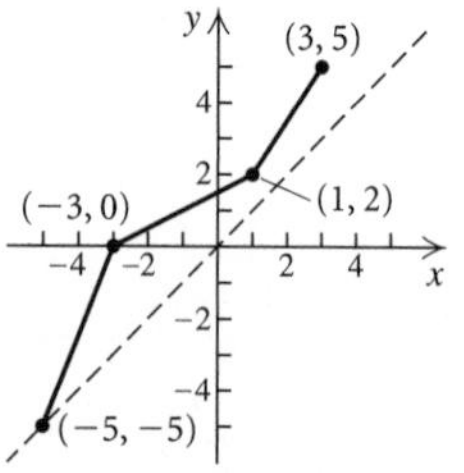

69. We reflect the graph of f across the line $y = x$. The reflections of the labeled points are $(-6, -2)$, $(1, -1)$, $(2, 0)$, and $(5.375, 1.5)$.

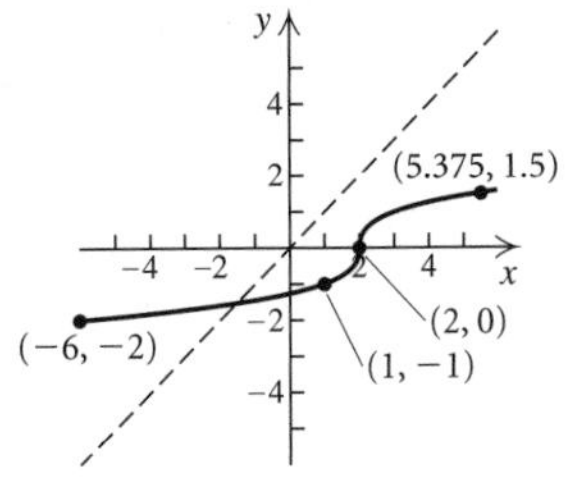

71. We reflect the graph of f across the line $y = x$.

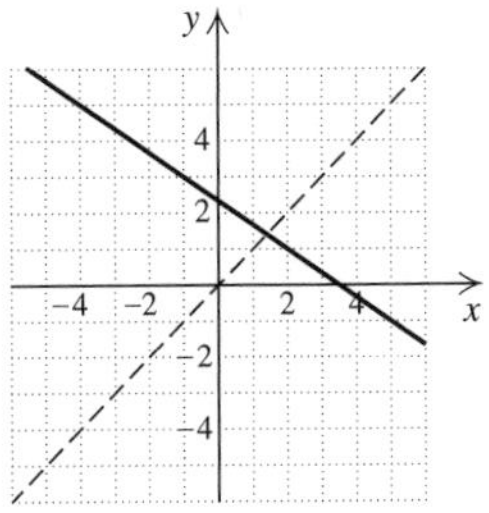

73. We find $(f^{-1}\circ f)(x)$ and $(f\circ f^{-1})(x)$ and check to see that each is x.

$(f^{-1}\circ f)(x) = f^{-1}(f(x)) = f^{-1}\left(\frac{7}{8}x\right) =$

$\frac{8}{7}\left(\frac{7}{8}x\right) = x$

$(f\circ f^{-1})(x) = f(f^{-1}(x)) = f\left(\frac{8}{7}x\right) = \frac{7}{8}\left(\frac{8}{7}x\right) = x$

75. We find $(f^{-1}\circ f)(x)$ and $(f\circ f^{-1})(x)$ and check to see that each is x.

$(f^{-1}\circ f)(x) = f^{-1}(f(x)) = f^{-1}\left(\frac{1-x}{x}\right) =$

$\frac{1}{\frac{1-x}{x}+1} = \frac{1}{\frac{1-x+x}{x}} = \frac{1}{\frac{1}{x}} = x$

$(f\circ f^{-1})(x) = f(f^{-1}(x)) = f\left(\frac{1}{x+1}\right) =$

$\frac{1-\frac{1}{x+1}}{\frac{1}{x+1}} = \frac{\frac{x+1-1}{x+1}}{\frac{1}{x+1}} = \frac{\frac{x}{x+1}}{\frac{1}{x+1}} = x$

77. $(f^{-1}\circ f)(x) = f^{-1}(f(x)) = \dfrac{5\left(\frac{2}{5}x+1\right)-5}{2} =$

$\frac{2x+5-5}{2} = \frac{2x}{2} = x$

$(f\circ f^{-1})(x) = f(f^{-1}(x) = \frac{2}{5}\left(\frac{5x-5}{2}\right)+1 =$

$x-1+1 = x$

79. Replace $f(x)$ with y: $y = 5x-3$

Interchange x and y: $x = 5y-3$

Solve for y: $x+3 = 5y$

$\frac{x+3}{5} = y$

Replace y with $f^{-1}(x)$: $f^{-1}(x) = \frac{x+3}{5}$, or $\frac{1}{5}x+\frac{3}{5}$

The domain and range of f are $(-\infty,\infty)$, so the domain and range of f^{-1} are also $(-\infty,\infty)$.

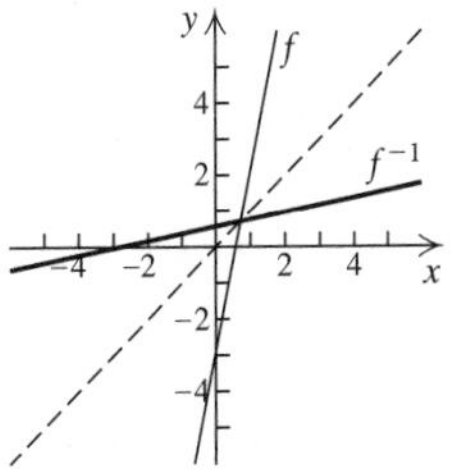

81. Replace $f(x)$ with y: $y = \frac{2}{x}$

Interchange x and y: $x = \frac{2}{y}$

Solve for y: $xy = 2$

$y = \frac{2}{x}$

Replace y with $f^{-1}(x)$: $f^{-1}(x) = \frac{2}{x}$

The domain and range of f are $(-\infty,0)\cup(0,\infty)$, so the domain and range of f^{-1} are also $(-\infty,0)\cup(0,\infty)$.

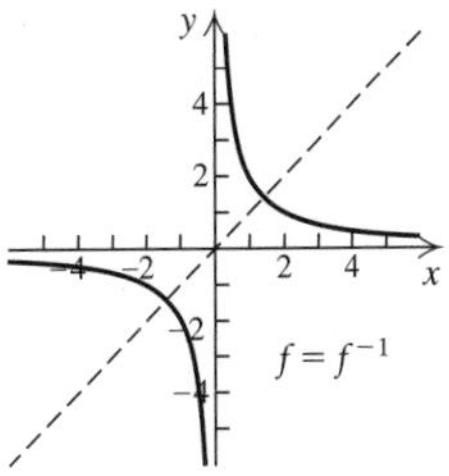

83. Replace $f(x)$ with y: $y = \frac{1}{3}x^3-2$

Interchange x and y: $x = \frac{1}{3}y^3-2$

Solve for y: $x+2 = \frac{1}{3}y^3$

$3x+6 = y^3$

$\sqrt[3]{3x+6} = y$

Replace y with $f^{-1}(x)$: $f^{-1}(x) = \sqrt[3]{3x+6}$

The domain and range of f are $(-\infty,\infty)$, so the domain and range of f^{-1} are also $(-\infty,\infty)$.

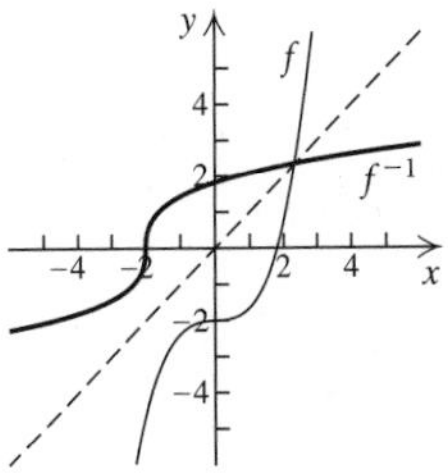

85. Replace $f(x)$ with y: $y = \dfrac{x+1}{x-3}$

Interchange x and y: $x = \dfrac{y+1}{y-3}$

Solve for y:
$$xy - 3x = y + 1$$
$$xy - y = 3x + 1$$
$$y(x-1) = 3x + 1$$
$$y = \frac{3x+1}{x-1}$$

Replace y with $f^{-1}(x)$: $f^{-1}(x) = \dfrac{3x+1}{x-1}$

The domain of f is $(-\infty, 3) \cup (3, \infty)$ and the range of f is $(-\infty, 1) \cup (1, \infty)$. Thus the domain of f^{-1} is $(-\infty, 1) \cup (1, \infty)$ and the range of f^{-1} is $(-\infty, 3) \cup (3, \infty)$.

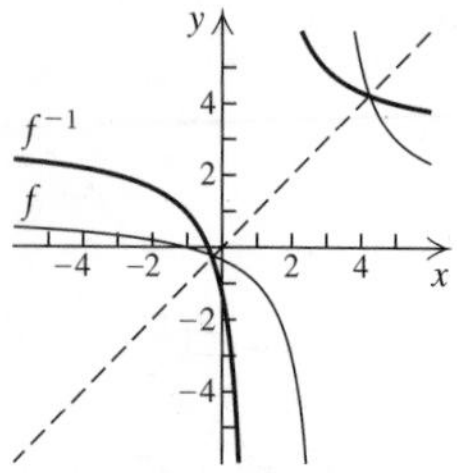

87. Since $f(f^{-1}(x)) = f^{-1}(f(x)) = x$, then $f(f^{-1}(5)) = 5$ and $f^{-1}(f(a)) = a$.

89. a) $g(x) = 2(x+12)$
$$g(6) = 2(6+12) = 2 \cdot 18 = 36$$
$$g(8) = 2(8+12) = 2 \cdot 20 = 40$$
$$g(10) = 2(10+12) = 2 \cdot 22 = 44$$
$$g(14) = 2(14+12) = 2 \cdot 26 = 52$$
$$g(18) = 2(18+12) = 2 \cdot 30 = 60$$

b) The graph passes the horizontal line test and thus has an inverse that is a function.

Replace $g(x)$ with y: $y = 2(x+12)$

Interchange x and y: $x = 2(y+12)$

Solve for y: $\dfrac{x-24}{2} = y$

Replace y with $g^{-1}(x)$: $g^{-1}(x) = \dfrac{x-24}{2}$, or $\dfrac{x}{2} - 12$

c) $g^{-1}(36) = \dfrac{36-24}{2} = \dfrac{12}{2} = 6$

$$g^{-1}(40) = \frac{40-24}{2} = \frac{16}{2} = 8$$
$$g^{-1}(44) = \frac{44-24}{2} = \frac{20}{2} = 10$$
$$g^{-1}(52) = \frac{52-24}{2} = \frac{28}{2} = 14$$
$$g^{-1}(60) = \frac{60-24}{2} = \frac{36}{2} = 18$$

91. $y_1 = 0.8x + 1.7$,
$y_2 = \dfrac{x-1.7}{0.8}$

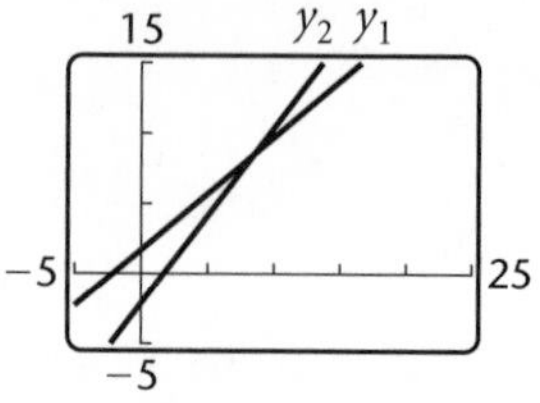

Both the domain and the range of f are the set of all real numbers. Then both the domain and the range of f^{-1} are also the set of all real numbers.

93. $y_1 = \frac{1}{2}x - 4$,
$y_2 = 2x + 8$

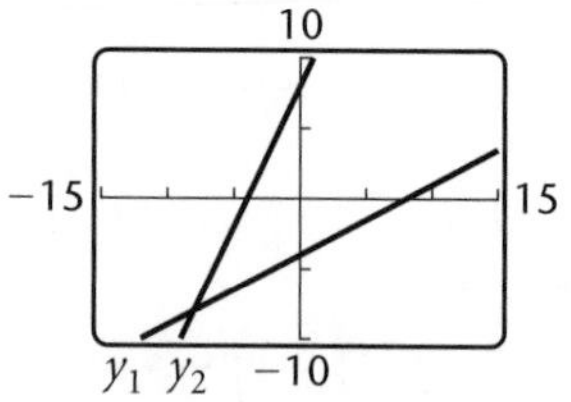

Both the domain and the range of f are the set of all real numbers. Then both the domain and the range of f^{-1} are also the set of all real numbers.

95. $y_1 = \sqrt{x-3}$,
$y_2 = x^2 + 3, x \geqslant 0$

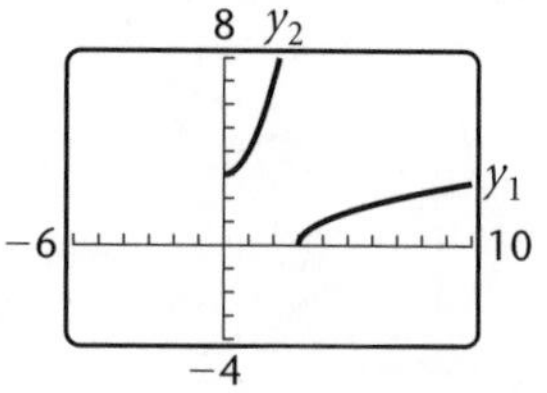

The domain of f is $[3, \infty)$ and the range of f is $[0, \infty)$. Then the domain of f^{-1} is $[0, \infty)$ and the range of f^{-1} is $[3, \infty)$.

97. $y_1 = x^2 - 4, x \geqslant 0$; $y_2 = \sqrt{4+x}$

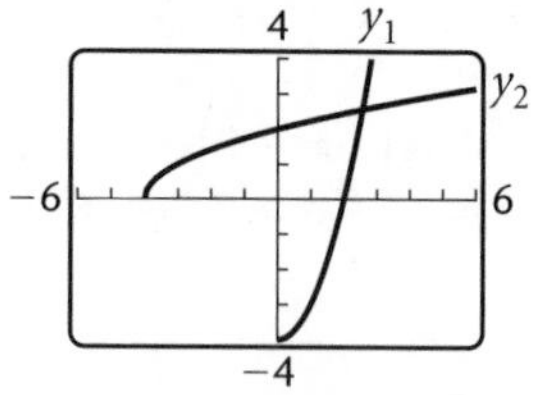

Since it is specified that $x \geq 0$, the domain of f is $[0, \infty)$. The range of f is $[-4, \infty)$. Then the domain of f^{-1} is $[-4, \infty)$ and the range of f^{-1} is $[0, \infty)$.

99. $y_1 = (3x - 9)^3,\ y_2 = \dfrac{\sqrt[3]{x} + 9}{3}$

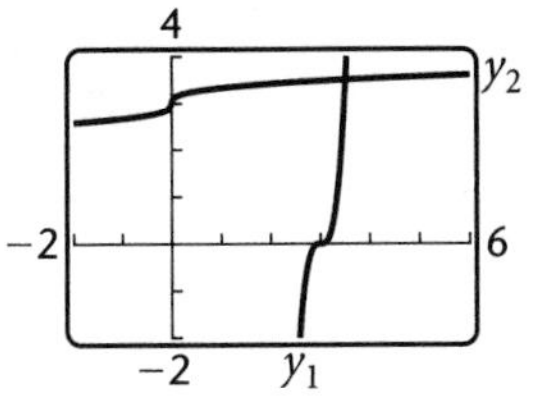

Both the domain and the range of f are the set of all real numbers. Then both the domain and the range of f^{-1} are also the set of all real numbers.

101. a) $D(r) = \dfrac{11r+5}{10}$

$$D(0) = \frac{11 \cdot 0 + 5}{10} = \frac{5}{10} = 0.5$$

$$D(10) = \frac{11 \cdot 10 + 5}{10} = \frac{115}{10} = 11.5$$

$$D(20) = \frac{11 \cdot 20 + 5}{10} = \frac{225}{10} = 22.5$$

$$D(50) = \frac{11 \cdot 50 + 5}{10} = \frac{555}{10} = 55.5$$

$$D(65) = \frac{11 \cdot 65 + 5}{10} = \frac{720}{10} = 72$$

b) Replace $D(r)$ with y: $y = \dfrac{11r+5}{10}$

Interchange r and y: $r = \dfrac{11y+5}{10}$

Solve for y: $10r = 11y + 5$

$$10r - 5 = 11y$$

$$\frac{10r-5}{11} = y$$

Replace y with $D^{-1}(r)$: $D^{-1}(r) = \dfrac{10r-5}{11}$

$D^{-1}(r)$ represents the speed, in miles per hour, that the car is traveling when the reaction distance is r feet.

c) $y_1 = \dfrac{11x+5}{10},\ y_2 = \dfrac{10x-5}{11}$

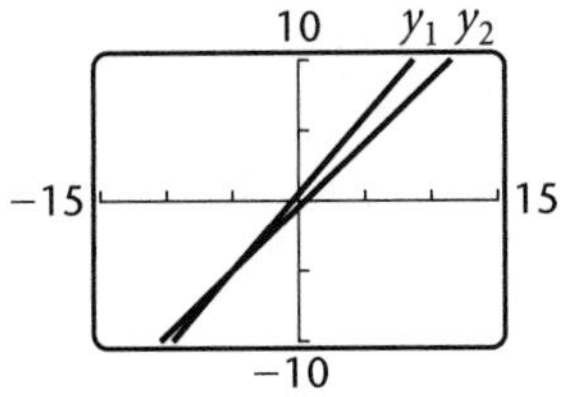

103. Discussion and Writing

105. The functions for which the coefficient of x^2 is negative have a maximum value. These are (b), (d), (f), and (h).

107. Since $|2| > 1$ the graph of $f(x) = 2x^2$ can be obtained by stretching the graph of $f(x) = x^2$ vertically. Since $0 < \left|\frac{1}{4}\right| < 1$, the graph of $f(x) = \frac{1}{4}x^2$ can be obtained by shrinking the graph of $y = x^2$ vertically. Thus the graph of $f(x) = 2x^2$, or (a) is narrower.

109. We can write (f) as $f(x) = -2[x - (-3)]^2 + 1$. Thus the graph of (f) has vertex $(-3, 1)$.

111. The graph of $f(x) = x^2 - 3$ is a parabola with vertex $(0, -3)$. If we consider x-values such that $x \geq 0$, then the graph is the right-hand side of the parabola and it passes the horizontal line test. We find the inverse of $f(x) = x^2 - 3,\ x \geq 0$.

Replace $f(x)$ with y: $y = x^2 - 3$

Interchange x and y: $x = y^2 - 3$

Solve for y: $x + 3 = y^2$

$$\sqrt{x+3} = y$$

(We take the principal square root, because $x \geq 0$ in the original equation.)

Replace y with $f^{-1}(x)$: $f^{-1}(x) = \sqrt{x+3}$ for all x in the range of $f(x)$, or $f^{-1}(x) = \sqrt{x+3},\ x \geq -3$.

Answers may vary. There are other restrictions that also make $f(x)$ one-to-one.

113. Answers may vary. $f(x) = \dfrac{3}{x}$, $f(x) = 1 - x$, $f(x) = x$.

115. If the graph $y = f(x)$ (or the graph of $y = f^{-1}(x)$) is symmetric with respect to the line $y = x$, then $f^{-1}(x) = f(x)$.

Exercise Set 4.2

1. $e^4 \approx 54.5982$

3. $e^{-2.458} \approx 0.0856$

5. $f(x) = -2^x - 1$

$f(0) = -2^0 - 1 = -1 - 1 = -2$

The only graph with y-intercept $(0, -2)$ is (f).

7. $f(x) = e^x + 3$

This is the graph of $f(x) = e^x$ shifted up 3 units. Then (e) is the correct choice.

9. $f(x) = 3^{-x} - 2$

$f(0) = 3^{-0} - 2 = 1 - 2 = -1$

Since the y-intercept is $(0, -1)$, the correct graph is (a) or (c). Check another point on the graph. $f(-1) = 3^{-(-1)} - 2 = 3 - 2 = 1$, so $(-1, 1)$ is on the graph. Thus (a) is the correct choice.

11. Graph $f(x) = 3^x$.

Compute some function values, plot the corresponding points, and connect them with a smooth curve.

x	$y = f(x)$	(x, y)
-3	$\frac{1}{27}$	$\left(-3, \frac{1}{27}\right)$
-2	$\frac{1}{9}$	$\left(-2, \frac{1}{9}\right)$
-1	$\frac{1}{3}$	$\left(-1, \frac{1}{3}\right)$
0	1	$(0, 1)$
1	3	$(1, 3)$
2	9	$(2, 9)$
3	27	$(3, 27)$

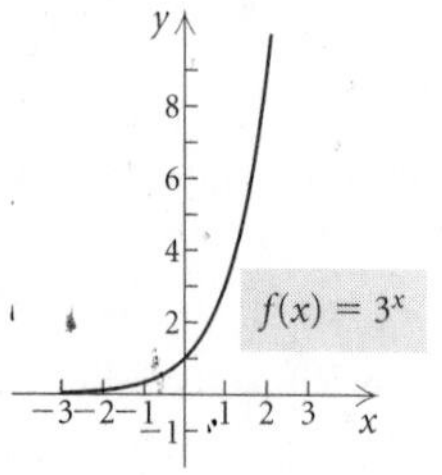

13. Graph $f(x) = 6^x$.

Compute some function values, plot the corresponding points, and connect them with a smooth curve.

x	$y = f(x)$	(x, y)
-3	$\frac{1}{216}$	$\left(-3, \frac{1}{216}\right)$
-2	$\frac{1}{36}$	$\left(-2, \frac{1}{36}\right)$
-1	$\frac{1}{6}$	$\left(-1, \frac{1}{6}\right)$
0	1	$(0, 1)$
1	6	$(1, 6)$
2	36	$(2, 36)$
3	216	$(3, 216)$

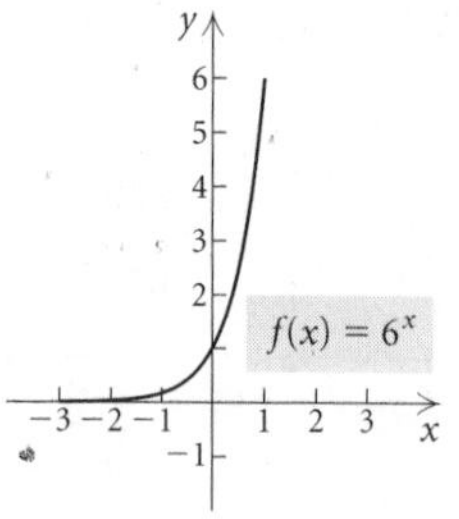

15. Graph $f(x) = \left(\frac{1}{4}\right)^x$.

Compute some function values, plot the corresponding points, and connect them with a smooth curve.

x	$y = f(x)$	(x, y)
-3	64	$(-3, 64)$
-2	16	$(-2, 16)$
-1	4	$(-1, 4)$
0	1	$(0, 1)$
1	$\frac{1}{4}$	$\left(1, \frac{1}{4}\right)$
2	$\frac{1}{16}$	$\left(2, \frac{1}{16}\right)$
3	$\frac{1}{64}$	$\left(3, \frac{1}{64}\right)$

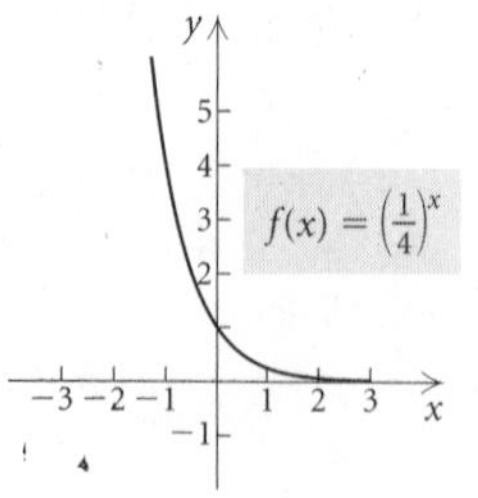

17. Graph $y = -2^x$.

x	y	(x, y)
-3	$-\frac{1}{8}$	$\left(-3, -\frac{1}{8}\right)$
-2	$-\frac{1}{4}$	$\left(-2, -\frac{1}{4}\right)$
-1	$-\frac{1}{2}$	$\left(-1, -\frac{1}{2}\right)$
0	-1	$(0, -1)$
1	-2	$(1, -2)$
2	-4	$(2, -4)$
3	-8	$(3, -8)$

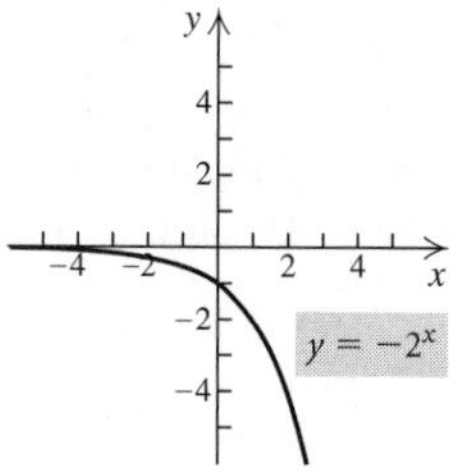

19. Graph $f(x) = -0.25^x + 4$.

x	$y = f(x)$	(x, y)
-3	-60	$(-3, -60)$
-2	-12	$(-2, -12)$
-1	0	$(-1, 0)$
0	3	$(0, 3)$
1	3.75	$(1, 3.75)$
2	3.94	$(2, 3.94)$
3	3.98	$(3, 3.98)$

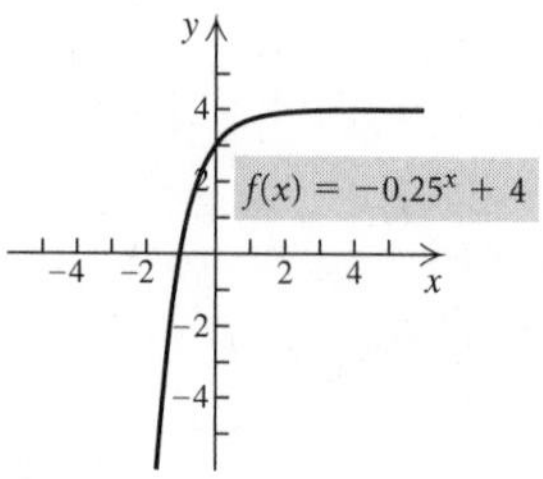

21. Graph $f(x) = 1 + e^{-x}$.

x	$y = f(x)$	(x, y)
-3	21.1	$(-3, 21.1)$
-2	8.4	$(-2, 8.4)$
-1	3.7	$(-1, 3.7)$
0	2	$(0, 2)$
1	1.4	$(1, 1.4)$
2	1.1	$(2, 1.1)$
3	1.0	$(3, 1.0)$

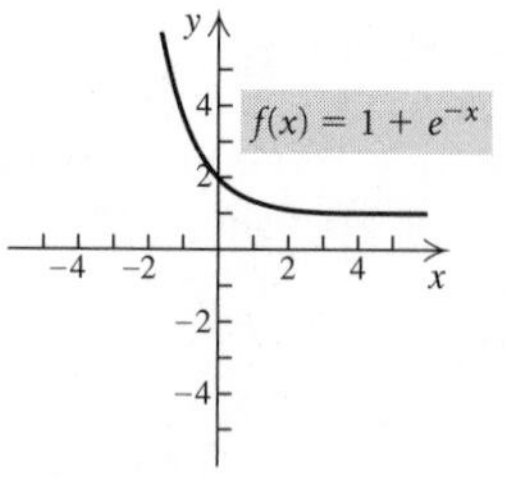

23. Graph $y = \frac{1}{4}e^x$.

Choose values for x and compute the corresponding y-values. Plot the points (x, y) and connect them with a smooth curve.

x	y	(x, y)
-3	0.0124	$(-3, 0.0124)$
-2	0.0338	$(-2, 0.0338)$
-1	0.0920	$(-1, 0.0920)$
0	0.25	$(0, 0.25)$
1	0.6796	$(1, 0.6796)$
2	1.8473	$(2, 1.8473)$
3	5.0214	$(3, 5.0214)$

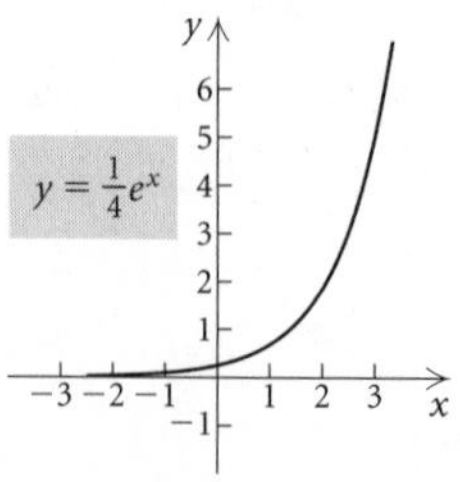

25. Graph $f(x) = 1 - e^{-x}$.

Compute some function values, plot the corresponding points, and connect them with a smooth curve.

x	y	(x, y)
-3	-19.0855	$(-3, -19.0855)$
-2	-6.3891	$(-2, -6.3891)$
-1	-1.7183	$(-1, -1.7183)$
0	0	$(0, 0)$
1	0.6321	$(1, 0.6321)$
2	0.8647	$(2, 0.8647)$
3	0.9502	$(3, 0.9502)$

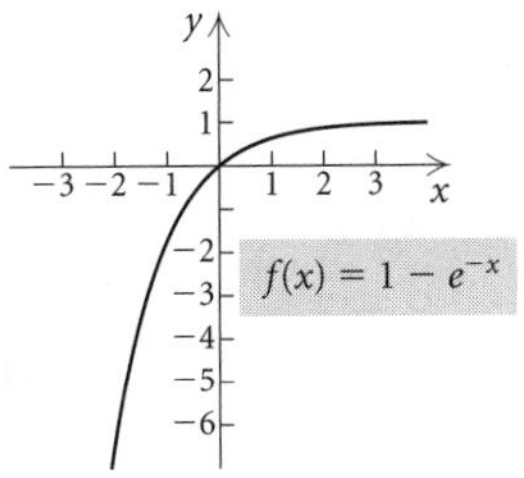

27. Shift the graph of $y = 2^x$ left 1 unit.

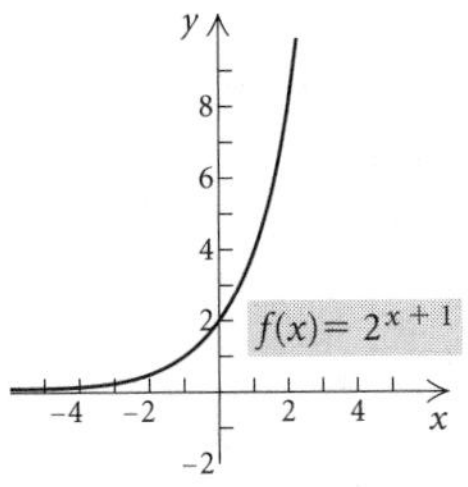

29. Shift the graph of $y = 2^x$ down 3 units.

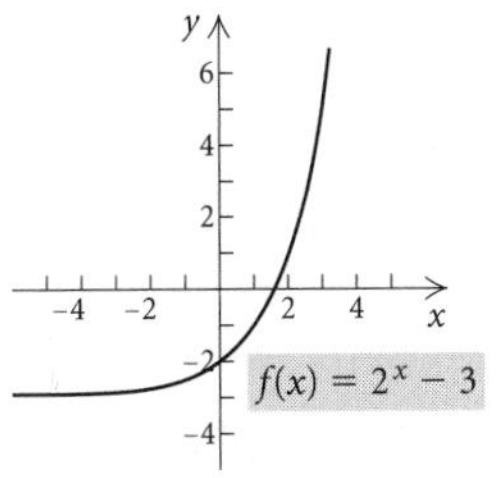

31. Reflect the graph of $y = 3^x$ across the y-axis, then across the x-axis, and then shift it up 4 units.

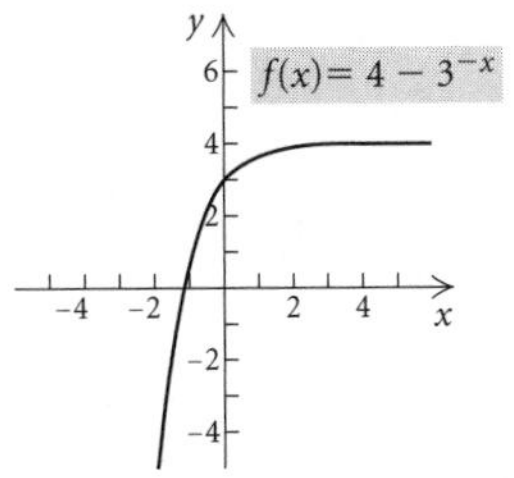

33. Shift the graph of $y = \left(\frac{3}{2}\right)^x$ right 1 unit.

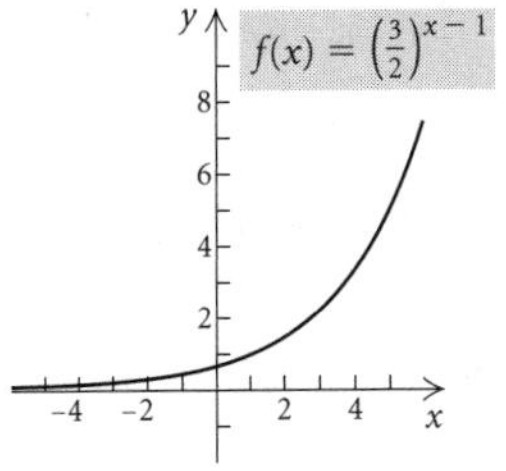

35. Shift the graph of $y = 2^x$ left 3 units and down 5 units.

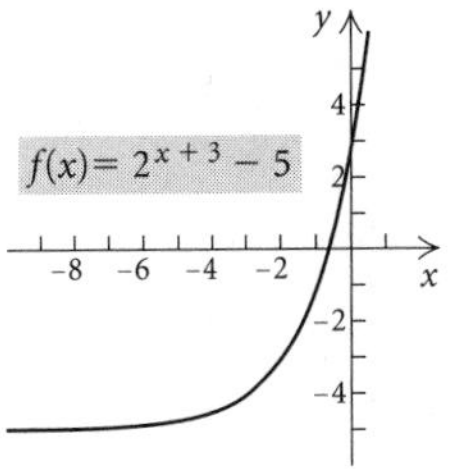

37. Shrink the graph of $y = e^x$ horizontally.

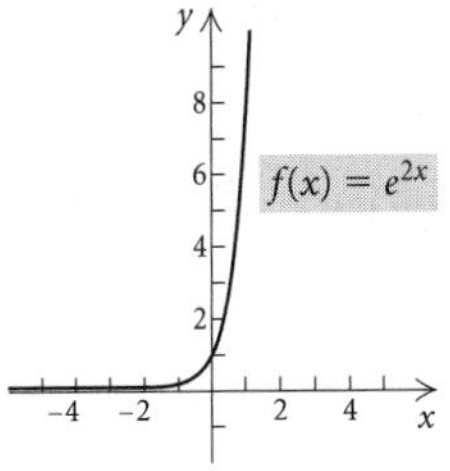

39. Shift the graph of $y = e^x$ left 1 unit and reflect it across the y-axis.

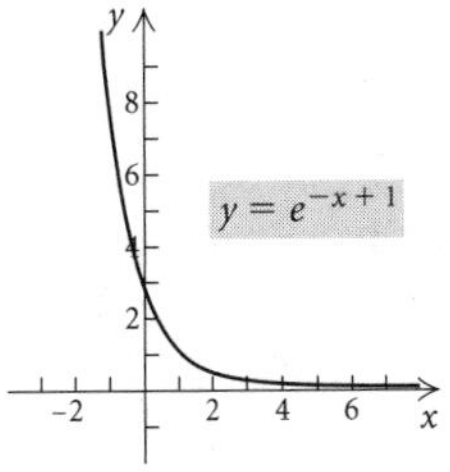

41. Reflect the graph of $y = e^x$ across the y-axis and then across the x-axis; shift it up 1 unit and then stretch it vertically.

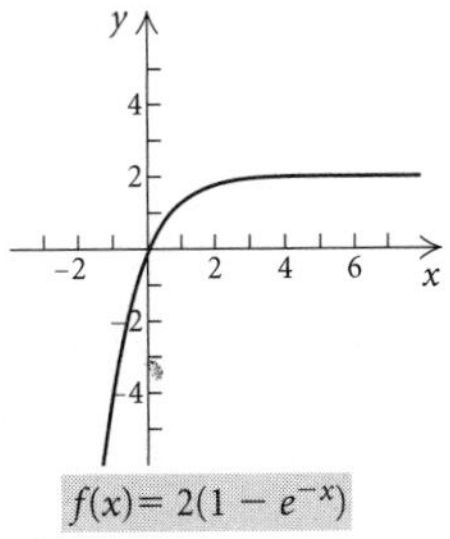

43. a) We use the formula $A = P\left(1+\dfrac{r}{n}\right)^{nt}$ and substitute 82,000 for P, 0.045 for r, and 4 for n.

$$A(t) = 82,000\left(1+\frac{0.045}{4}\right)^{4t} = 82,000(1.01125)^{4t}$$

b) $A(0) = 82,000(1.01125)^{4\cdot 0} = \$82,000$

$A(2) = 82,000(1.01125)^{4\cdot 2} \approx \$89,677.22$

$A(5) = 82,000(1.01125)^{4\cdot 5} \approx \$102,561.54$

$A(10) = 82,000(1.01125)^{4\cdot 10} \approx \$128,278.90$

45. We use the formula $A = P\left(1+\dfrac{r}{n}\right)^{nt}$ and substitute 3000 for P, 0.05 for r, and 4 for n.

$$A(t) = 3000\left(1+\frac{0.05}{4}\right)^{4t} = 3000(1.0125)^{4t}$$

On Jacob's sixteenth birthday, $t = 16 - 6 = 10$.

$A(10) = 3000(1.0125)^{4\cdot 10} = 4930.86$

When the CD matures \$4930.86 will be available.

47. We use the formula $A = P\left(1+\dfrac{r}{n}\right)^{nt}$ and substitute 3000 for P, 0.04 for r, 2 for n, and 2 for t.

$$A = 3000\left(1+\frac{0.04}{2}\right)^{2\cdot 2} \approx \$3247.30$$

49. We use the formula $A = P\left(1+\dfrac{r}{n}\right)^{nt}$ and substitute 120,000 for P, 0.025 for r, 1 for n, and 10 for t.

$$A = 120,000\left(1+\frac{0.025}{1}\right)^{1\cdot 10} \approx \$153,610.15$$

51. We use the formula $A = P\left(1+\dfrac{r}{n}\right)^{nt}$ and substitute 53,500 for P, 0.055 for r, 4 for n, and 6.5 for t.

$$A = 53,500\left(1+\frac{0.055}{4}\right)^{4(6.5)} \approx \$76,305.59$$

53. We use the formula $A = P\left(1+\dfrac{r}{n}\right)^{nt}$ and substitute 17,400 for P, 0.081 for r, 365 for n, and 5 for t.

$$A = 17,400\left(1+\frac{0.081}{365}\right)^{365\cdot 5} \approx \$26,086.69$$

55. a) $N(0) = 350,000\left(\dfrac{2}{3}\right)^{0} = 350,000$

$N(1) = 350,000\left(\dfrac{2}{3}\right)^{1} \approx 233,333$

$N(4) = 350,000\left(\dfrac{2}{3}\right)^{4} \approx 69,136$

$N(10) = 350,000\left(\dfrac{2}{3}\right)^{10} \approx 6070$

b)

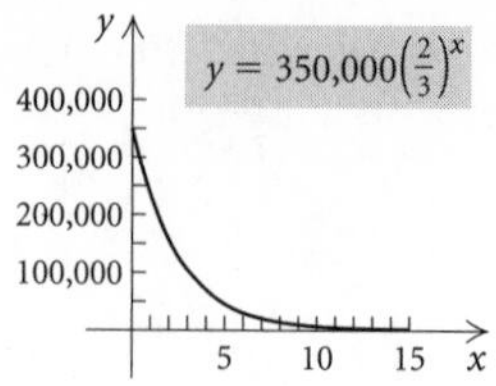

57. In 2003, $t = 2003 - 1998 = 5$.

$B(5) = 5.402(1.340)^5 \approx 23.3\%$

In 2004, $t = 2004 - 1998 = 6$.

$B(6) = 5.402(1.340)^6 \approx 31.3\%$

In 2005, $t = 2005 - 1998 = 7$.

$B(7) = 5.402(1.340)^7 \approx 41.9\%$

59. In 2003, $t = 2003 - 1997 = 6$.

$E(6) = 256.43(1.22)^6 \approx \$845.5$ million

$I(6) = 464.38(1.42)^6 \approx \$3807.2$ million

In 2005, $t = 2005 - 1997 = 8$.

$E(8) = 256.43(1.22)^8 \approx \$1258.5$ million

$I(8) = 256.43(1.42)^8 \approx \$7676.8$ million

In 2008, $t = 2008 - 1997 = 11$.

$E(11) = 256.43(1.22)^{11} \approx \$2285.2$ million

$I(11) = 464.38(1.42)^{11} \approx \$21,980.9$ million

61. $V(0) = 1800(0.8)^0 = \$1800$

$V(1) = 1800(0.8)^1 = \$1440$

$V(2) = 1800(0.8)^2 = \$1152$

$V(5) = 1800(0.8)^5 \approx \$589.82$

$V(10) = 1800(0.8)^{10} \approx \$193.27$

63. In 2005, $t = 2005 - 1981 = 24$.

$N(24) = 46.6(1.018)^{24} \approx 71.5$ billion cubic feet

In 2010, $t = 2010 - 1981 = 29$.

$N(29) = 46.6(1.018)^{29} \approx 78.2$ billion cubic feet

65. $f(25) = 100(1 - e^{-0.04(25)}) \approx 63\%$

67. Graph (c) is the graph of $y = 3^x - 3^{-x}$.

69. Graph (a) is the graph of $f(x) = -2.3^x$.

71. Graph (l) is the graph of $y = 2^{-|x|}$.

73. Graph (g) is the graph of $f(x) = (0.58)^x - 1$.

75. Graph (i) is the graph of $g(x) = e^{|x|}$.

77. Graph (k) is the graph of $y = 2^{-x^2}$.

79. Graph (m) is the graph of $g(x) = \dfrac{e^x - e^{-x}}{2}$.

81. Discussion and Writing

83. Discussion and Writing

85. $(1-4i)(7+6i) = 7+6i-28i-24i^2$
$= 7+6i-28i+24$
$= 31-22i$

87. $2x^2-13x-7=0$ Setting $f(x)=0$
$(2x+1)(x-7)=0$
$2x+1=0$ *or* $x-7=0$
$2x=-1$ *or* $x=7$
$x=-\frac{1}{2}$ *or* $x=7$

The zeros of the function are $-\frac{1}{2}$ and 7, and the x-intercepts are $\left(-\frac{1}{2},0\right)$ and $(7,0)$.

89. $x^4-x^2=0$ Setting $h(x)=0$
$x^2(x^2-1)=0$
$x^2(x+1)(x-1)=0$
$x^2=0$ *or* $x+1=0$ *or* $x-1=0$
$x=0$ *or* $x=-1$ *or* $x=1$

The zeros of the function are 0, -1, and 1, and the x-intercepts are $(0,0)$, $(-1,0)$, and $(1,0)$.

91. $x^3+6x^2-16x=0$
$x(x^2+6x-16)=0$
$x(x+8)(x-2)=0$
$x=0$ *or* $x+8=0$ *or* $x-2=0$
$x=0$ *or* $x=-8$ *or* $x=2$

The solutions are 0, -8, and 2.

93. $7^\pi \approx 451.8078726$ and $\pi^7 \approx 3020.293228$, so π^7 is larger.
$70^{80} \approx 4.054 \times 10^{147}$ and $80^{70} \approx 1.646 \times 10^{133}$, so 70^{80} is larger.

Exercise Set 4.3

1. Graph $x = 3^y$.

Choose values for y and compute the corresponding x-values. Plot the points (x,y) and connect them with a smooth curve.

x	y	(x,y)
$\frac{1}{27}$	-3	$\left(\frac{1}{27},-3\right)$
$\frac{1}{9}$	-2	$\left(\frac{1}{9},-2\right)$
$\frac{1}{3}$	-1	$\left(\frac{1}{3},-1\right)$
1	0	$(1,0)$
3	1	$(3,1)$
9	2	$(9,2)$
27	3	$(27,3)$

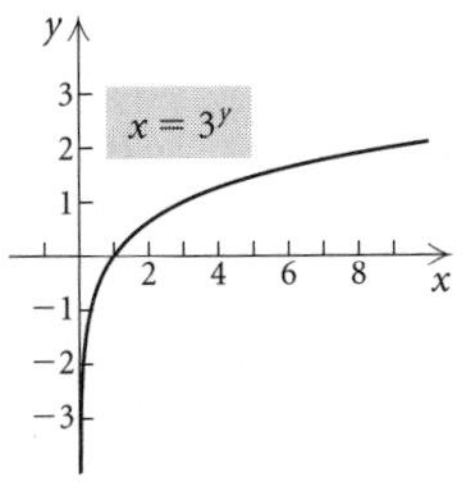

3. Graph $x = \left(\frac{1}{2}\right)^y$.

Choose values for y and compute the corresponding x-values. Plot the points (x,y) and connect them with a smooth curve.

x	y	(x,y)
8	-3	$(8,-3)$
4	-2	$(4,-2)$
2	-1	$(2,-1)$
1	0	$(1,0)$
$\frac{1}{2}$	1	$\left(\frac{1}{2},1\right)$
$\frac{1}{4}$	2	$\left(\frac{1}{4},2\right)$
$\frac{1}{8}$	3	$\left(\frac{1}{8},3\right)$

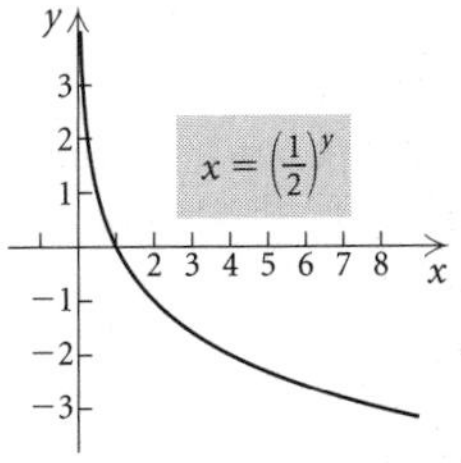

5. Graph $y = \log_3 x$.

The equation $y = \log_3 x$ is equivalent to $x = 3^y$. We can find ordered pairs that are solutions by choosing values for y and computing the corresponding x-values.

For $y=-2$, $x=3^{-2}=\frac{1}{9}$.

For $y=-1$, $x=3^{-1}=\frac{1}{3}$.

For $y=0$, $x=3^0=1$.

For $y=1$, $x=3^1=3$.

For $y=2$, $x=3^2=9$.

x, or 3^y	y
$\frac{1}{9}$	-2
$\frac{1}{3}$	-1
1	0
3	1
9	2

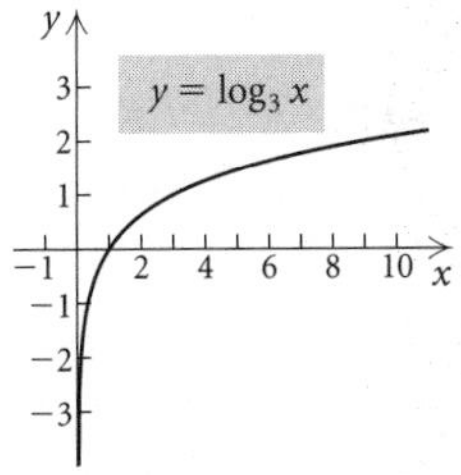

7. Graph $f(x) = \log x$.

Think of $f(x)$ as y. The equation $y = \log x$ is equivalent to $x = 10^y$. We can find ordered pairs that are solutions by choosing values for y and computing the corresponding x-values.

For $y=-2$, $x=10^{-2}=0.01$.

For $y=-1$, $x=10^{-1}=0.1$.

For $y=0$, $x=10^0=1$.

For $y=1$, $x=10^1=10$.

For $y=2$, $x=10^2=100$.

x, or 10^y	y
0.01	−2
0.1	−1
1	0
10	1
100	2

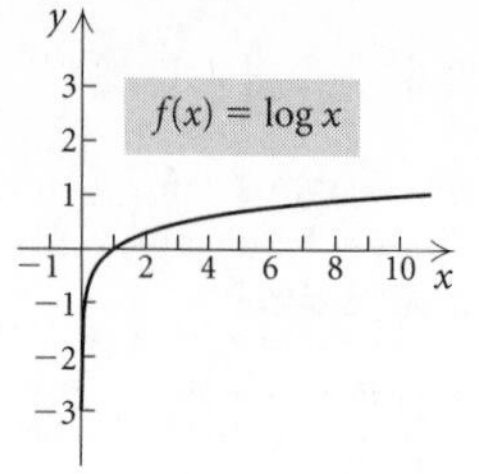

9. $\log_2 16 = 4$ because the exponent to which we raise 2 to get 16 is 4.

11. $\log_5 125 = 3$, because the exponent to which we raise 5 to get 125 is 3.

13. $\log 0.001 = -3$, because the exponent to which we raise 10 to get 0.001 is −3.

15. $\log_2 \frac{1}{4} = -2$, because the exponent to which we raise 2 to get $\frac{1}{4}$ is −2.

17. $\ln 1 = 0$, because the exponent to which we raise e to get 1 is 0.

19. $\log 10 = 1$, because the exponent to which we raise 10 to get 10 is 1.

21. $\log_5 5^4 = 4$, because the exponent to which we raise 5 to get 5^4 is 4.

23. $\log_3 \sqrt[4]{3} = \log_3 3^{1/4} = \frac{1}{4}$, because the exponent to which we raise 3 to get $3^{1/4}$ is $\frac{1}{4}$.

25. $\log 10^{-7} = -7$, because the exponent to which we raise 10 to get 10^{-7} is −7.

27. $\log_{49} 7 = \frac{1}{2}$, because the exponent to which we raise 49 to get 7 is $\frac{1}{2}$. $(49^{1/2} = \sqrt{49} = 7)$

29. $\ln e^{3/4} = \frac{3}{4}$, because the exponent to which we raise e to get $e^{3/4}$ is $\frac{3}{4}$.

31. $\log_4 1 = 0$, because the exponent to which we raise 4 to get 1 is 0.

33. $\ln \sqrt{e} = \ln e^{1/2} = \frac{1}{2}$, because the exponent to which we raise e to get $e^{1/2}$ is $\frac{1}{2}$.

35. The exponent is the logarithm.

$10^3 = 1000 \Rightarrow 3 = \log_{10} 1000$

The base remains the same.

37. The exponent is the logarithm.

$8^{1/3} = 2 \Rightarrow \log_8 2 = \frac{1}{3}$

The base remains the same.

39. $e^3 = t \Rightarrow \log_e t = 3$

41. $e^2 = 7.3891 \Rightarrow \log_e 7.3891 = 2$

43. $p^k = 3 \Rightarrow \log_p 3 = k$

45. The logarithm is the exponent.

$\log_5 5 = 1 \Rightarrow 5^1 = 5$

The base remains the same.

47. $\log 0.01 = -2$ is equivalent to $\log_{10} 0.01 = -2$.

The logarithm is the exponent.

$\log_{10} 0.01 = -2 \Rightarrow 10^{-2} = 0.01$

The base remains the same.

49. $\ln 30 = 3.4012 \Rightarrow e^{3.4012} = 30$

51. $\log_a M = -x \Rightarrow a^{-x} = M$

53. $\log_a T^3 = x \Rightarrow a^x = T^3$

55. $\log 3 \approx 0.4771$

57. $\log 532 \approx 2.7259$

59. $\log 0.57 \approx -0.2441$

61. $\log(-2)$ does not exist. (The calculator gives an error message.)

63. $\ln 2 \approx 0.6931$

65. $\ln 809.3 \approx 6.6962$

67. $\ln(-1.32)$ does not exist. (The calculator gives an error message.)

69. Let $a = 10$, $b = 4$, and $M = 100$ and substitute in the change-of-base formula.

$$\log_4 100 = \frac{\log_{10} 100}{\log_{10} 4} \approx 3.3219$$

71. Let $a = 10$, $b = 100$, and $M = 0.3$ and substitute in the change-of-base formula.

$$\log_{100} 0.3 = \frac{\log_{10} 0.3}{\log_{10} 100} \approx -0.2614$$

73. Let $a = 10$, $b = 200$, and $M = 50$ and substitute in the change-of-base formula.

$$\log_{200} 50 = \frac{\log_{10} 50}{\log_{10} 200} \approx 0.7384$$

75. Let $a = e$, $b = 3$, and $M = 12$ and substitute in the change-of-base formula.

$$\log_3 12 = \frac{\ln 12}{\ln 3} \approx 2.2619$$

77. Let $a = e$, $b = 100$, and $M = 15$ and substitute in the change-of-base formula.

$$\log_{100} 15 = \frac{\ln 15}{\ln 100} \approx 0.5880$$

79. Graph $y = 3^x$ and then reflect this graph across the line $y = x$ to get the graph of $y = \log_3 x$.

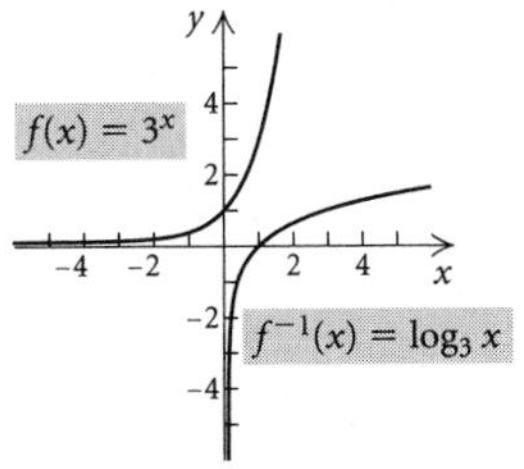

81. Graph $y = \log x$ and then reflect this graph across the line $y = x$ to get the graph of $y = 10^x$.

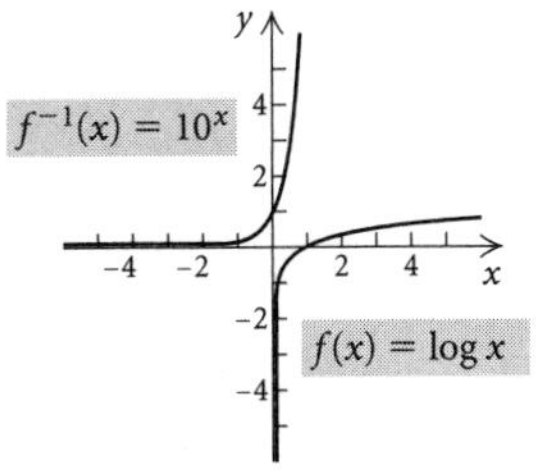

83. Shift the graph of $y = \log_2 x$ left 3 units.

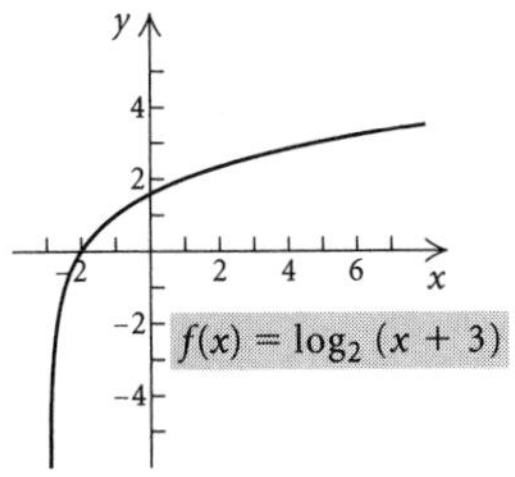

Domain: $(-3, \infty)$

Vertical asymptote: $x = -3$

85. Shift the graph of $y = \log_3 x$ down 1 unit.

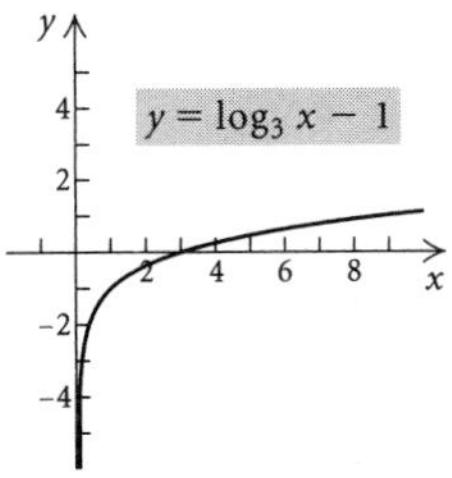

Domain: $(0, \infty)$

Vertical asymptote: $x = 0$

87. Stretch the graph of $y = \ln x$ vertically.

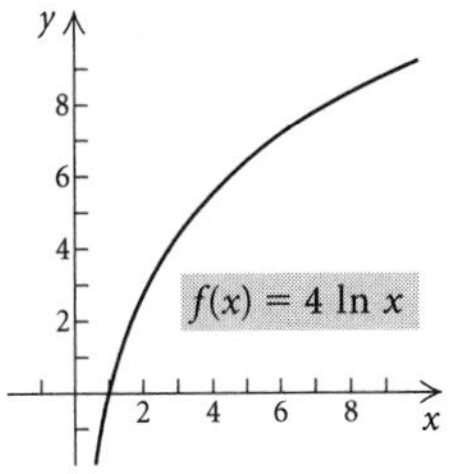

Domain: $(0, \infty)$

Vertical asymptote: $x = 0$

89. Reflect the graph of $y = \ln x$ across the x-axis and then shift it up 2 units.

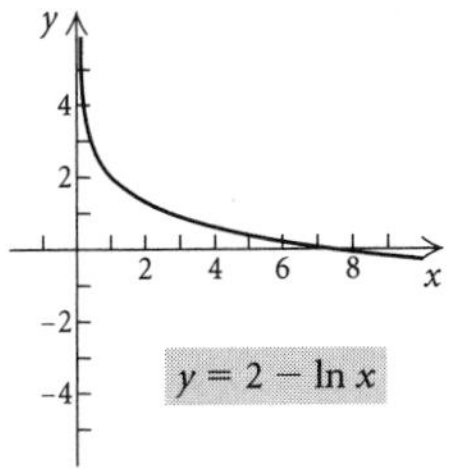

Domain: $(0, \infty)$

Vertical asymptote: $x = 0$

91. a) We substitute 711.5 for P, since P is in thousands.

$$w(711.5) = 0.37 \ln 711.5 + 0.05 \approx 2.5 \text{ ft/sec}$$

b) We substitute 478.4 for P, since P is in thousands.

$$w(478.4) = 0.37 \ln 478.4 + 0.05 \approx 2.3 \text{ ft/sec}$$

c) We substitute 277 for P, since P is in thousands.

$$w(277) = 0.37 \ln 277 + 0.05 \approx 2.1 \text{ ft/sec}$$

d) We substitute 113 for P, since P is in thousands.

$$w(113) = 0.37 \ln 113 + 0.05 \approx 1.8 \text{ ft/sec}$$

e) We substitute 416.5 for P, since P is in thousands.

$$w(416.5) = 0.37 \ln 416.5 + 0.05 \approx 2.3 \text{ ft/sec}$$

f) We substitute 328 for P, since P is in thousands.

$$w(328) = 0.37 \ln 328 + 0.05 \approx 2.2 \text{ ft/sec}$$

g) We substitute 8008.3 for P, since P is in thousands.

$$w(8008.3) = 0.37 \ln 8008.3 + 0.05 \approx 3.4 \text{ ft/sec}$$

h) We substitute 2896 for P, since P is in thousands.

$$w(2896) = 0.37 \ln 2896 + 0.05 \approx 3.0 \text{ ft/sec}$$

93. a) $S(0) = 78 - 15\log(0+1)$
$= 78 - 15\log 1$
$= 78 - 15\cdot 0$
$= 78\%$

b) $S(4) = 78 - 15\log(4+1)$
$= 78 - 15\log 5$
$\approx 78 - 15(0.698970)$
$\approx 67.5\%$

$S(24) = 78 - 15\log(24+1)$
$= 78 - 15\log 25$
$\approx 78 - 15(1.397940)$
$\approx 57\%$

95. a) $7 = -\log[H^+]$
$-7 = \log[H^+]$
$H^+ = 10^{-7}$ Using the definition of logarithm

b) $5.4 = -\log[H^+]$
$-5.4 = \log[H^+]$
$H^+ = 10^{-5.4}$ Using the definition of logarithm
$H^+ \approx 4.0\times 10^{-6}$

c) $3.2 = -\log[H^+]$
$-3.2 = \log[H^+]$
$H^+ = 10^{-3.2}$ Using the definition of logarithm
$H^+ \approx 6.3\times 10^{-4}$

d) $4.8 = -\log[H^+]$
$-4.8 = \log[H^+]$
$H^+ = 10^{-4.8}$ Using the definition of logarithm
$H^+ \approx 1.6\times 10^{-5}$

97. a) $L = 10\log\dfrac{2510\cdot I_0}{I_0}$
$= 10\log 2510$
≈ 34 decibels

b) $L = 10\log\dfrac{2,500,000\cdot I_0}{I_0}$
$= 10\log 2,500,000$
≈ 64 decibels

c) $L = 10\log\dfrac{10^6\cdot I_0}{I_0}$
$= 10\log 10^6$
$= 60$ decibels

d) $L = 10\log\dfrac{10^9\cdot I_0}{I_0}$
$= 10\log 10^9$
$= 90$ decibels

99. Discussion and Writing

101. $y = 6 = 0\cdot x + 6$

Slope: 0; y-intercept $(0, 6)$

103. $y = 2x - \dfrac{3}{13}$

Slope: 2, y-intercept: $\left(0, -\dfrac{3}{13}\right)$

105.
$$\begin{array}{r|rrrr} -5 & 1 & -6 & 3 & 10 \\ & & -5 & 55 & -290 \\ \hline & 1 & -11 & 58 & -280 \end{array}$$

The remainder is -280, so $f(-5) = -280$.

107. $f(x) = (x-\sqrt{7})(x+\sqrt{7})(x-0)$
$= (x^2-7)(x)$
$= x^3 - 7x$

109. Using the change-of-base formula, we get
$\dfrac{\log_5 8}{\log_2 8} = \log_2 8 = 3.$

111. $f(x) = \log_5 x^3$

x^3 must be positive. Since $x^3 > 0$ for $x > 0$, the domain is $(0, \infty)$.

113. $f(x) = \ln|x|$

$|x|$ must be positive. Since $|x| > 0$ for $x \neq 0$, the domain is $(-\infty, 0)\cup(0,\infty)$.

115. Graph $y = \log_2(2x+5) = \dfrac{\log(2x+5)}{\log 2}$. Observe that outputs are negative for inputs between $-\dfrac{5}{2}$ and -2. Thus, the solution set is $\left(-\dfrac{5}{2}, -2\right)$.

117. Graph (d) is the graph of $f(x) = \ln|x|$.

119. Graph (b) is the graph of $f(x) = \ln x^2$.

Exercise Set 4.4

1. Use the product rule.

$\log_3(81\cdot 27) = \log_3 81 + \log_3 27$

3. Use the product rule.

$\log_5(5\cdot 125) = \log_5 5 + \log_5 125$

5. Use the product rule.

$\log_t 8Y = \log_t 8 + \log_t Y$

7. Use the product rule.

$\ln xy = \ln x + \ln y$

9. Use the power rule.

$\log_b t^3 = 3\log_b t$

11. Use the power rule.

$\log y^8 = 8\log y$

13. Use the power rule.

$\log_c K^{-6} = -6\log_c K$

15. Use the power rule.

$\ln \sqrt[3]{4} = \ln 4^{1/3} = \frac{1}{3}\ln 4$

17. Use the quotient rule.

$\log_t \frac{M}{8} = \log_t M - \log_t 8$

19. Use the quotient rule.

$\log \frac{x}{y} = \log x - \log y$

21. Use the quotient rule.

$\ln \frac{r}{s} = \ln r - \ln s$

23. $\log_a 6xy^5z^4$

$= \log_a 6 + \log_a x + \log_a y^5 + \log_a z^4$ Product rule

$= \log_a 6 + \log_a x + 5\log_a y + 4\log_a z$ Power rule

25. $\log_b \frac{p^2q^5}{m^4b^9}$

$= \log_b p^2q^5 - \log_b m^4b^9$ Quotient rule

$= \log_b p^2 + \log_b q^5 - (\log_b m^4 + \log_b b^9)$ Product rule

$= \log_b p^2 + \log_b q^5 - \log_b m^4 - \log_b b^9$

$= \log_b p^2 + \log_b q^5 - \log_b m^4 - 9 \quad (\log_b b^9 = 9)$

$= 2\log_b p + 5\log_b q - 4\log_b m - 9$ Power rule

27. $\ln \frac{2}{3x^3y}$

$= \ln 2 - \ln 3x^3y$ Quotient rule

$= \ln 2 - (\ln 3 + \ln x^3 + \ln y)$ Product rule

$= \ln 2 - \ln 3 - \ln x^3 - \ln y$

$= \ln 2 - \ln 3 - 3\ln x - \ln y$ Power rule

29. $\log \sqrt{r^3t}$

$= \log(r^3t)^{1/2}$

$= \frac{1}{2}\log r^3t$ Power rule

$= \frac{1}{2}(\log r^3 + \log t)$ Product rule

$= \frac{1}{2}(3\log r + \log t)$ Power rule

$= \frac{3}{2}\log r + \frac{1}{2}\log t$

31. $\frac{1}{2}\log_a \frac{x^6}{p^5q^8}$

$= \frac{1}{2}[\log_a x^6 - \log_a(p^5q^8)]$ Quotient rule

$= \frac{1}{2}[\log_a x^6 - (\log_a p^5 + \log_a q^8)]$ Product rule

$= \frac{1}{2}(\log_a x^6 - \log_a p^5 - \log_a q^8)$

$= \frac{1}{2}(6\log_a x - 5\log_a p - 8\log_a q)$ Power rule

$= 3\log_a x - \frac{5}{2}\log_a p - 4\log_a q$

33. $\log_a \sqrt[4]{\frac{m^8n^{12}}{a^3b^5}}$

$= \frac{1}{4}\log_a \frac{m^8n^{12}}{a^3b^5}$ Power rule

$= \frac{1}{4}(\log_a m^8n^{12} - \log_a a^3b^5)$ Quotient rule

$= \frac{1}{4}[\log_a m^8 + \log_a n^{12} - (\log_a a^3 + \log_a b^5)]$ Product rule

$= \frac{1}{4}(\log_a m^8 + \log_a n^{12} - \log_a a^3 - \log_a b^5)$

$= \frac{1}{4}(\log_a m^8 + \log_a n^{12} - 3 - \log_a b^5)$ $(\log_a a^3 = 3)$

$= \frac{1}{4}(8\log_a m + 12\log_a n - 3 - 5\log_a b)$ Power rule

$= 2\log_a m + 3\log_a n - \frac{3}{4} - \frac{5}{4}\log_a b$

35. $\log_a 75 + \log_a 2$

$= \log_a(75 \cdot 2)$ Product rule

$= \log_a 150$

37. $\log 10{,}000 - \log 100$

$= \log \frac{10{,}000}{100}$ Quotient rule

$= \log 100$

$= 2$

39. $\frac{1}{2}\log n + 3\log m$

$= \log n^{1/2} + \log m^3$ Power rule

$= \log n^{1/2}m^3$, or Product rule

$\log m^3\sqrt{n}$ $\quad n^{1/2} = \sqrt{n}$

41. $\frac{1}{2}\log_a x + 4\log_a y - 3\log_a x$

$= \log_a x^{1/2} + \log_a y^4 - \log_a x^3$ Power rule

$= \log_a x^{1/2}y^4 - \log_a x^3$ Product rule

$= \log_a \frac{x^{1/2}y^4}{x^3}$ Quotient rule

$= \log_a x^{-5/2}y^4$, or $\log_a \frac{y^4}{x^{5/2}}$ Simplifying

43. $\ln x^2 - 2\ln\sqrt{x}$
$= \ln x^2 - \ln(\sqrt{x})^2$ Power rule
$= \ln x^2 - \ln x$ $[(\sqrt{x})^2 = x]$
$= \ln\frac{x^2}{x}$ Quotient rule
$= \ln x$

45. $\ln(x^2-4) - \ln(x+2)$
$= \ln\frac{x^2-4}{x+2}$ Quotient rule
$= \ln\frac{(x+2)(x-2)}{x+2}$ Factoring
$= \ln(x-2)$ Removing a factor of 1

47. $\log(x^2-5x-14) - \log(x^2-4)$
$= \log\frac{x^2-5x-14}{x^2-4}$ Quotient rule
$= \log\frac{(x+2)(x-7)}{(x+2)(x-2)}$ Factoring
$= \log\frac{x-7}{x-2}$ Removing a factor of 1

49. $\ln x - 3[\ln(x-5) + \ln(x+5)]$
$= \ln x - 3\ln[(x-5)(x+5)]$ Product rule
$= \ln x - 3\ln(x^2-25)$
$= \ln x - \ln(x^2-25)^3$ Power rule
$= \ln\frac{x}{(x^2-25)^3}$ Quotient rule

51. $\frac{3}{2}\ln 4x^6 - \frac{4}{5}\ln 2y^{10}$
$= \frac{3}{2}\ln 2^2x^6 - \frac{4}{5}\ln 2y^{10}$ Writing 4 as 2^2
$= \ln(2^2x^6)^{3/2} - \ln(2y^{10})^{4/5}$ Power rule
$= \ln(2^3x^9) - \ln(2^{4/5}y^8)$
$= \ln\frac{2^3x^9}{2^{4/5}y^8}$ Quotient rule
$= \ln\frac{2^{11/5}x^9}{y^8}$

53. $\log_a\frac{2}{11} = \log_a 2 - \log_a 11$ Quotient rule
$\approx 0.301 - 1.041$
≈ -0.74

55. $\log_a 98 = \log_a(7^2\cdot 2)$
$= \log_a 7^2 + \log_a 2$ Product rule
$= 2\log_a 7 + \log_a 2$ Power rule
$\approx 2(0.845) + 0.301$
≈ 1.991

57. $\frac{\log_a 2}{\log_a 7} \approx \frac{0.301}{0.845} \approx 0.356$

59. $\log_b 125 = \log_b 5^3$
$= 3\log_b 5$ Power rule
$\approx 3(1.609)$
≈ 4.827

61. $\log_b\frac{1}{6} = \log_b 1 - \log_b 6$ Quotient rule
$= \log_b 1 - \log_b(2\cdot 3)$
$= \log_b 1 - (\log_b 2 + \log_b 3)$ Product rule
$= \log_b 1 - \log_b 2 - \log_b 3$
$\approx 0 - 0.693 - 1.099$
≈ -1.792

63. $\log_b\frac{3}{b} = \log_b 3 - \log_b b$ Quotient rule
$\approx 1.099 - 1$
≈ 0.099

65. $\log_p p^3 = 3$ $(\log_a a^x = x)$

67. $\log_e e^{|x-4|} = |x-4|$ $(\log_a a^x = x)$

69. $3^{\log_3 4x} = 4x$ $(a^{\log_a x} = x)$

71. $10^{\log w} = w$ $(a^{\log_a x} = x)$

73. $\ln e^{8t} = 8t$ $(\log_a a^x = x)$

75. $\log_b\sqrt{b} = \log_b b^{1/2}$
$= \frac{1}{2}\log_b b$ Power rule
$= \frac{1}{2}\cdot 1$ $(\log_b b = 1)$
$= \frac{1}{2}$

77. Discussion and Writing

79. The degree of $f(x) = 5 - x^2 + x^4$ is 4, so the function is quartic.

81. $f(x) = -\frac{3}{4}$ is of the form $f(x) = mx + b$ $\left(\text{with } m = 0 \text{ and } b = -\frac{3}{4}\right)$, so it is a linear function. In fact, it is a constant function.

83. $f(x) = -\frac{3}{x}$ is of the form $f(x) = \frac{p(x)}{q(x)}$ where $p(x)$ and $q(x)$ are polynomials and $q(x)$ is not the zero polynomial, so $f(x)$ is a rational function.

85. The degree of $f(x) = -\frac{1}{3}x^3 - 4x^2 + 6x + 42$ is 3, so the function is cubic.

87. $f(x) = \frac{1}{2}x + 3$ is of the form $f(x) = mx + b$, so it is a linear function.

89. $5^{\log_5 8} = 2x$
$8 = 2x$ $(a^{\log_a x} = x)$
$4 = x$

The solution is 4.

91. $\log_a(x^2+xy+y^2)+\log_a(x-y)$
$= \log_a[(x^2+xy+y^2)(x-y)]$ Product rule
$= \log_a(x^3-y^3)$ Multiplying

93. $\log_a \dfrac{x-y}{\sqrt{x^2-y^2}}$
$= \log_a \dfrac{x-y}{(x^2-y^2)^{1/2}}$
$= \log_a(x-y)-\log_a(x^2-y^2)^{1/2}$ Quotient rule
$= \log_a(x-y)-\dfrac{1}{2}\log_a(x^2-y^2)$ Power rule
$= \log_a(x-y)-\dfrac{1}{2}\log_a[(x+y)(x-y)]$
$= \log_a(x-y)-\dfrac{1}{2}[\log_a(x+y)+\log_a(x-y)]$
Product rule
$= \log_a(x-y)-\dfrac{1}{2}\log_a(x+y)-\dfrac{1}{2}\log_a(x-y)$
$= \dfrac{1}{2}\log_a(x-y)-\dfrac{1}{2}\log_a(x+y)$

95. $\log_a \dfrac{\sqrt[4]{y^2z^5}}{\sqrt[4]{x^3z^{-2}}}$
$= \log_a \sqrt[4]{\dfrac{y^2z^5}{x^3z^{-2}}}$
$= \log_a \sqrt[4]{\dfrac{y^2z^7}{x^3}}$
$= \log_a \left(\dfrac{y^2z^7}{x^3}\right)^{1/4}$
$= \dfrac{1}{4}\log_a\left(\dfrac{y^2z^7}{x^3}\right)$ Power rule
$= \dfrac{1}{4}(\log_a y^2z^7-\log_a x^3)$ Quotient rule
$= \dfrac{1}{4}(\log_a y^2+\log_a z^7-\log_a x^3)$ Product rule
$= \dfrac{1}{4}(2\log_a y+7\log_a z-3\log_a x)$ Power rule
$= \dfrac{1}{4}(2\cdot 3+7\cdot 4-3\cdot 2)$
$= \dfrac{1}{4}\cdot 28$
$= 7$

97. $\log_a M-\log_a N=\log_a \dfrac{M}{N}$

This is the quotient rule, so it is true.

99. $\dfrac{\log_a M}{x}=\dfrac{1}{x}\log_a M=\log_a M^{1/x}$. The statement is true by the power rule.

101. $\log_a 8x=\log_a 8+\log_a x=\log_a x+\log_a 8$. The statement is true by the product rule and the commutative property of addition.

103. $\log_a\left(\dfrac{1}{x}\right)=\log_a x^{-1}=-1\cdot\log_a x=-1\cdot 2=-2$

105. We use the change-of-base formula.

$\log_{10}11\cdot\log_{11}12\cdot\log_{12}13\cdots$
$\log_{998}999\cdot\log_{999}1000$
$=\log_{10}11\cdot\dfrac{\log_{10}12}{\log_{10}11}\cdot\dfrac{\log_{10}13}{\log_{10}12}\cdots$
$\dfrac{\log_{10}999}{\log_{10}998}\cdot\dfrac{\log_{10}1000}{\log_{10}999}$
$=\dfrac{\log_{10}11}{\log_{10}11}\cdot\dfrac{\log_{10}12}{\log_{10}12}\cdots\dfrac{\log_{10}999}{\log_{10}999}\cdot\log_{10}1000$
$=\log_{10}1000$
$=3$

107. $\ln a-\ln b+xy=0$
$\ln a+\ln b=-xy$
$\ln ab=-xy$

Then, using the definition of a logarithm, we have $e^{-xy}=ab$.

109. $\log_a\left(\dfrac{x+\sqrt{x^2-5}}{5}\right)$
$=\log_a\left(\dfrac{x+\sqrt{x^2-5}}{5}\cdot\dfrac{x-\sqrt{x^2-5}}{x-\sqrt{x^2-5}}\right)$
$=\log_a\left(\dfrac{5}{5(x-\sqrt{x^2-5})}\right)=\log_a\left(\dfrac{1}{x-\sqrt{x^2-5}}\right)$
$=\log_a 1-\log_a(x-\sqrt{x^2-5})$
$=-\log_a(x-\sqrt{x^2-5})$

Exercise Set 4.5

1. $3^x=81$
$3^x=3^4$
$x=4$ The exponents are the same.

The solution is 4.

3. $2^{2x}=8$
$2^{2x}=2^3$
$2x=3$ The exponents are the same.
$x=\dfrac{3}{2}$

The solution is $\dfrac{3}{2}$.

5. $2^x=33$
$\log 2^x=\log 33$ Taking the common logarithm on both sides
$x\log 2=\log 33$ Power rule
$x=\dfrac{\log 33}{\log 2}$
$x\approx\dfrac{1.5185}{0.3010}$
$x\approx 5.044$

The solution is 5.044.

7.
$$\begin{aligned} 5^{4x-7} &= 125 \\ 5^{4x-7} &= 5^3 \\ 4x-7 &= 3 \\ 4x &= 10 \\ x &= \frac{10}{4} = \frac{5}{2} \end{aligned}$$

The solution is $\frac{5}{2}$.

9.
$$\begin{aligned} 27 &= 3^{5x}\cdot 9^{x^2} \\ 3^3 &= 3^{5x}\cdot (3^2)^{x^2} \\ 3^3 &= 3^{5x}\cdot 3^{2x^2} \\ 3^3 &= 3^{5x+2x^2} \\ 3 &= 5x+2x^2 \\ 0 &= 2x^2+5x-3 \\ 0 &= (2x-1)(x+3) \\ x &= \frac{1}{2} \quad or \quad x=-3 \end{aligned}$$

The solutions are -3 and $\frac{1}{2}$.

11.
$$\begin{aligned} 84^x &= 70 \\ \log 84^x &= \log 70 \\ x\log 84 &= \log 70 \\ x &= \frac{\log 70}{\log 84} \\ x &\approx \frac{1.8451}{1.9243} \\ x &\approx 0.959 \end{aligned}$$

The solution is 0.959.

13.
$$\begin{aligned} e^{-c} &= 5^{2c} \\ \ln e^{-c} &= \ln 5^{2c} \\ -c &= 2c\ \ln 5 \\ 0 &= c+2c\ \ln 5 \\ 0 &= c(1+2\ \ln 5) \\ 0 &= c \qquad \text{Dividing by } 1+2\ \ln 5 \end{aligned}$$

The solution is 0.

15.
$$\begin{aligned} e^t &= 1000 \\ \ln e^t &= \ln 1000 \\ t &= \ln 1000 \quad \text{Using } \log_a a^x = x \\ t &\approx 6.908 \end{aligned}$$

The solution is 6.908.

17.
$$\begin{aligned} e^{-0.03t} &= 0.08 \\ \ln e^{-0.03t} &= \ln 0.08 \\ -0.03t &= \ln 0.08 \\ t &= \frac{\ln 0.08}{-0.03} \\ t &\approx \frac{-2.5257}{-0.03} \\ t &\approx 84.191 \end{aligned}$$

The solution is 84.191.

19.
$$\begin{aligned} 3^x &= 2^{x-1} \\ \ln 3^x &= \ln 2^{x-1} \\ x\ln 3 &= (x-1)\ln 2 \\ x\ln 3 &= x\ln 2-\ln 2 \\ \ln 2 &= x\ln 2-x\ln 3 \\ \ln 2 &= x(\ln 2-\ln 3) \\ \frac{\ln 2}{\ln 2-\ln 3} &= x \\ \frac{0.6931}{0.6931-1.0986} &\approx x \\ -1.710 &\approx x \end{aligned}$$

The solution is -1.710.

21.
$$\begin{aligned} (3.9)^x &= 48 \\ \log(3.9)^x &= \log 48 \\ x\log 3.9 &= \log 48 \\ x &= \frac{\log 48}{\log 3.9} \\ x &\approx \frac{1.6812}{0.5911} \\ x &\approx 2.844 \end{aligned}$$

The solution is 2.844.

23.
$$\begin{aligned} e^x+e^{-x} &= 5 \\ e^{2x}+1 &= 5e^x \qquad \text{Multiplying by } e^x \\ e^{2x}-5e^x+1 &= 0 \qquad \text{This equation is quadratic in } e^x. \\ e^x &= \frac{5\pm\sqrt{21}}{2} \\ x &= \ln\left(\frac{5\pm\sqrt{21}}{2}\right) \approx \pm 1.567 \end{aligned}$$

The solutions are -1.567 and 1.567.

25.
$$\begin{aligned} \frac{e^x+e^{-x}}{e^x-e^{-x}} &= 3 \\ e^x+e^{-x} &= 3e^x-3e^{-x} \quad \text{Multiplying by } e^x-e^{-x} \\ 4e^{-x} &= 2e^x \quad \text{Subtracting } e^x \text{ and adding } e^{-x} \\ 2e^{-x} &= e^x \\ 2 &= e^{2x} \qquad \text{Multiplying by } e^x \\ \ln 2 &= \ln e^{2x} \\ \ln 2 &= 2x \\ \frac{\ln 2}{2} &= x \\ 0.347 &\approx x \end{aligned}$$

The solution is 0.347.

27.
$$\begin{aligned} \log_5 x &= 4 \\ x &= 5^4 \qquad \text{Writing an equivalent exponential equation} \\ x &= 625 \end{aligned}$$

The solution is 625.

29. $\log x = -4$ The base is 10.

$x = 10^{-4}$, or 0.0001

The solution is 0.0001.

31. $\ln x = 1$ The base is e.

$x = e^1 = e$

The solution is e.

33.
$$\begin{aligned} \log_2(10+3x) &= 5 \\ 2^5 &= 10+3x \\ 32 &= 10+3x \\ 22 &= 3x \\ \frac{22}{3} &= x \end{aligned}$$

The answer checks. The solution is $\frac{22}{3}$.

35. $\log x + \log(x-9) = 1$ The base is 10.
$$\begin{aligned} \log_{10}[x(x-9)] &= 1 \\ x(x-9) &= 10^1 \\ x^2 - 9x &= 10 \\ x^2 - 9x - 10 &= 0 \\ (x-10)(x+1) &= 0 \end{aligned}$$

$x = 10$ or $x = -1$

Check: For 10:

$\log x + \log(x-9) = 1$	
$\log 10 + \log(10-9)$	? 1
$\log 10 + \log 1$	
$1+0$	
1	1 TRUE

For -1:

$\log x + \log(x-9) = 1$	
$\log(-1) + \log(-1-9)$	? 1

The number -1 does not check, because negative numbers do not have logarithms. The solution is 10.

37. $\log_2(x+20) - \log_2(x+2) = \log_2 x$
$$\log_2 \frac{x+20}{x+2} = \log_2 x$$
$$\frac{x+20}{x+2} = x \quad \text{Using the property of logarithmic equality}$$
$$x + 20 = x^2 + 2x \quad \text{Multiplying by } x+2$$
$$0 = x^2 + x - 20$$
$$0 = (x+5)(x-4)$$

$x + 5 = 0$ *or* $x - 4 = 0$

$x = -5$ *or* $x = 4$

Check: For -5:

$\log_2(x+20) - \log_2(x+2) = \log_2 x$	
$\log_2(-5+20) - \log_2(-5+2)$	? $\log_2(-5)$

The number -5 does not check, because negative numbers do not have logarithms.

For 4:

$\log_2(x+20) - \log_2(x+2) = \log_2 x$	
$\log_2(4+20) - \log_2(4+2)$	? $\log_2 4$
$\log_2 24 - \log_2 6$	
$\log_2 \frac{24}{6}$	
$\log_2 4$	$\log_2 4$ TRUE

The solution is 4.

39. $\log_8(x+1) - \log_8 x = 2$
$$\log_8\left(\frac{x+1}{x}\right) = 2 \quad \text{Quotient rule}$$
$$\begin{aligned} \frac{x+1}{x} &= 8^2 \\ \frac{x+1}{x} &= 64 \\ x+1 &= 64x \\ 1 &= 63x \\ \frac{1}{63} &= x \end{aligned}$$

The answer checks. The solution is $\frac{1}{63}$.

41. $\log x + \log(x+4) = \log 12$
$$\log x(x+4) = \log 12$$
$$x(x+4) = 12 \quad \text{Using the property of logarithmic equality}$$
$$\begin{aligned} x^2 + 4x &= 12 \\ x^2 + 4x - 12 &= 0 \\ (x+6)(x-2) &= 0 \end{aligned}$$

$x + 6 = 0$ *or* $x - 2 = 0$

$x = -6$ *or* $x = 2$

Check: For -6:

$\log x + \log(x+4) = \log 12$	
$\log(-6) + \log(-6+4)$	? $\log 12$

The number -6 does not check, because negative numbers do not have logarithms.

For 2:

$\log x + \log(x+4) = \log 12$	
$\log 2 + \log(2+4)$	? $\log 12$
$\log 2 + \log 6$	
$\log(2 \cdot 6)$	
$\log 12$	$\log 12$ TRUE

The solution is 2.

43. $\log_4(x+3) + \log_4(x-3) = 2$

$$\log_4[(x+3)(x-3)] = 2 \quad \text{Product rule}$$
$$(x+3)(x-3) = 4^2$$
$$x^2 - 9 = 16$$
$$x^2 = 25$$
$$x = \pm 5$$

The number 5 checks, but -5 does not. The solution is 5.

45. $\log(2x+1) - \log(x-2) = 1$

$$\log\left(\frac{2x+1}{x-2}\right) = 1 \quad \text{Quotient rule}$$
$$\frac{2x+1}{x-2} = 10^1 = 10$$
$$2x + 1 = 10x - 20$$

Multiplying by $x - 2$

$$21 = 8x$$
$$\frac{21}{8} = x$$

The answer checks. The solution is $\frac{21}{8}$.

47. $\ln(x+8) + \ln(x-1) = 2\ln x$

$$\ln(x+8)(x-1) = \ln x^2$$
$$(x+8)(x-1) = x^2 \quad \text{Using the property of logarithmic equality}$$
$$x^2 + 7x - 8 = x^2$$
$$7x - 8 = 0$$
$$7x = 8$$
$$x = \frac{8}{7}$$

The answer checks. The solution is $\frac{8}{7}$.

49. $e^{7.2x} = 14.009$

Graph $y_1 = e^{7.2x}$ and $y_2 = 14.009$ and find the first coordinate of the point of intersection using the Intersect feature. The solution is 0.367.

51. $xe^{3x} - 1 = 3$

Graph $y_1 = xe^{3x} - 1$ and $y_2 = 3$ and find the first coordinate of the point of intersection using the Intersect feature. The solution is 0.621.

53. $4\ln(x+3.4) = 2.5$

Graph $y_1 = 4\ln(x+3.4)$ and $y_2 = 2.5$ and find the first coordinate of the point of intersection using the Intersect feature. The solution is -1.532.

55. $\log_8 x + \log_8(x+2) = 2$

Graph $y_1 = \frac{\log x}{\log 8} + \frac{\log(x+2)}{\log 8}$ and $y_2 = 2$ and find the first coordinate of the point of intersection using the intersect feature. The solution is 7.062.

57. $\log_5(x+7) - \log_5(2x-3) = 1$

Graph $y_1 = \frac{\log(x+7)}{\log 5} - \frac{\log(2x-3)}{\log 5}$ and $y_2 = 1$ and find the first coordinate of the point of intersection using the Intersect feature. The solution is 2.444.

59. Solving the first equation for y, we get $y = \frac{12.4 - 2.3x}{3.8}$. Graph $y_1 = \frac{12.4 - 2.3x}{3.8}$ and $y_2 = 1.1\ln(x - 2.05)$ and use the Intersect feature to find the point of intersection. It is $(4.093, 0.786)$.

61. Graph $y_1 = 2.3\ln(x+10.7)$ and $y_2 = 10e^{-0.007x^2}$ and use the Intersect feature to find the point of intersection. It is $(7.586, 6.684)$.

63. Discussion and Writing

65. $g(x) = x^2 - 6$

a) $-\frac{b}{2a} = -\frac{0}{2 \cdot 1} = 0$

$g(0) = 0^2 - 6 = -6$

The vertex is $(0, -6)$.

b) The axis of symmetry is $x = 0$.

c) Since the coefficient of the x^2-term is positive, the function has a minimum value. It is the second coordinate of the vertex, -6, and it occurs when $x = 0$.

67. $G(x) = -2x^2 - 4x - 7$

a) $-\frac{b}{2a} = -\frac{-4}{2(-2)} = -1$

$G(-1) = -2(-1)^2 - 4(-1) - 7 = -5$

The vertex is $(-1, -5)$.

b) The axis of symmetry is $x = -1$.

c) Since the coefficient of the x^2-term is negative, the function has a maximum value. It is the second coordinate of the vertex, -5, and it occurs when $x = -1$.

69. $\ln(\log x) = 0$

$$\log x = e^0$$
$$\log x = 1$$
$$x = 10^1 = 10$$

The answer checks. The solution is 10.

71. $\sqrt{\ln x} = \ln\sqrt{x}$

$$\sqrt{\ln x} = \frac{1}{2}\ln x \quad \text{Power rule}$$
$$\ln x = \frac{1}{4}(\ln x)^2 \quad \text{Squaring both sides}$$
$$0 = \frac{1}{4}(\ln x)^2 - \ln x$$

Let $u = \ln x$ and substitute.

$$\frac{1}{4}u^2 - u = 0$$
$$u\left(\frac{1}{4}u - 1\right) = 0$$

$u = 0 \quad or \quad \frac{1}{4}u - 1 = 0$

$u = 0 \quad or \quad \frac{1}{4}u = 1$

$u = 0 \quad or \quad u = 4$

$\ln x = 0 \quad or \quad \ln x = 4$

$x = e^0 = 1 \quad or \quad x = e^4 \approx 54.598$

Both answers check. The solutions are 1 and e^4, or 1 and 54.598.

73. $(\log_3 x)^2 - \log_3 x^2 = 3$

$(\log_3 x)^2 - 2\log_3 x - 3 = 0$

Let $u = \log_3 x$ and substitute:

$u^2 - 2u - 3 = 0$

$(u-3)(u+1) = 0$

$u = 3 \quad or \quad u = -1$

$\log_3 x = 3 \quad or \quad \log_3 x = -1$

$x = 3^3 \quad or \quad x = 3^{-1}$

$x = 27 \quad or \quad x = \frac{1}{3}$

Both answers check. The solutions are $\frac{1}{3}$ and 27.

75. $\ln x^2 = (\ln x)^2$

$2\ln x = (\ln x)^2$

$0 = (\ln x)^2 - 2\ln x$

Let $u = \ln x$ and substitute.

$0 = u^2 - 2u$

$0 = u(u-2)$

$u = 0 \quad or \quad u = 2$

$\ln x = 0 \quad or \quad \ln x = 2$

$x = 1 \quad or \quad x = e^2 \approx 7.389$

Both answers check. The solutions are 1 and e^2, or 1 and 7.389.

77. $5^{2x} - 3\cdot 5^x + 2 = 0$

$(5^x - 1)(5^x - 2) = 0$ This equation is quadratic in 5^x.

$5^x = 1 \quad or \quad 5^x = 2$

$\log 5^x = \log 1 \quad or \quad \log 5^x = \log 2$

$x\log 5 = 0 \quad or \quad x\log 5 = \log 2$

$x = 0 \quad or \quad x = \frac{\log 2}{\log 5} \approx 0.431$

The solutions are 0 and 0.431.

79. $\log_3 |x| = 2$

$|x| = 3^2$

$|x| = 9$

$x = -9 \quad or \quad x = 9$

Both answers check. The solutions are -9 and 9.

81. $\ln x^{\ln x} = 4$

$\ln x \cdot \ln x = 4$

$(\ln x)^2 = 4$

$\ln x = \pm 2$

$\ln x = -2 \quad or \quad \ln x = 2$

$x = e^{-2} \quad or \quad x = e^2$

$x \approx 0.135 \quad or \quad x \approx 7.389$

Both answers check. The solutions are e^{-2} and e^2, or 0.135 and 7.389.

83. $\frac{\sqrt{(e^{2x}\cdot e^{-5x})^{-4}}}{e^x \div e^{-x}} = e^7$

$\frac{\sqrt{e^{12x}}}{e^{x-(-x)}} = e^7$

$\frac{e^{6x}}{e^{2x}} = e^7$

$e^{4x} = e^7$

$4x = 7$

$x = \frac{7}{4}$

The solution is $\frac{7}{4}$.

85. $|\log_5 x| + 3\log_5 |x| = 4$

Note that we must have $x > 0$. First consider the case when $0 < x < 1$. When $0 < x < 1$, then $\log_5 x < 0$, so $|\log_5 x| = -\log_5 x$ and $|x| = x$. Thus we have:

$-\log_5 x + 3\log_5 x = 4$

$2\log_5 x = 4$

$\log_5 x^2 = 4$

$x^2 = 5^4$

$x = 5^2$

$x = 25$ (Recall that $x > 0$.)

25 cannot be a solution since we assumed $0 < x < 1$.

Now consider the case when $x > 1$. In this case $\log_5 x > 0$, so $|\log_5 x| = \log_5 x$ and $|x| = x$. Thus we have:

$\log_5 x + 3\log_5 x = 4$

$4\log_5 x = 4$

$\log_5 x = 1$

$x = 5$

This answer checks. The solution is 5.

87. $a = \log_8 225$, so $8^a = 225 = 15^2$.

$b = \log_2 15$, so $2^b = 15$.

Then $8^a = (2^b)^2$

$(2^3)^a = 2^{2b}$

$2^{3a} = 2^{2b}$

$3a = 2b$

$a = \frac{2}{3}b.$

89. $\log_2[\log_3(\log_4 x)] = 0$ yields $x = 64$.
$\log_3[\log_2(\log_4 y)] = 0$ yields $y = 16$.
$\log_4[\log_3(\log_2 z)] = 0$ yields $z = 8$.
Then $x + y + z = 64 + 16 + 8 = 88$.

Exercise Set 4.6

1. a) Substitute 6.2 for P_0 and 0.012 for k in $P(t) = P_0e^{kt}$. We have:

$P(t) = 6.2e^{0.012t}$, where $P(t)$ is in billions and t is the number of years after 2001.

b) In 2005, $t = 2005 - 2001 = 4$.

$P(4) = 6.2e^{0.012(4)} \approx 6.5$ billion

In 2010, $t = 2010 - 2001 = 9$.

$P(9) = 6.2e^{0.012(9)} \approx 6.9$ billion

c) Substitute 8 for $P(t)$ and solve for t.

$$8 = 6.2e^{0.012t}$$
$$\frac{8}{6.2} = e^{0.012t}$$
$$\ln\frac{8}{6.2} = \ln e^{0.012t}$$
$$\ln\frac{8}{6.2} = 0.012t$$
$$\frac{\ln\frac{8}{6.2}}{0.012} = t$$
$$21.2 \approx t$$

The world population will be 8 billion about 21.2 yr after 2001.

d) $T = \dfrac{\ln 2}{0.012} \approx 57.8$ yr

3. a) $T = \dfrac{\ln 2}{0.025} \approx 27.7$ yr

b) $k = \dfrac{\ln 2}{693} \approx 0.1\%$ per yr

c) $T = \dfrac{\ln 2}{0.033} \approx 21.0$ yr

d) $T = \dfrac{\ln 2}{0.002} \approx 346.6$ yr

e) $k = \dfrac{\ln 2}{46.2} \approx 1.5\%$ per yr

f) $k = \dfrac{\ln 2}{36.5} \approx 1.9\%$ per yr

g) $k = \dfrac{\ln 2}{0.009} \approx 77.0$ yr

h) $k = \dfrac{\ln 2}{99.0} \approx 0.7\%$ per yr

i) $k = \dfrac{\ln 2}{0.011} \approx 63.0$ yr

j) $k = \dfrac{\ln 2}{0.003} \approx 231.0$ yr

5.
$$P(t) = P_0e^{kt}$$
$$24,313,062,400 = 5,938,000e^{0.013t}$$
$$\frac{24,313,062,400}{5,938,000} = e^{0.013t}$$
$$\ln\left(\frac{24,313,062,400}{5,938,000}\right) = \ln e^{0.013t}$$
$$\ln\left(\frac{24,313,062,400}{5,938,000}\right) = 0.013t$$
$$\frac{\ln\left(\frac{24,313,062,400}{5,938,000}\right)}{0.013} = t$$
$$640 \approx t$$

There will be one person for every square yard of land about 640 yr after 2001.

7. a) Substitute 10,000 for P_0 and 5.4%, or 0.054 for k.

$P(t) = 10,000e^{0.054t}$

b) $P(1) = 10,000e^{0.054(1)} \approx \$10,555$

$P(2) = 10,000e^{0.054(2)} \approx \$11,140$

$P(5) = 10,000e^{0.054(5)} \approx \$13,100$

$P(10) = 10,000e^{0.054(10)} \approx \$17,160$

c) $T = \dfrac{\ln 2}{0.054} \approx 12.8$ yr

9. We use the function found in Example 5. If the mummy has lost 46% of its carbon-14 from an initial amount P_0, then $54\%P_0$, or $0.54P_0$ remains. We substitute in the function.

$$0.54P_0 = P_0e^{-0.00012t}$$
$$0.54 = e^{-0.00012t}$$
$$\ln 0.54 = \ln e^{-0.00012t}$$
$$\ln 0.54 = -0.00012t$$
$$\frac{\ln 0.54}{-0.00012} = t$$
$$5135 \approx t$$

The mummy is about 5135 years old.

11. a) $K = \dfrac{\ln 2}{3} \approx 0.231$, or 23.1% per min

b) $k = \dfrac{\ln 2}{22} \approx 0.0315$, or 3.15% per yr

c) $T = \dfrac{\ln 2}{0.096} \approx 7.2$ days

d) $T = \dfrac{\ln 2}{0.063} \approx 11$ yr

e) $k = \dfrac{\ln 2}{25} \approx 0.028$, or 2.8% per yr

f) $k = \dfrac{\ln 2}{4560} \approx 0.00015$, or 0.015% per yr

g) $k = \dfrac{\ln 2}{23,105} \approx 0.00003$, or 0.003% per yr

13. a) Substitute 2002 − 1984, or 18, for t; 3395 for P_0; and 145 for $P(18)$ in $P(t) = P_0e^{-kt}$ and solve for k.

$$145 = 3395e^{-18k}$$
$$\frac{145}{3395} = e^{-18k}$$
$$\ln\left(\frac{145}{3395}\right) = \ln e^{-18k}$$
$$\ln\left(\frac{145}{3395}\right) = -18k$$
$$\frac{\ln\left(\frac{145}{3395}\right)}{-18} = k$$
$$0.175 \approx k$$

The desired function is $P(t) = 3395e^{-0.175t}$, where $P(t)$ is in dollars and t is the number of years after 1984.

b) In 2004, $t = 2004 - 1984 = 20$.

$P(20) = 3395e^{-0.175(20)} \approx \$103$

In 2008, $t = 2008 - 1984 = 24$.

$P(24) = 3395e^{-0.175(24)} \approx \$51$

c)
$$39 = 3395e^{-0.175t}$$
$$\frac{39}{3395} = e^{-0.175t}$$
$$\ln\left(\frac{39}{3395}\right) = \ln e^{-0.175t}$$
$$\ln\left(\frac{39}{3395}\right) = -0.175t$$
$$\frac{\ln\left(\frac{39}{3395}\right)}{-0.175} = t$$
$$26 \approx t$$

At this decay rate, the price of a cellphone will be \$39 about 26 yr after 1984, or in 2010.

15. a) $N(0) = \dfrac{3500}{1 + 19.9e^{-0.6(0)}} \approx 167$

b) $N(2) = \dfrac{3500}{1 + 19.9e^{-0.6(2)}} \approx 500$

$N(5) = \dfrac{3500}{1 + 19.9e^{-0.6(5)}} \approx 1758$

$N(8) = \dfrac{3500}{1 + 19.9e^{-0.6(8)}} \approx 3007$

$N(12) = \dfrac{3500}{1 + 19.9e^{-0.6(12)}} \approx 3449$

$N(16) = \dfrac{3500}{1 + 19.9e^{-0.6(16)}} \approx 3495$

c) As $t \to \infty$, $N(t) \to 3500$; the number of people infected approaches 3500 but never actually reaches it.

17. To find k we substitute 105 for T_1, 0 for T_0, 5 for t, and 70 for $T(t)$ and solve for k.

$$70 = 0 + (105 - 0)e^{-5k}$$
$$70 = 105e^{-5k}$$
$$\frac{70}{105} = e^{-5k}$$
$$\ln\frac{70}{105} = \ln e^{-5k}$$
$$\ln\frac{70}{105} = -5k$$
$$\frac{\ln\frac{70}{105}}{-5} = k$$
$$0.081 \approx k$$

The function is $T(t) = 105e^{-0.081t}$.

Now we find $T(10)$.

$T(10) = 105e^{-0.081(10)} \approx 46.7\ ^\circ$F

19. To find k we substitute 43 for T_1, 68 for T_0, 12 for t, and 55 for $T(t)$ and solve for k.

$$55 = 68 + (43 - 68)e^{-12k}$$
$$-13 = -25e^{-12k}$$
$$0.52 = e^{-12k}$$
$$\ln 0.52 = \ln e^{-12k}$$
$$\ln 0.52 = -12k$$
$$0.0545 \approx k$$

The function is $T(t) = 68 - 25e^{-0.0545t}$.

Now we find $T(20)$.

$T(20) = 68 - 25e^{-0.0545(20)} \approx 59.6^\circ$F

21. a) $y = 4.195491964(1.025306189)^x$

We can convert this equation to an equation with base e, if desired.

$$y = 4.195491964e^{x(\ln 1.025306189)}$$
$$= 4.195491964e^{0.024991289x}$$

In each case x is the number of years after 2000 and y is in millions.

The coefficient of correlation r is approximately 0.9954. Since this is close to 1, the function is a good fit.

b)

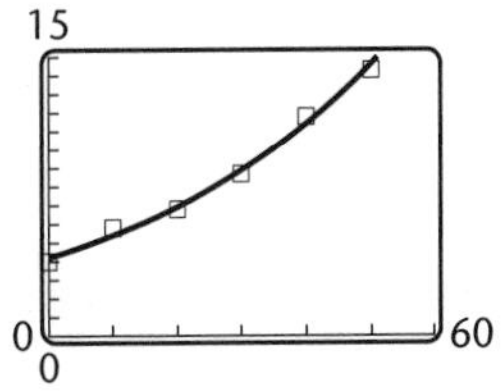

c) In 2005, $t = 2005 - 2000 = 5$.

$y = 4.195491964(1.025306189)^5 \approx 4.8$ million

In 2025, $t = 2025 - 2000 = 25$.

$y = 4.195491964(1.025306189)^{25} \approx 7.8$ million

In 2100, $t = 2100 - 2000 = 100$.

$y = 4.195491964(1.025306189)^{100} \approx 51.1$ million

23. a) 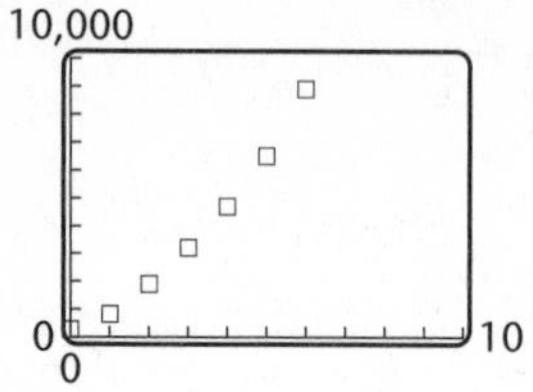

b) Linear: $y = 1429.214286x - 530.0714286$; $r^2 \approx 0.9641$

Quadratic: $y = 158.0952381x^2 + 480.6428571x + 260.4047619$; $R^2 \approx 0.9995$

Exponential: $y = 445.8787388(1.736315606)^x$; $r^2 \approx 0.9361$

The value of R^2 is highest for the quadratic function, so we determine that this function fits the data best.

c) 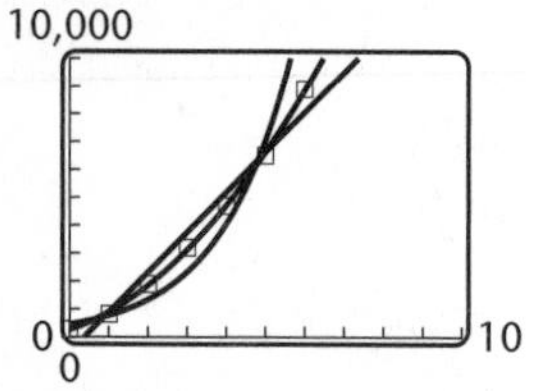

d) In 2010, $x = 2010 - 1996 = 14$.

For the linear function, when $x = 14$, $y \approx$ \$19,479 million, or \$19.479 billion.

For the quadratic function, when $x = 14$, $y \approx$ \$37,976 million, or \$37.976 billion.

For the exponential function, when $x = 14$, $y \approx$ \$1,009,295 million, or \$1009.295 billion.

Given the rate at which the revenues in the table are increasing, it appears that the quadratic function provides the most realistic prediction. Answers may vary.

25. a) Using the exponential regression feature on a graphing calculator, we get $y=21.13877717(1.038467095)^x$, where x is the number of years after 1980 and y is a percent.

b) In 2005, $x = 2005 - 1980 = 25$.

$y = 21.13877717(1.038467095)^{25} \approx 54.3\%$

In 2010, $x = 2010 - 1980 = 30$.

$y = 21.13877717(1.038467095)^{30} \approx 65.6\%$

c) Graph $y_1 = 21.13877717(1.038467095)^x$ and $y_2 = 70$ and find the first coordinate of the point of intersection of the graphs. It is approximately 31.7, so the percentage will first exceed 70% 32 yr after 1980, or in 2012.

27. Discussion and Writing

29. Multiplication principle for inequalities

31. Principle of zero products

33. Power rule

35.
$$\begin{aligned} P(t) &= P_0e^{kt} \\ 50,000 &= P_0e^{0.07(18)} \\ \frac{50,000}{e^{0.07(18)}} &= P_0 \\ \$14,182.70 &\approx P_0 \end{aligned}$$

37.
$$\begin{aligned} 480e^{-0.003p} &= 150e^{0.004p} \\ \frac{480}{150} &= \frac{e^{0.004p}}{e^{-0.003p}} \\ 3.2 &= e^{0.007p} \\ \ln 3.2 &= \ln e^{0.007p} \\ \ln 3.2 &= 0.007p \\ \frac{\ln 3.2}{0.007} &= p \\ \$166.16 &\approx p \end{aligned}$$

39.
$$\begin{aligned} i &= \frac{V}{R}\left[1 - e^{-(R/L)t}\right] \\ \frac{iR}{V} &= 1 - e^{-(R/L)t} \\ e^{-(R/L)t} &= 1 - \frac{iR}{V} \\ \ln e^{-(R/L)t} &= \ln\left(1 - \frac{iR}{V}\right) \\ -\frac{R}{L}t &= \ln\left(1 - \frac{iR}{V}\right) \\ t &= -\frac{L}{R}\left[\ln\left(1 - \frac{iR}{V}\right)\right] \end{aligned}$$

41.
$$\begin{aligned} y &= ae^x \\ \ln y &= \ln(ae^x) \\ \ln y &= \ln a + \ln e^x \\ \ln y &= \ln a + x \\ Y &= x + \ln a \end{aligned}$$

This function is of the form $y = mx + b$, so it is linear.

Chapter 5

Systems of Equations and Matrices

Exercise Set 5.1

1. Graph (c) is the graph of this system.

3. Graph (f) is the graph of this system.

5. Graph (b) is the graph of this system.

7. Graph $x + y = 2$ and $3x + y = 0$ and find the coordinates of the point of intersection.

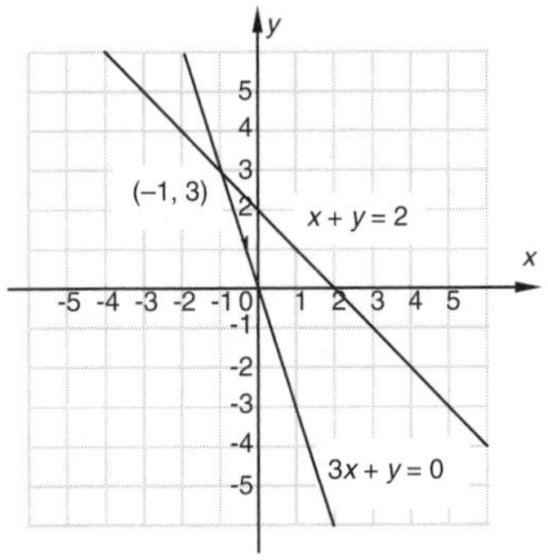

The solution is $(-1, 3)$.

9. Graph $x + 2y = 1$ and $x + 4y = 3$ and find the coordinates of the point of intersection.

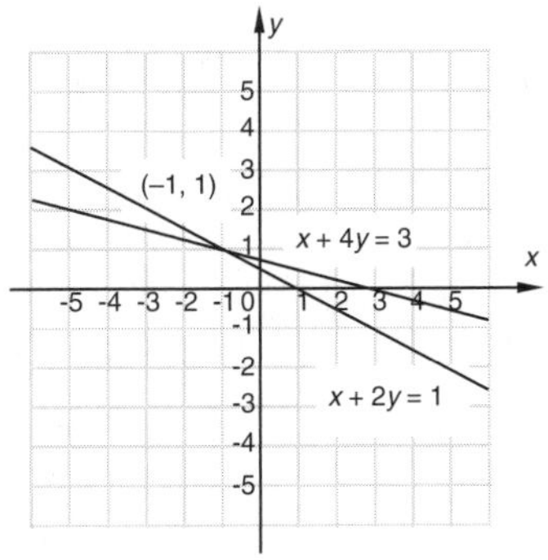

The solution is $(-1, 1)$.

11. Graph $y + 1 = 2x$ and $y - 1 = 2x$ and find the coordinates of the point of intersection.

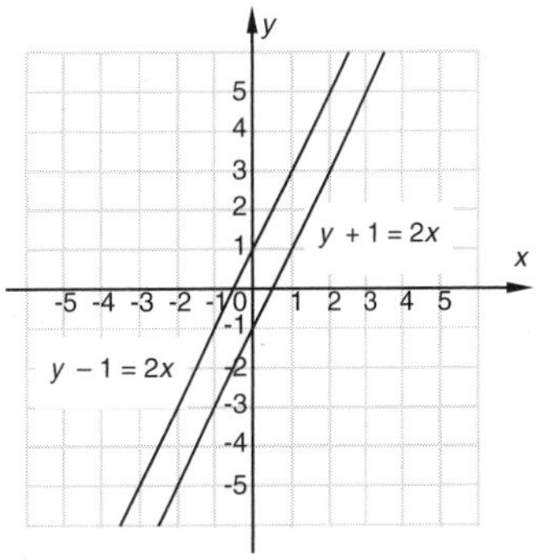

The graphs do not intersect, so there is no solution.

13. Graph $x - y = -6$ and $y = -2x$ and find the coordinates of the point of intersection.

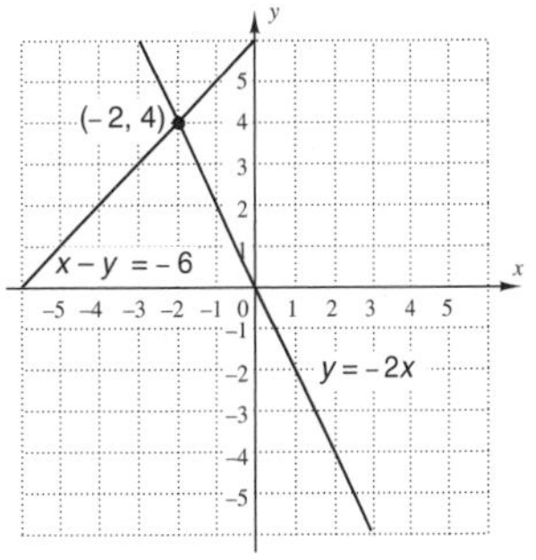

The solution is $(-2, 4)$.

15. Graph $2y = x - 1$ and $3x = 6y + 3$ and find the coordinates of the point of intersection.

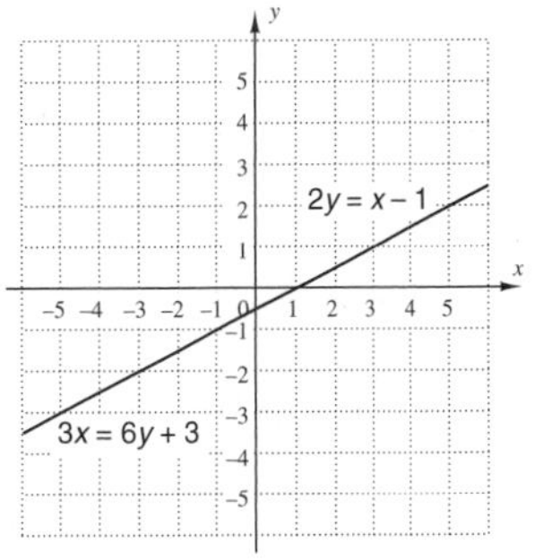

The graphs coincide so there are infinitely many solutions. Solving either equation for y, we get $y = \dfrac{x-1}{2}$, so the solutions can bae expressed as $\left(x, \dfrac{x-1}{2}\right)$. Similarly, solving either equation for x, we get $x = 2y + 1$, so the solutions can also be expressed as $(2y + 1, y)$.

17. $x + y = 9,\quad (1)$

$2x - 3y = -2\quad (2)$

Solve equation (1) for either x or y. We choose to solve for y.

$$y = 9 - x$$

Then substitute $9 - x$ for y in equation (2) and solve the resulting equation.

$$\begin{aligned}2x - 3(9 - x) &= -2\\ 2x - 27 + 3x &= -2\\ 5x - 27 &= -2\\ 5x &= 25\\ x &= 5\end{aligned}$$

Now substitute 5 for x in either equation (1) or (2) and solve for y.

$$\begin{aligned}5 + y &= 9 \quad \text{Using equation (1)}\\ y &= 4\end{aligned}$$

The solution is $(5, 4)$.

19. $x - 2y = 7,\quad (1)$

$x = y + 4\quad (2)$

Use equation (2) and substitute $y+4$ for x in equation (1). Then solve for y.

$$\begin{aligned}y + 4 - 2y &= 7\\ -y + 4 &= 7\\ -y &= 3\\ y &= -3\end{aligned}$$

Substitute -3 for y in equation (2) to find x.

$$x = -3 + 4 = 1$$

The solution is $(1, -3)$.

21. $y = 2x - 6,\quad (1)$

$5x - 3y = 16\quad (2)$

Use equation (1) and substitute $2x - 6$ for y in equation (2). Then solve for x.

$$\begin{aligned}5x - 3(2x - 6) &= 16\\ 5x - 6x + 18 &= 16\\ -x + 18 &= 16\\ -x &= -2\\ x &= 2\end{aligned}$$

Substitute 2 for x in equation (1) to find y.

$$y = 2 \cdot 2 - 6 = 4 - 6 = -2$$

The solution is $(2, -2)$.

23. $x - 5y = 4,\quad (1)$

$y = 7 - 2x\quad (2)$

Use equation (2) and substitute $7 - 2x$ for y in equation (1). Then solve for x.

$$\begin{aligned}x - 5(7 - 2x) &= 4\\ x - 35 + 10x &= 4\\ 11x - 35 &= 4\\ 11x &= 39\\ x &= \frac{39}{11}\end{aligned}$$

Substitute $\frac{39}{11}$ for x in equation (2) to find y.

$$y = 7 - 2 \cdot \frac{39}{11} = 7 - \frac{78}{11} = -\frac{1}{11}$$

The solution is $\left(\frac{39}{11}, -\frac{1}{11}\right)$.

25. $2x - 3y = 5,\quad (1)$

$5x + 4y = 1\quad (2)$

Solve one equation for either x or y. We choose to solve equation (1) for x.

$$\begin{aligned}2x - 3y &= 5\\ 2x &= 3y + 5\\ x &= \frac{3}{2}y + \frac{5}{2}\end{aligned}$$

Substitute $\frac{3}{2}y + \frac{5}{2}$ for x in equation (2) and solve for y.

$$\begin{aligned}5\left(\frac{3}{2}y + \frac{5}{2}\right) + 4y &= 1\\ \frac{15}{2}y + \frac{25}{2} + 4y &= 1\\ \frac{23}{2}y + \frac{25}{2} &= 1\\ \frac{23}{2}y &= -\frac{23}{2}\\ y &= -1\end{aligned}$$

Substitute -1 for y in either equation (1) or (2) and solve for x.

$$\begin{aligned}2x - 3(-1) &= 5 \quad \text{Using equation (1)}\\ 2x + 3 &= 5\\ 2x &= 2\\ x &= 1\end{aligned}$$

The solution is $(1, -1)$.

27. $x + 2y = 2,\quad (1)$

$4x + 4y = 5\quad (2)$

Solve one equation for either x or y. We choose to solve equation (1) for x since x has a coefficient of 1 in that equation.

$$\begin{aligned}x + 2y &= 2\\ x &= -2y + 2\end{aligned}$$

Substitute $-2y + 2$ for x in equation (2) and solve for y.

$$\begin{aligned}4(-2y + 2) + 4y &= 5\\ -8y + 8 + 4y &= 5\\ -4y + 8 &= 5\\ -4y &= -3\\ y &= \frac{3}{4}\end{aligned}$$

Substitute $\frac{3}{4}$ for y in either equation (1) or equation (2) and solve for x.

$x + 2y = 2$ Using equation (1)

$x + 2 \cdot \frac{3}{4} = 2$

$x + \frac{3}{2} = 2$

$x = \frac{1}{2}$

The solution is $\left(\frac{1}{2}, \frac{3}{4}\right)$.

29. $x + 2y = 7,$ (1)

$x - 2y = -5$ (2)

We add the equations to eliminate y.

$x + 2y = 7$

$x - 2y = -5$

$2x \quad = 2$ Adding

$x = 1$

Back-substitute in either equation and solve for y.

$1 + 2y = 7$ Using equation (1)

$2y = 6$

$y = 3$

The solution is $(1, 3)$. Since the system of equations has exactly one solution it is consistent and independent.

31. $x - 3y = 2,$ (1)

$6x + 5y = -34$ (2)

Multiply equation (1) by -6 and add it to equation (2) to eliminate x.

$-6x + 18y = -12$

$6x + 5y = -34$

$23y = -46$

$y = -2$

Back-substitute to find x.

$x - 3(-2) = 2$ Using equation (1)

$x + 6 = 2$

$x = -4$

The solution is $(-4, -2)$. Since the system of equations has exactly one solution it is consistent and independent.

33. $3x - 12y = 6,$ (1)

$2x - 8y = 4$ (2)

Multiply equation (1) by 2 and equation (2) by -3 and add.

$6x - 24y = 12$

$-6x + 24y = -12$

$0 = 0$

The equation $0 = 0$ is true for all values of x and y. Thus, the system of equations has infinitely many solutions. Solving either equation for y, we can write $y = \frac{1}{4}x - \frac{1}{2}$ so the solutions are ordered pairs of the form $\left(x, \frac{1}{4}x - \frac{1}{2}\right)$.

Equivalently, if we solve either equation for x we get $x = 4y + 2$ so the solutions can also be expressed as $(4y + 2, y)$. Since there are infinitely many solutions, the system of equations is consistent and dependent.

35. $2x = 5 - 3y,$ (1)

$4x = 11 - 7y$ (2)

We rewrite the equations.

$2x + 3y = 5,$ (1a)

$4x + 7y = 11$ (2a)

Multiply equation (2a) by -2 and add to eliminate x.

$-4x - 6y = -10$

$4x + 7y = 11$

$y = 1$

Back-substitute to find x.

$2x = 5 - 3 \cdot 1$ Using equation (1)

$2x = 2$

$x = 1$

The solution is $(1, 1)$. Since the system of equations has exactly one solution it is consistent and independent.

37. $0.3x - 0.2y = -0.9,$

$0.2x - 0.3y = -0.6$

First, multiply each equation by 10 to clear the decimals.

$3x - 2y = -9$ (1)

$2x - 3y = -6$ (2)

Now multiply equation (1) by 3 and equation (2) by -2 and add to eliminate y.

$9x - 6y = -27$

$-4x + 6y = 12$

$5x \quad = -15$

$x = -3$

Back-substitute to find y.

$3(-3) - 2y = -9$ Using equation (1)

$-9 - 2y = -9$

$-2y = 0$

$y = 0$

The solution is $(-3, 0)$. Since the system of equations has exactly one solution it is consistent and independent.

39. $\frac{1}{5}x + \frac{1}{2}y = 6,$ (1)

$\frac{3}{5}x - \frac{1}{2}y = 2$ (2)

We could multiply both equations by 10 to clear fractions, but since the y-coefficients differ only by sign we will just add to eliminate y.

$\frac{1}{5}x + \frac{1}{2}y = 6$

$\frac{3}{5}x - \frac{1}{2}y = 2$

$\frac{4}{5}x \quad = 8$

$x = 10$

Back-substitute to find y.

$$\frac{1}{5}\cdot 10+\frac{1}{2}y=6 \quad \text{Using equation (1)}$$

$$2+\frac{1}{2}y=6$$

$$\frac{1}{2}y=4$$

$$y=8$$

The solution is $(10, 8)$. Since the system of equations has exactly one solution it is consistent and independent.

41. ***Familiarize***. Let $x =$ the number of tons of ice consumed and $y =$ the number of tons of hot dogs consumed.

Translate. The amount of ice consumed was 50 times the amount of hot dogs consumed, by weight, so we have one equation:

$$x = 50y.$$

A second equation comes from the fact that a total of 204 tons of ice and hot dogs were consumed:

$$x + y = 204.$$

Carry out. We solve the system of equations

$$x = 50y, \quad (1)$$

$$x + y = 204. \quad (2)$$

Substitute $50y$ for x in equation (2) and solve for y.

$$50y + y = 204$$

$$51y = 204$$

$$y = 4$$

Back-substitute in equation (1) to find x.

$$x = 50\cdot 4 = 200$$

Check. 200 tons is 50 times 4 tons. Also, 4 tons + 200 tons = 204 tons, so the answer checks.

State. 200 tons of ice and 4 tons of hot dogs were consumed.

43. ***Familiarize***. Let $a =$ the cost of each adult's admission and $c =$ the cost of each child's admission.

Translate. One equation comes from the fact that an adult's admission is \$5.50 more than a child's:

$$a = c + 5.50.$$

A second equation comes from the fact that the total cost of 2 adult's admissions and 5 child's admissions is \$39:

$$2a + 5c = 39.$$

Carry out. We solve the system of equations

$$a = c + 5.50, \quad (1)$$

$$2a + 5c = 39. \quad (2)$$

Substitute $c + 5.50$ for a in equation (2) and solve for c.

$$2(c + 5.50) + 5c = 39$$

$$2c + 11 + 5c = 39$$

$$7c + 11 = 39$$

$$7c = 28$$

$$c = 4$$

Back-substitute in equation (1) to find a.

$$a = 4 + 5.50 = 9.50$$

Check. \$9.50 is \$5.50 more than \$4. Also, 2 adult's admissions cost 2(\$9.50), or \$19, and 5 child's admissions cost $5\cdot\$4$, or \$20. Then the total admission cost for 2 adults and 5 children is \$19 + \$20, or \$39. The answer checks.

State. An adult's admission costs \$9.50, and a child's admission costs \$4.

45. ***Familiarize***. Let $x =$ the number of video rentals and $y =$ the number of boxes of popcorn given away. Then the total cost of the rentals is $1\cdot x$, or x, and the total cost of the popcorn is $2y$.

Translate. The number of new members is the same as the number of incentives so we have one equation:

$$x + y = 48.$$

The total cost of the incentive was \$86. This gives us another equation:

$$x + 2y = 86.$$

Carry out. We solve the system of equations

$$x + y = 48, \quad (1)$$

$$x + 2y = 86. \quad (2)$$

Multiply equation (1) by -1 and add.

$$\begin{array}{r} -x - y = -48 \\ x + 2y = 86 \\ \hline y = 38 \end{array}$$

Back-substitute to find x.

$$x + 38 = 48 \quad \text{Using equation (1)}$$

$$x = 10$$

Check. When 10 rentals and 38 boxes of popcorn are given away, a total of 48 new members have signed up. Ten rentals cost the store \$10 and 38 boxes of popcorn cost $2\cdot 38$, or \$76, so the total cost of the incentives was \$10 + \$76, or \$86. The solution checks.

State. Ten rentals and 38 boxes of popcorn were given away.

47. ***Familiarize and Translate***. We use the system of equations given in the problem.

$$y = 70 + 2x \quad (1)$$

$$y = 175 - 5x, \quad (2)$$

Carry out. Substitute $175 - 5x$ for y in equation (1) and solve for x.

$$175 - 5x = 70 + 2x$$

$$105 = 7x \quad \text{Adding } 5x \text{ and subtracting 70}$$

$$15 = x$$

Back-substitute in either equation to find y. We choose equation (1).

$$y = 70 + 2\cdot 15 = 70 + 30 = 100$$

Check. Substituting 15 for x and 100 for y in both of the original equations yields true equations, so the solution checks. We could also check graphically by finding the point of intersection of equations (1) and (2).

State. The equilibrium point is $(15, \$100)$.

49. ***Familiarize and Translate***. We find the value of x for which $C = R$, where

$$C = 14x + 350,$$
$$R = 16.5x.$$

Carry out. When $C = R$ we have:

$$14x + 350 = 16.5x$$
$$350 = 2.5x$$
$$140 = x$$

Check. When $x = 140$, $C = 14 \cdot 140 + 350$, or 2310 and $R = 16.5(140)$, or 2310. Since $C = R$, the solution checks.

State. 140 units must be produced and sold in order to break even.

51. ***Familiarize and Translate***. We find the value of x for which $C = R$, where

$$C = 15x + 12,000,$$
$$R = 18x - 6000.$$

Carry out. When $C = R$ we have:

$$15x + 12,000 = 18x - 6000$$
$$18,000 = 3x \quad \text{Subtracting } 15x \text{ and adding } 6000$$
$$6000 = x$$

Check. When $x = 6000$, $C = 15 \cdot 6000 + 12,000$, or 102,000 and $R = 18 \cdot 6000 - 6000$, or 102,000. Since $C = R$, the solution checks.

State. 6000 units must be produced and sold in order to break even.

53. ***Familiarize***. Let x = the number of servings of spaghetti and meatballs required and y = the number of servings of iceberg lettuce required. Then x servings of spaghetti contain $260x$ Cal and $32x$ g of carbohydrates; y servings of lettuce contain $5y$ Cal and $1 \cdot y$ or y, g of carbohydrates.

Translate. One equation comes from the fact that 400 Cal are desired:

$$260x + 5y = 400.$$

A second equation comes from the fact that 50g of carbohydrates are required:

$$32x + y = 50.$$

Carry out. We solve the system

$$260x + 5y = 400, \quad (1)$$
$$32x + y = 50. \quad (2)$$

Multiply equation (2) by -5 and add.

$$260x + 5y = 400$$
$$-160x - 5y = -250$$
$$100x = 150$$
$$x = 1.5$$

Back-substitute to find y.

$$32(1.5) + y = 50 \quad \text{Using equation (2)}$$
$$48 + y = 50$$
$$y = 2$$

Check. 1.5 servings of spaghetti contain 260(1.5), or 390 Cal and 32(1.5), or 48 g of carbohydrates; 2 servings of lettuce contain $5 \cdot 2$, or 10 Cal and $1 \cdot 2$, or 2 g of carbohydrates. Together they contain $390 + 10$, or 400 Cal and $48 + 2$, or 50 g of carbohydrates. The solution checks.

State. 1.5 servings of spaghetti and meatballs and 2 servings of iceberg lettuce are required.

55. ***Familiarize***. It helps to make a drawing. Then organize the information in a table. Let x = the speed of the boat and y = the speed of the stream. The speed upstream is $x - y$. The speed downstream is $x + y$.

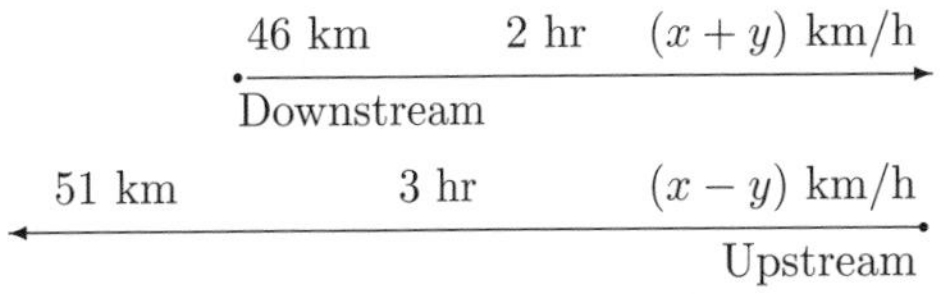

	Distance	Speed	Time
Downstream	46	$x+y$	2
Upstream	51	$x-y$	3

Translate. Using $d = rt$ in each row of the table, we get a system of equations.

$$46 = (x + y)2 \qquad x + y = 23, \quad (1)$$
or
$$51 = (x - y)3 \qquad x - y = 17 \quad (2)$$

Carry out. We begin by adding equations (1) and (2).

$$x + y = 23$$
$$x - y = 17$$
$$2x = 40$$
$$x = 20$$

Back-substitute to find y.

$$20 + y = 23 \quad \text{Using equation (1)}$$
$$y = 23$$

Check. The speed downstream is $20+3$, or 23 km/h. The distance traveled downstream in 2 hr is $23 \cdot 2$, or 46 km. The speed upstream is $20 - 3$, or 17 km/h. The distance traveled upstream in 3 hr is $17 \cdot 3$, or 51 km. The solution checks.

State. The speed of the boat is 20 km/h. The speed of the stream is 3 km/h.

57. ***Familiarize***. Let x = the amount invested at 7% and y = the amount invested at 9%. Then the interest from the investments is $7\%x$ and $9\%y$, or $0.07x$ and $0.09y$.

Translate.

The total investment is \$15,000.

$$x + y = 15,000$$

The total interest is \$1230.

$$0.07x + 0.09y = 1230$$

We have a system of equations:

$$x + y = 15,000,$$
$$0.07x + 0.09y = 1230$$

Multiplying the second equation by 100 to clear the decimals, we have:

$x + \quad y = 15,000, \quad (1)$

$7x + 9y = 123,000. \quad (2)$

Carry out. We begin by multiplying equation (1) by -7 and adding.

$$\begin{array}{r} -7x - 7y = -105,000 \\ 7x + 9y = 123,000 \\ \hline 2y = 18,000 \\ y = 9000 \end{array}$$

Back-substitute to find x.

$x + 9000 = 15,000$ Using equation (1)

$x = 6000$

Check. The total investment is $6000+$9000, or $15,000. The total interest is $0.07(\$6000) + 0.09(\$9000)$, or $\$420 + \$810$, or $1230. The solution checks.

State. $6000 was invested at 7% and $9000 was invested at 9%.

59. ***Familiarize***. Let x = the number of pounds of French roast coffee used and y = the number of pounds of Kenyan coffee. We organize the information in a table.

	French roast	Kenyan	Mixture
Amount	x	y	10 lb
Price per pound	$9.00	$7.50	$8.40
Total cost	$9x	$7.50y	$8.40(10), or $84

Translate. The first and third rows of the table give us a system of equations.

$x + \quad y = 10,$

$9x + 7.5y = 84$

Multiply the second equation by 10 to clear the decimals.

$x + \quad y = 10, \quad (1)$

$90x + 75y = 840 \quad (2)$

Carry out. Begin by multiplying equation (1) by -75 and adding.

$$\begin{array}{r} -75x - 75y = -750 \\ 90x + 75y = 840 \\ \hline 15x \qquad = 90 \\ x = 6 \end{array}$$

Back-substitute to find y.

$6 + y = 10$ Using equation (1)

$y = 4$

Check. The total amount of coffee in the mixture is $6+4$, or 10 lb. The total value of the mixture is $6(\$9)+4(\$7.50)$, or $\$54 + \$30$, or $84. The solution checks.

State. 6 lb of French roast coffee and 4 lb of Kenyan coffee should be used.

61. ***Familiarize***. Let x = the monthly sales, C = the earnings with the straight-commission plan, and S = the earnings with the salary-plus-commission plan. Then 8% of sales is represented by $8\%x$, or $0.08x$, and 1% of sales is represented by $1\%x$, or $0.01x$.

Translate.

Straight commission pays 8% of sales.

$C = 0.08x$

Salary plus commission pays $1500 plus 1% of sales.

$S = 1500 + 0.01x$

Carry out. We find the value of x for which $C = S$. We have:

$0.08x = 1500 + 0.01x$

$0.07x = 1500$

$x \approx 21,428.57$

Check. When $x \approx 21,428.57$, $C \approx 0.08(21,428.57) \approx 1714.29$ and $S \approx 1500 + 0.01(21,428.57) \approx 1714.29$. Since $C = S$, the solution checks.

State. The two plans pay the same amount for monthly sales of about $21,428.57.

63. Left to the student

65. a) $b(x) = 0.1714285714x + 63.48571429;$

$c(x) = 1.007142857x + 47.92857143$

b) Graph $y_1 = b(x)$ and $y_2 = c(x)$ and find the first coordinate of the point of intersection of the graphs. It is approximately 18.6, so we estimate that chicken consumption will equal beef consumption about 19 yr after 1995.

67. Discussion and Writing

69. ***Familiarize***. Let d = the number of DVDs shipped to retailers in the first quarter of 2002, in millions. Then a 93% increase over this number is $d + 0.93d$, or $1.93d$.

Translate.

Number of DVDs shipped in first quarter of 2003	is	a 93% increase over number shipped in first quarter of 2002.
↓	↓	↓
232	=	1.93d

Carry out. We solve the equation.

$232 = 1.93d$

$120 \approx d$ Dividing by 1.93

Check. 93% of 120 million is about 112 million, and 120 million + 112 million = 232 million. The answer checks.

State. About 120 million DVDs were shipped to retailers in the first quarter of 2002.

71. Substituting 15 for $f(x)$, we solve the following equation.

$15 = x^2 - 4x + 3$

$0 = x^2 - 4x - 12$

$0 = (x - 6)(x + 2)$

$x - 6 = 0$ *or* $x + 2 = 0$

$x = 6$ *or* $x = -2$

If the output is 15, the input is 6 or -2.

73. Substituting 8 for $f(x)$, we solve the following equation.

$$8 = x^2 - 4x + 3$$
$$0 = x^2 - 4x - 5$$
$$0 = (x - 5)(x + 1)$$

$x - 5 = 0$ *or* $x + 1 = 0$

$x = 5$ *or* $x = -1$

Given an output of 8, the corresponding inputs are 5 and -1.

75. ***Familiarize***. Let x = the time spent jogging and y = the time spent walking. Then Nancy jogs $8x$ km and walks $4y$ km. We organize the information in a table.

Translate.

The total time is 1 hr.

$$x + y = 1$$

The total distance is 6 km.

$$8x + 4y = 6$$

Carry out. Solve the system

$$x + y = 1, \quad (1)$$
$$8x + 4y = 6. \quad (2)$$

Multiply equation (1) by -4 and add.

$$\begin{aligned} -4x - 4y &= -4 \\ 8x + 4y &= 6 \\ \hline 4x \quad &= 2 \\ x &= \frac{1}{2} \end{aligned}$$

This is the time we need to find the distance spent jogging, so we could stop here. However, we will not be able to check the solution unless we find y also so we continue. We back-substitute.

$$\frac{1}{2} + y = 1 \quad \text{Using equation (1)}$$
$$y = \frac{1}{2}$$

Then the distance jogged is $8 \cdot \frac{1}{2}$, or 4 km.

Check. The total time is $\frac{1}{2}$ hr $+ \frac{1}{2}$ hr, or 1 hr. The total distance is 4 km + 2 km, or 6 km. The solution checks.

State. Nancy jogged 4 km on each trip.

77. ***Familiarize and Translate***. We let x and y represent the speeds of the trains. Organize the information in a table. Using $d = rt$, we let $3x$, $2y$, $1.5x$, and $3y$ represent the distances the trains travel.

First situation:

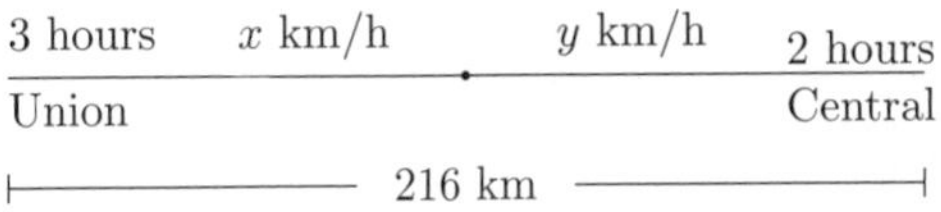

Second situation:

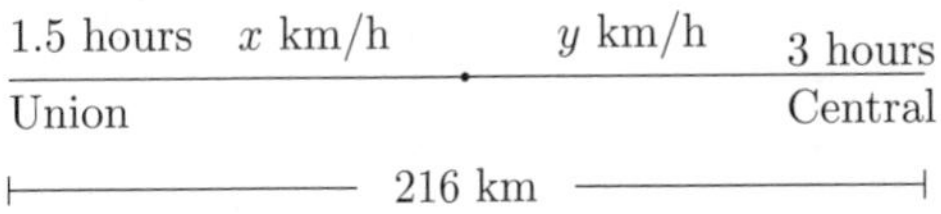

	Distance traveled in first situation	Distance traveled in second situation
Train_1 (from Union to Central)	$3x$	$1.5x$
Train_2 (from Central to Union)	$2y$	$3y$
Total	216	216

The total distance in each situation is 216 km. Thus, we have a system of equations.

$$3x + 2y = 216, \quad (1)$$
$$1.5x + 3y = 216 \quad (2)$$

Carry out. Multiply equation (2) by -2 and add.

$$\begin{aligned} 3x + 2y &= 216 \\ -3x - 6y &= -432 \\ \hline -4y &= -216 \\ y &= 54 \end{aligned}$$

Back-substitute to find x.

$$3x + 2 \cdot 54 = 216 \quad \text{Using equation (1)}$$
$$3x + 108 = 216$$
$$3x = 108$$
$$x = 36$$

Check. If $x = 36$ and $y = 54$, the total distance the trains travel in the first situation is $3 \cdot 36 + 2 \cdot 54$, or 216 km. The total distance they travel in the second situation is $1.5 \cdot 36 + 3 \cdot 54$, or 216 km. The solution checks.

State. The speed of the first train is 36 km/h. The speed of the second train is 54 km/h.

79. Substitute the given solutions in the equation $Ax + By = 1$ to get a system of equations.

$$3A - B = 1, \quad (1)$$
$$-4A - 2B = 1 \quad (2)$$

Multiply equation (1) by -2 and add.

$$\begin{aligned} -6A + 2B &= -2 \\ -4A - 2B &= 1 \\ \hline -10A \quad &= -1 \\ A &= \frac{1}{10} \end{aligned}$$

Back-substitute to find B.

$$3\left(\frac{1}{10}\right) - B = 1 \quad \text{Using equation (1)}$$
$$\frac{3}{10} - B = 1$$
$$-B = \frac{7}{10}$$
$$B = -\frac{7}{10}$$

We have $A = \frac{1}{10}$ and $B = -\frac{7}{10}$.

81. ***Familiarize***. Let x and y represent the number of gallons of gasoline used in city driving and in highway driving, respectively. Then $46x$ and $51y$ represent the number of miles driven in the city and on the highway, respectively.

Translate. The fact that 13 gal of gasoline were used gives us one equation:

$$x + y = 13.$$

A second equation comes from the fact that the car is driven 621 mile:

$$46x + 51y = 621.$$

Carry out. We solve the system of equations

$$x + y = 13, \quad (1)$$
$$46x + 51y = 621. \quad (2)$$

Multiply equation (1) by -46 and add.

$$-46x - 46y = -598$$
$$46x + 51y = 621$$
$$5y = 23$$
$$y = 4.6$$

Back-substitute to find x.

$$x + 4.6 = 13$$
$$x = 8.4$$

Then in the city the car is driven 46(8.4), or 386.4 mi; on the highway it is driven 51(4.6), or 234.6 mi.

Check. The number of gallons of gasoline used is 8.4+4.6, or 13. The number of miles driven is 386.4+234.6, or 621. The answer checks.

State. The car was driven 386.4 mi in the city and 234.6 mi on the highway.

Exercise Set 5.2

1.
$$x + y + z = 2, \quad (1)$$
$$6x - 4y + 5z = 31, \quad (2)$$
$$5x + 2y + 2z = 13 \quad (3)$$

Multiply equation (1) by -6 and add it to equation (2). We also multiply equation (1) by -5 and add it to equation (3).

$$x + y + z = 2 \quad (1)$$
$$-10y - z = 19 \quad (4)$$
$$-3y - 3z = 3 \quad (5)$$

Multiply the last equation by 10 to make the y-coefficient a multiple of the y-coefficient in equation (4).

$$x + y + z = 2 \quad (1)$$
$$-10y - z = 19 \quad (4)$$
$$-30y - 30z = 30 \quad (6)$$

Multiply equation (4) by -3 and add it to equation (6).

$$x + y + z = 2 \quad (1)$$
$$-10y - z = 19 \quad (4)$$
$$-27z = -27 \quad (7)$$

Solve equation (7) for z.

$$-27z = -27$$
$$z = 1$$

Back-substitute 1 for z in equation (4) and solve for y.

$$-10y - 1 = 19$$
$$-10y = 20$$
$$y = -2$$

Back-substitute 1 for z for -2 and y in equation (1) and solve for x.

$$x + (-2) + 1 = 2$$
$$x - 1 = 2$$
$$x = 3$$

The solution is $(3, -2, 1)$.

3.
$$x - y + 2z = -3 \quad (1)$$
$$x + 2y + 3z = 4 \quad (2)$$
$$2x + y + z = -3 \quad (3)$$

Multiply equation (1) by -1 and add it to equation (2). We also multiply equation (1) by -2 and add it to equation (3).

$$x - y + 2z = -3 \quad (1)$$
$$3y + z = 7 \quad (4)$$
$$3y - 3z = 3 \quad (5)$$

Multiply equation (4) by -1 and add it to equation (5).

$$x - y + 2z = -3 \quad (1)$$
$$3y + z = 7 \quad (4)$$
$$-4z = -4 \quad (6)$$

Solve equation (6) for z.

$$-4z = -4$$
$$z = 1$$

Back-substitute 1 for z in equation (4) and solve for y.

$$3y + 1 = 7$$
$$3y = 6$$
$$y = 2$$

Back-substitute 1 for z and 2 for y in equation (1) and solve for x.

$$x - 2 + 2 \cdot 1 = -3$$
$$x = -3$$

The solution is $(-3, 2, 1)$.

5. $x + 2y - z = 5$, (1)
$2x - 4y + z = 0$, (2)
$3x + 2y + 2z = 3$ (3)

Multiply equation (1) by -2 and add it to equation (2). Also, multiply equation (1) by -3 and add it to equation (3).

$x + 2y - z = 5$, (1)
$-8y + 3z = -10$, (4)
$-4y + 5z = -12$ (5)

Multiply equation (5) by 2 to make the y-coefficient a multiple of the y-coefficient of equation (4).

$x + 2y - z = 5$, (1)
$-8y + 3z = -10$, (4)
$-8y + 10z = -24$ (6)

Multiply equation (4) by -1 and add it to equation (6).

$x + 2y - z = 5$, (1)
$-8y + 3z = -10$, (4)
$7z = -14$ (7)

Solve equation (7) for z.

$$7z = -14$$
$$z = -2$$

Back-substitute -2 for z in equation (4) and solve for y.

$$-8y + 3(-2) = -10$$
$$-8y - 6 = -10$$
$$-8y = -4$$
$$y = \frac{1}{2}$$

Back-substitute $\frac{1}{2}$ for y and -2 for z in equation (1) and solve for x.

$$x + 2 \cdot \frac{1}{2} - (-2) = 5$$
$$x + 1 + 2 = 5$$
$$x = 2$$

The solution is $\left(2, \frac{1}{2}, -2\right)$.

7. $x + 2y - z = -8$, (1)
$2x - y + z = 4$, (2)
$8x + y + z = 2$ (3)

Multiply equation (1) by -2 and add it to equation (2). Also, multiply equation (1) by -8 and add it to equation (3).

$x + 2y - z = -8$, (1)
$-5y + 3z = 20$, (4)
$-15y + 9z = 66$ (5)

Multiply equation (4) by -3 and add it to equation (5).

$x + 2y - z = -8$, (1)
$-5y + 3z = 20$, (4)
$0 = 6$ (6)

Equation (6) is false, so the system of equations has no solution.

9. $2x + y - 3z = 1$, (1)
$x - 4y + z = 6$, (2)
$4x - 7y - z = 13$ (3)

Interchange equations (1) and (2).

$x - 4y + z = 6$, (2)
$2x + y - 3z = 1$, (1)
$4x - 7y - z = 13$ (3)

Multiply equation (2) by -2 and add it to equation (1). Also, multiply equation (2) by -4 and add it to equation (3).

$x - 4y + z = 6$, (2)
$9y - 5z = -11$, (4)
$9y - 5z = -11$ (5)

Multiply equation (4) by -1 and add it to equation (5).

$x - 4y + z = 6$, (1)
$9y - 5z = -11$, (4)
$0 = 0$ (6)

The equation $0 = 0$ tells us that equation (3) of the original system is dependent on the first two equations. The system of equations has infinitely many solutions and is equivalent to

$2x + y - 3z = 1$, (1)
$x - 4y + z = 6$. (2)

To find an expression for the solutions, we first solve equation (4) for either y or z. We choose to solve for z.

$$9y - 5z = -11$$
$$-5z = -9y - 11$$
$$z = \frac{9y + 11}{5}$$

Back-substitute in equation (2) to find an expression for x in terms of y.

$$x - 4y + \frac{9y + 11}{5} = 6$$
$$x - 4y + \frac{9}{5}y + \frac{11}{5} = 6$$
$$x = \frac{11}{5}y + \frac{19}{5} = \frac{11y + 19}{5}$$

The solutions are given by $\left(\frac{11y + 19}{5}, y, \frac{9y + 11}{5}\right)$, where y is any real number.

11. $4a + 9b = 8$, (1)
$8a + 6c = -1$, (2)
$6b + 6c = -1$ (3)

Multiply equation (1) by -2 and add it to equation (2).

$4a + 9b = 8$, (1)
$-18b + 6c = -17$, (4)
$6b + 6c = -1$ (3)

Multiply equation (3) by 3 to make the b-coefficient a multiple of the b-coefficient in equation (4).

$$\begin{aligned} 4a + 9b \quad &= 8, \quad (1)\\ -18b + 6c &= -17, \quad (4)\\ 18b + 18c &= -3 \quad (5) \end{aligned}$$

Add equation (4) to equation (5).

$$\begin{aligned} 4a + 9b \quad &= 8, \quad (1)\\ -18b + 6c &= -17, \quad (4)\\ 24c &= -20 \quad (6) \end{aligned}$$

Solve equation (6) for c.

$$24c = -20$$
$$c = -\frac{20}{24} = -\frac{5}{6}$$

Back-substitute $-\frac{5}{6}$ for c in equation (4) and solve for b.

$$\begin{aligned} -18b + 6c &= -17\\ -18b + 6\left(-\frac{5}{6}\right) &= -17\\ -18b - 5 &= -17\\ -18b &= -12\\ b &= \frac{12}{18} = \frac{2}{3} \end{aligned}$$

Back-substitute $\frac{2}{3}$ for b in equation (1) and solve for a.

$$\begin{aligned} 4a + 9b &= 8\\ 4a + 9\cdot\frac{2}{3} &= 8\\ 4a + 6 &= 8\\ 4a &= 2\\ a &= \frac{1}{2} \end{aligned}$$

The solution is $\left(\frac{1}{2}, \frac{2}{3}, -\frac{5}{6}\right)$.

13.
$$\begin{aligned} 2x \qquad + z &= 1, \quad (1)\\ 3y - 2z &= 6, \quad (2)\\ x - 2y \qquad &= -9 \quad (3) \end{aligned}$$

Interchange equations (1) and (3).

$$\begin{aligned} x - 2y \qquad &= -9, \quad (3)\\ 3y - 2z &= 6, \quad (2)\\ 2x \qquad + z &= 1 \quad (1) \end{aligned}$$

Multiply equation (3) by -2 and add it to equation (1).

$$\begin{aligned} x - 2y \qquad &= -9, \quad (3)\\ 3y - 2z &= 6, \quad (2)\\ 4y + z &= 19 \quad (4) \end{aligned}$$

Multiply equation (4) by 3 to make the y-coefficient a multiple of the y-coefficient in equation (2).

$$\begin{aligned} x - 2y \qquad &= -9, \quad (3)\\ 3y - 2z &= 6, \quad (2)\\ 12y + 3z &= 57 \quad (5) \end{aligned}$$

Multiply equation (2) by -4 and add it to equation (5).

$$\begin{aligned} x - 2y \qquad &= -9, \quad (3)\\ 3y - 2z &= 6, \quad (2)\\ 11z &= 33 \quad (6) \end{aligned}$$

Solve equation (6) for z.

$$11z = 33$$
$$z = 3$$

Back-substitute 3 for z in equation (2) and solve for y.

$$\begin{aligned} 3y - 2z &= 6\\ 3y - 2\cdot 3 &= 6\\ 3y - 6 &= 6\\ 3y &= 12\\ y &= 4 \end{aligned}$$

Back-substitute 4 for y in equation (3) and solve for x.

$$\begin{aligned} x - 2y &= -9\\ x - 2\cdot 4 &= -9\\ x - 8 &= -9\\ x &= -1 \end{aligned}$$

The solution is $(-1, 4, 3)$.

15.
$$\begin{aligned} w + x + y + z &= 2 \quad (1)\\ w + 2x + 2y + 4z &= 1 \quad (2)\\ -w + x - y - z &= -6 \quad (3)\\ -w + 3x + y - z &= -2 \quad (4) \end{aligned}$$

Multiply equation (1) by -1 and add to equation (2). Add equation (1) to equation (3) and to equation (4).

$$\begin{aligned} w + x + y + z &= 2 \quad (1)\\ x + y + 3z &= -1 \quad (5)\\ 2x \qquad &= -4 \quad (6)\\ 4x + 2y \qquad &= 0 \quad (7) \end{aligned}$$

Solve equation (6) for x.

$$2x = -4$$
$$x = -2$$

Back-substitute -2 for x in equation (7) and solve for y.

$$\begin{aligned} 4(-2) + 2y &= 0\\ -8 + 2y &= 0\\ 2y &= 8\\ y &= 4 \end{aligned}$$

Back-substitute -2 for x and 4 for y in equation (5) and solve for z.

$$\begin{aligned} -2 + 4 + 3z &= -1\\ 3z &= -3\\ z &= -1 \end{aligned}$$

Back-substitute -2 for x, 4 for y, and -1 for z in equation (1) and solve for w.

$$\begin{aligned} w - 2 + 4 - 1 &= 2\\ w &= 1 \end{aligned}$$

The solution is $(1, -2, 4, -1)$.

17. ***Familiarize.*** Let x = the number of orders under 10 lb, y = the number of orders from 10 lb up to 15 lb, and z = the number of orders of 15 lb or more. Then the total shipping charges for each category of order are \$$3x$, \$$5y$, and \$$7.50z$.

Translate.

The total number of orders was 150.

$$x + y + z = 150$$

Total shipping charges were \$680.

$$3x + 5y + 7.5z = 680$$

The number of orders under 10 lb was three times the number of orders weighing 15 lb or more.

$$x = 3z$$

We have a system of equations

$$\begin{aligned} x + y + z &= 150, & x + y + z &= 150,\\ 3x + 5y + 7.5z &= 680, \quad \text{or} & 30x + 50y + 75z &= 6800,\\ x &= 3z & x - 3z &= 0 \end{aligned}$$

Carry out. Solving the system of equations, we get $(60, 70, 20)$.

Check. The total number of orders is $60+70+20$, or 150. The total shipping charges are $\$3 \cdot 60 + \$5 \cdot 70 + \$7.50(20)$, or \$680. The number of orders under 10 lb, 60, is three times the number of orders weighing over 15 lb, 20. The solution checks.

State. There were 60 packages under 10 lb, 70 packages from 10 lb up to 15 lb, and 20 packages weighing 15 lb or more.

19. ***Familiarize.*** Let x, y, and z represent the number of servings of ground beef, baked potato, and strawberries required, respectively. One serving of ground beef contains $245x$ Cal, $0x$ or 0 g of carbohydrates, and $9x$ mg of calcium. One baked potato contains $145y$ Cal, $34y$ g of carbohydrates, and $8y$ mg of calcium. One serving of strawberries contains $45z$ Cal, $10z$ g of carbohydrates, and $21z$ mg of calcium.

Translate.

The total number of calories is 485.

$$245x + 145y + 45z = 485$$

A total of 41.5 g of carbohydrates is required.

$$34y + 10z = 41.5$$

A total of 35 mg of calcium is required.

$$9x + 8y + 21z = 35$$

We have a system of equations.

$$\begin{aligned} 245x + 145y + 45z &= 485,\\ 34y + 10z &= 41.5,\\ 9x + 8y + 21z &= 35 \end{aligned}$$

Carry out. Solving the system of equations, we get $(1.25, 1, 0.75)$.

Check. 1.25 servings of ground beef contains 306.25 Cal, no carbohydrates, and 11.25 mg of calcium; 1 baked potato contains 145 Cal, 34 g of carbohydrates, and 8 mg of calcium; 0.75 servings of strawberries contains 33.75 Cal, 7.5 g of carbohydrates, and 15.75 mg of calcium. Thus, there are a total of $306.25 + 145 + 33.75$, or 485 Cal, $34 + 7.5$, or 41.5 g of carbohydrates, and $11.25 + 8 + 15.75$, or 35 mg of calcium. The solution checks.

State. 1.25 servings of ground beef, 1 baked potato, and 0.75 serving of strawberries are required.

21. ***Familiarize.*** Let x, y, and z represent the amounts invested at 3%, 4%, and 6%, respectively. Then the annual interest from the investments is $3\%x$, $4\%y$, and $6\%z$, or $0.03x$, $0.04y$, and $0.06z$.

Translate.

A total of \$5000 was invested.

$$x + y + z = 5000$$

The total interest is \$243.

$$0.03x + 0.04y + 0.06z = 243$$

The amount invested at 6% is \$1500 more than the amount invested at 3%.

$$z = x + 1500$$

We have a system of equations.

$$\begin{aligned} x + y + z &= 5000,\\ 0.03x + 0.04y + 0.06z &= 243,\\ z &= x + 1500 \end{aligned}$$

or

$$\begin{aligned} x + y + z &= 5000,\\ 3x + 4y + 6z &= 24,300,\\ -x + z &= 1500 \end{aligned}$$

Carry out. Solving the system of equations, we get $(1300, 900, 2800)$.

Check. The total investment was \$1300+\$900+\$2800, or \$5000. The total interest was $0.03(\$1300) + 0.04(\$900) + 0.06(\$2800) = \$39 + \$36 + \$168$, or \$243. The amount invested at 6%, \$2800, is \$1500 more than the amount invested at 3%, \$1300. The solution checks.

State. \$1300 was invested at 3%, \$900 at 4%, and \$2800 at 6%.

23. ***Familiarize.*** Let x, y, and z represent the prices of orange juice, a raisin bagel, and a cup of coffee, respectively. The new price for orange juice is $x + 50\%x$, or $x + 0.5x$, or $1.5x$; the new price of a bagel is $y + 20\%y$, or $y + 0.2y$, or $1.2y$.

Translate.

Orange juice, a raisin bagel, and a cup of coffee cost \$3.

$$x + y + x = 3$$

After the price increase, orange juice, a raisin bagel, and a cup of coffee will cost \$3.75.

$$1.5x + 1.2y + z = 3.75$$

After the price increases, orange juice will cost twice as much as coffee.

$$1.5x = 2z$$

We have a system of equations.

$$\begin{aligned} x+y+z&=3, & x+\quad y+\quad z&=3,\\ 1.5x+1.2y+z&=3.75, \text{ or } & 150x+120y+100z&=375,\\ 1.5x&=2z & 15x\qquad -\ 20z&=0 \end{aligned}$$

Carry out. Solving the system of equations, we get $(1, 1.25, 0.75)$.

Check. If orange juice costs \$1, a bagel costs \$1.25, and a cup of coffee costs \$0.75, then together they cost \$1 + \$1.25 + \$0.75, or \$3. After the price increases orange juice will cost 1.5(\$1), or \$1.50 and a bagel will cost 1.2(\$1.25) or \$1.50. Then orange juice, a bagel, and coffee will cost \$1.50 + \$1.50 + \$0.75, or \$3.75. After the price increase the price of orange juice, \$1.50, will be twice the price of coffee, \$0.75. The solution checks.

State. Before the increase orange juice costs \$1, a raisin bagel cost \$1.25, and a cup of coffee cost \$0.75.

25. ***Familiarize.*** Let x, y, and z represent the volume of passenger traffic by private automobile, by bus, and by railroads, respectively, in billions of passenger-miles.

Translate.

The total volume of passenger traffic was 1899 billion passenger-miles.

$$x+y+z=1899$$

The volume of bus traffic was 21 billion passenger-miles more than the volume of railroad traffic.

$$y=z+21$$

The volume of bus traffic was 1815 billion passenger-miles less than the volume of traffic by private automobile.

$$y=x-1815$$

We have a system of equations.

$$\begin{aligned} x+y+z&=1899, & x+y+z&=1899,\\ y&=z+21, \quad\text{or} & y-z&=21,\\ y&=x-1815 & -x\quad +y&=-1815 \end{aligned}$$

Carry out. Solving the system of equations, we get $(1850, 35, 14)$.

Check. The total volume is $1850+35+14$, or 1899 billion passenger-miles. The volume of bus traffic, 35 billion passenger-miles, is 21 billion passenger-miles more than the volume of railroad traffic, 14 billion passenger-miles. The volume of bus traffic, 35 billion passenger-miles, is 1815 billion passenger-miles less than the volume of traffic by private automobile, 1850 billion passenger-miles. The solution checks.

State. The volume of traffic by private automobile was 1850 billion passenger-miles, by bus was 35 billion passenger-miles, and by railroad was 14 billion passenger-miles.

27. ***Familiarize.*** Let x, y, and z represent the number of par-3, par-4, and par-5 holes, respectively. A golfer who shoots par on every hole has a score of $3x$ from the par-3 holes, $4y$ from the par-4 holes, and $5z$ from the par-5 holes.

Translate.

The total number of holes is 18.

$$x+y+z=18$$

A golfer who shoots par on every hole has a score of 72.

$$3x+4y+5z=72$$

The sum of the number of par-3 holes and the number of par-5 holes is 8.

$$x+z=8$$

We have a system of equations.

$$\begin{aligned} x+\ y+\ z&=18,\\ 3x+4y+5z&=72,\\ x\qquad +\ z&=8 \end{aligned}$$

Carry out. We solve the system. The solution is $(4, 10, 4)$.

Check. The total number of holes is $4+10+4$, or 18. A golfer who shoots par on every hole has a score of $3\cdot4+4\cdot10+5\cdot4$, or 72. The sum of the number of par-3 holes and the number of par-5 holes is $4+4$, or 8. The solution checks.

State. There are 4 par-3 holes, 10 par-4 holes, and 4 par-5 holes.

29. a) Substitute the data points $(0, 237)$, $(5, 200)$, and $(11, 224)$ in the function $f(x)=ax^2+bx+c$.

$$237=a\cdot0^2+b\cdot0+c$$
$$200=a\cdot5^2+b\cdot5+c$$
$$224=a\cdot11^2+b\cdot11+c$$

We have a system of equations.

$$\begin{aligned} c&=237,\\ 25a+5b+c&=200,\\ 121a+11b+c&=224 \end{aligned}$$

Solving the system of equations, we get $\left(\frac{57}{55}, -\frac{692}{55}, 237\right)$, so $f(x)=\frac{57}{55}x^2-\frac{692}{55}x+237$, where $f(x)$ is in thousands and x is the number of years after 1990.

b) In 2008, $x=2008-1990$, or 18.

$$f(18)=\frac{57}{55}(18)^2-\frac{692}{55}(18)+237\approx346$$

There will be about 346 thousand marriages in California in 2008.

31. a) Substitute the data points $(0, 594)$, $(10, 577)$, and $(15, 593)$ in the function $f(x)=ax^2+bx+c$.

$$594=a\cdot0^2+b\cdot0+c$$
$$577=a\cdot10^2+b\cdot10+c$$
$$593=a\cdot15^2+b\cdot15+c$$

We have a system of equations.

$$\begin{aligned} c&=594,\\ 100a+10b+c&=577,\\ 225a+15b+c&=593 \end{aligned}$$

Solving the system of equations, we get $\left(\frac{49}{150}, -\frac{149}{30}, 594\right)$, so $f(x)=\frac{49}{150}x^2-\frac{149}{30}x+594$, where x is the number of years after 1985.

b) In 2007, $x = 2007 - 1985$, or 22.

$$f(22) = \frac{49}{150}(22)^2 - \frac{149}{30}(22) + 594 \approx 643.$$

The per capita consumption of dairy products in 2007 will be about 643 lb.

33. a) Using the quadratic regression feature on a graphing calculator, we have $f(x) = 0.1793514633x^2 - 11.15232206x + 468.8939939$, where x is the number of years after 1920.

b) In 2006, $x = 2006 - 1920$, or 86; $f(86) \approx 836$, so we estimate that there will be about 836 morning newspapers in 2006.

In 2009, $x = 2009 - 1920$, or 89; $f(89) \approx 897$, so we estimate that there will be about 897 morning newspapers in 2009.

35. Discussion and Writing

37. Perpendicular

39. A vertical line

41. A rational function

43. A vertical asymptote

45.
$$\frac{2}{x} - \frac{1}{y} - \frac{3}{z} = -1,$$
$$\frac{2}{x} - \frac{1}{y} + \frac{1}{z} = -9,$$
$$\frac{1}{x} + \frac{2}{y} - \frac{4}{z} = 17$$

First substitute u for $\frac{1}{x}$, v for $\frac{1}{y}$, and w for $\frac{1}{z}$ and solve for u, v, and w.

$$2u - v - 3w = -1,$$
$$2u - v + w = -9,$$
$$u + 2v - 4w = 17$$

Solving this system we get $(-1, 5, -2)$.

If $u = -1$, and $u = \frac{1}{x}$, then $-1 = \frac{1}{x}$, or $x = -1$.

If $v = 5$ and $v = \frac{1}{y}$, then $5 = \frac{1}{y}$, or $y = \frac{1}{5}$.

If $w = -2$ and $w = \frac{1}{z}$, then $-2 = \frac{1}{z}$, or $z = -\frac{1}{2}$.

The solution of the original system is $\left(-1, \frac{1}{5} - \frac{1}{2}\right)$.

47. Label the angle measures at the tips of the stars a, b, c, d, and e. Also label the angles of the pentagon p, q, r, s, and t.

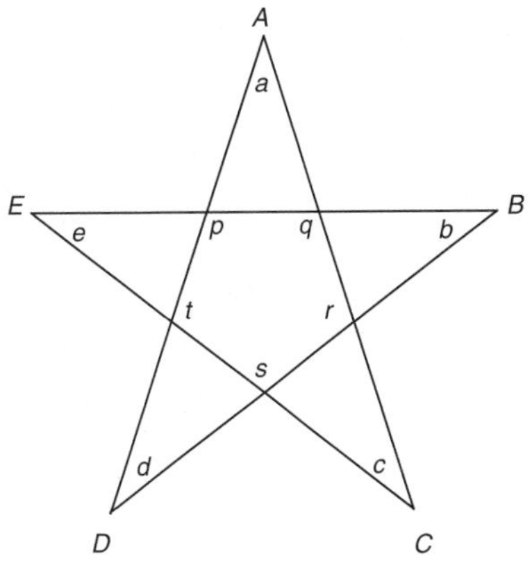

Using the geometric fact that the sum of the angle measures of a triangle is 180°, we get 5 equations.

$$p + b + d = 180$$
$$q + c + e = 180$$
$$r + a + d = 180$$
$$s + b + e = 180$$
$$t + a + c = 180$$

Adding these equations, we get

$$(p + q + r + s + t) + 2a + 2b + 2c + 2d + 2e = 5(180).$$

The sum of the angle measures of any convex polygon with n sides is given by the formula $S = (n - 2)180$. Thus $p + q + r + s + t = (5 - 2)180$, or 540. We substitute and solve for $a + b + c + d + e$.

$$540 + 2(a + b + c + d + e) = 900$$
$$2(a + b + c + d + e) = 360$$
$$a + b + c + d + e = 180$$

The sum of the angle measures at the tips of the star is 180°.

49. Substituting, we get

$$A + \frac{3}{4}B + 3C = 12,$$
$$\frac{4}{3}A + B + 2C = 12,$$
$$2A + B + C = 12, \text{ or}$$

$$4A + 3B + 12C = 48,$$
$$4A + 3B + 6C = 36, \quad \text{Clearing fractions}$$
$$2A + B + C = 12.$$

Solving the system of equations, we get $(3, 4, 2)$. The equation is $3x + 4y + 2z = 12$.

51. Substituting, we get

$$59 = a(-2)^3 + b(-2)^2 + c(-2) + d,$$
$$13 = a(-1)^3 + b(-1)^2 + c(-1) + d,$$
$$-1 = a \cdot 1^3 + b \cdot 1^2 + c \cdot 1 + d,$$
$$-17 = a \cdot 2^3 + b \cdot 2^2 + c \cdot 2 + d, \text{ or}$$

$$\begin{aligned}-8a + 4b - 2c + d &= 59,\\ -a + b - c + d &= 13,\\ a + b + c + d &= -1,\\ 8a + 4b + 2c + d &= -17.\end{aligned}$$

Solving the system of equations, we get $(-4, 5, -3, 1)$, so $y = -4x^3 + 5x^2 - 3x + 1$.

53. ***Familiarize and Translate***. Let a, s, and c represent the number of adults, students, and children in attendance, respectively.

The total attendance was 100.

$$a + s + c = 100$$

The total amount of money taken in was \$100.

(Express 50 cents as $\frac{1}{2}$ dollar.)

$$10a + 3s + \frac{1}{2}c = 100$$

The resulting system is

$$\begin{aligned}a + s + c &= 100,\\ 10a + 3s + \frac{1}{2}c &= 100.\end{aligned}$$

Carry out. Multiply the first equation by -3 and add it to the second equation to obtain $7a - \frac{5}{2}c = -200$ or $a = \frac{5}{14}(c - 80)$ where $(c-80)$ is a positive multiple of 14 (because a must be a positive integer). That is $(c - 80) = k \cdot 14$ or $c = 80 + k \cdot 14$, where k is a positive integer. If $k > 1$, then $c > 100$. This is impossible since the total attendance is 100. Thus $k = 1$, so $c = 80 + 1 \cdot 14 = 94$. Then $a = \frac{5}{14}(94 - 80) = \frac{5}{14} \cdot 14 = 5$, and $5 + s + 94 = 10$, or $s = 1$.

Check. The total attendance is $5 + 1 + 94$, or 100.

The total amount of money taken in was $\$10 \cdot 5 + \$3 \cdot 1 + \$\frac{1}{2} \cdot 94 = \$100$. The result checks.

State. There were 5 adults, 1 student, and 94 children in attendance.

Exercise Set 5.3

1. The matrix has 3 rows and 2 columns, so its order is 3×2.

3. The matrix has 1 row and 4 columns, so its order is 1×4.

5. The matrix has 3 rows and 3 columns, so its order is 3×3.

7. We omit the variables and replace the equals signs with a vertical line.

$$\left[\begin{array}{cc|c} 2 & -1 & 7 \\ 1 & 4 & -5 \end{array}\right]$$

9. We omit the variables, writing zeros for the missing terms, and replace the equals signs with a vertical line.

$$\left[\begin{array}{ccc|c} 1 & -2 & 3 & 12 \\ 2 & 0 & -4 & 8 \\ 0 & 3 & 1 & 7 \end{array}\right]$$

11. Insert variables and replace the vertical line with equals signs.

$$\begin{aligned}3x - 5y &= 1,\\ x + 4y &= -2\end{aligned}$$

13. Insert variables and replace the vertical line with equals signs.

$$\begin{aligned}2x + y - 4z &= 12,\\ 3x \quad + 5z &= -1,\\ x - y + z &= 2\end{aligned}$$

15. $4x + 2y = 11,$
$3x - y = 2$

Write the augmented matrix. We will use Gaussian elimination.

$$\left[\begin{array}{cc|c} 4 & 2 & 11 \\ 3 & -1 & 2 \end{array}\right]$$

Multiply row 2 by 4 to make the first number in row 2 a multiple of 4.

$$\left[\begin{array}{cc|c} 4 & 2 & 11 \\ 12 & -4 & 8 \end{array}\right]$$

Multiply row 1 by -3 and add it to row 2.

$$\left[\begin{array}{cc|c} 4 & 2 & 11 \\ 0 & -10 & -25 \end{array}\right]$$

Multiply row 1 by $\frac{1}{4}$ and row 2 by $-\frac{1}{10}$.

$$\left[\begin{array}{cc|c} 1 & \frac{1}{2} & \frac{11}{4} \\ 0 & 1 & \frac{5}{2} \end{array}\right]$$

Write the system of equations that corresponds to the last matrix.

$$x + \frac{1}{2}y = \frac{11}{4}, \quad (1)$$
$$y = \frac{5}{2} \quad (2)$$

Back-substitute in equation (1) and solve for x.

$$\begin{aligned}x + \frac{1}{2} \cdot \frac{5}{2} &= \frac{11}{4}\\ x + \frac{5}{4} &= \frac{11}{4}\\ x &= \frac{6}{4} = \frac{3}{2}\end{aligned}$$

The solution is $\left(\frac{3}{2}, \frac{5}{2}\right)$.

17. $5x - 2y = -3,$

$2x + 5y = -24$

Write the augmented matrix. We will use Gaussian elimination.

$$\left[\begin{array}{cc|c} 5 & -2 & -3 \\ 2 & 5 & -24 \end{array}\right]$$

Multiply row 2 by 5 to make the first number in row 2 a multiple of 5.

$$\left[\begin{array}{cc|c} 5 & -2 & -3 \\ 10 & 25 & -120 \end{array}\right]$$

Multiply row 1 by -2 and add it to row 2.

$$\left[\begin{array}{cc|c} 5 & -2 & -3 \\ 0 & 29 & -114 \end{array}\right]$$

Multiply row 1 by $\frac{1}{5}$ and row 2 by $\frac{1}{29}$.

$$\left[\begin{array}{cc|c} 1 & -\frac{2}{5} & -\frac{3}{5} \\ 0 & 1 & -\frac{114}{29} \end{array}\right]$$

Write the system of equations that corresponds to the last matrix.

$$x - \frac{2}{5}y = -\frac{3}{5}, \quad (1)$$

$$y = -\frac{114}{29} \quad (2)$$

Back-substitute in equation (1) and solve for x.

$$x - \frac{2}{5}\left(-\frac{114}{29}\right) = -\frac{3}{5}$$

$$x + \frac{228}{145} = -\frac{3}{5}$$

$$x = -\frac{315}{145} = -\frac{63}{29}$$

The solution is $\left(-\frac{63}{29}, -\frac{114}{29}\right)$.

19. $3x + 4y = 7,$

$-5x + 2y = 10$

Write the augmented matrix. We will use Gaussian elimination.

$$\left[\begin{array}{cc|c} 3 & 4 & 7 \\ -5 & 2 & 10 \end{array}\right]$$

Multiply row 2 by 3 to make the first number in row 2 a multiple of 3.

$$\left[\begin{array}{cc|c} 3 & 4 & 7 \\ -15 & 6 & 30 \end{array}\right]$$

Multiply row 1 by 5 and add it to row 2.

$$\left[\begin{array}{cc|c} 3 & 4 & 7 \\ 0 & 26 & 65 \end{array}\right]$$

Multiply row 1 by $\frac{1}{3}$ and row 2 by $\frac{1}{26}$.

$$\left[\begin{array}{cc|c} 1 & \frac{4}{3} & \frac{7}{3} \\ 0 & 1 & \frac{5}{2} \end{array}\right]$$

Write the system of equations that corresponds to the last matrix.

$$x + \frac{4}{3}y = \frac{7}{3}, \quad (1)$$

$$y = \frac{5}{2} \quad (2)$$

Back-substitute in equation (1) and solve for x.

$$x + \frac{4}{3} \cdot \frac{5}{2} = \frac{7}{3}$$

$$x + \frac{10}{3} = \frac{7}{3}$$

$$x = -\frac{3}{3} = -1$$

The solution is $\left(-1, \frac{5}{2}\right)$.

21. $3x + 2y = 6,$

$2x - 3y = -9$

Write the augmented matrix. We will use Gauss-Jordan elimination.

$$\left[\begin{array}{cc|c} 3 & 2 & 6 \\ 2 & -3 & -9 \end{array}\right]$$

Multiply row 2 by 3 to make the first number in row 2 a multiple of 3.

$$\left[\begin{array}{cc|c} 3 & 2 & 6 \\ 6 & -9 & -27 \end{array}\right]$$

Multiply row 1 by -2 and add it to row 2.

$$\left[\begin{array}{cc|c} 3 & 2 & 6 \\ 0 & -13 & -39 \end{array}\right]$$

Multiply row 2 by $-\frac{1}{13}$.

$$\left[\begin{array}{cc|c} 3 & 2 & 6 \\ 0 & 1 & 3 \end{array}\right]$$

Multiply row 2 by -2 and add it to row 1.

$$\left[\begin{array}{cc|c} 3 & 0 & 0 \\ 0 & 1 & 3 \end{array}\right]$$

Multiply row 1 by $\frac{1}{3}$.

$$\left[\begin{array}{cc|c} 1 & 0 & 0 \\ 0 & 1 & 3 \end{array}\right]$$

We have $x = 0$, $y = 3$. The solution is $(0, 3)$.

23. $x - 3y = 8,$
$2x - 6y = 3$

Write the augmented matrix.

$$\left[\begin{array}{cc|c} 1 & -3 & 8 \\ 2 & -6 & 3 \end{array}\right]$$

Multiply row 1 by -2 and add it to row 2.

$$\left[\begin{array}{cc|c} 1 & -3 & 8 \\ 0 & 0 & -13 \end{array}\right]$$

The last row corresponds to the false equation $0 = -13$, so there is no solution.

25. $-2x + 6y = 4,$
$3x - 9y = -6$

Write the augmented matrix.

$$\left[\begin{array}{cc|c} -2 & 6 & 4 \\ 3 & -9 & -6 \end{array}\right]$$

Multiply row 1 by $-\frac{1}{2}$.

$$\left[\begin{array}{cc|c} 1 & -3 & -2 \\ 3 & -9 & -6 \end{array}\right]$$

Multiply row 1 by -3 and add it to row 2.

$$\left[\begin{array}{cc|c} 1 & -3 & -2 \\ 0 & 0 & 0 \end{array}\right]$$

The last row corresponds to the equation $0 = 0$ which is true for all values of x and y. Thus, the system of equations is dependent and is equivalent to the first equation $-2x + 6y = 4$, or $x - 3y = -2$. Solving for x, we get $x = 3y - 2$. Then the solutions are of the form $(3y - 2, y)$, where y is any real number.

27. $x + 2y - 3z = 9,$
$2x - y + 2z = -8,$
$3x - y - 4z = 3$

Write the augmented matrix. We will use Gauss-Jordan elimination.

$$\left[\begin{array}{ccc|c} 1 & 2 & -3 & 9 \\ 2 & -1 & 2 & -8 \\ 3 & -1 & -4 & 3 \end{array}\right]$$

Multiply row 1 by -2 and add it to row 2. Also, multiply row 1 by -3 and add it to row 3.

$$\left[\begin{array}{ccc|c} 1 & 2 & -3 & 9 \\ 0 & -5 & 8 & -26 \\ 0 & -7 & 5 & -24 \end{array}\right]$$

Multiply row 2 by $-\frac{1}{5}$ to get a 1 in the second row, second column.

$$\left[\begin{array}{ccc|c} 1 & 2 & -3 & 9 \\ 0 & 1 & -\frac{8}{5} & \frac{26}{5} \\ 0 & -7 & 5 & -24 \end{array}\right]$$

Multiply row 2 by -2 and add it to row 1. Also, multiply row 2 by 7 and add it to row 3.

$$\left[\begin{array}{ccc|c} 1 & 0 & \frac{1}{5} & -\frac{7}{5} \\ 0 & 1 & -\frac{8}{5} & \frac{26}{5} \\ 0 & 0 & -\frac{31}{5} & \frac{62}{5} \end{array}\right]$$

Multiply row 3 by $-\frac{5}{31}$ to get a 1 in the third row, third column.

$$\left[\begin{array}{ccc|c} 1 & 0 & \frac{1}{5} & -\frac{7}{5} \\ 0 & 1 & -\frac{8}{5} & \frac{26}{5} \\ 0 & 0 & 1 & -2 \end{array}\right]$$

Multiply row 3 by $-\frac{1}{5}$ and add it to row 1. Also, multiply row 3 by $\frac{8}{5}$ and add it to row 2.

$$\left[\begin{array}{ccc|c} 1 & 0 & 0 & -1 \\ 0 & 1 & 0 & 2 \\ 0 & 0 & 1 & -2 \end{array}\right]$$

We have $x = -1$, $y = 2$, $z = -2$. The solution is $(-1, 2, -2)$.

29. $4x - y - 3z = 1,$
$8x + y - z = 5,$
$2x + y + 2z = 5$

Write the augmented matrix. We will use Gauss-Jordan elimination.

$$\left[\begin{array}{ccc|c} 4 & -1 & -3 & 1 \\ 8 & 1 & -1 & 5 \\ 2 & 1 & 2 & 5 \end{array}\right]$$

First interchange rows 1 and 3 so that each number below the first number in the first row is a multiple of that number.

$$\left[\begin{array}{rrr|r} 2 & 1 & 2 & 5 \\ 8 & 1 & -1 & 5 \\ 4 & -1 & -3 & 1 \end{array}\right]$$

Multiply row 1 by -4 and add it to row 2. Also, multiply row 1 by -2 and add it to row 3.

$$\left[\begin{array}{rrr|r} 2 & 1 & 2 & 5 \\ 0 & -3 & -9 & -15 \\ 0 & -3 & -7 & -9 \end{array}\right]$$

Multiply row 2 by -1 and add it to row 3.

$$\left[\begin{array}{rrr|r} 2 & 1 & 2 & 5 \\ 0 & -3 & -9 & -15 \\ 0 & 0 & 2 & 6 \end{array}\right]$$

Multiply row 2 by $-\frac{1}{3}$ to get a 1 in the second row, second column.

$$\left[\begin{array}{rrr|r} 2 & 1 & 2 & 5 \\ 0 & 1 & 3 & 5 \\ 0 & 0 & 2 & 6 \end{array}\right]$$

Multiply row 2 by -1 and add it to row 1.

$$\left[\begin{array}{rrr|r} 2 & 0 & -1 & 0 \\ 0 & 1 & 3 & 5 \\ 0 & 0 & 2 & 6 \end{array}\right]$$

Multiply row 3 by $\frac{1}{2}$ to get a 1 in the third row, third column.

$$\left[\begin{array}{rrr|r} 2 & 0 & -1 & 0 \\ 0 & 1 & 3 & 5 \\ 0 & 0 & 1 & 3 \end{array}\right]$$

Add row 3 to row 1. Also multiply row 3 by -3 and add it to row 2.

$$\left[\begin{array}{rrr|r} 2 & 0 & 0 & 3 \\ 0 & 1 & 0 & -4 \\ 0 & 0 & 1 & 3 \end{array}\right]$$

Finally, multiply row 1 by $\frac{1}{2}$.

$$\left[\begin{array}{rrr|r} 1 & 0 & 0 & \frac{3}{2} \\ 0 & 1 & 0 & -4 \\ 0 & 0 & 1 & 3 \end{array}\right]$$

We have $x = \frac{3}{2}$, $y = -4$, $z = 3$. The solution is $\left(\frac{3}{2}, -4, 3\right)$.

31. $x - 2y + 3z = 4,$
$3x + y - z = 0,$
$2x + 3y - 5z = 1$

Write the augmented matrix. We will use Gaussian elimination.

$$\left[\begin{array}{rrr|r} 1 & -2 & 3 & -4 \\ 3 & 1 & -1 & 0 \\ 2 & 3 & -5 & 1 \end{array}\right]$$

Multiply row 1 by -3 and add it to row 2. Also, multiply row 1 by -2 and add it to row 3.

$$\left[\begin{array}{rrr|r} 1 & -2 & 3 & -4 \\ 0 & 7 & -10 & 12 \\ 0 & 7 & -11 & 9 \end{array}\right]$$

Multiply row 2 by -1 and add it to row 3.

$$\left[\begin{array}{rrr|r} 1 & -2 & 3 & -4 \\ 0 & 7 & -10 & 12 \\ 0 & 0 & -1 & -3 \end{array}\right]$$

Multiply row 2 by $\frac{1}{7}$ and multiply row 3 by -1.

$$\left[\begin{array}{rrr|r} 1 & -2 & 3 & -4 \\ 0 & 1 & -\frac{10}{7} & \frac{12}{7} \\ 0 & 0 & 1 & 3 \end{array}\right]$$

Now write the system of equations that corresponds to the last matrix.

$$\begin{aligned} x - 2y + 3z &= -4, \quad (1) \\ y - \frac{10}{7}z &= \frac{12}{7}, \quad (2) \\ z &= 3 \quad (3) \end{aligned}$$

Back-substitute 3 for z in equation (2) and solve for y.

$$\begin{aligned} y - \frac{10}{7}\cdot 3 &= \frac{12}{7} \\ y - \frac{30}{7} &= \frac{12}{7} \\ y &= \frac{42}{7} = 6 \end{aligned}$$

Back-substitute 6 for y and 3 for z in equation (1) and solve for x.

$$\begin{aligned} x - 2\cdot 6 + 3\cdot 3 &= -4 \\ x - 3 &= -4 \\ x &= -1 \end{aligned}$$

The solution is $(-1, 6, 3)$.

33. $2x - 4y - 3z = 3,$
$x + 3y + z = -1,$
$5x + y - 2z = 2$

Write the augmented matrix.

$$\left[\begin{array}{rrr|r} 2 & -4 & -3 & 3 \\ 1 & 3 & 1 & -1 \\ 5 & 1 & -2 & 2 \end{array}\right]$$

Interchange the first two rows to get a 1 in the first row, first column.

$$\left[\begin{array}{rrr|r} 1 & 3 & 1 & -1 \\ 2 & -4 & -3 & 3 \\ 5 & 1 & -2 & 2 \end{array}\right]$$

Multiply row 1 by -2 and add it to row 2. Also, multiply row 1 by -5 and add it to row 3.

$$\left[\begin{array}{rrr|r} 1 & 3 & 1 & -1 \\ 0 & -10 & -5 & 5 \\ 0 & -14 & -7 & 7 \end{array}\right]$$

Multiply row 2 by $-\frac{1}{10}$ to get a 1 in the second row, second column.

$$\left[\begin{array}{rrr|r} 1 & 3 & 1 & -1 \\ 0 & 1 & \frac{1}{2} & -\frac{1}{2} \\ 0 & -14 & -7 & 7 \end{array}\right]$$

Multiply row 2 by 14 and add it to row 3.

$$\left[\begin{array}{rrr|r} 1 & 3 & 1 & -1 \\ 0 & 1 & \frac{1}{2} & -\frac{1}{2} \\ 0 & 0 & 0 & 0 \end{array}\right]$$

The last row corresponds to the equation $0 = 0$. This indicates that the system of equations is dependent. It is equivalent to

$$x + 3y + z = -1,$$
$$y + \frac{1}{2}z = -\frac{1}{2}$$

We solve the second equation for y.

$$y = -\frac{1}{2}z - \frac{1}{2}$$

Substitute for y in the first equation and solve for x.

$$x + 3\left(-\frac{1}{2}z - \frac{1}{2}\right) + z = -1$$
$$x - \frac{3}{2}z - \frac{3}{2} + z = -1$$
$$x = \frac{1}{2}z + \frac{1}{2}$$

The solution is $\left(\frac{1}{2}z + \frac{1}{2}, -\frac{1}{2}z - \frac{1}{2}, z\right)$, where z is any real number.

35. $p + q + r = 1,$

$p + 2q + 3r = 4,$

$4p + 5q + 6r = 7$

Write the augmented matrix.

$$\left[\begin{array}{rrr|r} 1 & 1 & 1 & 1 \\ 1 & 2 & 3 & 4 \\ 4 & 5 & 6 & 7 \end{array}\right]$$

Multiply row 1 by -1 and add it to row 2. Also, multiply row 1 by -4 and add it to row 3.

$$\left[\begin{array}{rrr|r} 1 & 1 & 1 & 1 \\ 0 & 1 & 2 & 3 \\ 0 & 1 & 2 & 3 \end{array}\right]$$

Multiply row 2 by -1 and add it to row 3.

$$\left[\begin{array}{rrr|r} 1 & 1 & 1 & 1 \\ 0 & 1 & 2 & 3 \\ 0 & 0 & 0 & 0 \end{array}\right]$$

The last row corresponds to the equation $0 = 0$. This indicates that the system of equations is dependent. It is equivalent to

$$p + q + r = 1,$$
$$q + 2r = 3.$$

We solve the second equation for q.

$$q = -2r + 3$$

Substitute for y in the first equation and solve for p.

$$p - 2r + 3 + r = 1$$
$$p - r + 3 = 1$$
$$p = r - 2$$

The solution is $(r - 2, -2r + 3, r)$, where r is any real number.

37. $a + b - c = 7,$

$a - b + c = 5,$

$3a + b - c = -1$

Write the augmented matrix.

$$\left[\begin{array}{rrr|r} 1 & 1 & -1 & 7 \\ 1 & -1 & 1 & 5 \\ 3 & 1 & -1 & -1 \end{array}\right]$$

Multiply row 1 by -1 and add it to row 2. Also, multiply row 1 by -3 and add it to row 3.

$$\left[\begin{array}{rrr|r} 1 & 1 & -1 & 7 \\ 0 & -2 & 2 & -2 \\ 0 & -2 & 2 & -22 \end{array}\right]$$

Multiply row 2 by -1 and add it to row 3.

$$\left[\begin{array}{rrr|r} 1 & 1 & -1 & 7 \\ 0 & -2 & 2 & -2 \\ 0 & 0 & 0 & -20 \end{array}\right]$$

The last row corresponds to the false equation $0 = -20$. Thus, the system of equations has no solution.

39. $-2w + 2x + 2y - 2z = -10,$
$w + x + y + z = -5,$
$3w + x - y + 4z = -2,$
$w + 3x - 2y + 2z = -6$

Write the augmented matrix. We will use Gaussian elimination.

$$\left[\begin{array}{rrrr|r} -2 & 2 & 2 & -2 & -10 \\ 1 & 1 & 1 & 1 & -5 \\ 3 & 1 & -1 & 4 & -2 \\ 1 & 3 & -2 & 2 & -6 \end{array}\right]$$

Interchange rows 1 and 2.

$$\left[\begin{array}{rrrr|r} 1 & 1 & 1 & 1 & -5 \\ -2 & 2 & 2 & -2 & -10 \\ 3 & 1 & -1 & 4 & -2 \\ 1 & 3 & -2 & 2 & -6 \end{array}\right]$$

Multiply row 1 by 2 and add it to row 2. Multiply row 1 by -3 and add it to row 3. Multiply row 1 by -1 and add it to row 4.

$$\left[\begin{array}{rrrr|r} 1 & 1 & 1 & 1 & -5 \\ 0 & 4 & 4 & 0 & -20 \\ 0 & -2 & -4 & 1 & 13 \\ 0 & 2 & -3 & 1 & -1 \end{array}\right]$$

Interchange rows 2 and 3.

$$\left[\begin{array}{rrrr|r} 1 & 1 & 1 & 1 & -5 \\ 0 & -2 & -4 & 1 & 13 \\ 0 & 4 & 4 & 0 & -20 \\ 0 & 2 & -3 & 1 & -1 \end{array}\right]$$

Multiply row 2 by 2 and add it to row 3. Add row 2 to row 4.

$$\left[\begin{array}{rrrr|r} 1 & 1 & 1 & 1 & -5 \\ 0 & -2 & -4 & 1 & 13 \\ 0 & 0 & -4 & 2 & 6 \\ 0 & 0 & -7 & 2 & 12 \end{array}\right]$$

Multiply row 4 by 4.

$$\left[\begin{array}{rrrr|r} 1 & 1 & 1 & 1 & -5 \\ 0 & -2 & -4 & 1 & 13 \\ 0 & 0 & -4 & 2 & 6 \\ 0 & 0 & -28 & 8 & 48 \end{array}\right]$$

Multiply row 3 by -7 and add it to row 4.

$$\left[\begin{array}{rrrr|r} 1 & 1 & 1 & 1 & -5 \\ 0 & -2 & -4 & 1 & 13 \\ 0 & 0 & -4 & 2 & 6 \\ 0 & 0 & 0 & -6 & 6 \end{array}\right]$$

Multiply row 2 by $-\frac{1}{2}$, row 3 by $-\frac{1}{4}$, and row 6 by $-\frac{1}{6}$.

$$\left[\begin{array}{rrrr|r} 1 & 1 & 1 & 1 & -5 \\ 0 & 1 & 2 & -\frac{1}{2} & -\frac{13}{2} \\ 0 & 0 & 1 & -\frac{1}{2} & -\frac{3}{2} \\ 0 & 0 & 0 & 1 & -1 \end{array}\right]$$

Write the system of equations that corresponds to the last matrix.

$$w + x + y + z = -5, \quad (1)$$
$$x + 2y - \frac{1}{2}z = -\frac{13}{2}, \quad (2)$$
$$y - \frac{1}{2}z = -\frac{3}{2}, \quad (3)$$
$$z = -1 \quad (4)$$

Back-substitute in equation (3) and solve for y.

$$y - \frac{1}{2}(-1) = -\frac{3}{2}$$
$$y + \frac{1}{2} = -\frac{3}{2}$$
$$y = -2$$

Back-substitute in equation (2) and solve for x.

$$x + 2(-2) - \frac{1}{2}(-1) = -\frac{13}{2}$$
$$x - 4 + \frac{1}{2} = -\frac{13}{2}$$
$$x = -3$$

Back-substitute in equation (1) and solve for w.

$$w - 3 - 2 - 1 = -5$$
$$w = 1$$

The solution is $(1, -3, -2, -1)$.

41. ***Familiarize.*** Let $x =$ the number of hours the Houlihans were out before 11 P.M. and $y =$ the number of hours after 11 P.M. Then they pay the babysitter \$$5x$ before 11 P.M. and \$$7.50y$ after 11 P.M.

Translate.

The Houlihans were out for a total of 5 hr.

$$x + y = 5$$

They paid the sitter a total of \$30.

$$5x + 7.5y = 30$$

Carry out. Use Gaussian elimination or Gauss-Jordan elimination to solve the system of equations.

$$x + y = 5,$$
$$5x + 7.5y = 30.$$

The solution is $(3, 2)$. The coordinate $y = 2$ indicates that the Houlihans were out 2 hr after 11 P.M., so they came home at 1 A.M.

Check. The total time is $3 + 2$, or 5 hr. The total pay is $\$5 \cdot 3 + \$7.50(2)$, or $\$15 + \$15$, or \$30. The solution checks.

State. The Houlihans came home at 1 A.M.

43. ***Familiarize***. Let x, y, and z represent the amounts borrowed at 8%, 10%, and 12%, respectively. Then the annual interest is $8\%x$, $10\%y$, and $12\%z$, or $0.08x$, $0.1y$, and $0.12z$.

Translate.

The total amount borrowed was \$30,000.

$$x + y + z = 30,000$$

The total annual interest was \$3040.

$$0.08x + 0.1y + 0.12z = 3040$$

The total amount borrowed at 8% and 10% was twice the amount borrowed at 12%.

$$x + y = 2z$$

We have a system of equations.

$$x + y + z = 30,000,$$
$$0.08x + 0.1y + 0.12z = 3040,$$
$$x + y = 2z, \text{ or}$$

$$\begin{aligned} x + \quad y + \quad z &= 30,000,\\ 0.08x + 0.1y + 0.12z &= 3040,\\ x + \quad y - \quad 2z &= 0 \end{aligned}$$

Carry out. Using Gaussian elimination or Gauss-Jordan elimination, we find that the solution is $(8000, 12,000, 10,000)$.

Check. The total amount borrowed was \$8000+\$12,000+\$10,000, or \$30,000. The total annual interest was $0.08(\$8000) + 0.1(\$12,000)+$ $0.12(\$10,000)$, or \$640 + \$1200 + \$1200, or \$3040. The total amount borrowed at 8% and 10%, \$8000 + \$12,000 or \$20,000, was twice the amount borrowed at 12%, \$10,000. The solution checks.

State. The amounts borrowed at 8%, 10%, and 12% were \$8000, \$12,000 and \$10,000, respectively.

45. Discussion and Writing

47. The function has a variable in the exponent, so it is an exponential function.

49. The function is the quotient of two polynomials, so it is a rational function.

51. The function is of the form $f(x) = \log_a x$, so it is logarithmic.

53. The function is of the form $f(x) = mx + b$, so it is linear.

55. Substitute to find three equations.

$$12 = a(-3)^2 + b(-3) + c$$
$$-7 = a(-1)^2 + b(-1) + c$$
$$-2 = a \cdot 1^2 + b \cdot 1 + c$$

We have a system of equations.

$$\begin{aligned} 9a - 3b + c &= 12,\\ a - \quad b + c &= -7,\\ a + \quad b + c &= -2 \end{aligned}$$

Write the augmented matrix. We will use Gaussian elimination.

$$\left[\begin{array}{rrr|r} 9 & -3 & 1 & 12\\ 1 & -1 & 1 & -7\\ 1 & 1 & 1 & -2 \end{array}\right]$$

Interchange the first two rows.

$$\left[\begin{array}{rrr|r} 1 & -1 & 1 & -7\\ 9 & -3 & 1 & 12\\ 1 & 1 & 1 & -2 \end{array}\right]$$

Multiply row 1 by -9 and add it to row 2. Also, multiply row 1 by -1 and add it to row 3.

$$\left[\begin{array}{rrr|r} 1 & -1 & 1 & -7\\ 0 & 6 & -8 & 75\\ 0 & 2 & 0 & 5 \end{array}\right]$$

Interchange row 2 and row 3.

$$\left[\begin{array}{rrr|r} 1 & -1 & 1 & -7\\ 0 & 2 & 0 & 5\\ 0 & 6 & -8 & 75 \end{array}\right]$$

Multiply row 2 by -3 and add it to row 3.

$$\left[\begin{array}{rrr|r} 1 & -1 & 1 & -7\\ 0 & 2 & 0 & 5\\ 0 & 0 & -8 & 60 \end{array}\right]$$

Multiply row 2 by $\frac{1}{2}$ and row 3 by $-\frac{1}{8}$.

$$\left[\begin{array}{rrr|r} 1 & -1 & 1 & -7\\ 0 & 1 & 0 & \frac{5}{2}\\ 0 & 0 & 1 & -\frac{15}{2} \end{array}\right]$$

Write the system of equations that corresponds to the last matrix.

$$\begin{aligned} x - y + z &= -7,\\ y &= \frac{5}{2},\\ z &= -\frac{15}{2} \end{aligned}$$

Back-substitute $\frac{5}{2}$ for y and $-\frac{15}{2}$ for z in the first equation and solve for x.

$$x - \frac{5}{2} - \frac{15}{2} = -7$$
$$x - 10 = -7$$
$$x = 3$$

The solution is $\left(3, \frac{5}{2}, -\frac{15}{2}\right)$, so the equation is $y = 3x^2 + \frac{5}{2}x - \frac{15}{2}$.

57. $\begin{bmatrix} 1 & 5 \\ 3 & 2 \end{bmatrix}$

Multiply row 1 by -3 and add it to row 2.

$\begin{bmatrix} 1 & 5 \\ 0 & -13 \end{bmatrix}$

Multiply row 2 by $-\dfrac{1}{13}$.

$\begin{bmatrix} 1 & 5 \\ 0 & 1 \end{bmatrix}$ Row-echelon form

Multiply row 2 by -5 and add it to row 1.

$\begin{bmatrix} 1 & 0 \\ 0 & 1 \end{bmatrix}$ Reduced row-echelon form

59. $y = x + z,$

$3y + 5z = 4,$

$x + 4 = y + 3z,$ or

$x - y + z = 0,$

$3y + 5z = 4,$

$x - y - 3z = -4$

Write the augmented matrix. We will use Gauss-Jordan elimination.

$\left[\begin{array}{rrr|r} 1 & -1 & 1 & 0 \\ 0 & 3 & 5 & 4 \\ 1 & -1 & -3 & -4 \end{array}\right]$

Multiply row 1 by -1 and add it to row 3.

$\left[\begin{array}{rrr|r} 1 & -1 & 1 & 0 \\ 0 & 3 & 5 & 4 \\ 0 & 0 & -4 & -4 \end{array}\right]$

Multiply row 3 by $-\dfrac{1}{4}$.

$\left[\begin{array}{rrr|r} 1 & -1 & 1 & 0 \\ 0 & 3 & 5 & 4 \\ 0 & 0 & 1 & 1 \end{array}\right]$

Multiply row 3 by -1 and add it to row 1. Also, multiply row 3 by -5 and add it to row 2.

$\left[\begin{array}{rrr|r} 1 & -1 & 0 & -1 \\ 0 & 3 & 0 & -1 \\ 0 & 0 & 1 & 1 \end{array}\right]$

Multiply row 2 by $\dfrac{1}{3}$.

$\left[\begin{array}{rrr|r} 1 & -1 & 0 & -1 \\ 0 & 1 & 0 & -\frac{1}{3} \\ 0 & 0 & 1 & 1 \end{array}\right]$

Add row 2 to row 1.

$\left[\begin{array}{rrr|r} 1 & 0 & 0 & -\frac{4}{3} \\ 0 & 1 & 0 & -\frac{1}{3} \\ 0 & 0 & 1 & 1 \end{array}\right]$

Read the solution from the last matrix. It is $\left(-\dfrac{4}{3}, -\dfrac{1}{3}, 1\right)$.

61. $x - 4y + 2z = 7,$

$3x + y + 3z = -5$

Write the augmented matrix.

$\left[\begin{array}{rrr|r} 1 & -4 & 2 & 7 \\ 3 & 1 & 3 & -5 \end{array}\right]$

Multiply row 1 by -3 and add it to row 2.

$\left[\begin{array}{rrr|r} 1 & -4 & 2 & 7 \\ 0 & 13 & -3 & -26 \end{array}\right]$

Multiply row 2 by $\dfrac{1}{13}$.

$\left[\begin{array}{rrr|r} 1 & -4 & 2 & 7 \\ 0 & 1 & -\frac{3}{13} & -2 \end{array}\right]$

Write the system of equations that corresponds to the last matrix.

$x - 4y + 2z = 7,$

$y - \dfrac{3}{13}z = -2$

Solve the second equation for y.

$y = \dfrac{3}{13}z - 2$

Substitute in the first equation and solve for x.

$x - 4\left(\dfrac{3}{13}z - 2\right) + 2z = 7$

$x - \dfrac{12}{13}z + 8 + 2z = 7$

$x = -\dfrac{14}{13}z - 1$

The solution is $\left(-\dfrac{14}{13}z - 1, \dfrac{3}{13}z - 2, z\right)$, where z is any real number.

63. $4x + 5y = 3,$
$-2x + y = 9,$
$3x - 2y = -15$

Write the augmented matrix.

$$\left[\begin{array}{rr|r} 4 & 5 & 3 \\ -2 & 1 & 9 \\ 3 & -2 & -15 \end{array}\right]$$

Multiply row 2 by 2 and row 3 by 4.

$$\left[\begin{array}{rr|r} 4 & 5 & 3 \\ -4 & 2 & 18 \\ 12 & -8 & -60 \end{array}\right]$$

Add row 1 to row 2. Also, multiply row 1 by -3 and add it to row 3.

$$\left[\begin{array}{rr|r} 4 & 5 & 3 \\ 0 & 7 & 21 \\ 0 & -23 & -69 \end{array}\right]$$

Multiply row 2 by $\frac{1}{7}$ and row 3 by $-\frac{1}{23}$.

$$\left[\begin{array}{rr|r} 4 & 5 & 3 \\ 0 & 1 & 3 \\ 0 & 1 & 3 \end{array}\right]$$

Multiply row 2 by -1 and add it to row 3.

$$\left[\begin{array}{rr|r} 4 & 5 & 3 \\ 0 & 1 & 3 \\ 0 & 0 & 0 \end{array}\right]$$

The last row corresponds to the equation $0 = 0$. Thus we have a dependent system that is equivalent to

$4x + 5y = 3,$ (1)

$y = 3.$ (2)

Back-substitute in equation (1) to find x.

$4x + 5 \cdot 3 = 3$

$4x + 15 = 3$

$4x = -12$

$x = -3$

The solution is $(-3, 3)$.

Exercise Set 5.4

1. $\begin{bmatrix} 5 & x \end{bmatrix} = \begin{bmatrix} y & -3 \end{bmatrix}$

Corresponding entries of the two matrices must be equal. Thus we have $5 = y$ and $x = -3$.

3. $\begin{bmatrix} 3 & 2x \\ y & -8 \end{bmatrix} = \begin{bmatrix} 3 & -2 \\ 1 & -8 \end{bmatrix}$

Corresponding entries of the two matrices must be equal. Thus, we have:

$2x = -2$ and $y = 1$

$x = -1$ and $y = 1$

5. $$\mathbf{A} + \mathbf{B} = \begin{bmatrix} 1 & 2 \\ 4 & 3 \end{bmatrix} + \begin{bmatrix} -3 & 5 \\ 2 & -1 \end{bmatrix} = \begin{bmatrix} 1+(-3) & 2+5 \\ 4+2 & 3+(-1) \end{bmatrix} = \begin{bmatrix} -2 & 7 \\ 6 & 2 \end{bmatrix}$$

7. $$\mathbf{E} + \mathbf{O} = \begin{bmatrix} 1 & 3 \\ 2 & 6 \end{bmatrix} + \begin{bmatrix} 0 & 0 \\ 0 & 0 \end{bmatrix} = \begin{bmatrix} 1+0 & 3+0 \\ 2+0 & 6+0 \end{bmatrix} = \begin{bmatrix} 1 & 3 \\ 2 & 6 \end{bmatrix}$$

9. $$3\mathbf{F} = 3\begin{bmatrix} 3 & 3 \\ -1 & -1 \end{bmatrix} = \begin{bmatrix} 3 \cdot 3 & 3 \cdot 3 \\ 3 \cdot (-1) & 3 \cdot (-1) \end{bmatrix} = \begin{bmatrix} 9 & 9 \\ -3 & -3 \end{bmatrix}$$

11. $$3\mathbf{F} = 3\begin{bmatrix} 3 & 3 \\ -1 & -1 \end{bmatrix} = \begin{bmatrix} 9 & 9 \\ -3 & -3 \end{bmatrix},$$

$$2\mathbf{A} = 2\begin{bmatrix} 1 & 2 \\ 4 & 3 \end{bmatrix} = \begin{bmatrix} 2 & 4 \\ 8 & 6 \end{bmatrix}$$

$$3\mathbf{F} + 2\mathbf{A} = \begin{bmatrix} 9 & 9 \\ -3 & -3 \end{bmatrix} + \begin{bmatrix} 2 & 4 \\ 8 & 6 \end{bmatrix} = \begin{bmatrix} 9+2 & 9+4 \\ -3+8 & -3+6 \end{bmatrix} = \begin{bmatrix} 11 & 13 \\ 5 & 3 \end{bmatrix}$$

13. $$\mathbf{B} - \mathbf{A} = \begin{bmatrix} -3 & 5 \\ 2 & -1 \end{bmatrix} - \begin{bmatrix} 1 & 2 \\ 4 & 3 \end{bmatrix} = \begin{bmatrix} -3 & 5 \\ 2 & -1 \end{bmatrix} + \begin{bmatrix} -1 & -2 \\ -4 & -3 \end{bmatrix}$$

$[\mathbf{B} - \mathbf{A} = \mathbf{B} + (-\mathbf{A})]$

$$= \begin{bmatrix} -3+(-1) & 5+(-2) \\ 2+(-4) & -1+(-3) \end{bmatrix} = \begin{bmatrix} -4 & 3 \\ -2 & -4 \end{bmatrix}$$

15. $\mathbf{BA} = \begin{bmatrix} -3 & 5 \\ 2 & -1 \end{bmatrix} \begin{bmatrix} 1 & 2 \\ 4 & 3 \end{bmatrix}$

$= \begin{bmatrix} -3\cdot 1+5\cdot 4 & -3\cdot 2+5\cdot 3 \\ 2\cdot 1+(-1)4 & 2\cdot 2+(-1)3 \end{bmatrix}$

$= \begin{bmatrix} 17 & 9 \\ -2 & 1 \end{bmatrix}$

17. $\mathbf{CD} = \begin{bmatrix} 1 & -1 \\ -1 & 1 \end{bmatrix} \begin{bmatrix} 1 & 1 \\ 1 & 1 \end{bmatrix}$

$= \begin{bmatrix} 1\cdot 1+(-1)\cdot 1 & 1\cdot 1+(-1)\cdot 1 \\ -1\cdot 1+1\cdot 1 & -1\cdot 1+1\cdot 1 \end{bmatrix}$

$= \begin{bmatrix} 0 & 0 \\ 0 & 0 \end{bmatrix}$

19. $\mathbf{AI} = \begin{bmatrix} 1 & 2 \\ 4 & 3 \end{bmatrix} \begin{bmatrix} 1 & 0 \\ 0 & 1 \end{bmatrix}$

$= \begin{bmatrix} 1\cdot 1+2\cdot 0 & 1\cdot 0+2\cdot 1 \\ 4\cdot 1+3\cdot 0 & 4\cdot 0+3\cdot 1 \end{bmatrix}$

$= \begin{bmatrix} 1 & 2 \\ 4 & 3 \end{bmatrix}$

21. $\begin{bmatrix} -1 & 0 & 7 \\ 3 & -5 & 2 \end{bmatrix} \begin{bmatrix} 6 \\ -4 \\ 1 \end{bmatrix}$

$= \begin{bmatrix} -1\cdot 6+0(-4)+7\cdot 1 \\ 3\cdot 6+(-5)(-4)+2\cdot 1 \end{bmatrix}$

$= \begin{bmatrix} 1 \\ 40 \end{bmatrix}$

23. $\begin{bmatrix} -2 & 4 \\ 5 & 1 \\ -1 & -3 \end{bmatrix} \begin{bmatrix} 3 & -6 \\ -1 & 4 \end{bmatrix}$

$= \begin{bmatrix} -2\cdot 3+4(-1) & -2(-6)+4\cdot 4 \\ 5\cdot 3+1(-1) & 5(-6)+1\cdot 4 \\ -1\cdot 3+(-3)(-1) & -1(-6)+(-3)\cdot 4 \end{bmatrix}$

$= \begin{bmatrix} -10 & 28 \\ 14 & -26 \\ 0 & -6 \end{bmatrix}$

25. $\begin{bmatrix} 1 \\ -5 \\ 3 \end{bmatrix} \begin{bmatrix} -6 & 5 & 8 \\ 0 & 4 & -1 \end{bmatrix}$

This product is not defined because the number of columns of the first matrix, 1, is not equal to the number of rows of the second matrix, 2.

27. $\begin{bmatrix} 1 & -4 & 3 \\ 0 & 8 & 0 \\ -2 & -1 & 5 \end{bmatrix} \begin{bmatrix} 3 & 0 & 0 \\ 0 & -4 & 0 \\ 0 & 0 & 1 \end{bmatrix}$

$= \begin{bmatrix} 3+0+0 & 0+16+0 & 0+0+3 \\ 0+0+0 & 0-32+0 & 0+0+0 \\ -6+0+0 & 0+4+0 & 0+0+5 \end{bmatrix}$

$= \begin{bmatrix} 3 & 16 & 3 \\ 0 & -32 & 0 \\ -6 & 4 & 5 \end{bmatrix}$

29. a) $\mathbf{B} = \begin{bmatrix} 150 & 80 & 40 \end{bmatrix}$

b) $\$150 + 5\% \cdot \$150 = 1.05(\$150) = \$157.50$

$\$80 + 5\% \cdot \$80 = 1.05(\$80) = \$84$

$\$40 + 5\% \cdot \$40 = 1.05(\$40) = \$42$

We write the matrix that corresponds to these amounts.

$\mathbf{R} = \begin{bmatrix} 157.5 & 84 & 42 \end{bmatrix}$

c) $\mathbf{B}+\mathbf{R} = \begin{bmatrix} 150 & 80 & 40 \end{bmatrix} + \begin{bmatrix} 157.5 & 84 & 42 \end{bmatrix}$

$= \begin{bmatrix} 307.5 & 164 & 82 \end{bmatrix}$

The entries represent the total budget for each type of expenditure for June and July.

31. a) $\mathbf{C} = \begin{bmatrix} 140 & 27 & 3 & 13 & 64 \end{bmatrix}$

$\mathbf{P} = \begin{bmatrix} 180 & 4 & 11 & 24 & 662 \end{bmatrix}$

$\mathbf{B} = \begin{bmatrix} 50 & 5 & 1 & 82 & 20 \end{bmatrix}$

b) $\mathbf{C} + 2\mathbf{P} + 3\mathbf{B}$

$= \begin{bmatrix} 140 & 27 & 3 & 13 & 64 \end{bmatrix} +$
$\begin{bmatrix} 360 & 8 & 22 & 48 & 1324 \end{bmatrix} +$
$\begin{bmatrix} 150 & 15 & 3 & 246 & 60 \end{bmatrix}$

$= \begin{bmatrix} 650 & 50 & 28 & 307 & 1448 \end{bmatrix}$

The entries represent the total nutritional value of one serving of chicken, 1 cup of potato salad, and 3 broccoli spears.

33. a) $\mathbf{M} = \begin{bmatrix} 45.29 & 6.63 & 10.94 & 7.42 & 8.01 \\ 53.78 & 4.95 & 9.83 & 6.16 & 12.56 \\ 47.13 & 8.47 & 12.66 & 8.29 & 9.43 \\ 51.64 & 7.12 & 11.57 & 9.35 & 10.72 \end{bmatrix}$

b) $\mathbf{N} = \begin{bmatrix} 65 & 48 & 93 & 57 \end{bmatrix}$

c) $\mathbf{NM} =$

$\begin{bmatrix} 12{,}851.86 & 1862.1 & 3019.81 & 2081.9 & 2611.56 \end{bmatrix}$

d) The entries of **NM** represent the total cost, in cents, of each item for the day's meals.

35. a) $\mathbf{S} = \begin{bmatrix} 8 & 15 \\ 6 & 10 \\ 4 & 3 \end{bmatrix}$

b) $\mathbf{C} = \begin{bmatrix} 3 & 1.5 & 2 \end{bmatrix}$

c) $\mathbf{CS} = \begin{bmatrix} 41 & 66 \end{bmatrix}$

d) The entries of **CS** represent the total cost, in dollars, of ingredients for each coffee shop.

37. a) $\mathbf{P} = \begin{bmatrix} 6 & 4.5 & 5.2 \end{bmatrix}$

b) $\mathbf{PS} = \begin{bmatrix} 6 & 4.5 & 5.2 \end{bmatrix} \begin{bmatrix} 8 & 15 \\ 6 & 10 \\ 4 & 3 \end{bmatrix}$

$= \begin{bmatrix} 95.8 & 150.6 \end{bmatrix}$

The profit from Mugsey's Coffee Shop is \$95.80, and the profit from The Coffee Club is \$150.60.

39. $2x - 3y = 7,$

$x + 5y = -6$

Write the coefficients on the left in a matrix. Then write the product of that matrix and the column matrix containing the variables, and set the result equal to the column matrix containing the constants on the right.

$$\begin{bmatrix} 2 & -3 \\ 1 & 5 \end{bmatrix}\begin{bmatrix} x \\ y \end{bmatrix} = \begin{bmatrix} 7 \\ -6 \end{bmatrix}$$

41. $x + y - 2z = 6,$

$3x - y + z = 7,$

$2x + 5y - 3z = 8$

Write the coefficients on the left in a matrix. Then write the product of that matrix and the column matrix containing the variables, and set the result equal to the column matrix containing the constants on the right.

$$\begin{bmatrix} 1 & 1 & -2 \\ 3 & -1 & 1 \\ 2 & 5 & -3 \end{bmatrix}\begin{bmatrix} x \\ y \\ z \end{bmatrix} = \begin{bmatrix} 6 \\ 7 \\ 8 \end{bmatrix}$$

43. $3x - 2y + 4z = 17,$

$2x + y - 5z = 13$

Write the coefficients on the left in a matrix. Then write the product of that matrix and the column matrix containing the variables, and set the result equal to the column matrix containing the constants on the right.

$$\begin{bmatrix} 3 & -2 & 4 \\ 2 & 1 & -5 \end{bmatrix}\begin{bmatrix} x \\ y \\ z \end{bmatrix} = \begin{bmatrix} 17 \\ 13 \end{bmatrix}$$

45. $-4w + x - y + 2z = 12,$

$w + 2x - y - z = 0,$

$-w + x + 4y - 3z = 1,$

$2w + 3x + 5y - 7z = 9$

Write the coefficients on the left in a matrix. Then write the product of that matrix and the column matrix containing the variables, and set the result equal to the column matrix containing the constants on the right.

$$\begin{bmatrix} -4 & 1 & -1 & 2 \\ 1 & 2 & -1 & -1 \\ -1 & 1 & 4 & -3 \\ 2 & 3 & 5 & -7 \end{bmatrix}\begin{bmatrix} w \\ x \\ y \\ z \end{bmatrix} = \begin{bmatrix} 12 \\ 0 \\ 1 \\ 9 \end{bmatrix}$$

47. Discussion and Writing

49. No; see Exercise 17, for example.

51. $f(x) = x^2 - x - 6$

a) $-\dfrac{b}{2a} = -\dfrac{-1}{2 \cdot 1} = \dfrac{1}{2}$

$$f\left(\frac{1}{2}\right) = \left(\frac{1}{2}\right)^2 - \frac{1}{2} - 6 = -\frac{25}{4}$$

The vertex is $\left(\dfrac{1}{2}, -\dfrac{25}{4}\right)$.

b) The axis of symmetry is $x = \dfrac{1}{2}$.

c) Since the coefficient of x^2 is positive, the function has a minimum value. It is the second coordinate of the vertex, $-\dfrac{25}{4}$.

d) Plot some points and draw the graph of the function.

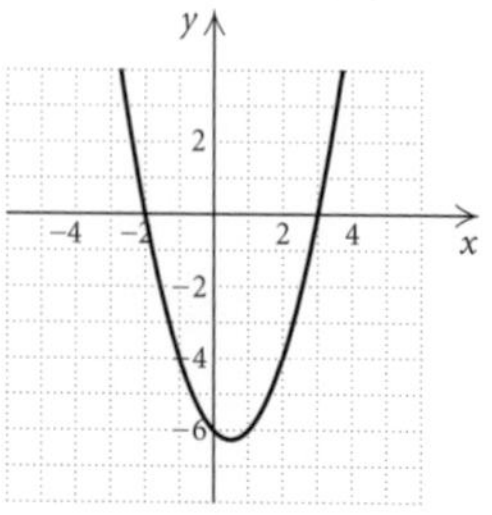

$f(x) = x^2 - x - 6$

53. $f(x) = -x^2 - 3x + 2$

a) $-\dfrac{b}{2a} = -\dfrac{-3}{2(-1)} = -\dfrac{3}{2}$

$$f\left(-\frac{3}{2}\right) = -\left(-\frac{3}{2}\right)^2 - 3\left(-\frac{3}{2}\right) + 2 = \frac{17}{4}$$

The vertex is $\left(-\dfrac{3}{2}, \dfrac{17}{4}\right)$.

b) The axis of symmetry is $x = -\dfrac{3}{2}$.

c) Since the coefficient of x^2 is negative, the function has a maximum value. It is the second coordinate of the vertex, $\dfrac{17}{4}$.

d) Plot some points and draw the graph of the function.

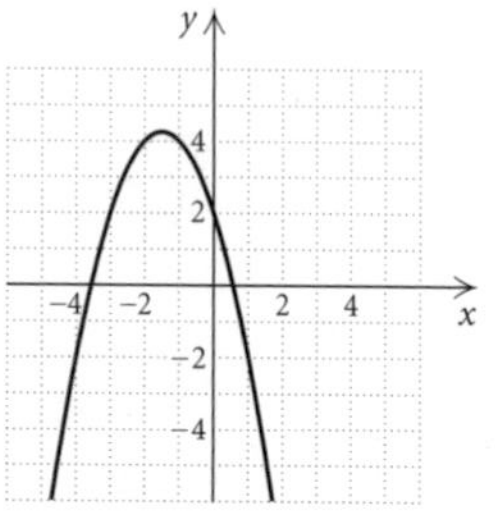

$f(x) = -x^2 - 3x + 2$

55. $\mathbf{A} = \begin{bmatrix} -1 & 0 \\ 2 & 1 \end{bmatrix}, \mathbf{B} = \begin{bmatrix} 1 & -1 \\ 0 & 2 \end{bmatrix}$

$$(\mathbf{A}+\mathbf{B})(\mathbf{A}-\mathbf{B}) = \begin{bmatrix} 0 & -1 \\ 2 & 3 \end{bmatrix}\begin{bmatrix} -2 & 1 \\ 2 & -1 \end{bmatrix}$$

$$= \begin{bmatrix} -2 & 1 \\ 2 & -1 \end{bmatrix}$$

$\mathbf{A}^2 - \mathbf{B}^2$

$$= \begin{bmatrix} -1 & 0 \\ 2 & 1 \end{bmatrix}\begin{bmatrix} -1 & 0 \\ 2 & 1 \end{bmatrix} - \begin{bmatrix} 1 & -1 \\ 0 & 2 \end{bmatrix}\begin{bmatrix} 1 & -1 \\ 0 & 2 \end{bmatrix}$$

$$= \begin{bmatrix} 1 & 0 \\ 0 & 1 \end{bmatrix} - \begin{bmatrix} 1 & -3 \\ 0 & 4 \end{bmatrix}$$

$$= \begin{bmatrix} 0 & 3 \\ 0 & -3 \end{bmatrix}$$

Thus $(\mathbf{A}+\mathbf{B})(\mathbf{A}-\mathbf{B}) \neq \mathbf{A}^2 - \mathbf{B}^2$.

57. In Exercise 55 we found that $(\mathbf{A}+\mathbf{B})(\mathbf{A}-\mathbf{B}) = \begin{bmatrix} -2 & 1 \\ 2 & -1 \end{bmatrix}$

and we also found $\mathbf{A}^2$ and $\mathbf{B}^2$.

$$\mathbf{BA} = \begin{bmatrix} 1 & -1 \\ 0 & 2 \end{bmatrix}\begin{bmatrix} -1 & 0 \\ 2 & 1 \end{bmatrix} = \begin{bmatrix} -3 & -1 \\ 4 & 2 \end{bmatrix}$$

$$\mathbf{AB} = \begin{bmatrix} -1 & 0 \\ 2 & 1 \end{bmatrix}\begin{bmatrix} 1 & -1 \\ 0 & 2 \end{bmatrix} = \begin{bmatrix} -1 & 1 \\ 2 & 0 \end{bmatrix}$$

$$\mathbf{A}^2 + \mathbf{BA} - \mathbf{AB} - \mathbf{B}^2$$
$$= \begin{bmatrix} 1 & 0 \\ 0 & 1 \end{bmatrix} + \begin{bmatrix} -3 & -1 \\ 4 & 2 \end{bmatrix} - \begin{bmatrix} -1 & 1 \\ 2 & 0 \end{bmatrix} - \begin{bmatrix} 1 & -3 \\ 0 & 4 \end{bmatrix}$$
$$= \begin{bmatrix} -2 & 1 \\ 2 & -1 \end{bmatrix}$$

Thus $(\mathbf{A}+\mathbf{B})(\mathbf{A}-\mathbf{B}) = \mathbf{A}^2 + \mathbf{BA} - \mathbf{AB} - \mathbf{B}^2$.

59. See the answer section in the text.

61. See the answer section in the text.

63. See the answer section in the text.

Exercise Set 5.5

1. $\mathbf{BA} = \begin{bmatrix} 7 & 3 \\ 2 & 1 \end{bmatrix}\begin{bmatrix} 1 & -3 \\ -2 & 7 \end{bmatrix} = \begin{bmatrix} 1 & 0 \\ 0 & 1 \end{bmatrix}$

$\mathbf{AB} = \begin{bmatrix} 1 & -3 \\ -2 & 7 \end{bmatrix}\begin{bmatrix} 7 & 3 \\ 2 & 1 \end{bmatrix} = \begin{bmatrix} 1 & 0 \\ 0 & 1 \end{bmatrix}$

Since $\mathbf{BA} = \mathbf{I} = \mathbf{AB}$, $\mathbf{B}$ is the inverse of $\mathbf{A}$.

3. $\mathbf{BA} = \begin{bmatrix} 2 & 3 & 2 \\ 3 & 3 & 4 \\ 1 & 1 & 1 \end{bmatrix}\begin{bmatrix} -1 & -1 & 6 \\ 1 & 0 & -2 \\ 1 & 0 & -3 \end{bmatrix} = \begin{bmatrix} 3 & -2 & 0 \\ 4 & -3 & 0 \\ 1 & -1 & 1 \end{bmatrix}$

Since $\mathbf{BA} \neq \mathbf{I}$, $\mathbf{B}$ is not the inverse of $\mathbf{A}$.

5. $\mathbf{A} = \begin{bmatrix} 3 & 2 \\ 5 & 3 \end{bmatrix}$

Write the augmented matrix.

$\left[\begin{array}{cc|cc} 3 & 2 & 1 & 0 \\ 5 & 3 & 0 & 1 \end{array}\right]$

Multiply row 2 by 3.

$\left[\begin{array}{cc|cc} 3 & 2 & 1 & 0 \\ 15 & 9 & 0 & 3 \end{array}\right]$

Multiply row 1 by -5 and add it to row 2.

$\left[\begin{array}{cc|cc} 3 & 2 & 1 & 0 \\ 0 & -1 & -5 & 3 \end{array}\right]$

Multiply row 2 by 2 and add it to row 1.

$\left[\begin{array}{cc|cc} 3 & 0 & -9 & 6 \\ 0 & -1 & -5 & 3 \end{array}\right]$

Multiply row 1 by $\frac{1}{3}$ and row 2 by -1.

$\left[\begin{array}{cc|cc} 1 & 0 & -3 & 2 \\ 0 & 1 & 5 & -3 \end{array}\right]$

Then $\mathbf{A}^{-1} = \begin{bmatrix} -3 & 2 \\ 5 & -3 \end{bmatrix}$.

7. $\mathbf{A} = \begin{bmatrix} 6 & 9 \\ 4 & 6 \end{bmatrix}$

Write the augmented matrix.

$\left[\begin{array}{cc|cc} 6 & 9 & 1 & 0 \\ 4 & 6 & 0 & 1 \end{array}\right]$

Multiply row 2 by 3.

$\left[\begin{array}{cc|cc} 6 & 9 & 1 & 0 \\ 12 & 18 & 0 & 3 \end{array}\right]$

Multiply row 1 by -2 and add it to row 2.

$\left[\begin{array}{cc|cc} 6 & 9 & 1 & 0 \\ 0 & 0 & -2 & 3 \end{array}\right]$

We cannot obtain the identity matrix on the left since the second row contains only zeros to the left of the vertical line. Thus, $\mathbf{A}^{-1}$ does not exist.

9. $\mathbf{A} = \begin{bmatrix} 4 & -3 \\ 1 & -2 \end{bmatrix}$

Write the augmented matrix.

$\left[\begin{array}{cc|cc} 4 & -3 & 1 & 0 \\ 1 & -2 & 0 & 1 \end{array}\right]$

Interchange the rows.

$\left[\begin{array}{cc|cc} 1 & -2 & 0 & 1 \\ 4 & -3 & 1 & 0 \end{array}\right]$

Multiply row 1 by -4 and add it to row 2.

$\left[\begin{array}{cc|cc} 1 & -2 & 0 & 1 \\ 0 & 5 & 1 & -4 \end{array}\right]$

Multiply row 2 by $\frac{1}{5}$.

$\left[\begin{array}{cc|cc} 1 & -2 & 0 & 1 \\ 0 & 1 & \frac{1}{5} & -\frac{4}{5} \end{array}\right]$

Multiply row 2 by 2 and add it to row 1.

$\left[\begin{array}{cc|cc} 1 & 0 & \frac{2}{5} & -\frac{3}{5} \\ 0 & 1 & \frac{1}{5} & -\frac{4}{5} \end{array}\right]$

Then $\mathbf{A}^{-1} = \begin{bmatrix} \frac{2}{5} & -\frac{3}{5} \\ \frac{1}{5} & -\frac{4}{5} \end{bmatrix}$.

11. $\mathbf{A} = \begin{bmatrix} 3 & 1 & 0 \\ 1 & 1 & 1 \\ 1 & -1 & 2 \end{bmatrix}$

Write the augmented matrix.

$\left[\begin{array}{ccc|ccc} 3 & 1 & 0 & 1 & 0 & 0 \\ 1 & 1 & 1 & 0 & 1 & 0 \\ 1 & -1 & 2 & 0 & 0 & 1 \end{array}\right]$

Interchange the first two rows.

$$\left[\begin{array}{ccc|ccc} 1 & 1 & 1 & 0 & 1 & 0 \\ 3 & 1 & 0 & 1 & 0 & 0 \\ 1 & -1 & 2 & 0 & 0 & 1 \end{array}\right]$$

Multiply row 1 by -3 and add it to row 2. Also, multiply row 1 by -1 and add it to row 3.

$$\left[\begin{array}{ccc|ccc} 1 & 1 & 1 & 0 & 1 & 0 \\ 0 & -2 & -3 & 1 & -3 & 0 \\ 0 & -2 & 1 & 0 & -1 & 1 \end{array}\right]$$

Multiply row 2 by $-\dfrac{1}{2}$.

$$\left[\begin{array}{ccc|ccc} 1 & 1 & 1 & 0 & 1 & 0 \\ 0 & 1 & \frac{3}{2} & -\frac{1}{2} & \frac{3}{2} & 0 \\ 0 & -2 & 1 & 0 & -1 & 1 \end{array}\right]$$

Multiply row 2 by -1 and add it to row 1. Also, multiply row 2 by 2 and add it to row 3.

$$\left[\begin{array}{ccc|ccc} 1 & 0 & -\frac{1}{2} & \frac{1}{2} & -\frac{1}{2} & 0 \\ 0 & 1 & \frac{3}{2} & -\frac{1}{2} & \frac{3}{2} & 0 \\ 0 & 0 & 4 & -1 & 2 & 1 \end{array}\right]$$

Multiply row 3 by $\dfrac{1}{4}$.

$$\left[\begin{array}{ccc|ccc} 1 & 0 & -\frac{1}{2} & \frac{1}{2} & -\frac{1}{2} & 0 \\ 0 & 1 & \frac{3}{2} & -\frac{1}{2} & \frac{3}{2} & 0 \\ 0 & 0 & 1 & -\frac{1}{4} & \frac{1}{2} & \frac{1}{4} \end{array}\right]$$

Multiply row 3 by $\dfrac{1}{2}$ and add it to row 1. Also, multiply row 3 by $-\dfrac{3}{2}$ and add it to row 2.

$$\left[\begin{array}{ccc|ccc} 1 & 0 & 0 & \frac{3}{8} & -\frac{1}{4} & \frac{1}{8} \\ 0 & 1 & 0 & -\frac{1}{8} & \frac{3}{4} & -\frac{3}{8} \\ 0 & 0 & 1 & -\frac{1}{4} & \frac{1}{2} & \frac{1}{4} \end{array}\right]$$

Then $\mathbf{A}^{-1} = \begin{bmatrix} \frac{3}{8} & -\frac{1}{4} & \frac{1}{8} \\ -\frac{1}{8} & \frac{3}{4} & -\frac{3}{8} \\ -\frac{1}{4} & \frac{1}{2} & \frac{1}{4} \end{bmatrix}$.

13. $\mathbf{A} = \begin{bmatrix} 1 & -4 & 8 \\ 1 & -3 & 2 \\ 2 & -7 & 10 \end{bmatrix}$

Write the augmented matrix.

$$\left[\begin{array}{ccc|ccc} 1 & -4 & 8 & 1 & 0 & 0 \\ 1 & -3 & 2 & 0 & 1 & 0 \\ 2 & -7 & 10 & 0 & 0 & 1 \end{array}\right]$$

Multiply row 1 by -1 and add it to row 2. Also, multiply row 1 by -2 and add it to row 3.

$$\left[\begin{array}{ccc|ccc} 1 & -4 & 8 & 1 & 0 & 0 \\ 0 & 1 & -6 & -1 & 1 & 0 \\ 0 & 1 & -6 & -2 & 0 & 1 \end{array}\right]$$

Since the second and third rows are identical left of the vertical line, it will not be possible to obtain the identity matrix on the left side. Thus, $\mathbf{A}^{-1}$ does not exist.

15. $\mathbf{A} = \begin{bmatrix} 2 & 3 & 2 \\ 3 & 3 & 4 \\ -1 & -1 & -1 \end{bmatrix}$

Write the augmented matrix.

$$\left[\begin{array}{ccc|ccc} 2 & 3 & 2 & 1 & 0 & 0 \\ 3 & 3 & 4 & 0 & 1 & 0 \\ -1 & -1 & -1 & 0 & 0 & 1 \end{array}\right]$$

Interchange rows 1 and 3.

$$\left[\begin{array}{ccc|ccc} -1 & -1 & -1 & 0 & 0 & 1 \\ 3 & 3 & 4 & 0 & 1 & 0 \\ 2 & 3 & 2 & 1 & 0 & 0 \end{array}\right]$$

Multiply row 1 by 3 and add it to row 2. Also, multiply row 1 by 2 and add it to row 3.

$$\left[\begin{array}{ccc|ccc} -1 & -1 & -1 & 0 & 0 & 1 \\ 0 & 0 & 1 & 0 & 1 & 3 \\ 0 & 1 & 0 & 1 & 0 & 2 \end{array}\right]$$

Multiply row 1 by -1.

$$\left[\begin{array}{ccc|ccc} 1 & 1 & 1 & 0 & 0 & -1 \\ 0 & 0 & 1 & 0 & 1 & 3 \\ 0 & 1 & 0 & 1 & 0 & 2 \end{array}\right]$$

Interchange rows 2 and 3.

$$\left[\begin{array}{ccc|ccc} 1 & 1 & 1 & 0 & 0 & -1 \\ 0 & 1 & 0 & 1 & 0 & 2 \\ 0 & 0 & 1 & 0 & 1 & 3 \end{array}\right]$$

Multiply row 2 by -1 and add it to row 1.

$$\left[\begin{array}{ccc|ccc} 1 & 0 & 1 & -1 & 0 & -3 \\ 0 & 1 & 0 & 1 & 0 & 2 \\ 0 & 0 & 1 & 0 & 1 & 3 \end{array}\right]$$

Multiply row 3 by -1 and add it to row 1.

$$\left[\begin{array}{ccc|ccc} 1 & 0 & 0 & -1 & -1 & -6 \\ 0 & 1 & 0 & 1 & 0 & 2 \\ 0 & 0 & 1 & 0 & 1 & 3 \end{array}\right]$$

Then $\mathbf{A}^{-1} = \begin{bmatrix} -1 & -1 & -6 \\ 1 & 0 & 2 \\ 0 & 1 & 3 \end{bmatrix}$.

17. $\mathbf{A} = \begin{bmatrix} 1 & 2 & -1 \\ -2 & 0 & 1 \\ 1 & -1 & 0 \end{bmatrix}$

Write the augmented matrix.

$$\left[\begin{array}{ccc|ccc} 1 & 2 & -1 & 1 & 0 & 0 \\ -2 & 0 & 1 & 0 & 1 & 0 \\ 1 & -1 & 0 & 0 & 0 & 1 \end{array}\right]$$

Multiply row 1 by 2 and add it to row 2. Also, multiply row 1 by -1 and add it to row 3.

$$\left[\begin{array}{ccc|ccc} 1 & 2 & -1 & 1 & 0 & 0 \\ 0 & 4 & -1 & 2 & 1 & 0 \\ 0 & -3 & 1 & -1 & 0 & 1 \end{array}\right]$$

Add row 3 to row 1 and also to row 2.

$$\left[\begin{array}{ccc|ccc} 1 & -1 & 0 & 0 & 0 & 1 \\ 0 & 1 & 0 & 1 & 1 & 1 \\ 0 & -3 & 1 & -1 & 0 & 1 \end{array}\right]$$

Add row 2 to row 1. Also, multiply row 2 by 3 and add it to row 3.

$$\left[\begin{array}{ccc|ccc} 1 & 0 & 0 & 1 & 1 & 2 \\ 0 & 1 & 0 & 1 & 1 & 1 \\ 0 & 0 & 1 & 2 & 3 & 4 \end{array}\right]$$

Then $\mathbf{A}^{-1} = \begin{bmatrix} 1 & 1 & 2 \\ 1 & 1 & 1 \\ 2 & 3 & 4 \end{bmatrix}$.

19. $\mathbf{A} = \begin{bmatrix} 1 & 3 & -1 \\ 0 & 2 & -1 \\ 1 & 1 & 0 \end{bmatrix}$

Write the augmented matrix.

$$\left[\begin{array}{ccc|ccc} 1 & 3 & -1 & 1 & 0 & 0 \\ 0 & 2 & -1 & 0 & 1 & 0 \\ 1 & 1 & 0 & 0 & 0 & 1 \end{array}\right]$$

Multiply row 1 by -1 and add it to row 3.

$$\left[\begin{array}{ccc|ccc} 1 & 3 & -1 & 1 & 0 & 0 \\ 0 & 2 & -1 & 0 & 1 & 0 \\ 0 & -2 & 1 & -1 & 0 & 1 \end{array}\right]$$

Add row 3 to row 1 and also to row 2.

$$\left[\begin{array}{ccc|ccc} 1 & 1 & 0 & 0 & 0 & 0 \\ 0 & 0 & 0 & -1 & 1 & 1 \\ 0 & -2 & 1 & -1 & 0 & 1 \end{array}\right]$$

Since the second row consists only of zeros to the left of the vertical line, it will not be possible to obtain the identity matrix on the left side. Thus, $\mathbf{A}^{-1}$ does not exist.

21. $\mathbf{A} = \begin{bmatrix} 1 & 2 & 3 & 4 \\ 0 & 1 & 3 & -5 \\ 0 & 0 & 1 & -2 \\ 0 & 0 & 0 & -1 \end{bmatrix}$

Write the augmented matrix.

$$\left[\begin{array}{cccc|cccc} 1 & 2 & 3 & 4 & 1 & 0 & 0 & 0 \\ 0 & 1 & 3 & -5 & 0 & 1 & 0 & 0 \\ 0 & 0 & 1 & -2 & 0 & 0 & 1 & 0 \\ 0 & 0 & 0 & -1 & 0 & 0 & 0 & 1 \end{array}\right]$$

Multiply row 4 by -1.

$$\left[\begin{array}{cccc|cccc} 1 & 2 & 3 & 4 & 1 & 0 & 0 & 0 \\ 0 & 1 & 3 & -5 & 0 & 1 & 0 & 0 \\ 0 & 0 & 1 & -2 & 0 & 0 & 1 & 0 \\ 0 & 0 & 0 & 1 & 0 & 0 & 0 & -1 \end{array}\right]$$

Multiply row 4 by -4 and add it to row 1. Multiply row 4 by 5 and add it to row 2. Also, multiply row 4 by 2 and add it to row 3.

$$\left[\begin{array}{cccc|cccc} 1 & 2 & 3 & 0 & 1 & 0 & 0 & 4 \\ 0 & 1 & 3 & 0 & 0 & 1 & 0 & -5 \\ 0 & 0 & 1 & 0 & 0 & 0 & 1 & -2 \\ 0 & 0 & 0 & 1 & 0 & 0 & 0 & -1 \end{array}\right]$$

Multiply row 3 by -3 and add it to row 1 and to row 2.

$$\left[\begin{array}{cccc|cccc} 1 & 2 & 0 & 0 & 1 & 0 & -3 & 10 \\ 0 & 1 & 0 & 0 & 0 & 1 & -3 & 1 \\ 0 & 0 & 1 & 0 & 0 & 0 & 1 & -2 \\ 0 & 0 & 0 & 1 & 0 & 0 & 0 & -1 \end{array}\right]$$

Multiply row 2 by -2 and add it to row 1.

$$\left[\begin{array}{cccc|cccc} 1 & 0 & 0 & 0 & 1 & -2 & 3 & 8 \\ 0 & 1 & 0 & 0 & 0 & 1 & -3 & 1 \\ 0 & 0 & 1 & 0 & 0 & 0 & 1 & -2 \\ 0 & 0 & 0 & 1 & 0 & 0 & 0 & -1 \end{array}\right]$$

Then $\mathbf{A}^{-1} = \begin{bmatrix} 1 & -2 & 3 & 8 \\ 0 & 1 & -3 & 1 \\ 0 & 0 & 1 & -2 \\ 0 & 0 & 0 & -1 \end{bmatrix}$.

23. $\mathbf{A} = \begin{bmatrix} 1 & -14 & 7 & 38 \\ -1 & 2 & 1 & -2 \\ 1 & 2 & -1 & -6 \\ 1 & -2 & 3 & 6 \end{bmatrix}$

Write the augmented matrix.

$$\left[\begin{array}{cccc|cccc} 1 & -14 & 7 & 38 & 1 & 0 & 0 & 0 \\ -1 & 2 & 1 & -2 & 0 & 1 & 0 & 0 \\ 1 & 2 & -1 & -6 & 0 & 0 & 1 & 0 \\ 1 & -2 & 3 & 6 & 0 & 0 & 0 & 1 \end{array}\right]$$

Add row 1 to row 2. Also, multiply row 1 by -1 and add it to row 3 and to row 4.

$$\left[\begin{array}{cccc|cccc} 1 & -14 & 7 & 38 & 1 & 0 & 0 & 0 \\ 0 & -12 & 8 & 36 & 1 & 1 & 0 & 0 \\ 0 & 16 & -8 & -44 & -1 & 0 & 1 & 0 \\ 0 & 12 & -4 & -32 & -1 & 0 & 0 & 1 \end{array}\right]$$

Add row 2 to row 4.

$$\left[\begin{array}{cccc|cccc} 1 & -14 & 7 & 38 & 1 & 0 & 0 & 0 \\ 0 & -12 & 8 & 36 & 1 & 1 & 0 & 0 \\ 0 & 16 & -8 & -44 & -1 & 0 & 1 & 0 \\ 0 & 0 & 4 & 4 & 0 & 1 & 0 & 1 \end{array}\right]$$

Multiply row 4 by $\frac{1}{4}$.

$$\left[\begin{array}{cccc|cccc} 1 & -14 & 7 & 38 & 1 & 0 & 0 & 0 \\ 0 & -12 & 8 & 36 & 1 & 1 & 0 & 0 \\ 0 & 16 & -8 & -44 & -1 & 0 & 1 & 0 \\ 0 & 0 & 1 & 1 & 0 & \frac{1}{4} & 0 & \frac{1}{4} \end{array}\right]$$

Multiply row 4 by -38 and add it to row 1. Multiply row 4 by -36 and add it to row 2. Also, multiply row 4 by 44 and add it to row 3.

$$\left[\begin{array}{cccc|cccc} 1 & -14 & -31 & 0 & 1 & -\frac{19}{2} & 0 & -\frac{19}{2} \\ 0 & -12 & -28 & 0 & 1 & -8 & 0 & -9 \\ 0 & 16 & 36 & 0 & -1 & 11 & 1 & 11 \\ 0 & 0 & 1 & 1 & 0 & \frac{1}{4} & 0 & \frac{1}{4} \end{array}\right]$$

Multiply row 3 by $\frac{1}{36}$.

$$\left[\begin{array}{cccc|cccc} 1 & -14 & -31 & 0 & 1 & -\frac{19}{2} & 0 & -\frac{19}{2} \\ 0 & -12 & -28 & 0 & 1 & -8 & 0 & -9 \\ 0 & \frac{4}{9} & 1 & 0 & -\frac{1}{36} & \frac{11}{36} & \frac{1}{36} & \frac{11}{36} \\ 0 & 0 & 1 & 1 & 0 & \frac{1}{4} & 0 & \frac{1}{4} \end{array}\right]$$

Multiply row 3 by 31 and add it to row 1. Multiply row 3 by 28 and add it to row 2. Also, multiply row 3 by -1 and add it to row 4.

$$\left[\begin{array}{cccc|cccc} 1 & -\frac{2}{9} & 0 & 0 & \frac{5}{36} & -\frac{1}{36} & \frac{31}{36} & -\frac{1}{36} \\ 0 & \frac{4}{9} & 0 & 0 & \frac{2}{9} & \frac{5}{9} & \frac{7}{9} & -\frac{4}{9} \\ 0 & \frac{4}{9} & 1 & 0 & -\frac{1}{36} & \frac{11}{36} & \frac{1}{36} & \frac{11}{36} \\ 0 & -\frac{4}{9} & 0 & 1 & \frac{1}{36} & -\frac{1}{18} & -\frac{1}{36} & -\frac{1}{18} \end{array}\right]$$

Multiply row 2 by $\frac{1}{2}$ and add it to row 1. Also, multiply row 2 by -1 and add it to row 3. Add row 2 to row 4.

$$\left[\begin{array}{cccc|cccc} 1 & 0 & 0 & 0 & \frac{1}{4} & \frac{1}{4} & \frac{5}{4} & -\frac{1}{4} \\ 0 & \frac{4}{9} & 0 & 0 & \frac{2}{9} & \frac{5}{9} & \frac{7}{9} & -\frac{4}{9} \\ 0 & 0 & 1 & 0 & -\frac{1}{4} & -\frac{1}{4} & -\frac{3}{4} & \frac{3}{4} \\ 0 & 0 & 0 & 1 & \frac{1}{4} & \frac{1}{2} & \frac{3}{4} & -\frac{1}{2} \end{array}\right]$$

Multiply row 2 by $\frac{9}{4}$.

$$\left[\begin{array}{cccc|cccc} 1 & 0 & 0 & 0 & \frac{1}{4} & \frac{1}{4} & \frac{5}{4} & -\frac{1}{4} \\ 0 & 1 & 0 & 0 & \frac{1}{2} & \frac{5}{4} & \frac{7}{4} & -1 \\ 0 & 0 & 1 & 0 & -\frac{1}{4} & -\frac{1}{4} & -\frac{3}{4} & \frac{3}{4} \\ 0 & 0 & 0 & 1 & \frac{1}{4} & \frac{1}{2} & \frac{3}{4} & -\frac{1}{2} \end{array}\right]$$

Then $\mathbf{A}^{-1} = \begin{bmatrix} \frac{1}{4} & \frac{1}{4} & \frac{5}{4} & -\frac{1}{4} \\ \frac{1}{2} & \frac{5}{4} & \frac{7}{4} & -1 \\ -\frac{1}{4} & -\frac{1}{4} & -\frac{3}{4} & \frac{3}{4} \\ \frac{1}{4} & \frac{1}{2} & \frac{3}{4} & -\frac{1}{2} \end{bmatrix}$, or

$$\begin{bmatrix} 0.25 & 0.25 & 1.25 & -0.25 \\ 0.5 & 1.25 & 1.75 & -1 \\ -0.25 & -0.25 & -0.75 & 0.75 \\ 0.25 & 0.5 & 0.75 & -0.5 \end{bmatrix}.$$

25. Write an equivalent matrix equation, $\mathbf{AX} = \mathbf{B}$.

$$\begin{bmatrix} 11 & 3 \\ 7 & 2 \end{bmatrix}\begin{bmatrix} x \\ y \end{bmatrix} = \begin{bmatrix} -4 \\ 5 \end{bmatrix}$$

Then we have $\mathbf{X} = \mathbf{A}^{-1}\mathbf{B}$.

$$\begin{bmatrix} x \\ y \end{bmatrix} = \begin{bmatrix} 2 & -3 \\ -7 & 11 \end{bmatrix}\begin{bmatrix} -4 \\ 5 \end{bmatrix} = \begin{bmatrix} -23 \\ 83 \end{bmatrix}$$

The solution is $(-23, 83)$.

27. Write an equivalent matrix equation, $\mathbf{AX} = \mathbf{B}$.

$$\begin{bmatrix} 3 & 1 & 0 \\ 2 & -1 & 2 \\ 1 & 1 & 1 \end{bmatrix}\begin{bmatrix} x \\ y \\ z \end{bmatrix} = \begin{bmatrix} 2 \\ -5 \\ 5 \end{bmatrix}$$

Then we have $\mathbf{X} = \mathbf{A}^{-1}\mathbf{B}$.

$$\begin{bmatrix} x \\ y \\ z \end{bmatrix} = \frac{1}{9}\begin{bmatrix} 3 & 1 & -2 \\ 0 & -3 & 6 \\ -3 & 2 & 5 \end{bmatrix}\begin{bmatrix} 2 \\ -5 \\ 5 \end{bmatrix} = \frac{1}{9}\begin{bmatrix} -9 \\ 45 \\ 9 \end{bmatrix} = \begin{bmatrix} -1 \\ 5 \\ 1 \end{bmatrix}$$

The solution is $(-1, 5, 1)$.

29. $4x + 3y = 2,$
$x - 2y = 6$

Write an equivalent matrix equation, $\mathbf{AX} = \mathbf{B}$.

$$\begin{bmatrix} 4 & 3 \\ 1 & -2 \end{bmatrix}\begin{bmatrix} x \\ y \end{bmatrix} = \begin{bmatrix} 2 \\ 6 \end{bmatrix}$$

Then $\mathbf{X} = \mathbf{A}^{-1}\mathbf{B} = \begin{bmatrix} \frac{2}{11} & \frac{3}{11} \\ \frac{1}{11} & -\frac{4}{11} \end{bmatrix}\begin{bmatrix} 2 \\ 6 \end{bmatrix} = \begin{bmatrix} 2 \\ -2 \end{bmatrix}$.

The solution is $(2, -2)$.

31. $5x + y = 2,$
$3x - 2y = -4$

Write an equivalent matrix equation, $\mathbf{AX} = \mathbf{B}$.

$$\begin{bmatrix} 5 & 1 \\ 3 & -2 \end{bmatrix}\begin{bmatrix} x \\ y \end{bmatrix} = \begin{bmatrix} \frac{2}{13} & \frac{1}{13} \\ \frac{3}{13} & -\frac{5}{13} \end{bmatrix}\begin{bmatrix} 2 \\ -4 \end{bmatrix} = \begin{bmatrix} 2 \\ -4 \end{bmatrix}$$

Then $\mathbf{X} = \mathbf{A}^{-1}\mathbf{B} = \begin{bmatrix} 0 \\ 2 \end{bmatrix}$.

The solution is $(0, 2)$.

33. $x + z = 1,$
$2x + y = 3,$
$x - y + z = 4$

Write an equivalent matrix equation, $\mathbf{AX} = \mathbf{B}$.

$$\begin{bmatrix} 1 & 0 & 1 \\ 2 & 1 & 0 \\ 1 & -1 & 1 \end{bmatrix}\begin{bmatrix} x \\ y \\ z \end{bmatrix} = \begin{bmatrix} 1 \\ 3 \\ 4 \end{bmatrix}$$

Then $\mathbf{X} = \mathbf{A}^{-1}\mathbf{B} = \begin{bmatrix} -\frac{1}{2} & \frac{1}{2} & \frac{1}{2} \\ 1 & 0 & -1 \\ \frac{3}{2} & -\frac{1}{2} & -\frac{1}{2} \end{bmatrix}\begin{bmatrix} 1 \\ 3 \\ 4 \end{bmatrix} = \begin{bmatrix} 3 \\ -3 \\ -2 \end{bmatrix}$.

The solution is $(3, -3, -2)$.

35. $2x + 3y + 4z = 2,$
$x - 4y + 3z = 2,$
$5x + y + z = -4$

Write an equivalent matrix equation, $\mathbf{AX} = \mathbf{B}$.

$$\begin{bmatrix} 2 & 3 & 4 \\ 1 & -4 & 3 \\ 5 & 1 & 1 \end{bmatrix}\begin{bmatrix} x \\ y \\ z \end{bmatrix} = \begin{bmatrix} 2 \\ 2 \\ -4 \end{bmatrix}$$

Then $\mathbf{X}=\mathbf{A}^{-1}\mathbf{B}=\begin{bmatrix} -\frac{1}{16} & \frac{1}{112} & \frac{25}{112} \\ \frac{1}{8} & -\frac{9}{56} & -\frac{1}{56} \\ \frac{3}{16} & \frac{13}{112} & -\frac{11}{112} \end{bmatrix}\begin{bmatrix} 2 \\ 2 \\ -4 \end{bmatrix}=\begin{bmatrix} -1 \\ 0 \\ 1 \end{bmatrix}$.

The solution is $(-1, 0, 1)$.

37. $2w - 3x + 4y - 5z = 0,$

$3w - 2x + 7y - 3z = 2,$

$w + x - y + z = 1,$

$-w - 3x - 6y + 4z = 6$

Write an equivalent matrix equation, $\mathbf{AX} = \mathbf{B}$.

$$\begin{bmatrix} 2 & -3 & 4 & -5 \\ 3 & -2 & 7 & -3 \\ 1 & 1 & -1 & 1 \\ -1 & -3 & -6 & 4 \end{bmatrix}\begin{bmatrix} w \\ x \\ y \\ z \end{bmatrix} = \begin{bmatrix} 0 \\ 2 \\ 1 \\ 6 \end{bmatrix}$$

Then $\mathbf{X} = \mathbf{A}^{-1}\mathbf{B} = \frac{1}{203}\begin{bmatrix} 26 & 11 & 127 & 9 \\ -8 & -19 & 39 & -34 \\ -37 & 39 & -48 & -5 \\ -55 & 47 & -11 & 20 \end{bmatrix}\begin{bmatrix} 0 \\ 2 \\ 1 \\ 6 \end{bmatrix} = \begin{bmatrix} 1 \\ -1 \\ 0 \\ 1 \end{bmatrix}$.

The solution is $(1, -1, 0, 1)$.

39. ***Familiarize.*** Let x = the number of hot dogs sold and y = the number of sausages.

Translate.

The total number of items sold was 145.

$x + y = 145$

The number of hot dogs sold is 45 more than the number of sausages.

$x = y + 45$

We have a system of equations:

$x + y = 145, \qquad x + y = 145,$

or

$x = y + 45, \qquad x - y = 45.$

Carry out. Write an equivalent matrix equation, $\mathbf{AX} = \mathbf{B}$.

$$\begin{bmatrix} 1 & 1 \\ 1 & -1 \end{bmatrix}\begin{bmatrix} x \\ y \end{bmatrix} = \begin{bmatrix} 145 \\ 45 \end{bmatrix}$$

Then $\mathbf{X} = \mathbf{A}^{-1}\mathbf{B}=\begin{bmatrix} \frac{1}{2} & \frac{1}{2} \\ \frac{1}{2} & -\frac{1}{2} \end{bmatrix}\begin{bmatrix} 145 \\ 45 \end{bmatrix} = \begin{bmatrix} 95 \\ 50 \end{bmatrix}$, so the solution is $(95, 50)$.

Check. The total number of items is $95 + 50$, or 145. The number of hot dogs, 95, is 45 more than the number of sausages. The solution checks.

State. Stefan sold 95 hot dogs and 50 Italian sausages.

41. ***Familiarize.*** Let x, y, and z represent the prices of one ton of topsoil, mulch, and pea gravel, respectively.

Translate.

Four tons of topsoil, 3 tons of mulch, and 6 tons of pea gravel costs \$2825.

$4x + 3y + 6z = 2825$

Five tons of topsoil, 2 tons of mulch, and 5 tons of pea gravel costs \$2663.

$5x + 2y + 5z = 2663$

Pea gravel costs \$17 less per ton than topsoil.

$z = x - 17$

We have a system of equations.

$4x + 3y + 6z = 2825,$

$5x + 2y + 5z = 2663,$

$z = x - 17,$ or

$4x + 3y + 6z = 2825,$

$5x + 2y + 5z = 2663,$

$x \qquad - z = 17$

Carry out. Write an equivalent matrix equation, $\mathbf{AX} = \mathbf{B}$.

$$\begin{bmatrix} 4 & 3 & 6 \\ 5 & 2 & 5 \\ 1 & 0 & -1 \end{bmatrix}\begin{bmatrix} x \\ y \\ z \end{bmatrix} = \begin{bmatrix} 2825 \\ 2663 \\ 17 \end{bmatrix}$$

Then $\mathbf{X} = \mathbf{A}^{-1}\mathbf{B} = \begin{bmatrix} -\frac{1}{5} & \frac{3}{10} & \frac{3}{10} \\ 1 & -1 & 1 \\ -\frac{1}{5} & \frac{3}{10} & -\frac{7}{10} \end{bmatrix}\begin{bmatrix} 2825 \\ 2663 \\ 17 \end{bmatrix} = \begin{bmatrix} 239 \\ 179 \\ 222 \end{bmatrix}$, so the solution is $(239, 179, 222)$.

Check. Four tons of topsoil, 3 tons of mulch, and 6 tons of pea gravel costs $4 \cdot \$239 + 3 \cdot \$179 + 6 \cdot \$222$, or $\$956 + \$537 + \$1332$, or \$2825. Five tons of topsoil, 2 tons of mulch, and 5 tons of pea gravel costs $5 \cdot \$239 + 2 \cdot \$179 + 5 \cdot \$222$, or $\$1195 + \$358 + \$1110$, or \$2663. The price of pea gravel, \$222, is \$17 less than the price of topsoil, \$239. The solution checks.

State. The price of topsoil is \$239 per ton, of mulch is \$179 per ton, and of pea gravel is \$222 per ton.

43. Left to the student

45. Left to the student

47. Discussion and Writing

49.

-2	1	-6	4	-8
		-2	16	-40
	1	-8	20	-48

$f(-2) = -48$

51. $2x^2 + x = 7$

$2x^2 + x - 7 = 0$

$a = 2,\ b = 1,\ c = -7$

$$x = \frac{-b \pm \sqrt{b^2 - 4ac}}{2a}$$
$$= \frac{-1 \pm \sqrt{1^2 - 4 \cdot 2 \cdot (-7)}}{2 \cdot 2} = \frac{-1 \pm \sqrt{1+56}}{4}$$
$$= \frac{-1 \pm \sqrt{57}}{4}$$

The solutions are $\frac{-1+\sqrt{57}}{4}$ and $\frac{-1-\sqrt{57}}{4}$, or $\frac{-1 \pm \sqrt{57}}{4}$.

53.

$\sqrt{2x+1} - 1 = \sqrt{2x-4}$

$(\sqrt{2x+1} - 1)^2 = (\sqrt{2x-4})^2$ Squaring both sides

$2x + 1 - 2\sqrt{2x+1} + 1 = 2x - 4$

$2x + 2 - 2\sqrt{2x+1} = 2x - 4$

$2 - 2\sqrt{2x+1} = -4$ Subtracting $2x$

$-2\sqrt{2x+1} = -6$ Subtracting 2

$\sqrt{2x+1} = 3$ Dividing by -2

$(\sqrt{2x+1})^2 = 3^2$ Squaring both sides

$2x + 1 = 9$

$2x = 8$

$x = 4$

The number 4 checks. It is the solution.

55. $f(x) = x^3 - 3x^2 - 6x + 8$

We use synthetic division to find one factor. We first try $x - 1$.

$$\begin{array}{r|rrrr} 1 & 1 & -3 & -6 & 8 \\ & & 1 & -2 & -8 \\ \hline & 1 & -2 & -8 & 0 \end{array}$$

Since $f(1) = 0$, $x - 1$ is a factor of $f(x)$. We have $f(x) = (x-1)(x^2-2x-8)$. Factoring the trinomial we get $f(x) = (x-1)(x-4)(x+2)$.

57. $\mathbf{A} = [x]$

Write the augmented matrix.

$$\left[\begin{array}{c|c} x & 1 \end{array}\right]$$

Multiply by $\frac{1}{x}$.

$$\left[\begin{array}{c|c} 1 & \frac{1}{x} \end{array}\right]$$

Then $\mathbf{A}^{-1}$ exists if and only if $x \neq 0$. $\mathbf{A}^{-1} = \left[\frac{1}{x}\right]$.

59. $\mathbf{A} = \begin{bmatrix} 0 & 0 & x \\ 0 & y & 0 \\ z & 0 & 0 \end{bmatrix}$

Write the augmented matrix.

$$\left[\begin{array}{ccc|ccc} 0 & 0 & x & 1 & 0 & 0 \\ 0 & y & 0 & 0 & 1 & 0 \\ z & 0 & 0 & 0 & 0 & 1 \end{array}\right]$$

Interchange row 1 and row 3.

$$\left[\begin{array}{ccc|ccc} z & 0 & 0 & 0 & 0 & 1 \\ 0 & y & 0 & 0 & 1 & 0 \\ 0 & 0 & x & 1 & 0 & 0 \end{array}\right]$$

Multiply row 1 by $\frac{1}{z}$, row 2 by $\frac{1}{y}$, and row 3 by $\frac{1}{x}$.

$$\left[\begin{array}{ccc|ccc} 1 & 0 & 0 & 0 & 0 & \frac{1}{z} \\ 0 & 1 & 0 & 0 & \frac{1}{y} & 0 \\ 0 & 0 & 1 & \frac{1}{x} & 0 & 0 \end{array}\right]$$

Then $\mathbf{A}^{-1}$ exists if and only if $x \neq 0$ and $y \neq 0$ and $z \neq 0$, or if and only if $xyz \neq 0$.

$$\mathbf{A}^{-1} = \begin{bmatrix} 0 & 0 & \frac{1}{z} \\ 0 & \frac{1}{y} & 0 \\ \frac{1}{x} & 0 & 0 \end{bmatrix}$$

Exercise Set 5.6

1. $\begin{vmatrix} -2 & -\sqrt{5} \\ -\sqrt{5} & 3 \end{vmatrix} = -2 \cdot 3 - (-\sqrt{5})(-\sqrt{5}) = -6 - 5 = -11$

3. $\begin{vmatrix} x & 4 \\ x & x^2 \end{vmatrix} = x \cdot x^2 - x \cdot 4 = x^3 - 4x$

5. We will expand across the first row. We could have chosen any other row or column just as well.

$$\begin{vmatrix} 3 & 1 & 2 \\ -2 & 3 & 1 \\ 3 & 4 & -6 \end{vmatrix}$$

$$= 3(-1)^{1+1}\begin{vmatrix} 3 & 1 \\ 4 & -6 \end{vmatrix} + 1 \cdot (-1)^{1+2}\begin{vmatrix} -2 & 1 \\ 3 & -6 \end{vmatrix} + 2(-1)^{1+3}\begin{vmatrix} -2 & 3 \\ 3 & 4 \end{vmatrix}$$

$$= 3 \cdot 1[3(-6) - 4 \cdot 1] + 1(-1)[-2(-6) - 3 \cdot 1] + 2 \cdot 1(-2 \cdot 4 - 3 \cdot 3)$$

$$= 3(-22) - (9) + 2(-17)$$

$$= -109$$

7. We will expand down the second column. We could have chosen any other row or column just as well.

$$\begin{vmatrix} x & 0 & -1 \\ 2 & x & x^2 \\ -3 & x & 1 \end{vmatrix}$$

$$= 0(-1)^{1+2}\begin{vmatrix} 2 & x^2 \\ -3 & 1 \end{vmatrix} + x(-1)^{2+2}\begin{vmatrix} x & -1 \\ -3 & 1 \end{vmatrix} +$$

$$x(-1)^{3+2}\begin{vmatrix} x & -1 \\ 2 & x^2 \end{vmatrix}$$

$$= 0(-1)[2\cdot 1-(-3)x^2]+x\cdot 1[x\cdot 1-(-3)(-1)]+$$
$$x(-1)[x\cdot x^2 - 2(-1)]$$
$$= 0 + x(x-3) - x(x^3+2)$$
$$= x^2 - 3x - x^4 - 2x = -x^4 + x^2 - 5x$$

9. $\mathbf{A} = \begin{bmatrix} 7 & -4 & -6 \\ 2 & 0 & -3 \\ 1 & 2 & -5 \end{bmatrix}$

M_{11} is the determinant of the matrix formed by deleting the first row and first column of $\mathbf{A}$:

$$M_{11} = \begin{vmatrix} 0 & -3 \\ 2 & -5 \end{vmatrix} = 0(-5) - 2(-3) = 0 + 6 = 6$$

M_{32} is the determinant of the matrix formed by deleting the third row and second column of $\mathbf{A}$:

$$M_{32} = \begin{vmatrix} 7 & -6 \\ 2 & -3 \end{vmatrix} = 7(-3) - 2(-6) = -21 + 12 = -9$$

M_{22} is the determinant of the matrix formed by deleting the second row and second column of $\mathbf{A}$:

$$M_{22} = \begin{vmatrix} 7 & -6 \\ 1 & -5 \end{vmatrix} = 7(-5) - 1(-6) = -35 + 6 = -29$$

11. In Exercise 9 we found that $M_{11} = 6$.

$A_{11} = (-1)^{1+1}M_{11} = 1\cdot 6 = 6$

In Exercise 9 we found that $M_{32} = -9$.

$A_{32} = (-1)^{3+2}M_{32} = -1(-9) = 9$

In Exercise 9 we found that $M_{22} = -29$.

$A_{22} = (-1)^{2+2}(-29) = 1(-29) = -29$

13. $\mathbf{A} = \begin{bmatrix} 7 & -4 & -6 \\ 2 & 0 & -3 \\ 1 & 2 & -5 \end{bmatrix}$

$$|\mathbf{A}|$$
$$= 2A_{21} + 0A_{22} + (-3)A_{23}$$
$$= 2(-1)^{2+1}\begin{vmatrix} -4 & -6 \\ 2 & -5 \end{vmatrix} + 0 + (-3)(-1)^{2+3}\begin{vmatrix} 7 & -4 \\ 1 & 2 \end{vmatrix}$$
$$= 2(-1)[-4(-5) - 2(-6)] + 0 +$$
$$(-3)(-1)[7\cdot 2 - 1(-4)]$$
$$= -2(32) + 0 + 3(18) = -64 + 0 + 54$$
$$= -10$$

15. $\mathbf{A} = \begin{bmatrix} 7 & -4 & -6 \\ 2 & 0 & -3 \\ 1 & 2 & -5 \end{bmatrix}$

$$|\mathbf{A}|$$
$$= -6A_{13} + (-3)A_{23} + (-5)A_{33}$$
$$= -6(-1)^{1+3}\begin{vmatrix} 2 & 0 \\ 1 & 2 \end{vmatrix} + (-3)(-1)^{2+3}\begin{vmatrix} 7 & -4 \\ 1 & 2 \end{vmatrix} +$$
$$(-5)(-1)^{3+3}\begin{vmatrix} 7 & -4 \\ 2 & 0 \end{vmatrix}$$
$$= -6\cdot 1(2\cdot 2 - 1\cdot 0) + (-3)(-1)[7\cdot 2 - 1(-4)] +$$
$$-5\cdot 1(7\cdot 0 - 2(-4))$$
$$= -6(4) + 3(18) - 5(8) = -24 + 54 - 40$$
$$= -10$$

17. $\mathbf{A} = \begin{bmatrix} 1 & 0 & 0 & -2 \\ 4 & 1 & 0 & 0 \\ 5 & 6 & 7 & 8 \\ -2 & -3 & -1 & 0 \end{bmatrix}$

M_{41} is the determinant of the matrix formed by deleting the fourth row and the first column of $\mathbf{A}$.

$$M_{41} = \begin{bmatrix} 0 & 0 & -2 \\ 1 & 0 & 0 \\ 6 & 7 & 8 \end{bmatrix}$$

We will expand M_{41} across the first row.

$$M_{41} = 0(-1)^{1+1}\begin{vmatrix} 0 & 0 \\ 7 & 8 \end{vmatrix} + 0(-1)^{1+2}\begin{vmatrix} 1 & 0 \\ 6 & 8 \end{vmatrix} +$$
$$(-2)(-1)^{3+1}\begin{vmatrix} 1 & 0 \\ 6 & 7 \end{vmatrix}$$
$$= 0 + 0 + (-2)(1)(1\cdot 7 - 6\cdot 0)$$
$$= 0 + 0 - 2(7) = -14$$

M_{33} is the determinant of the matrix formed by deleting the third row and the third column of $\mathbf{A}$.

$$M_{33} = \begin{bmatrix} 1 & 0 & -2 \\ 4 & 1 & 0 \\ -2 & -3 & 0 \end{bmatrix}$$

We will expand M_{33} down the third column.

$$M_{33} = -2(-1)^{1+3}\begin{vmatrix} 4 & 1 \\ -2 & -3 \end{vmatrix} + 0(-1)^{2+3}\begin{vmatrix} 1 & 0 \\ -2 & -3 \end{vmatrix} +$$
$$0(-1)^{3+3}\begin{vmatrix} 1 & 0 \\ 4 & 1 \end{vmatrix}$$
$$= -2(1)[4(-3) - (-2)(1)] + 0 + 0$$
$$= -2(-10) + 0 + 0 = 20$$

19. $\mathbf{A} = \begin{bmatrix} 1 & 0 & 0 & -2 \\ 4 & 1 & 0 & 0 \\ 5 & 6 & 7 & 8 \\ -2 & -3 & -1 & 0 \end{bmatrix}$

$$A_{24} = (-1)^{2+4}M_{24} = 1\cdot M_{24} = M_{24}$$
$$= \begin{vmatrix} 1 & 0 & 0 \\ 5 & 6 & 7 \\ -2 & -3 & -1 \end{vmatrix}$$

We will expand across the first row.

$$\begin{vmatrix} 1 & 0 & 0 \\ 5 & 6 & 7 \\ -2 & -3 & -1 \end{vmatrix}$$

$$= 1(-1)^{1+1}\begin{vmatrix} 6 & 7 \\ -3 & -1 \end{vmatrix} + 0(-1)^{1+2}\begin{vmatrix} 5 & 7 \\ -2 & -1 \end{vmatrix} +$$

$$0(-1)^{1+3}\begin{vmatrix} 5 & 6 \\ -2 & -3 \end{vmatrix}$$

$$= 1 \cdot 1[6(-1) - (-3)(7)] + 0 + 0$$

$$= 1(15) = 15$$

$$A_{43} = (-1)^{4+3}M_{43} = -1 \cdot M_{43}$$

$$= -1 \cdot \begin{vmatrix} 1 & 0 & -2 \\ 4 & 1 & 0 \\ 5 & 6 & 8 \end{vmatrix}$$

We will expand across the first row.

$$-1 \cdot \begin{vmatrix} 1 & 0 & -2 \\ 4 & 1 & 0 \\ 5 & 6 & 8 \end{vmatrix}$$

$$= -1\Bigg[1(-1)^{1+1}\begin{vmatrix} 1 & 0 \\ 6 & 8 \end{vmatrix} + 0(-1)^{1+2}\begin{vmatrix} 4 & 0 \\ 5 & 8 \end{vmatrix} +$$

$$(-2)(-1)^{1+3}\begin{vmatrix} 4 & 1 \\ 5 & 6 \end{vmatrix}\Bigg]$$

$$= -1[1 \cdot 1(1 \cdot 8 - 6 \cdot 0) + 0 + (-2) \cdot 1(4 \cdot 6 - 5 \cdot 1)]$$

$$= -1[1(8) + 0 - 2(19)]$$

$$= -1(8 - 38) = -1(-30)$$

$$= 30$$

21. $\mathbf{A} = \begin{bmatrix} 1 & 0 & 0 & -2 \\ 4 & 1 & 0 & 0 \\ 5 & 6 & 7 & 8 \\ -2 & -3 & -1 & 0 \end{bmatrix}$

$|\mathbf{A}|$

$$= 1 \cdot A_{11} + 0 \cdot A_{12} + 0 \cdot A_{13} + (-2)A_{14}$$

$$= A_{11} + (-2)A_{14}$$

$$= (-1)^{1+1}\begin{vmatrix} 1 & 0 & 0 \\ 6 & 7 & 8 \\ -3 & -1 & 0 \end{vmatrix} +$$

$$(-2)(-1)^{1+4}\begin{vmatrix} 4 & 1 & 0 \\ 5 & 6 & 7 \\ -2 & -3 & -1 \end{vmatrix}$$

$$= \begin{vmatrix} 1 & 0 & 0 \\ 6 & 7 & 8 \\ -3 & -1 & 0 \end{vmatrix} + 2\begin{vmatrix} 4 & 1 & 0 \\ 5 & 6 & 7 \\ -2 & -3 & -1 \end{vmatrix}$$

We will expand each determinant across the first row. We have:

$$1(-1)^{1+1}\begin{vmatrix} 7 & 8 \\ -1 & 0 \end{vmatrix} + 0 + 0 +$$

$$2\left[4(-1)^{1+1}\begin{vmatrix} 6 & 7 \\ -3 & -1 \end{vmatrix} + 1(-1)^{1+2}\begin{vmatrix} 5 & 7 \\ -2 & -1 \end{vmatrix} + 0\right]$$

$$= 1 \cdot 1[7 \cdot 0 - (-1)8] + 2[4 \cdot 1[6(-1) - (-3) \cdot 7] +$$

$$1(-1)[5(-1) - (-2) \cdot 7]$$

$$= 1(8) + 2[4(15) - 1(9)] = 8 + 2(51)$$

$$= 8 + 102 = 110$$

23. $-2x + 4y = 3,$

$3x - 7y = 1$

$$D = \begin{vmatrix} -2 & 4 \\ 3 & -7 \end{vmatrix} = -2(-7) - 3 \cdot 4 = 14 - 12 = 2$$

$$D_x = \begin{vmatrix} 3 & 4 \\ 1 & -7 \end{vmatrix} = 3(-7) - 1 \cdot 4 = -21 - 4 = -25$$

$$D_y = \begin{vmatrix} -2 & 3 \\ 3 & 1 \end{vmatrix} = -2 \cdot 1 - 3 \cdot 3 = -2 - 9 = -11$$

$$x = \frac{D_x}{D} = \frac{-25}{2} = -\frac{25}{2}$$

$$y = \frac{D_y}{D} = \frac{-11}{2} = -\frac{11}{2}$$

The solution is $\left(-\frac{25}{2}, -\frac{11}{2}\right)$.

25. $2x - y = 5,$

$x - 2y = 1$

$$D = \begin{vmatrix} 2 & -1 \\ 1 & -2 \end{vmatrix} = 2(-2) - 1(-1) = -4 + 1 = -3$$

$$D_x = \begin{vmatrix} 5 & -1 \\ 1 & -2 \end{vmatrix} = 5(-2) - 1(-1) = -10 + 1 = -9$$

$$D_y = \begin{vmatrix} 2 & 5 \\ 1 & 1 \end{vmatrix} = 2 \cdot 1 - 1 \cdot 5 = 2 - 5 = -3$$

$$x = \frac{D_x}{D} = \frac{-9}{-3} = 3$$

$$y = \frac{D_y}{D} = \frac{-3}{-3} = 1$$

The solution is $(3, 1)$.

27. $2x + 9y = -2,$

$4x - 3y = 3$

$$D = \begin{vmatrix} 2 & 9 \\ 4 & -3 \end{vmatrix} = 2(-3) - 4 \cdot 9 = -6 - 36 = -42$$

$$D_x = \begin{vmatrix} -2 & 9 \\ 3 & -3 \end{vmatrix} = -2(-3) - 3 \cdot 9 = 6 - 27 = -21$$

$$D_y = \begin{vmatrix} 2 & -2 \\ 4 & 3 \end{vmatrix} = 2 \cdot 3 - 4(-2) = 6 + 8 = 14$$

$$x = \frac{D_x}{D} = \frac{-21}{-42} = \frac{1}{2}$$
$$y = \frac{D_y}{D} = \frac{14}{-42} = -\frac{1}{3}$$

The solution is $\left(\frac{1}{2}, -\frac{1}{3}\right)$.

29. $2x + 5y = 7,$
$3x - 2y = 1$

$$D = \begin{vmatrix} 2 & 5 \\ 3 & -2 \end{vmatrix} = 2(-2) - 3 \cdot 5 = -4 - 15 = -19$$

$$D_x = \begin{vmatrix} 7 & 5 \\ 1 & -2 \end{vmatrix} = 7(-2) - 1 \cdot 5 = -14 - 5 = -19$$

$$D_y = \begin{vmatrix} 2 & 7 \\ 3 & 1 \end{vmatrix} = 2 \cdot 1 - 3 \cdot 7 = 2 - 21 = -19$$

$$x = \frac{D_x}{D} = \frac{-19}{-19} = 1$$
$$y = \frac{D_y}{D} = \frac{-19}{-19} = 1$$

The solution is $(1, 1)$.

31. $3x + 2y - z = 4,$
$3x - 2y + z = 5,$
$4x - 5y - z = -1$

$$D = \begin{vmatrix} 3 & 2 & -1 \\ 3 & -2 & 1 \\ 4 & -5 & -1 \end{vmatrix} = 42$$

$$D_x = \begin{vmatrix} 4 & 2 & -1 \\ 5 & -2 & 1 \\ -1 & -5 & -1 \end{vmatrix} = 63$$

$$D_y = \begin{vmatrix} 3 & 4 & -1 \\ 3 & 5 & 1 \\ 4 & -1 & -1 \end{vmatrix} = 39$$

$$D_z = \begin{vmatrix} 3 & 2 & 4 \\ 3 & -2 & 5 \\ 4 & -5 & -1 \end{vmatrix} = 99$$

$$x = \frac{D_x}{D} = \frac{63}{42} = \frac{3}{2}$$

$$y = \frac{D_y}{D} = \frac{39}{42} = \frac{13}{14}$$

$$z = \frac{D_z}{D} = \frac{99}{42} = \frac{33}{14}$$

The solution is $\left(\frac{3}{2}, \frac{13}{14}, \frac{33}{14}\right)$.

(Note that we could have used Cramer's rule to find only two of the values and then used substitution to find the remaining value.)

33. $3x + 5y - z = -2,$
$x - 4y + 2z = 13,$
$2x + 4y + 3z = 1$

$$D = \begin{vmatrix} 3 & 5 & -1 \\ 1 & -4 & 2 \\ 2 & 4 & 3 \end{vmatrix} = -67$$

$$D_x = \begin{vmatrix} -2 & 5 & -1 \\ 13 & -4 & 2 \\ 1 & 4 & 3 \end{vmatrix} = -201$$

$$D_y = \begin{vmatrix} 3 & -2 & -1 \\ 1 & 13 & 2 \\ 2 & 1 & 3 \end{vmatrix} = 134$$

$$D_z = \begin{vmatrix} 3 & 5 & -2 \\ 1 & -4 & 13 \\ 2 & 4 & 1 \end{vmatrix} = -67$$

$$x = \frac{D_x}{D} = \frac{-201}{-67} = 3$$

$$y = \frac{D_y}{D} = \frac{134}{-67} = -2$$

$$z = \frac{D_z}{D} = \frac{-67}{-67} = 1$$

The solution is $(3, -2, 1)$.

(Note that we could have used Cramer's rule to find only two of the values and then used substitution to find the remaining value.)

35. $x - 3y - 7z = 6,$
$2x + 3y + z = 9,$
$4x + y = 7$

$$D = \begin{vmatrix} 1 & -3 & -7 \\ 2 & 3 & 1 \\ 4 & 1 & 0 \end{vmatrix} = 57$$

$$D_x = \begin{vmatrix} 6 & -3 & -7 \\ 9 & 3 & 1 \\ 7 & 1 & 0 \end{vmatrix} = 57$$

$$D_y = \begin{vmatrix} 1 & 6 & -7 \\ 2 & 9 & 1 \\ 4 & 7 & 0 \end{vmatrix} = 171$$

$$D_z = \begin{vmatrix} 1 & -3 & 6 \\ 2 & 3 & 9 \\ 4 & 1 & 7 \end{vmatrix} = -114$$

$$x = \frac{D_x}{D} = \frac{57}{57} = 1$$

$$y = \frac{D_y}{D} = \frac{171}{57} = 3$$

$$z = \frac{D_z}{D} = \frac{-114}{57} = -2$$

The solution is $(1, 3, -2)$.

(Note that we could have used Cramer's rule to find only two of the values and then used substitution to find the remaining value.)

37.
$$\begin{aligned} 6y + 6z &= -1, \\ 8x \qquad + 6z &= -1, \\ 4x + 9y \qquad &= 8 \end{aligned}$$

$$D = \begin{vmatrix} 0 & 6 & 6 \\ 8 & 0 & 6 \\ 4 & 9 & 0 \end{vmatrix} = 576$$

$$D_x = \begin{vmatrix} -1 & 6 & 6 \\ -1 & 0 & 6 \\ 8 & 9 & 0 \end{vmatrix} = 288$$

$$D_y = \begin{vmatrix} 0 & -1 & 6 \\ 8 & -1 & 6 \\ 4 & 8 & 0 \end{vmatrix} = 384$$

$$D_z = \begin{vmatrix} 0 & 6 & -1 \\ 8 & 0 & -1 \\ 4 & 9 & 8 \end{vmatrix} = -480$$

$$x = \frac{D_x}{D} = \frac{288}{576} = \frac{1}{2}$$

$$y = \frac{D_y}{D} = \frac{384}{576} = \frac{2}{3}$$

$$z = \frac{D_z}{D} = \frac{-480}{576} = -\frac{5}{6}$$

The solution is $\left(\frac{1}{2}, \frac{2}{3}, -\frac{5}{6}\right)$.

(Note that we could have used Cramer's rule to find only two of the values and then used substitution to find the remaining value.)

39. Left to the student

41. Enter matrix **A** and use the "det(" option from the MATRIX MATH menu.

$|\mathbf{A}| = 110$

43. Left to the student

45. Discussion and Writing

47. The graph of $f(x) = 3x+2$ is shown below. Since it passes the horizontal-line test, the function is one-to-one.

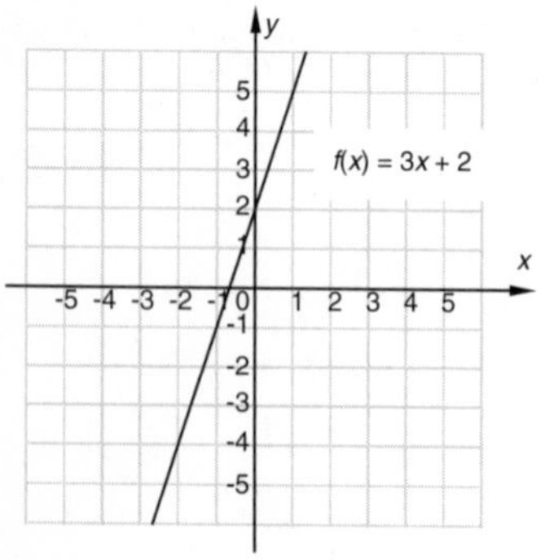

We find a formula for $f^{-1}(x)$.

Replace $f(x)$ with y: $y = 3x + 2$

Interchange x and y: $x = 3y + 2$

Solve for y: $y = \frac{x-2}{3}$

Replace y with $f^{-1}(x)$: $f^{-1}(x) = \frac{x-2}{3}$

49. The graph of $f(x) = |x| + 3$ is shown below. It fails the horizontal-line test, so it is not one-to-one.

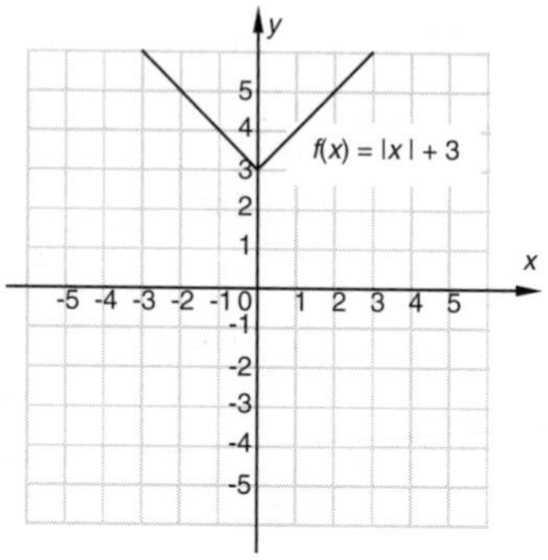

51. $(3-4i) - (-2-i) = 3 - 4i + 2 + i =$
$(3+2) + (-4+1)i = 5 - 3i$

53. $(1-2i)(6+2i) = 6 + 2i - 12i - 4i^2 =$
$6 + 2i - 12i + 4 = 10 - 10i$

55.
$$\begin{vmatrix} x & 5 \\ -4 & x \end{vmatrix} = 24$$

$x \cdot x - (-4)(5) = 24$ Evaluating the determinant

$$\begin{aligned} x^2 + 20 &= 24 \\ x^2 &= 4 \\ x &= \pm 2 \end{aligned}$$

The solutions are -2 and 2.

57.
$$\begin{vmatrix} x & -3 \\ -1 & x \end{vmatrix} \geq 0$$

$$\begin{aligned} x \cdot x - (-1)(-3) &\geq 0 \\ x^2 - 3 &\geq 0 \end{aligned}$$

We solve the related equation.

$$\begin{aligned} x^2 - 3 &= 0 \\ x^2 &= 3 \\ x &= \pm\sqrt{3} \end{aligned}$$

The numbers $-\sqrt{3}$ and $\sqrt{3}$ divide the x-axis into three intervals. We let $f(x) = x^2 - 3$ and test a value in each interval.

$(-\infty, -\sqrt{3}):\ f(-2) = (-2)^2 - 3 = 1 > 0$

$(-\sqrt{3}, \sqrt{3}):\ f(0) = 0^2 - 3 = -3 < 0$

$(\sqrt{3}, \infty):\ f(2) = 2^2 - 3 = 1 > 0$

The function is positive in $(-\infty, -\sqrt{3})$, and $(\sqrt{3}, \infty)$. We also include the endpoints of the intervals since the inequality symbol is $\geq$. The solution set is $\{x | x \leq -\sqrt{3} \text{ or } x \geq \sqrt{3}\}$, or $(-\infty, -\sqrt{3}] \cup [\sqrt{3}, \infty)$.

59. $$\begin{vmatrix} x+3 & 4 \\ x-3 & 5 \end{vmatrix} = -7$$

$$(x+3)(5)-(x-3)(4) = -7$$
$$5x+15-4x+12 = -7$$
$$x+27 = -7$$
$$x = -34$$

The solution is -34.

61. $$\begin{vmatrix} 2 & x & 1 \\ 1 & 2 & -1 \\ 3 & 4 & -2 \end{vmatrix} = -6$$

$$-x-2 = -6 \quad \text{Evaluating the determinant}$$
$$-x = -4$$
$$x = 4$$

The solution is 4.

63. Answers may vary.

$$\begin{vmatrix} L & -W \\ 2 & 2 \end{vmatrix}$$

65. Answers may vary.

$$\begin{vmatrix} a & b \\ -b & a \end{vmatrix}$$

67. Answers may vary.

$$\begin{vmatrix} 2\pi r & 2\pi r \\ -h & r \end{vmatrix}$$

Exercise Set 5.7

1. Graph (f) is the graph of $y > x$.

3. Graph (h) is the graph of $y \leq x-3$.

5. Graph (g) is the graph of $2x+y<4$.

7. Graph (b) is the graph of $2x-5y>10$.

9. Graph: $y > 2x$

1. We first graph the related equation $y = 2x$. We draw the line dashed since the inequality symbol is $>$.
2. To determine which half-plane to shade, test a point not on the line. We try $(1,1)$ and substitute:

$$\begin{array}{c|c} \multicolumn{2}{c}{y > 2x} \\ \hline 1 & 2\cdot 1 \\ 1 & 2 \end{array} \quad \text{FALSE}$$

Since $1 > 2$ is false, $(1,1)$ is not a solution, nor are any points in the half-plane containing $(1,1)$. The points in the opposite half-plane are solutions, so we shade that half-plane and obtain the graph.

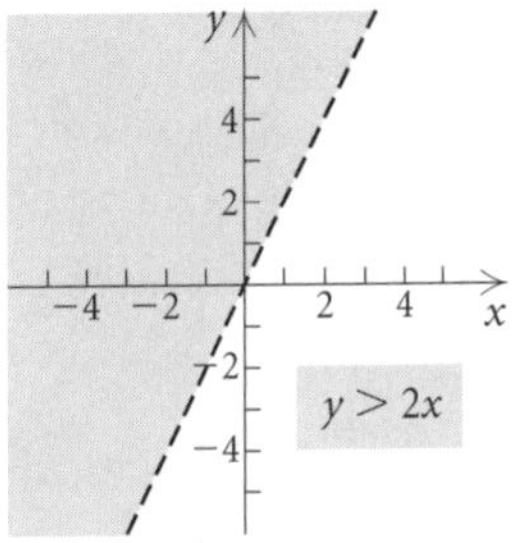

11. Graph: $y + x \geq 0$

1. First graph the related equation $y + x = 0$. Draw the line solid since the inequality is $\geq$.
2. Next determine which half-plane to shade by testing a point not on the line. Here we use $(2,2)$ as a check.

$$\begin{array}{c|c} \multicolumn{2}{c}{y+x \geq 0} \\ \hline 2+2 & 0 \\ 4 & 0 \end{array} \quad \text{TRUE}$$

Since $4 \geq 0$ is true, $(2,2)$ is a solution. Thus shade the half-plane containing $(2,2)$.

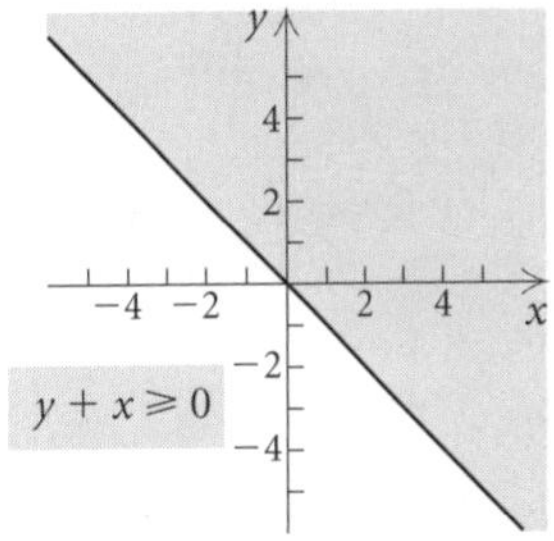

13. Graph: $y > x-3$

1. We first graph the related equation $y = x-3$. Draw the line dashed since the inequality symbol is $>$.
2. To determine which half-plane to shade, test a point not on the line. We try $(0,0)$.

$$\begin{array}{c|c} \multicolumn{2}{c}{y > x-3} \\ \hline 0 & 0-3 \\ 0 & -3 \end{array} \quad \text{TRUE}$$

Since $0 > -3$ is true, $(0,0)$ is a solution. Thus we shade the half-plane containing $(0,0)$.

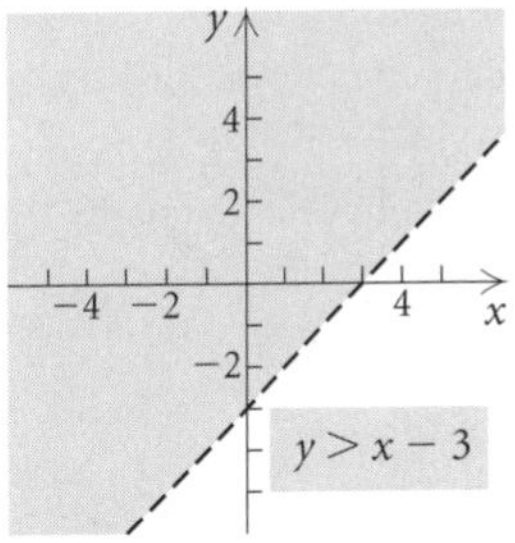

15. Graph: $x + y < 4$

1. First graph the related equation $x + y = 4$. Draw the line dashed since the inequality is $<$.
2. To determine which half-plane to shade, test a point not on the line. We try $(0, 0)$.

$$\begin{array}{r|l} \multicolumn{2}{c}{x + y < 4} \\ \hline 0 + 0 & ?\ 4 \\ 0 & 4 \ \text{TRUE} \end{array}$$

Since $0 < 4$ is true, $(0, 0)$ is a solution. Thus shade the half-plane containing $(0, 0)$.

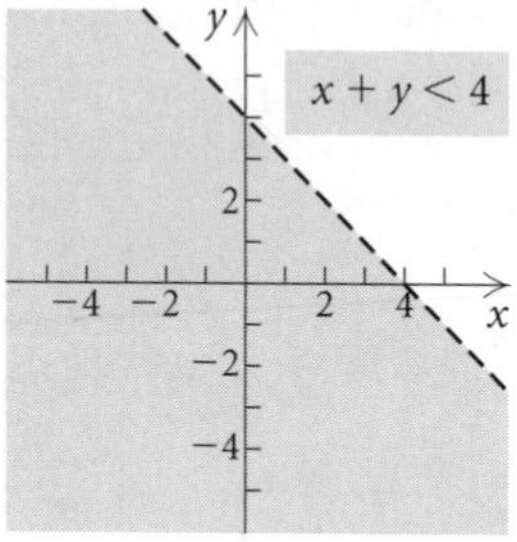

17. Graph: $3x - 2y \leq 6$

1. First graph the related equation $3x - 2y = 6$. Draw the line solid since the inequality is $\leq$.
2. To determine which half-plane to shade, test a point not on the line. We try $(0, 0)$.

$$\begin{array}{r|l} \multicolumn{2}{c}{3x - 2y \leq 6} \\ \hline 3(0) - 2(0) & ?\ 6 \\ 0 & 6 \ \text{TRUE} \end{array}$$

Since $0 \leq 6$ is true, $(0, 0)$ is a solution. Thus shade the half-plane containing $(0, 0)$.

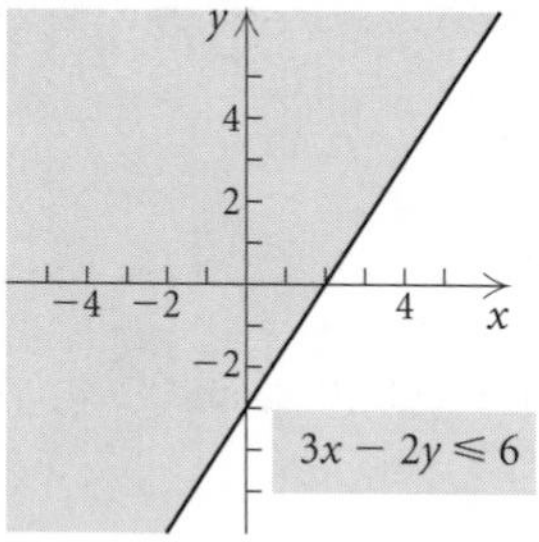

19. Graph: $3y + 2x \geq 6$

1. First graph the related equation $3y + 2x = 6$. Draw the line solid since the inequality is $\geq$.
2. To determine which half-plane to shade, test a point not on the line. We try $(0, 0)$.

$$\begin{array}{r|l} \multicolumn{2}{c}{3y + 2x \geq 6} \\ \hline 3 \cdot 0 + 2 \cdot 0 & ?\ 6 \\ 0 & 6 \ \text{FALSE} \end{array}$$

Since $0 \geq 6$ is false, $(0, 0)$ is not a solution. We shade the half-plane which does not contain $(0, 0)$.

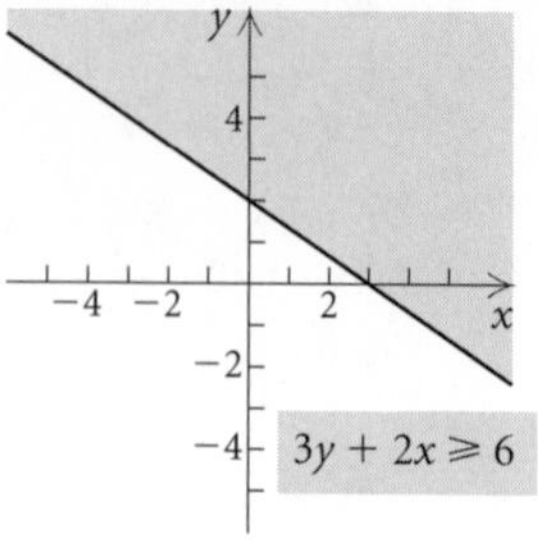

21. Graph: $3x - 2 \leq 5x + y$

$$-2 \leq 2x + y \quad \text{Adding } -3x$$

1. First graph the related equation $2x + y = -2$. Draw the line solid since the inequality is $\leq$.
2. To determine which half-plane to shade, test a point not on the line. We try $(0, 0)$.

$$\begin{array}{r|l} \multicolumn{2}{c}{2x + y \geq -2} \\ \hline 2(0) + 0 & ?\ -2 \\ 0 & -2 \ \text{TRUE} \end{array}$$

Since $0 \geq -2$ is true, $(0, 0)$ is a solution. Thus shade the half-plane containing the origin.

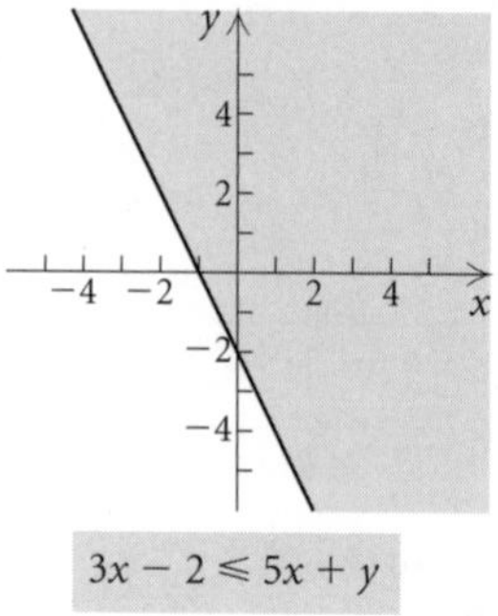

23. Graph: $x < -4$

1. We first graph the related equation $x = -4$. Draw the line dashed since the inequality is $<$.
2. To determine which half-plane to shade, test a point not on the line. We try $(0, 0)$.

$$\begin{array}{l} x < -4 \\ \hline 0\ ?\ -4 \ \text{FALSE} \end{array}$$

Since $0 < -4$ is false, $(0, 0)$ is not a solution. Thus, we shade the half-plane which does not contain the origin.

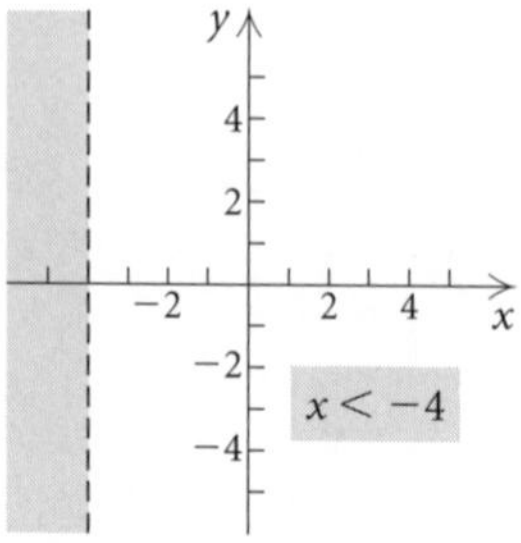

25. Graph: $y > -3$

1. First we graph the related equation $y = -3$. Draw the line dashed since the inequality is $>$.
2. To determine which half-plane to shade we test a point not on the line. We try $(0, 0)$.

   $$\begin{array}{c|c} y > -3 & \\ \hline 0 \ ? \ -3 & \text{TRUE} \end{array}$$

   Since $0 > -3$ is true, $(0, 0)$ is a solution. We shade the half-plane containing $(0, 0)$.

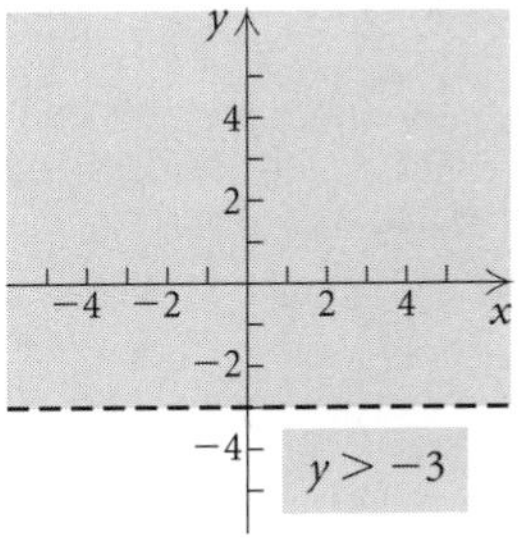

27. Graph: $-4 < y < -1$

This is a conjunction of two inequalities

$4 < y$ *and* $y < -1$.

We can graph $-4 < y$ and $y < -1$ separately and then graph the intersection, or region in both solution sets.

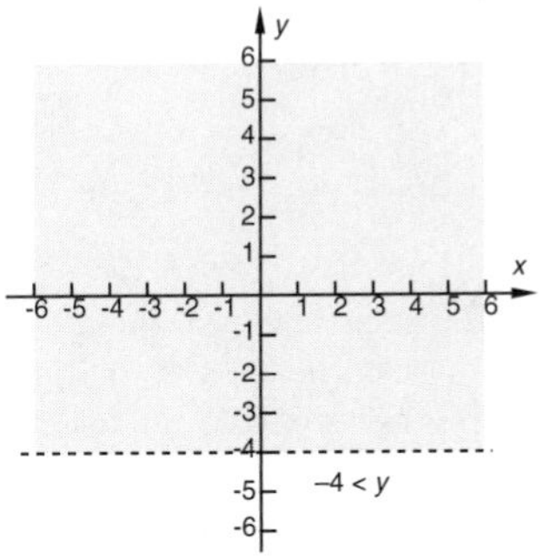

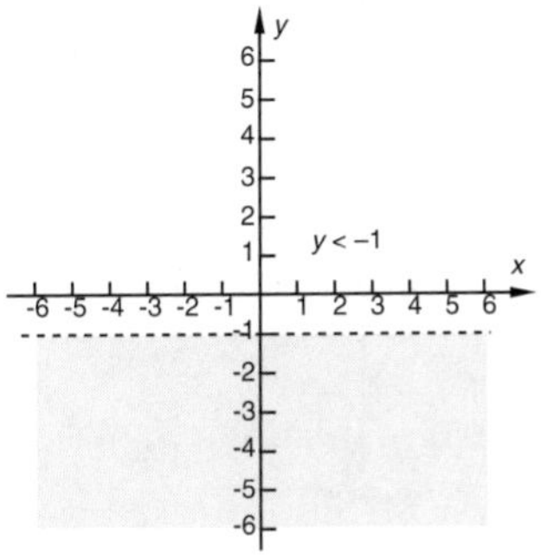

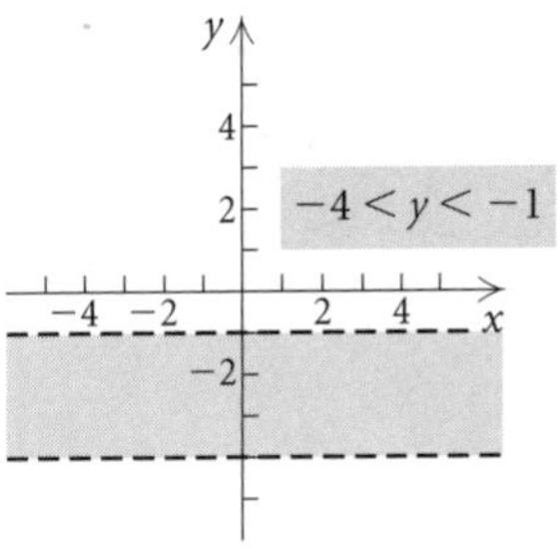

29. Graph: $y \geq |x|$

1. Graph the related equation $y = |x|$. Draw the line solid since the inequality symbol is $\geq$.
2. To determine the region to shade, observe that the solution set consists of all ordered pairs (x, y) where the second coordinate is greater than or equal to the absolute value of the first coordinate. We see that the solutions are the points on or above the graph of $y = |x|$.

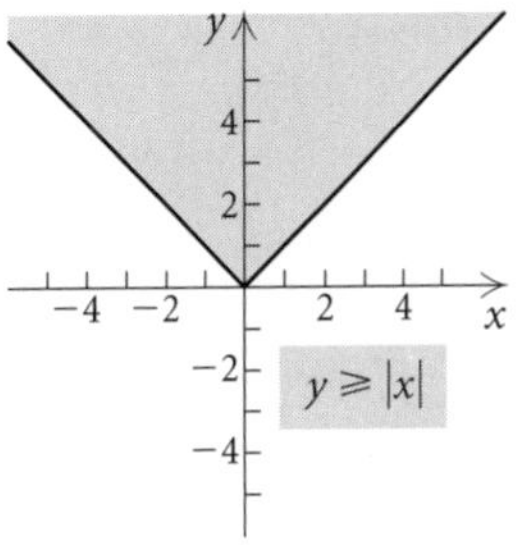

31. Graph (f) is the correct graph.

33. Graph (a) is the correct graph.

35. Graph (b) is the correct graph.

37. First we find the related equations. One line goes through $(0, 4)$ and $(4, 0)$. We find its slope:

$$m = \frac{0-4}{4-0} = \frac{-4}{4} = -1$$

This line has slope -1 and y-intercept $(0, 4)$, so its equation is $y = -x + 4$.

The other line goes through $(0, 0)$ and $(1, 3)$. We find the slope.

$$m = \frac{3-0}{1-0} = 3$$

This line has slope 3 and y-intercept $(0, 0)$, so its equation is $y = 3x + 0$, or $y = 3x$.

Observing the shading on the graph and the fact that the lines are solid, we can write the system of inqualities as

$$y \leq -x + 4,$$
$$y \leq 3x.$$

Answers may vary.

39. The equation of the vertical line is $x = 2$ and the equation of the horizontal line is $y = -1$. The lines are dashed and the shaded area is to the left of the vertical line and above the horizontal line, so the system of inequalities can be written

$$x < 2,$$
$$y > -1.$$

41. First we find the related equations. One line goes through $(0,3)$ and $(3,0)$. We find its slope:

$$m = \frac{0-3}{3-0} = \frac{-3}{3} = -1$$

This line has slope -1 and y-intercept $(0,3)$, so its equation is $y = -x + 3$.

The other line goes through $(0,1)$ and $(1,2)$. We find its slope:

$$m = \frac{2-1}{1-0} = \frac{1}{1} = 1$$

This line has slope 1 and y-intercept $(0,1)$, so its equation is $y = x + 1$.

Observe that both lines are solid and that the shading lies below both lines, to the right of the y-axis, and above the x-axis. We can write this system of inequalities as

$$y \le -x + 3,$$
$$y \le x + 1,$$
$$x \ge 0,$$
$$y \ge 0.$$

43. Graph: $y \le x$,

$\qquad y \ge 3 - x$

We graph the related equations $y = x$ and $y = 3 - x$ using solid lines. The arrows at the ends of the lines indicate the half-plane containing the solution set for each inequality. Shade the region common to both solution sets.

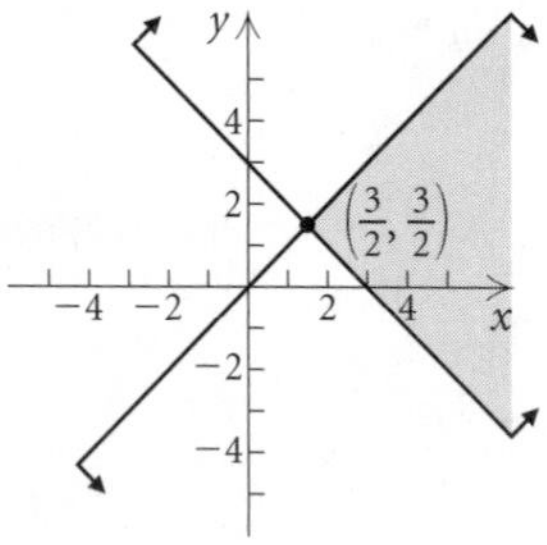

We find the vertex $\left(\frac{3}{2}, \frac{3}{2}\right)$ by solving the system

$$y = x,$$
$$y = 3 - x.$$

45. Graph: $y \ge x$,

$\qquad y \le x - 4$

We graph the related equations $y = x$ and $y = x - 4$ using solid lines. The arrows at the ends of the lines indicate the half-plane containing the solution set for each inequality. There is not a region common to both solution sets, so there are no vertices.

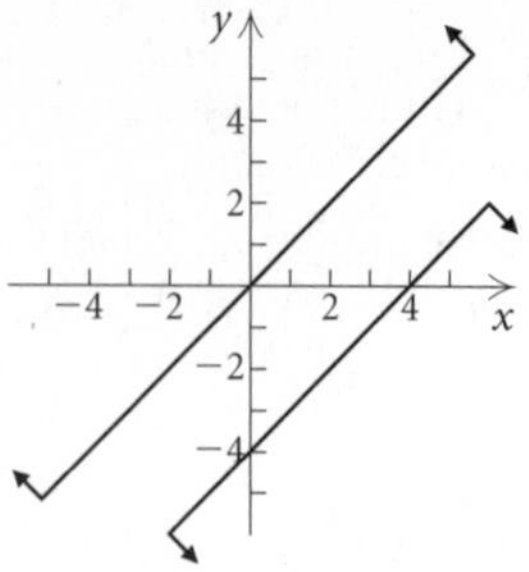

47. Graph: $y \ge -3$,

$\qquad x \ge 1$

We graph the related equations $y = -3$ and $x = 1$ using solid lines. The arrows at the ends of the lines indicate the half-plane containing the solution set for each inequality. Shade the region common to both solution sets.

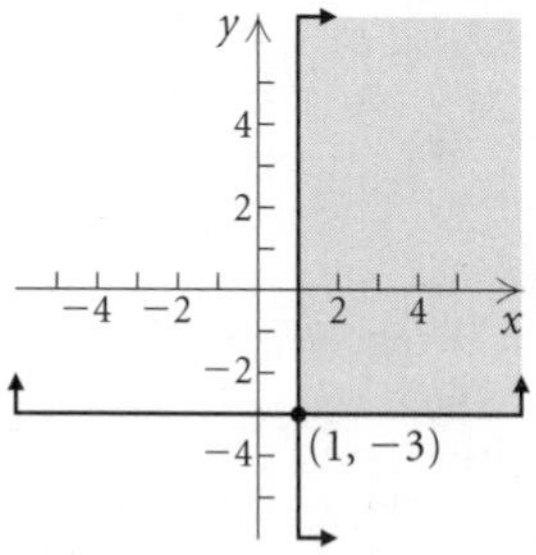

We find the vertex $(1, -3)$ by solving the system

$$y = -3,$$
$$x = 1.$$

49. Graph: $x \le 3$,

$\qquad y \ge 2 - 3x$

We graph the related equations $x = 3$ and $y = 2 - 3x$ using solid lines. The arrows at the ends of the lines indicate the half-plane containing the solution set for each inequality. Shade the region common to both solution sets.

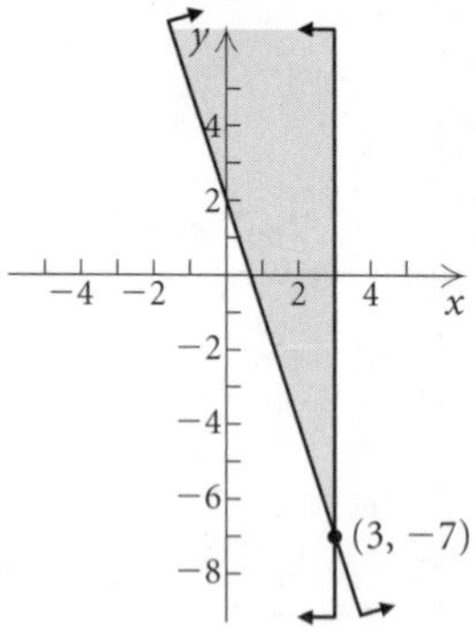

We find the vertex $(3, -7)$ by solving the system

$$x = 3,$$
$$y = 2 - 3x.$$

51. Graph: $x + y \le 1$,

$\qquad x - y \le 2$

We graph the related equations $x + y = 1$ and $x - y = 2$ using solid lines. The arrows at the ends of the lines indicate the half-plane containing the solution set for each inequality. Shade the region common to both solution sets.

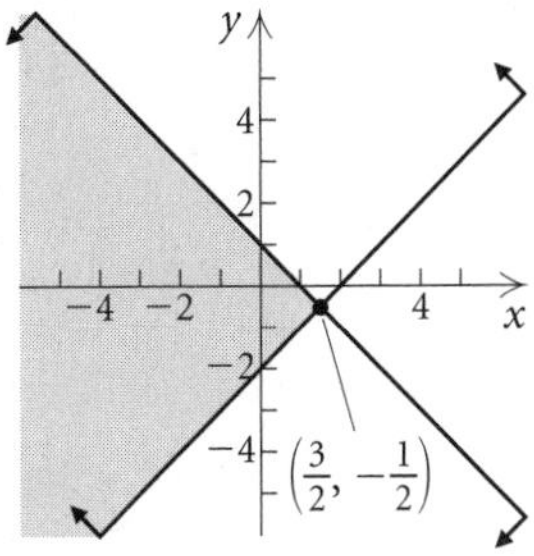

We find the vertex $\left(\frac{3}{2}, -\frac{1}{2}\right)$ by solving the system

$$x + y = 1,$$
$$x - y = 2.$$

53. Graph: $2y - x \le 2$,

$$y + 3x \ge -1$$

We graph the related equations $2y - x = 2$ and $y + 3x = -1$ using solid lines. The arrows at the ends of the lines indicate the half-plane containing the solution set for each inequality. Shade the region common to both solution sets.

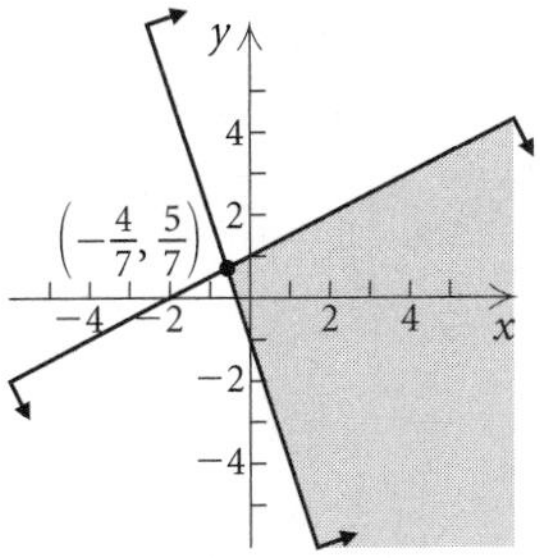

We find the vertex $\left(-\frac{4}{7}, \frac{5}{7}\right)$ by solving the system

$$2y - x = 2,$$
$$y + 3x = -1.$$

55. Graph: $x - y \le 2$,

$$x + 2y \ge 8,$$
$$y \le 4$$

We graph the related equations $x - y = 2$, $x + 2y = 8$, and $y = 4$ using solid lines. The arrows at the ends of the lines indicate the half-plane containing the solution set for each inequality. Shade the region common to all three solution sets.

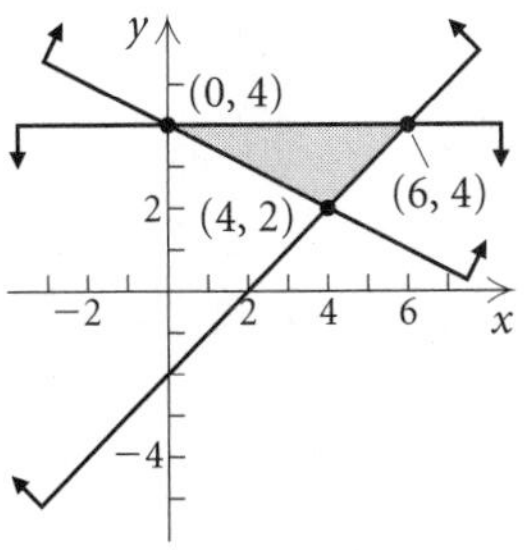

We find the vertex $(0, 4)$ by solving the system

$$x + 2y = 8,$$
$$y = 4.$$

We find the vertex $(6, 4)$ by solving the system

$$x - y = 2,$$
$$y = 4.$$

We find the vertex $(4, 2)$ by solving the system

$$x - y = 2,$$
$$x + 2y = 8.$$

57. Graph: $4x - 3y \ge -12$,

$$4x + 3y \ge -36,$$
$$y \le 0,$$
$$x \le 0$$

Shade the intersection of the graphs of the four inequalities.

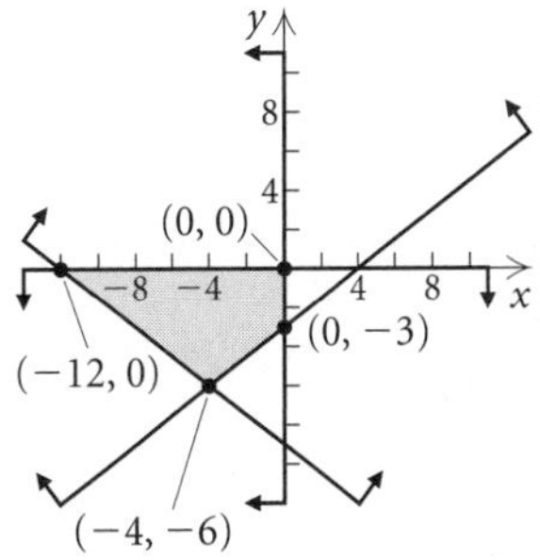

We find the vertex $(-12, 0)$ by solving the system

$$4y + 3x = -36,$$
$$y = 0.$$

We find the vertex $(0, 0)$ by solving the system

$$y = 0,$$
$$x = 0.$$

We find the vertex $(0, -3)$ by solving the system

$$4y - 3x = -12,$$
$$x = 0.$$

We find the vertex $(-4, -6)$ by solving the system

$$4y - 3x = -12,$$
$$4y + 3x = -36.$$

59. Graph: $3x + 4y \ge 12$,

$$5x + 6y \le 30,$$
$$1 \le x \le 3$$

Shade the intersection of the graphs of the given inequalities.

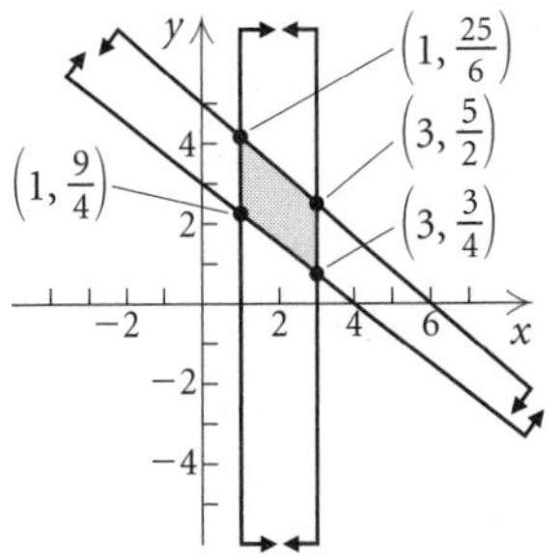

We find the vertex $\left(1, \dfrac{25}{6}\right)$ by solving the system

$$5x + 6y = 30,$$
$$x = 1.$$

We find the vertex $\left(3, \dfrac{5}{2}\right)$ by solving the system

$$5x + 6y = 30,$$
$$x = 3.$$

We find the vertex $\left(3, \dfrac{3}{4}\right)$ by solving the system

$$3x + 4y = 12,$$
$$x = 3.$$

We find the vertex $\left(1, \dfrac{9}{4}\right)$ by solving the system

$$3x + 4y = 12,$$
$$x = 1.$$

61. Find the maximum and minimum values of
$P = 17x - 3y + 60$, subject to

$$6x + 8y \le 48,$$
$$0 \le y \le 4,$$
$$0 \le x \le 3.$$

Graph the system of inequalities and determine the vertices.

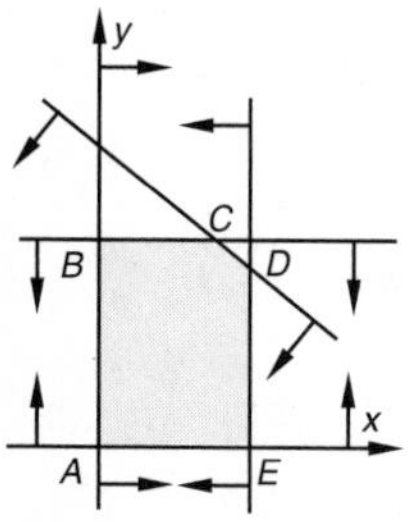

Vertex A: $(0, 0)$

Vertex B:
We solve the system $x = 0$ and $y = 4$. The coordinates of point B are $(0, 4)$.

Vertex C:
We solve the system $6x + 8y = 48$ and $y = 4$. The coordinates of point C are $\left(\dfrac{8}{3}, 4\right)$.

Vertex D:
We solve the system $6x + 8y = 48$ and $y = 7$. The coordinates of point D are $\left(7, \dfrac{3}{4}\right)$.

Vertex E:
We solve the system $x = 7$ and $y = 0$. The coordinates of point E are $(7, 0)$.

Evaluate the objective function P at each vertex.

Vertex	$P = 17x - 3y + 60$
$A(0, 0)$	$17 \cdot 0 - 3 \cdot 0 + 60 = 60$
$B(0, 4)$	$17 \cdot 0 - 3 \cdot 4 + 60 = 48$
$C\left(\dfrac{8}{3}, 3\right)$	$17 \cdot \dfrac{8}{3} - 3 \cdot 4 + 60 = 66\dfrac{2}{3}$
$D\left(7, \dfrac{3}{4}\right)$	$17 \cdot 7 - 3 \cdot \dfrac{3}{4} + 60 = 176\dfrac{3}{4}$
$E(7, 0)$	$17 \cdot 7 - 3 \cdot 0 + 60 = 179$

The maximum value of P is 179 when $x = 7$ and $y = 0$.

The minimum value of P is 48 when $x = 0$ and $y = 4$.

63. Find the maximum and minimum values of
$F = 5x + 36y$, subject to

$$5x + 3y \le 34,$$
$$3x + 5y \le 30,$$
$$x \ge 0,$$
$$y \ge 0.$$

Graph the system of inequalities and find the vertices.

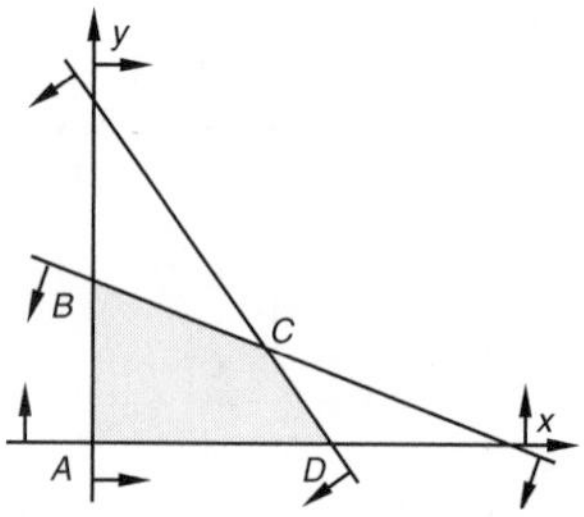

Vertex A: $(0, 0)$

Vertex B:
We solve the system $3x + 5y = 30$ and $x = 0$. The coordinates of point B are $(0, 6)$.

Vertex C:
We solve the system $5x + 3y = 34$ and $3x + 5y = 30$. The coordinates of point C are $(5, 3)$.

Vertex D:
We solve the system $5x + 3y = 34$ and $y = 0$. The coordinates of point D are $\left(\dfrac{34}{5}, 0\right)$.

Evaluate the objective function F at each vertex.

Vertex	$F = 5x + 36y$
$A(0, 0)$	$5 \cdot 0 + 36 \cdot 0 + = 0$
$B(0, 6)$	$5 \cdot 0 + 36 \cdot 6 = 216$
$C(5, 3)$	$5 \cdot 5 + 39 \cdot 3 = 133$
$D\left(\dfrac{34}{5}, 0\right)$	$5 \cdot \dfrac{34}{5} + 36 \cdot 0 = 34$

The maximum value of F is 216 when $x = 0$ and $y = 6$.

The minimum value of F is 0 when $x = 0$ and $y = 0$.

65. Let $x =$ the number of jumbo biscuits and $y =$ the number of regular biscuits to be made per day. The income I is given by

$$I = 0.10x + 0.08y$$

subject to the constrains

$$x + y \le 200,$$
$$2x + y \le 300,$$
$$x \ge 0,$$
$$y \ge 0.$$

We graph the system of inequalities, determine the vertices, and find the value if I at each vertex.

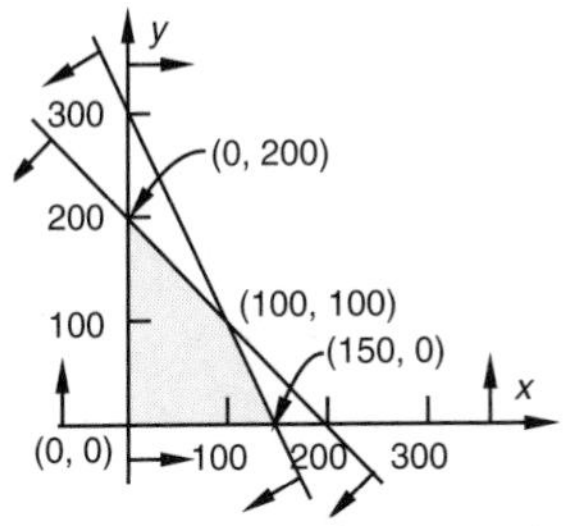

Vertex	$I = 0.10x + 0.08y$
$(0, 0)$	$0.10(0) + 0.08(0) = 0$
$(0, 200)$	$0.10(0) + 0.08(200) = 16$
$(100, 100)$	$0.10(100) + 0.08(100) = 18$
$(150, 0)$	$0.10(150) + 0.08(0) = 15$

The company will have a maximum income of \$18 when 100 of each type of biscuit is made.

67. Let x = the number of units of lumber and y = the number of units of plywood produced per week. The profit P is given by

$$P = 20x + 30y$$

subject to the constraints

$$x + y \le 400,$$
$$x \ge 100,$$
$$y \ge 150.$$

We graph the system of inequalities, determine the vertices and find the value of P at each vertex.

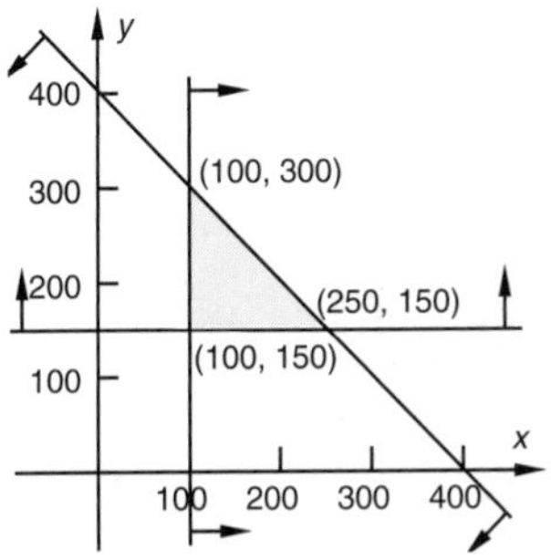

Vertex	$P = 20x + 30y$
$(100, 150)$	$20 \cdot 100 + 30 \cdot 150 = 6500$
$(100, 300)$	$20 \cdot 100 + 30 \cdot 300 = 11,000$
$(250, 150)$	$20 \cdot 250 + 30 \cdot 150 = 9500$

The maximum profit of \$11,000 is achieved by producing 100 units of lumber and 300 units of plywood.

69. Let x = the number of sacks of soybean meal to be used and y = the number of sacks of oats. The minimum cost is given by

$$C = 15x + 5y$$

subject to the constraints

$$50x + 15y \ge 120,$$
$$8x + 5y \ge 24,$$
$$5x + y \ge 10,$$
$$x \ge 0,$$
$$y \ge 0.$$

Graph the system of inequalities, determine the vertices, and find the value of C at each vertex.

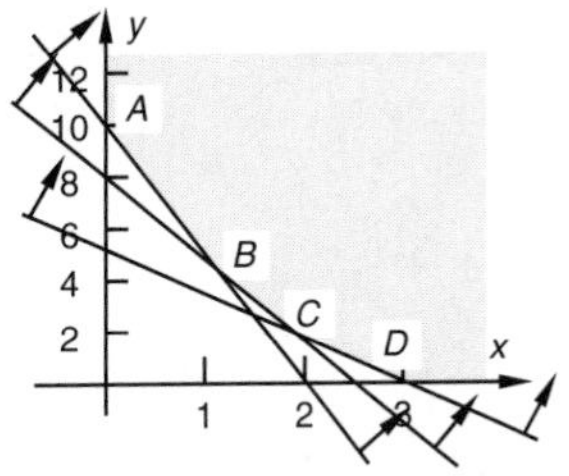

Vertex	$C = 15x + 5y$
$A(0, 10)$	$15 \cdot 0 + 5 \cdot 10 = 50$
$B\left(\frac{6}{5}, 4\right)$	$15 \cdot \frac{6}{5} + 5 \cdot 4 = 38$
$C\left(\frac{24}{13}, \frac{24}{13}\right)$	$15 \cdot \frac{24}{13} + 5 \cdot \frac{24}{13} = 36\frac{12}{13}$
$D(3, 0)$	$15 \cdot 3 + 5 \cdot 0 = 45$

The minimum cost of $\$36\frac{12}{13}$ is achieved by using $\frac{24}{13}$, or $1\frac{11}{13}$ sacks of soybean meal and $\frac{24}{13}$, or $1\frac{11}{13}$ sacks of oats.

71. Let x = the amount invested in corporate bonds and y = the amount invested in municipal bonds. The income I is given by

$$I = 0.08x + 0.075y$$

subject to the constrains

$$x + y \le 40,000,$$
$$6000 \le x \le 22,000,$$
$$y \le 30,000.$$

We graph the system of inequalities, determine the vertices, and find the value of I at each vertex.

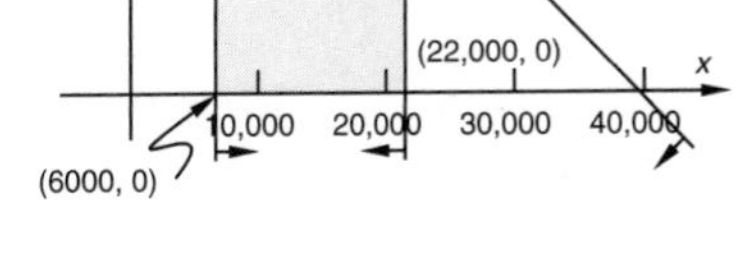

Vertex	$I = 0.08x + 0.075y$
$(6000, 0)$	480
$(6000, 30,000)$	2730
$(10,000, 30,000)$	3050
$(22,000, 18,000)$	3110
$(22,000, 0)$	1760

The maximum income of \$3110 occurs when \$22,000 is invested in corporate bonds and \$18,000 is invested in municipal bonds.

73. Let x = the number of P_1 airplanes and y = the number of P_2 airplanes to be used. The operating cost C, in thousands of dollars, is given by

$$C = 12x + 10y$$

subject to the constraints

$$\begin{aligned} 40x + 80y &\geq 2000, \\ 40x + 30y &\geq 1500, \\ 120x + 40y &\geq 2400, \\ x &\geq 0, \\ y &\geq 0. \end{aligned}$$

Graph the system of inequalities, determine the vertices, and find the value of C at each vertex.

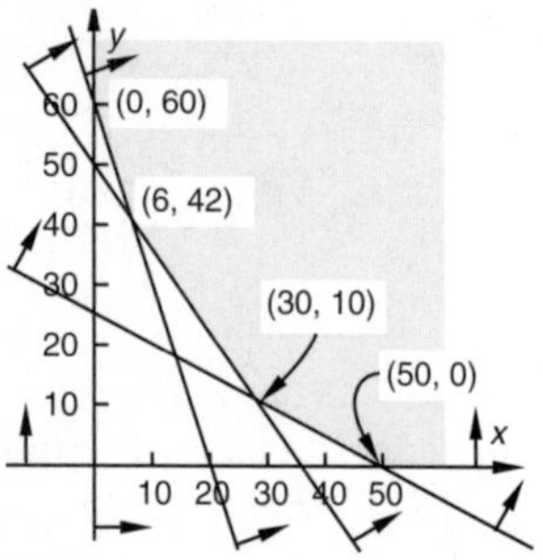

Vertex	$C = 12x + 10y$
$(0, 60)$	$12 \cdot 0 + 10 \cdot 60 = 600$
$(6, 42)$	$12 \cdot 6 + 10 \cdot 42 = 492$
$(30, 10)$	$12 \cdot 30 + 10 \cdot 10 = 460$
$(50, 0)$	$12 \cdot 50 + 10 \cdot 0 = 600$

The minimum cost of \$460 thousand is achieved using 30 P_1's and 10 P_2's.

75. Let x = the number of knit suits and y = the number of worsted suits made. The profit is given by

$$P = 34x + 31y$$

subject to

$$\begin{aligned} 2x + 4y &\leq 20, \\ 4x + 2y &\leq 16, \\ x &\geq 0, \\ y &\geq 0. \end{aligned}$$

Graph the system of inequalities, determine the vertices, and find the value of P at each vertex.

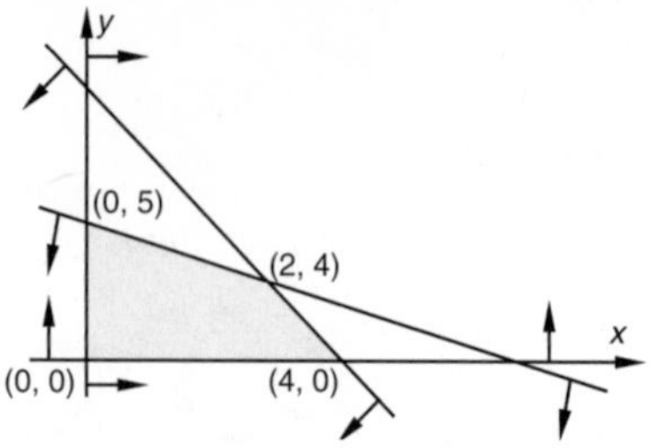

Vertex	$P = 34x + 31y$
$(0, 0)$	$34 \cdot 0 + 31 \cdot 0 = 0$
$(0, 5)$	$34 \cdot 0 + 31 \cdot 5 = 155$
$(2, 4)$	$34 \cdot 2 + 31 \cdot 4 = 192$
$(4, 0)$	$34 \cdot 4 + 31 \cdot 0 = 136$

The maximum profit per day is \$192 when 2 knit suits and 4 worsted suits are made.

77. Let x = the number of pounds of meat and y = the number of pounds of cheese in the diet in a week. The cost is given by

$$C = 3.50x + 4.60y$$

subject to

$$\begin{aligned} 2x + 3y &\geq 12, \\ 2x + y &\geq 6, \\ x &\geq 0, \\ y &\geq 0. \end{aligned}$$

Graph the system of inequalities, determine the vertices, and find the value of C at each vertex.

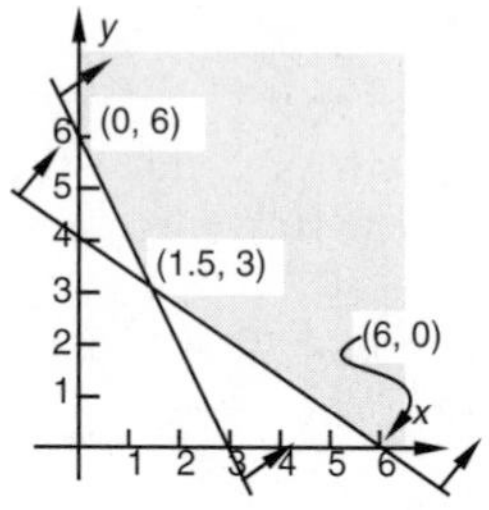

Vertex	$C = 3.50x + 4.60y$
$(0, 6)$	$3.50(0) + 4.60(6) = 27.60$
$(1.5, 3)$	$3.50(1.5) + 4.60(3) = 19.05$
$(6, 0)$	$3.50(6) + 4.60(0) = 21.00$

The minimum weekly cost of \$19.05 is achieved when 1.5 lb of meat and 3 lb of cheese are used.

79. Let x = the number of animal A and y = the number of animal B. The total number of animals is given by

$$T = x + y$$

subject to

$$\begin{aligned} x + 0.2y &\leq 600, \\ 0.5x + y &\leq 525, \\ x &\geq 0, \\ y &\geq 0. \end{aligned}$$

Graph the system of inequalities, determine the vertices, and find the value of T at each vertex.

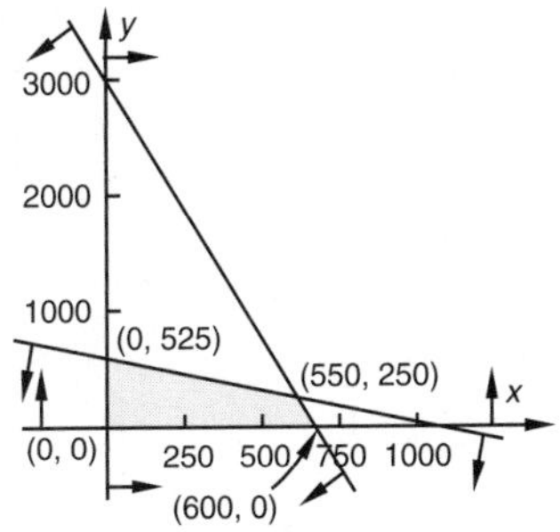

Vertex	$T = x + y$
$(0, 0)$	$0 + 0 = 0$
$(0, 525)$	$0 + 525 = 525$
$(550, 250)$	$550 + 250 = 800$
$(600, 0)$	$600 + 0 = 600$

The maximum total number of 800 is achieved when there are 550 of A and 250 of B.

81. Left to the student

83. Discussion and Writing

85. $-5 \le x + 2 < 4$

$-7 \le x < 2$ Subtracting 2

The solution set is $\{x| -7 \le x < 2\}$, or $[-7, 2)$.

87. $x^2 - 2x \le 3$ Polynomial inequality

$x^2 - 2x - 3 \le 0$

$x^2 - 2x - 3 = 0$ Related equation

$(x + 1)(x - 3) = 0$ Factoring

Using the principle of zero products or by observing the graph of $y = x^2 - 2x - 3$, we see that the solutions of the related equation are -1 and 3. These numbers divide the x-axis into the intervals $(-\infty, -1)$, $(-1, 3)$, and $(3, \infty)$. We let $f(x) = x^2 - 2x - 3$ and test a value in each interval.

$(-\infty, -1)$: $f(-2) = 5 > 0$

$(-1, 3)$: $f(0) = -3 < 0$

$(3, \infty)$: $f(4) = 5 > 0$

Function values are negative on $(-1, 3)$. This can also be determined from the graph of $y = x^2 - 2x - 3$. Since the inequality symbol is $\le$, the endpoints of the interval must be included in the solution set. It is $\{x| -1 \le x \le 3\}$ or $[-1, 3]$.

89. Graph: $y \ge x^2 - 2$,

$y \le 2 - x^2$

First graph the related equations $y = x^2 - 2$ and $y = 2 - x^2$ using solid lines. The solution set consists of the region above the graph of $y = x^2 - 2$ and below the graph of $y = 2 - x^2$.

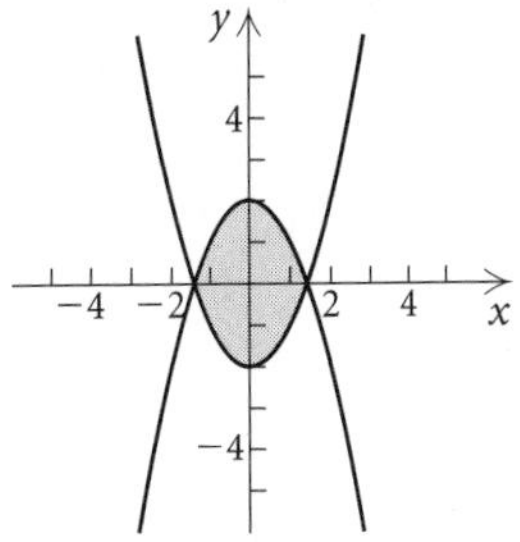

91. See the answer section in the text.

93. See the answer section in the text.

95. Let x = the number of less expensive speaker assemblies and y = the number of more expensive assemblies. The income is given by

$$I = 350x + 600y$$

subject to

$$y \le 44$$
$$x + y \le 60,$$
$$x + 2y \le 90,$$
$$x \ge 0,$$
$$y \ge 0.$$

Graph the system of inequalities, determine the vertices, and find the value of I at each vertex.

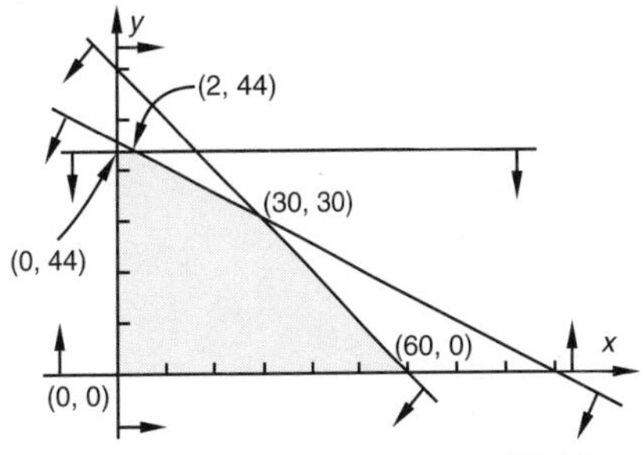

Vertex	$I = 350x + 600y$
$(0, 0)$	$350 \cdot 0 + 600 \cdot 0 = 0$
$(0, 44)$	$350 \cdot 0 + 600 \cdot 44 = 26,400$
$(2, 44)$	$350 \cdot 2 + 600 \cdot 44 = 27,100$
$(30, 30)$	$350 \cdot 30 + 600 \cdot 30 = 28,500$
$(60, 0)$	$350 \cdot 60 + 600 \cdot 0 = 21,000$

The maximum income of \$28,500 is achieved when 30 less expensive and 30 more expensive assemblies are made.

Exercise Set 5.8

1. $$\frac{x+7}{(x-3)(x+2)} = \frac{A}{x-3} + \frac{B}{x+2}$$

$$\frac{x+7}{(x-3)(x+2)} = \frac{A(x+2) + B(x-3)}{(x-3)(x+2)} \quad \text{Adding}$$

Equate the numerators:

$x + 7 = A(x + 2) + B(x - 3)$

Let $x + 2 = 0$, or $x = -2$. Then we get

$$-2+7 = 0+B(-2-3)$$
$$5 = -5B$$
$$-1 = B$$

Next let $x-3=0$, or $x=3$. Then we get

$$3+7 = A(3+2)+0$$
$$10 = 5A$$
$$2 = A$$

The decomposition is as follows:

$$\frac{2}{x-3} - \frac{1}{x+2}$$

3. $\dfrac{7x-1}{6x^2-5x+1}$

$= \dfrac{7x-1}{(3x-1)(2x-1)}$ Factoring the denominator

$= \dfrac{A}{3x-1} + \dfrac{B}{2x-1}$

$= \dfrac{A(2x-1)+B(3x-1)}{(3x-1)(2x-1)}$ Adding

Equate the numerators:

$$7x-1 = A(2x-1)+B(3x-1)$$

Let $2x-1=0$, or $x=\dfrac{1}{2}$. Then we get

$$7\left(\frac{1}{2}\right)-1 = 0+B\left(3\cdot\frac{1}{2}-1\right)$$
$$\frac{5}{2} = \frac{1}{2}B$$
$$5 = B$$

Next let $3x-1=0$, or $x=\dfrac{1}{3}$. We get

$$7\left(\frac{1}{3}\right)-1 = A\left(2\cdot\frac{1}{3}-1\right)$$
$$\frac{7}{3}-1 = A\left(\frac{2}{3}-1\right)$$
$$\frac{4}{3} = -\frac{1}{3}A$$
$$-4 = A$$

The decomposition is as follows:

$$-\frac{4}{3x-1} + \frac{5}{2x-1}$$

5. $\dfrac{3x^2-11x-26}{(x^2-4)(x+1)}$

$= \dfrac{3x^2-11x-26}{(x+2)(x-2)(x+1)}$ Factoring the denominator

$= \dfrac{A}{x+2} + \dfrac{B}{x-2} + \dfrac{C}{x+1}$

$= \dfrac{A(x-2)(x+1)+B(x+2)(x+1)+C(x+2)(x-2)}{(x+2)(x-2)(x+1)}$ Adding

Equate the numerators:

$$3x^2-11x-26 = A(x-2)(x+1)+ B(x+2)(x+1)+C(x+2)(x-2)$$

Let $x+2=0$ or $x=-2$. Then we get

$$3(-2)^2-11(-2)-26 = A(-2-2)(-2+1)+0+0$$
$$12+22-26 = A(-4)(-1)$$
$$8 = 4A$$
$$2 = A$$

Next let $x-2=0$, or $x=2$. Then, we get

$$3\cdot 2^2-11\cdot 2-26 = 0+B(2+2)(2+1)+0$$
$$12-22-26 = B\cdot 4\cdot 3$$
$$-36 = 12B$$
$$-3 = B$$

Finally let $x+1=0$, or $x=-1$. We get

$$3(-1)^2-11(-1)-26 = 0+0+C(-1+2)(-1-2)$$
$$3+11-26 = C(1)(-3)$$
$$-12 = -3C$$
$$4 = C$$

The decomposition is as follows:

$$\frac{2}{x+2} - \frac{3}{x-2} + \frac{4}{x+1}$$

7. $\dfrac{9}{(x+2)^2(x-1)}$

$= \dfrac{A}{x+2} + \dfrac{B}{(x+2)^2} + \dfrac{C}{x-1}$

$= \dfrac{A(x+2)(x-1)+B(x-1)+C(x+2)^2}{(x+2)^2(x-1)}$ Adding

Equate the numerators:

$$9 = A(x+2)(x-1)+B(x-1)+C(x+2)^2 \quad (1)$$

Let $x-1=0$, or $x=1$. Then, we get

$$9 = 0+0+C(1+2)^2$$
$$9 = 9C$$
$$1 = C$$

Next let $x+2=0$, or $x=-2$. Then, we get

$$9 = 0+B(-2-1)+0$$
$$9 = -3B$$
$$-3 = B$$

To find A we first simplify equation (1).

$$9 = A(x^2+x-2)+B(x-1)+C(x^2+4x+4)$$
$$= Ax^2+Ax-2A+Bx-B+Cx^2+4Cx+4C$$
$$= (A+C)x^2+(A+B+4C)x+(-2A-B+4C)$$

Then we equate the coefficients of x^2.

$$0 = A+C$$
$$0 = A+1 \quad \text{Substituting 1 for } C$$
$$-1 = A$$

The decomposition is as follows:

$$-\frac{1}{x+2} - \frac{3}{(x+2)^2} + \frac{1}{x-1}$$

9. $\dfrac{2x^2+3x+1}{(x^2-1)(2x-1)}$

$=\dfrac{2x^2+3x+1}{(x+1)(x-1)(2x-1)}$ Factoring the denominator

$=\dfrac{A}{x+1}+\dfrac{B}{x-1}+\dfrac{C}{2x-1}$

$=\dfrac{A(x-1)(2x-1)+B(x+1)(2x-1)+C(x+1)(x-1)}{(x+1)(x-1)(2x-1)}$ Adding

Equate the numerators:

$2x^2+3x+1=A(x-1)(2x-1)+B(x+1)(2x-1)+C(x+1)(x-1)$

Let $x+1=0$, or $x=-1$. Then, we get

$$2(-1)^2+3(-1)+1=A(-1-1)[2(-1)-1]+0+0$$
$$2-3+1=A(-2)(-3)$$
$$0=6A$$
$$0=A$$

Next let $x-1=0$, or $x=1$. Then, we get

$$2\cdot1^2+3\cdot1+1=0+B(1+1)(2\cdot1-1)+0$$
$$2+3+1=B\cdot2\cdot1$$
$$6=2B$$
$$3=B$$

Finally we let $2x-1=0$, or $x=\dfrac{1}{2}$. We get

$$2\left(\frac{1}{2}\right)^2+3\left(\frac{1}{2}\right)+1=0+0+C\left(\frac{1}{2}+1\right)\left(\frac{1}{2}-1\right)$$
$$\frac{1}{2}+\frac{3}{2}+1=C\cdot\frac{3}{2}\cdot\left(-\frac{1}{2}\right)$$
$$3=-\frac{3}{4}C$$
$$-4=C$$

The decomposition is as follows:

$\dfrac{3}{x-1}-\dfrac{4}{2x-1}$

11. $\dfrac{x^4-3x^3-3x^2+10}{(x+1)^2(x-3)}$

$=\dfrac{x^4-3x^3-3x^2+10}{x^3-x^2-5x-3}$ Multiplying the denominator

Since the degree of the numerator is greater than the degree of the denominator, we divide.

$$\begin{array}{r} x-\ \ 2\qquad\qquad\qquad\\ x^3-x^2-5x-3\,\overline{)\,x^4-3x^3-3x^2+\ 0x+10}\\ \underline{x^4-\ x^3-5x^2-\ 3x\qquad}\\ -2x^3+2x^2+\ 3x+10\\ \underline{-2x^3+2x^2+10x+\ 6}\\ -\ 7x+\ 4 \end{array}$$

The original expression is thus equivalent to the following:

$x-2+\dfrac{-7x+4}{x^3-x^2-5x-3}$

We proceed to decompose the fraction.

$\dfrac{-7x+4}{(x+1)^2(x-3)}$

$=\dfrac{A}{x+1}+\dfrac{B}{(x+1)^2}+\dfrac{C}{x-3}$

$=\dfrac{A(x+1)(x-3)+B(x-3)+C(x+1)^2}{(x+1)^2(x-3)}$ Adding

Equate the numerators:

$-7x+4=A(x+1)(x-3)+B(x-3)+C(x+1)^2$ (1)

Let $x-3=0$, or $x=3$. Then, we get

$$-7\cdot3+4=0+0+C(3+1)^2$$
$$-17=16C$$
$$-\frac{17}{16}=C$$

Let $x+1=0$, or $x=-1$. Then, we get

$$-7(-1)+4=0+B(-1-3)+0$$
$$11=-4B$$
$$-\frac{11}{4}=B$$

To find A we first simplify equation (1).

$-7x+4$

$=A(x^2-2x-3)+B(x-3)+C(x^2+2x+1)$

$=Ax^2-2Ax-3A+Bx-3B+Cx^2-2Cx+C$

$=(A+C)x^2+(-2A+B-2C)x+(-3A-3B+C)$

Then equate the coefficients of x^2.

$0=A+C$

Substituting $-\dfrac{17}{16}$ for C, we get $A=\dfrac{17}{16}$.

The decomposition is as follows:

$\dfrac{17/16}{x+1}-\dfrac{11/4}{(x+1)^2}-\dfrac{17/16}{x-3}$

The original expression is equivalent to the following:

$x-2+\dfrac{17/16}{x+1}-\dfrac{11/4}{(x+1)^2}-\dfrac{17/16}{x-3}$

13. $\dfrac{-x^2+2x-13}{(x^2+2)(x-1)}$

$=\dfrac{Ax+B}{x^2+2}+\dfrac{C}{x-1}$

$=\dfrac{(Ax+B)(x-1)+C(x^2+2)}{(x^2+2)(x-1)}$ Adding

Equate the numerators:

$-x^2+2x-13=(Ax+B)(x-1)+C(x^2+2)$ (1)

Let $x-1=0$, or $x=1$. Then we get

$$-1^2+2\cdot1-13=0+C(1^2+2)$$
$$-1+2-13=C(1+2)$$
$$-12=3C$$
$$-4=C$$

To find A and B we first simplify equation (1).

$-x^2+2x-13$

$= Ax^2-Ax+Bx-B+Cx^2+2C$

$= (A+C)x^2+(-A+B)x+(-B+2C)$

Equate the coefficients of x^2:

$-1 = A+C$

Substituting -4 for C, we get $A=3$.

Equate the constant terms:

$-13 = -B+2C$

Substituting -4 for C, we get $B=5$.

The decomposition is as follows:

$$\frac{3x+5}{x^2+2} - \frac{4}{x-1}$$

15. $\dfrac{6+26x-x^2}{(2x-1)(x+2)^2}$

$$= \frac{A}{2x-1} + \frac{B}{x+2} + \frac{C}{(x+2)^2}$$

$$= \frac{A(x+2)^2+B(2x-1)(x+2)+C(2x-1)}{(2x-1)(x+2)^2} \quad \text{Adding}$$

Equate the numerators:

$$6+26x-x^2 = A(x+2)^2+B(2x-1)(x+2)+ C(2x-1) \quad (1)$$

Let $2x-1=0$, or $x=\dfrac{1}{2}$. Then, we get

$$6+26\cdot\frac{1}{2}-\left(\frac{1}{2}\right)^2 = A\left(\frac{1}{2}+2\right)^2+0+0$$

$$6+13-\frac{1}{4} = A\left(\frac{5}{2}\right)^2$$

$$\frac{75}{4} = \frac{25}{4}A$$

$$3 = A$$

Let $x+2=0$, or $x=-2$. We get

$$6+26(-2)-(-2)^2 = 0+0+C[2(-2)-1]$$

$$6-52-4 = -5C$$

$$-50 = -5C$$

$$10 = C$$

To find B we first simplify equation (1).

$6+26x-x^2$

$= A(x^2+4x+4)+B(2x^2+3x-2)+C(2x-1)$

$= Ax^2+4Ax+4A+2Bx^2+3Bx-2B+2Cx-C$

$= (A+2B)x^2+(4A+3B+2C)x+(4A-2B-C)$

Equate the coefficients of x^2:

$-1 = A+2B$

Substituting 3 for A, we obtain $B=-2$.

The decomposition is as follows:

$$\frac{3}{2x-1} - \frac{2}{x+2} + \frac{10}{(x+2)^2}$$

17. $\dfrac{6x^3+5x^2+6x-2}{2x^2+x-1}$

Since the degree of the numerator is greater than the degree of the denominator, we divide.

$$\begin{array}{r} 3x+\ \ 1 \\ 2x^2+x-1 \overline{\smash{\big)}\, 6x^3+5x^2+6x-2} \\ \underline{6x^3+3x^2-3x} \\ 2x^2+9x-2 \\ \underline{2x^2+\ x-1} \\ 8x-1 \end{array}$$

The original expression is equivalent to

$$3x+1+\frac{8x-1}{2x^2+x-1}$$

We proceed to decompose the fraction.

$$\frac{8x-1}{2x^2+x-1} = \frac{8x-1}{(2x-1)(x+1)} \quad \text{Factoring the denominator}$$

$$= \frac{A}{2x-1}+\frac{B}{x+1}$$

$$= \frac{A(x+1)+B(2x-1)}{(2x-1)(x+1)} \quad \text{Adding}$$

Equate the numerators:

$8x-1 = A(x+1)+B(2x-1)$

Let $x+1=0$, or $x=-1$. Then we get

$$8(-1)-1 = 0+B[2(-1)-1]$$

$$-8-1 = B(-2-1)$$

$$-9 = -3B$$

$$3 = B$$

Next let $2x-1=0$, or $x=\dfrac{1}{2}$. We get

$$8\left(\frac{1}{2}\right)-1 = A\left(\frac{1}{2}+1\right)+0$$

$$4-1 = A\left(\frac{3}{2}\right)$$

$$3 = \frac{3}{2}A$$

$$2 = A$$

The decomposition is

$$\frac{2}{2x-1}+\frac{3}{x+1}.$$

The original expression is equivalent to

$$3x+1+\frac{2}{2x-1}+\frac{3}{x+1}.$$

19. $\dfrac{2x^2-11x+5}{(x-3)(x^2+2x-5)}$

$$= \frac{A}{x-3}+\frac{Bx+C}{x^2+2x-5}$$

$$= \frac{A(x^2+2x-5)+(Bx+C)(x-3)}{(x-3)(x^2+2x-5)} \quad \text{Adding}$$

Equate the numerators:

$$2x^2-11x+5 = A(x^2+2x-5)+ (Bx+C)(x-3) \quad (1)$$

Let $x-3=0$, or $x=3$. Then, we get

$$2 \cdot 3^2 - 11 \cdot 3 + 5 = A(3^2 + 2 \cdot 3 - 5) + 0$$
$$18 - 33 + 5 = A(9 + 6 - 5)$$
$$-10 = 10A$$
$$-1 = A$$

To find B and C, we first simplify equation (1).

$$2x^2 - 11x + 5 = Ax^2 + 2Ax - 5A + Bx^2 - 3Bx + Cx - 3C$$
$$= (A + B)x^2 + (2A - 3B + C)x + (-5A - 3C)$$

Equate the coefficients of x^2:

$2 = A + B$

Substituting -1 for A, we get $B = 3$.

Equate the constant terms:

$5 = -5A - 3C$

Substituting -1 for A, we get $C = 0$.

The decomposition is as follows:

$$-\frac{1}{x-3} + \frac{3x}{x^2 + 2x - 5}$$

21. $\dfrac{-4x^2 - 2x + 10}{(3x+5)(x+1)^2}$

The decomposition looks like

$$\frac{A}{3x+5} + \frac{B}{x+1} + \frac{C}{(x+1)^2}.$$

Add and equate the numerators.

$$-4x^2 - 2x + 10$$
$$= A(x+1)^2 + B(3x+5)(x+1) + C(3x+5)$$
$$= A(x^2 + 2x + 1) + B(3x^2 + 8x + 5) + C(3x + 5)$$

or

$$-4x^2 - 2x + 10$$
$$= (A + 3B)x^2 + (2A + 8B + 3C)x + (A + 5B + 5C)$$

Then equate corresponding coefficients.

$-4 = A + 3B$	Coefficients of x^2-terms
$-2 = 2A + 8B + 3C$	Coefficients of x-terms
$10 = A + 5B + 5C$	Constant terms

We solve this system of three equations and find $A = 5$, $B = -3$, $C = 4$.

The decomposition is

$$\frac{5}{3x+5} - \frac{3}{x+1} + \frac{4}{(x+1)^2}.$$

23. $\dfrac{36x+1}{12x^2 - 7x - 10} = \dfrac{36x+1}{(4x-5)(3x+2)}$

The decomposition looks like

$$\frac{A}{4x-5} + \frac{B}{3x+2}.$$

Add and equate the numerators.

$$36x + 1 = A(3x + 2) + B(4x - 5)$$

or $36x + 1 = (3A + 4B)x + (2A - 5B)$

Then equate corresponding coefficients.

$36 = 3A + 4B$	Coefficients of x-terms
$1 = 2A - 5B$	Constant terms

We solve this system of equations and find $A = 8$ and $B = 3$.

The decomposition is

$$\frac{8}{4x-5} + \frac{3}{3x+2}.$$

25. $\dfrac{-4x^2 - 9x + 8}{(3x^2+1)(x-2)}$

The decomposition looks like

$$\frac{Ax+B}{3x^2+1} + \frac{C}{x-2}.$$

Add and equate the numerators.

$$-4x^2 - 9x + 8$$
$$= (Ax + B)(x - 2) + C(3x^2 + 1)$$
$$= Ax^2 - 2Ax + Bx - 2B + 3Cx^2 + C$$

or

$$-4x^2 - 9x + 8$$
$$= (A + 3C)x^2 + (-2A + B)x + (-2B + C)$$

Then equate corresponding coefficients.

$-4 = A + 3C$	Coefficients of x^2-terms
$-9 = -2A + B$	Coefficients of x-terms
$8 = -2B + C$	Constant terms

We solve this system of equations and find $A = 2$, $B = -5$, $C = -2$.

The decomposition is

$$\frac{2x-5}{3x^2+1} - \frac{2}{x-2}.$$

27. Discussion and Writing

29. Discussion and Writing

31. $f(x) = x^3 + x^2 - 3x - 2$

We use synthetic division to factor the polynomial. Using the possibilities found by the rational zeros theorem we find that $x + 2$ is a factor:

-2	1	1	-3	-2
		-2	2	2
	1	-1	-1	0

We have $x^3 + x^2 - 3x - 2 = (x + 2)(x^2 - x - 1)$.

$$x^3 + x^2 - 3x - 2 = 0$$
$$(x + 2)(x^2 - x - 1) = 0$$
$$x + 2 = 0 \quad or \quad x^2 - x - 1 = 0$$

The solution of the first equation is -2. We use the quadratic formula to solve the second equation.

$$x = \frac{-b \pm \sqrt{b^2 - 4ac}}{2a}$$
$$= \frac{-(-1) \pm \sqrt{(-1)^2 - 4 \cdot 1 \cdot (-1)}}{2 \cdot 1}$$
$$= \frac{1 \pm \sqrt{5}}{2}$$

The solutions are -2, $\dfrac{1+\sqrt{5}}{2}$ and $\dfrac{1-\sqrt{5}}{2}$.

33. $f(x) = x^3 + 5x^2 + 5x - 3$

$$\begin{array}{r|rrrr} -3 & 1 & 5 & 5 & -3 \\ & & -3 & -6 & 3 \\ \hline & 1 & 2 & -1 & 0 \end{array}$$

$$x^3 + 5x^2 + 5x - 3 = 0$$
$$(x+3)(x^2+2x-1) = 0$$
$$x + 3 = 0 \quad or \quad x^2 + 2x - 1 = 0$$

The solution of the first equation is -3. We use the quadratic formula to solve the second equation.

$$\begin{aligned} x &= \frac{-b \pm \sqrt{b^2 - 4ac}}{2a} \\ &= \frac{-2 \pm \sqrt{2^2 - 4 \cdot 1 \cdot (-1)}}{2 \cdot 1} = \frac{-2 \pm \sqrt{8}}{2} \\ &= \frac{-2 \pm 2\sqrt{2}}{2} = \frac{2(-1 \pm \sqrt{2})}{2} \\ &= -1 \pm \sqrt{2} \end{aligned}$$

The solutions are -3, $-1 + \sqrt{2}$, and $-1 - \sqrt{2}$.

35. $\dfrac{x}{x^4 - a^4}$

$= \dfrac{x}{(x^2+a^2)(x+a)(x-a)}$ Factoring the denominator

$= \dfrac{Ax+B}{x^2+a^2} + \dfrac{C}{x+a} + \dfrac{D}{x-a}$

$= [(Ax+B)(x+a)(x-a) + C(x^2+a^2)(x-a) +$
$D(x^2+a^2)(x+a)]/[(x^2+a^2)(x+a)(x-a)]$

Equate the numerators:

$$x = (Ax+B)(x+a)(x-a) + C(x^2+a^2)(x-a) + D(x^2+a^2)(x+a)$$

Let $x - a = 0$, or $x = a$. Then, we get

$$\begin{aligned} a &= 0 + 0 + D(a^2+a^2)(a+a) \\ a &= D(2a^2)(2a) \\ a &= 4a^3 D \\ \frac{1}{4a^2} &= D \end{aligned}$$

Let $x + a = 0$, or $x = -a$. We get

$$\begin{aligned} -a &= 0 + C[(-a)^2 + a^2](-a-a) + 0 \\ -a &= C(2a^2)(-2a) \\ -a &= -4a^3 C \\ \frac{1}{4a^2} &= C \end{aligned}$$

Equate the coefficients of x^3:

$0 = A + C + D$

Substituting $\dfrac{1}{4a^2}$ for C and for D, we get

$A = -\dfrac{1}{2a^2}$.

Equate the constant terms:

$0 = -Ba^2 - Ca^3 + Da^3$

Substitute $\dfrac{1}{4a^2}$ for C and for D. Then solve for B.

$$\begin{aligned} 0 &= -Ba^2 - \frac{1}{4a^2} \cdot a^3 + \frac{1}{4a^2} \cdot a^3 \\ 0 &= -Ba^2 \\ 0 &= B \end{aligned}$$

The decomposition is as follows:

$$-\frac{\frac{1}{2a^2}x}{x^2+a^2} + \frac{\frac{1}{4a^2}}{x+a} + \frac{\frac{1}{4a^2}}{x-a}$$

37. $\dfrac{1 + \ln x^2}{(\ln x + 2)(\ln x - 3)^2} = \dfrac{1 + 2\ln x}{(\ln x + 2)(\ln x - 3)^2}$

Let $u = \ln x$. Then we have:

$$\begin{aligned} &\frac{1+2u}{(u+2)(u-3)^2} \\ &= \frac{A}{u+2} + \frac{B}{u-3} + \frac{C}{(u-3)^2} \\ &= \frac{A(u3)^2 + B(u+2)(u-3) + C(u+2)}{(u+2)(u-3)^2} \end{aligned}$$

Equate the numerators:

$1 + 2u = A(u-3)^2 + B(u+2)(u-3) + C(u+2)$

Let $u - 3 = 0$, or $u = 3$.

$$\begin{aligned} 1 + 2 \cdot 3 &= 0 + 0 + C(5) \\ 7 &= 5C \\ \frac{7}{5} &= C \end{aligned}$$

Let $u + 2 = 0$, or $u = -2$.

$$\begin{aligned} 1 + 2(-2) &= A(-2-3)^2 + 0 + 0 \\ -3 &= 25A \\ -\frac{3}{25} &= A \end{aligned}$$

To find B, we equate the coefficients of u^2:

$0 = A + B$

Substituting $-\dfrac{3}{25}$ for A and solving for B, we get $B = \dfrac{3}{25}$.

The decomposition of $\dfrac{1+2u}{(u+2)(u-3)^2}$ is as follows:

$$-\frac{3}{25(u+2)} + \frac{3}{25(u-3)} + \frac{7}{5(u-3)^2}$$

Substituting $\ln x$ for u we get

$$-\frac{3}{25(\ln x + 2)} + \frac{3}{25(\ln x - 3)} + \frac{7}{5(\ln x - 3)^2}.$$

Chapter 6

Conic Sections

Exercise Set 6.1

1. Graph (f) is the graph of $x^2 = 8y$.

3. Graph (b) is the graph of $(y-2)^2 = -3(x+4)$.

5. Graph (d) is the graph of $13x^2 - 8y - 9 = 0$.

7. $x^2 = 20y$

$x^2 = 4 \cdot 5 \cdot y$ Writing $x^2 = 4py$

Vertex: $(0, 0)$

Focus: $(0, 5)$ $[(0, p)]$

Directrix: $y = -5$ $(y = -p)$

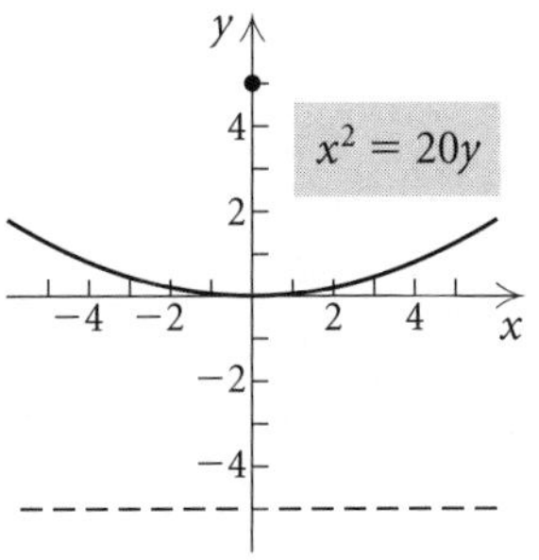

9. $y^2 = -6x$

$y^2 = 4\left(-\frac{3}{2}\right)x$ Writing $y^2 = 4px$

Vertex: $(0, 0)$

Focus: $\left(-\frac{3}{2}, 0\right)$ $[(p, 0)]$

Directrix: $x = -\left(-\frac{3}{2}\right) = \frac{3}{2}$ $(x = -p)$

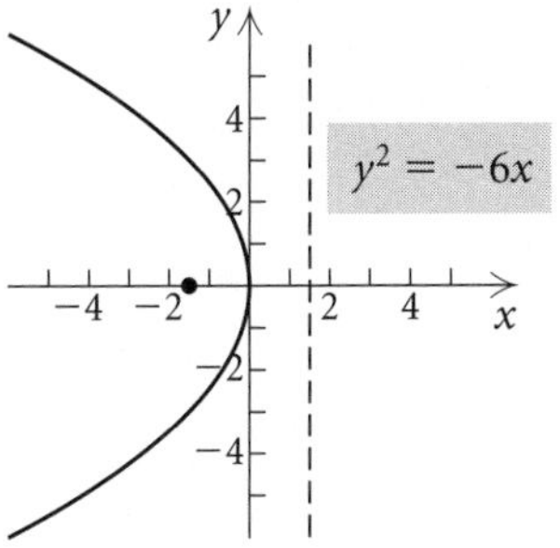

11. $x^2 - 4y = 0$

$x^2 = 4y$

$x^2 = 4 \cdot 1 \cdot y$ Writing $x^2 = 4py$

Vertex: $(0, 0)$

Focus: $(0, 1)$ $[(0, p)]$

Directrix: $y = -1$ $(y = -p)$

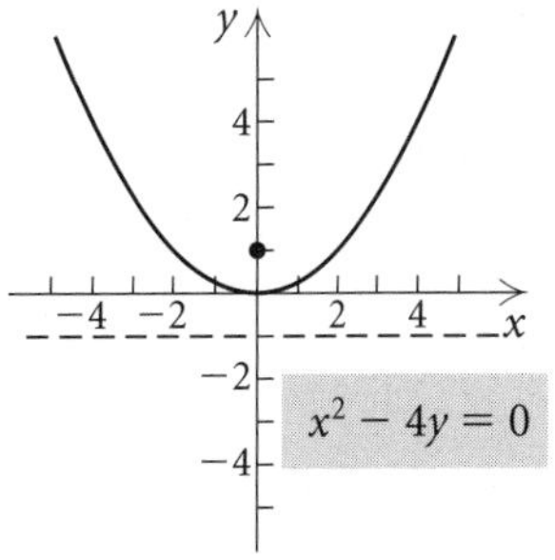

13. $x = 2y^2$

$y^2 = \frac{1}{2}x$

$y^2 = 4 \cdot \frac{1}{8} \cdot x$ Writing $y^2 = 4px$

Vertex: $(0, 0)$

Focus: $\left(\frac{1}{8}, 0\right)$

Directrix: $x = -\frac{1}{8}$

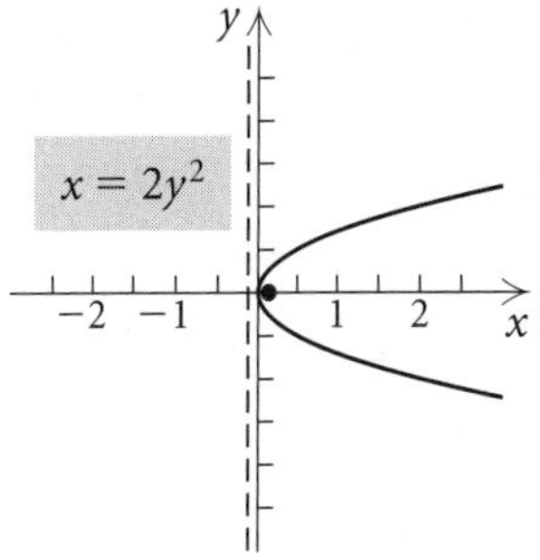

15. Since the directrix, $x = -4$, is a vertical line, the equation is of the form $(y-k)^2 = 4p(x-h)$. The focus, $(4, 0)$, is on the x-axis so the line of symmetry is the x-axis and $p = 4$. The vertex, (h, k), is the point on the x-axis midway between the directrix and the focus. Thus, it is $(0, 0)$. We have

$$(y-k)^2 = 4p(x-h)$$
$$(y-0)^2 = 4 \cdot 4(x-0) \quad \text{Substituting}$$
$$y^2 = 16x.$$

17. Since the directrix, $y = \pi$, is a horizontal line, the equation is of the form $(x-h)^2 = 4p(y-k)$. The focus, $(0, -\pi)$, is on the y-axis so the line of symmetry is the y-axis and $p = -\pi$. The vertex (h, k) is the point on the y-axis midway between the directrix and the focus. Thus, it is $(0, 0)$. We have

$$(x-h)^2 = 4p(y-k)$$
$$(x-0)^2 = 4(-\pi)(y-0) \quad \text{Substituting}$$
$$x^2 = -4\pi y$$

19. Since the directrix, $x = -4$, is a vertical line, the equation is of the form $(y-k)^2 = 4p(x-h)$. The focus, $(3, 2)$, is on the horizontal line $y = 2$, so the line of symmetry is $y = 2$. The vertex is the point on the line $y = 2$ that is midway between the directrix and the focus. That is, it is the midpoint of the segment from $(-4, 2)$ to $(3, 2)$: $\left(\frac{-4+3}{2}, \frac{2+2}{2}\right)$, or $\left(-\frac{1}{2}, 2\right)$. Then $h = -\frac{1}{2}$ and the directrix is $x = h - p$, so we have

$$\begin{aligned} x &= h - p \\ -4 &= -\frac{1}{2} - p \\ -\frac{7}{2} &= -p \\ \frac{7}{2} &= p. \end{aligned}$$

Now we find the equation of the parabola.

$$\begin{aligned} (y-k)^2 &= 4p(x-h) \\ (y-2)^2 &= 4\left(\frac{7}{2}\right)\left[x - \left(-\frac{1}{2}\right)\right] \\ (y-2)^2 &= 14\left(x + \frac{1}{2}\right) \end{aligned}$$

21. $(x+2)^2 = -6(y-1)$

$[x-(-2)]^2 = 4\left(-\frac{3}{2}\right)(y-1) \quad [(x-h)^2 = 4p(y-k)]$

Vertex: $(-2, 1) \quad [(h, k)]$

Focus: $\left(-2, 1 + \left(-\frac{3}{2}\right)\right)$, or $\left(-2, -\frac{1}{2}\right)$

$[(h, k+p)]$

Directrix: $y = 1 - \left(-\frac{3}{2}\right) = \frac{5}{2} \quad (y = k - p)$

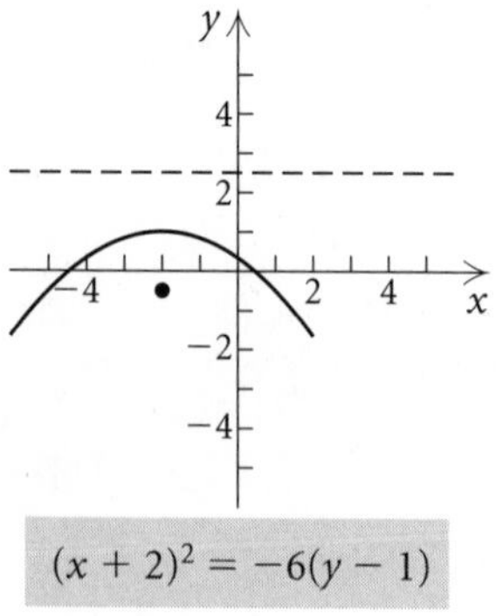

23. $x^2 + 2x + 2y + 7 = 0$

$$\begin{aligned} x^2 + 2x &= -2y - 7 \\ (x^2 + 2x + 1) &= -2y - 7 + 1 = -2y - 6 \\ (x+1)^2 &= -2(y+3) \\ [x - (-1)]^2 &= 4\left(-\frac{1}{2}\right)[y - (-3)] \end{aligned}$$

$[(x-h)^2 = 4p(y-k)]$

Vertex: $(-1, -3) \quad [(h, k)]$

Focus: $\left(-1, -3 + \left(-\frac{1}{2}\right)\right)$, or $\left(-1, -\frac{7}{2}\right)$

$[(h, k+p)]$

Directrix: $y = -3 - \left(-\frac{1}{2}\right) = -\frac{5}{2} \quad (y = k - p)$

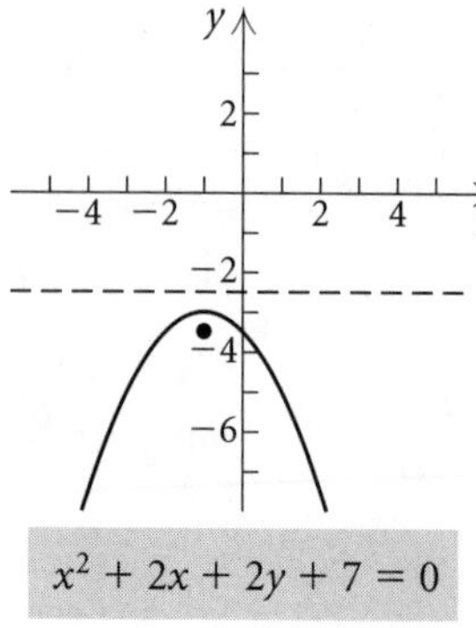

25. $x^2 - y - 2 = 0$

$$\begin{aligned} x^2 &= y + 2 \\ (x - 0)^2 &= 4 \cdot \frac{1}{4} \cdot [y - (-2)] \end{aligned}$$

$[(x-h)^2 = 4p(y-k)]$

Vertex: $(0, -2) \quad [(h, k)]$

Focus: $\left(0, -2 + \frac{1}{4}\right)$, or $\left(0, -\frac{7}{4}\right) \quad [(h, k+p)]$

Directrix: $y = -2 - \frac{1}{4} = -\frac{9}{4} \quad (y = k - p)$

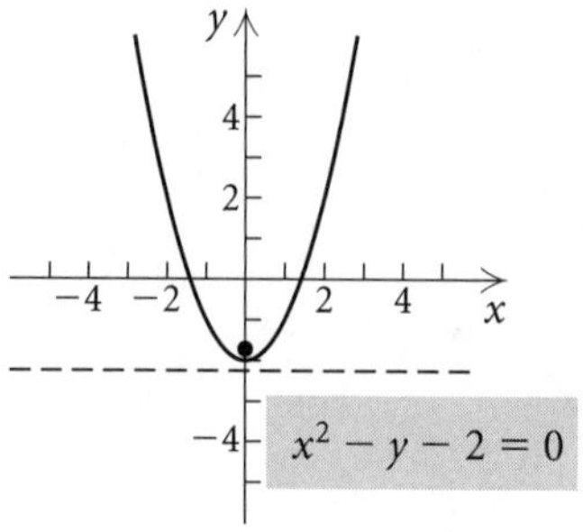

27.

$$\begin{aligned} y &= x^2 + 4x + 3 \\ y - 3 &= x^2 + 4x \\ y - 3 + 4 &= x^2 + 4x + 4 \\ y + 1 &= (x+2)^2 \\ 4 \cdot \frac{1}{4} \cdot [y - (-1)] &= [x - (-2)]^2 \end{aligned}$$

$[(x-h)^2 = 4p(y-k)]$

Vertex: $(-2, -1) \quad [(h, k)]$

Focus: $\left(-2, -1 + \frac{1}{4}\right)$, or $\left(-2, -\frac{3}{4}\right) \quad [(h, k+p)]$

Directrix: $y = -1 - \frac{1}{4} = -\frac{5}{4} \quad (y = k - p)$

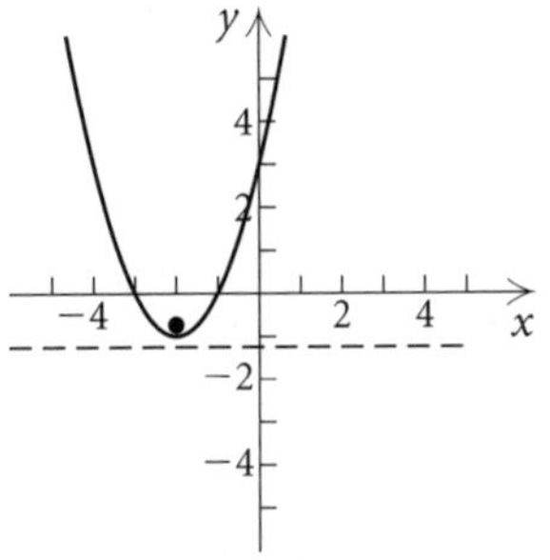

$y = x^2 + 4x + 3$

29. $y^2 - y - x + 6 = 0$

$$y^2 - y = x - 6$$

$$y^2 - y + \frac{1}{4} = x - 6 + \frac{1}{4}$$

$$\left(y - \frac{1}{2}\right)^2 = x - \frac{23}{4}$$

$$\left(y - \frac{1}{2}\right)^2 = 4 \cdot \frac{1}{4}\left(x - \frac{23}{4}\right)$$

$$[(y-k)^2 = 4p(x-h)]$$

Vertex: $\left(\frac{23}{4}, \frac{1}{2}\right)$ $[(h, k)]$

Focus: $\left(\frac{23}{4} + \frac{1}{4}, \frac{1}{2}\right)$, or $\left(6, \frac{1}{2}\right)$ $[(h+p, k)]$

Directrix: $x = \frac{23}{4} - \frac{1}{4} = \frac{22}{4}$ or $\frac{11}{2}$ $(x = h - p)$

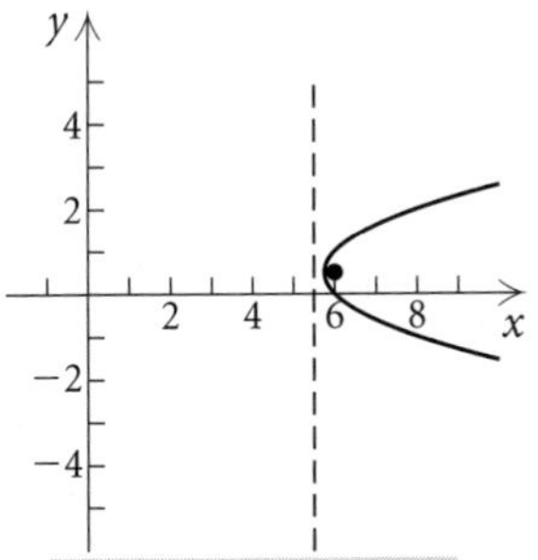

$y^2 - y - x + 6 = 0$

31. a) The vertex is $(0, 0)$. The focus is $(4, 0)$, so $p = 4$. The parabola has a horizontal axis of symmetry so the equation is of the form $y^2 = 4px$. We have

$$y^2 = 4px$$

$$y^2 = 4 \cdot 4 \cdot x$$

$$y^2 = 16x$$

b) We make a drawing.

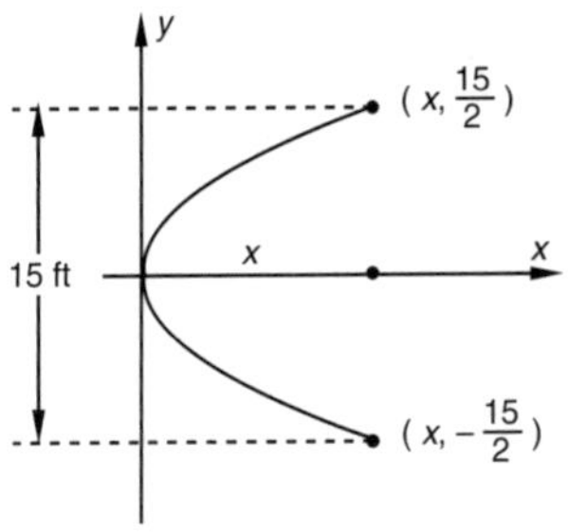

The depth of the satellite dish at the vertex is x where $\left(x, \frac{15}{2}\right)$ is a point on the parabola.

$$y^2 = 16x$$

$$\left(\frac{15}{2}\right)^2 = 16x \quad \text{Substituting } \frac{15}{2} \text{ for } y$$

$$\frac{225}{4} = 16x$$

$$\frac{225}{64} = x, \text{ or}$$

$$3\frac{33}{64} = x$$

The depth of the satellite dish at the vertex is $3\frac{33}{64}$ ft.

33. We position a coordinate system with the origin at the vertex and the x-axis on the parabola's axis of symmetry.

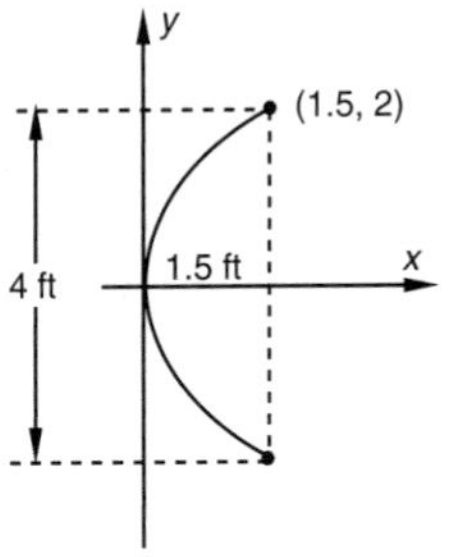

The parabola is of the form $y^2 = 4px$ and a point on the parabola is $\left(1.5, \frac{4}{2}\right)$, or $(1.5, 2)$.

$$y^2 = 4px$$

$$2^2 = 4 \cdot p \cdot (1.5) \quad \text{Substituting}$$

$$4 = 6p$$

$$\frac{4}{6} = p, \text{ or}$$

$$\frac{2}{3} = p$$

Since the focus is at $(p, 0)$, or $\left(\frac{2}{3}, 0\right)$, the focus is $\frac{2}{3}$ ft, or 8 in., from the vertex.

35. Vertex: $(0.867, 0.348)$

Focus: $(0.867, -0.190)$

Directrix: $y = 0.887$

37. Discussion and Writing

39. When we let $y = 0$ and solve for x, the only equation for which $x = \frac{2}{3}$ is (h), so only equation (h) has x-intercept $\left(\frac{2}{3}, 0\right)$.

41. Note that equation (g) is equivalent to $y = 2x - \frac{7}{4}$ and equation (h) is equivalent to $y = -\frac{1}{2}x + \frac{1}{3}$. When we look at the equations in the form $y = mx+b$, we see that $m > 0$ for (a), (b), (f), and (g) so these equations have positive slope, or slant up front left to right.

43. When we look at the equations in the form $y = mx+b$ (See Exercise 41.), only (b) has $m = \frac{1}{3}$ so only (b) has slope $\frac{1}{3}$.

45. Parallel lines have the same slope and different y-intercepts. When we look at the equations in the form $y = mx + b$ (See Exercise 41.), we see that (a) and (g) represent parallel lines.

47. A parabola with a vertical axis of symmetry has an equation of the type $(x - h)^2 = 4p(y - k)$.

Solve for p substituting $(-1, 2)$ for (h, k) and $(-3, 1)$ for (x, y).

$$[-3 - (-1)]^2 = 4p(1 - 2)$$
$$4 = -4p$$
$$-1 = p$$

The equation of the parabola is

$$[x - (-1)]^2 = 4(-1)(y - 2), \text{ or}$$
$$(x + 1)^2 = -4(y - 2).$$

49. Position a coordinate system as shown below with the y-axis on the parabola's axis of symmetry.

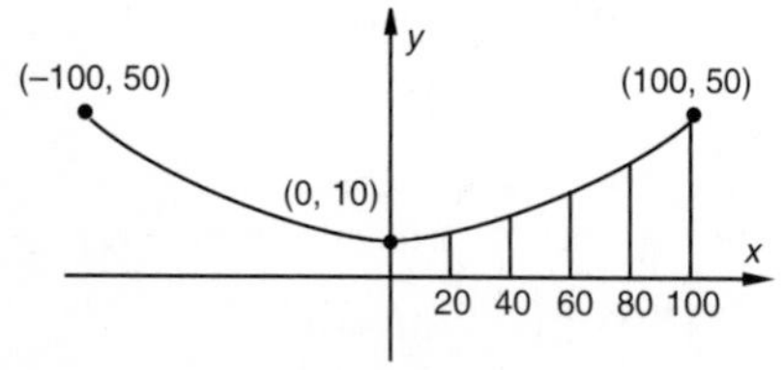

The equation of the parabola is of the form $(x - h)^2 = 4p(y - k)$. Substitute 100 for x, 50 for y, 0 for h, and 10 for k and solve for p.

$$(x - h)^2 = 4p(y - k)$$
$$(100 - 0)^2 = 4p(50 - 10)$$
$$10,000 = 160p$$
$$\frac{250}{4} = p$$

Then the equation is

$$x^2 = 4\left(\frac{250}{4}\right)(y - 10), \text{ or}$$
$$x^2 = 250(y - 10).$$

To find the lengths of the vertical cables, find y when $x = 0$, 20, 40, 60, 80, and 100.

When $x = 0$: $0^2 = 250(y - 10)$
$$0 = y - 10$$
$$10 = y$$

When $x = 20$: $20^2 = 250(y - 10)$
$$400 = 250(y - 10)$$
$$1.6 = y - 10$$
$$11.6 = y$$

When $x = 40$: $40^2 = 250(y - 10)$
$$1600 = 250(y - 10)$$
$$6.4 = y - 10$$
$$16.4 = y$$

When $x = 60$: $60^2 = 250(y - 10)$
$$3600 = 250(y - 10)$$
$$14.4 = y - 10$$
$$24.4 = y$$

When $x = 80$: $80^2 = 250(y - 10)$
$$6400 = 250(y - 10)$$
$$25.6 = y - 10$$
$$35.6 = y$$

When $x = 100$, we know from the given information that $y = 50$.

The lengths of the vertical cables are 10 ft, 11.6 ft, 16.4 ft, 24.4 ft, 35.6 ft, and 50 ft.

Exercise Set 6.2

1. Graph (b) is the graph of $x^2 + y^2 = 5$.

3. Graph (d) is the graph of $x^2 + y^2 - 6x + 2y = 6$.

5. Graph (a) is the graph of $x^2 + y^2 - 5x + 3y = 0$.

7. Complete the square twice.

$$x^2 + y^2 - 14x + 4y = 11$$
$$x^2 - 14x + y^2 + 4y = 11$$
$$x^2 - 14x + 49 + y^2 + 4y + 4 = 11 + 49 + 4$$
$$(x - 7)^2 + (y + 2)^2 = 64$$
$$(x - 7)^2 + [y - (-2)]^2 = 8^2$$

Center: $(7, -2)$

Radius: 8

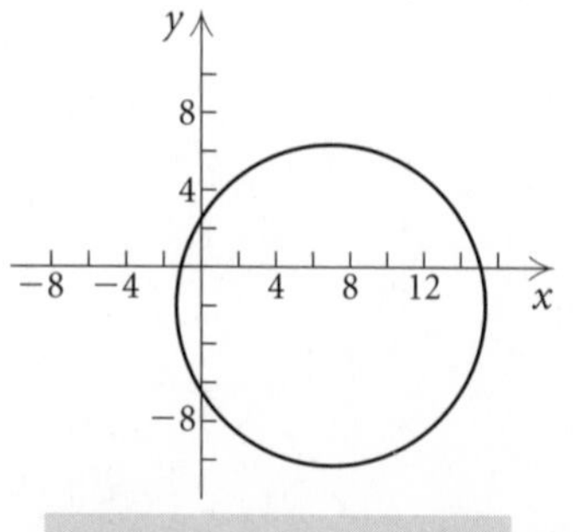

$x^2 + y^2 - 14x + 4y = 11$

9. Complete the square twice.

$$\begin{aligned} x^2+y^2+6x-2y &= 6 \\ x^2+6x+y^2-2y &= 6 \\ x^2+6x+9+y^2-2y+1 &= 6+9+1 \\ (x+3)^2+(y-1)^2 &= 16 \\ [x-(-3)]^2+(y-1)^2 &= 4^2 \end{aligned}$$

Center: $(-3, 1)$

Radius: 4

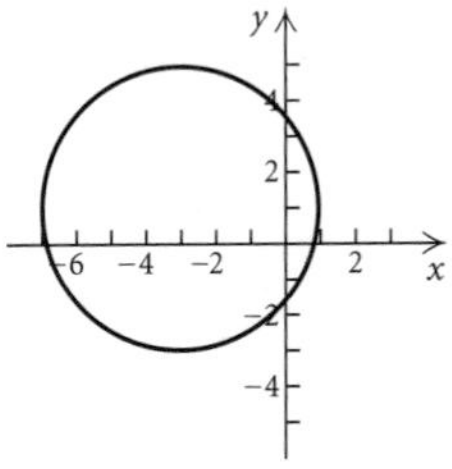

$x^2 + y^2 + 6x - 2y = 6$

11. Complete the square twice.

$$\begin{aligned} x^2+y^2+4x-6y-12 &= 0 \\ x^2+4x+y^2-6y &= 12 \\ x^2+4x+4+y^2-6y+9 &= 12+4+9 \\ (x+2)^2+(y-3)^2 &= 25 \\ [x-(-2)]^2+(y-3)^2 &= 5^2 \end{aligned}$$

Center: $(-2, 3)$

Radius: 5

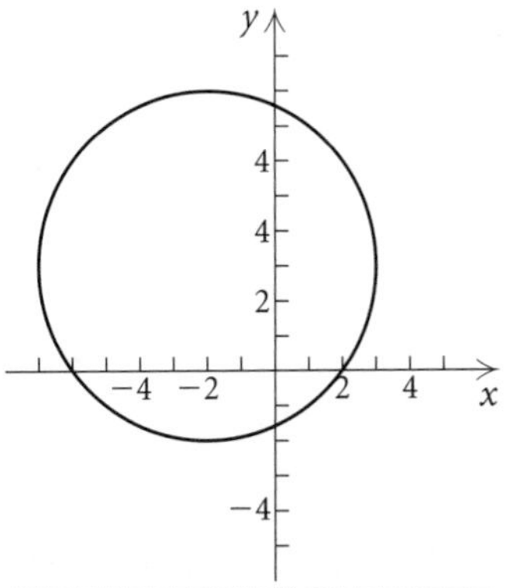

$x^2 + y^2 + 4x - 6y - 12 = 0$

13. Complete the square twice.

$$\begin{aligned} x^2+y^2-6x-8y+16 &= 0 \\ x^2-6x+y^2-8y &= -16 \\ x^2-6x+9+y^2-8y+16 &= -16+9+16 \\ (x-3)^2+(y-4)^2 &= 9 \\ (x-3)^2+(y-4)^2 &= 3^2 \end{aligned}$$

Center: $(3, 4)$

Radius: 3

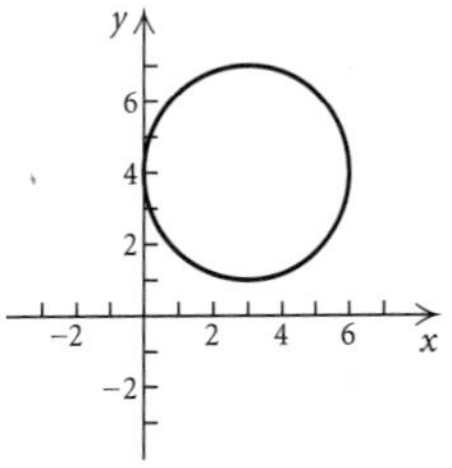

$x^2 + y^2 - 6x - 8y + 16 = 0$

15. Complete the square twice.

$$\begin{aligned} x^2+y^2+6x-10y &= 0 \\ x^2+6x+y^2-10y &= 0 \\ x^2+6x+9+y^2-10y+25 &= 0+9+25 \\ (x+3)^2+(y-5)^2 &= 34 \\ [x-(-3)]^2+(y-5)^2 &= (\sqrt{34})^2 \end{aligned}$$

Center: $(-3, 5)$

Radius: $\sqrt{34}$

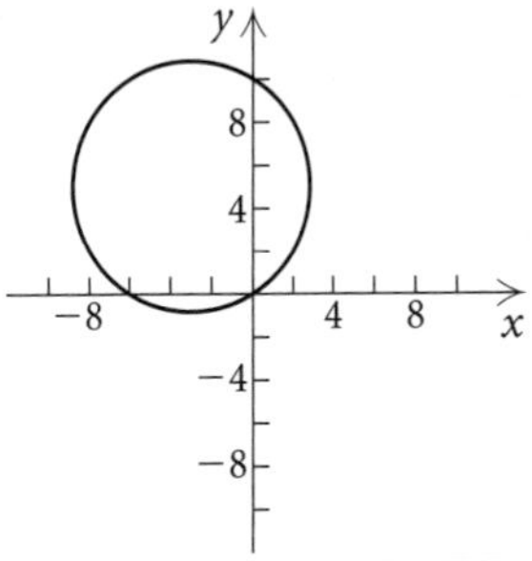

$x^2 + y^2 + 6x - 10y = 0$

17. Complete the square twice.

$$\begin{aligned} x^2+y^2-9x &= 7-4y \\ x^2-9x+y^2+4y &= 7 \\ x^2-9x+\frac{81}{4}+y^2+4y+4 &= 7+\frac{81}{4}+4 \\ \left(x-\frac{9}{2}\right)^2+(y+2)^2 &= \frac{125}{4} \\ \left(x-\frac{9}{2}\right)^2+[y-(-2)]^2 &= \left(\frac{5\sqrt{5}}{2}\right)^2 \end{aligned}$$

Center: $\left(\frac{9}{2}, -2\right)$

Radius: $\frac{5\sqrt{5}}{2}$

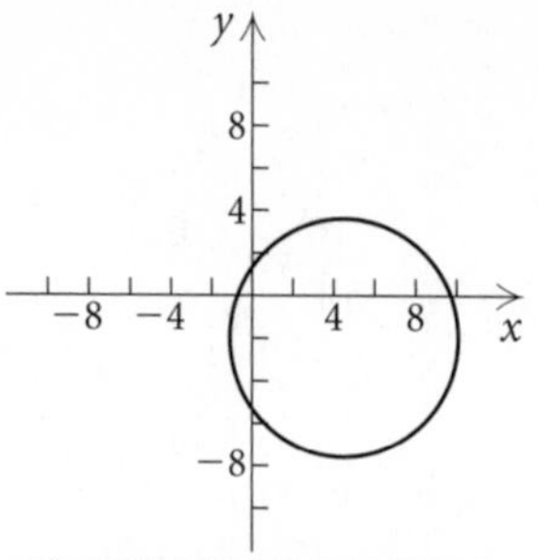

$x^2 + y^2 - 9x = 7 - 4y$

19. Graph (c) is the graph of $16x^2 + 4y^2 = 64$.

21. Graph (d) is the graph of $x^2 + 9y^2 - 6x + 90y = -225$.

23. $\dfrac{x^2}{4} + \dfrac{y^2}{1} = 1$

$\dfrac{x^2}{2^2} + \dfrac{y^2}{1^2} = 1$ Standard form

$a = 2$, $b = 1$

The major axis is horizontal, so the vertices are $(-2, 0)$ and $(2, 0)$. Since we know that $c^2 = a^2 - b^2$, we have $c^2 = 4 - 1 = 3$, so $c = \sqrt{3}$ and the foci are $(-\sqrt{3}, 0)$ and $(\sqrt{3}, 0)$.

To graph the ellipse, plot the vertices. Note also that since $b = 1$, the y-intercepts are $(0, -1)$ and $(0, 1)$. Plot these points as well and connect the four plotted points with a smooth curve.

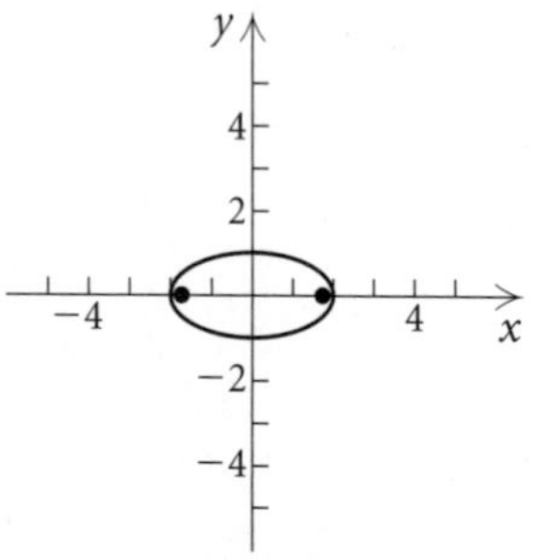

$\dfrac{x^2}{4} + \dfrac{y^2}{1} = 1$

25. $16x^2 + 9y^2 = 144$

$\dfrac{x^2}{9} + \dfrac{y^2}{16} = 1$ Dividing by 144

$\dfrac{x^2}{3^2} + \dfrac{y^2}{4^2} = 1$ Standard form

$a = 4$, $b = 3$

The major axis is vertical, so the vertices are $(0, -4)$ and $(0, 4)$. Since $c^2 = a^2 - b^2$, we have $c^2 = 16 - 9 = 7$, so $c = \sqrt{7}$ and the foci are $(0, -\sqrt{7})$ and $(0, \sqrt{7})$.

To graph the ellipse, plot the vertices. Note also that since $b = 3$, the x-intercepts are $(-3, 0)$ and $(3, 0)$. Plot these points as well and connect the four plotted points with a smooth curve.

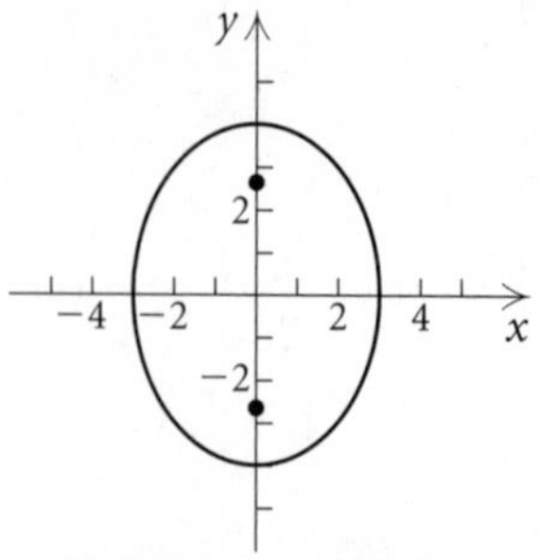

$16x^2 + 9y^2 = 144$

27. $2x^2 + 3y^2 = 6$

$\dfrac{x^2}{3} + \dfrac{y^2}{2} = 1$

$\dfrac{x^2}{(\sqrt{3})^2} + \dfrac{y^2}{(\sqrt{2})^2} = 1$

$a = \sqrt{3}$, $b = \sqrt{2}$

The major axis is horizontal, so the vertices are $(-\sqrt{3}, 0)$ and $(\sqrt{3}, 0)$. Since $c^2 = a^2 - b^2$, we have $c^2 = 3 - 2 = 1$, so $c = 1$ and the foci are $(-1, 0)$ and $(1, 0)$.

To graph the ellipse, plot the vertices. Note also that since $b = \sqrt{2}$, the y-intercepts are $(0, -\sqrt{2})$ and $(0, \sqrt{2})$. Plot these points as well and connect the four plotted points with a smooth curve.

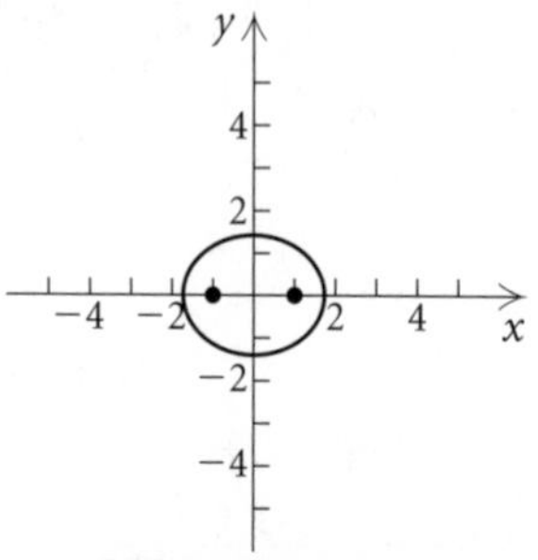

$2x^2 + 3y^2 = 6$

29. $4x^2 + 9y^2 = 1$

$\dfrac{x^2}{\frac{1}{4}} + \dfrac{y^2}{\frac{1}{9}} = 1$

$\dfrac{x^2}{\left(\frac{1}{2}\right)^2} + \dfrac{y^2}{\left(\frac{1}{3}\right)^2} = 1$

$a = \dfrac{1}{2}$, $b = \dfrac{1}{3}$

The major axis is horizontal, so the vertices are $\left(-\dfrac{1}{2}, 0\right)$ and $\left(\dfrac{1}{2}, 0\right)$. Since $c^2 = a^2 - b^2$, we have $c^2 = \dfrac{1}{4} - \dfrac{1}{9} = \dfrac{5}{36}$, so $c = \dfrac{\sqrt{5}}{6}$ and the foci are $\left(-\dfrac{\sqrt{5}}{6}, 0\right)$ and $\left(\dfrac{\sqrt{5}}{6}, 0\right)$.

To graph the ellipse, plot the vertices. Note also that since $b = \frac{1}{3}$, the y-intercepts are $\left(0, -\frac{1}{3}\right)$ and $\left(0, \frac{1}{3}\right)$. Plot these points as well and connect the four plotted points with a smooth curve.

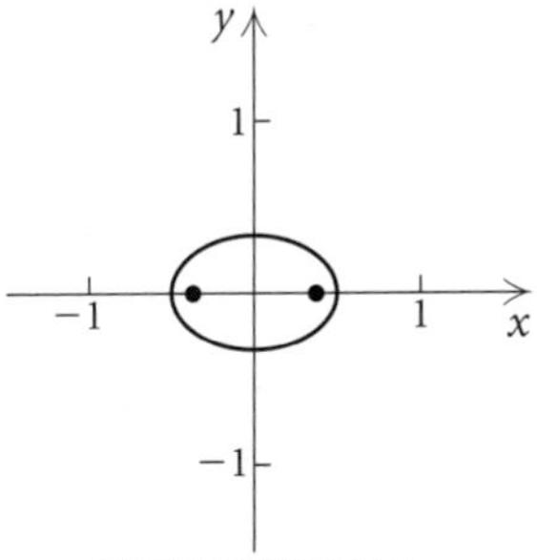

$4x^2 + 9y^2 = 1$

31. The vertices are on the x-axis, so the major axis is horizontal. We have $a = 7$ and $c = 3$, so we can find b^2:

$$c^2 = a^2 - b^2$$
$$3^2 = 7^2 - b^2$$
$$b^2 = 49 - 9 = 40$$

Write the equation:

$$\frac{x^2}{a^2} + \frac{y^2}{b^2} = 1$$
$$\frac{x^2}{49} + \frac{y^2}{40} = 1$$

33. The vertices, $(0, -8)$ and $(0, 8)$, are on the y-axis, so the major axis is vertical and $a = 8$. Since the vertices are equidistant from the origin, the center of the ellipse is at the origin. The length of the minor axis is 10, so $b = 10/2$, or 5.

Write the equation:

$$\frac{x^2}{b^2} + \frac{y^2}{a^2} = 1$$
$$\frac{x^2}{5^2} + \frac{y^2}{8^2} = 1$$
$$\frac{x^2}{25} + \frac{y^2}{64} = 1$$

35. The foci, $(-2, 0)$ and $(2, 0)$ are on the x-axis, so the major axis is horizontal and $c = 2$. Since the foci are equidistant from the origin, the center of the ellipse is at the origin. The length of the major axis is 6, so $a = 6/2$, or 3. Now we find b^2:

$$c^2 = a^2 - b^2$$
$$2^2 = 3^2 - b^2$$
$$4 = 9 - b^2$$
$$b^2 = 5$$

Write the equation:

$$\frac{x^2}{a^2} + \frac{y^2}{b^2} = 1$$
$$\frac{x^2}{9} + \frac{y^2}{5} = 1$$

37. $$\frac{(x-1)^2}{9} + \frac{(y-2)^2}{4} = 1$$
$$\frac{(x-1)^2}{3^2} + \frac{(y-2)^2}{2^2} = 1 \quad \text{Standard form}$$

The center is $(1, 2)$. Note that $a = 3$ and $b = 2$. The major axis is horizontal so the vertices are 3 units left and right of the center:

$(1 - 3, 2)$ and $(1 + 3, 2)$, or $(-2, 2)$ and $(4, 2)$.

We know that $c^2 = a^2 - b^2$, so $c^2 = 9 - 4 = 5$ and $c = \sqrt{5}$. Then the foci are $\sqrt{5}$ units left and right of the center:

$(1 - \sqrt{5}, 2)$ and $(1 + \sqrt{5}, 2)$.

To graph the ellipse, plot the vertices. Since $b = 2$, two other points on the graph are 2 units below and above the center:

$(1, 2 - 2)$ and $(1, 2 + 2)$ or $(1, 0)$ and $(1, 4)$

Plot these points also and connect the four plotted points with a smooth curve.

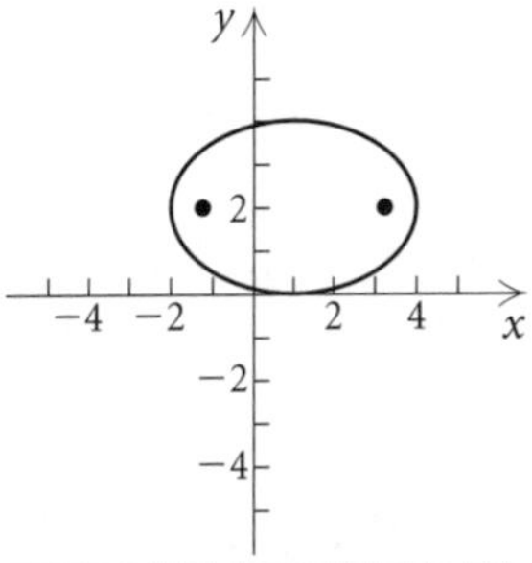

$\frac{(x-1)^2}{9} + \frac{(y-2)^2}{4} = 1$

39. $$\frac{(x+3)^2}{25} + \frac{(y-5)^2}{36} = 1$$
$$\frac{[x-(-3)]^2}{5^2} + \frac{(y-5)^2}{6^2} = 1 \quad \text{Standard form}$$

The center is $(-3, 5)$. Note that $a = 6$ and $b = 5$. The major axis is vertical so the vertices are 6 units below and above the center:

$(-3, 5 - 6)$ and $(-3, 5 + 6)$, or $(-3, -1)$ and $(-3, 11)$.

We know that $c^2 = a^2 - b^2$, so $c^2 = 36 - 25 = 11$ and $c = \sqrt{11}$. Then the foci are $\sqrt{11}$ units below and above the vertex:

$(-3, 5 - \sqrt{11})$ and $(-3, 5 + \sqrt{11})$.

To graph the ellipse, plot the vertices. Since $b = 5$, two other points on the graph are 5 units left and right of the center:

$(-3 - 5, 5)$ and $(-3 + 5, 5)$, or $(-8, 5)$ and $(2, 5)$

Plot these points also and connect the four plotted points with a smooth curve.

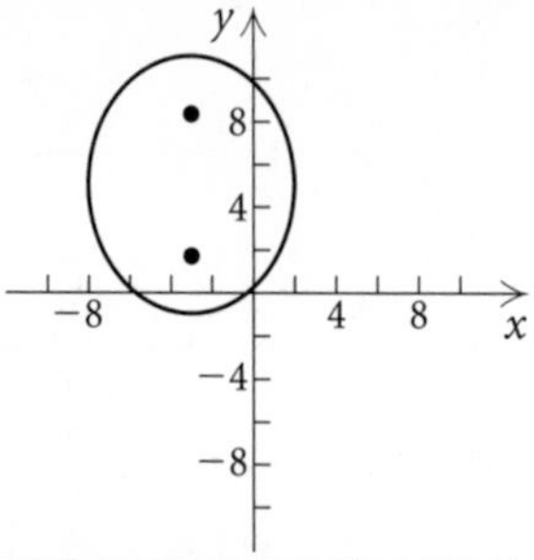

$$\frac{(x+3)^2}{25} + \frac{(y-5)^2}{36} = 1$$

41.
$$3(x+2)^2 + 4(y-1)^2 = 192$$
$$\frac{(x+2)^2}{64} + \frac{(y-1)^2}{48} = 1 \quad \text{Dividing by 192}$$
$$\frac{[x-(-2)]^2}{8^2} + \frac{(y-1)^2}{(\sqrt{48})^2} = 1 \quad \text{Standard form}$$

The center is $(-2, 1)$. Note that $a = 8$ and $b = \sqrt{48}$, or $4\sqrt{3}$. The major axis is horizontal so the vertices are 8 units left and right of the center:

$(-2-8, 1)$ and $(-2+8, 1)$, or $(-10, 1)$ and $(6, 1)$.

We know that $c^2 = a^2 - b^2$, so $c^2 = 64 - 48 = 16$ and $c = 4$. Then the foci are 4 units left and right of the center:

$(-2-4, 1)$ and $(-2+4, 1)$ or $(-6, 1)$ and $(2, 1)$.

To graph the ellipse, plot the vertices. Since $b = 4\sqrt{3} \approx 6.928$, two other points on the graph are about 6.928 units below and above the center:

$(-2, 1-6.928)$ and $(-2, 1+6.928)$, or

$(-2, -5.928)$ and $(-2, 7.928)$.

Plot these points also and connect the four plotted points with a smooth curve.

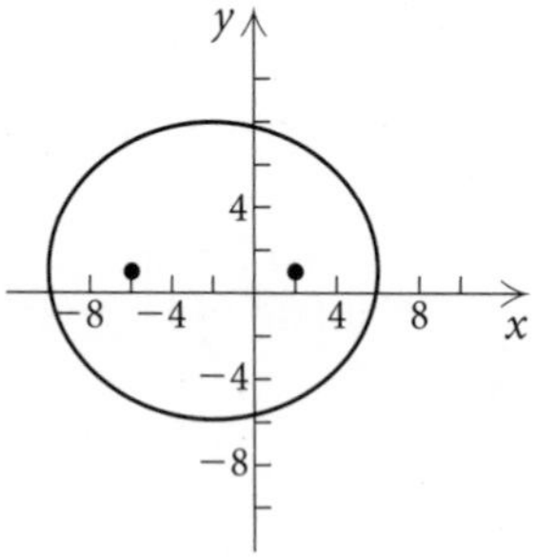

$$3(x+2)^2 + 4(y-1)^2 = 192$$

43. Begin by completing the square twice.

$$4x^2 + 9y^2 - 16x + 18y - 11 = 0$$
$$4x^2 - 16x + 9y^2 + 18y = 11$$
$$4(x^2 - 4x) + 9(y^2 + 2y) = 11$$
$$4(x^2 - 4x + 4) + 9(y^2 + 2y + 1) = 11 + 4 \cdot 4 + 9 \cdot 1$$
$$4(x-2)^2 + 9(y+1)^2 = 36$$
$$\frac{(x-2)^2}{9} + \frac{(y+1)^2}{4} = 1$$
$$\frac{(x-2)^2}{3^2} + \frac{[y-(-1)]^2}{2^2} = 1$$

The center is $(2, -1)$. Note that $a = 3$ and $b = 2$. The major axis is horizontal so the vertices are 3 units left and right of the center:

$(2-3, -1)$ and $(2+3, -1)$, or $(-1, -1)$ and $(5, -1)$.

We know that $c^2 = a^2 - b^2$, so $c^2 = 9 - 4 = 5$ and $c = \sqrt{5}$. Then the foci are $\sqrt{5}$ units left and right of the center:

$(2-\sqrt{5}, -1)$ and $(2+\sqrt{5}, -1)$.

To graph the ellipse, plot the vertices. Since $b = 2$, two other points on the graph are 2 units below and above the center:

$(2, -1-2)$ and $(2, -1+2)$, or $(2, -3)$ and $(2, 1)$.

Plot these points also and connect the four plotted points with a smooth curve.

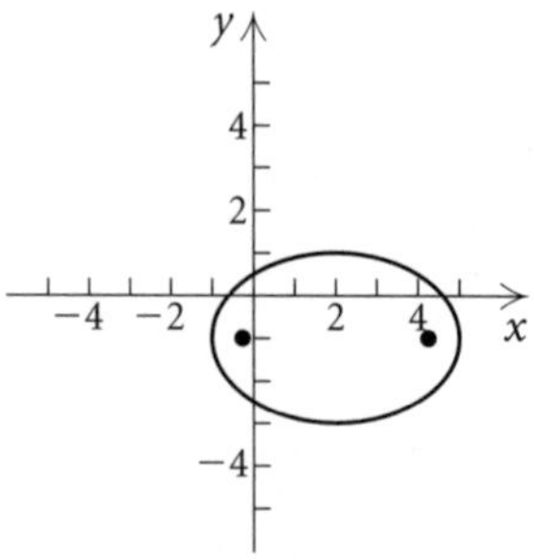

$$4x^2 + 9y^2 - 16x + 18y - 11 = 0$$

45. Begin by completing the square twice.

$$4x^2 + y^2 - 8x - 2y + 1 = 0$$
$$4x^2 - 8x + y^2 - 2y = -1$$
$$4(x^2 - 2x) + y^2 - 2y = -1$$
$$4(x^2 - 2x + 1) + y^2 - 2y + 1 = -1 + 4 \cdot 1 + 1$$
$$4(x-1)^2 + (y-1)^2 = 4$$
$$\frac{(x-1)^2}{1} + \frac{(y-1)^2}{4} = 1$$
$$\frac{(x-1)^2}{1^2} + \frac{(y-1)^2}{2^2} = 1$$

The center is $(1, 1)$. Note that $a = 2$ and $b = 1$. The major axis is vertical so the vertices are 2 units below and above the center:

$(1, 1-2)$ and $(1, 1+2)$, or $(1, -1)$ and $(1, 3)$.

We know that $c^2 = a^2 - b^2$, so $c^2 = 4 - 1 = 3$ and $c = \sqrt{3}$. Then the foci are $\sqrt{3}$ units below and above the center:

$(1, 1-\sqrt{3})$ and $(1, 1+\sqrt{3})$.

To graph the ellipse, plot the vertices. Since $b = 1$, two other points on the graph are 1 unit left and right of the center:

$(1-1, 1)$ and $(1+1, 1)$ or $(0, 1)$ and $(2, 1)$.

Plot these points also and connect the four plotted points with a smooth curve.

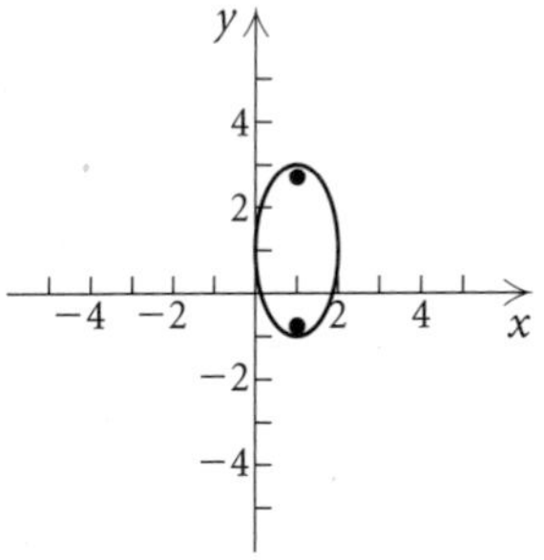

$4x^2 + y^2 - 8x - 2y + 1 = 0$

47. The ellipse in Example 4 is flatter than the one in Example 2, so the ellipse in Example 2 has the smaller eccentricity.

We compute the eccentricities: In Example 2, $c = 3$ and $a = 5$, so $e = c/a = 3/5 = 0.6$. In Example 4, $c = 2\sqrt{3}$ and $a = 4$, so $e = c/a = 2\sqrt{3}/4 \approx 0.866$. These computations confirm that the ellipse in Example 2 has the smaller eccentricity.

49. Since the vertices, $(0, -4)$ and $(0, 4)$ are on the y-axis and are equidistant from the origin, we know that the major axis of the ellipse is vertical, its center is at the origin, and $a = 4$. Use the information that $e = 1/4$ to find c:

$$e = \frac{c}{a}$$

$$\frac{1}{4} = \frac{c}{4} \quad \text{Substituting}$$

$$c = 1$$

Now $c^2 = a^2 - b^2$, so we can find b^2:

$$1^2 = 4^2 - b^2$$

$$1 = 16 - b^2$$

$$b^2 = 15$$

Write the equation of the ellipse:

$$\frac{x^2}{b^2} + \frac{y^2}{a^2} = 1$$

$$\frac{x^2}{15} + \frac{y^2}{16} = 1$$

51. From the figure in the text we see that the center of the ellipse is $(0, 0)$, the major axis is horizontal, the vertices are $(-50, 0)$ and $(50, 0)$, and one y-intercept is $(0, 12)$. Then $a = 50$ and $b = 12$. The equation is

$$\frac{x^2}{a^2} + \frac{y^2}{b^2} = 1$$

$$\frac{x^2}{50^2} + \frac{y}{12^2} = 1$$

$$\frac{x^2}{2500} + \frac{y^2}{144} = 1.$$

53. Position a coordinate system as shown below where 1 unit $= 10^7$ mi.

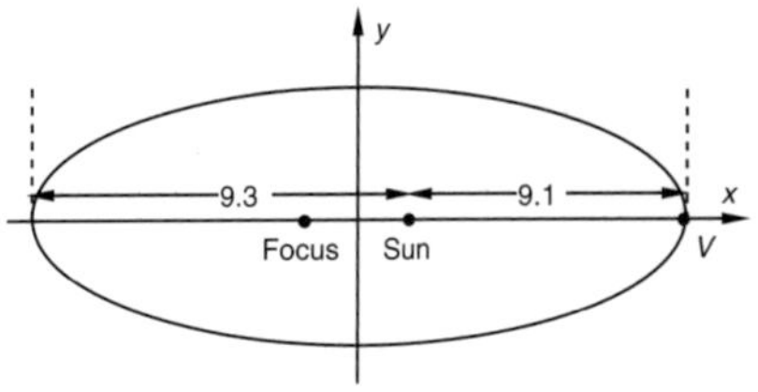

The length of the major axis is $9.3 + 9.1$, or 18.4. Then the distance from the center of the ellipse (the origin) to V is $18.4/2$, or 9.2. Since the distance from the sun to V is 9.1, the distance from the sun to the center is $9.2 - 9.1$, or 0.1. Then the distance from the sun to the other focus is twice this distance:

$$2(0.1 \times 10^7 \text{ mi}) = 0.2 \times 10^7 \text{ mi}$$

$$= 2 \times 10^6 \text{ mi}$$

55. Center: $(2.003, -1.005)$

Vertices: $(-1.017, -1.005)$, $(5.023, -1.005)$

57. Discussion and Writing

59. midpoint

61. y-intercept

63. remainder

65. parabola

67. The center of the ellipse is the midpoint of the segment connecting the vertices:

$$\left(\frac{3+3}{2}, \frac{-4+6}{2}\right), \text{ or } (3, 1).$$

Now a is the distance from the origin to a vertex. We use the vertex $(3, 6)$.

$$a = \sqrt{(3-3)^2 + (6-1)^2} = 5$$

Also b is one-half the length of the minor axis.

$$b = \frac{\sqrt{(5-1)^2 + (1-1)^2}}{2} = \frac{4}{2} = 2$$

The vertices lie on the vertical line $x = 3$, so the major axis is vertical. We write the equation of the ellipse.

$$\frac{(x-h)^2}{b^2} + \frac{(y-k)^2}{a^2} = 1$$

$$\frac{(x-3)^2}{4} + \frac{(y-1)^2}{25} = 1$$

69. The center is the midpoint of the segment connecting the vertices:

$$\left(\frac{-3+3}{0}, \frac{0+0}{0}\right), \text{ or } (0, 0).$$

Then $a = 3$ and since the vertices are on the x-axis, the major axis is horizontal. The equation is of the form $\frac{x^2}{a^2} + \frac{y^2}{b^2} = 1$.

Substitute 3 for a, 2 for x, and $\frac{22}{3}$ for y and solve for b^2.

$$\frac{4}{9} + \frac{\frac{484}{9}}{b^2} = 1$$
$$\frac{4}{9} + \frac{484}{9b^2} = 1$$
$$4b^2 + 484 = 9b^2$$
$$484 = 5b^2$$
$$\frac{484}{5} = b^2$$

Then the equation is $\frac{x^2}{9} + \frac{y^2}{484/5} = 1$.

71. Position a coordinate system as shown.

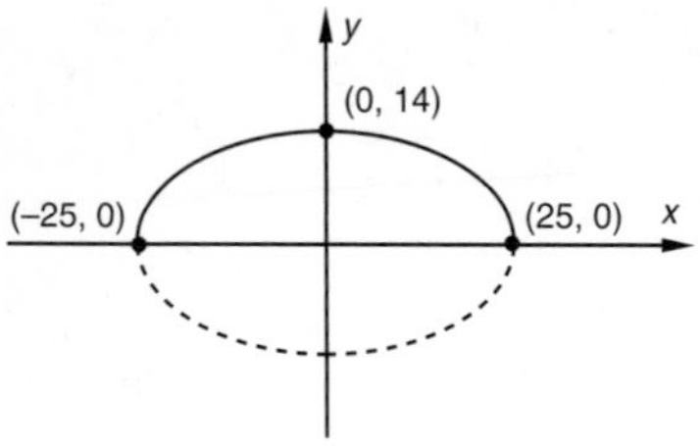

The equation of the ellipse is

$$\frac{x^2}{25^2} + \frac{y^2}{14^2} = 1$$
$$\frac{x^2}{625} + \frac{y^2}{196} = 1.$$

A point 6 ft from the riverbank corresponds to $(25-6, 0)$, or $(19, 0)$ or to $(-25+6, 0)$, or $(-19, 0)$. Substitute either 19 or -19 for x and solve for y, the clearance.

$$\frac{19^2}{625} + \frac{y^2}{196} = 1$$
$$\frac{y^2}{196} = 1 - \frac{361}{625}$$
$$y^2 = 196\left(1 - \frac{361}{625}\right)$$
$$y \approx 9.1$$

The clearance 6 ft from the riverbank is about 9.1 ft.

Exercise Set 6.3

1. Graph (b) is the graph of $\frac{x^2}{25} - \frac{y^2}{9} = 1$.

3. Graph (c) is the graph of $\frac{(y-1)^2}{16} - \frac{(x+3)^2}{1} = 1$.

5. Graph (a) is the graph of $25x^2 - 16y^2 = 400$.

7. The vertices are equidistant from the origin and are on the y-axis, so the center is at the origin and the transverse axis is vertical. Since $c^2 = a^2 + b^2$, we have $5^2 = 3^2 + b^2$ so $b^2 = 16$.

The equation is of the form $\frac{y^2}{a^2} - \frac{x^2}{b^2} = 1$, so we have $\frac{y^2}{9} - \frac{x^2}{16} = 1$.

9. The asymptotes pass through the origin, so the center is the origin. The given vertex is on the x-axis, so the transverse axis is horizontal. Since $\frac{b}{a}x = \frac{3}{2}x$ and $a = 2$, we have $b = 3$. The equation is of the form $\frac{x^2}{a^2} - \frac{y^2}{b^2} = 1$, so we have $\frac{x^2}{2^2} - \frac{y^2}{3^2} = 1$, or $\frac{x^2}{4} - \frac{y^2}{9} = 1$.

11. $\frac{x^2}{4} - \frac{y^2}{4} = 1$

$\frac{x^2}{2^2} - \frac{y^2}{2^2} = 1$ Standard form

The center is $(0, 0)$; $a = 2$ and $b = 2$. The transverse axis is horizontal so the vertices are $(-2, 0)$ and $(2, 0)$. Since $c^2 = a^2 + b^2$, we have $c^2 = 4 + 4 = 8$ and $c = \sqrt{8}$, or $2\sqrt{2}$. Then the foci are $(-2\sqrt{2}, 0)$ and $(2\sqrt{2}, 0)$.

Find the asymptotes:

$$y = \frac{b}{a}x \text{ and } y = -\frac{b}{a}x$$
$$y = \frac{2}{2}x \text{ and } y = -\frac{2}{2}x$$
$$y = x \text{ and } y = -x$$

To draw the graph sketch the asymptotes, plot the vertices, and draw the branches of the hyperbola outward from the vertices toward the asymptotes.

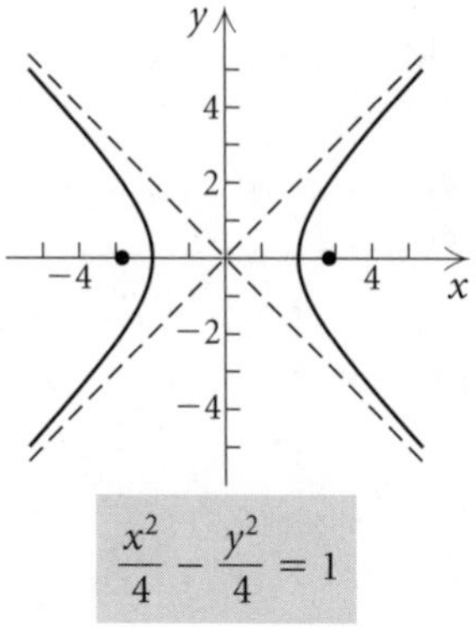

13. $\frac{(x-2)^2}{9} - \frac{(y+5)^2}{1} = 1$

$\frac{(x-2)^2}{3^2} - \frac{[y-(-5)]^2}{1^2} = 1$ Standard form

The center is $(2, -5)$; $a = 3$ and $b = 1$. The transverse axis is horizontal, so the vertices are 3 units left and right of the center:

$(2-3, -5)$ and $(2+3, -5)$, or $(-1, -5)$ and $(5, -5)$.

Since $c^2 = a^2 + b^2$, we have $c^2 = 9 + 1 = 10$ and $c = \sqrt{10}$. Then the foci are $\sqrt{10}$ units left and right of the center:

$$(2-\sqrt{10}, -5) \text{ and } (2+\sqrt{10}, -5).$$

Find the asymptotes:

$y - k = \frac{b}{a}(x - h)$ and $y - k = -\frac{b}{a}(x - h)$

$y - (-5) = \frac{1}{3}(x - 2)$ and $y - (-5) = -\frac{1}{3}(x - 2)$

$y + 5 = \frac{1}{3}(x - 2)$ and $y + 5 = -\frac{1}{3}(x - 2)$, or

$y = \frac{1}{3}x - \frac{17}{3}$ and $y = -\frac{1}{3}x - \frac{13}{3}$

Sketch the asymptotes, plot the vertices, and draw the graph.

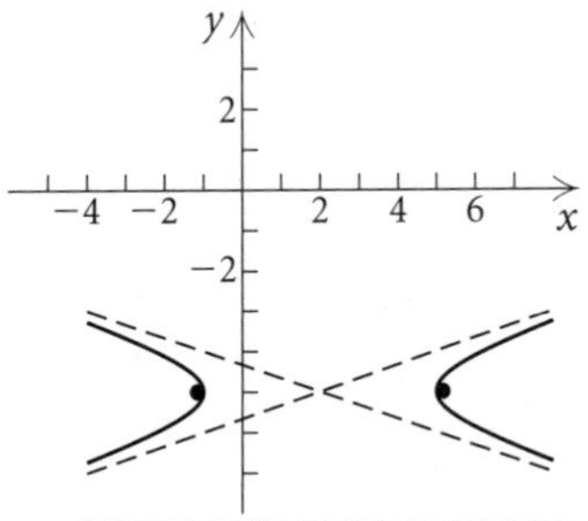

$$\frac{(x-2)^2}{9} - \frac{(y+5)^2}{1} = 1$$

15. $\frac{(y+3)^2}{4} - \frac{(x+1)^2}{16} = 1$

$\frac{[y-(-3)]^2}{2^2} - \frac{[x-(-1)]^2}{4^2} = 1$ Standard form

The center is $(-1, -3)$; $a = 2$ and $b = 4$. The transverse axis is vertical, so the vertices are 2 units below and above the center:

$(-1, -3 - 2)$ and $(1, -3 + 2)$, or $(-1, -5)$ and $(-1, -1)$.

Since $c^2 = a^2 + b^2$, we have $c^2 = 4 + 16 = 20$ and $c = \sqrt{20}$, or $2\sqrt{5}$. Then the foci are $2\sqrt{5}$ units below and above of the center:

$(-1, -3 - 2\sqrt{5})$ and $(-1, -3 + 2\sqrt{5})$.

Find the asymptotes:

$y - k = \frac{a}{b}(x - h)$ and $y - k = -\frac{a}{b}(x - h)$

$y - (-3) = \frac{2}{4}(x - (-1))$ and $y - (-3) = -\frac{2}{4}(x - (-1))$

$y + 3 = \frac{1}{2}(x + 1)$ and $y + 3 = -\frac{1}{2}(x + 1)$, or

$y = \frac{1}{2}x - \frac{5}{2}$ and $y = -\frac{1}{2}x - \frac{7}{2}$

Sketch the asymptotes, plot the vertices, and draw the graph.

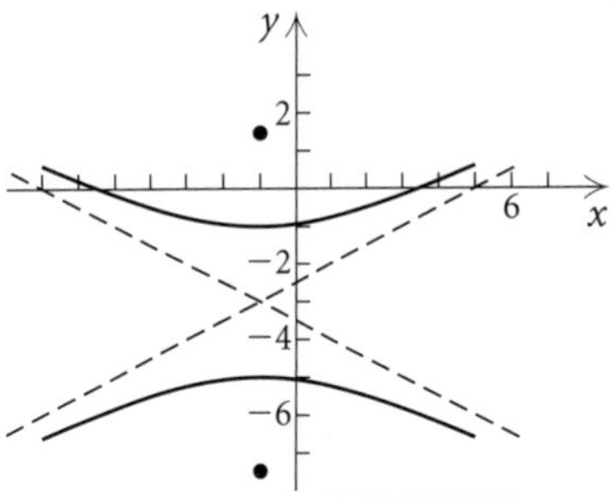

$$\frac{(y+3)^2}{4} - \frac{(x+1)^2}{16} = 1$$

17. $x^2 - 4y^2 = 4$

$\frac{x^2}{4} - \frac{y^2}{1} = 1$

$\frac{x^2}{2^2} - \frac{y^2}{1^2} = 1$ Standard form

The center is $(0, 0)$; $a = 2$ and $b = 1$. The transverse axis is horizontal, so the vertices are $(-2, 0)$ and $(2, 0)$. Since $c^2 = a^2 + b^2$, we have $c^2 = 4 + 1 = 5$ and $c = \sqrt{5}$. Then the foci are $(-\sqrt{5}, 0)$ and $(\sqrt{5}, 0)$.

Find the asymptotes:

$y = \frac{b}{a}x$ and $y = -\frac{b}{a}x$

$y = \frac{1}{2}x$ and $y = -\frac{1}{2}x$

Sketch the asymptotes, plot the vertices, and draw the graph.

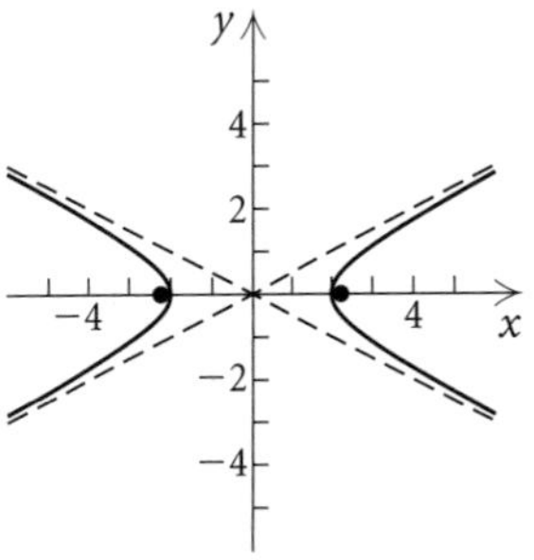

$$x^2 - 4y^2 = 4$$

19. $9y^2 - x^2 = 81$

$\frac{y^2}{9} - \frac{x^2}{81} = 1$

$\frac{y^2}{3^2} - \frac{x^2}{9^2} = 1$ Standard form

The center is $(0, 0)$; $a = 3$ and $b = 9$. The transverse axis is vertical, so the vertices are $(0, -3)$ and $(0, 3)$. Since $c^2 = a^2 + b^2$, we have $c^2 = 9 + 81 = 90$ and $c = \sqrt{90}$, or $3\sqrt{10}$. Then the foci are $(0, -3\sqrt{10})$ and $(0, 3\sqrt{10})$.

Find the asymptotes:

$$y = \frac{a}{b}x \text{ and } y = -\frac{a}{b}x$$

$$y = \frac{3}{9}x \text{ and } y = -\frac{3}{9}x$$

$$y = \frac{1}{3}x \text{ and } y = -\frac{1}{3}x$$

Sketch the asymptotes, plot the vertices, and draw the graph.

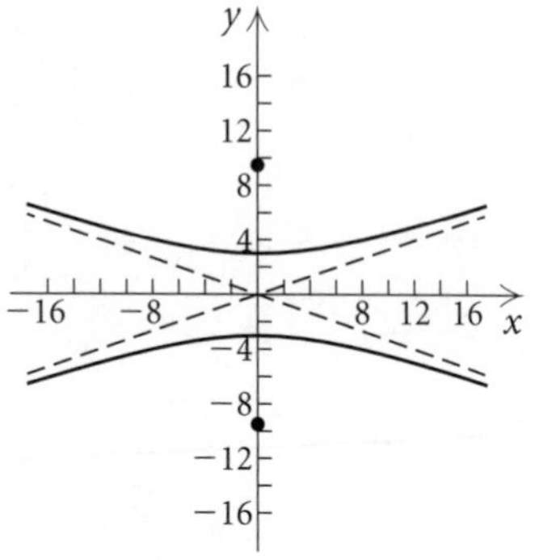

$9y^2 - x^2 = 81$

21.

$$x^2 - y^2 = 2$$

$$\frac{x^2}{2} - \frac{y^2}{2} = 1$$

$$\frac{x^2}{(\sqrt{2})^2} - \frac{y^2}{(\sqrt{2})^2} = 1 \quad \text{Standard form}$$

The center is $(0,0)$; $a = \sqrt{2}$ and $b = \sqrt{2}$. The transverse axis is horizontal, so the vertices are $(-\sqrt{2}, 0)$ and $(\sqrt{2}, 0)$. Since $c^2 = a^2 + b^2$, we have $c^2 = 2 + 2 = 4$ and $c = 2$. Then the foci are $(-2, 0)$ and $(2, 0)$.

Find the asymptotes:

$$y = \frac{b}{a}x \quad \text{and } y = -\frac{b}{a}x$$

$$y = \frac{\sqrt{2}}{\sqrt{2}}x \text{ and } y = -\frac{\sqrt{2}}{\sqrt{2}}x$$

$$y = x \quad \text{and } y = -x$$

Sketch the asymptotes, plot the vertices, and draw the graph.

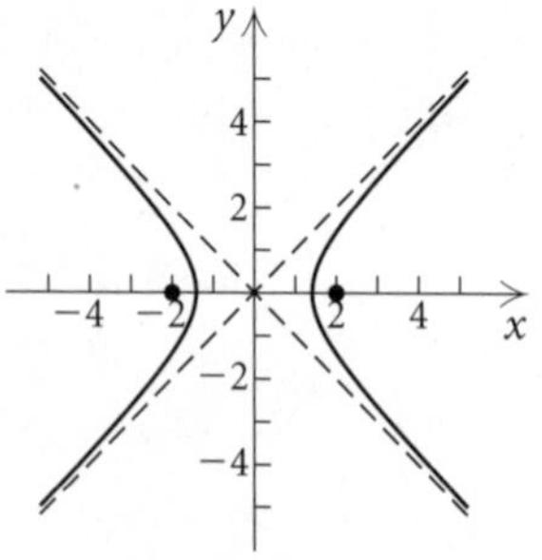

$x^2 - y^2 = 2$

23.

$$y^2 - x^2 = \frac{1}{4}$$

$$\frac{y^2}{1/4} - \frac{x^2}{1/4} = 1$$

$$\frac{y^2}{(1/2)^2} - \frac{x^2}{(1/2)^2} = 1 \quad \text{Standard form}$$

The center is $(0,0)$; $a = \frac{1}{2}$ and $b = \frac{1}{2}$. The transverse axis is vertical, so the vertices are $\left(0, -\frac{1}{2}\right)$ and $\left(0, \frac{1}{2}\right)$. Since $c^2 = a^2 + b^2$, we have $c^2 = \frac{1}{4} + \frac{1}{4} = \frac{1}{2}$ and $c = \sqrt{\frac{1}{2}}$, or $\frac{\sqrt{2}}{2}$. Then the foci are $\left(0, -\frac{\sqrt{2}}{2}\right)$ and $\left(0, \frac{\sqrt{2}}{2}\right)$.

Find the asymptotes:

$$y = \frac{a}{b}x \quad \text{and } y = -\frac{a}{b}x$$

$$y = \frac{1/2}{1/2}x \text{ and } y = -\frac{1/2}{1/2}x$$

$$y = x \quad \text{and } y = -x$$

Sketch the asymptotes, plot the vertices, and draw the graph.

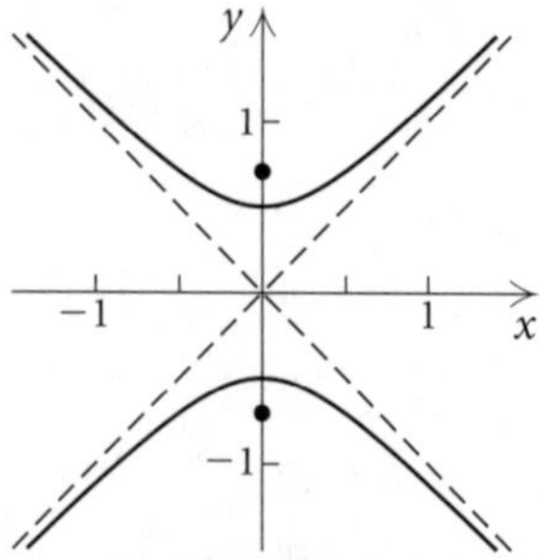

$y^2 - x^2 = \frac{1}{4}$

25. Begin by completing the square twice.

$$x^2 - y^2 - 2x - 4y - 4 = 0$$

$$(x^2 - 2x) - (y^2 + 4y) = 4$$

$$(x^2 - 2x + 1) - (y^2 + 4y + 4) = 4 + 1 - 1 \cdot 4$$

$$(x - 1)^2 - (y + 2)^2 = 1$$

$$\frac{(x-1)^2}{1^2} - \frac{[y - (-2)]^2}{1^2} = 1 \quad \text{Standard form}$$

The center is $(1, -2)$; $a = 1$ and $b = 1$. The transverse axis is horizontal, so the vertices are 1 unit left and right of the center:

$(1 - 1, -2)$ and $(1 + 1, -2)$ or $(0, -2)$ and $(2, -2)$

Since $c^2 = a^2 + b^2$, we have $c^2 = 1 + 1 = 2$ and $c = \sqrt{2}$. Then the foci are $\sqrt{2}$ units left and right of the center:

$$(1 - \sqrt{2}, -2) \text{ and } (1 + \sqrt{2}, -2).$$

Find the asymptotes:

$$y-k=\frac{b}{a}(x-h) \text{ and } \quad y-k=-\frac{b}{a}(x-h)$$

$$y-(-2)=\frac{1}{1}(x-1) \text{ and } y-(-2)=-\frac{1}{1}(x-1)$$

$$y+2=x-1 \quad \text{and} \quad y+2=-(x-1), \text{ or}$$

$$y=x-3 \quad \text{and} \quad y=-x-1$$

Sketch the asymptotes, plot the vertices, and draw the graph.

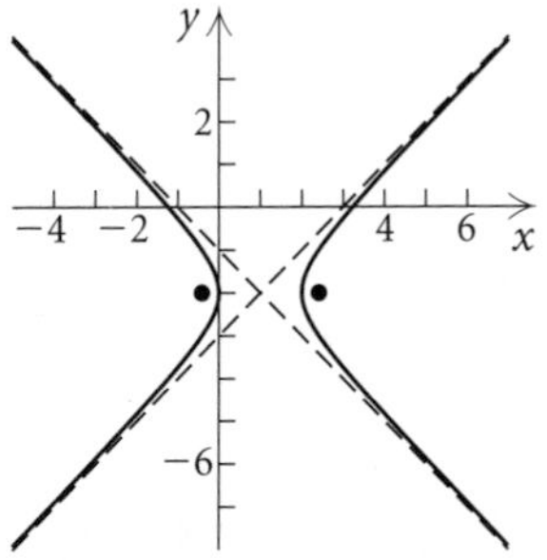

$x^2-y^2-2x-4y-4=0$

27. Begin by completing the square twice.

$$36x^2-y^2-24x+6y-41=0$$

$$(36x^2-24x)-(y^2-6y)=41$$

$$36\left(x^2-\frac{2}{3}x\right)-(y^2-6y)=41$$

$$36\left(x^2-\frac{2}{3}x+\frac{1}{9}\right)-(y^2-6y+9)=41+36\cdot\frac{1}{9}-1\cdot 9$$

$$36\left(x-\frac{1}{3}\right)^2-(y-3)^2=36$$

$$\frac{\left(x-\frac{1}{3}\right)^2}{1}-\frac{(y-3)^2}{36}=1$$

$$\frac{\left(x-\frac{1}{3}\right)^2}{1^2}-\frac{(y-3)^2}{6^2}=1 \quad \text{Standard form}$$

The center is $\left(\frac{1}{3},3\right)$; $a=1$ and $b=6$. The transverse axis is horizontal, so the vertices are 1 unit left and right of the center:

$\left(\frac{1}{3}-1,3\right)$ and $\left(\frac{1}{3}+1,3\right)$ or $\left(-\frac{2}{3},3\right)$ and $\left(\frac{4}{3},3\right)$.

Since $c^2=a^2+b^2$, we have $c^2=1+36=37$ and $c=\sqrt{37}$. Then the foci are $\sqrt{37}$ units left and right of the center:

$$\left(\frac{1}{3}-\sqrt{37},3\right) \text{ and } \left(\frac{1}{3}+\sqrt{37},3\right).$$

Find the asymptotes:

$$y-k=\frac{b}{a}(x-h) \quad \text{and } y-k=-\frac{b}{a}(x-h)$$

$$y-3=\frac{6}{1}\left(x-\frac{1}{3}\right) \text{ and } y-3=-\frac{6}{1}\left(x-\frac{1}{3}\right)$$

$$y-3=6\left(x-\frac{1}{3}\right) \text{ and } y-3=-6\left(x-\frac{1}{3}\right), \text{ or}$$

$$y=6x+1 \quad \text{and} \quad y=-6x+5$$

Sketch the asymptotes, plot the vertices, and draw the graph.

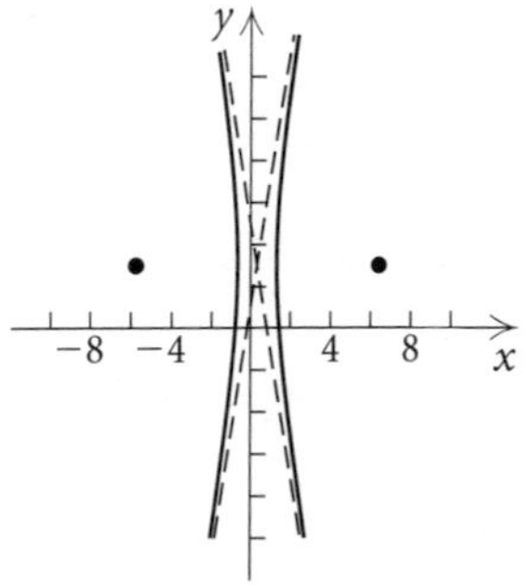

$36x^2-y^2-24x+6y-41=0$

29. Begin by completing the square twice.

$$9y^2-4x^2-18y+24x-63=0$$

$$9(y^2-2y)-4(x^2-6x)=63$$

$$9(y^2-2y+1)-4(x^2-6x+9)=63+9\cdot1-4\cdot9$$

$$9(y-1)^2-4(x-3)^2=36$$

$$\frac{(y-1)^2}{4}-\frac{(x-3)^2}{9}=1$$

$$\frac{(y-1)^2}{2^2}-\frac{(x-3)^2}{3^2}=1 \quad \text{Standard form}$$

The center is $(3,1)$; $a=2$ and $b=3$. The transverse axis is vertical, so the vertices are 2 units below and above the center:

$(3,1-2)$ and $(3,1+2)$, or $(3,-1)$ and $(3,3)$.

Since $c^2=a^2+b^2$, we have $c^2=4+9=13$ and $c=\sqrt{13}$. Then the foci are $\sqrt{13}$ units below and above the center:

$$(3,1-\sqrt{13}) \text{ and } (3,1+\sqrt{13}).$$

Find the asymptotes:

$$y-k=\frac{a}{b}(x-h) \text{ and } y-k=-\frac{a}{b}(x-h)$$

$$y-1=\frac{2}{3}(x-3) \text{ and } y-1=-\frac{2}{3}(x-3), \text{ or}$$

$$y=\frac{2}{3}x-1 \quad \text{and} \quad y=-\frac{2}{3}x+3$$

Sketch the asymptotes, plot the vertices, and draw the graph.

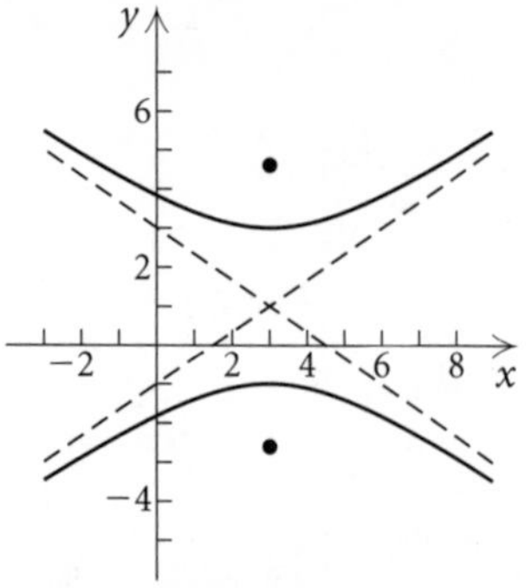

$9y^2 - 4x^2 - 18y + 24x - 63 = 0$

31. Begin by completing the square twice.

$$x^2 - y^2 - 2x - 4y = 4$$
$$(x^2 - 2x + 1) - (y^2 + 4y + 4) = 4 + 1 - 4$$
$$(x-1)^2 - (y+2)^2 = 1$$
$$\frac{(x-1)^2}{1^2} - \frac{[y-(-2)]^2}{1^2} = 1 \quad \text{Standard form}$$

The center is $(1, -2)$; $a = 1$ and $b = 1$. The transverse axis is horizontal, so the vertices are 1 unit left and right of the center:

$(1 - 1, -2)$ and $(1 + 1, -2)$, or $(0, -2)$ and $(2, -2)$.

Since $c^2 = a^2 + b^2$, we have $c^2 = 1 + 1 = 2$ and $c = \sqrt{2}$. Then the foci are $\sqrt{2}$ units left and right of the center:

$$(1 - \sqrt{2}, -2) \text{ and } (1 + \sqrt{2}, -2).$$

Find the asymptotes:

$$y - k = \frac{b}{a}(x - h) \text{ and } \quad y - k = -\frac{b}{a}(x - h)$$
$$y - (-2) = \frac{1}{1}(x - 1) \text{ and } y - (-2) = -\frac{1}{1}(x - 1)$$
$$y + 2 = x - 1 \quad \text{and} \quad y + 2 = -(x - 1), \text{ or}$$
$$y = x - 3 \quad \text{and} \quad y = -x - 1$$

Sketch the asymptotes, plot the vertices, and draw the graph.

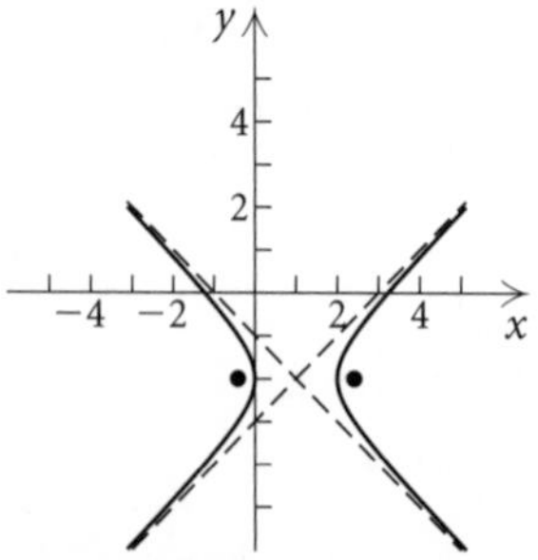

$x^2 - y^2 - 2x - 4y = 4$

33. Begin by completing the square twice.

$$y^2 - x^2 - 6x - 8y - 29 = 0$$
$$(y^2 - 8y + 16) - (x^2 + 6x + 9) = 29 + 16 - 9$$
$$(y-4)^2 - (x+3)^2 = 36$$
$$\frac{(y-4)^2}{36} - \frac{(x+3)^2}{36} = 1$$
$$\frac{(y-4)^2}{6^2} - \frac{[x-(-3)]^2}{6^2} = 1 \quad \text{Standard form}$$

The center is $(-3, 4)$; $a = 6$ and $b = 6$. The transverse axis is vertical, so the vertices are 6 units below and above the center:

$(-3, 4 - 6)$ and $(-3, 4 + 6)$, or $(-3, -2)$ and $(-3, 10)$.

Since $c^2 = a^2 + b^2$, we have $c^2 = 36+36 = 72$ and $c = \sqrt{72}$, or $6\sqrt{2}$. Then the foci are $6\sqrt{2}$ units below and above the center:

$$(-3, 4 - 6\sqrt{2}) \text{ and } (-3, 4 + 6\sqrt{2}).$$

Find the asymptotes:

$$y - k = \frac{a}{b}(x - h) \quad \text{and} \quad y - k = -\frac{a}{b}(x - h)$$
$$y - 4 = \frac{6}{6}(x - (-3)) \text{ and } y - 4 = -\frac{6}{6}(x - (-3))$$
$$y - 4 = x + 3 \quad \text{and} \quad y - 4 = -(x + 3), \text{ or}$$
$$y = x + 7 \quad \text{and} \quad y = -x + 1$$

Sketch the asymptotes, plot the vertices, and draw the graph.

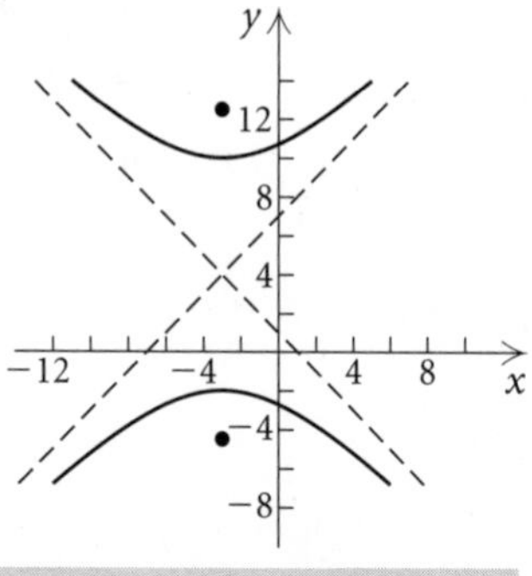

$y^2 - x^2 - 6x - 8y - 29 = 0$

35. The hyperbola in Example 3 is wider than the one in Example 2, so the hyperbola in Example 3 has the larger eccentricity.

Compute the eccentricities: In Example 2, $c = 5$ and $a = 4$, so $e = 5/4$, or 1.25. In Example 3, $c = \sqrt{5}$ and $a = 1$, so $e = \sqrt{5}/1 \approx 2.24$. These computations confirm that the hyperbola in Example 3 has the larger eccentricity.

37. The center is the midpoint of the segment connecting the vertices:

$$\left(\frac{3-3}{2}, \frac{7+7}{2}\right), \text{ or } (0, 7).$$

The vertices are on the horizontal line $y = 7$, so the transverse axis is horizontal. Since the vertices are 3 units left and right of the center, $a = 3$.

Find c:

$$e = \frac{c}{a} = \frac{5}{3}$$

$$\frac{c}{3} = \frac{5}{3} \quad \text{Substituting 3 for } a$$

$$c = 5$$

Now find b^2:

$$c^2 = a^2 + b^2$$

$$5^2 = 3^2 + b^2$$

$$16 = b^2$$

Write the equation:

$$\frac{(x-h)^2}{a^2} - \frac{(y-k)^2}{b^2} = 1$$

$$\frac{x^2}{9} - \frac{(y-7)^2}{16} = 1$$

39.

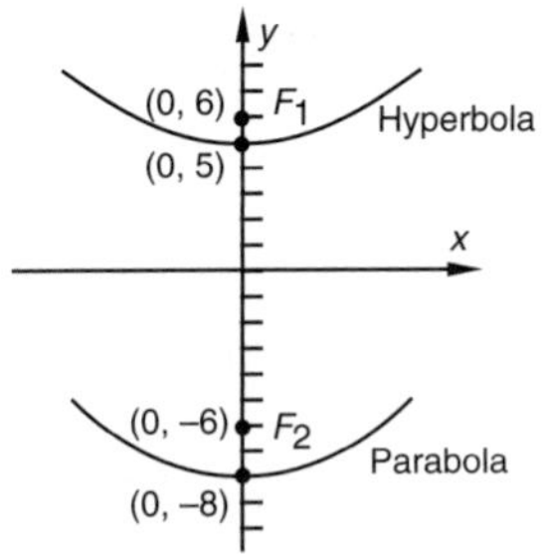

One focus is 6 units above the center of the hyperbola, so $c = 6$. One vertex is 5 units above the center, so $a = 5$. Find b^2:

$$c^2 = a^2 + b^2$$

$$6^2 = 5^2 + b^2$$

$$11 = b^2$$

Write the equation:

$$\frac{y^2}{a^2} - \frac{x^2}{b^2} = 1$$

$$\frac{y^2}{25} - \frac{x^2}{11} = 1$$

41. Center: $(-1.460, -0.957)$

Vertices: $(-2.360, -0.957)$, $(-0.560, -0.957)$

Asymptotes: $y = -1.429x - 3.043$, $y = 1.429x + 1.129$

43. Discussion and Writing

45. a) The graph of $f(x) = 2x - 3$ is shown below.

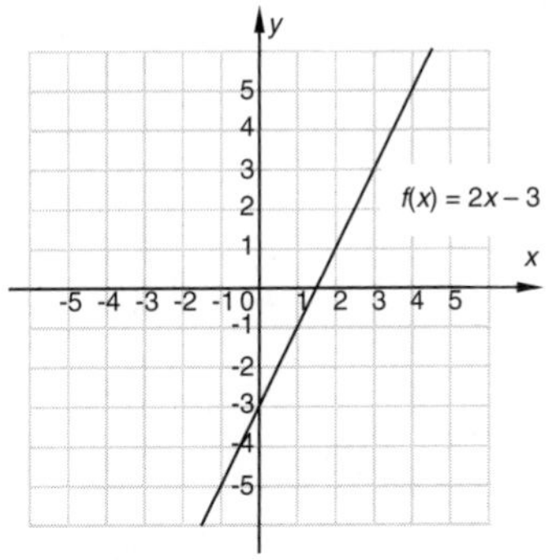

Since there is no horizontal line that crosses the graph more than once, the function is one-to-one.

b) Replace $f(x)$ with y: $y = 2x - 3$

Interchange x and y: $x = 2y - 3$

Solve for y: $x + 3 = 2y$

$$\frac{x+3}{2} = y$$

Replace y with $f^{-1}(x)$: $f^{-1}(x) = \dfrac{x+3}{2}$

47. a) The graph of $f(x) = \dfrac{5}{x-1}$ is shown below.

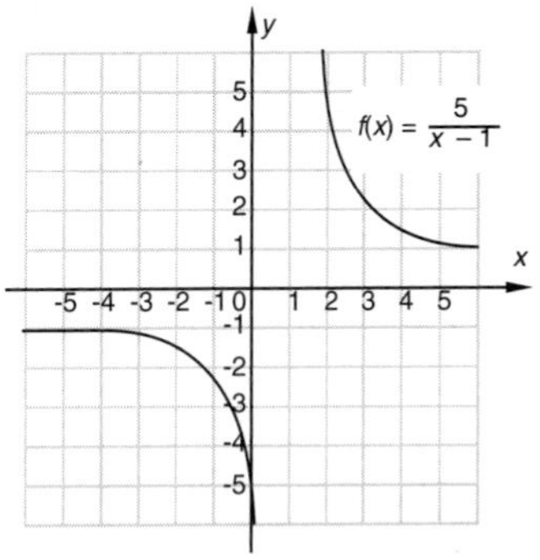

Since there is no horizontal line that crosses the graph more than once, the function is one-to-one.

b) Replace $f(x)$ with y: $y = \dfrac{5}{x-1}$

Interchange x and y: $x = \dfrac{5}{y-1}$

Solve for y: $x(y-1) = 5$

$$y - 1 = \frac{5}{x}$$

$$y = \frac{5}{x} + 1$$

Replace y with $f^{-1}(x)$: $f^{-1} = \dfrac{5}{x} + 1$, or $\dfrac{5+x}{x}$

49.

$$\begin{array}{rl} x + y = 5, & (1) \\ x - y = 7 & (2) \\ \hline 2x \quad = 12 & \text{Adding} \\ x = 6 & \end{array}$$

Back-substitute in either equation (1) or (2) and solve for y. We use equation (1).

$$6 + y = 5$$

$$y = -1$$

The solution is $(6, -1)$.

51. $2x - 3y = 7$, (1)

$3x + 5y = 1$ (2)

Multiply equation (1) by 5 and equation (2) by 3 and add to eliminate y.

$$\begin{array}{r} 10x - 15y = 35 \\ 9x + 15y = 3 \\ \hline 19x \quad = 38 \\ x = 2 \end{array}$$

Back-substitute and solve for y.

$$3 \cdot 2 + 5y = 1 \quad \text{Using equation (2)}$$
$$5y = -5$$
$$y = -1$$

The solution is $(2, -1)$.

53. The center is the midpoint of the segment connecting $(3, -8)$ and $(3, -2)$:

$$\left(\frac{3+3}{2}, \frac{-8-2}{2}\right), \text{ or } (3, -5).$$

The vertices are on the vertical line $x = 3$ and are 3 units above and below the center so the transverse axis is vertical and $a = 3$. Use the equation of an asymptote to find b:

$$y - k = \frac{a}{b}(x - h)$$
$$y + 5 = \frac{3}{b}(x - 3)$$
$$y = \frac{3}{b}x - \frac{9}{b} - 5$$

This equation corresponds to the asymptote $y = 3x - 14$, so $\frac{3}{b} = 3$ and $b = 1$.

Write the equation of the hyperbola:

$$\frac{(y-k)^2}{a^2} - \frac{(x-h)^2}{b^2} = 1$$
$$\frac{(y+5)^2}{9} - \frac{(x-3)^2}{1} = 1$$

55. S and T are the foci of the hyperbola, so $c = 300/2 = 150$.

$200 \text{ microseconds} \cdot \dfrac{0.186 \text{ mi}}{1 \text{ microsecond}} = 37.2 \text{ mi}$, the difference of the ships' distances from the foci. That is, $2a = 37.2$, so $a = 18.6$.

Find b^2:

$$c^2 = a^2 + b^2$$
$$150^2 = 18.6^2 + b^2$$
$$22{,}154.04 = b^2$$

Then the equation of the hyperbola is

$$\frac{x^2}{18.6^2} - \frac{y^2}{22{,}154.04} = 1, \text{ or } \frac{x^2}{345.96} - \frac{y^2}{22{,}154.04} = 1.$$

Exercise Set 6.4

1. The correct graph is (e).

3. The correct graph is (c).

5. The correct graph is (b).

7. $x^2 + y^2 = 25, \quad (1)$

$y - x = 1 \quad (2)$

First solve equation (2) for y.

$y = x + 1 \quad (3)$

Then substitute $x + 1$ for y in equation (1) and solve for x.

$$x^2 + y^2 = 25$$
$$x^2 + (x+1)^2 = 25$$
$$x^2 + x^2 + 2x + 1 = 25$$
$$2x^2 + 2x - 24 = 0$$
$$x^2 + x - 12 = 0 \quad \text{Multiplying by } \frac{1}{2}$$
$$(x+4)(x-3) = 0 \quad \text{Factoring}$$
$$x + 4 = 0 \quad \text{or} \quad x - 3 = 0 \quad \text{Principle of zero products}$$
$$x = -4 \quad \text{or} \quad x = 3$$

Now substitute these numbers into equation (3) and solve for y.

$$y = -4 + 1 = -3$$
$$y = 3 + 1 = 4$$

The pairs $(-4, -3)$ and $(3, 4)$ check, so they are the solutions.

9. $4x^2 + 9y^2 = 36, \quad (1)$

$3y + 2x = 6 \quad (2)$

First solve equation (2) for y.

$$3y = -2x + 6$$
$$y = -\frac{2}{3}x + 2 \quad (3)$$

Then substitute $-\frac{2}{3}x + 2$ for y in equation (1) and solve for x.

$$4x^2 + 9y^2 = 36$$
$$4x^2 + 9\left(-\frac{2}{3}x + 2\right)^2 = 36$$
$$4x^2 + 9\left(\frac{4}{9}x^2 - \frac{8}{3}x + 4\right) = 36$$
$$4x^2 + 4x^2 - 24x + 36 = 36$$
$$8x^2 - 24x = 0$$
$$x^2 - 3x = 0$$
$$x(x-3) = 0$$
$$x = 0 \quad \text{or} \quad x = 3$$

Now substitute these numbers in equation (3) and solve for y.

$$y = -\frac{2}{3} \cdot 0 + 2 = 2$$
$$y = -\frac{2}{3} \cdot 3 + 2 = 0$$

The pairs $(0, 2)$ and $(3, 0)$ check, so they are the solutions.

11. $x^2 + y^2 = 25, \quad (1)$

$y^2 = x + 5 \quad (2)$

We substitute $x + 5$ for y^2 in equation (1) and solve for x.

$$x^2 + y^2 = 25$$
$$x^2 + (x+5) = 25$$
$$x^2 + x - 20 = 0$$
$$(x+5)(x-4) = 0$$

$x+5=0$ or $x-4=0$

$x=-5$ or $x=4$

We substitute these numbers for x in either equation (1) or equation (2) and solve for y. Here we use equation (2).

$y^2=-5+5=0$ and $y=0$.

$y^2=4+5=9$ and $y=\pm 3$.

The pairs $(-5,0)$, $(4,3)$ and $(4,-3)$ check. They are the solutions.

13. $x^2+y^2=9$, (1)

$x^2-y^2=9$ (2)

Here we use the elimination method.

$$\begin{array}{rcll} x^2+y^2 &=& 9 & (1) \\ x^2-y^2 &=& 9 & (2) \\ \hline 2x^2 &=& 18 & \text{Adding} \\ x^2 &=& 9 & \\ x &=& \pm 3 & \end{array}$$

If $x=3$, $x^2=9$, and if $x=-3$, $x^2=9$, so substituting 3 or -3 in equation (1) gives us

$$x^2+y^2=9$$
$$9+y^2=9$$
$$y^2=0$$
$$y=0.$$

The pairs $(3,0)$ and $(-3,0)$ check. They are the solutions.

15. $y^2-x^2=9$ (1)

$2x-3=y$ (2)

Substitute $2x-3$ for y in equation (1) and solve for x.

$$y^2-x^2=9$$
$$(2x-3)^2-x^2=9$$
$$4x^2-12x+9-x^2=9$$
$$3x^2-12x=0$$
$$x^2-4x=0$$
$$x(x-4)=0$$

$x=0$ or $x=4$

Now substitute these numbers into equation (2) and solve for y.

If $x=0$, $y=2\cdot 0-3=-3$.

If $x=4$, $y=2\cdot 4-3=5$.

The pairs $(0,-3)$ and $(4,5)$ check. They are the solutions.

17. $y^2=x+3$, (1)

$2y=x+4$ (2)

First solve equation (2) for x.

$2y-4=x$ (3)

Then substitute $2y-4$ for x in equation (1) and solve for y.

$$y^2=x+3$$
$$y^2=(2y-4)+3$$
$$y^2=2y-1$$
$$y^2-2y+1=0$$
$$(y-1)(y-1)=0$$

$y-1=0$ or $y-1=0$

$y=1$ or $y=1$

Now substitute 1 for y in equation (3) and solve for x.

$$2\cdot 1-4=x$$
$$-2=x$$

The pair $(-2,1)$ checks. It is the solution.

19. $x^2+y^2=25$, (1)

$xy=12$ (2)

First we solve equation (2) for y.

$$xy=12$$
$$y=\frac{12}{x}$$

Then we substitute $\frac{12}{x}$ for y in equation (1) and solve for x.

$$x^2+y^2=25$$
$$x^2+\left(\frac{12}{x}\right)^2=25$$
$$x^2+\frac{144}{x^2}=25$$
$$x^4+144=25x^2 \quad \text{Multiplying by } x^2$$
$$x^4-25x^2+144=0$$
$$u^2-25u+144=0 \quad \text{Letting } u=x^2$$
$$(u-9)(u-16)=0$$

$u=9$ or $u=16$

We now substitute x^2 for u and solve for x.

$x^2=9$ or $x^2=16$

$x=\pm 3$ or $x=\pm 4$

Since $y=12/x$, if $x=3$, $y=4$; if $x=-3$, $y=-4$; if $x=4$, $y=3$; and if $x=-4$, $y=-3$. The pairs $(3,4)$, $(-3,-4)$, $(4,3)$, and $(-4,-3)$ check. They are the solutions.

21. $x^2+y^2=4$, (1)

$16x^2+9y^2=144$ (2)

$$\begin{array}{rcll} -9x^2-9y^2 &=& -36 & \text{Multiplying (1) by } -9 \\ 16x^2+9y^2 &=& 144 & \\ \hline 7x^2 &=& 108 & \text{Adding} \end{array}$$

$$x^2=\frac{108}{7}$$
$$x=\pm\sqrt{\frac{108}{7}}=\pm 6\sqrt{\frac{3}{7}}$$
$$x=\pm\frac{6\sqrt{21}}{7} \quad \text{Rationalizing the denominator}$$

Substituting $\frac{6\sqrt{21}}{7}$ or $-\frac{6\sqrt{21}}{7}$ for x in equation (1) gives us

$$\frac{36 \cdot 21}{49} + y^2 = 4$$

$$y^2 = 4 - \frac{108}{7}$$

$$y^2 = -\frac{80}{7}$$

$$y = \pm\sqrt{-\frac{80}{7}} = \pm 4i\sqrt{\frac{5}{7}}$$

$$y = \pm\frac{4i\sqrt{35}}{7}. \quad \text{Rationalizing the denominator}$$

The pairs $\left(\frac{6\sqrt{21}}{7}, \frac{4i\sqrt{35}}{7}\right)$, $\left(\frac{6\sqrt{21}}{7}, -\frac{4i\sqrt{35}}{7}\right)$, $\left(-\frac{6\sqrt{21}}{7}, \frac{4i\sqrt{35}}{7}\right)$, and $\left(-\frac{6\sqrt{21}}{7}, -\frac{4i\sqrt{35}}{7}\right)$ check. They are the solutions.

23. $x^2 + 4y^2 = 25$, (1)

$x + 2y = 7$ (2)

First solve equation (2) for x.

$x = -2y + 7$ (3)

Then substitute $-2y + 7$ for x in equation (1) and solve for y.

$$x^2 + 4y^2 = 25$$
$$(-2y+7)^2 + 4y^2 = 25$$
$$4y^2 - 28y + 49 + 4y^2 = 25$$
$$8y^2 - 28y + 24 = 0$$
$$2y^2 - 7y + 6 = 0$$
$$(2y-3)(y-2) = 0$$

$y = \frac{3}{2}$ or $y = 2$

Now substitute these numbers in equation (3) and solve for x.

$$x = -2 \cdot \frac{3}{2} + 7 = 4$$
$$x = -2 \cdot 2 + 7 = 3$$

The pairs $\left(4, \frac{3}{2}\right)$ and $(3, 2)$ check, so they are the solutions.

25. $x^2 - xy + 3y^2 = 27$, (1)

$x - y = 2$ (2)

First solve equation (2) for y.

$x - 2 = y$ (3)

Then substitute $x - 2$ for y in equation (1) and solve for x.

$$x^2 - xy + 3y^2 = 27$$
$$x^2 - x(x-2) + 3(x-2)^2 = 27$$
$$x^2 - x^2 + 2x + 3x^2 - 12x + 12 = 27$$
$$3x^2 - 10x - 15 = 0$$

$$x = \frac{-(-10) \pm \sqrt{(-10)^2 - 4(3)(-15)}}{2 \cdot 3}$$

$$x = \frac{10 \pm \sqrt{100+180}}{6} = \frac{10 \pm \sqrt{280}}{6}$$

$$x = \frac{10 \pm 2\sqrt{70}}{6} = \frac{5 \pm \sqrt{70}}{3}$$

Now substitute these numbers in equation (3) and solve for y.

$$y = \frac{5+\sqrt{70}}{3} - 2 = \frac{-1+\sqrt{70}}{3}$$

$$y = \frac{5-\sqrt{70}}{3} - 2 = \frac{-1-\sqrt{70}}{3}$$

The pairs $\left(\frac{5+\sqrt{70}}{3}, \frac{-1+\sqrt{70}}{3}\right)$ and $\left(\frac{5-\sqrt{70}}{3}, \frac{-1-\sqrt{70}}{3}\right)$ check, so they are the solutions.

27. $x^2 + y^2 = 16$, $\quad$ $x^2 + y^2 = 16$, (1)

or

$y^2 - 2x^2 = 10$ $\quad$ $-2x^2 + y^2 = 10$ (2)

Here we use the elimination method.

$$\begin{array}{rl} 2x^2 + 2y^2 = 32 & \text{Multiplying (1) by 2} \\ -2x^2 + y^2 = 10 & \\ \hline 3y^2 = 42 & \text{Adding} \\ y^2 = 14 & \\ y = \pm\sqrt{14} & \end{array}$$

Substituting $\sqrt{14}$ or $-\sqrt{14}$ for y in equation (1) gives us

$$x^2 + 14 = 16$$
$$x^2 = 2$$
$$x = \pm\sqrt{2}$$

The pairs $(-\sqrt{2}, -\sqrt{14})$, $(-\sqrt{2}, \sqrt{14})$, $(\sqrt{2}, -\sqrt{14})$, and $(\sqrt{2}, \sqrt{14})$ check. They are the solutions.

29. $x^2 + y^2 = 5$, (1)

$xy = 2$ (2)

First we solve equation (2) for y.

$$xy = 2$$
$$y = \frac{2}{x}$$

Then we substitute $\frac{2}{x}$ for y in equation (1) and solve for x.

$$x^2 + y^2 = 5$$
$$x^2 + \left(\frac{2}{x}\right)^2 = 5$$
$$x^2 + \frac{4}{x^2} = 5$$
$$x^4 + 4 = 5x^2 \quad \text{Multiplying by } x^2$$
$$x^4 - 5x^2 + 4 = 0$$
$$u^2 - 5u + 4 = 0 \quad \text{Letting } u = x^2$$
$$(u-4)(u-1) = 0$$

$u = 4$ or $u = 1$

We now substitute x^2 for u and solve for x.

$x^2 = 4$ or $x^2 = 1$

$x = \pm 2$ $\quad$ $x = \pm 1$

Since $y = 2/x$, if $x = 2$, $y = 1$; if $x = -2$, $y = -1$; if $x = 1$, $y = 2$; and if $x = -1$, $y = -2$. The pairs $(2, 1)$, $(-2, -1)$, $(1, 2)$, and $(-1, -2)$ check. They are the solutions.

31. $3x+y=7$ (1)
$4x^2+5y=56$ (2)

First solve equation (1) for y.

$$3x+y=7$$
$$y=7-3x \quad (3)$$

Next substitute $7-3x$ for y in equation (2) and solve for x.

$$4x^2+5y=56$$
$$4x^2+5(7-3x)=56$$
$$4x^2+35-15x=56$$
$$4x^2-15x-21=0$$

Using the quadratic formula, we find that

$x=\dfrac{15-\sqrt{561}}{8}$ or $x=\dfrac{15+\sqrt{561}}{8}$.

Now substitute these numbers into equation (3) and solve for y.

If $x=\dfrac{15-\sqrt{561}}{8}$, $y=7-3\left(\dfrac{15-\sqrt{561}}{8}\right)$, or $\dfrac{11+3\sqrt{561}}{8}$.

If $x=\dfrac{15+\sqrt{561}}{8}$, $y=7-3\left(\dfrac{15+\sqrt{561}}{8}\right)$, or $\dfrac{11-3\sqrt{561}}{8}$.

The pairs $\left(\dfrac{15-\sqrt{561}}{8},\dfrac{11+3\sqrt{561}}{8}\right)$ and $\left(\dfrac{15+\sqrt{561}}{8},\dfrac{11-3\sqrt{561}}{8}\right)$ check and are the solutions.

33. $a+b=7,$ (1)
$ab=4$ (2)

First solve equation (1) for a.

$a=-b+7$ (3)

Then substitute $-b+7$ for a in equation (2) and solve for b.

$$(-b+7)b=4$$
$$-b^2+7b=4$$
$$0=b^2-7b+4$$
$$b=\frac{-(-7)\pm\sqrt{(-7)^2-4\cdot 1\cdot 4}}{2\cdot 1}$$
$$b=\frac{7\pm\sqrt{33}}{2}$$

Now substitute these numbers in equation (3) and solve for a.

$$a=-\left(\frac{7+\sqrt{33}}{2}\right)+7=\frac{7-\sqrt{33}}{2}$$
$$a=-\left(\frac{7-\sqrt{33}}{2}\right)+7=\frac{7+\sqrt{33}}{2}$$

The pairs $\left(\dfrac{7-\sqrt{33}}{2},\dfrac{7+\sqrt{33}}{2}\right)$ and $\left(\dfrac{7+\sqrt{33}}{2},\dfrac{7-\sqrt{33}}{2}\right)$ check, so they are the solutions.

35. $x^2+y^2=13,$ (1)
$xy=6$ (2)

First we solve Equation (2) for y.

$$xy=6$$
$$y=\frac{6}{x}$$

Then we substitute $\dfrac{6}{x}$ for y in equation (1) and solve for x.

$$x^2+y^2=13$$
$$x^2+\left(\frac{6}{x}\right)^2=13$$
$$x^2+\frac{36}{x^2}=13$$
$$x^4+36=13x^2 \quad \text{Multiplying by } x^2$$
$$x^4-13x^2+36=0$$
$$u^2-13u+36=0 \quad \text{Letting } u=x^2$$
$$(u-9)(u-4)=0$$
$$u=9 \quad \text{or} \quad u=4$$

We now substitute x^2 for u and solve for x.

$$x^2=9 \quad \text{or} \quad x^2=4$$
$$x=\pm 3 \quad \text{or} \quad x=\pm 2$$

Since $y=6/x$, if $x=3$, $y=2$; if $x=-3$, $y=-2$; if $x=2$, $y=3$; and if $x=-2$, $y=-3$. The pairs $(3,2)$, $(-3,-2)$, $(2,3)$, and $(-2,-3)$ check. They are the solutions.

37. $x^2+y^2+6y+5=0$ (1)
$x^2+y^2-2x-8=0$ (2)

Using the elimination method, multiply equation (2) by -1 and add the result to equation (1).

$$x^2+y^2+6y+5=0 \quad (1)$$
$$-x^2-y^2+2x+8=0 \quad (2)$$
$$\overline{2x+6y+13=0} \quad (3)$$

Solve equation (3) for x.

$$2x+6y+13=0$$
$$2x=-6y-13$$
$$x=\frac{-6y-13}{2}$$

Substitute $\dfrac{-6y-13}{2}$ for x in equation (1) and solve for y.

$$x^2+y^2+6y+5=0$$
$$\left(\frac{-6y-13}{2}\right)^2+y^2+6y+5=0$$
$$\frac{36y^2+156y+169}{4}+y^2+6y+5=0$$
$$36y^2+156y+169+4y^2+24y+20=0$$
$$40y^2+180y+189=0$$

Using the quadratic formula, we find that

$y=\dfrac{-45\pm 3\sqrt{15}}{20}$. Substitute $\dfrac{-45\pm 3\sqrt{15}}{20}$ for y in

$x = \dfrac{-6y-13}{2}$ and solve for x.

If $y = \dfrac{-45+3\sqrt{15}}{20}$, then

$$x = \frac{-6\left(\dfrac{-45+3\sqrt{15}}{20}\right)-13}{2} = \frac{5-9\sqrt{15}}{20}.$$

If $y = \dfrac{-45-3\sqrt{15}}{20}$, then

$$x = \frac{-6\left(\dfrac{-45-3\sqrt{15}}{20}\right)-13}{2} = \frac{5+9\sqrt{15}}{20}.$$

The pairs $\left(\dfrac{5+9\sqrt{15}}{20}, \dfrac{-45-3\sqrt{15}}{20}\right)$ and $\left(\dfrac{5-9\sqrt{15}}{20}, \dfrac{-45+3\sqrt{15}}{20}\right)$ check and are the solutions.

39. $2a+b=1, \quad (1)$

$b = 4-a^2 \quad (2)$

Equation (2) is already solved for b. Substitute $4-a^2$ for b in equation (1) and solve for a.

$$\begin{aligned} 2a+4-a^2 &= 1 \\ 0 &= a^2-2a-3 \\ 0 &= (a-3)(a+1) \end{aligned}$$

$a=3 \quad \text{or} \quad a=-1$

Substitute these numbers in equation (2) and solve for b.

$b = 4-3^2 = -5$

$b = 4-(-1)^2 = 3$

The pairs $(3,-5)$ and $(-1,3)$ check. They are the solutions.

41. $a^2+b^2=89, \quad (1)$

$a-b=3 \quad (2)$

First solve equation (2) for a.

$a = b+3 \quad (3)$

Then substitute $b+3$ for a in equation (1) and solve for b.

$$\begin{aligned} (b+3)^2+b^2 &= 89 \\ b^2+6b+9+b^2 &= 89 \\ 2b^2+6b-80 &= 0 \\ b^2+3b-40 &= 0 \\ (b+8)(b-5) &= 0 \end{aligned}$$

$b=-8$ or $b=5$

Substitute these numbers in equation (3) and solve for a.

$a = -8+3 = -5$

$a = 5+3 = 8$

The pairs $(-5,-8)$ and $(8,5)$ check. They are the solutions.

43. $xy-y^2 = 2, \quad (1)$

$2xy-3y^2 = 0 \quad (2)$

$$\begin{aligned} -2xy+2y^2 &= -4 \quad \text{Multiplying (1) by } -2 \\ 2xy-3y^2 &= 0 \\ \hline -y^2 &= -4 \quad \text{Adding} \\ y^2 &= 4 \\ y &= \pm 2 \end{aligned}$$

We substitute for y in equation (1) and solve for x.

When $y=2$: $\quad x\cdot 2-2^2 = 2$

$$\begin{aligned} 2x-4 &= 2 \\ 2x &= 6 \\ x &= 3 \end{aligned}$$

When $y=-2$: $\quad x(-2)-(-2)^2 = 2$

$$\begin{aligned} -2x-4 &= 2 \\ -2x &= 6 \\ x &= -3 \end{aligned}$$

The pairs $(3,2)$ and $(-3,-2)$ check. They are the solutions.

45. $m^2-3mn+n^2+1 = 0, \quad (1)$

$3m^2-mn+3n^2 = 13 \quad (2)$

$m^2-3mn+n^2 = -1 \quad (3) \quad \text{Rewriting (1)}$

$3m^2-mn+3n^2 = 13 \quad (2)$

$$\begin{aligned} -3m^2+9mn-3n^2 &= 3 \quad \text{Multiplying (3) by } -3 \\ 3m^2-mn+3n^2 &= 13 \\ \hline 8mn &= 16 \\ mn &= 2 \\ n &= \frac{2}{m} \quad (4) \end{aligned}$$

Substitute $\dfrac{2}{m}$ for n in equation (1) and solve for m.

$$\begin{aligned} m^2-3m\left(\frac{2}{m}\right)+\left(\frac{2}{m}\right)^2+1 &= 0 \\ m^2-6+\frac{4}{m^2}+1 &= 0 \\ m^2-5+\frac{4}{m^2} &= 0 \\ m^4-5m^2+4 &= 0 \quad \text{Multiplying by } m^2 \end{aligned}$$

Substitute u for m^2.

$$\begin{aligned} u^2-5u+4 &= 0 \\ (u-4)(u-1) &= 0 \end{aligned}$$

$u=4 \quad \textit{or} \quad u=1$

$m^2=4 \quad \textit{or} \quad m^2=1$

$m=\pm 2 \quad \textit{or} \quad m=\pm 1$

Substitute for m in equation (4) and solve for n.

When $m=2$, $n=\dfrac{2}{2}=1$.

When $m=-2$, $n=\dfrac{2}{-2}=-1$.

When $m=1$, $n=\dfrac{2}{1}=2$.

When $m=-1$, $n=\dfrac{2}{-1}=-2$.

The pairs $(2,1)$, $(-2,-1)$, $(1,2)$, and $(-1,-2)$ check. They are the solutions.

47. $x^2+y^2=5$, (1)

$x-y=8$ (2)

First solve equation (2) for x.

$x=y+8$ (3)

Then substitute $y+8$ for x in equation (1) and solve for y.

$$(y+8)^2+y^2=5$$
$$y^2+16y+64+y^2=5$$
$$2y^2+16y+59=0$$
$$y=\frac{-16\pm\sqrt{(16)^2-4(2)(59)}}{2\cdot 2}$$
$$y=\frac{-16\pm\sqrt{-216}}{4}$$
$$y=\frac{-16\pm 6i\sqrt{6}}{4}$$
$$y=-4\pm\frac{3}{2}i\sqrt{6}$$

Now substitute these numbers in equation (3) and solve for x.

$$x=-4+\frac{3}{2}i\sqrt{6}+8=4+\frac{3}{2}i\sqrt{6}$$
$$x=-4-\frac{3}{2}i\sqrt{6}+8=4-\frac{3}{2}i\sqrt{6}$$

The pairs $\left(4+\frac{3}{2}i\sqrt{6},-4+\frac{3}{2}i\sqrt{6}\right)$ and $\left(4-\frac{3}{2}i\sqrt{6},-4-\frac{3}{2}i\sqrt{6}\right)$ check. They are the solutions.

49. $a^2+b^2=14$, (1)

$ab=3\sqrt{5}$ (2)

Solve equation (2) for b.

$$b=\frac{3\sqrt{5}}{a}$$

Substitute $\dfrac{3\sqrt{5}}{a}$ for b in equation (1) and solve for a.

$$a^2+\left(\frac{3\sqrt{5}}{a}\right)^2=14$$
$$a^2+\frac{45}{a^2}=14$$
$$a^4+45=14a^2$$
$$a^4-14a^2+45=0$$
$$u^2-14u+45=0 \quad \text{Letting } u=a^2$$
$$(u-9)(u-5)=0$$
$$u=9 \quad \textit{or} \quad u=5$$
$$a^2=9 \quad \textit{or} \quad a^2=5$$
$$a=\pm 3 \quad \textit{or} \quad a=\pm\sqrt{5}$$

Since $b=3\sqrt{5}/a$, if $a=3$, $b=\sqrt{5}$; if $a=-3$, $b=-\sqrt{5}$; if $a=\sqrt{5}$, $b=3$; and if $a=-\sqrt{5}$, $b=-3$. The pairs $(3,\sqrt{5})$, $(-3,-\sqrt{5})$, $(\sqrt{5},3)$, $(-\sqrt{5},-3)$ check. They are the solutions.

51. $x^2+y^2=25$, (1)

$9x^2+4y^2=36$ (2)

$$-4x^2-4y^2=-100 \quad \text{Multiplying (1) by } -4$$
$$\underline{9x^2+4y^2=36}$$
$$5x^2\quad =-64$$
$$x^2=-\frac{64}{5}$$
$$x=\pm\sqrt{\frac{-64}{5}}=\pm\frac{8i}{\sqrt{5}}$$
$$x=\pm\frac{8i\sqrt{5}}{5} \quad \text{Rationalizing the denominator}$$

Substituting $\dfrac{8i\sqrt{5}}{5}$ or $-\dfrac{8i\sqrt{5}}{5}$ for x in equation (1) and solving for y gives us

$$-\frac{64}{5}+y^2=25$$
$$y^2=\frac{189}{5}$$
$$y=\pm\sqrt{\frac{189}{5}}=\pm 3\sqrt{\frac{21}{5}}$$
$$y=\pm\frac{3\sqrt{105}}{5}. \quad \text{Rationalizing the denominator}$$

The pairs $\left(\frac{8i\sqrt{5}}{5},\frac{3\sqrt{105}}{5}\right)$, $\left(-\frac{8i\sqrt{5}}{5},\frac{3\sqrt{105}}{5}\right)$, $\left(\frac{8i\sqrt{5}}{5},-\frac{3\sqrt{105}}{5}\right)$, and $\left(-\frac{8i\sqrt{5}}{5},-\frac{3\sqrt{105}}{5}\right)$ check.

They are the solutions.

53. $5y^2-x^2=1$, (1)

$xy=2$ (2)

Solve equation (2) for x.

$$x=\frac{2}{y}$$

Substitute $\dfrac{2}{y}$ for x in equation (1) and solve for y.

$$5y^2-\left(\frac{2}{y}\right)^2=1$$
$$5y^2-\frac{4}{y^2}=1$$
$$5y^4-4=y^2$$
$$5y^4-y^2-4=0$$
$$5u^2-u-4=0 \quad \text{Letting } u=y^2$$
$$(5u+4)(u-1)=0$$

$$5u + 4 = 0 \quad or \quad u - 1 = 0$$
$$u = -\frac{4}{5} \quad or \quad u = 1$$
$$y^2 = -\frac{4}{5} \quad or \quad y^2 = 1$$
$$y = \pm\frac{2i}{\sqrt{5}} \quad or \quad y = \pm 1$$
$$y = \pm\frac{2i\sqrt{5}}{5} \quad or \quad y = \pm 1$$

Since $x = 2/y$, if $y = \frac{2i\sqrt{5}}{5}$, $x = \frac{2}{\frac{2i\sqrt{5}}{5}} = \frac{5}{i\sqrt{5}} =$

$\frac{5}{i\sqrt{5}} \cdot \frac{-i\sqrt{5}}{-i\sqrt{5}} = -i\sqrt{5}$; if $y = -\frac{2i\sqrt{5}}{5}$,

$x = \frac{2}{-\frac{2i\sqrt{5}}{5}} = i\sqrt{5}$;

if $y = 1$, $x = 2/1 = 2$; if $y = -1$, $x = 2/-1 = -2$.

The pairs $\left(-i\sqrt{5}, \frac{2i\sqrt{5}}{5}\right)$, $\left(i\sqrt{5}, -\frac{2i\sqrt{5}}{5}\right)$, $(2,1)$ and $(-2,-1)$ check. They are the solutions.

55. ***Familiarize.*** We first make a drawing. We let l and w represent the length and width, respectively.

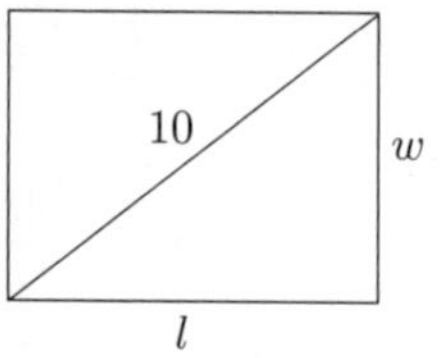

Translate. The perimeter is 28 cm.

$2l + 2w = 28$, or $l + w = 14$

Using the Pythagorean theorem we have another equation.

$l^2 + w^2 = 10^2$, or $l^2 + w^2 = 100$

Carry out. We solve the system:

$l + w = 14, \quad (1)$

$l^2 + w^2 = 100 \quad (2)$

First solve equation (1) for w.

$w = 14 - l \quad (3)$

Then substitute $14 - l$ for w in equation (2) and solve for l.

$$l^2 + w^2 = 100$$
$$l^2 + (14 - l)^2 = 100$$
$$l^2 + 196 - 28l + l^2 = 100$$
$$2l^2 - 28l + 96 = 0$$
$$l^2 - 14l + 48 = 0$$
$$(l - 8)(l - 6) = 0$$

$l = 8$ or $l = 6$

If $l = 8$, then $w = 14 - 8$, or 6. If $l = 6$, then $w = 14 - 6$, or 8. Since the length is usually considered to be longer than the width, we have the solution $l = 8$ and $w = 6$, or $(8, 6)$.

Check. If $l = 8$ and $w = 6$, then the perimeter is $2\cdot 8 + 2\cdot 6$, or 28. The length of a diagonal is $\sqrt{8^2 + 6^2}$, or $\sqrt{100}$, or 10. The numbers check.

State. The length is 8 cm, and the width is 6 cm.

57. ***Familiarize.*** We first make a drawing. Let l = the length and w = the width of the brochure.

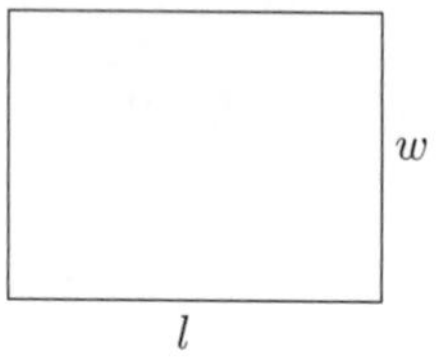

Translate.

Area: $lw = 20$

Perimeter: $2l + 2w = 18$, or $l + w = 9$

Carry out. We solve the system:

Solve the second equation for l: $l = 9 - w$

Substitute $9 - w$ for l in the first equation and solve for w.

$$(9 - w)w = 20$$
$$9w - w^2 = 20$$
$$0 = w^2 - 9w + 20$$
$$0 = (w - 5)(w - 4)$$

$w = 5$ or $w = 4$

If $w = 5$, then $l = 9 - w$, or 4. If $w = 4$, then $l = 9 - 4$, or 5. Since length is usually considered to be longer than width, we have the solution $l = 5$ and $w = 4$, or $(5, 4)$.

Check. If $l = 5$ and $w = 4$, the area is $5 \cdot 4$, or 20. The perimeter is $2 \cdot 5 + 2 \cdot 4$, or 18. The numbers check.

State. The length of the brochure is 5 in. and the width is 4 in.

59. ***Familiarize.*** We first make a drawing. Let l = the length and w = the width.

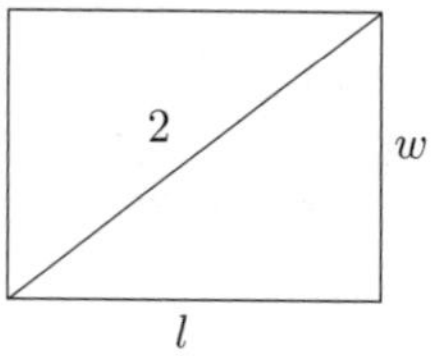

Translate.

Area: $lw = \sqrt{3} \quad (1)$

From the Pythagorean theorem: $l^2 + w^2 = 2^2 \quad (2)$

Carry out. We solve the system of equations.

We first solve equation (1) for w.

$$lw = \sqrt{3}$$
$$w = \frac{\sqrt{3}}{l}$$

Then we substitute $\frac{\sqrt{3}}{l}$ for w in equation 2 and solve for l.

$$l^2 + \left(\frac{\sqrt{3}}{l}\right)^2 = 4$$

$$l^2 + \frac{3}{l^2} = 4$$

$$l^4 + 3 = 4l^2$$

$$l^4 - 4l^2 + 3 = 0$$

$$u^2 - 4u + 3 = 0 \quad \text{Letting } u = l^2$$

$$(u-3)(u-1) = 0$$

$$u = 3 \quad \text{or} \quad u = 1$$

We now substitute l^2 for u and solve for l.

$$l^2 = 3 \quad \text{or} \quad l^2 = 1$$

$$l = \pm\sqrt{3} \quad \text{or} \quad l = \pm 1$$

Measurements cannot be negative, so we only need to consider $l = \sqrt{3}$ and $l = 1$. Since $w = \sqrt{3}/l$, if $l = \sqrt{3}$, $w = 1$ and if $l = 1$, $w = \sqrt{3}$. Length is usually considered to be longer than width, so we have the solution $l = \sqrt{3}$ and $w = 1$, or $(\sqrt{3}, 1)$.

Check. If $l = \sqrt{3}$ and $w = 1$, the area is $\sqrt{3} \cdot 1 = \sqrt{3}$. Also $(\sqrt{3})^2 + 1^2 = 3 + 1 = 4 = 2^2$. The numbers check.

State. The length is $\sqrt{3}$ m, and the width is 1 m.

61. ***Familiarize.*** We make a drawing of the dog run. Let $l =$ the length and $w =$ the width.

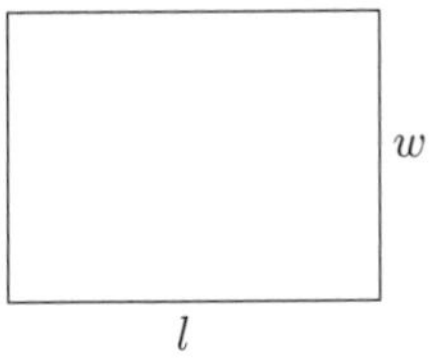

Since it takes 210 yd of fencing to enclose the run, we know that the perimeter is 210 yd.

Translate.

Perimeter: $2l + 2w = 210$, or $l + w = 105$

Area: $lw = 2250$

Carry out. We solve the system:

Solve the first equation for l: $l = 105 - w$

Substitute $105 - w$ for l in the second equation and solve for w.

$$(105 - w)w = 2250$$

$$105w - w^2 = 2250$$

$$0 = w^2 - 105w + 2250$$

$$0 = (w - 30)(w - 75)$$

$$w = 30 \quad \text{or} \quad w = 75$$

If $w = 30$, then $l = 105 - 30$, or 75. If $w = 75$, then $l = 105 - 75$, or 30. Since length is usually considered to be longer than width, we have the solution $l = 75$ and $w = 30$, or $(75, 30)$.

Check. If $l = 75$ and $w = 30$, the perimeter is $2 \cdot 75 + 2 \cdot 30$, or 210. The area is 75(30), or 2250. The numbers check.

State. The length is 75 yd and the width is 30 yd.

63. ***Familiarize.*** We let $x =$ the length of a side of one test plot and $y =$ the length of a side of the other plot. Make a drawing.

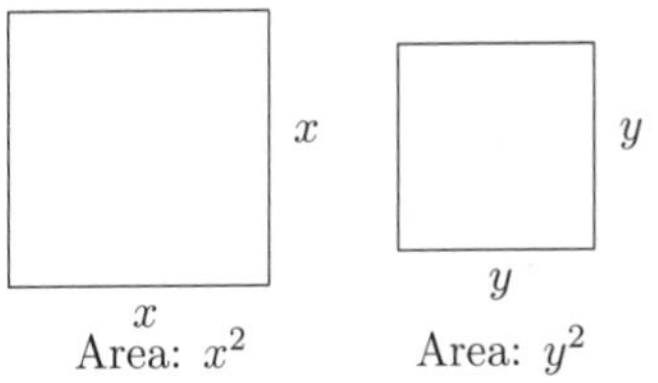

Translate.

The sum of the areas is 832 ft^2.

$$\underbrace{x^2 + y^2}_{\text{The sum of the areas}} \;\underbrace{=}_{\text{is}}\; \underbrace{832}_{832 \text{ ft}^2}$$

The difference of the areas is 320 ft^2.

$$\underbrace{x^2 - y^2}_{\text{The difference of the areas}} \;\underbrace{=}_{\text{is}}\; \underbrace{320}_{320 \text{ ft}^2}$$

Carry out. We solve the system of equations.

$$x^2 + y^2 = 832$$

$$x^2 - y^2 = 320$$

$$2x^2 = 1152 \quad \text{Adding}$$

$$x^2 = 576$$

$$x = \pm 24$$

Since measurements cannot be negative, we consider only $x = 24$. Substitute 24 for x in the first equation and solve for y.

$$24^2 + y^2 = 832$$

$$576 + y^2 = 832$$

$$y^2 = 256$$

$$y = \pm 16$$

Again, we consider only the positive value, 16. The possible solution is $(24, 16)$.

Check. The areas of the test plots are 24^2, or 576, and 16^2, or 256. The sum of the areas is $576 + 256$, or 832. The difference of the areas is $576 - 256$, or 320. The values check.

State. The lengths of the test plots are 24 ft and 16 ft.

65. Find the points of intersection of $y_1 = \ln x + 2$ and $y_2 = x^2$. They are $(1.564, 2.448)$ and $(0.138, 0.019)$.

67. Find the point of intersection of $y_1 = e^x - 1$ and $y_2 = -3x + 4$. It is $(0.871, 1.388)$.

69. Find the points of intersection of $y_1 = e^x$ and $y_2 = x + 2$. They are $(1.146, 3.146)$ and $(-1.841, 0.159)$.

71. Graph $y_1 = \sqrt{19,380,510.36 - x^2}$,

$y_2 = -\sqrt{19,380,510.36 - x^2}$, and

$y_3 = 27,941.25x/6.125$ and find the points of intersection. They are $(0.965, 4402.33)$ and $(-0.965, -4402.33)$.

73. Graph $y_1 = \sqrt{\dfrac{14.5x^2 - 64.5}{13.5}}$,

$y_2 = -\sqrt{\dfrac{14.5x^2 - 64.5}{13.5}}$, and $y_3 = (5.5x - 12.3)/6.3$ and find the points of intersection. They are $(2.112, -0.109)$ and $(-13.041, -13.337)$.

75. Graph $y_1 = \sqrt{\dfrac{56,548 - 0.319x^2}{2688.7}}$,

$y_2 = -\sqrt{\dfrac{56,548 - 0.319x^2}{2688.7}}$,

$y_3 = \sqrt{\dfrac{0.306x^2 - 43,452}{2688.7}}$,

and $y_4 = -\sqrt{\dfrac{0.306x^2 - 43,452}{2688.7}}$ and find the points of intersection. They are $(400, 1.431)$, $(-400, 1.431)$, $(400, -1.431)$, and $(-400, -1.431)$.

77. Discussion and Writing

79.
$$2^{3x} = 64$$
$$2^{3x} = 2^6$$
$$3x = 6$$
$$x = 2$$

The solution is 2.

81.
$$\log_3 x = 4$$
$$x = 3^4$$
$$x = 81$$

The solution is 81.

83. $(x - h)^2 + (y - k)^2 = r^2$

If $(2, 4)$ is a point on the circle, then

$(2 - h)^2 + (4 - k)^2 = r^2$.

If $(3, 3)$ is a point on the circle, then

$(3 - h)^2 + (3 - k)^2 = r^2$.

Thus

$$(2 - h)^2 + (4 - k)^2 = (3 - h)^2 + (3 - k)^2$$
$$4 - 4h + h^2 + 16 - 8k + k^2 =$$
$$9 - 6h + h^2 + 9 - 6k + k^2$$
$$-4h - 8k + 20 = -6h - 6k + 18$$
$$2h - 2k = -2$$
$$h - k = -1$$

If the center (h, k) is on the line $3x - y = 3$, then $3h - k = 3$.

Solving the system

$$h - k = -1,$$
$$3h - k = 3$$

we find that $(h, k) = (2, 3)$.

Find r^2, substituting $(2, 3)$ for (h, k) and $(2, 4)$ for (x, y). We could also use $(3, 3)$ for (x, y).

$$(x - h)^2 + (y - k)^2 = r^2$$
$$(2 - 2)^2 + (4 - 3)^2 = r^2$$
$$0 + 1 = r^2$$
$$1 = r^2$$

The equation of the circle is $(x - 2)^2 + (y - 3)^2 = 1$.

85. The equation of the ellipse is of the form $\dfrac{x^2}{a^2} + \dfrac{y^2}{b^2} = 1$. Substitute $\left(1, \dfrac{\sqrt{3}}{2}\right)$ and $\left(\sqrt{3}, \dfrac{1}{2}\right)$ for (x, y) to get two equations.

$$\frac{1^2}{a^2} + \frac{\left(\frac{\sqrt{3}}{2}\right)^2}{b^2} = 1, \quad or \quad \frac{1}{a^2} + \frac{3}{4b^2} = 1$$

$$\frac{(\sqrt{3})^2}{a^2} + \frac{\left(\frac{1}{2}\right)^2}{b^2} = 1, \quad or \quad \frac{3}{a^2} + \frac{1}{4b^2} = 1$$

Substitute u for $\dfrac{1}{a^2}$ and v for $\dfrac{1}{b^2}$.

$$u + \frac{3}{4}v = 1, \qquad 4u + 3v = 4,$$
$$or$$
$$3u + \frac{1}{4}v = 1 \qquad 12u + v = 4$$

Solving for u and v, we get $u = \dfrac{1}{4}$, $v = 1$. Then $u = \dfrac{1}{a^2} = \dfrac{1}{4}$, so $a^2 = 4$; $v = \dfrac{1}{b^2} = 1$, so $b^2 = 1$.

Then the equation of the ellipse is

$\dfrac{x^2}{4} + \dfrac{y^2}{1} = 1$, or $\dfrac{x^2}{4} + y^2 = 1$.

87. $(x - h)^2 + (y - k)^2 = r^2$ Standard form

Substitute $(4, 6)$, $(-6, 2)$, and $(1, -3)$ for (x, y).

$$(4 - h)^2 + (6 - k)^2 = r^2 \quad (1)$$
$$(-6 - h)^2 + (2 - k)^2 = r^2 \quad (2)$$
$$(1 - h)^2 + (-3 - k)^2 = r^2 \quad (3)$$

Thus

$(4 - h)^2 + (6 - k)^2 = (-6 - h)^2 + (2 - k)^2$, or

$5h + 2k = 3$

and

$(4 - h)^2 + (6 - k)^2 = (1 - h)^2 + (-3 - k)^2$, or

$h + 3k = 7$.

We solve the system

$$5h + 2k = 3,$$
$$h + 3k = 7.$$

Solving we get $h = -\dfrac{5}{13}$ and $k = \dfrac{32}{13}$. Substituting these values in equation (1), (2), or (3), we find that $r^2 = \dfrac{5365}{169}$.

The equation of the circle is

$$\left(x + \frac{5}{13}\right)^2 + \left(y - \frac{32}{13}\right)^2 = \frac{5365}{169}.$$

89. See the answer section in the text.

91. ***Familiarize.*** Let x and y represent the numbers.

Translate.

The square of a certain number exceeds twice the square of another number by $\dfrac{1}{8}$.

$$x^2 = 2y^2 + \frac{1}{8}$$

The sum of the squares is $\frac{5}{16}$.

$$x^2 + y^2 = \frac{5}{16}$$

Carry out. We solve the system.

$$x^2 - 2y^2 = \frac{1}{8}, \quad (1)$$

$$x^2 + y^2 = \frac{5}{16} \quad (2)$$

$$x^2 - 2y^2 = \frac{1}{8},$$

$$2x^2 + 2y^2 = \frac{5}{8} \quad \text{Multiplying (2) by 2}$$

$$3x^2 = \frac{6}{8}$$

$$x^2 = \frac{1}{4}$$

$$x = \pm\frac{1}{2}$$

Substitute $\pm\frac{1}{2}$ for x in (2) and solve for y.

$$\left(\pm\frac{1}{2}\right)^2 + y^2 = \frac{5}{16}$$

$$\frac{1}{4} + y^2 = \frac{5}{16}$$

$$y^2 = \frac{1}{16}$$

$$y = \pm\frac{1}{4}$$

We get $\left(\frac{1}{2}, \frac{1}{4}\right)$, $\left(-\frac{1}{2}, \frac{1}{4}\right)$, $\left(\frac{1}{2}, -\frac{1}{4}\right)$ and $\left(-\frac{1}{2}, -\frac{1}{4}\right)$.

Check. It is true that $\left(\pm\frac{1}{2}\right)^2$ exceeds twice $\left(\pm\frac{1}{4}\right)^2$ by $\frac{1}{8}$: $\frac{1}{4} = 2\left(\frac{1}{16}\right) + \frac{1}{8}$

Also $\left(\pm\frac{1}{2}\right)^2 + \left(\pm\frac{1}{4}\right)^2 = \frac{5}{16}$. The pairs check.

State. The numbers are $\frac{1}{2}$ and $\frac{1}{4}$ or $-\frac{1}{2}$ and $\frac{1}{4}$ or $\frac{1}{2}$ and $-\frac{1}{4}$ or $-\frac{1}{2}$ and $-\frac{1}{4}$.

93. See the answer section in the text.

95. $x^3 + y^3 = 72, \quad (1)$

$x + y = 6 \quad (2)$

Solve equation (2) for y: $y = 6 - x$

Substitute for y in equation (1) and solve for x.

$$x^3 + (6 - x)^3 = 72$$

$$x^3 + 216 - 108x + 18x^2 - x^3 = 72$$

$$18x^2 - 108x + 144 = 0$$

$$x^2 - 6x + 8 = 0 \quad \text{Multiplying by } \frac{1}{18}$$

$$(x - 4)(x - 2) = 0$$

$x = 4$ or $x = 2$

If $x = 4$, then $y = 6 - 4 = 2$.

If $x = 2$, then $y = 6 - 2 = 4$.

The pairs $(4, 2)$ and $(2, 4)$ check.

97. $p^2 + q^2 = 13, \quad (1)$

$\frac{1}{pq} = -\frac{1}{6} \quad (2)$

Solve equation (2) for p.

$$\frac{1}{q} = -\frac{p}{6}$$

$$-\frac{6}{q} = p$$

Substitute $-6/q$ for p in equation (1) and solve for q.

$$\left(-\frac{6}{q}\right)^2 + q^2 = 13$$

$$\frac{36}{q^2} + q^2 = 13$$

$$36 + q^4 = 13q^2$$

$$q^4 - 13q^2 + 36 = 0$$

$$u^2 - 13u + 36 = 0 \quad \text{Letting } u = q^2$$

$$(u - 9)(u - 4) = 0$$

$u = 9$ or $u = 4$

$x^2 = 9$ or $x^2 = 4$

$x = \pm 3$ or $x = \pm 2$

Since $p = -6/q$, if $q = 3$, $p = -2$; if $q = -3$, $p = 2$; if $q = 2$, $p = -3$; and if $q = -2$, $p = 3$. The pairs $(-2, 3)$, $(2, -3)$, $(-3, 2)$, and $(3, -2)$ check. They are the solutions.

99. $5^{x+y} = 100,$

$3^{2x-y} = 1000$

$(x + y)\log 5 = 2,$ Taking logarithms and

$(2x - y)\log 3 = 3$ simplifying

$x\log 5 + y\log 5 = 2, \quad (1)$

$2x\log 3 - y\log 3 = 3 \quad (2)$

Multiply equation (1) by $\log 3$ and equation (2) by $\log 5$ and add.

$$x\log 3 \cdot \log 5 + y\log 3 \cdot \log 5 = 2\log 3$$

$$2x\log 3 \cdot \log 5 - y\log 3 \cdot \log 5 = 3\log 5$$

$$3x\log 3 \cdot \log 5 = 2\log 3 + 3\log 5$$

$$x = \frac{2\log 3 + 3\log 5}{3\log 3 \cdot \log 5}$$

Substitute in (1) to find y.

$$\frac{2\log 3 + 3\log 5}{3\log 3 \cdot \log 5} \cdot \log 5 + y\log 5 = 2$$

$$y\log 5 = 2 - \frac{2\log 3 + 3\log 5}{3\log 3}$$

$$y\log 5 = \frac{6\log 3 - 2\log 3 - 3\log 5}{3\log 3}$$

$$y\log 5 = \frac{4\log 3 - 3\log 5}{3\log 3}$$

$$y = \frac{4\log 3 - 3\log 5}{3\log 3 \cdot \log 5}$$

The pair $\left(\dfrac{2\log 3 + 3\log 5}{3\log 3 \cdot \log 5}, \dfrac{4\log 3 - 3\log 5}{3\log 3 \cdot \log 5}\right)$ checks. It is the solution.

Chapter 7

Sequences, Series, and Combinatorics

Exercise Set 7.1

1. $a_n = 4n - 1$

$a_1 = 4 \cdot 1 - 1 = 3,$

$a_2 = 4 \cdot 2 - 1 = 7,$

$a_3 = 4 \cdot 3 - 1 = 11,$

$a_4 = 4 \cdot 4 - 1 = 15;$

$a_{10} = 4 \cdot 10 - 1 = 39;$

$a_{15} = 4 \cdot 15 - 1 = 59$

3. $a_n = \dfrac{n}{n-1}$, $n \geq 2$

The first 4 terms are a_2, a_3, a_4, and a_5:

$a_2 = \dfrac{2}{2-1} = 2,$

$a_3 = \dfrac{3}{3-1} = \dfrac{3}{2},$

$a_4 = \dfrac{4}{4-1} = \dfrac{4}{3},$

$a_5 = \dfrac{5}{5-1} = \dfrac{5}{4};$

$a_{10} = \dfrac{10}{10-1} = \dfrac{10}{9};$

$a_{15} = \dfrac{15}{15-1} = \dfrac{15}{14}$

5. $a_n = \dfrac{n^2-1}{n^2+1},$

$a_1 = \dfrac{1^2-1}{1^2+1} = 0,$

$a_2 = \dfrac{2^2-1}{2^2+1} = \dfrac{3}{5},$

$a_3 = \dfrac{3^2-1}{3^2+1} = \dfrac{8}{10} = \dfrac{4}{5},$

$a_4 = \dfrac{4^2-1}{4^2+1} = \dfrac{15}{17};$

$a_{10} = \dfrac{10^2-1}{10^2+1} = \dfrac{99}{101};$

$a_{15} = \dfrac{15^2-1}{15^2+1} = \dfrac{224}{226} = \dfrac{112}{113}$

7. $a_n = (-1)^n n^2$

$a_1 = (-1)^1 1^2 = -1,$

$a_2 = (-1)^2 2^2 = 4,$

$a_3 = (-1)^3 3^2 = -9,$

$a_4 = (-1)^4 4^2 = 16;$

$a_{10} = (-1)^{10} 10^2 = 100;$

$a_{15} = (-1)^{15} 15^2 = -225$

9. $a_n = 5 + \dfrac{(-2)^{n+1}}{2^n}$

$a_1 = 5 + \dfrac{(-2)^{1+1}}{2^1} = 5 + \dfrac{4}{2} = 7,$

$a_2 = 5 + \dfrac{(-2)^{2+1}}{2^2} = 5 + \dfrac{-8}{4} = 3,$

$a_3 = 5 + \dfrac{(-2)^{3+1}}{2^3} = 5 + \dfrac{16}{8} = 7,$

$a_4 = 5 + \dfrac{(-2)^{4+1}}{2^4} = 5 + \dfrac{-32}{16} = 3;$

$a_{10} = 5 + \dfrac{(-2)^{10+1}}{2^{10}} = 5 + \dfrac{-1 \cdot 2^{11}}{2^{10}} = 3;$

$a_{15} = 5 + \dfrac{(-2)^{15+1}}{2^{15}} = 5 + \dfrac{2^{16}}{2^{15}} = 7$

11. $a_n = 5n - 6$

$a_8 = 5 \cdot 8 - 6 = 40 - 6 = 34$

13. $a_n = (2n+3)^2$

$a_6 = (2 \cdot 6 + 3)^2 = 225$

15. $a_n = 5n^2(4n - 100)$

$a_{11} = 5(11)^2(4 \cdot 11 - 100) = 5(121)(-56) =$
$-33,880$

17. $a_n = \ln e^n$

$a_{67} = \ln e^{67} = 67$

19. $2, 4, 6, 8, 10, \ldots$

These are the even integers, so the general term might be $2n$.

21. $-2, 6, -18, 54, \ldots$

We can see a pattern if we write the sequence as

$-1 \cdot 2 \cdot 1, 1 \cdot 2 \cdot 3, -1 \cdot 2 \cdot 9, 1 \cdot 2 \cdot 27, \ldots$

The general term might be $(-1)^n 2(3)^{n-1}$.

23. $\dfrac{2}{3}, \dfrac{3}{4}, \dfrac{4}{5}, \dfrac{5}{6}, \dfrac{6}{7}, \ldots$

These are fractions in which the denominator is 1 greater than the numerator. Also, each numerator is 1 greater than the preceding numerator. The general term might be $\dfrac{n+1}{n+2}$.

25. $1 \cdot 2, 2 \cdot 3, 3 \cdot 4, 4 \cdot 5, \ldots$

These are the products of pairs of consecutive natural numbers. The general term might be $n(n+1)$.

27. 0, log 10, log 100, log 1000, . . .

We can see a pattern if we write the sequence as

log 1, log 10, log 100, log 1000, . . .

The general term might be $\log 10^{n-1}$. This is equivalent to $n-1$.

29. 1, 2, 3, 4, 5, 6, 7, . . .

$S_3 = 1+2+3 = 6$

$S_7 = 1+2+3+4+5+6+7 = 28$

31. 2, 4, 6, 8, . . .

$S_4 = 2+4+6+8 = 20$

$S_5 = 2+4+6+8+10 = 30$

33. $$\sum_{k=1}^{5} \frac{1}{2k} = \frac{1}{2\cdot 1}+\frac{1}{2\cdot 2}+\frac{1}{2\cdot 3}+\frac{1}{2\cdot 4}+\frac{1}{2\cdot 5}$$
$$= \frac{1}{2}+\frac{1}{4}+\frac{1}{6}+\frac{1}{8}+\frac{1}{10}$$
$$= \frac{60}{120}+\frac{30}{120}+\frac{20}{120}+\frac{15}{120}+\frac{12}{120}$$
$$= \frac{137}{120}$$

35. $$\sum_{i=0}^{6} 2^i = 2^0+2^1+2^2+2^3+2^4+2^5+2^6$$
$$= 1+2+4+8+16+32+64$$
$$= 127$$

37. $$\sum_{k=7}^{10} \ln k = \ln 7+\ln 8+\ln 9+\ln 10 =$$
$$\ln(7\cdot 8\cdot 9\cdot 10) = \ln 5040 \approx 8.5252$$

39. $$\sum_{k=1}^{8} \frac{k}{k+1} = \frac{1}{1+1}+\frac{2}{2+1}+\frac{3}{3+1}+\frac{4}{4+1}+$$
$$\frac{5}{5+1}+\frac{6}{6+1}+\frac{7}{7+1}+\frac{8}{8+1}$$
$$= \frac{1}{2}+\frac{2}{3}+\frac{3}{4}+\frac{4}{5}+\frac{5}{6}+\frac{6}{7}+\frac{7}{8}+\frac{8}{9}$$
$$= \frac{15{,}551}{2520}$$

41. $$\sum_{i=1}^{5} (-1)^i$$
$$= (-1)^1+(-1)^2+(-1)^3+(-1)^4+(-1)^5$$
$$= -1+1-1+1-1$$
$$= -1$$

43. $$\sum_{k=1}^{8} (-1)^{k+1}3k$$
$$= (-1)^2 3\cdot 1+(-1)^3 3\cdot 2+(-1)^4 3\cdot 3+$$
$$(-1)^5 3\cdot 4+(-1)^6 3\cdot 5+(-1)^7 3\cdot 6+$$
$$(-1)^8 3\cdot 7+(-1)^9 3\cdot 8$$
$$= 3-6+9-12+15-18+21-24$$
$$= -12$$

45. $$\sum_{k=0}^{6} \frac{2}{k^2+1} = \frac{2}{0^2+1}+\frac{2}{1^2+1}+\frac{2}{2^2+1}+\frac{2}{3^2+1}+$$
$$\frac{2}{4^2+1}+\frac{2}{5^2+1}+\frac{2}{6^2+1}$$
$$= 2+1+\frac{2}{5}+\frac{2}{10}+\frac{2}{17}+\frac{2}{26}+\frac{2}{37}$$
$$= 2+1+\frac{2}{5}+\frac{1}{5}+\frac{2}{17}+\frac{1}{13}+\frac{2}{37}$$
$$= \frac{157{,}351}{40{,}885}$$

47. $$\sum_{k=0}^{5} (k^2-2k+3)$$
$$= (0^2-2\cdot 0+3)+(1^2-2\cdot 1+3)+$$
$$(2^2-2\cdot 2+3)+(3^2-2\cdot 3+3)+$$
$$(4^2-2\cdot 4+3)+(5^2-2\cdot 5+3)$$
$$= 3+2+3+6+11+18$$
$$= 43$$

49. $$\sum_{i=0}^{10} \frac{2i}{2^i+1}$$
$$= \frac{2^0}{2^0+1}+\frac{2^1}{2^1+1}+\frac{2^2}{2^2+1}+\frac{2^3}{2^3+1}+\frac{2^4}{2^4+1}+$$
$$\frac{2^5}{2^5+1}+\frac{2^6}{2^6+1}+\frac{2^7}{2^7+1}+\frac{2^8}{2^8+1}+\frac{2^9}{2^9+1}+$$
$$\frac{2^{10}}{2^{10}+1}$$
$$= \frac{1}{2}+\frac{2}{3}+\frac{4}{5}+\frac{8}{9}+\frac{16}{17}+\frac{32}{33}+\frac{64}{65}+\frac{128}{129}+$$
$$\frac{256}{257}+\frac{512}{513}+\frac{1024}{1025}$$
$$\approx 9.736$$

51. 5 + 10 + 15 + 20 + 25+ . . .

This is a sum of multiples of 5, and it is an infinite series. Sigma notation is

$$\sum_{k=1}^{\infty} 5k.$$

53. $2-4+8-16+32-64$

This is a sum of powers of 2 with alternating signs. Sigma notation is

$$\sum_{k=1}^{6} (-1)^{k+1}2k, \text{ or } \sum_{k=1}^{6} (-1)^{k-1}2k$$

55. $$-\frac{1}{2}+\frac{2}{3}-\frac{3}{4}+\frac{4}{5}-\frac{5}{6}+\frac{6}{7}$$

This is a sum of fractions in which the denominator is one greater than the numerator. Also, each numerator is 1 greater than the preceding numerator and the signs alternate. Sigma notation is

$$\sum_{k=1}^{6} (-1)^k \frac{k}{k+1}.$$

57. $4 - 9 + 16 - 25 + \ldots + (-1)^n n^2$

This is a sum of terms of the form $(-1)^k k^2$, beginning with $k = 2$ and continuing through $k = n$. Sigma notation is

$$\sum_{k=2}^{n} (-1)^k k^2.$$

59. $\frac{1}{1 \cdot 2} + \frac{1}{2 \cdot 3} + \frac{1}{3 \cdot 4} + \frac{1}{4 \cdot 5} + \ldots$

This is a sum of fractions in which the numerator is 1 and the denominator is a product of two consecutive integers. The larger integer in each product is the smaller integer in the succeeding product. It is an infinite series. Sigma notation is

$$\sum_{k=1}^{\infty} \frac{1}{k(k+1)}.$$

61. $a_1 = 4, \quad a_{k+1} = 1 + \frac{1}{a_k}$

$$a_2 = 1 + \frac{1}{4} = 1\frac{1}{4}, \text{ or } \frac{5}{4}$$

$$a_3 = 1 + \frac{1}{\frac{5}{4}} = 1 + \frac{4}{5} = 1\frac{4}{5}, \text{ or } \frac{9}{5}$$

$$a_4 = 1 + \frac{1}{\frac{9}{5}} = 1 + \frac{5}{9} = 1\frac{5}{9}, \text{ or } \frac{14}{9}$$

63. $a_1 = 6561, \quad a_{k+1} = (-1)^k \sqrt{a_k}$

$a_2 = (-1)^1 \sqrt{6561} = -81$

$a_3 = (-1)^2 \sqrt{-81} = 9i$

$a_4 = (-1)^3 \sqrt{9i} = -3\sqrt{i}$

65. $a_1 = 2, \quad a_{k+1} = a_k + a_{k-1}$

$a_2 = 3$

$a_3 = 3 + 2 = 5$

$a_4 = 5 + 3 = 8$

67. a) $a_1 = \$1000(1.062)^1 = \$1062$

$a_2 = \$1000(1.062)^2 \approx \$1127.84$

$a_3 = \$1000(1.062)^3 \approx \$1197.77$

$a_4 = \$1000(1.062)^4 \approx \$1272.03$

$a_5 = \$1000(1.062)^5 \approx \$1350.90$

$a_6 = \$1000(1.062)^6 \approx \$1434.65$

$a_7 = \$1000(1.062)^7 \approx \$1523.60$

$a_8 = \$1000(1.062)^8 \approx \$1618.07$

$a_9 = \$1000(1.062)^9 \approx \$1718.39$

$a_{10} = \$1000(1.062)^{10} \approx \$1824.93$

b) $a_{20} = \$1000(1.062)^{20} \approx \$3330.35$

69. Find each term by multiplying the preceding term by 2. Find 17 terms, beginning with $a_1 = 1$, since there are 16 fifteen minute periods in 4 hr.

1, 2, 4, 8, 16, 32, 64, 128, 256, 512, 1024,

2048, 4096, 8192, 16,384, 32,768, 65,536

71. $a_1 = 1$ (Given)

$a_2 = 1$ (Given)

$a_3 = a_2 + a_1 = 1 + 1 = 2$

$a_4 = a_3 + a_2 = 2 + 1 = 3$

$a_5 = a_4 + a_3 = 3 + 2 = 5$

$a_6 = a_5 + a_4 = 5 + 3 = 8$

$a_7 = a_6 + a_5 = 8 + 5 = 13$

73. See the answer section in the text.

75. See the answer section in the text.

77. a)

n	Un
15	27.25
16	26.108
17	25.002
18	23.932
19	22.898
20	21.9
21	20.938
22	20.012
23	19.122
24	18.268

b) From the table in part (a), we know that $a_{16} = 26.108 \approx 26$ and $a_{23} = 19.122 \approx 19$. Using a table set in Ask mode we find that $a_{50} = 8.7 \approx 9$, $a_{75} = 22.45 \approx 22$, and $a_{85} = 34.25 \approx 34$.

79. Discussion and Writing

81. ***Familiarize***. Let x and y represent the amount of individual income taxes collected by the federal government in 2001 and 2002, respectively, in billions of dollars.

Translate. A total of \$1943.5 billion was collected in 2001 and 2002, so we have one equation:

$x + y = 1943.5$

We also know that the amount collected in 2002 was \$45.1 billion less than the amount collected in 2001. This gives us another equation:

$y = x - 45.1$

We have a system of equations:

$x + y = 1943.5,$

$y = x - 45.1$

Carry out. We use the substitution method.

$$\begin{aligned} x + (x - 45.1) &= 1943.5 \\ 2x - 45.1 &= 1943.5 \\ 2x &= 1988.6 \\ x &= 994.3 \end{aligned}$$

Back-substitute to find y.

$y = 994.3 - 45.1 = 949.2$

Check. The total amount collected is \$994.3 billion + \$949.2 billion, or \$1943.5 billion. Also, the amount collected in 2002, \$949.2 billion, is \$45.1 billion less than

\$994.3 billion, the amount collected in 2001. The answer checks.

State. In 2001 \$994.3 billion was collected, and \$949.2 billion was collected in 2002.

83. We complete the square twice.

$$x^2 + y^2 + 5x - 8y = 2$$
$$x^2 + 5x + y^2 - 8y = 2$$
$$x^2 + 5x + \frac{25}{4} + y^2 - 8y + 16 = 2 + \frac{25}{4} + 16$$
$$\left(x + \frac{5}{2}\right)^2 + (y-4)^2 = \frac{97}{4}$$
$$\left[x - \left(-\frac{5}{2}\right)\right]^2 + (y-4)^2 = \left(\frac{\sqrt{97}}{2}\right)^2$$

The center is $\left(-\frac{5}{2}, 4\right)$ and the radius is $\frac{\sqrt{97}}{2}$.

85. $a_n = i^n$

$a_1 = i$

$a_2 = i^2 = -1$

$a_3 = i^3 = -i$

$a_4 = i^4 = 1$

$a_5 = i^5 = i^4 \cdot i = i;$

$S_5 = i - 1 - i + 1 + i = i$

87. $S_n = \ln 1 + \ln +2 \ln 3 + \cdots + \ln n$

$= \ln(1 \cdot 2 \cdot 3 \cdots n)$

Exercise Set 7.2

1. 3, 8, 13, 18, . . .

$a_1 = 3$

$d = 5 \quad (8 - 3 = 5,\ 13 - 8 = 5,\ 18 - 13 = 5)$

3. 9, 5, 1, −3, . . .

$a_1 = 9$

$d = -4 \quad (5-9 = -4,\ 1-5 = -4,\ -3-1 = -4)$

5. $\frac{3}{2}, \frac{9}{4}, 3, \frac{15}{4}, \ldots$

$a_1 = \frac{3}{2}$

$d = \frac{3}{4} \quad \left(\frac{9}{4} - \frac{3}{2} = \frac{3}{4}, 3 - \frac{9}{4} = \frac{3}{4}\right)$

7. $a_1 = \$316$

$d = -\$3 \quad (\$313 - \$316 = -\$3,$
$\$310 - \$313 = -\$3,\ \$307 - \$310 = -\$3)$

9. 2, 6, 10, . . .

$a_1 = 2,\ d = 4,\ \text{and } n = 12$

$a_n = a_1 + (n-1)d$

$a_{12} = 2 + (12-1)4 = 2 + 11 \cdot 4 = 2 + 44 = 46$

11. $3, \frac{7}{3}, \frac{5}{3}, \ldots$

$a_1 = 3,\ d = -\frac{2}{3},\ \text{and } n = 14$

$a_n = a_1 + (n-1)d$

$a_{14} = 3 + (14-1)\left(-\frac{2}{3}\right) = 3 - \frac{26}{3} = -\frac{17}{3}$

13. \$2345.78, \$2967.54, \$3589.30, . . .

$a_1 = \$2345.78,\ d = \$621.76,\ \text{and } n = 10$

$a_n = a_1 + (n-1)d$

$a_{10} = \$2345.78 + (10-1)(\$621.76) = \$7941.62$

15. $a_1 = 0.07,\ d = 0.05$

$a_n = a_1 + (n-1)d$

Let $a_n = 1.67$, and solve for n.

$1.67 = 0.07 + (n-1)(0.05)$

$1.67 = 0.07 + 0.05n - 0.05$

$1.65 = 0.05n$

$33 = n$

The 33rd term is 1.67.

17. $a_1 = 3,\ d = -\frac{2}{3}$

$a_n = a_1 + (n-1)d$

Let $a_n = -27$, and solve for n.

$-27 = 3 + (n-1)\left(-\frac{2}{3}\right)$

$-81 = 9 + (n-1)(-2)$

$-81 = 9 - 2n + 2$

$-92 = -2n$

$46 = n$

The 46th term is −27.

19. $a_n = a_1 + (n-1)d$

$33 = a_1 + (8-1)4$ Substituting 33 for a_8, 8 for n, and 4 for d

$33 = a_1 + 28$

$5 = a_1$

(Note that this procedure is equivalent to subtracting d from a_8 seven times to get a_1: $33 - 7(4) = 33 - 28 = 5$)

21. $a_n = a_1 + (n-1)d$

$-507 = 25 + (n-1)(-14)$

$-507 = 25 - 14n + 14$

$-546 = -14n$

$39 = n$

23. $\dfrac{25}{3} + 15d = \dfrac{95}{6}$

$$15d = \frac{45}{6}$$

$$d = \frac{1}{2}$$

$$a_1 = \frac{25}{3} - 16\left(\frac{1}{2}\right) = \frac{25}{3} - 8 = \frac{1}{3}$$

The first five terms of the sequence are $\dfrac{1}{3}, \dfrac{5}{6}, \dfrac{4}{3}, \dfrac{11}{6}, \dfrac{7}{3}$.

25. $5 + 8 + 11 + 14 + \ldots$

Note that $a_1 = 5$, $d = 3$, and $n = 20$. First we find a_{20}:

$$a_n = a_1 + (n-1)d$$
$$a_{20} = 5 + (20-1)3$$
$$= 5 + 19 \cdot 3 = 62$$

Then

$$S_n = \frac{n}{2}(a_1 + a_n)$$
$$S_{20} = \frac{20}{2}(5 + 62)$$
$$= 10(67) = 670.$$

27. The sum is $2+4+6+\ldots+798+800$. This is the sum of the arithmetic sequence for which $a_1 = 2$, $a_n = 800$, and $n = 400$.

$$S_n = \frac{n}{2}(a_1 + a_n)$$
$$S_{400} = \frac{400}{2}(2 + 800) = 200(802) = 160,400$$

29. The sum is $7 + 14 + 21 + \ldots + 91 + 98$. This is the sum of the arithmetic sequence for which $a_1 = 7$, $a_n = 98$, and $n = 14$.

$$S_n = \frac{n}{2}(a_1 + a_n)$$
$$S_{14} = \frac{14}{2}(7 + 98) = 7(105) = 735$$

31. First we find a_{20}:

$$a_n = a_1 + (n-1)d$$
$$a_{20} = 2 + (20-1)5$$
$$= 2 + 19 \cdot 5 = 97$$

Then

$$S_n = \frac{n}{2}(a_1 + a_n)$$
$$S_{20} = \frac{20}{2}(2 + 97)$$
$$= 10(99) = 990.$$

33. $\displaystyle\sum_{k=1}^{40} (2k+3)$

Write a few terms of the sum:

$$5 + 7 + 9 + \ldots + 83$$

This is a series coming from an arithmetic sequence with $a_1 = 5$, $n = 40$, and $a_{40} = 83$. Then

$$S_n = \frac{n}{2}(a_1 + a_n)$$
$$S_{40} = \frac{40}{2}(5 + 83)$$
$$= 20(88) = 1760$$

35. $\displaystyle\sum_{k=0}^{19} \frac{k-3}{4}$

Write a few terms of the sum:

$$-\frac{3}{4} - \frac{1}{2} - \frac{1}{4} + 0 + \frac{1}{4} + \ldots + 4$$

Since k goes from 0 through 19, there are 20 terms. Thus, this is equivalent to a series coming from an arithmetic sequence with $a_1 = -\dfrac{3}{4}$, $n = 20$, and $a_{20} = 4$. Then

$$S_n = \frac{n}{2}(a_1 + a_n)$$
$$S_{20} = \frac{20}{2}\left(-\frac{3}{4} + 4\right)$$
$$= 10 \cdot \frac{13}{4} = \frac{65}{2}.$$

37. $\displaystyle\sum_{k=12}^{57} \frac{7-4k}{13}$

Write a few terms of the sum:

$$-\frac{41}{13} - \frac{45}{13} - \frac{49}{13} - \ldots - \frac{221}{13}$$

Since k goes from 12 through 57, there are 46 terms. Thus, this is equivalent to a series coming from an arithmetic sequence with $a_1 = -\dfrac{41}{13}$, $n = 46$, and $a_{46} = -\dfrac{221}{13}$. Then

$$S_n = \frac{n}{2}(a_1 + a_n)$$
$$S_{46} = \frac{46}{2}\left(-\frac{41}{13} - \frac{221}{13}\right)$$
$$= 23\left(-\frac{262}{13}\right) = -\frac{6026}{13}.$$

39. ***Familiarize***. We go from 50 poles in a row, down to six poles in the top row, so there must be 45 rows. We want the sum $50 + 49 + 48 + \ldots + 6$. Thus we want the sum of an arithmetic sequence. We will use the formula $S_n = \dfrac{n}{2}(a_1 + a_n)$.

Translate. We want to find the sum of the first 45 terms of an arithmetic sequence with $a_1 = 50$ and $a_{45} = 6$.

Carry out. Substituting into the formula, we have

$$S_{45} = \frac{45}{2}(50 + 6)$$
$$= \frac{45}{2} \cdot 56 = 1260$$

Check. We can do the calculation again, or we can do the entire addition:

$50 + 49 + 48 + \ldots + 6$.

State. There will be 1260 poles in the pile.

41. We first find how many plants will be in the last row.

Familiarize. The sequence is 35, 31, 27, ... It is an arithmetic sequence with $a_1 = 35$ and $d = -4$. Since each row must contain a positive number of plants, we must determine how many times we can add -4 to 35 and still have a positive result.

Translate. We find the largest integer x for which $35 + x(-4) > 0$. Then we evaluate the expression $35 - 4x$ for that value of x.

Carry out. We solve the inequality.

$$35 - 4x > 0$$
$$35 > 4x$$
$$\frac{35}{4} > x$$
$$8\frac{3}{4} > x$$

The integer we are looking for is 8. Thus $35 - 4x = 35 - 4(8) = 3$.

Check. If we add -4 to 35 eight times we get 3, a positive number, but if we add -4 to 35 more than eight times we get a negative number.

State. There will be 3 plants in the last row.

Next we find how many plants there are altogether.

Familiarize. We want to find the sum 35+31+27+. . .+3. We know $a_1 = 35$ $a_n = 3$, and, since we add -4 to 35 eight times, $n = 9$. (There are 8 terms after a_1, for a total of 9 terms.) We will use the formula $S_n = \frac{n}{2}(a_1 + a_n)$.

Translate. We want to find the sum of the first 9 terms of an arithmetic sequence in which $a_1 = 35$ and $a_9 = 3$.

Carry out. Substituting into the formula, we have

$$S_9 = \frac{9}{2}(35 + 3)$$
$$= \frac{9}{2} \cdot 38 = 171$$

Check. We can check the calculations by doing them again. We could also do the entire addition:

$35 + 31 + 27 + . . . + 3$.

State. There are 171 plants altogether.

43. ***Familiarize***. We have a sequence 10, 20, 30, . . . It is an arithmetic sequence with $a_1 = 10$, $d = 10$, and $n = 31$.

Translate. We want to find $S_n = \frac{n}{2}(a_1 + a_n)$ where $a_n = a_1 + (n-1)d$, $a_1 = 10$, $d = 10$, and $n = 31$.

Carry out. First we find a_{31}.

$a_{31} = 10 + (31 - 1)10 = 10 + 30 \cdot 10 = 310$

Then $S_{31} = \frac{31}{2}(10 + 310) = \frac{31}{2} \cdot 320 = 4960$.

Check. We can do the calculation again, or we can do the entire addition:

$10 + 20 + 30 + . . . +310$.

State. A total of 4960¢, or \$49.60 is saved.

45. ***Familiarize***. We have arithmetic sequence with $a_1 = 28$, $d = 4$, and $n = 20$.

Translate. We want to find $S_n = \frac{n}{2}(a_1 + a_n)$ where $a_n = a_1 + (n-1)d$, $a_1 = 28$, $d = 4$, and $n = 20$.

Carry out. First we find a_{20}.

$a_{20} = 28 + (20 - 1)4 = 104$

Then $S_{20} = \frac{20}{2}(28 + 104) = 10 \cdot 132 = 1320$.

Check. We can do the calculations again, or we can do the entire addition:

$28 + 32 + 36 + . . . 104$.

State. There are 1320 seats in the first balcony.

47. Yes; $d = 6 - 3 = 9 - 6 = 3n - 3(n-1) = 3$.

49. Discussion and Writing

51.
$$2x + y + 3z = 12$$
$$x - 3y - 2z = -1$$
$$5x + 2y - 4z = -4$$

We will use Gauss-Jordan elimination with matrices. First we write the augmented matrix.

$$\left[\begin{array}{ccc|c} 2 & 1 & 3 & 12 \\ 1 & -3 & -2 & -1 \\ 5 & 2 & -4 & -4 \end{array}\right]$$

Next we interchange the first two rows.

$$\left[\begin{array}{ccc|c} 1 & -3 & -2 & -1 \\ 2 & 1 & 3 & 12 \\ 5 & 2 & -4 & -4 \end{array}\right]$$

Now multiply the first row by -2 and add it to the second row. Also multiply the first row by -5 and add it to the third row.

$$\left[\begin{array}{ccc|c} 1 & -3 & -2 & -1 \\ 0 & 7 & 7 & 14 \\ 0 & 17 & 6 & 1 \end{array}\right]$$

Multiply the second row by $\frac{1}{7}$.

$$\left[\begin{array}{ccc|c} 1 & -3 & -2 & -1 \\ 0 & 1 & 1 & 2 \\ 0 & 17 & 6 & 1 \end{array}\right]$$

Multiply the second row by 3 and add it to the first row. Also multiply the second row by -17 and add it to the third row.

$$\left[\begin{array}{ccc|c} 1 & 0 & 1 & 5 \\ 0 & 1 & 1 & 2 \\ 0 & 0 & -11 & -33 \end{array}\right]$$

Multiply the third row by $-\frac{1}{11}$.

$$\left[\begin{array}{ccc|c} 1 & 0 & 1 & 5 \\ 0 & 1 & 1 & 2 \\ 0 & 0 & 1 & 3 \end{array}\right]$$

Multiply the third row by -1 and add it to the first row and also to the second row.

$$\left[\begin{array}{ccc|c} 1 & 0 & 0 & 2 \\ 0 & 1 & 0 & -1 \\ 0 & 0 & 1 & 3 \end{array}\right]$$

Now we can read the solution from the matrix. It is $(2, -1, 3)$.

53. The vertices are on the y-axis, so the transverse axis is vertical and $a = 5$. The length of the minor axis is 4, so $b = 4/2 = 2$. The equation is

$$\frac{x^2}{4} + \frac{y^2}{25} = 1.$$

55. $S_n = \frac{n}{2}(1 + 2n - 1) = n^2$

57. Let $d =$ the common difference. Then $a_4 = a_2 + 2d$, or

$$10p + q = 40 - 3q + 2d$$
$$10p + 4q - 40 = 2d$$
$$5p + 2q - 20 = d.$$

Also, $a_1 = a_2 - d$, so we have

$$a_1 = 40 - 3q - (5p + 2q - 20)$$
$$= 40 - 3q - 5p - 2q + 20$$
$$= 60 - 5p - 5q.$$

59. $4, m_1, m_2, m_3, 1$

We look for m_1, m_2, and m_3 such that $4, m_1, m_2, m_3, 13$ is an arithmetic sequence. In this case, $a_1 = 4$, $n = 5$, and $a_5 = 12$. First we find d:

$$a_n = a_1 + (n - 1)d$$
$$12 = 4 + (5 - 1)d$$
$$12 = 4 + 4d$$
$$8 = 4d$$
$$2 = d$$

Then we have

$$m_1 = a_1 + d = 4 + 2 = 6$$
$$m_2 = m_1 + d = 6 + 2 = 8$$
$$m_3 = m_2 + d = 8 + 2 = 10$$

61. $4, m_1, m_2, m_3, m_4, 13$

We look for m_1, m_2, m_3, and m_4 such that $4, m_1, m_2, m_3, m_4, 13$ is an arithmetic sequence. In this case $a_1 = 4$, $n = 6$, and $a_6 = 13$. First we find d.

$$a_n = a_1 + (n - 1)d$$
$$13 = 4 + (6 - 1)d$$
$$9 = 5d$$
$$1\frac{4}{5} = d$$

Then we have

$$m_1 = a_1 + d = 4 + 1\frac{4}{5} = 5\frac{4}{5},$$
$$m_2 = m_1 + d = 5\frac{4}{5} + 1\frac{4}{5} = 6\frac{8}{5} = 7\frac{3}{5},$$
$$m_3 = m_2 + d = 7\frac{3}{5} + 1\frac{4}{5} = 8\frac{7}{5} = 9\frac{2}{5},$$
$$m_4 = m_3 + d = 9\frac{2}{5} + 1\frac{4}{5} = 10\frac{6}{5} = 11\frac{1}{5}.$$

63. $1, 1 + d, 1 + 2d, \ldots, 50$ has n terms and $S_n = 459$.

Find n:

$$459 = \frac{n}{2}(1 + 50)$$
$$18 = n$$

Find d:

$$50 = 1 + (18 - 1)d$$
$$\frac{49}{17} = d$$

The sequence has a total of 18 terms, so we insert 16 arithmetic means between 1 and 50 with $d = \frac{49}{17}$.

65.

$$m = p + d$$
$$m = q - d$$
$$2m = p + q \quad \text{Adding}$$
$$m = \frac{p + q}{2}$$

Exercise Set 7.3

1. $2, 4, 8, 16, \ldots$

$$\frac{4}{2} = 2,\ \frac{8}{4} = 2,\ \frac{16}{8} = 2$$
$$r = 2$$

3. $1, -1, 1, -1, \ldots$

$$\frac{-1}{1} = -1,\ \frac{1}{-1} = -1,\ \frac{-1}{1} = -1$$
$$r = -1$$

5. $\frac{2}{3}, -\frac{4}{3}, \frac{8}{3}, -\frac{16}{3}, \ldots$

$$\frac{-\frac{4}{3}}{\frac{2}{3}} = -2,\ \frac{\frac{8}{3}}{-\frac{4}{3}} = -2,\ \frac{-\frac{16}{3}}{\frac{8}{3}} = -2$$
$$r = -2$$

7. $\frac{0.6275}{6.275} = 0.1,\ \frac{0.06275}{0.6275} = 0.1$

$$r = 0.1$$

9. $\frac{\frac{5a}{2}}{5} = \frac{a}{2},\ \frac{\frac{5a^2}{4}}{\frac{5a}{2}} = \frac{a}{2},\ \frac{\frac{5a^3}{8}}{\frac{5a}{4}} = \frac{a}{2}$

$$r = \frac{a}{2}$$

11. 2, 4, 8, 16, . . .

$a_1 = 2$, $n = 7$, and $r = \frac{4}{2}$, or 2.

We use the formula $a_n = a_1 r^{n-1}$.

$$a_7 = 2(2)^{7-1} = 2 \cdot 2^6 = 2 \cdot 64 = 128$$

13. 2, $2\sqrt{3}$, 6, . . .

$a_1 = 2$, $n = 9$, and $r = \frac{2\sqrt{3}}{2}$, or $\sqrt{3}$

$$a_n = a_1 r^{n-1}$$

$$a_9 = 2(\sqrt{3})^{9-1} = 2(\sqrt{3})^8 = 2 \cdot 81 = 162$$

15. $\frac{7}{625}, -\frac{7}{25}, \ldots$

$a_1 = \frac{7}{625}$, $n = 23$, and $r = \frac{-\frac{7}{25}}{\frac{7}{625}} = -25$.

$$a_n = a_1 r^{n-1}$$

$$a_{23} = \frac{7}{625}(-25)^{23-1} = \frac{7}{625}(-25)^{22}$$

$$= \frac{7}{25^2} \cdot 25^2 \cdot 25^{20} = 7(25)^{20}, \text{ or } 7(5)^{40}$$

17. 1, 3, 9, . . .

$a_1 = 1$ and $r = \frac{3}{1}$, or 3

$$a_n = a_1 r^{n-1}$$

$$a_n = 1(3)^{n-1} = 3^{n-1}$$

19. 1, −1, 1, −1, . . .

$a_1 = 1$ and $r = \frac{-1}{1} = -1$

$$a_n = a_1 r^{n-1}$$

$$a_n = 1(-1)^{n-1} = (-1)^{n-1}$$

21. $\frac{1}{x}, \frac{1}{x^2}, \frac{1}{x^2}, \ldots$

$a_1 = \frac{1}{x}$ and $r = \frac{\frac{1}{x^2}}{\frac{1}{x}} = \frac{1}{x}$

$$a_n = a_1 r^{n-1}$$

$$a_n = \frac{1}{x}\left(\frac{1}{x}\right)^{n-1} = \frac{1}{x} \cdot \frac{1}{x^{n-1}} = \frac{1}{x^{1+n-1}} = \frac{1}{x^n}$$

23. $6 + 12 + 24 + \ldots$

$a_1 = 6$, $n = 7$, and $r = \frac{12}{6}$, or 2

$$S_n = \frac{a_1(1 - r^n)}{1 - r}$$

$$S_7 = \frac{6(1 - 2^7)}{1 - 2} = \frac{6(1 - 128)}{-1} = \frac{6(-127)}{-1} = 762$$

25. $\frac{1}{18} - \frac{1}{6} + \frac{1}{2} - \ldots$

$a_1 = \frac{1}{18}$, $n = 9$, and $r = \frac{-\frac{1}{6}}{\frac{1}{18}} = -\frac{1}{6} \cdot \frac{18}{1} = -3$

$$S_n = \frac{a_1(1 - r^n)}{1 - r}$$

$$S_9 = \frac{\frac{1}{18}\left[1-(-3)^9\right]}{1 - (-3)} = \frac{\frac{1}{18}(1 + 19,683)}{4}$$

$$\frac{\frac{1}{18}(19,684)}{4} = \frac{1}{18}(19,684)\left(\frac{1}{4}\right) = \frac{4921}{18}$$

27. $4 + 2 + 1 + \ldots$

$|r| = \left|\frac{2}{4}\right| = \left|\frac{1}{2}\right| = \frac{1}{2}$, and since $|r| < 1$, the series does have a sum.

$$S_\infty = \frac{a_1}{1 - r} = \frac{4}{1 - \frac{1}{2}} = \frac{4}{\frac{1}{2}} = 4 \cdot \frac{2}{1} = 8$$

29. $25 + 20 + 16 + \ldots$

$|r| = \left|\frac{20}{25}\right| = \left|\frac{4}{5}\right| = \frac{4}{5}$, and since $|r| < 1$, the series does have a sum.

$$S_\infty = \frac{a_1}{1 - r} = \frac{25}{1 - \frac{4}{5}} = \frac{25}{\frac{1}{5}} = 25 \cdot \frac{5}{1} = 125$$

31. $8 + 40 + 200 + \ldots$

$|r| = \left|\frac{40}{8}\right| = |5| = 5$, and since $|r| > 1$ the series does not have a sum.

33. $0.6 + 0.06 + 0.006 + \ldots$

$|r| = \left|\frac{0.06}{0.6}\right| = |0.1| = 0.1$, and since $|r| < 1$, the series does have a sum.

$$S_\infty = \frac{a_1}{1 - r} = \frac{0.6}{1 - 0.1} = \frac{0.6}{0.9} = \frac{6}{9} = \frac{2}{3}$$

35. $\sum_{k=1}^{11} 15\left(\frac{2}{3}\right)^k$

$a_1 = 15 \cdot \frac{2}{3}$ or 10; $|r| = \left|\frac{2}{3}\right| = \frac{2}{3}$, $n = 11$

$$S_{11} = \frac{10\left[1 - \left(\frac{2}{3}\right)^{11}\right]}{1 - \frac{2}{3}} = \frac{10\left[1 - \frac{2048}{177,147}\right]}{\frac{1}{3}}$$

$$= 10 \cdot \frac{175,099}{177,147} \cdot 3$$

$$= \frac{1,750,990}{59,049}, \text{ or } 29\frac{38,569}{59,049}$$

37. $\sum_{k=1}^{\infty}\left(\frac{1}{2}\right)^{k-1}$

$$a_1 = 1,\ |r| = \left|\frac{1}{2}\right| = \frac{1}{2}$$

$$S_\infty = \frac{a_1}{1-r} = \frac{1}{1-\frac{1}{2}} = \frac{1}{\frac{1}{2}} = 2$$

39. $\sum_{k=1}^{\infty} 12.5^k$

Since $|r| = 12.5 > 1$, the sum does not exist.

41. $\sum_{k=1}^{\infty} \$500(1.11)^{-k}$

$$a_1 = \$500(1.11)^{-1},\ \text{or}\ \frac{\$500}{1.11};\ |r| = |1.11^{-1}| = \frac{1}{1.11}$$

$$S_\infty = \frac{a_1}{1-r} = \frac{\frac{\$500}{1.11}}{1-\frac{1}{1.11}} = \frac{\frac{\$500}{1.11}}{\frac{0.11}{1.11}} \approx \$4545.\overline{45}$$

43. $\sum_{k=1}^{\infty} 16(0.1)^{k-1}$

$$a_1 = 16,\ |r| = |0.1| = 0.1$$

$$S_\infty = \frac{a_1}{1-r} = \frac{16}{1-0.1} = \frac{16}{0.9} = \frac{160}{9}$$

45. $0.131313\ldots = 0.13 + 0.0013 + 0.000013 + \ldots$

This is an infinite geometric series with $a_1 = 0.13$.

$$|r| = \left|\frac{0.0013}{0.13}\right| = |0.01| = 0.01 < 1, \text{ so the series has a limit.}$$

$$S_\infty = \frac{a_1}{1-r} = \frac{0.13}{1-0.01} = \frac{0.13}{0.99} = \frac{13}{99}$$

47. We will find fractional notation for $0.999\overline{9}$ and then add 8.

$0.999\overline{9} = 0.9 + 0.09 + 0.009 + 0.0009 + \ldots$

This is an infinite geometric series with $a_1 = 0.9$.

$$|r| = \left|\frac{0.09}{0.9}\right| = |0.1| = 0.1 < 1, \text{ so the series has a limit.}$$

$$S_\infty = \frac{a_1}{1-r} = \frac{0.9}{1-0.1} = \frac{0.9}{0.9} = 1$$

Then $8.999\overline{9} = 8 + 1 = 9$.

49. $3.4125\overline{125} = 3.4 + 0.0125\overline{125}$

We will find fractional notation for $0.0125\overline{125}$ and then add 3.4, or $\frac{34}{10}$, or $\frac{17}{5}$.

$0.0125\overline{125} = 0.0125 + 0.0000125 + \ldots$

This is an infinite geometric series with $a_1 = 0.0125$.

$|r| = \left|\frac{0.0000125}{0.0125}\right| = |0.001| = 0.001 < 1$, so the series has a limit.

$$S_\infty = \frac{a_1}{1-r} = \frac{0.0125}{1-0.001} = \frac{0.0125}{0.999} = \frac{125}{9990}$$

$$\text{Then } \frac{17}{5} + \frac{125}{9990} = \frac{33,966}{9990} + \frac{125}{9990} = \frac{34,091}{9990}$$

51. a) ***Familiarize***. The rebound distances form a geometric sequence:

$$\frac{1}{4}\times 16,\ \left(\frac{1}{4}\right)^2 \times 16,\ \left(\frac{1}{4}\right)^3 \times 16, \ldots,$$

$$\text{or } 4,\quad \frac{1}{4}\times 4,\quad \left(\frac{1}{4}\right)^2 \times 4, \ldots$$

The height of the 6th rebound is the 6th term of the sequence.

Translate. We will use the formula $a_n = a_1 r^{n-1}$, with $a_1 = 4$, $r = \frac{1}{4}$, and $n = 6$:

$$a_6 = 4\left(\frac{1}{4}\right)^{6-1}$$

Carry out. We calculate to obtain $a_6 = \frac{1}{256}$.

Check. We can do the calculation again.

State. It rebounds $\frac{1}{256}$ ft the 6th time.

b) $S_\infty = \frac{a}{1-r} = \frac{4}{1-\frac{1}{4}} = \frac{4}{\frac{3}{4}} = \frac{16}{3}$ ft, or $5\frac{1}{3}$ ft

53. a) ***Familiarize***. The rebound distances form a geometric sequence:

$$0.6\times 200,\ (0.6)^2\times 200,\ (0.6)^3\times 200, \ldots,$$

or $120,\ 0.6\times 120,\ (0.6)^2\times 120, \ldots$

The total rebound distance after 9 rebounds is the sum of the first 9 terms of this sequence.

Translate. We will use the formula

$S_n = \frac{a_1(1-r^n)}{1-r}$ with $a_1 = 120$, $r = 0.6$, and $n = 9$.

Carry out.

$$S_9 = \frac{120[1-(0.6)^9]}{1-0.6} \approx 297$$

Check. We repeat the calculation.

State. The bungee jumper has traveled about 297 ft upward after 9 rebounds.

b) $S_\infty = \frac{a_1}{1-r} = \frac{120}{1-0.6} = 300$ ft

55. ***Familiarize***. The amount of the annuity is the geometric series

$\$1000 + \$1000(1.032) + \$1000(1.032)^2 + \ldots + \$1000(1.032)^{17}$, where $a_1 = \$1000$, $r = 1.032$, and $n = 18$.

Translate. Using the formula

$$S_n = \frac{a_1(1-r^n)}{1-r}$$

we have

$$S_{18} = \frac{\$1000[1-(1.032)^{18}]}{1-1.032}$$

Carry out. We carry out the computation and get $S_{18} \approx \$23,841.50$.

Check. Repeat the calculations.

State. The amount of the annuity is \$23,841.50.

57. ***Familiarize.*** The amounts owed at the beginning of successive years form a geometric sequence:

$\$120,000,\ (1.12)\$120,000,\ (1.12)^2\$120,000,\ \ldots$

The amount to be repaid at the end of 13 years is the amount owed at the beginning of the 14th year.

Translate. Use the formula $a_n = a_1 r^{n-1}$ with $a_1 = 120,000$, $r = 1.12$, and $n = 14$:

$$a_{14} = 120,000(1.12)^{14-1}$$

Carry out. We perform the calculation, obtaining $a_{14} \approx \$523,619.17$.

Check. Repeat the calculation.

State. At the end of 13 years, \$523,619.17 will be repaid.

59. ***Familiarize.*** The total effect on the economy is the sum of an infinite geometric series

$\$13,000,000,000 + \$13,000,000,000(0.85) + \$13,000,000,000(0.85)^2 + \ldots$

with $a_1 = \$13,000,000,000$ and $r = 0.85$.

Translate. Using the formula

$$S_\infty = \frac{a_1}{1-r}$$

we have

$$S_\infty = \frac{\$13,000,000,000}{1-0.85}.$$

Carry out. Perform the calculation:

$S_\infty \approx \$86,666,666,667.$

Check. Repeat the calculation.

State. The total effect on the economy is \$86,666,666,667.

61. Left to the student

63. Discussion and Writing

65. $f(x) = x^2$, $g(x) = 4x + 5$

$(f \circ g)(x) = f(g(x)) = f(4x+5) = (4x+5)^2 = 16x^2 + 40x + 25$

$(g \circ f)(x) = g(f(x)) = g(x^2) = 4x^2 + 5$

67.
$$5^x = 35$$
$$\ln 5^x = \ln 35$$
$$x \ln 5 = \ln 35$$
$$x = \frac{\ln 35}{\ln 5}$$
$$x \approx 2.209$$

69. See the answer section in the text.

71. a) If the sequence is arithmetic, then $a_2 - a_1 = a_3 - a_2$.

$$x + 7 - (x+3) = 4x - 2 - (x+7)$$
$$x = \frac{13}{3}$$

The three given terms are $\frac{13}{3} + 3 = \frac{22}{3}$, $\frac{13}{3} + 7 = \frac{34}{3}$, and $4 \cdot \frac{13}{3} - 2 = \frac{46}{3}$.

Then $d = \frac{12}{3}$, or 4, so the fourth term is $\frac{46}{3} + \frac{12}{3} = \frac{58}{3}$.

b) If the sequence is geometric, then $a_2/a_1 = a_3/a_2$.

$$\frac{x+7}{x+3} = \frac{4x-2}{x+7}$$
$$x = -\frac{11}{3} \text{ or } x = 5$$

For $x = -\frac{11}{3}$: The three given terms are $-\frac{11}{3} + 3 = -\frac{2}{3}$, $-\frac{11}{3} + 7 = \frac{10}{3}$, and $4\left(-\frac{11}{3}\right) - 2 = -\frac{50}{3}$.

Then $r = -5$, so the fourth term is $-\frac{50}{3}(-5) = \frac{250}{3}$.

For $x = 5$: The three given terms are $5 + 3 = 8$, $5 + 7 = 12$, and $4 \cdot 5 - 2 = 18$. Then $r = \frac{3}{2}$, so the fourth term is $18 \cdot \frac{3}{2} = 27$.

73. $x^2 - x^3 + x^4 - x^5 + \ldots$

This is a geometric series with $a_1 = x^2$ and $r = -x$.

$$S_n = \frac{a_1(1-r^n)}{1-r} = \frac{x^2(1-(-x)^n)}{1-(-x)} = \frac{x^2(1-(-x)^n)}{1+x}$$

75. See the answer section in the text.

77. ***Familiarize.*** The length of a side of the first square is 16 cm. The length of a side of the next square is the length of the hypotenuse of a right triangle with legs 8 cm and 8 cm, or $8\sqrt{2}$ cm. The length of a side of the next square is the length of the hypotenuse of a right triangle with legs $4\sqrt{2}$ cm and $4\sqrt{2}$ cm, or 8 cm. The areas of the squares form a sequence:

$(16)^2,\ (8\sqrt{2})^2,\ (8)^2,\ \ldots,$ or

$256,\ 128,\ 64,\ \ldots.$

This is a geometric sequence with $a_1 = 256$ and $r = \frac{1}{2}$.

Translate. We find the sum of the infinite geometric series $256 + 128 + 64 + \ldots$.

$$S_\infty = \frac{a_1}{1-r}$$
$$S_\infty = \frac{256}{1-\frac{1}{2}}$$

Carry out. We calculate to obtain $S_\infty = 512$.

Check. We can do the calculation again.

State. The sum of the areas is 512 cm^2.

Exercise Set 7.4

1. $n^2 < n^3$

$1^2 < 1^3$, $2^2 < 2^3$, $3^2 < 3^3$, $4^2 < 4^3$, $5^2 < 5^3$

The first statement is false, and the others are true.

3. A polygon of n sides has $\dfrac{n(n-3)}{2}$ diagonals.

A polygon of 3 sides has $\dfrac{3(3-3)}{2}$ diagonals.

A polygon of 4 sides has $\dfrac{4(4-3)}{2}$ diagonals.

A polygon of 5 sides has $\dfrac{5(5-3)}{2}$ diagonals.

A polygon of 6 sides has $\dfrac{6(6-3)}{2}$ diagonals.

A polygon of 7 sides has $\dfrac{7(7-3)}{2}$ diagonals.

Each of these statements is true.

5. - 25. See the answer section in the text.

27. Discussion and Writing

29.
$$\begin{aligned} x + y + z &= 3, \quad (1)\\ 2x - 3y - 2z &= 5, \quad (2)\\ 3x + 2y + 2z &= 8 \quad (3)\end{aligned}$$

We will use Gaussian elimination. First multiply equation (1) by -2 and add it to equation (2). Also multiply equation (1) by -3 and add it to equation (3).

$$\begin{aligned} x + y + z &= 3\\ -5y - 4z &= -1\\ -y - z &= -1\end{aligned}$$

Now multiply the last equation above by 5 to make the y-coefficient a multiple of the y-coefficient in the equation above it.

$$\begin{aligned} x + y + z &= 3 \quad (1)\\ -5y - 4z &= -1 \quad (4)\\ -5y - 5z &= -5 \quad (5)\end{aligned}$$

Multiply equation (4) by -1 and add it to equation (3).

$$\begin{aligned} x + y + z &= 3 \quad (1)\\ -5y - 4z &= -1 \quad (4)\\ -z &= -4 \quad (6)\end{aligned}$$

Now solve equation (6) for z.

$$\begin{aligned} -z &= -4\\ z &= 4\end{aligned}$$

Back-substitute 4 for z in equation (4) and solve for y.

$$\begin{aligned} -5y - 4\cdot 4 &= -1\\ -5y - 16 &= -1\\ -5y &= 15\\ y &= -3\end{aligned}$$

Finally, back-substitute -3 for y and 4 for z in equation (1) and solve for x.

$$\begin{aligned} x - 3 + 4 &= 3\\ x + 1 &= 3\\ x &= 2\end{aligned}$$

The solution is $(2, -3, 4)$.

31. ***Familiarize***. Let x, y, and z represent the amounts invested at 1.5%, 2%, and 3%, respectively.

Translate. We know that simple interest for one year was \$104. This gives us one equation:

$$0.015x + 0.02y + 0.03z = 104$$

The amount invested at 2% is twice the amount invested at 1.5%:

$$y = 2x, \text{ or } -2x + y = 0$$

There is \$400 more invested at 3% than at 2%:

$$z = y + 400, \text{ or } -y + z = 400$$

We have a system of equations:

$$\begin{aligned} 0.015x + 0.02y + 0.03z &= 104,\\ -2x + y \qquad &= 0\\ -y + z &= 400\end{aligned}$$

Carry out. Solving the system of equations, we get $(800, 1600, 2000)$.

Check. Simple interest for one year would be 0.015(\$800)+0.02(\$1600)+0.03(\$2000), or \$12+\$32+\$60, or \$104. The amount invested at 2%, \$1600, is twice \$800, the amount invested at 1.5%. The amount invested at 3%, \$2000, is \$400 more than \$1600, the amount invested at 2%. The answer checks.

State. Martin invested \$800 at 1.5%, \$1600 at 2%, and \$2000 at 3%.

33. - 41.

Exercise Set 7.5

1. ${}_6P_6 = 6! = 6\cdot 5\cdot 4\cdot 3\cdot 2\cdot 1 = 720$

3. Using formula (1), we have

${}_{10}P_7 = 10\cdot 9\cdot 8\cdot 7\cdot 6\cdot 5\cdot 4 = 604,800.$

Using formula (2), we have

${}_{10}P_7 = \dfrac{10!}{(10-7)!} = \dfrac{10!}{3!} = \dfrac{10\cdot 9\cdot 8\cdot 7\cdot 6\cdot 5\cdot 4\cdot 3!}{3!} =$
$604,800.$

5. $5! = 5\cdot 4\cdot 3\cdot 2\cdot 1 = 120$

7. $0!$ is defined to be 1.

9. $\dfrac{9!}{5!} = \dfrac{9\cdot 8\cdot 7\cdot 6\cdot 5!}{5!} = 9\cdot 8\cdot 7\cdot 6 = 3024$

11. $(8-3)! = 5! = 5\cdot 4\cdot 3\cdot 2\cdot 1 = 120$

13. $\dfrac{10!}{7!3!} = \dfrac{10\cdot 9\cdot 8\cdot 7!}{7!3\cdot 2\cdot 1} = \dfrac{10\cdot 3\cdot 3\cdot 4\cdot 2}{3\cdot 2\cdot 1} =$
$10\cdot 3\cdot 4 = 120$

15. Using formula (2), we have

${}_8P_0 = \dfrac{8!}{(8-0)!} = \dfrac{8!}{8!} = 1.$

17. Using a calculator, we find
$_{52}P_4 = 6,497,400$

19. Using formula (1), we have $_nP_3 = n(n-1)(n-2)$.
Using formula (2), we have

$$_nP_3 = \frac{n!}{(n-3)!} = \frac{n(n-1)(n-2)(n-3)!}{(n-3)!} =$$
$$n(n-1)(n-2).$$

21. Using formula (1), we have $_nP_1 = n$.
Using formula (2), we have

$$_nP_1 = \frac{n!}{(n-1)!} = \frac{n(n-1)!}{(n-1)!} = n.$$

23. $_6P_6 = 6! = 720$

25. $_9P_9 = 9! = 362,880$

27. $_9P_4 = 9 \cdot 8 \cdot 7 \cdot 6 = 3024$

29. Without repetition: $_5P_5 = 5! = 120$
With repetition: $5^5 = 3125$

31. BUSINESS: 1 B, 1 U, 3 S's, 1 I, 1 N, 1 E, a total of 8.

$$= \frac{8!}{1! \cdot 1! \cdot 3! \cdot 1! \cdot 1! \cdot 1!}$$
$$= \frac{8!}{3!} = \frac{8 \cdot 7 \cdot 6 \cdot 5 \cdot 4 \cdot 3!}{3!} = 8 \cdot 7 \cdot 6 \cdot 5 \cdot 4 = 6720$$

BIOLOGY: 1 B, 1 I, 2 0's, 1 L, 1 G, 1 Y, a total of 7.

$$= \frac{7!}{1! \cdot 1! \cdot 2! \cdot 1! \cdot 1! \cdot 1!}$$
$$= \frac{7!}{2!} = \frac{7 \cdot 6 \cdot 5 \cdot 4 \cdot 3 \cdot 2!}{2!} = 7 \cdot 6 \cdot 5 \cdot 4 \cdot 3 = 2520$$

MATHEMATICS: 2 M's, 2 A's, 2 T's, 1 H, 1 E, 1 I, 1 C, 1 S, a total of 11.

$$= \frac{11!}{2! \cdot 2! \cdot 2! \cdot 1! \cdot 1! \cdot 1! \cdot 1! \cdot 1!}$$
$$= \frac{11!}{2! \cdot 2! \cdot 2!} = \frac{11 \cdot 10 \cdot 9 \cdot 8 \cdot 7 \cdot 6 \cdot 5 \cdot 4 \cdot 3 \cdot 2!}{2! \cdot 2! \cdot 2!}$$
$$= \frac{11 \cdot 10 \cdot 9 \cdot 8 \cdot 7 \cdot 6 \cdot 5 \cdot 4 \cdot 3}{2 \cdot 1 \cdot 2 \cdot 1}$$
$$= 4,989,600$$

33. The first number can be any of the eight digits other than 0 and 1. The remaining 6 numbers can each be any of the ten digits 0 through 9. We have

$$8 \cdot 10^6 = 8,000,000$$

Accordingly, there can be 8,000,000 telephone numbers within a given area code before the area needs to be split with a new area code.

35. $a^2b^3c^4 = a \cdot a \cdot b \cdot b \cdot b \cdot c \cdot c \cdot c \cdot c$

There are 2 a's, 3 b's, and 4 c's, for a total of 9. We have

$$\frac{9!}{2! \cdot 3! \cdot 4!}$$
$$= \frac{9 \cdot 8 \cdot 7 \cdot 6 \cdot 5 \cdot 4!}{2 \cdot 1 \cdot 3 \cdot 2 \cdot 1 \cdot 4!} = \frac{9 \cdot 8 \cdot 7 \cdot 6 \cdot 5}{2 \cdot 3 \cdot 2} = 1260.$$

37. a) $_6P_5 = 6 \cdot 5 \cdot 4 \cdot 3 \cdot 2 = 720$

b) $6^5 = 7776$

c) The first letter can only be D. The other four letters are chosen from A, B, C, E, F without repetition. We have

$$1 \cdot _5P_4 = 1 \cdot 5 \cdot 4 \cdot 3 \cdot 2 = 120.$$

d) The first letter can only be D. The second letter can only be E. The other three letters are chosen from A, B, C, F without repetition. We have

$$1 \cdot 1 \cdot _4P_3 = 1 \cdot 1 \cdot 4 \cdot 3 \cdot 2 = 24.$$

39. a) Since repetition is allowed, each of the 5 digits can be chosen in 10 ways. The number of zip-codes possible is $10 \cdot 10 \cdot 10 \cdot 10 \cdot 10$, or 100,000.

b) Since there are 100,000 possible zip-codes, there could be 100,000 post offices.

41. a) Since repetition is allowed, each digit can be chosen in 10 ways. There can be $10 \cdot 10 \cdot 10 \cdot 10 \cdot 10 \cdot 10 \cdot 10 \cdot 10 \cdot 10$, or 1,000,000,000 social security numbers.

b) Since more than 285 million social security numbers are possible, each person can have a social security number.

43. Discussion and Writing

45.
$$x^2 + x - 6 = 0$$
$$(x+3)(x-2) = 0$$
$$x + 3 = 0 \quad or \quad x - 2 = 0$$
$$x = -3 \quad or \quad x = 2$$

The solutions are -3 and 2.

47. $f(x) = x^3 - 4x^2 - 7x + 10$

We use synthetic division to find one factor of the polynomial. We try $x - 1$.

$$\begin{array}{r|rrrr} 1 & 1 & -4 & -7 & 10 \\ & & 1 & -3 & -10 \\ \hline & 1 & -3 & -10 & 0 \end{array}$$

$$x^3 - 4x^2 - 7x + 10 = 0$$
$$(x-1)(x^2 - 3x - 10) = 0$$
$$(x-1)(x-5)(x+2) = 0$$
$$x - 1 = 0 \quad or \quad x - 5 = 0 \quad or \quad x + 2 = 0$$
$$x = 1 \quad or \quad x = 5 \quad or \quad x = -2$$

The solutions are -2, 1, and 5.

49.
$$_nP_4 = 8 \cdot _{n-1}P_3$$
$$\frac{n!}{(n-4)!} = 8 \cdot \frac{(n-1)!}{(n-1-3)!}$$
$$\frac{n!}{(n-4)!} = 8 \cdot \frac{(n-1)!}{(n-4)!}$$
$$n! = 8 \cdot (n-1)! \qquad \text{Multiplying by } (n-4)!$$
$$n(n-1)! = 8 \cdot (n-1)!$$
$$n = 8 \qquad \text{Dividing by } (n-1)!$$

51.

$$ {}_nP_4 = 8 \cdot {}_nP_3 $$

$$ \frac{n!}{(n-4)!} = 8 \cdot \frac{n!}{(n-3)!} $$

$$ (n-3)! = 8(n-4)! \quad \text{Multiplying by } \frac{(n-4)!(n-3)!}{n!} $$

$$ (n-3)(n-4)! = 8(n-4)! $$

$$ n-3 = 8 \quad \text{Dividing by } (n-4)! $$

$$ n = 11 $$

53. There is one losing team per game. In order to leave one tournament winner there must be $n-1$ losers produced in $n-1$ games.

Exercise Set 7.6

1.
$$ {}_{13}C_2 = \frac{13!}{2!(13-2)!} = \frac{13!}{2!11!} = \frac{13\cdot 12\cdot 11!}{2\cdot 1\cdot 11!} = \frac{13\cdot 12}{2\cdot 1} = \frac{13\cdot 6\cdot 2}{2\cdot 1} = 78 $$

3.
$$ \binom{13}{11} = \frac{13!}{11!(13-11)!} = \frac{13!}{11!2!} = 78 \quad \text{(See Exercise 1.)} $$

5.
$$ \binom{7}{1} = \frac{7!}{1!(7-1)!} = \frac{7!}{1!6!} = \frac{7\cdot 6!}{1\cdot 6!} = 7 $$

7.
$$ \frac{{}_5P_3}{3!} = \frac{5\cdot 4\cdot 3}{3!} = \frac{5\cdot 4\cdot 3}{3\cdot 2\cdot 1} = \frac{5\cdot 2\cdot 2\cdot 3}{3\cdot 2\cdot 1} = 5\cdot 2 = 10 $$

9.
$$ \binom{6}{0} = \frac{6!}{0!(6-0)!} = \frac{6!}{0!6!} = \frac{6!}{6!\cdot 1} = 1 $$

11.
$$ \binom{6}{2} = \frac{6\cdot 5}{2\cdot 1} = 15 $$

13. $\binom{n}{r} = \binom{n}{n-r}$, so

$$ \binom{7}{0} + \binom{7}{1} + \binom{7}{2} + \binom{7}{3} + \binom{7}{4} + \binom{7}{5} + \binom{7}{6} + \binom{7}{7} $$

$$ = 2\left[\binom{7}{0} + \binom{7}{1} + \binom{7}{2} + \binom{7}{3}\right] $$

$$ = 2\left[\frac{7!}{7!0!} + \frac{7!}{6!1!} + \frac{7!}{5!2!} + \frac{7!}{4!3!}\right] $$

$$ = 2(1+7+21+35) = 2\cdot 64 = 128 $$

15. We will use form (1).

$$ {}_{52}C_4 = \frac{52!}{4!(52-4)!} = \frac{52\cdot 51\cdot 50\cdot 49\cdot 48!}{4\cdot 3\cdot 2\cdot 1\cdot 48!} = \frac{52\cdot 51\cdot 50\cdot 49}{4\cdot 3\cdot 2\cdot 1} = 270,725 $$

17. We will use form (2).

$$ \binom{27}{11} = \frac{27\cdot 26\cdot 25\cdot 24\cdot 23\cdot 22\cdot 21\cdot 20\cdot 19\cdot 18\cdot 17}{11\cdot 10\cdot 9\cdot 8\cdot 7\cdot 6\cdot 5\cdot 4\cdot 3\cdot 2\cdot 1} = 13,037,895 $$

19.
$$ \binom{n}{1} = \frac{n!}{1!(n-1)!} = \frac{n(n-1)!}{1!(n-1)!} = n $$

21.
$$ \binom{m}{m} = \frac{m!}{m!(m-m)!} = \frac{m!}{m!0!} = 1 $$

23.
$$ {}_{23}C_4 = \frac{23!}{4!(23-4)!} = \frac{23!}{4!19!} = \frac{23\cdot 22\cdot 21\cdot 20\cdot 19!}{4\cdot 3\cdot 2\cdot 1\cdot 19!} = \frac{23\cdot 22\cdot 21\cdot 20}{4\cdot 3\cdot 2\cdot 1} = \frac{23\cdot 2\cdot 11\cdot 3\cdot 7\cdot 4\cdot 5}{4\cdot 3\cdot 2\cdot 1} = 8855 $$

25.
$$ {}_{13}C_{10} = \frac{13!}{10!(13-10)!} = \frac{13!}{10!3!} = \frac{13\cdot 12\cdot 11\cdot 10!}{10!\cdot 3\cdot 2\cdot 1} = \frac{13\cdot 12\cdot 11}{3\cdot 2\cdot 1} = \frac{13\cdot 3\cdot 2\cdot 2\cdot 11}{3\cdot 2\cdot 1} = 286 $$

27. Since two points determine a line and no three of these 8 points are colinear, we need to find the number of combinations of 8 points taken 2 at a time, ${}_8C_2$.

$$\begin{aligned} {}_8C_2 = \binom{8}{2} &= \frac{8!}{2!(8-2)!} \\ &= \frac{8\cdot 7\cdot 6!}{2\cdot 1\cdot 6!} = \frac{4\cdot 2\cdot 7}{2\cdot 1} \\ &= 28 \end{aligned}$$

Thus 28 lines are determined.

Since three noncolinear points determine a triangle, we need to find the number of combinations of 8 points taken 3 at a time, ${}_8C_3$.

$$\begin{aligned} {}_8C_3 = \binom{8}{3} &= \frac{8!}{3!(8-3)!} \\ &= \frac{8\cdot 7\cdot 6\cdot 5!}{3\cdot 2\cdot 1\cdot 5!} = \frac{8\cdot 7\cdot 3\cdot 2}{3\cdot 2\cdot 1} \\ &= 56 \end{aligned}$$

Thus 56 triangles are determined.

29. ${}_{52}C_5 = 2,598,960$

31. a) ${}_{31}P_2 = 930$

b) $31 \cdot 31 = 961$

c) ${}_{31}C_2 = 465$

33. Discussion and Writing

35.
$$\begin{aligned} 2x^2 - x &= 3 \\ 2x^2 - x - 3 &= 0 \\ (2x-3)(x+1) &= 0 \end{aligned}$$
$$2x - 3 = 0 \quad or \quad x + 1 = 0$$
$$2x = 3 \quad or \quad x = -1$$
$$x = \frac{3}{2} \quad or \quad x = -1$$

The solutions are $\frac{3}{2}$ and -1.

37.
$$\begin{aligned} x^3 + 3x^2 - 10x &= 24 \\ x^3 + 3x^2 - 10x - 24 &= 0 \end{aligned}$$

We use synthetic division to find one factor of the polynomial on the left side of the equation. We try $x - 3$.

$$\begin{array}{r|rrrr} 3 & 1 & 3 & -10 & -24 \\ & & 3 & 18 & 24 \\ \hline & 1 & 6 & 8 & 0 \end{array}$$

Now we have:

$$\begin{aligned} (x-3)(x^2+6x+8) &= 0 \\ (x-3)(x+2)(x+4) &= 0 \end{aligned}$$
$$x - 3 = 0 \quad or \quad x + 2 = 0 \quad or \quad x + 4 = 0$$
$$x = 3 \quad or \quad x = -2 \quad or \quad x = -4$$

The solutions are -4, -2, and 3.

39. There are 13 diamonds, and we choose 5. We have ${}_{13}C_5 = 1287$.

41. Playing once: ${}_nC_2$

Playing twice: $2 \cdot {}_n C_2$

43.
$$\begin{aligned} \binom{n}{n-2} &= 6 \\ \frac{n!}{(n-(n-2))!(n-2)!} &= 6 \\ \frac{n!}{2!(n-2)!} &= 6 \\ \frac{n(n-1)(n-2)!}{2\cdot 1\cdot (n-2)!} &= 6 \\ \frac{n(n-1)}{2} &= 6 \\ n(n-1) &= 12 \\ n^2 - n &= 12 \\ n^2 - n - 12 &= 0 \\ (n-4)(n+3) &= 0 \end{aligned}$$
$$n = 4 \quad \text{or} \quad n = -3$$

Only 4 checks. The solution is 4.

45.
$$\begin{aligned} \binom{n+2}{4} &= 6 \cdot \binom{n}{2} \\ \frac{(n+2)!}{(n+2-4)!4!} &= 6 \cdot \frac{n!}{(n-2)!2!} \\ \frac{(n+2)!}{(n-2)!4!} &= 6 \cdot \frac{n!}{(n-2)!2!} \\ \frac{(n+2)!}{4!} &= 6 \cdot \frac{n!}{2!} \quad \text{Multiplying by } (n-2)! \\ 4! \cdot \frac{(n+2)!}{4!} &= 4! \cdot 6 \cdot \frac{n!}{2!} \\ (n+2)! &= 72 \cdot n! \\ (n+2)(n+1)n! &= 72 \cdot n! \\ (n+2)(n+1) &= 72 \quad \text{Dividing by } n! \\ n^2 + 3n + 2 &= 72 \\ n^2 + 3n - 70 &= 0 \\ (n+10)(n-7) &= 0 \end{aligned}$$
$$n = -10 \quad \text{or} \quad n = 7$$

Only 7 checks. The solution is 7.

47. See the answer section in the text.

Exercise Set 7.7

1. Expand: $(x+5)^4$.

We have $a = x$, $b = 5$, and $n = 4$.

Pascal's triangle method: Use the fifth row of Pascal's triangle.

1 4 6 4 1

$$\begin{aligned} &(x+5)^4 \\ &= 1\cdot x^4 + 4\cdot x^3\cdot 5 + 6\cdot x^2\cdot 5^2 + \\ &\quad 4\cdot x\cdot 5^3 + 1\cdot 5^4 \\ &= x^4 + 20x^3 + 150x^2 + 500x + 625 \end{aligned}$$

Factorial notation method:

$(x+5)^4$

$= \binom{4}{0}x^4 + \binom{4}{1}x^3 \cdot 5 + \binom{4}{2}x^2 \cdot 5^2 +$

$\binom{4}{3}x \cdot 5^3 + \binom{4}{4}5^4$

$= \frac{4!}{0!4!}x^4 + \frac{4!}{1!3!}x^3 \cdot 5 + \frac{4!}{2!2!}x^2 \cdot 5^2 +$

$\frac{4!}{3!1!}x \cdot 5^3 + \frac{4!}{4!0!}5^4$

$= x^4 + 20x^3 + 150x^2 + 500x + 625$

3. Expand: $(x-3)^5$.

We have $a = x$, $b = -3$, and $n = 5$.

Pascal's triangle method: Use the sixth row of Pascal's triangle.

1 5 10 10 5 1

$(x-3)^5$

$= 1 \cdot x^5 + 5x^4(-3) + 10x^3(-3)^2 + 10x^2(-3)^3 +$

$5x(-3)^4 + 1 \cdot (-3)^5$

$= x^5 - 15x^4 + 90x^3 - 270x^2 + 405x - 243$

Factorial notation method:

$(x-3)^5$

$= \binom{5}{0}x^5 + \binom{5}{1}x^4(-3) + \binom{5}{2}x^3(-3)^2 +$

$\binom{5}{3}x^2(-3)^3 + \binom{5}{4}x(-3)^4 + \binom{5}{5}(-3)^5$

$= \frac{5!}{0!5!}x^5 + \frac{5!}{1!4!}x^4(-3) + \frac{5!}{2!3!}x^3(9) +$

$\frac{5!}{3!2!}x^2(-27) + \frac{5!}{4!1!}x(81) + \frac{5!}{5!0!}(-243)$

$= x^5 - 15x^4 + 90x^3 - 270x^2 + 405x - 243$

5. Expand: $(x-y)^5$.

We have $a = x$, $b = -y$, and $n = 5$.

Pascal's triangle method: We use the sixth row of Pascal's triangle.

1 5 10 10 5 1

$(x-y)^5$

$= 1 \cdot x^5 + 5x^4(-y) + 10x^3(-y)^2 + 10x^2(-y)^3 +$

$5x(-y)^4 + 1 \cdot (-y)^5$

$= x^5 - 5x^4y + 10x^3y^2 - 10x^2y^3 + 5xy^4 - y^5$

Factorial notation method:

$(x-y)^5$

$= \binom{5}{0}x^5 + \binom{5}{1}x^4(-y) + \binom{5}{2}x^3(-y)^2 +$

$\binom{5}{3}x^2(-y)^3 + \binom{5}{4}x(-y)^4 + \binom{5}{5}(-y)^5$

$= \frac{5!}{0!5!}x^5 + \frac{5!}{1!4!}x^4(-y) + \frac{5!}{2!3!}x^3(y^2) +$

$\frac{5!}{3!2!}x^2(-y^3) + \frac{5!}{4!1!}x(y^4) + \frac{5!}{5!0!}(-y^5)$

$= x^5 - 5x^4y + 10x^3y^2 - 10x^2y^3 + 5xy^4 - y^5$

7. Expand: $(5x+4y)^6$.

We have $a = 5x$, $b = 4y$, and $n = 6$.

Pascal's triangle method: Use the seventh row of Pascal's triangle.

1 6 15 20 15 6 1

$(5x+4y)^6$

$= 1 \cdot (5x)^6 + 6 \cdot (5x)^5(4y) + 15(5x)^4(4y)^2 +$

$20(5x)^3(4y)^3 + 15(5x)^2(4y)^4 + 6(5x)(4y)^5 +$

$1 \cdot (4y)^6$

$= 15,625x^6 + 75,000x^5y + 150,000x^4y^2 +$

$160,000x^3y^3 + 96,000x^2y^4 + 30,720xy^5 + 4096y^6$

Factorial notation method:

$(5x+4y)^6$

$= \binom{6}{0}(5x)^6 + \binom{6}{1}(5x)^5(4y) +$

$\binom{6}{2}(5x)^4(4y)^2 + \binom{6}{3}(5x)^3(4y)^3 +$

$\binom{6}{4}(5x)^2(4y)^4 + \binom{6}{5}(5x)(4y)^5 + \binom{6}{6}(4y)^6$

$= \frac{6!}{0!6!}(15,625x^6) + \frac{6!}{1!5!}(3125x^5)(4y) +$

$\frac{6!}{2!4!}(625x^4)(16y^2) + \frac{6!}{3!3!}(125x^3)(64y^3) +$

$\frac{6!}{4!2!}(25x^2)(256y^4) + \frac{6!}{5!1!}(5x)(1024y^5) +$

$\frac{6!}{6!0!}(4096y^6)$

$= 15,625x^6 + 75,000x^5y + 150,000x^4y^2 +$

$160,000x^3y^3 + 96,000x^2y^4 + 30,720xy^5 +$

$4096y^6$

9. Expand: $\left(2t + \frac{1}{t}\right)^7$.

We have $a = 2t$, $b = \frac{1}{t}$, and $n = 7$.

Pascal's triangle method: Use the eighth row of Pascal's triangle.

1 7 21 35 35 21 7 1

$$\left(2t+\frac{1}{t}\right)^7$$
$$= 1\cdot(2t)^7 + 7(2t)^6\left(\frac{1}{t}\right) + 21(2t)^5\left(\frac{1}{t}\right)^2 +$$
$$35(2t)^4\left(\frac{1}{t}\right)^3 + 35(2t)^3\left(\frac{1}{t}\right)^4 + 21(2t)^2\left(\frac{1}{t}\right)^5 +$$
$$7(2t)\left(\frac{1}{t}\right)^6 + 1\cdot\left(\frac{1}{t}\right)^7$$
$$= 128t^7 + 7\cdot 64t^6\cdot\frac{1}{t} + 21\cdot 32t^5\cdot\frac{1}{t^2} +$$
$$35\cdot 16t^4\cdot\frac{1}{t^3} + 35\cdot 8t^3\cdot\frac{1}{t^4} + 21\cdot 4t^2\cdot\frac{1}{t^5} +$$
$$7\cdot 2t\cdot\frac{1}{t^6} + \frac{1}{t^7}$$
$$= 128t^7 + 448t^5 + 672t^3 + 560t + 280t^{-1} +$$
$$84t^{-3} + 14t^{-5} + t^{-7}$$

Factorial notation method:

$$\left(2t+\frac{1}{t}\right)^7$$
$$= \binom{7}{0}(2t)^7 + \binom{7}{1}(2t)^6\left(\frac{1}{t}\right) +$$
$$\binom{7}{2}(2t)^5\left(\frac{1}{t}\right)^2 + \binom{7}{3}(2t)^4\left(\frac{1}{t}\right)^3 +$$
$$\binom{7}{4}(2t)^3\left(\frac{1}{t}\right)^4 + \binom{7}{5}(2t)^2\left(\frac{1}{t}\right)^5 +$$
$$\binom{7}{6}(2t)\left(\frac{1}{t}\right)^6 + \binom{7}{7}\left(\frac{1}{t}\right)^7$$
$$= \frac{7!}{0!7!}(128t^7) + \frac{7!}{1!6!}(64t^6)\left(\frac{1}{t}\right) + \frac{7!}{2!5!}(32t^5)\left(\frac{1}{t^2}\right) +$$
$$\frac{7!}{3!4!}(16t^4)\left(\frac{1}{t^3}\right) + \frac{7!}{4!3!}(8t^3)\left(\frac{1}{t^4}\right) +$$
$$\frac{7!}{5!2!}(4t^2)\left(\frac{1}{t^5}\right) + \frac{7!}{6!1!}(2t)\left(\frac{1}{t^6}\right) + \frac{7!}{7!0!}\left(\frac{1}{t^7}\right)$$
$$= 128t^7 + 448t^5 + 672t^3 + 560t + 280t^{-1} +$$
$$84t^{-3} + 14t^{-5} + t^{-7}$$

11. Expand: $(x^2-1)^5$.

We have $a = x^2$, $b = -1$, and $n = 5$.

Pascal's triangle method: Use the sixth row of Pascal's triangle.

1 5 10 10 5 1

$$(x^2-1)^5$$
$$= 1\cdot(x^2)^5 + 5(x^2)^4(-1) + 10(x^2)^3(-1)^2 +$$
$$10(x^2)^2(-1)^3 + 5(x^2)(-1)^4 + 1\cdot(-1)^5$$
$$= x^{10} - 5x^8 + 10x^6 - 10x^4 + 5x^2 - 1$$

Factorial notation method:

$$(x^2-1)^5$$
$$= \binom{5}{0}(x^2)^5 + \binom{5}{1}(x^2)^4(-1) +$$
$$\binom{5}{2}(x^2)^3(-1)^2 + \binom{5}{3}(x^2)^2(-1)^3 +$$
$$\binom{5}{4}(x^2)(-1)^4 + \binom{5}{5}(-1)^5$$
$$= \frac{5!}{0!5!}(x^{10}) + \frac{5!}{1!4!}(x^8)(-1) + \frac{5!}{2!3!}(x^6)(1) +$$
$$\frac{5!}{3!2!}(x^4)(-1) + \frac{5!}{4!1!}(x^2)(1) + \frac{5!}{5!0!}(-1)$$
$$= x^{10} - 5x^8 + 10x^6 - 10x^4 + 5x^2 - 1$$

13. Expand: $(\sqrt{5}+t)^6$.

We have $a = \sqrt{5}$, $b = t$, and $n = 6$.

Pascal's triangle method: We use the seventh row of Pascal's triangle:

1 6 15 20 15 6 1

$$(\sqrt{5}+t)^6 = 1\cdot(\sqrt{5})^6 + 6(\sqrt{5})^5(t) +$$
$$15(\sqrt{5})^4(t^2) + 20(\sqrt{5})^3(t^3) +$$
$$15(\sqrt{5})^2(t^4) + 6\sqrt{5}t^5 + 1\cdot t^6$$
$$= 125 + 150\sqrt{5}\,t + 375t^2 + 100\sqrt{5}\,t^3 +$$
$$75t^4 + 6\sqrt{5}\,t^5 + t^6$$

Factorial notation method:

$$(\sqrt{5}+t)^6 = \binom{6}{0}(\sqrt{5})^6 + \binom{6}{1}(\sqrt{5})^5(t) +$$
$$\binom{6}{2}(\sqrt{5})^4(t^2) + \binom{6}{3}(\sqrt{5})^3(t^3) +$$
$$\binom{6}{4}(\sqrt{5})^2(t^4) + \binom{6}{5}(\sqrt{5})(t^5) +$$
$$\binom{6}{6}(t^6)$$
$$= \frac{6!}{0!6!}(125) + \frac{6!}{1!5!}(25\sqrt{5})t + \frac{6!}{2!4!}(25)(t^2) +$$
$$\frac{6!}{3!3!}(5\sqrt{5})(t^3) + \frac{6!}{4!2!}(5)(t^4) +$$
$$\frac{6!}{5!1!}(\sqrt{5})(t^5) + \frac{6!}{6!0!}(t^6)$$
$$= 125 + 150\sqrt{5}\,t + 375t^2 + 100\sqrt{5}\,t^3 +$$
$$75t^4 + 6\sqrt{5}\,t^5 + t^6$$

15. Expand: $\left(a-\frac{2}{a}\right)^9$.

We have $a = a$, $b = -\frac{2}{a}$, and $n = 9$.

Pascal's triangle method: Use the tenth row of Pascal's triangle.

1 9 36 84 126 126 84 36 9 1

$\left(a-\frac{2}{a}\right)^9 = 1\cdot a^9+9a^8\left(-\frac{2}{a}\right)+36a^7\left(-\frac{2}{a}\right)^2+$

$84a^6\left(-\frac{2}{a}\right)^3+126a^5\left(-\frac{2}{a}\right)^4+$

$126a^4\left(-\frac{2}{a}\right)^5+84a^3\left(-\frac{2}{a}\right)^6+$

$36a^2\left(-\frac{2}{a}\right)^7+9a\left(-\frac{2}{a}\right)^8+1\cdot\left(-\frac{2}{a}\right)^9$

$= a^9-18a^7+144a^5-672a^3+2016a-$

$4032a^{-1}+5376a^{-3}-4608a^{-5}+$

$2304a^{-7}-512a^{-9}$

Factorial notation method:

$\left(a-\frac{2}{a}\right)^9$

$=\binom{9}{0}a^9+\binom{9}{1}a^8\left(-\frac{2}{a}\right)+\binom{9}{2}a^7\left(-\frac{2}{a}\right)^2+$

$\binom{9}{3}a^6\left(-\frac{2}{a}\right)^3+\binom{9}{4}a^5\left(-\frac{2}{a}\right)^4+$

$\binom{9}{5}a^4\left(-\frac{2}{a}\right)^5+\binom{9}{6}a^3\left(-\frac{2}{a}\right)^6+$

$\binom{9}{7}a^2\left(-\frac{2}{a}\right)^7+\binom{9}{8}a\left(-\frac{2}{a}\right)^8+$

$\binom{9}{9}\left(-\frac{2}{a}\right)^9$

$=\frac{9!}{9!0!}a^9+\frac{9!}{8!1!}a^8\left(-\frac{2}{a}\right)+\frac{9!}{7!2!}a^7\left(\frac{4}{a^2}\right)+$

$\frac{9!}{6!3!}a^6\left(-\frac{8}{a^3}\right)+\frac{9!}{5!4!}a^5\left(\frac{16}{a^4}\right)+$

$\frac{9!}{4!5!}a^4\left(-\frac{32}{a^5}\right)+\frac{9!}{3!6!}a^3\left(\frac{64}{a^6}\right)+$

$\frac{9!}{2!7!}a^2\left(-\frac{128}{a^7}\right)+\frac{9!}{1!8!}a\left(\frac{256}{a^8}\right)+$

$\frac{9!}{0!9!}\left(-\frac{512}{a^9}\right)$

$= a^9-9(2a^7)+36(4a^5)-84(8a^3)+126(16a)-$

$126(32a^{-1})+84(64a^{-3})-36(128a^{-5})+$

$9(256a^{-7})-512a^{-9}$

$= a^9-18a^7+144a^5-672a^3+2016a-4032a^{-1}+$

$5376a^{-3}-4608a^{-5}+2304a^{-7}-512a^{-9}$

17. $(\sqrt{2}+1)^6-(\sqrt{2}-1)^6$

First, expand $(\sqrt{2}+1)^6$.

$(\sqrt{2}+1)^6 = \binom{6}{0}(\sqrt{2})^6+\binom{6}{1}(\sqrt{2})^5(1)+$

$\binom{6}{2}(\sqrt{2})^4(1)^2+\binom{6}{3}(\sqrt{2})^3(1)^3+$

$\binom{6}{4}(\sqrt{2})^2(1)^4+\binom{6}{5}(\sqrt{2})(1)^5+$

$\binom{6}{6}(1)^6$

$=\frac{6!}{6!0!}\cdot 8+\frac{6!}{5!1!}\cdot 4\sqrt{2}+\frac{6!}{4!2!}\cdot 4+$

$\frac{6!}{3!3!}\cdot 2\sqrt{2}+\frac{6!}{2!4!}\cdot 2+\frac{6!}{1!5!}\cdot\sqrt{2}+\frac{6!}{0!6!}$

$=8+24\sqrt{2}+60+40\sqrt{2}+30+6\sqrt{2}+1$

$=99+70\sqrt{2}$

Next, expand $(\sqrt{2}-1)^6$.

$(\sqrt{2}-1)^6$

$=\binom{6}{0}(\sqrt{2})^6+\binom{6}{1}(\sqrt{2})^5(-1)+$

$\binom{6}{2}(\sqrt{2})^4(-1)^2+\binom{6}{3}(\sqrt{2})^3(-1)^3+$

$\binom{6}{4}(\sqrt{2})^2(-1)^4+\binom{6}{5}(\sqrt{2})(-1)^5+$

$\binom{6}{6}(-1)^6$

$=\frac{6!}{6!0!}\cdot 8-\frac{6!}{5!1!}\cdot 4\sqrt{2}+\frac{6!}{4!2!}\cdot 4-\frac{6!}{3!3!}\cdot 2\sqrt{2}+$

$\frac{6!}{2!4!}\cdot 2-\frac{6!}{1!5!}\cdot\sqrt{2}+\frac{6!}{0!6!}$

$=8-24\sqrt{2}+60-40\sqrt{2}+30-6\sqrt{2}+1$

$=99-70\sqrt{2}$

$(\sqrt{2}+1)^6-(\sqrt{2}-1)^6$

$=(99+70\sqrt{2})-(99-70\sqrt{2})$

$=99+70\sqrt{2}-99+70\sqrt{2}$

$=140\sqrt{2}$

19. Expand: $(x^{-2}+x^2)^4$.

We have $a=x^{-2}$, $b=x^2$, and $n=4$.

Pascal's triangle method: Use the fifth row of Pascal's triangle.

1 4 6 4 1.

$(x^{-2}+x^2)^4$

$=1\cdot(x^{-2})^4+4(x^{-2})^3(x^2)+6(x^{-2})^2(x^2)^2+$

$4(x^{-2})(x^2)^3+1\cdot(x^2)^4$

$=x^{-8}+4x^{-4}+6+4x^4+x^8$

Factorial notation method:

$(x^{-2}+x^2)^4$

$$= \binom{4}{0}(x^{-2})^4 + \binom{4}{1}(x^{-2})^3(x^2) + \binom{4}{2}(x^{-2})^2(x^2)^2 + \binom{4}{3}(x^{-2})(x^2)^3 + \binom{4}{4}(x^2)^4$$

$$= \frac{4!}{4!0!}(x^{-8}) + \frac{4!}{3!1!}(x^{-6})(x^2) + \frac{4!}{2!2!}(x^{-4})(x^4) + \frac{4!}{1!3!}(x^{-2})(x^6) + \frac{4!}{0!4!}(x^8)$$

$$= x^{-8} + 4x^{-4} + 6 + 4x^4 + x^8$$

21. Find the 3rd term of $(a+b)^7$.

First, we note that $3 = 2+1$, $a = a$, $b = b$, and $n = 7$. Then the 3rd term of the expansion of $(a+b)^7$ is

$$\binom{7}{2}a^{7-2}b^2, \text{ or } \frac{7!}{2!5!}a^5b^2, \text{ or } 21a^5b^2.$$

23. Find the 6th term of $(x-y)^{10}$.

First, we note that $6 = 5+1$, $a = x$, $b = -y$, and $n = 10$. Then the 6th term of the expansion of $(x-y)^{10}$ is

$$\binom{10}{5}x^5(-y)^5, \text{ or } -252x^5y^5.$$

25. Find the 12th term of $(a-2)^{14}$.

First, we note that $12 = 11+1$, $a = a$, $b = -2$, and $n = 14$. Then the 12th term of the expansion of $(a-2)^{14}$ is

$$\binom{14}{11}a^{14-11}\cdot(-2)^{11} = \frac{14!}{3!11!}a^3(-2048)$$
$$= 364a^3(-2048)$$
$$= -745,472a^3$$

27. Find the 5th term of $(2x^3-\sqrt{y})^8$.

First, we note that $5 = 4+1$, $a = 2x^3$, $b = -\sqrt{y}$, and $n = 8$. Then the 5th term of the expansion of $(2x^3-\sqrt{y})^8$ is

$$\binom{8}{4}(2x^3)^{8-4}(-\sqrt{y})^4$$
$$= \frac{8!}{4!4!}(2x^3)^4(-\sqrt{y})^4$$
$$= 70(16x^{12})(y^2)$$
$$= 1120x^{12}y^2$$

29. The expansion of $(2u-3v^2)^{10}$ has 11 terms so the 6th term is the middle term. Note that $6 = 5+1$, $a = 2u$, $b = -3v^2$, and $n = 10$. Then the 6th term of the expansion of $(2u-3v^2)^{10}$ is

$$\binom{10}{5}(2u)^{10-5}(-3v^2)^5$$
$$= \frac{10!}{5!5!}(2u)^5(-3v^2)^5$$
$$= 252(32u^5)(-243v^{10})$$
$$= -1,959,552u^5v^{10}$$

31. The number of subsets is 2^7, or 128

33. The number of subsets is 2^{24}, or 16,777,216.

35. The term of highest degree of $(x^5+3)^4$ is the first term, or

$$\binom{4}{0}(x^5)^{4-0}3^0 = \frac{4!}{4!0!}x^{20} = x^{20}.$$

Therefore, the degree of $(x^5+3)^4$ is 20.

37. We use factorial notation. Note that $a = 3$, $b = i$, and $n = 5$.

$(3+i)^5$

$$= \binom{5}{0}(3^5) + \binom{5}{1}(3^4)(i) + \binom{5}{2}(3^3)(i^2) + \binom{5}{3}(3^2)(i^3) + \binom{5}{4}(3)(i^4) + \binom{5}{5}(i^5)$$

$$= \frac{5!}{0!5!}(243) + \frac{5!}{1!4!}(81)(i) + \frac{5!}{2!3!}(27)(-1) + \frac{5!}{3!2!}(9)(-i) + \frac{5!}{4!1!}(3)(1) + \frac{5!}{5!0!}(i)$$

$$= 243 + 405i - 270 - 90i + 15 + i$$
$$= -12 + 316i$$

39. We use factorial notation. Note that $a = \sqrt{2}$, $b = -i$, and $n = 4$.

$$(\sqrt{2}-i)^4 = \binom{4}{0}(\sqrt{2})^4 + \binom{4}{1}(\sqrt{2})^3(-i) + \binom{4}{2}(\sqrt{2})^2(-i)^2 + \binom{4}{3}(\sqrt{2})(-i)^3 + \binom{4}{4}(-i)^4$$

$$= \frac{4!}{0!4!}(4) + \frac{4!}{1!3!}(2\sqrt{2})(-i) + \frac{4!}{2!2!}(2)(-1) + \frac{4!}{3!1!}(\sqrt{2})(i) + \frac{4!}{4!0!}(1)$$

$$= 4 - 8\sqrt{2}i - 12 + 4\sqrt{2}i + 1$$
$$= -7 - 4\sqrt{2}i$$

41. $(a-b)^n = \binom{n}{0}a^n(-b)^0 + \binom{n}{1}a^{n-1}(-b)^1 +$

$\binom{n}{2}a^{n-2}(-b)^2 + \cdots +$

$\binom{n}{n-1}a^1(-b)^{n-1} + \binom{n}{n}a^0(-b)^n$

$= \binom{n}{0}(-1)^0 a^n b^0 + \binom{n}{1}(-1)^1 a^{n-1}b^1 +$

$\binom{n}{2}(-1)^2 a^{n-2}b^2 + \cdots +$

$\binom{n}{n-1}(-1)^{n-1}a^1 b^{n-1} +$

$\binom{n}{n}(-1)^n a^0 b^n$

$= \sum_{k=0}^{n}\binom{n}{k}(-1)^k a^{n-k}b^k$

43. $\dfrac{(x+h)^n - x^n}{h}$

$= \dfrac{\binom{n}{0}x^n + \binom{n}{1}x^{n-1}h + \cdots + \binom{n}{n}h^n - x^n}{h}$

$= \binom{n}{1}x^{n-1} + \binom{n}{2}x^{n-2}h + \cdots + \binom{n}{n}h^{n-1}$

$= \sum_{k=1}^{n}\binom{n}{k}x^{n-k}h^{k-1}$

45. Discussion and Writing

47. $(fg)(x) = f(x)g(x) = (x^2+1)(2x-3) =$
$2x^3 - 3x^2 + 2x - 3$

49. $(g \circ f)(x) = g(f(x)) = g(x^2+1) = 2(x^2+1) - 3 =$
$2x^2 + 2 - 3 = 2x^2 - 1$

51. $\sum_{k=0}^{4}\binom{4}{k}5^{4-k}x^k = 64$

The left side of the equation is sigma notation for $(5+x)^4$, so we have:

$(5+x)^4 = 64$

$5 + x = \pm 2\sqrt{2}$ Taking the 4th root on both sides

$x = -5 \pm 2\sqrt{2}$

The real solutions are $-5 \pm 2\sqrt{2}$.

If we also observe that $(2\sqrt{2}i)^4 = 64$, we also find the imaginary solutions $-5 \pm 2\sqrt{2}i$.

53. $\sum_{k=0}^{4}\binom{4}{k}(-1)^k x^{4-k}6^k = \sum_{k=0}^{4}\binom{4}{k}x^{4-k}(-6)^k$, so

the left side of the equation is sigma notation for $(x-6)^4$. We have:

$(x-6)^4 = 81$

$x - 6 = \pm 3$ Taking the 4th root on both sides

$x - 6 = 3$ or $x - 6 = -3$

$x = 9$ or $x = 3$

The solutions are 9 and 3.

If we also observe that $(3i)^4 = 81$, we also find the imaginary solutions $6 \pm 3i$.

55. The expansion of $(x^2 - 6y^{3/2})^6$ has 7 terms, so the 4th term is the middle term.

$\binom{6}{3}(x^2)^3(-6y^{3/2})^3 = \dfrac{6!}{3!3!}(x^6)(-216y^{9/2}) =$
$-4320x^6y^{9/2}$

57. The $(k+1)$st term of $\left(\sqrt[3]{x} - \dfrac{1}{\sqrt{x}}\right)^7$ is

$\binom{7}{k}(\sqrt[3]{x})^{7-k}\left(-\dfrac{1}{\sqrt{x}}\right)^k$. The term containing $\dfrac{1}{x^{1/6}}$ is the term in which the sum of the exponents is $-1/6$. That is,

$$\left(\frac{1}{3}\right)(7-k) + \left(-\frac{1}{2}\right)(k) = -\frac{1}{6}$$

$$\frac{7}{3} - \frac{k}{3} - \frac{k}{2} = -\frac{1}{6}$$

$$-\frac{5k}{6} = -\frac{15}{6}$$

$$k = 3$$

Find the $(3+1)$st, or 4th term.

$\binom{7}{3}(\sqrt[3]{x})^4\left(-\dfrac{1}{\sqrt{x}}\right)^3 = \dfrac{7!}{4!3!}(x^{4/3})(-x^{-3/2}) =$

$-35x^{-1/6}$, or $-\dfrac{35}{x^{1/6}}$.

59. ${}_{100}C_0 + {}_{100}C_1 + \cdots + {}_{100}C_{100}$ is the total number of subsets of a set with 100 members, or 2^{100}.

61. $\sum_{k=0}^{23}\binom{23}{k}(\log_a x)^{23-k}(\log_a t)^k =$

$(\log_a x + \log_a t)^{23} = [\log_a(xt)]^{23}$

63. See the answer section in the text.

Exercise Set 7.8

1. a) We use Principle P.

For 1: $P = \dfrac{18}{100}$, or 0.18

For 2: $P = \dfrac{24}{100}$, or 0.24

For 3: $P = \dfrac{23}{100}$, or 0.23

For 4: $P = \dfrac{23}{100}$, or 0.23

For 5: $P = \dfrac{12}{100}$, or 0.12

b) Opinions may vary, but it seems that people tend not to select the first or last numbers.

3. The company can expect 78% of the 15,000 pieces of advertising to be opened and read. We have:

$78\%(15,000) = 0.78(15,000) = 11,700.$

5. a) The consonants with the 5 greatest numbers of occurrences are the 5 consonants with the greatest probability of occurring. They are T, S, R, N, and L.

b) E is the vowel with the greatest number of occurrences, so E is the vowel with the greatest probability of occurring.

c) Yes

7. a) Since there are 14 equally likely ways of selecting a marble from a bag containing 4 red marbles and 10 green marbles, we have, by Principle P,

$P(\text{selecting a red marble}) = \frac{4}{14} = \frac{2}{7}.$

b) Since there are 14 equally likely ways of selecting a marble from a bag containing 4 red marbles and 10 green marbles, we have, by Principle P,

$P(\text{selecting a green marble}) = \frac{10}{14} = \frac{5}{7}.$

c) Since there are 14 equally likely ways of selecting a marble from a bag containing 4 red marbles and 10 green marbles, we have, by Principle P,

$P(\text{selecting a purple marble}) = \frac{0}{14} = 0.$

d) Since there are 14 equally likely ways of selecting a marble from a bag containing 4 red marbles and 10 green marbles, we have, by Principle P,

$P(\text{selecting a red or a green marble}) =$

$\frac{4+10}{14} = 1.$

9. The total number of coins is $7+5+10$, or 22 and the total number of coins to be drawn is $4+3+1$, or 8. The number of ways of selecting 8 coins from a group of 22 is ${}_{22}C_8$. Four dimes can be selected in ${}_7C_4$ ways, 3 nickels in ${}_5C_3$ ways, and 1 quarter in ${}_{10}C_1$ ways.

$P(\text{selecting 4 dimes, 3 nickels, and 1 quarter}) =$

$\frac{{}_7C_4 \cdot {}_5C_3 \cdot {}_{10}C_1}{{}_{22}C_8}$, or $\frac{350}{31,977}$

11. The number of ways of selecting 5 cards from a deck of 52 cards is ${}_{52}C_5$. Three sevens can be selected in ${}_4C_3$ ways and 2 kings in ${}_4C_2$ ways.

$P(\text{drawing 3 sevens and 2 kings}) = \frac{{}_4C_3 \cdot {}_4C_2}{{}_{52}C_5}$, or

$\frac{1}{108,290}.$

13. The number of ways of selecting 5 cards from a deck of 52 cards is ${}_{52}C_5$. Since 13 of the cards are spades, then 5 spades can be drawn in ${}_{13}C_5$ ways

$P(\text{drawing 5 spades}) = \frac{{}_{13}C_5}{{}_{52}C_5} = \frac{1287}{2,598,960} =$

$\frac{33}{66,640}$

15. a) HHH, HHT, HTH, HTT, THH, THT, TTH, TTT

b) Three of the 8 outcomes have exactly one head. Thus, $P(\text{exactly one head}) = \frac{3}{8}.$

c) Seven of the 8 outcomes have exactly 0, 1, or 2 heads. Thus, $P(\text{at most two heads}) = \frac{7}{8}.$

d) Seven of the 8 outcomes have 1, 2, or 3 heads. Thus, $P(\text{at least one head}) = \frac{7}{8}.$

e) Three of the 8 outcomes have exactly two tails. Thus, $P(\text{exactly two tails}) = \frac{3}{8}.$

17. The roulette wheel contains 38 equally likely slots. Eighteen of the 38 slots are colored black. Thus, by Principle P,

$P(\text{the ball falls in a black slot}) = \frac{18}{38} = \frac{9}{19}.$

19. The roulette wheel contains 38 equally likely slots. Only 1 slot is numbered 0. Then, by Principle P,

$P(\text{the ball falls in the 0 slot}) = \frac{1}{38}.$

21. The roulette wheel contains 38 equally likely slots. Thirty-six of the slots are colored red or black. Then, by Principle P,

$P(\text{the ball falls in a red or a black slot}) = \frac{36}{38} = \frac{18}{19}.$

23. The roulette wheel contains 38 equally likely slots. Eighteen of the slots are odd-numbered. Then, by Principle P,

$P(\text{the ball falls in a an odd-numbered slot}) =$

$\frac{18}{38} = \frac{9}{19}.$

25. a), b) Answers may vary

27. Discussion and Writing

29. one-to-one

31. zero

33. inverse variation

35. geometric sequence

37. Consider a suit

A K Q J 10 9 8 7 6 5 4 3 2

A straight flush can be any of the following combinations in the same suit.

K	Q	J	10	9
Q	J	10	9	8
J	10	9	8	7
10	9	8	7	6
9	8	7	6	5
8	7	6	5	4
7	6	5	4	3
6	5	4	3	2
5	4	3	2	A

Remember a straight flush does not include A K Q J 10 which is a royal flush.

a) Since there are 9 straight flushes per suit, there are 36 straight flushes in all 4 suits.

b) Since 2,598,960, or ${}_{52}C_5$, poker hands can be dealt from a standard 52-card deck and 36 of those hands are straight flushes, the probability of getting a straight flush is $\frac{36}{2,598,960}$, or about 1.39×10^{-5}.

39. a) There are 13 ways to select a denomination. Then from that denomination there are ${}_4C_3$ ways to pick 3 of the 4 cards in that denomination. Now there are 12 ways to select any one of the remaining 12 denominations and ${}_4C_2$ ways to pick 2 cards from the 4 cards in that denomination. Thus the number of full houses is $(13 \cdot {}_4C_3) \cdot (12 \cdot {}_4C_2)$ or 3744.

b) $\frac{3744}{{}_{52}C_5} = \frac{3744}{2,598,960} \approx 0.00144$

41. a) There are 4 ways to select a suit and then $\binom{13}{5}$ ways to choose 5 cards from that suit. But these combinations include hands with all the cards in sequence, so we subtract the 4 royal flushes (Exercise 28) and the 36 straight flushes (Exercise 29). Thus there are $4 \cdot \binom{13}{5} - 4 - 36$, or 5108 flushes.

b) $\frac{5108}{{}_{52}C_5} = \frac{5108}{2,598,960} \approx 0.00197$

43. a) There are 10 sets of 5 consecutive cards:

A K Q J 10
K Q J 10 9
.
.
.
5 4 3 2 A

In each of these 10 sets there are 4 ways to choose (from 4 suits) each of the 5 cards. These combinations include the 4 royal flushes and the 36 straight flushes, both of which consist of 5 cards of the *same suit* in sequence.

Thus there are $10 \cdot 4 \cdot 4 \cdot 4 \cdot 4 \cdot 4 - 4 - 36$, or 10,200 straights.

b) $\frac{10,200}{{}_{52}C_5} = \frac{10,200}{2,598,960} \approx 0.00392$